Sachar Paulus
Norbert Pohlmann
Helmut Reimer

ISSE 2006 –
Securing Electronic Business Processes

W0235304

vieweg-it

www.vieweg.de

Sachar Paulus
Norbert Pohlmann
Helmut Reimer

ISSE 2006 – Securing Electronic Business Processes

Highlights of the Information Security Solutions Europe 2006 Conference

With 130 illustrations

vieweg

Bibliographic information published by Die Deutsche Nationalibliothek
Die Deutsche Nationalbibliothek lists this publication in the Deutsche Nationalbibliographie;
detailed bibliographic data is available in the Internet at <http://dnb.d-nb.de>.

Many of designations used by manufacturers and sellers to distinguish their
products are claimed as trademarks.

1st edition October 2006

All rights reserved
© Friedr. Vieweg & Sohn Verlag | GWV Fachverlage GmbH, Wiesbaden 2006

Editorial office: Günter Schulz / Andrea Broßler

Vieweg is a company of Springer Science+Business Media.
www.vieweg.de

Cover design: Ulrike Weigel, www.CorporateDesignGroup.de
Typesetting: Oliver Reimer, Ilmenau
Printing and binding: LegoPrint SpA, Lavis
Printed on acid-free paper
Printed in Italy

ISBN-10 3-8348-0213-1
ISBN-13 978-3-8348-0213-2

Contents

Identity Management, Biometrics, PKI-Solutions, Network Security _____ 149

Awareness Raising, Compliance, Data Protection, Cyberspace Regulation _____ 375

Preface

ENISA is proud to be working with eema, TeleTrusT, ISCOM (the Italian Institute for Communications and Information Technologies) and the German Federal Ministry of the Interior as well as the German Federal Office for Information Security for this year's 8th annual Information Security Solutions Europe Conference.

The aim of ISSE has always been to support the development of a European information security culture. ENISA is committed to this goal, in our work to assist and advise the European Commission, Member States as well as business community on network, information security and legislative requirements and we are delighted to support ISSE again this year.

The security of communication networks and information systems is of increasing concern. In order to face today's complex information security challenges it is clear that working collaboratively with one another is the key to generating new strategies to address these problems. It has been an exciting opportunity to facilitate this collaboration at ISSE 2006, and pull together the wealth of industry knowledge, information and research that we hold in Europe, and across the globe.

The success of this event in generating ideas and frank, lively debate around the complex topic of IT security is due also to the independent, varied nature of the programme, which was selected by world-wide industry specialists.

Some of the key topics explored at this year's conference have been chosen as the basis for this book, which is an invaluable reference point for anyone involved in the IT security industry.

We hope that you will find it a thought-provoking and informative read.

Andrea Pirotti, Executive Director, ENISA

About this Book

The Information Security Solutions Europe Conference (ISSE) was started in 1999 by eema and TeleTrusT with the support of the European Commission and the German Federal Ministry of Technology and Economics. Today the annual conference is a fixed event in every IT security professional's calendar.

The integration of security in IT applications was initially driven only by the actual security issues considered important by experts in the field; currently, however, the economic aspects of the corresponding solutions are the most important factor in deciding their success. ISSE offers a suitable podium for the discussion of the relationship between these considerations and for the presentation of the practical implementation of concepts with their technical, organisational and economic parameters.

From the beginning ISSE has been carefully prepared. The organisers succeeded in giving the conference a profile that combines a scientifically sophisticated and interdisciplinary discussion of IT security solutions while presenting pragmatic approaches for overcoming current IT security problems.

An enduring documentation of the presentations given at the conference which is available to every interested person thus became important. This year sees the publication of the third ISSE book – another mark of the event's success – and with about 50 carefully edited papers it bears witness to the quality of the conference.

An international programme committee is responsible for the selection of the conference contributions and the composition of the programme:
- **Ronny Bjones,** Microsoft (Belgium)
- **Alfred Büllesbach,** Daimler Chrysler (Germany)
- **Lucas Cardholm,** Ernst&Young (Sweden)
- **Roger Dean,** eema (UK)
- **Marijke De Soete,** Security4Biz (Belgium)
- **Jos Dumortier,** KU Leuven (Belgium)
- **Walter Fumy,** Siemens (Germany)
- **Boaz Gelbord,** ENISA (Greece)
- **David Goodman,** eema (UK)
- **Michael Hange,** Federal Office for Information Security (Germany)
- **John Hermans,** KPMG (Netherlands)
- **Jeremy Hilton,** Cardiff University (UK)
- **Alison James,** eema (UK)
- **Frank Jorissen,** SafeBoot (Belgium)
- **Matt Landrock,** Cryptomathic (Denmark)
- **Tim Mertens,** ENISA (Greece)
- **Andreas Mitrakas,** ENISA (Greece)
- **David Naccache,** ENS (France)
- **Sachar Paulus,** SAP (Germany)

- **Daniele Perucchini,** Fondazione Ugo Bordoni (Italy)
- **Attila Péterfalvi,** Parliamentary Commissioner for Data Protection and Freedom of Information (Hungary)
- **Norbert Pohlmann,** University of Applied Sciences Gelsenkirchen (Germany)
- **Bart Preneel,** KU Leuven (Belgium)
- **Helmut Reimer,** TeleTrusT (Germany)
- **Paolo Rossini,** Telsy Italia (Italy)
- **Wolfgang Schneider,** Fraunhofer SIT (Germany)
- **Robert Temple,** BT (UK)

The editors have endeavoured to allocate the contributions in these proceedings – which differ from the structure of the conference programme – to topic areas which cover the interests of the readers.

Sachar Paulus   *Norbert Pohlmann*   *Helmut Reimer*

eema (www.eema.org):	TeleTrusT (www.teletrust.de):
Established in 1987, eema is an independent association of IT professionals, businesses and governments providing business and technical networking opportunities at both local and regional levels in the broad areas associated with digital identity and its applications, such as security. Our mission is to stimulate the growth and effectiveness of our members' business in these areas through increased market awareness, cooperation and opportunity creation.	In the 16 years of its existence TeleTrusT has evolved into a competence network for applied Cryptography and Biometrics with over 90 institutional members.
	The TeleTrusT working groups produce results which create an advantageous framework for trustworthy solutions of daily business processes as well as contributing to their acceptance.
We aim to bring over 1,500 member representatives together in a neutral environment for education and networking puposes. We enable members to share experiences and best practice by holding meetings and conferences, by facilitating working groups who produce reports on topical subjects, and by helping members to connect with the right person to help them solve business issues or develop beneficial business relationships. All work produced by members is available free to other members, and previous papers include: Towards Understanding Identity, Role Based Access Control – a Users Guide, Secure e-mail within a Corporate Environment and Secure e-mail between Organisations.	TeleTrusT brings together the interests of users and vendors. Thus vendors can satisfy the users' demands more effectively with marketable products and services, in which scalable security mechanisms are implemented.
	TeleTrusT seeks and cultivates the cooperation with other organisations with similar objectives – in Germany and internationally. Thus ISSE has been organised in cooperation with EEMA, ENISA and ISCOM in Rome this year.
	For further information contact: sophie.hellmann@teletrust.de
For more information contact: alison.james@eema.org.	

ISCOM:
On the Way for ICT Security in Italy

The Istituto Superiore delle Comunicazioni e delle Tecnologie dell'Informazione (ISCOM) was established in 1907 as a technical-scientific department belonging to the Italian Communication Ministry. Considering its role as a nonpartisan public institution, the Institute's value added in terms of reliability and expertise is the aspect which characterizes the technical support and consultancy services it provides to businesses and entities in the TLC sector. The role of ISCOM in providing services to ICT Companies, government agencies and users is manifold, spanning from experimental and research activities to specialized training and education in the TLC field.

One of ISCOM's main missions is its proactive role in national and international law-making activities, in order to ensure greater transparency and better access to services for users, manufacturers and TLC network administrators alike.

As far as research is concerned, ISCOM is essentially focused on developing and improving TLC and IT related services. Hence, activities involve almost all areas in these fields, from telephony to television, to signal processing and treatment, from network architecture to service implementation.

ISCOM runs the Post-Graduate Specialization School in TLC (which began its activity in 1923), which provides higher education in electronic communication and information technologies; it also provides technical training and updating courses on electronic communications and information technologies, security, multimedia applications, and Quality of Service to both Ministry and government staff in general, to enhance their technical know-how and skills.

ISCOM works with several Certification Bodies to verify and control Corporate Quality System compliance with UNI EN ISO 9000 standards, is involved in monitoring Accredited Laboratory compliance with UNI CEI EN ISO/IEC 17025 rules and is a Notified Body for activities envisaged by Legislative Decree n. 269 of May 9, 2001. It is also a Notified Body under the EU Directive on radio equipment and telecommunications terminal equipment as well as a Competent Body and Notified Body on electromagnetic compatibility. In 2002, the Institute became the International Certification Body for the TETRA MoU.

Among all the numerous ISCOM fields of activity, ICT security is getting an increasing relevance. Here, ISCOM plays a leading role in various contexts, some of which are briefly summarized below:

- Due to his widely recognized non-partisan role, a government decree dated october 30, 2003 appointed ISCOM the Certification Body within the Italian certification scheme for commercial security systems and products. The Certification Body supervises all the activities carried out within the certification scheme, which operates according to the international evaluation criteria ITSEC and Common Criteria.

- ISCOM is an Evaluation Center (Ce.Va.) for ICT systems and products dealing with classified data. The center, the only one belonging to the Italian Public Administration which has been accredited by the Autorità Nazionale per la Sicurezza (ANS), carries out evaluation activities according to ITSEC and Common Criteria.

- ISCOM runs the Training Center on ICT Security for Public Administration personnel. The Training Center provides training and raises awareness amongst government employees on ICT security, through the development of a centralized and coordinated Training and Awareness-Raising Plan aimed at disseminating security principles and methodologies throughout the Administration.

- The Institute acts as promoter and leader of several initiatives aimed at raising the national level of ICT security, by gathering the expertise of the major subjects operating in the ICT field. Among these initiatives we can recall the redaction of three guidelines, in English and Italian, on *"The quality of service in ICT networks"*, *"Risk analysis and protection strategies for network security"* and *"Network security in critical infrastructures"*, carried out with the contribution of experts from institutions and industry. Six more guidelines are being released; these will be focused on deepenings on risk analysis, on the outsourcing of security services, on QoS in UMTS, on QoS in broadband networks, on local emergency handling and on security certification. Moreover, ISCOM has promoted the creation of ISAC on network security, currently involving all the major Italian network operating companies.

ISCOM hosting of ISSE 2006 is a further prove of our desire to play a role in fostering the European information security debate. We look forward to a great opportunity for the exchange of ideas and experiences.

Luisa Franchina,

PhD, General Director of Istituto Superiore delle Comunicazioni
E delle Tecnologie dell'Informazione

RFID
e-ID Cards
Trusted Computing
Interoperability

Radio Frequency Identification (RFID) and Data Protection Legal Issues[*]

Zoi Talidou

Hellenic Data Protection Authority
Legal Auditor
Kifisias 1-3, Athens
ztalidou@dpa.gr

Abstract

Radio Frequency Identification (RFID) Technology uses radio waves to identify automatically, wire-lessly, contact less and without visibility objects which, or people who have an RFID tag attached. It is being used in many sectors but raises data-protection concerns. The reasons for that are the world-wide unique identifier, the possibility of unnoticed remote reading, and the profiling through sporadic surveillance. For these reasons RFID-technology introduces new legal issues that have to be discussed: what is personal data, who is responsible for the data processing, whether the data-transmission is tele-communication, whether it presents a new way of direct marketing or if it constitutes an automatic decision.

In the early 1970s fears about loss of privacy and worries concerning data protection were focused on large, centrally held data-bases containing files about named or numbered individuals processed by huge computers situated in big rooms. As the Web, its attendant search engines and the inter-link abil-ity of many databases in various networks have developed, the concept of "files" became trivial. Now the emerging RFID technology contributes to the realisation of the Ambient Intelligence Environment, where intelligent objects communicate with each other by exchanging information and taking deci-sions. That introduces us to the next step of the "Internet of the things". Technology innovation and the impact of its usage stress a rethinking and re-examining of the traditional legal principles and legal instruments in the field of data protection.

1 What RFIDs are all about

Radio Frequency Identification (RFID) Technology belongs to the broad category of auto-matic identification technologies[1] and uses radio waves to automatically identify wirelessly, contact less and without visibility[2] objects which, or people who have an RFID tag attached. It consists of two parts: **a tag** that contains an identification number and **a reader** who works as a scanner. This number usually acts as an input to further data processing[3]. A typical RFID tag consists of a small integrated circuit attached to a radio antenna, capable of transmitting a unique serial number. The tag can easily be embedded onto or into (textile-) products, onto their packages or even direct implanted beneath human's skin. RFID tags can be active, semi-

---

[*] This paper is based on a report conducted for LEGAL-IST

[1] What is RFID?, RFID Journal, available at: http://www.rfidjournal.com/article/articleprint/1339/-1/129/

[2] See http://en.wikipedia.org/wiki/Rfid.

[3] *Hennig, Ladkin, Sieker,* Privacy Enhancing Technology Concepts for RFID Technology Scrutinised, p.1.

active or passive. *Passive Tags* do not have a power source; they simply reflect back energy coming from the reader antenna[4]. *Active RFID* tags on the other hand, have their own internal power source that allows them having longer range and larger memories than passive tags, as well as the ability to store additional information sent by the transceiver. A typical **reader** is a device that has one or more antennas that emit radio waves and receive signals back from the tag. This RFID reader is a data-collection instrument, and a transmitter or broadcaster of information, as it sends its data through the information network. The databases connected to these networks hold, use and disclose the gathered information.

The innovation of RFID tags is that they provide for unique identification of each tagged unit whereas bar codes are identical for every unit of the same product[5]. Prices of RFID are dropping. Many postulate that they will be the essential drivers of ubiquitous computing and will introduce the so-called "Internet of the things".

2 Use of RFID technology

2.1 Retail/Consumer Goods Sector

Companies across the retail and consumer packaged goods supply chains have been among the early adopters of RFID and Electronic Product Code (EPC) technologies. The use of this new technology is connected to the EPC Discovery Service, an aggregate database of tag "sightings" collected from independent readers. Anyone with access EPC Discovery can monitor or track the movement of a particular RFID-tagged item. The retail industry is using passive tags that implement no protection against unauthorised access to the information held. Hence the EPC can be read out directly by any RFID-reader from a six to eight meters distance[6].

2.2 Manufacturing Sector

RFID technology can increase productivity and reduce costs by enabling to track inventory, reusable containers, work in process and finished products: they can manage parts inventory with active RFID, improve the tracking of work in process, reduce parts defects, and increase factory productivity by using active RFID tags. In some cases, RFIDs aim in such seemingly simple tasks as ensuring that the right label goes on a product or that a box contains everything it should. In other cases, RFID is put through more complex uses as tracking an item through every workstation and recording every tool that performed an operation on it. This information can be used to quickly identify potential problems and correct them before they show up in the product. RFID can furthermore save companies a great amount of money spent on replacing lost tools, that can be easily traced through the tags.

---

[4] The basic of RFID Technology, RFID Journal, available at: http://www.rfidjournal.com/article/articleprint/1337/-1/129/

[5] See *International Conference of Data Protection & Privacy Commissioners,* Resolution on Radio-Frequency Identification, (Nov. 20, 2003) p. 2, available at: http://www.privacyconference2003org/resolutions/res5.DOC.

[6] Auto-ID Centre (2003): Technical report 860MHz-930MHz Class I Radio Frequency Identification Tag Radio Frequency & Logical Communication Interface Specification Candidate Recommendation, Version 1.0.1., MIT, USA, available at: http://interval.hu-berlin.de/downloads/rfid/chipklassen/4_candidate_recommendation_1_0_1.pdf

2.3 Recycling & waste management

The EPC tags may be used to automatically sort recyclable material and will also identify manufacturer, type and weight of disposable material (the manufacturer of a product that will eventually constitute hazardous waste may ultimate have to pay for its safe disposal).

2.4 Transportation/Logistics Sector

Transportation and logistic companies are already tagging product for their customers. Some of them are still examining how they can benefit internally, by improving the utilization of containers and chassis with RFID tracking. Logistics hubs can benefit from a real-time locating system, and they can improve the visibility of cargo in transit and cargo security with electronic seals.

2.5 Libraries

Libraries began using RFID systems to replace their electro-magnetic and bar code systems in the late 1990s. RFID technology in libraries promises to relieve repetitive strain injury, speed patron self-checkout, make possible comprehensive inventory and automated sorting, retrieve hidden items and support security. Many libraries (more than 130 in North America and the Stadtbibliothek of the city Wien[7]) are starting to tag every item in their collections with RFID tags. But current library RFID tags do not prevent unauthorised reading of tag data[8].

2.6 Tracking of animals (dogs, cows and sheep)

Pets can be implanted with small chips so that they may be returned to their owners if lost. They can also be used to satisfy the need to track herds and to be able to recognize when an animal is missing and, if the animal has died, locate its body[9]. Beside that, request on safe handling with animals as a result of repeated outbreaks of epidemics is pointing out electronic animal tracking through RFID as a significant solution. Following successful animal tracking trials[10], the European Council of Ministers (ECM) has adopted a law[11] throughout Europe requiring the individual electronic tagging of sheep and goats using RFID technology. Besides RFID tags are used for to identify big pets, such as dogs over 20 kilograms. Several laws at the European level make the wear of such a tag compulsory, that will have to contain at least following data: unique number for the chip, data of the pet and data of the owner of the pet.

---

[7] http://www.ekz.de/2110.html

[8] See *Molnar, Wagner,* Privacy and Security in Library RFID issues, practices and architectures, CCS'04, October 25-29 2004, Washington, DC, USA, p. 218, available at: http://www.cs.berkeley.edu/molnar/library.pdf

[9] See http://www.rfidgazette.org/asset_tracking/.

[10] See *Balch, Feldman, Wilson,* Assessment of a RFID System for Animal Tracking, The BORG Lab, Georgia Institute of Technology, Atlanta, 1.10.2004, available at: http://www.cc.gatech.edu/~storm/Feldman2004TR.pdf

[11] Council Regulation (EC) No 644/2005 of 27 April 2005 authorising a special identification system for bovine animals kept for cultural and historical purposes on approved premises as provided for in Regulation (EC) No 1760/2000 of the European Parliament and of the Council, available at: http://europa.eu.int/eur-lex/lex/LexUriServ/site/de/oj/2005/l_107/l_10720050428de00180019.pdf

2.7 Health Care Sector

Hospitals plan to deploy RFID to identify patients, call up records, reduce medical errors and improve overall productivity. A pilot project has started in July 2005 in clinical centre of Saarbrücken, where thousand of patients receive by admission a bracelet with an RFID tag on which the patient identifier is stored. Physicians and nurses may access the patient identifier and data stored on a database through a wireless network. The project is based on a solution already deployed in Jacobi Medical Centre, New York[12].

2.8 Tracking of people (schools, prisons, VIP clubs)

A group of children in Yokohama City in Japan wears active tags to keep them safe on their way to and from school[13]. Each child participating to the programme wears a bracelet with a RFID tag. Existing Wi-Fi access points used by the city for wireless Internet access work as RFID readers that receive signals send by the tags. The system can also be set up to notify parents or guardians automatically via e-mail on a cell phone or PC if a child passes a specific Wi-Fi access point on the way to or from the school. The VIP Baja Beach Club in Barcelona offers it's VIP clients the opportunity to have a syringe-injected RFID microchip implanted in their upper arms: this chip gives them special access to VIP lounges, but also acts as a debit account, from which they can pay for drinks[14]. A new tracking system has been developed which provides real-time identification and tracking of inmates and officers[15]. It handles common prison complexities such as a multi-floor, mixed indoor/outdoor environment, as well as the need for cell-level accuracy. The tag immediately detects any attempt to remove or tamper with it. The Los Angeles County jail system has reportedly engaged in a pilot project to use RFID technology to track inmates at the Pitchess Detention Centre in Castaic[16].

2.9 Passports and Ids

In May 2004 the International Civil Aviation Organisation (ICAO) adopted specifications for machine readable travel documents (MRTD) which demands for digital storage of the pass photo[17]. In compliance with the recommendations of the ICAO the Council of the European Union adopted on 13/12/2004 a regulation[18] mandating the inclusion of both facial image and fingerprints in future passports and travel documents issued by EU Member States. The new regulation aims at better protecting EU passports against falsification, at enabling better identification of passport holders and at harmonising security standard features used in the production of passports and travel documents issued by Member States[19]. As a result in November 2005 Germany introduced the first e-passport[20], equipped with biometric data stored on a

---

[12] Computer mit Augen und Ohren, at: Frankfurter Allgemeine Zeitung, 14.01.2006, p. 18.

[13] http://www.rfidjournal.com/article/articleprint/2050/-1/1/

[14] See http://news.bbc.co.uk/2/hi/technology/3697940.stm; http://www.heise.de/newsticker/meldung/53789

[15] See http://www.technologynewsdaily.com/node/1900.

[16] See http://www.socaltech.com/fullstory/0001952.html.

[17] Available at: http://www.icao.int/cgi/goto_m.pl?/icao/en/strategic_objectives.htm.

[18] Council Regulation 2252/2004 on standards for security features and biometrics in passports and travel documents issued by Member States, OJ L 385, available at: http://europa.eu.int/eur-lex/lex/LexUriServ /site/en/oj/2004/l_385/l_38520041229en00010006.pdf

[19] See e-government of the European Union news available at: http://europa.eu.int/idabc/en/document/3669/330.

[20] http://www.epass.de/

RFID tag. In Italy the Foreign Affairs Ministry issued on 17th January 2006 a decree concerning the introduction of a new electronic passport that will include biometric data contained in RFID chips[21]. The European Central Bank was moving forward with plans to embed RFID tags as thin as a human hair into the fibres of Euro bank notes by 2005[22]. Hitachi Ltd. has developed a RFID chip that requires no external antenna and makes possible the embedding of tracking and identification chips in bank notes, tickets and other paper products[23]. But now it is still uncertain whether they will force this plan or not because, according to new statements, RFID technology is not safe enough to combat monetary counterfeit[24].

2.10 Transportation: e-pass, e-plate, e-ticket

Many countries, including Greece, have developed RFID-based Electronic Toll Collection systems for a variety of highways and bridges. As a vehicle equipped with a RFID transponder enters a toll plaza equipped to accept RFID toll collection the radio frequency emitted by the electronic reader will activate the transponder. The transponder then sends out account or identification information pertaining to the vehicle. The information is received by the reader and through the antenna sent to the host computer system. The toll is then deducted from the account associated to that vehicle and the driver is signaled to proceed. The tags can be read at a speed of 100 miles per hour. Their use is simplifying the toll-collection procedure and so cutting traffic jams and the resulting levels of smog at toll booths. It is definitely clear, that these systems, once they are not designed to function anonymously, create a huge database recording the precise time and location of every toll crossing by every tagged car. For instance, the Greek "Taxes-Code for Books" poses the obligation of collecting and retaining for 6 years following data: name, residence, taxation-number, taxation authority, date of entrance, hour and exact point of entrance of the highway/bridge user. The purpose of this data processing is limited to the performance of the contract between the toll collectors and their subscribers. Nevertheless of great importance is to establish policies that will prevent toll-crossing information from being used for purposes unrelated to traffic management. So that ETC databases are not routinely used by law enforcement agencies to track the movement of suspect cars and by both divorce lawyers and labor lawyers to track the movements of people under investigation.

The British government is preparing to test new high-tech license plates containing microchips capable of transmitting unique vehicle identification numbers and other data to readers more than 300 feet away. United States are initiating their own tests of the plates, which incorporate radio frequency identification to make vehicles trackable. Greece is in the very beginning of creating working groups with representatives of both governmental and private sector/university actors for planning their developement and eventually their deployment.

---

[21] See www.statewatch.org/news/2006/feb/08italy-biometric-passports.htm. Very critical: *Juels / Molnar / Wagner*, Security and Privacy Issues in E-Passports, IEE SecureComm 2005, available at: www.cs.berkeley.edu /~dmolnar/papers/papers.html; *Rieback, Crispo, Tanenbaum*, Is your cat infected with a computer virus?, 2006, available at: www.rfidvirus.org/papers/percom.06.pdf; *Schulzki / Haddouti*, Neue Reisepässe: Mit Sicherheit teuer, available at: http://www.sicherheit-heute.de/index.php?cccpage=Verkehr

[22] See *Yoshida*, Euro Bank Notes to Embed RFID Chips by 2005, EETimes, 19.12.2001, available at: http://www.eetimes.com/story/OEG20011219S0016

[23] See http://www.computerworld.com/mobiletopics/mobile/story/0,10801,84543,00.html.

[24] See http://www.zeit.de/zeit-wissen/2006/01/Falschgeld.xml.

The public transportation network of big cities like London, Helsinki, Peking are already using e-ticket. We are talking about a chip-card, used as a rechargable ticket, which will permit the passangers of easier and faster entrance of the transportation means and the public transport companies to avoid fare dodger and to use easier and faster the system of dynamic prices.

3 Legal Implications

From the applications of RFID technology, as described above, following categories of RFID-tags arrear: We have the tags that contain only an item number. Their use is in giving information for the identification of an item. Through the linking of the RFID tag number with a products database one can find out what kind of item this is. Supposing the item information is linked to the purchaser during the payment procedure and further stored to a customers' database one may create customers' purchase profiles. Supposing the item information can be associated to a person either because this person is currently visible or this person is identifiable by other means, for instance with its RFID identification card (i.e. passport) or employee's card, this all may lead to a person's identification for various purposes (customers' profiling, surveillance of workers at workplace). The second category concerns tags that contain an identification number which reveals the identity of a person after the matching of the information contained on the tag with a backend data-base, which holds the information concerning the identity of the person. However the stronger relation to a person is to be found in the RFID tags of the third category. On these tags personal data are directly stored. They are normally active tags and contain information like name, age, nationality and so on. According to that following legal implications may arise.

3.1 Infringement of the right to privacy and data protection

RFIDs tag may be related to personal information. Data protection and the information self-determination is a precious fundamental right that should be protected from the technical development, if this proceeds without taking into account the conformity to main constitutional values and rights. It should be assured that the right to privacy and to data protection will not turn into a caprice of the individual but will still remain an obligation of the democratic society.

3.1.1 Identification and profiling of a person

RFID tags consist of a unique identification number. The use of the tag is to enable identifying and tracking every single item. Everyone who carries at least one so-tagged item is possible to get allocated and tracked. RFID tags function as a unique identifier and the growing interoperability of the system makes allocating and tracking possible worldwide. Beyond that, the link-ability of RFID technology to other databases and their supersets-archives can facilitate the identification process. RFID information can be used independent from information of other sources. But the facileness of the combination of both turns it into a main threat to privacy. As we saw in the application of RFID technology in the retail sector, once tagged objects are owned by persons, it is possible to be related to them. The ability of tracking objects might become an ability to track individuals. Using RFID-Technology retailers might track customers within their shops in order to create profiles of movement which can be used to improve marketing strategies. One should mention that this is possible only by connecting the information obtained by the tagged object that individuals carry with them and their customer or credit cards that they submit at the purchase point. Only in that matter the data stored on the EPC tag relates to the person carrying it. In shopping malls several shops might interlink tracks and analyse the popularity of different parts of the centres by analysing the favourite shopping routes of customers that have already been identified by one of the shops in the mall. The advantage of it is a better management and promotion policy to increase consumption.

3.1.2 Unnoticed remote reading without line-of-sight

RFID tags can be read without line-of-sight and without overt evidence that they are being read. In addition their small size and their ability of working without any energy supply make them appropriate to be installed hidden. The problem is that radio waves allow data to be processed over a given distance without any need for a direct line-of-sight link with the chip and without the data subject having to take an active part in the process. In other words, data processing can take place without the knowledge of the data subject. Any data on RFID transponders that have not been destroyed or deleted can be read by visible or even invisible readers. The unnoticed remote reading may indeed be used for various purposes without the knowledge of the person in question, for instance for unnoticed surveillance of workers, unnoticed profiling of one's consuming preferences etc.

3.1.3 Use of RFID technology for law enforcement purposes

The state might have an interest on making use of personal data obtained through RFID applications for law enforcement purposes. Here all the applications mentioned above can be used by the Law Enforcement Authorities, under the conditions that every national legislation allow this, for the puropses of prevention, investigation and prosecution of criminal offences. We could imagine the interest of these authorities for the exact identification of the owner of a consumer good related to a criminal offence, or the lists of the movement of cars passing through the toll-controls, the tracking of people carrying RFID enabled IDs or passports, or even RFID implanted tags. Even the use of RFID tags in banknotes can be highly problematic in this perspective. Through RFIDs it will be possible to determine which banknotes were withdrawn by whom from which automatic teller machine, or where those banknotes were then used to buy certain products or services.

3.2 Infringement of the right to personality

RFID technology will contribute to the realisation of the Ubiquitous Computing: in a world of ubiquitous services the interaction of humans with computers should step behind and help us enter a digital world without realising it. The citizens must be fully aware of the innovation and of the data-processing procedures that enable this phenomenon but at the same time concerns them instantaneous[25]. Within a densely populated world of smart and intelligent but invisible communication and computation devices, no single part of our lives will per default be able to seclude itself from digitalisation[26]. Nevertheless one should always be able to retrace the data-processing procedures and have the right to switch onto an "of-line" world. If there is no possibility to do so, this will affect the free expression of the personality of a human being.

---

[25] See *Langheinrich*, Die Privatsphäre im Ubiquitous Computing - Datenschutzaspekte der RFID-Technologie, available at: http://www.vs.inf.ethz.ch/publ/papers/langhein2004rfid.pdf

[26] *Langheinrich*, Privacy by Design-Principles of Privacy-Aware Ubiquitous Computing, p. 7 available at: http://www.vs.inf.ethz.ch/publ/papers/privacy-principles.pdf

3.3   Infringement of the right to human dignity

RFID systems introduce for the first time a new dimension of availability of trustworthy data about objects and about the movement of these objects in real time. They improve the congruence between real and virtual life[27]. Consequently one could say that we enter a new era where the co-existence of two cognitive dimensions takes place while there is no assurance that the new technological aspects that lead us over are faultless. Beside the sociological aspect of this observation, there is a legal impact too: complete reliance on technical systems and on-going dependency on them can turn into discrimination of individuals and breach of their constitutional rights. Here one could think of an obligation to carry RFID because there is no other way of acting in a future society. For instance we could imagine of future toll-controll systems using only RFID technology, where the right of travelling anonymous simply does not exist. The nature of RFID technology, identifying by sending information will first affect the right to privacy and to data protection of the individuals. However, the range of use of the new technology and the intensity of its application could contribute to the establishment of an environment, which does not respect basic values of a democratic society and fundamental constitutional rights. In this regard, the Japanese program for the children (see sec. 3.1.8) might breach children's right to privacy and dignity by treating them like cattle or a piece of inventory and by familiarizing them with an environment and a world of absolute surveillance.

3.4   Unfair competition

The interoperability of RFID systems is to be evaluated positively from a business perspective: for a sustainable model, a retailer should avoid having to implement several different tag readers in order to scan tags produced by various manufacturers. Inexpensive tags simply do not have the memory to store lists of readers that can authenticate themselves to the tag, in order to avoid unwanted reading of tags; and they don't have the power to call out to an enterprise server to get this information from a database[28]. So they are exposed to unauthorised reading by competitors, for instance if a rival enters the shop of a competitor and "scans" by a mobile reader its inventory. In this respect concerns appear regarding unfair competition practices.

3.5   Labour law

The deployment of RFID technology for the improvement of manufacturing, the supply and the logistics chain or for the end-customer service in the retail sector may raise implications for the employees. Besides, the use of the same RFID tags for other purposes, such as the surveillance of employees which is already mentioned above, this technology may affect the health of employees in terms of possible radiation emitted during the data communication between tag and reader. It might also lead to cutting personnel as a result of rationalisation through the use of the technology. Such issues shall be treated as any other similar technology which is introduced at the workplace. For instance, according to national legislation in question prior approval by the workers' council might be necessary for the deployment of RFID

---

[27] See *German Federal Authority for Information Systems Security* (Bundesamt für Sicherheit in der Informationstechnik), Security Aspects and Prospective Applications of RFID Systems, 2005, p. 85, available at: http://www.bsi.bund.de/fachthem/rfid/RIKCHA_englisch.pdf

[28] For more details concerning authentication in the RFID technology see *Marlena Erdos,* RFID and authenticity of goods, p. 137, in: *Simson Garfinke /, Beth, Rosenberg,* RFID Applications, Security and Privacy, 2006

technology[29]. Moreover, as for any other technology deployed within the workplace, the employer has a duty to monitor any negative effects to employees' health and take the appropriate counter-measures.

4 Existing and proposed Legislation

Responding to worried constituents state legislators across the USA have already proposed new legislation that would limit the use of RFID technologies in businesses, schools, governments and other applications. This initial response varies widely from state to state: Utah recently reviewed its laws on unauthorised access to networks and added wireless networks as it previously only addressed wire line networks: it clarifies that computer crimes laws apply to wireless networks. Virginia's law authorises research relating to methods of electronic toll collection. Also provides that data generated by automated electronic toll-collection systems on use of toll facilities can only be disclosed when so required by order of a court. Wyoming authorises telepharmacies to use automated inventory control including radio frequency tags. In many other states there exist pending legislature on RFID technology, which sometimes just seek to require only labelling and notice that RFID is in use, while in other cases like the California's approach would most tightly regulate the technology itself, including prohibitions of certain applications and technology-specific security requirements[30].

At the European level the legislator did not take any initiative yet. Currently the subgroup "RFID and the interpretation of the term personal data" of the Article 29 Data Protection Working Party aims to specify and point out the legal implication of this new technology on the data protection rights of European citizens.

At national level worthy to mention is Paragraph 6c of the German Federal Data Protection Law (BDSG is the German abbreviation), which applies to mobile data-storing and data processing devices. Recently new interpretations[31] emerge, which consider RFID tags as such a mobile device and consequently extend the applicability of this provision to the RFID technology as well. Aim of the new provision is to make the use of these devises transparent[32]: it designs exhaustively both, the obligation of the controllers to give information to the data subjects and the right of access of the latter to the data concerned. It also requires that the communication processing, which takes place on the mobile devices, should be clearly recognisable for the data subject.

5 Open Legal Issues

5.1 Do RFID tags contain personal data

At a first glance, RFID products IDs look to be anonymous. But this data becomes person-related as soon as someone engages this product: it gets into contact with a customer willing

---

[29] The German Kaufhof AG has prior agreed with the employee's Council the exact purposes of RFID tags within its stores and its obligations regarding employees' health safety and a temporary prohibition of personnel reduction as a result of the use of RFID technology: RFID in Pilotphase – Gesamtvereinbarung bei der Kaufhof Warenhaus AG, in: RDV 2005, pp. 185

[30] US privacy legislature related to RFID available at: http://www.ncsl.org/programs/lis/privacy/rfid05.htm.

[31] See *Claus Mauricio Lahner,* Anwendung des § 6 c BDSG auf RFID, available at DuD 2004, p. 723.

[32] See *Bizer* in *Spiros Simitis,* BDSG-Kommentar, 2003, § 6 c, p. 599.

to buy it. This is a new person-relatable quality: the role of the tag is to bring the product and the consumer to a retraceable contact and to maintain it. The Data Protection Directive 95/46/EC sets out the general principles for the processing of personal data. In article 2 (a) defines the term "personal data" however in a very broad manner: "*any information relating to any identified or identifiable person*". This also means that a person can be identified indirectly by reference to an identification number such as the one of RFID tag[33]. From the moment a person can make a link between the "anonymous RFID tag" and a person, even indirectly, Directive 95/46/EC is applicable. The data subject can be identified at an associative level because of the possibility of identifying her/him without difficulty due to the large mass of information surrounding her/him or stored about her/him. The perception of personal data has to be re-analysed in regard to specific characteristics of the RFID technology[34].

5.2 Applicability of Directive 2002/58/EC

When the RFID applications are not in use just for the organizational needs of a company but are settled in places that can be approached easily from everybody so that the data processing concerns the citizens and so touches their rights one should examine whether the transmission of data through radio frequencies can be considered as *telecommunication*: In this case the question is whether Directive 2002/58[35] on privacy and electronic communications is applicable. The main points that are crucial for the discussion of the applicability of the Directive are following:

- article 5 point 3 concerning the *hidden identifiers* such as cookies for Internet
- article 9 concerning the *location data*
- article 13 concerning the *direct marketing*

One should take into account that according Article 3 of 58/2002 EC the provisions of the Directive apply only to the processing of personal data in connection with the provisions of *publicly available electronic communications services in public communications networks*. Either we analyze these terms very broadly so that an RFID system can be considered as such a public electronic communication network or we appeal to similar provisions taken on board of the Directive 95/46 EC. In Article 17 a supplementary provision should be added to provide for the adequate safeguards that contain all the three provisions of the E-privacy Directive mentioned above.

Direct marketing with item-level tagging: It is to be settled down in which cases and under which conditions RFID technology can be used for the purposes of direct marketing (e.g. prior consent, opportunity to object of Art. 13 Directive 2002/58), and to appoint the safeguards and the appropriate measures this will be prohibited.

Location data: According to Art. 2 (c) Directive 2002/58 "location data" means any data processed in an electronic communications network, indicating the geographic position of the terminal equipment of a user of a publicly available electronic communications services. The

---

[33] See *Keuleers, Ewout,* Reconciling RFID technology with data protection principles, Droit Nouvelles Technologies, April 2005, p. 2.

[34] *Article 29 Data Protection Working Party,* Working document on data protection issues related to RFID technology, WP 105, January 19, 2005, available at: http://europa.eu.int/comm/justice_home/fsj/privacy/docs/wpdocs/2005wp105_en.pdf

[35] OJ 2002 L 201/37.

data getting processed by RFID tags are location data, considering the fact that the readers that retrieve them are locally suited in a certain location in the network. That means that people's movements, and potentially their associations, can be tracked via a tag associated with them just as the widest application of RFID technology is to track items and consequently individuals. Art. 9 Directive 2002/58 though stresses the need to inform the data subject of the type of location data which will be processed, of the purposes and the duration of the processing and whether data will be transmitted to third parties, so that they give to it.

5.3 Prior-checking

One should examine whether according to Article 20 of the Directive 95/46 specific operations performed with RFID technology are subjects to prior checking because they present specific risks and whether this can be replaced by the process of *Privacy Impact Assessment (PIA)*. The latter can become an integral part of business process and can be made from the legislation of the Member States to a mandatory process.

6 Guidelines

6.1 Legal Guidelines to the deployers of RFID technology

Data Protection Legislation in generally authorises the processing of personal data if data subjects consent to their data being processed, unless justified by a superior public or private interest or if there is a legal basis for the data to be processed. Consent is only valid if the purpose, place and manner of the data processing have been specified. The principle of good faith presupposes that data subjects are informed in a transparent manner.

Notice and consent – The right to know whether a product contains an EPC RFID tag, and whether an RFID reader is being used in a public place. Participation in an RFID application should be strictly voluntary. Collection of data under informed consent means covert capture of information should not be permitted. Informed consent is recognised as the primary tool available to individuals to protect their privacy from technological invasion.

Choice – The right to have the RFID tag in a purchased product deactivated without cost. Furthermore this means the right to RFID alternatives if the citizens decide to opt-out or "kill" the RFID tags and the right not to be discriminated by deny of use of this technology. We will have to ensure that for instance the option to return a product from which the RFID tag was removed or to travel on a particular road without using the RFID toll-system will still remain

Data Quality Principle – Stipulates that personal data should be relevant to the purposes for which they are to be used and should be accurate, complete and up-to-date.

Purpose Limitation Principle – The purposes for which personal data are collected should be specified not later than at the time of data collection and the subsequent use limited to the fulfilment of those purposes. Personal data should not be disclosed, made available or otherwise used for purposes other than those specified under the preceding purpose specification principle except with consent or by legal authority.

Security Safeguards– Personal data should be protected by reasonable security safeguards against such risks as loss or unauthorised access to personal data, destruction, use, modification or disclosure.

Right of access – An individual should have the right to ascertain or confirm whether a data controller has data relating to him or her and to challenge that data.

6.2 Technical recommendations

Apart from these fundamental data-protection-principles that should be taken into account and should be embedded in a future RFID legislation[36], a provision should be also established that facilitates the proper data-security measure based on the one of the technical solutions below.

Kill-Order Solution: The most common solution to the RFID privacy problem is to disable the tag at the point of sail by sending a "kill" command, the so called kill solution. Even though deactivated tags cannot be read anymore, this solution has several technical and economic drawbacks: This cannot be implemented to all tag functions, for instance to library book tags or toll road subscriptions. Deactivation of the tag at the point of sale ensures the privacy of the consumer (if the tag is properly killed) but it prevents natural post-purchase services such as warranty, access to product support, advanced recycling and waste management, advanced home applications, and all the other applications in the two last phases of the RFID-tag life cycle.

The blocker tag: It is a cheap passive RFID device that can simulate many ordinary RFID tags simultaneously. When carried by a consumer, a blocker tag thus blocks RFID readers. It can do so universally by simulating all possible RFID tags. Or a blocker tag can block selectively by simulating only selected subsets of ID codes, such as those by a particular manufacturer, or those in a designated "privacy zone"[37].

Encryption-Solution: Encryption of the data being transmitted is one method of protecting against anyone eavesdropping on communication via the air interface. It is a way of insuring that information namely personal data carried in an RFID tag will not be read by an unauthorised reader. The use of encryption can be used on tags on books in libraries but also in the retail supply chain for protecting retailers from potential surveillance by other rivals[38]. One should certainly take into account that not all of the tags support strong cryptographic procedures which exclude them from being strong protected from unauthorised retrieving of data. For the moment even specialists[39] insist on storing content data in a backend database and just a unique number on the tag that will be associated to the database as the most effective way of avoiding eavesdropping.

Privacy Bit (proposal by RSA security): it represents a simple and cost-effective way of mitigating the problems of RFID privacy while preserving the consumer benefits of RFID. A privacy bit is a single logical bit resident in the memory of an RFID tag. It indicates the privacy properties of the tag. A tag's privacy bit might be *off*, indicating that the tag is freely subject to scanning, or it may be *on*, indicating that the tag's information cannot be scanned. The operation of changing the privacy bit should naturally require authorization via an RFID-tag-specific PIN. The RFID readers will be able to scan the tags either private or public: if the privacy-bit is on, only private scanning will be permitted, while when it is off both. This assure that the consumers will still enjoy the wide range of innovative end-user applications in the areas of home automation and ambient intelligence environments through controlled ac-

---

[36] See as a reference the proposal of an "RFID Bill of rights" available at: http://www.leginfo.ca.gov/cgi-bin/postquery.

[37] See *Juels, Rivest, Szydlo,* The Blocker Tag: Selective blocking of RFID tags for consumer privacy, p. 1.

[38] See *Jonathan Collins*, Tag Encryption for Libraries, available at: http://www.rfidjournal.com/article /articleprint/1027/-1/1.

[39] See Security aspects and prospective applications of RFID systems, BSI, p. 46, available at: http://www.bsi.de/fachthem/rfid/RIKCHA_englisch_Layout.pdf.

tivity of the tags after they pass the point of sail, without surrendering their privacy rights. And the crucial point for data protection is that the control of their data will be in their hands.

7 Conclusions – Recommendations

First conceived in 1948, Radio Frequency Identification has taken many years for the technology to mature to the point where it is sufficient affordable and reliable for widespread use[40]. The use of RFID technology for different purposes in increasingly more sectors and in various applications of everyday life may benefit business, individuals and public services. With increasing use comes increasing concern on privacy and security. Clearly there is considerable work to be undertaken before RFID becomes as pervasive as bar codes. Two instruments could be put in force in order to work uncertainties and find out appropriate results: either amend and redefine the aforementioned Articles of the two Directives, or adopt a Position Paper concerning the particularisation and implementation of already existing data protection instruments in the specific sector of RFID systems (Directives 95/46, 58/2002, "Data Retention").

References

Article 29 Data Protection Working Party, Results of the Public Consultation on Article 29 Working Document 105 on Data Protection Issues Related to RFID Technology, WP 111, 28 September, 2005, available at:
http://europa.eu.int/comm/justice_home/fsj/privacy/docs/wpdocs/2005/wp111_en.pdf

Article 29 Data Protection Working Party, Working document on data protection issues related to RFID technology, WP 105, January 19, 2005, available at:
http://europa.eu.int/comm/justice_home/fsj/privacy/docs/wpdocs/2005/wp105_en.pdf

Auto-ID Centre (2003): Technical report 860MHz-930MHz Class I Radio Frequency Identification Tag Radio Frequency & Logical Communication Interface Specification Candidate Recommendation, Version 1.0.1., MIT, USA, available at:
http://interval.hu-berlin.de/downloads/rfid/chipklassen/4_candidate_recommendation_1_0_1.pdf

Balch / Feldman / Wilson, Assessment of a RFID System for Animal Tracking, The BORG Lab, Georgia Institute of Technology, Atlanta, Oct. 1 2004, available at:
http://www.cc.gatech.edu/~storm/Feldman2004TR.pdf

Collins, Jonathan, Tag Encryption for Libraries, available at:
http://www.rfidjournal.com/article/articleprint/1027/-1/1

Council Regulation 2252/2004 on standards for security features and biometrics in passports and travel documents issued by Member States, OJ L 385, available at:
http://europa.eu.int/eur-lex/lex/LexUriServ/site/en/oj/2004/l_385/l_38520041229en00010006.pdf

Council Regulation 644/2005/EC of 27 April 2005 authorising a special identification system for bovine animals kept for cultural and historical purposes on approved premises as provided for in Regulation (EC) No 1760/2000 of the European Parliament and the Council, 2005, OJ 107, p. 18

---

[40] See *C.M. Roberts,* Radio Frequency Identification (RFID), Computer & Security, 2006, p. 18.

EPCglobal „Electronic Product Code" available at:
    www.epcglobalus.org/Network/Electronic%20Product%20Code.html

Erdos, Marlena, RFID and authenticity of goods, p. 137, in: *Simson Garfinke /, Beth, Rosenberg,* RFID Applications, Security and Privacy, 2006

Garfinkel, Simson / Rosenberg, Beth, RFID Applications, Security and Privacy, 2006, p. 533

German Association for the promotion of the public and not-public data traffic, (Verein zur Foerderung des oeffentlichen und nicht oeffentlichen Datenverkehrs e.V.) (FOEBUD), available at: http://www.foebud.org/rfid/positionspapier.pdf

German Federal Authority for Information Systems Security (Bundesamt für Sicherheit in der Informationstechnik), Security Aspects and Prospective Applications of RFID Systems, 2005, available at: http://www.bsi.bund.de/fachthem/rfid/RIKCHA_englisch.pdf

Hennig / Ladkin /, Sieker, Privacy Enhancing Technology Concepts for RFID Technology Scrutinised, p.1

International Conference of Data Protection & Privacy Commissioners, Resolution on Radio-Frequency Identification, (Nov. 20, 2003) p. 2, available at: http://www.privacyconference2003org/resolutions/res5.DOC

Italian Data Protection Authority, Smart (RFID) Tags: Safeguards applying to their use, March 2005, available at: http://www.garanteprivacy.it/garante/doc.jsp?ID=1121107

Juels / Molnar / Wagner, Security and Privacy Issues in E-Passports, IEE SecureComm 2005, available at: www.cs.berkeley.edu/~dmolnar/papers/papers.html

Juels / Rivest / Szydlo, The Blocker Tag: Selective blocking of RFID tags for consumer privacy, p. 1

Keuleers, Ewout, Reconciling RFID technology with data protection principles, Droit Nouvelles Technologies, April 2005, p. 2

Lahner, Claus Mauricio, Anwendung des par. 6c BDSG auf RFID, in: DuD 2004, p. 723

Langheinrich, Die Privatsphäre im Ubiquitous Computing - Datenschutzaspekte der RFID-Technologie, available at: http://www.vs.inf.ethz.ch/publ/papers/langhein2004rfid.pdf

Langheinrich, Privacy by Design-Principles of Privacy-Aware Ubiquitous Computing, p. 7 available at: http://www.vs.inf.ethz.ch/publ/papers/privacy-principles.pdf

Molnar / Wagner, Privacy and Security in Library RFID issues, practices and architectures, CCS'04, October 25-29 2004, Washington, DC, USA, p. 210, available at: http://www.cs.berkeley.edu/molnar/library.pdf

Rieback, Crispo, Tanenbaum, Is your cat infected with a computer virus?, 2006, available at: www.rfidvirus.org/papers/percom.06.pdf

Roberts, C.M,. Radio Frequency Identification (RFID), Computer & Security, 2006, p. 18

Schulzki / Haddouti, Neue Reisepässe: Mit Sicherheit teuer, available at: http://www.sicherheit-heute.de/index.php?cccpage=Verkehr

U.S. Food and Drug Administration, Combating counterfeit Drugs, A Report of the Food and Drug Administration, February 2004, available at: www.fda.gov/oc/initiatives/counterfeit/report02_04.html

Yoshida, Euro Bank Notes to Embed RFID Chips by 2005, EETimes, 19.12.2001, available at: http://www.eetimes.com/story/OEG20011219S0016

e-ID and Smartcards – Current Status, Hopeful Developments and Best Practices

Graham Williamson

Internet Commerce Australia
graham.williamson@inca.com.au

Abstract

Smartcards were first deployed in the early 1980s but it was not until the early 1990's that they were deployed in large numbers. During the 90's the number of smartcards in circulation grew exponentially. They are now in widespread use in credit card, ticketing and mobile phone applications. But they have yet to be deployed in large numbers in identification applications.

There are several reasons for this but the lack of standards has hindered the deployment of smartcards in e-ID applications. Without standards interoperability between card schemes is severely hampered which limits the benefit that an ID card scheme operator can realise.

The situation is changing, however, and the development of standards is progressing well. We are now seeing the publication of guidance on deploying e-ID smartcards that are interoperable with other card schemes. This bodes well for the expanded use of smartcards in the identification sector.

1 Background

A prerequisite for the widespread adoption of smartcard technology is the development and publication of standards. This is illustrated by the areas in which smartcards are most widely used:

1.1 Financial Sector

In the Financial sector the use of the EMV standards is now widespread. This means that a credit card issued in the USA can be used to make transactions in Rome, with the cardholder paying the bill a month later in the US.

The EMV standards spawned the development of EFTPOS devices including the messaging protocols, card handling protocols, session encryption requirements and PIN management. This allows an Australian EFTPOS card tendered in London to dispense cash in the local currency.

The Financial sector has made smartcards work to fulfil consumer expectations. Without standards it would have been impossible for the widespread use of smartcards to occur. If there was no standard for the way to establish secure sessions the current array of keypad card readers could not operate; without standards ATMs that capture the card to avoid tearing would not exist and without standards it would be impossible to design a two-factor authentication mechanism to ensure cardholders provide their PINs before a transaction is committed.

1.2 Mobile Phone Sector

In the mobile phone sector one of the elements that differentiates the GSM market from the CDMA market is the use of SIMs. This has been a factor in the widespread deployment of

GSM as opposed to the relatively limited use of CDMA. The GSM memorandum of understanding defines how a SIM card in the UK phone should work in Malaysia, so that a phone call can be made, with the call costs appearing a month later on the user's regular phone bill. The phone industry has anticipated customer needs and has largely filled their expectations.

(It is interesting to note that the industry has failed to learn from history and are currently developing multiple standards for high capacity SIMs needed for multi-media functionality.)

1.3 Ticketing

In the ticketing sector, standards development has occurred in some geographies but it has not been as prevalent as in the financial or mobile phone sectors. Vendors of ticketing systems have little incentive to promote interoperability between schemes, preferring to keep their systems proprietary. Customers have failed to force vendors to adopt open architectures because most system deployments have been driven by project expediencies rather than by developing the best solution for scheme operators or the travelling public.

To be fair, other than in Europe, the ticketing scheme business model does not warrant large-scale interoperability between schemes. For instance, there are few requirements for a visitor from Brisbane to be able to use their TransLink card on a tram in Melbourne. There is more of a requirement for a visitor from London to be able to user their oyster card in Rome. It is hardly surprising that in Europe, the ITSO has worked hard to ensure that compatibility between schemes is technically possible even if the ticketing system vendors do not promote it.

It is interesting to note that the picture is now changing with the deployment of 2nd & 3rd generation schemes. Customers are now demanding more open ticketing architectures and are fuelling the standards development debate.

Another influence of note is coming from the banks. It has not gone unnoticed that some card schemes maintain a significant "float" of funds on deposit that cardholders debit when they travel. The banks, until lately, have been unable to handle small financial transaction without the addition of high fees. With the advent of "touch and go" technology, card operators are enabling banks to take a share of this market. Ticketing applications will soon debit cardholder's accounts directly and small transactions will occur without two-factor authentication (note the EFTPOS definitions, originally enabled by the EMV standards, have allowed this to occur).

This means that a ticketing application on a bankcard is entirely possible; it is frustrated only by the current proprietary nature of these ticketing schemes. The banks are likely to add their influence to standards adoption and it is expected that an expansion of the ITSO and/or Calypso standards development activity will occur.

1.4 Identification

In the e-ID space however interoperability is not so advanced. There are no international standards yet in place.

The USA is at the forefront of standards development with their experience with the Common Access Card. The Personal Identification Verification standards of FIPS201 and the smartcard methodology of NIST 6887 are now being internationalised in ISO24727 which shows promise as a card interoperability standard.

1.5 Convergence

Although the standardisation work is currently focussed on the use of smartcards for identification purposes, much of the methodology associated with the card design is common to all cards. This means that we can expect to see, over the next five years, convergence between card schemes and a blurring of the current division between the various sectors in which smartcards are used. The first will be between the financial cards and e-ID cards since they both have an identification requirement. But, as seen above, convergence between ticketing cards and financial cards is already taking place and if mobile phones become the ubiquitous payment device as currently promised by the marketplace – placing an e-ID applet and an EMV applet on a SIM card might soon be commonplace.

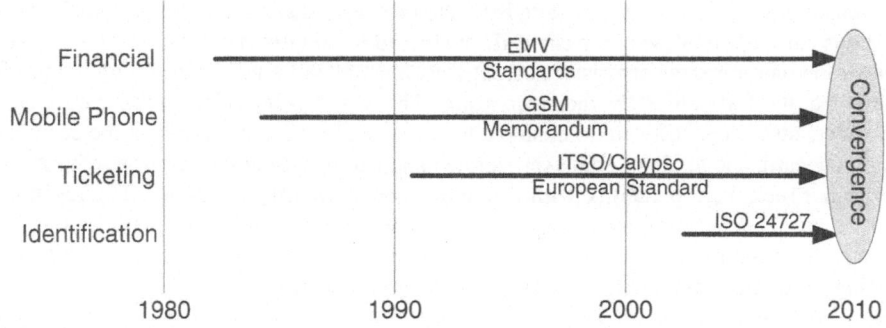

Fig 1: Smartcard Development Timeline

2 Experience with e-ID

It is true to say that the current experience with e-ID cards has been less than inspiring. Two schemes that have been at the frontier of nation-wide e-ID card deployment are the US Department of Defence Common Access Card (CAC) and the Belgian e-ID card scheme.

2.1 US Federal Government Initiatives

The USA has been at the forefront of standards development for e-ID cards for some time. They began with their experience with the Common Access Card (CAC). The CAC came out of the realisation that many government agencies were issuing smartcards for their staff, but the schemes were incompatible. In some cases contractors were required to apply to multiple scheme operators for access cards to more than one facility. In order to reduce the escalating cost of closed card schemes in different geographies and between the services, the common access card defined a common card structure for access control to e-ID smartcards.

This led to the development of NIST 6887 document, the first to define a complete smartcard model. This document provided a model for a comprehensive multi-application smartcard that provided facilities to enhance interoperability. A common card capability container provided the ability for the card to be interrogated to reveal the applications that resided on it.

But at the same time as the NIST 6887 initiative was maturing as a US standard for the deployment of smartcards, a Department of Homeland Security directive instigated the development of a Personal Identification Verification (PIV) mechanism to allow compliant e-ID cards to provide cardholder identification details. A separate initiative under the FIPS 201 program defined the PIV requirements specifying how a smartcard should respond to an identity verification request.

A new NIST initiative was then commenced to support the initialisation of the PIV. This has led to the ISO24727 standards development which is an ambitious program to formalise a structure for a PIV-compliant card with capabilities to support various identity-based functionality within a standard smartcard definition. The experience with NIST 6887 is assisting in the development of ISO24727 which shows promise as the first true smartcard interoperability standard.

2.2 Belgian Government Cards

The Belgian e-ID initiative is an example of the problems that arise in a standards void. The scheme is currently deploying a basic e-ID smartcard to all citizens in the country. When advised of the date for their card issuance, citizens must attend a government enrolment office to complete the formalities for their smartcard. The program provides a smartcard reader to cardholders and client software to enable citizens to read their card, to verify the accuracy of data on the card, and to alter certain self-service applications. In doing this, the scheme operators did not seek interoperability with Belgium's social security smartcard. The result is the two card management programs cannot be co-resident on the cardholder's PC. Not only are Belgians on social security required to carry two government smartcards, they must also be sufficiently computer literate to be able to read their smartcards.

3 The Issues

There are multiple challenges to the introduction of an e-ID card, but the most important are interoperability and privacy.

3.1 Interoperability

Interoperability greatly increases the utilization of an e-ID card and significantly reduces the inconvenience users will experience with the cards they utilise. Banks have realized this with the combination of credit card facilities, bankcard features and ATM access on a single smartcard. Much work has been invested in back-end integration to allow one bank's card to be accepted by associated banks. This means that the cardholder has to carry only one card and remember one PIN for their banking needs.

The same is required for the e-ID card. A single card should allow the cardholder to gain access to a building, provide identify at the company's HR office and grant access to computer facilities.

The ability for an e-ID card scheme to interoperate with another scheme is a substantial benefit that will often justify the initiative. Without interoperability the economic justification for a scheme might be questionable; with interoperability card scheme costs can be spread over multiple applications. This also means that cardholders will gain benefits beyond the core application provided by the scheme operator.

Just as standardisation in the financial sector means that a credit card can be used for EFTPOS transactions, the same is true for e-ID cards. Multiple applications on the same card will heighten the usefulness of the card making it more likely that the cardholder will carry the card. Card scheme operators will benefit from the potential spread of card costs over multiple applications.

3.1.1 ISO 24727

The nascent ISO 24727 standard seeks to provide a comprehensive model for a smartcard development. It is aimed at multi-application cards such as Javacards or MULTOS cards. The intent is to allow the scheme operator to decide at what level they wish to communicated with the card. There are three basic levels:

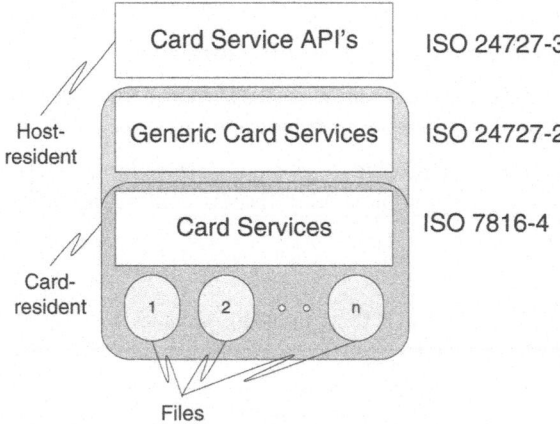

Fig 2: ISO 24727 Architecture

At the lowest level communication with the card can adhere to standard APDUs that are supported by all smartcards.

At the next level the standard recommends a set of calls that all compliant cards will support. These will initially be via host applications that will communicate with the standard card services. When fully compliant smartcards come on the market the generic card services as defined in the standard will be available directly from the card. Level 2 commands define the way in which a connection to the card can be established, the commands to be used for data loading, creation, selection and deletion, and the way in which cryptographic services can be used. The command set also supports a Differential Identity Service which describes how identify data can be created, retrieved, updated and deleted.

At level 3 compliant smartcard host systems will provide a standard command set to which card scheme applications can interface. The standard assumes that these system calls will remain host-based. Level 3 is still in development and it is expected that a number of sophisticated calls will be defined to perform standard card service tasks.

It is standards such as this that enable interoperability. With the knowledge that compliant cards will support the same command sets, card scheme developers can define functions for their cards that will allow other card schemes to interoperate. This is particularly important for e-ID cards. An identification application should allow all compliant cards to access cardholder identification information to the extent permitted by the scheme operator.

3.2 Privacy

A related challenge is that of privacy. It is the one issue that has the potential to derail a smartcard project. An attempt to introduce a smartcard in Ontario, Canada was terminated in 2001 because of privacy issues. The agencies involved could not agree on a mechanism to adequately protect the privacy of their constituents. The inability to satisfactorily address privacy issues resulted in the initiative being shelved after a sunk cost of $12M.

Privacy considerations include:

- what cardholder information can be collected and retained?
- how will cardholder information be kept secure?
- how will cardholder information be kept current?
- how will a cardholder be able to verify their information?

Card scheme operators fail to address these issues at their peril. Operators must be honest in their dealing with the public and ensure their processes are transparent.

Fortunately the technology is quite able to accommodate multiple levels of access to card information. Most multi-application cards adopt access controls as defined under the Global Platform program.

A subset is as follows:

Table 1: Authentication Classes

Access control rule	Description
Always	The corresponding service can be provided without restrictions.
External authenticate	The corresponding service can be provided only after a "get challenge" and subsequent "external authenticate APDUs."
PIN protected	The corresponding service is provided if and only if the verification code of the PIN associated with the service has been provided in the current card session.
External authenticate or PIN	Either one of the two controls gives access to the service. This allows for a cardholder validation when a PIN pad is available and for an external authentication when no PIN pad is available. Or, this provides an authentication method when the application cannot be trusted to perform an external authentication and to protect the external authentication key.
Update once	A target object can only be updated once during its lifetime.
Secure channel (ISO)	The corresponding service can be provided through a secure channel managed by an ISO [ISO4],[ISO8] secure messaging layer.

PIN protected data requires the cardholder to input their PIN before the data can be accessed. Data protected under an external authenticate mechanism typically requires a card reader containing the appropriate key in order for the data to be read.

These access controls, provided they are implemented correctly, allow scheme operators to provide the required privacy protection.

3.2.1 Example: Australian Driver Licence Smartcard

The New Queensland Driver Licence is a good example of the implementation of card access security to protect individual's privacy.

In Australia driver license administration is a state-level activity. This means that when the Queensland state government embarked upon a project to issue a smartcard driver licence it was necessary to gain agreement with the other states and territories on interoperability requirements. This led to the establishment of the Smartcard Licence Interoperability Protocol (SLIP) under the auspices of the national Austroads organization.

It is this organisation that will decide which applications will be mandatory and which optional applications can be provided by the states. It will also decide on the access control rules to be supported.

The following is a subset of the standard Global Platform access control rules as applied to driver licence card data:

Table 2: Data mapping to Authentication Classes

Card Container	Access control rule	Attributes
Card public information	Always	Card serial number Smartcard issue date Card scheme operator Data model version #
Card holder public information	Always	Card holder name Digital signature
Cardholder biometrics	External authenticate	Digital photograph Digitised signature Fingerprint template
Cardholder private attribute	PIN or external authenticate	Gender Date of birth Address
Card holder licence information	PIN or external authenticate	Licence number Conditions Driver Class (1..N) Effective date Expiry Date Jurisdiction
Emergency contact information	PIN or external authenticate	Contact name Contact address Contact phone number 1 Contact phone number 2 Donor status
Digital certificate	always	Digital certificate 3k

Note: the above access control rules provide the capability protect data. However, any implementation of an e-ID scheme requires the appropriate use of these controls to achieve the required privacy protection. In the driver licence application it is recognised that the driver licence is often used as an identity document. If the driver license number is used by relying parties it could be possible for the agencies or companies using the card to form transaction profiles on cardholders. This is of particular concern in situations in which the card is used for electronic transactions.

To this end the Queensland card will expressly prohibit other government agencies, or commercial parties relying on the card, to use the driver licence number in their internal applications. The card will carry a cardholder number which each relying entity will be required to map to their own internal customer number scheme. This will frustrate any attempt to form a transaction profile on card users.

4 Conclusion

To properly exploit the capabilities of e-ID cards standards development must mature. This is occurring, and the speed at which the ISO24727 standard has reached draft stage is impressive. This is largely the result of the previous work by NIST on the smartcard initiatives.

In Australia much work has been expended on the smartcard licence interoperability protocol (SLIP) that seeks to gain agreement from all jurisdictions (5 states and 2 territories).

All states and territories have participated in the definition of the data model and supported access control. Key management still needs definition with distribution of keys for externally authenticated data. Two states are leading the work to define these attributes.

The SLIP definition will seek to influence the development of ISO24727 to include applications that the driver licence will need in order to be a compliant identity document and will likely mandate the standard as the access protocol to the driver license smartcard.

Standards development is therefore of seminal importance to the adoption of e-ID smartcards. It will save scheme developers significant time in the design and development of their schemes. It will also significantly benefit users who will no longer need to carry multiple cards and remember different PINs for different identification functions.

References

ISO/IEC FDIS 24727-1 Integrated circuit card programming interfaces – Part 1 Architecture

ISO/IEC FCD 24727-2 Integrated circuit card programming interfaces – Part 2 Generic Card Interfaces

ISO/IEC CD 24727-3 Integrated circuit card programming interfaces – Part 1 Application Interface

European Citizen Card Combined with Travel Document Function, Convergence or Divergence?

Detlef Houdeau

Senior Director Business Development
Infineon Technologies AG
Neubiberg near Munich, Germany
detlef.houdeau@infineon.com

Abstract

Since 2.5 year is a new application standard for the European citizen card in development. Data structure, transport protocol, interoperability and the issuing are the pillar of this card and there application for e-government services. The article start an early analysing about the expected implementation in EU member states. In the conclusion is shown, that the standardisation work lag behind the government request for implementation. The current solutions are more divergent in the solution themselves and for the combination with the upcoming digital travel documents.

1 Introduction

The EU Commission has decided in October 2004, that the next generation of travel documents and the new border process must increase security and fraud protection as part of the European Homeland Security program. Harmonized technology and synchronized timeframe enabled this approach. The EU regulation 2252/200 [1] defined the roadmap for technology and implementation. European Homeland Security program started a technology wave over Europe, with the elements

- digital identity
- biometrics and
- PKI

The focus of this regulation is the electronic passport, the data structure, the security architecture, the biometrics and the communication. By October 2006, 33 countries (27 VWP-Countries, 5 non-VWP-countries and USA) will have started with the issuing of electronic passports [2]. In Europe this captures 100% of the member countries, worldwide 30% of the countries with MRZ-passports.

Many governments of the EU member nations think of issuing also a national electronic ID (e-ID) card, after the ePassport is implemented and in use. Two reasons are keys for this approach:

- Re-use of infrastructure
  (data capturing, PKI, IT-network, border control system)
- increase security at border control

In Europe, about 20% of residents have passports and about 80% to 90% of residents hold ID cards. For border control in Europe, the ID card is the typical travel document. For increasing security at border control the e-Passport in combination with the e-ID card for EU residents are required.

In autumn 2005, the EU Commission published the recommendation for minimum security standards for such national e-ID card programs in its regulation 14351/2005.

These travel programs are typically controlled by Ministry of Interior (MoI) in each member nation. This contain visa documents, immigration cards, national ID-cards and international passports

A complete other discussion has run during the last six to seven years on national level in the government corner Ministry of Economics (MoE). The main focus is cost reduction and increasing of government services. One module of this discussion is the changing of the communication location from the government office with face-to- face to the home PC in combination with the online authentication and commu-nication via internet. The new name was found with "e-Government". For this online-authentication technology was a new identification media requested, called citizen card. Since springtime 2004, there is a new application standard in progress, see CEN/TC 224 and CEN/TS 15480 (CEN = Comité Européen de Normalisation). Harmonized data structure, security architecture and interoperability are on the scope.

The standardisation work on European Citizen Card (ECC) could be closed till 2007 with the work share:

- Part 1: Physical, Electrical and Transport Protocol Characteristics
- Part 2: Logical Data Structures and Security Services
- Part 3: ECC interoperability using and application interface
- Part 4: Recommendations for ECC issuance, operation and use.

The next points analyse the current situation in EU member nations.

2 The EU nation strategies and the new ECC-Standard

National e-Card programs are not synchronized with the standardisation work. Some national programs have started early and have non-standardized solution in place, like Finland (Start 2003), Belgium (Start 2005) [3], Sweden (Start 2005) [4], and Austria (Start 2005) [5].In other countries are the decisions published for a citizen card function and e-government service based on the new upcoming CEN-Standard. For example, the governments in France and Germany have announced this approach .In many countries the decision has not been made yet and/or published, like in UK, Spain, Italy and Netherlands.

3 Selected card interface for ECC

Under ISO there are the two interfaces possible: a) ISO 7816 = contact based and b) ISO 14443 = contact-less. Some countries would follow the contact-based interface, like Finland, Italy, Belgium, Sweden, and Austria. France and Germany would take the contact-less approach. In many countries is the decision not made and/or published.

4 ECC and the "carrier"

France has announced a special citizen card (Carte de Vie Quotidienne = CVQ) on one carrier and the national e-ID (Identité Nationale Electronique Sécurisée = INES) on a second carrier. Italy has started under the name Carta Nationale Servici (CNS) an e-ID-card pilot in 2005/6.The decision for an own carrier or a "host"-carrier is not made. Germany, Austria, and Sweden have announced the "host"-carrier approach:

- Austria: ECC on social security card [5]
- Sweden: ECC on national e-ID card [4]
- Germany: ECC on national e-ID card [6]

In many countries are these decisions not made and/or published

5 ECC and addressable memory space

Some countries have in the upcoming e-ID card a microcontroller only for the ECC function. This is the case in Sweden and France. Other countries would take one micro-Controller which contains ECC and other data set:

- Germany: ECC + ICAO data set [6]
- Belgium: ECC + national e-ID data set [3]
- Finland: ECC + national e-ID data set
- Austria: ECC + social data set [5]

In many countries are these decisions not made/or published.

6 The legal framework for the ECC

In Germany is the "Gesetz über Rahmenbedingungen für elektronische Signaturen"(SigG) since 16th of Mai 2001 in place, with the last changing on 4th of January 2005. This defines:

- Electronic signature
- Advanced electronic signature
- Qualified electronic signature

Till November 2001 is the German regulation established (SigV).

In other countries is the legal situation unclear.

7 ECC and the challenge for the supplier industry, for example the semiconductor producer

To develop, qualify and certify the microcontroller for this market right in time. To support software development companies and system integrators. To foster field trial, interoperability and conformity tests.

8 Conclusion

The standardisation works lag behind the government request for implementation. The standardisation work would freeze till CY 2007. The development of the solution and implementation based on this new application standard is possible at earliest 2008.

For the key technologies, such as digital identity, online authentication and signing it is recommended to work out the same definition and create the same legal framework in each member country.

The European citizen card could be one pillar of a multiapplication card system in the future.

From the industry point of view, we recommend the combination of the national electronic ID-card with the European citizen card on one carrier with the three basic (pillar) functions

- visible optical identity
- travel function (ICAO standard)
- e-Government services (CEN standard),

to increase the convenience for the citizen in there daily life and reduce the acceptance of such new digital identity document. To follow international standards reduce specification money, time and effort, minimize technology risks and create more supplier for the governments. This opens the door for national (and international) interoperability tests of components, like cards and card-reader.

References

[1] EU-Regulation, see http://europa.eu.int/eur-lex/lex/LexUriServ /LexUriServ.do?uri=CELEX:32004R2252:EN:HTML

[2] Keesing Journal of Documents and Identity, Annual Report 2005 – 2006

[3] Information brochure of the Belgian ID card, see http://www.rijksregister.fgov.be/cie /brochure/05145_bz_leaflet_fr.pdf

[4] Information about the Swedish ID card, see http://www.polisen.se /Inter/nodeid=36624&pageversion=1.html

[5] DIN-Workshop Multiapplicationcard, on July, 13th and 14th, 2006, Berlin, Germany; Presentation from Prof. Posch, Austria, Chancellor of the Confederation Bureau

[6] Global Security Forum, on July, 6th and 7th, Vienna, Austria, see http://www.global-security-forum.com; Presentation from Andreas Reisen, Ministry of Interior, Germany

Glossary

e-ID	electronic ID-card
PKI	Public Key Infrastructure
CEN	Comité Européen de Normalisation
ECC	Européen Citizen Card
INES	Identité Nationale Electronique Sécurisée
CVQ	Carte de Vie Quotidienne
VWP	Visa Waiver Program
MRZ	Machine Readable Zone
IT	Information Technology
ISO	International Standardisation Organisation
CNS	Carta Nationale Servici

Physical Unclonable Functions
for enhanced security of tokens and tags

Pim Tuyls · Boris Škorić

Philips Research, The Netherlands
{pim.tuyls | boris.skoric}@philips.com

Abstract

Security tokens and RFID-tags are playing an increasingly important role in the authentication of persons and devices, e.g. controlling access to services and protecting the value of goods and digital content. In order to provide the required security level they are used in combination with a cryptographic algorithm. State of the art algorithms are so sophisticated nowadays that they are virtually immune against mathematical attacks. Hence, the offered security level essentially depends on the secrecy of the employed keys. Several studies have shown that the secrecy of keys stored in memory is not guaranteed when physical attacks are used.

Recently, Physical Unclonable Functions (PUFs) were introduced as an identification tool to build secure tokens. In this paper, we extend this setting and show how PUFs can be used for generating and storing keys in a way that is secure even against physical attacks. This enables new strong security devices such as unclonable tokens, secure key storage devices and unclonable RFID-tags. These are briefly described together with some applications.

1 Introduction

In our society information, content and knowledge is becoming increasingly important. Often this information has some value and is therefore an attractive target for attackers. In order to protect the value of the information or content appropriate protection measures have to be applied on the devices where the information is stored or on the communication links over which such information is communicated. Such protection is provided, amongst others, by cryptographic algorithms. Those algorithms use a secret key and their security depends critically on the secrecy of the key.

The security of many cryptographic algorithms is well understood. State of the art cryptographic algorithms and protocols guarantee that only a negligible amount of information on the secret keys can be obtained from eavesdropping on communications. Hence, when the device can be considered as a black-box in which the secret key is stored and to which an attacker has no access, cryptographic protection is sufficient.

It was shown at several places that the black-box assumption does not hold in real life. Attackers have successfully demonstrated how secret keys can be extracted from devices by performing physical attacks. More importantly, they showed that in many cases such attacks are relatively simple. As a consequence, many attackers often choose to attack the hardware in which a key is stored instead of attacking the cryptographic algorithms used to protect the communication link. Cost-effective protection of secret keys against physical attacks in general and against invasive attacks in particular is a long-standing and challenging problem.

S. Paulus, N. Pohlmann, H. Reimer (Editors): Securing Electronic Business Processes, Vieweg (2006), 30-37

Physical Unclonable Functions (PUFs) [PRTG2002] have been proposed to solve this problem. A PUF is a physical system with a unique, random-looking input-output relation. Unclonability means that it is infeasible to produce either a physical copy or a mathematical model that simulates the behaviour of the system. A final property of PUFs is their inherent tamper resistance. An attacker who tries to attack a PUF will damage it in such a way that its input-output behaviour is completely changed. Physical systems that are produced by an uncontrolled production process, e.g. by mixing several substances, turn out to be good candidates for PUFs.

A 'Controlled PUF' (CPUF) [GCvDD2002a] is a PUF whose input and output are completely controlled by a layer of control electronics. The control layer is inseparably bound to the PUF in such a way that removal will damage the PUF. By preventing direct access to the PUF, and by cryptographically manipulating the input and output, the control layer strengthens the security.

In this paper we first give an overview of PUF hardware and then describe three applications of PUFs. In Section 3.1 we describe a token equipped with a PUF and list the advantages that it offers. The way in which a PUF can be used to build a secure key storage device is explained in Section 3.2. Finally in Section 3.3 we show how a secure key storage device can be implemented on an RFID-tag to make it unclonable and suitable for anti-counterfeiting purposes.

2 Physical realisations

Several physical systems are known on which PUFs can be based. The main types are optical PUFs [PRTG2002,Pap2001,STO2005], coating PUFs [TS2005], silicon PUFs [Gas2003, GCvDD2002b] and acoustic PUFs [TS2005]. We briefly discuss coating PUFs and optical PUFs.

2.1 Coating PUFs

The idea of using an 'active coating' was originally proposed in [Pos1998] and further developed in the context of PUFs in [TS2005] and [TSSW$^+$2006]. Coating PUFs are integrated with an IC (see Figure 1). The IC is covered with a protective (opaque) coating doped with random dielectric particles. By random dielectric particles, we mean several kinds of particles of random size and shape with a relative dielectric constant ε_r differing from the dielectric constant of the coating matrix. An array of metal sensors lies directly beneath the passivation layer. Because of the presence of the coating material with its random dielectric properties, the sensor wires with the material in between behave as a capacitor with a random capacitance value. The measured capacitance values are converted into a bit string which can be used as an identifier or a key.

Coating PUFs have the advantage of possessing a high degree of integration. The matrix containing the random particles can be part of a tamper-resistance coating. A coating PUF additionally has the advantage that it is easily turned into a Controlled PUF (CPUF), as it is inseparably bound to the underlying IC.

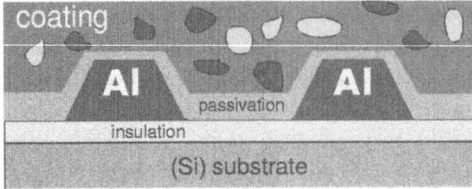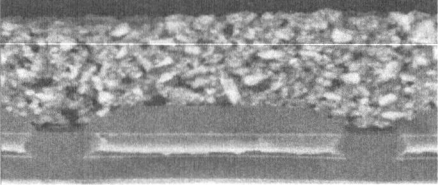

Figure 1: Left: Schematic cross-section of a coating PUF.
Right: Scanning Electron Microscope image.

2.2 Optical PUFs

Optical PUFs consist of a transparent material (e.g. glass) containing randomly distributed light scattering particles (e.g. air bubbles, plastic or aluminium). They exploit the uniqueness of speckle patterns that result from multiple scattering of laser light in a disordered optical medium. The challenge is a laser beam directed at the PUF. The response is a speckle pattern (see Figure 2). The pattern is a function of the internal structure of the PUF, the wave length of the laser, its angle of incidence, focal distance and other characteristics of the wave front.

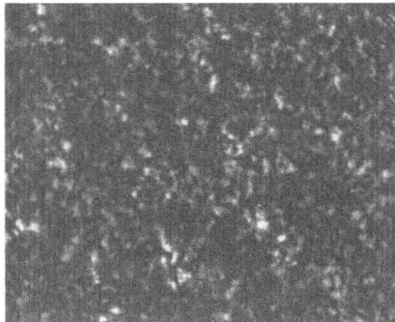

Figure 2: Example of a speckle pattern.

Optical probing of the PUF is difficult because the light diffusion obscures the locations of the scatterers. At this moment the best physical techniques can probe diffusive materials up to a depth of approximately 10 scattering lengths [MDR2001]. Moreover, even if an attacker learns the positions of all the scatterers, this knowledge is of limited use to him. If he tries to make a physical copy of the PUF, he runs into the problem that precise positioning of a large number of scatterers is an arduous process. It would seem easier to make an "electronic" clone, i.e. a device that simply computes the correct responses to all challenges in real time or looks them up in a database, without bothering with physical reproduction. However, even this turns out to be extremely hard, since it requires accurate optical modelling of multiple coherent scattering.

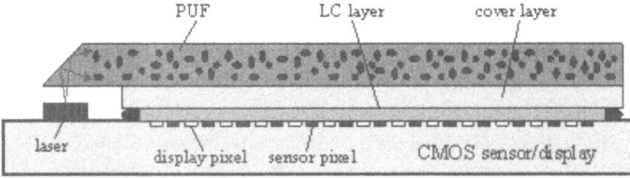

Figure 3: Integrated optical PUF containing a laser, a PUF, a challenging mechanism and sensors.

An optical PUF can be employed (i) as a separate physical component, to be challenged by a special reader device containing a laser and a camera, or (ii) as a Controlled PUF, if it is properly integrated into an inseparable package together with the laser, challenging mechanism and camera. Figure 3 schematically shows a highly integrated implementation of an optical PUF. The CMOS sensor has detector pixels as well as switchable 'display' pixels. The display pixels are used to locally switch the Liquid Crystal (LC) layer between two phase rotation states, e.g. no rotation and 45° rotation. The configuration of the display pixels forms a challenge. The optical PUF is situated in the top layer. The laser light enters the PUF, and the light is eventually scattered downward. There it may directly enter a detector pixel. Alternatively, it hits a display pixel, where it partly gets absorbed, and partly scatters with a phase rotation depending on the LC state. At each detector pixel all contributions from the various scattering paths are added coherently.

3 Overview of PUF applications

From a security perspective the uniqueness of the responses and unclonability of the PUF are very useful properties. Because of these properties, PUFs can be used as unique identifiers [Bau1983,3DAS,Kir2004, BCJP⁺2005], means of tamper-detection and/or as a cost-effective source for key generation (common randomness) between two parties [TS2005, STO2005]. The latter is very useful for authenticating objects and persons.

3.1 PUF-Based Tokens

PUFs with a large number of Challenge-Response Pairs (CRPs), such as optical PUFs, are well suited for authentication tokens. In its simplest and cheapest form, the token contains only a PUF and a serial number. The token can be inserted into a reader able to read the identifier and to measure the challenge-response behaviour of the PUF. The reader is connected to a database.

Typically there are two phases: *enrolment* and *verification*. During the enrolment phase, a number of challenges is chosen randomly for each token, and the corresponding PUF responses are measured and then stored, e.g. in a database or, if the token has an EEPROM, in encrypted/hashed form in the EEPROM. During the verification phase, the PUF is subjected to one or more of the enrolled challenges. The verifier checks the response against the enrolled response data. The same CRP is never used twice.

Several secure protocols based on CRPs have been worked out in [TS2005, GCvDD2002a, Gas2003]. In the simplest case eavesdroppers can easily see the PUF responses in plaintext. In more sophisticated protocols PUF responses are used to encrypt nonces or to generate Message Authentication Codes. The latter protocols have the advantage that the token holder and the verifier end up with a shared secret which they use as a session key for a secure transaction.

3.2 Secure Key Storage

Many hardware devices, such as DVD players and Trusted Platform Modules, need access to secret 'Device Keys' that are stored somewhere inside the device. Often these Device Keys are unique for each device. Hence, they have to be stored in the digital memory in a separate process during or after manufacture. Special protective measures must be taken to ensure that attackers cannot read this memory, not even with invasive means such as a Focused Ion Beam (FIB).

Regarding protection of memories against read-out, we make the following observation. Keys stored in digital memory (such as ROM or EEPROM) are stored as strings of zeros and ones. Attackers can employ known physical attacks to probe the content of the memory, even when the IC is not active. In order to protect stored keys against invasive physical attacks, we propose that *no key shall be stored in digital form in the memory of a device*. Since there is no digital key in the memory, it can not be directly attacked.

Instead, we propose to generate the key K only at the time when it is needed. The key is extracted from a *tamper evident* physical structure, integrated with the IC, by applying a challenge, measuring the response and carrying out the reconstruction phase of the helper data algorithm [LT2003] implemented on the IC. In the case of coating PUFs, the IC extracts the key from the coating covering it, as described in Section 2.1.

Since the key is extracted from coating measurements, and measurements on a physical structure are inherently noisy, the responses can not be directly used as a secret key. This implies that we need a helper data algorithm/fuzzy extractor [LT2003,DRS2004] for key reconstruction. A helper data algorithm consists of a pair of algorithms (G,W) and two phases: an *enrolment* and a *reconstruction* phase (see Figure 4). We use the following notation: x denotes the measurement value of a response during the enrolment phase, while y denotes the corresponding value during the reconstruction phase. During enrolment, the key K is randomly chosen from a uniform distribution. The helper data algorithm W is used during the enrolment phase and creates the helper data w based on x and K. The helper data is stored in the EEPROM of the IC. The algorithm $G(.,.)$ is used during the key reconstruction phase for reconstruction of the key K as follows: $K=G(y,w)$, where w is read from the EEPROM.

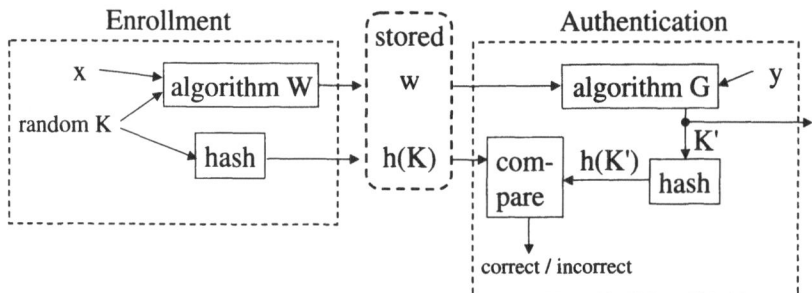

Figure 4: The helper data scheme

We have developed an IC equipped with a coating PUF having 30 capacitance sensors lying underneath the coating. We have shown that from each of the sensor measurements we can derive 3 bits in a reliable way. In total a string of 90 bits is derived. Taking the noise into account, this leads to a secure key of 66 bits[1]. Additionally, we have performed several invasive attacks on the IC with a Focused Ion Beam. Such an attack causes clearly visible errors in the measured capacitance values (see Figure 5). Hence the attack is detected by the IC. This detection can be used to let the chip shut down. Furthermore, it was shown that the damage even destroys the key. In case of an 128-bit AES key, after a FIB attack the attacker still faces a computation complexity in the order of 2^{72} to find the key.

---

[1] We note that when more sensors are put on the IC, longer keys can be constructed.

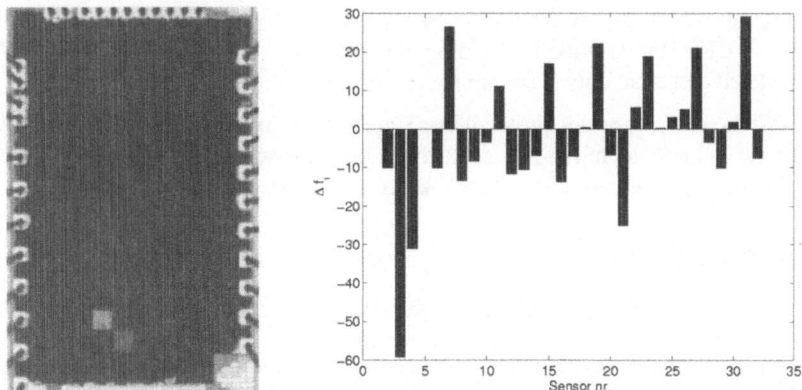

Figure 5: Left: Top view of a coated IC that has been attacked with a Gallium Focused Ion Beam. Right: Differences between the capacitance values before and after the FIB attack.

3.3 Unclonable RFID-Tags

RFID tags are small devices, consisting of an antenna connected to a micro-chip. They are used for identification purposes in many applications nowadays. It is expected that they will enable many new applications and link the physical and the virtual world in the near future. Since the processing power of these devices is low, they are often in the line of fire when security and privacy are concerned.

An emerging application for RFID tags is to prevent *counterfeiting* of goods. This is done by embedding a tag with authentic reference information into a product or into the seal of its package. An attacker who aims to counterfeit the product has to make a copy of the tag. This is called a *cloning* attack. A cloning attack can be performed in two ways:

1. The attacker attacks the protocols between a tag and a reader (either actively or passively) and tries to retrieve the tag's secrets (reference information) or

2. The attacker performs a physical attack on the tag (optical attack on the memory, Focused Ion Beam attack,...) and retrieves the secrets in this way.

Once the attacker has retrieved the secret reference information stored in the tag, she stores those data in new tags which she then embeds into counterfeit products. A legitimate RFID reader cannot tell an authentic tag from a cloned one, and hence cannot distinguish between authentic and counterfeit products.

In order to make an RFID tag unclonable, it is equipped with a coating PUF as described in Section 2. During enrolment a secret key K is derived from the PUF using the techniques explained in Section 3.2. Then a cryptographically secure commitment C_K is computed. Finally, the product issuer signs the commitment C_K with his secret key sk: $\sigma(C_K)$. The commitment C_K and the signature $\sigma(C_K)$ are stored in the tag's EEPROM.

In order to verify the authenticity of a product, a reader runs the following protocol with the tag that is embedded in the product.

1. The tag reads the public data CK, σ(CK) from EEPROM and sends them to the reader.

2. The reader checks the signature σ(CK) by using the public key pk associated with the secret key sk. If the signature is ok, the reader proceeds; otherwise the product is considered fake.

3. The tag proves to the reader that it knows the secret key K corresponding to the commitment CK. This is done by running a secure identification protocol. The product is considered authentic only if the tag passes this test.

In [TB2006] the security of this protocol was rigorously proven. Moreover it was shown there that when the Schnorr identification protocol is used for secure identification, the complete protocol can be implemented in less than 10k gates, which is feasible on a tag.

4 Conclusion

In this paper we have described Physical Unclonable Functions (PUFs) and explained their use for security purposes. We have investigated three applications in more detail. Firstly, we explained how PUFs are used to build an unclonable token. Secondly, we have shown how coating PUFs are used to build hardware that is resistant against invasive physical attacks. Finally, we have shown how RFID-Tags can be made suitable for anti-counterfeiting purposes by integrating them with a coating PUF.

References

[3DAS]   Unicate BV's '3DAS' system, http://www.andreae.com/Unicate/Appendix \%201.htm, 1999.

[Bau1983]   Bauder D.W: *An Anti-Counterfeiting Concept for Currency*. Systems Research Report PTK-11990, Sandia National Laboratories, 1983.

[BCJP+2005]   Buchanan J.D.R., Cowburn R.P., Jausovec A., Petit D., Seem P., Xiong G., Atkinson D., Fenton K., Allwood D.A., Bryan M.T.: *Forgery: 'Fingerprinting' documents and packaging*. Nature 436 (28 Jul 2005), Brief Communications, p.475.

[DRS2004]   Dodis Y., Reyzin M., Smith A.: *Fuzzy Extractors: How to generate strong keys from biometrics and other noisy data*. In: Cachin and Camenisch, (Eds.): Proceedings of Eurocrypt 2004, Lecture Notes in Computer Science, volume 3027, Springer-Verlag, 2004, p. 523-540.

[Gas2003]   Gassend B.: *Physical Random Functions*, Master's Thesis, MIT 2003.

[GCvDD2002a]   Gassend B., Clarke D., van Dijk M., Devadas S.: *Controlled Physical Random Functions*. Proc. 18th Annual Computer Security Applications Conf., Dec. 2002.

[GCvDD2002b]   Gassend B., Clarke D., van Dijk M., Devadas S.: *Silicon Physical Random Functions*, Proc. 9th ACM Conf. on Computer and Communications Security, Nov. 2002.

[Kir2004]   Kirovski D.,: A Point-Subset Compression Algorithm for Fiber-based Certificates of Authenticity, IEEE Proc. ISIT 2004, p.173.

[LT2003]   Linnartz J.P., Tuyls. P.: *New Shielding Functions to Enhance Privacy and Prevent Misuse of Biometric Templates*, Proc. 4th International Conference on Audio and Video based Biometric Person Authentication (2003), LNCS 2688, Springer-Verlag, p. 238-250.

[MDR2001]   Magnor M., Dorn P., Rudolph W.: *Simulation of confocal microscopy through scattering media with and without time gating*, J.Opt.Soc.Am. B, Vol. 19, no. 11 (2001), p. 1695-1700.

[Pap2001]   Pappu R.: *Physical One-Way Functions*. Ph.D. thesis, MIT 2001.

[Pos1998]   Posch R.: *Protecting Devices by Active Coating*, Journal of Universal Computer Science, vol.4, no.7 (1998), p.652-668.

[PRTG2002]   Pappu R., Recht B., Taylor J., Gershenfeld N.: *Physical One-Way Functions*, Science Vol. 297, Sept 2002, p.2026.

[STO2005]   Škorić B., Tuyls P., Ophey W.: *Robust key extraction from Physical Uncloneable Functions*. In: Ioannidis, Keromytis, Yung (Eds.): Proc. ACNS 2005, LNCS 3531, p.407-422.

[TB2006]   Tuyls P., Batina L.: *RFID-Tags for Anti-Counterfeiting*, In D. Pointcheval (ed.): 'Topics in Cryptology' - CT-RSA 2006, The Cryptographers' Track at the RSA Conference, LNCS 3860, Springer-Verlag, p. 115-131.

[TS2005]   Tuyls P., Škorić B.: *Secret Key Generation from Classical Physics*. In: S. Mukherjee et al (Eds.): 'AmIware: Hardware Technology Drivers of Ambient Intelligence', Philips Research Book Series Vol. 5, Kluwer, 2005., p. 421-447.

[TSSW+2006]   Tuyls P., Škorić B., Schrijen G.J., Wolters R., van Geloven J., Verhaegh N., Kretschman H.: *Read-proof hardware from protective coatings*, accepted at CHES 2006.

Hardware Security Features for Secure Embedded Devices

Helena Handschuh[1] · Elena Trichina [2]

[1]Spansion EMEA, 7 avenue Georges Pompidou
F-92593 Levallois-Perret, France
Helena.Handschuh@spansion.com

[2]Spansion International Inc., Willi-Brandt-Allee 4
D-81829 Munich, Germany
Elena.Trichina@spansion.com

Abstract

Secure embedded Devices for the mobile, financial and automotive markets require more and more security features to resist today's field attacks. At the software level, side-channel attacks such as timing
attacks, power attacks, electro-magnetic attacks and radio-frequency attacks on embedded devices
have been described for a number of years now, and numerous adequate security countermeasures
have been published and implemented by most manufacturers. At the hardware level, the story is completely different. Manufacturers have been aware of physical security issues and invasive/side-channel
attacks for quite some time, but protecting embedded chips against such attacks requires quite some
architectural knowledge and needs to be addressed at the design level. Countermeasures can hardly be
added after the fact.

1 Introduction

In this paper we provide a state-of-the-art overview of hardware security features for secure
embedded devices such as smart cards. In the first part of the paper we describe typical hardware attack techniques and equipment required for reverse-engineering the chip layout and
extracting static secrets from the chip. The main steps in such invasive attacks are chip de-
capsulation by etching, probing, e-beam attacks and focused ion beam attacks. We also deal
with another category of threats which relate to the fact that an attacker may try to influence
the behaviour of the chip while running a sensitive computation. These attacks are called fault
attacks and aim at retrieving secrets used at run-time. They use lasers, X-rays, or even simple
white light flashes.

Another widespread practice among chip manufacturers is a move towards secure system on
chip (SoC) solutions by implementing cryptographic algorithms in hardware. Of course, a
cryptographic accelerator with embedded memory that stores and processes secret keys increases the security level of the device by making attacks much more difficult. However,
"keeping secrets in hardware" is still not a guarantee that they stay secure! At some stage a
co-processor will still have to process secret information "in clear". If this information can be
monitored in a non-invasive way then recovering the key is still possible. In the second part
of the paper we give a number of examples when otherwise beautifully designed cryptographic accelerators might fail to keep secrets if the thought of protection against side channel

S. Paulus, N. Pohlmann, H. Reimer (Editors): Securing Electronic Business Processes, Vieweg (2006), 38-44

attacks was not among the initial design criteria and where the weakness was indeed the datapath itself. We also outline some of the countermeasures at the micro-architecture level that evolved during the last decade and evaluate their effectiveness in the "real world" and when submitted to an "evaluation lab".

2 Physical Attacks on Secure Hardware

2.1 Invasive Techniques

In this section we provide an overview of the main techniques used for invasive attacks. These include chip de-capsulation by etching, probing, e-beam attacks and focused ion beam attacks.

- Chip de-capsulation by etching allows exposing the hardwired logic and memory of the chip. Dry etching refers to the removal of semiconductor material by exposing the material to a bombardment of ions that dislodge portions of the material from the exposed surface. Wet etching is the removal of material by immersing the wafer in a liquid bath of chemical etchant. Both techniques can be applied to achieve the required exposure.

- Probing requires a setup with extremely thin micro-probes or needles which are stitched into a target memory cell or bus line and allows reading the transitions on the bus or the contents of a very specific memory location on the chip. Typically up to 5 or 7 needles can be operated concurrently on the same chip without functionally destroying it. Another way to probe is to use an e-beam coupled with a detector which measures the reflected secondary electrons when the chip is bombarded with electrons and thereby allows to measure if the bus is carrying along a one or a zero.

- Focused ion beams typically bombard an exposed chip with ions and are used to drill holes into certain specific locations in order to cut tracks or disconnect hardwired lines. This allows disabling functional sections of the chip such as random number generators or security sensors as if they never existed. Focused ion beams can also deposit new material to connect tracks and to create new links which hadn't been there before. For example, mechanically blown fuses can be reconstructed this way or large probe pads can be manufactured locally.

Another class of attacks includes invasive attacks which aim at generating random transient computation faults at run-time. These subsequently allow to recover secrets by offline cryptanalytical methods. Typical equipement for such fault attacks include lasers, X-ray machines or simple white light flashes which shine light with different wavelengths onto the chip and sometimes produce the desired effect. Faults may also be a consequence of glitches on the voltage supply or other environmental stress on the chip.

2.2 Hardware Countermeasures

As attacks and threats are being published, manufacturers constantly add new hardware security features on their products. Even though most manufacturers do not publish their designs and keep their security features private, in the following we provide some insight into secure silicon design principles.

- Hardware security sensors detect abnormal environmental conditions such as out-of-range operating temperature, clock frequency or external power supply glitches. They also detect when the chip is flashed with white light, UV or X-rays and take corrective actions such as shutting down the chip or forcing it to reset and clear all sensitive data. This is particularly suited against fault attacks due to external stress.

- Another useful idea is to isolate the internal clock from the external clock supply to disallow random clock glitches and thus to stop fault attacks on the clock itself.

- A protective conductive shield or grid is sometimes placed on top of the chip in order to protect it against physical removal of the passivation layer to avoid invasive attacks using heavier equipment.

- Glue logic design spreads different memory blocks and logical functions all over the chip such that it becomes highly unlikely to be able to reverse-engineer the chip layout. Close-up views of older chips allowed to distinguish different logical components on them. Today, these blocks do not have any distinguishing features any more and cannot easily be localized on a decapsulated chip.

- Dynamic data and address scrambling protect against probing individual ROM, RAM or EEPROM memory cells or external data buses. As a matter of fact, even if probing succeeds, the attacker does not know what he is actually looking at. Scrambling algorithms are still using mostly linear operations, since these need to be hardwired into the chip, but given that few input-output pairs of texts are available to the attacker in the sense of cryptanalysis, this may still be sufficient protection for current generations of chips.

- For further protection against probing attacks, data busses are best buried under several independent metal layers and a submicron scale is used wherever possible.

- Latest flash memory provides an additional technological barrier in the sense that it is much denser (90 downto 65nm technology) than other types of memory and thus much more difficult to read out. Preliminary evaluations of such flash memories seem to indicate invasive attacks are becoming increasingly difficult to set up and current methodologies remain basically ineffective.

3 SoC and Cryptographic Coprocessors

Implementing cryptographic algorithm in SoC results in a black box that has several observable physical properties such as power consumption, electromagnetic radiation, time required to complete an operation... This side-channel information can be measured when the device processes secret information, and the measurements can be used for attacking the secret key. This fact has been known since the early days of smart cards and has been discreetly addressed in patents such as [FS95] that proposed to mask power consumption signals while reading and writing logical zeroes or ones by adding to a circuit so called simulation cells built in such a way that they consume current substantially equal to those of memory cells. With the publications [K96] and [KJJ99], the genie has been let out of the bottle; and ever since there is a race between a growing sophistication of hardware side channel attacks and countermeasures.

3.1 Attacks on Public Key Coprocessors

Paul Kocher's publication [K96] became so influential because it presented to a general public for the first time a practical attack that used side channel information to determine a part of the cipher key. In this attack "by carefully measuring the amount of time required for private key operations", the bits of the key were revealed experimentally. The attack was based on the fact that ALUs in modern microcontrollers are optimized for square and multiply operations, so that squares take much less time than multiply operations. Most of the public key cryptographic schemes are based on modular exponentiation, and modular exponentiation normally would use a binary algorithm which scans a key bit by bit, and if the bit is set to 0 then only modular squaring is performed, otherwise the square operation is followed by a multiply. Since multiply takes more time than square, the observed time difference reveals the bits of the key!

This type of attacks, where the secret information is revealed directly by measurements, is called simple side channel analysis attacks. These attacks are intuitive for both, attackers and designers, and defence against them is relatively easy. Unfortunately, there is a type of side channel attacks that is based on the property inherent in circuits built with the standard static CMOS logic style which is the most established method for implementing custom hardware. So-called Differential Power Analysis (DPA) attacks rely on the fact that the power consumption of the circuit depends on the data that it processes, as described below.

Overall, there are three factors contributing to a total power consumption P of the CMOS gate, namely static power due to leakage currents (P_{sta}), short-circuit power due to non ideal switching characteristics (P_{sc}), and the dynamic power consumed by charging or discharging output load (P_{dyn}): $P = P_{sta} + P_{sc} + P_{dyn}$. If the contributions of P_{sta} and P_{sc} are neglected, this equation can be simplified to $P \sim P_{dyn} = a\, f\, C_L\, V_{DD}^2$.

The supply voltage V_{DD} and the operation frequency f can be considered constant for a given circuit. The load capacitance C_L driven by the circuit is in effect determined by the netlist of the circuit. The activity factor a is determined by the data that is being processed by the circuit. This means that as soon as a cryptographic key is being processed, the circuit's power consumption depends to a certain degree on the key value.

DPA attacks target this specific moment of execution of the algorithm. Of course, only a small part of the key is being attacked at once, the length of the attacked subkey being chosen so that a manageable number K of possible values (permutations) exists. Using a simple model of the circuit (for example, models based on Hamming weights or on Hamming distances), for every possible value from the set K, S samples are processed (simulated) and the hypothetical power consumption is calculated.

Then the power consumption of the real circuit is measured while it processes the same S samples with a chosen but unknown subkey. Statistical methods are used to correlate the power measurement results to a set of hypothetical power consumption expectations for various values of the subkey from the set of all possible permutations obtained at the simulation step. In a successful attack, the correct subkey hypothesis will show a "significantly higher" correlation to the measured power than all other subkey hypotheses.

Initially most of the successful real-life published attacks targeted implementations of cryptographic algorithms on relatively simple microcontrollers; for a typical ASIC implementation composed of few hundreds of thousands of gates to determine the exact shape of the power supply current seemed to be impossible. However, in 1999 the confirmation that differential power analysis attacks on cryptographic hardware is indeed possible appeared in [MDS99] where the authors developed attack techniques on a binary method of modular exponentiation widely used in RSA algorithm. In order to confirm that the attack worked in real life, an experiment was conducted using a smartcard equipped with a Montgomery multiplication circuit to speed up modular reduction. The experiment carried out on 64-bit long data and modulus demonstrated that with statistical methods it was indeed possible to distinguish the bias signal for correct and incorrect guesses of the exponent bit due to minor variations in power consumption between squaring and multiplication even if they were performed in a uniform way on a special-purpose multiplier. The variations were due entirely to differences in processed data which are equal for squaring and different for multiplication.

The countermeasures for RSA are fortunately on an algorithmic, software level:

- Masking a message with a random value v_i prior to exponentiation (and unmasking it after exponentiation with $v_f = (v_i^{-1})^e \bmod N$ in order to preclude an attacker from predicting intermediate results

- Blinding an exponent by, for example, randomly splitting it into two shares and executing exponentiation first with one, and then with another share

- Randomization of exponentiation algorithm itself

3.2 Attacks on Secret Key Accelerators

For secret key accelerators the situation differs: no software countermeasures can be added to a hardware cipher. On the other hand, usually such a cipher is a very small, difficult to locate part of a large SoC, and rather than observing an instantaneous power consumption at the cipher output at a precise moment, what can be measured is the power consumption of the entire ASIC during a clock period. Specialized evaluation labs probably can conduct attacks anyway; and in 2004 an academic publication described a real attack on a competent, albeit designed by graduate students, ASIC implementation of Advanced Encryption Standard [OGOP04]. The attack exploited a specific feature of the datapath itself, where in order to optimize performance, the result of the initialization operation that XOR-s 128-bits of a plaintext with 128-bits of the secret key, was written into a register at the rising edge of the second clock cycle. Hence, it was enough to measure power consumption of the AES core during the first two clock cycles since these data contained information which was directly related to the attacked key. Even with a 128-bit datapath the attackers could successfully use "divide and conquer" techniques by targeting only the first 8 bits of the key and minimizing the effect of the power signal that was unrelated to the first 8 bits by carefully selecting input data and by treating unrelated signal as noise.

This was an attack on registers, somewhat similar to traditional attacks on microprocessors. However, a year later a new powerful attack targeted the intermediate results that occur only at the outputs of logic gates [MPO05]. The Byte Substitution operation (so-called S-box) in the first round of the AES has been chosen as an ideal target for an attack. The result of the S-box is calculated based on one byte of a plaintext (controlled by an attacker) and one byte of the cipher key, and the operation has an interesting property that helps in conducting statistical attacks, namely, a 1 bit change in the S-box input results into changes of approximately half of the bits of the S-box output. The attacked AES co-processor however, did not write the output into registers but used them directly as inputs in the subsequent operation. Therefore, intermediate results occurred only at the output of logic gates in the S-box implementation.

The transitions occurring at logic gates are very difficult to predict because logic gates switch their output potentially several times per clock cycle. In order to assess the power consumption of the combinational circuit, the complete "glass box" simulation based on a back-annotated netlist of the attacked part of the AES circuit was conducted for all possible input transitions, and for each simulation the number of transitions that occurred at the interesting part was counted using a specially developed tool. The statistics calculated on these results have been used to predict the outputs of logic gates of a real circuit. Although the preprocessing stage included acquisitions of millions of power traces to collect statistics, the final attack revealed 8-bits of the key with only 25,000 measurements.

Although attacks carried out in both described examples are not likely to occur in the field, they still illustrate one important principal: the countermeasures for secret key ciphers must be built-in, not add-on. The far from exhaustive list includes:

- Countermeasures that aim to prevent an attacker from predicting accurately the time when certain data are processed in a certain way. These include randomization of external clock by clock skipping or alternatively using internal self-timed clocks with randomized frequency modulation or clock jitter. At a system architecture level, asynchronous self-timed circuits were proposed as well as techniques similar to multithreading with threads randomly selected

- Countermeasures that increase noise to signal ratio of the measurements by using random register and network pre-charging, random register re-naming, insertion of operations on random data interleaved with real operations with or without duplication of hardware, and by simply adding a noise source such as LFSR

- Countermeasures that de-correlate the power signal and processed data by masking all data with random values. Several alternative masking schemes were proposed for AES, from algorithmic level multiplicative masking to a gate level substitution of each gate in the data path with a "masked equivalent", as in the first published industrial AES core with a gate-level masking [TKL05]

- Countermeasures that aim to decrease signal to noise ratio by equalizing dynamic power dissipation while processing zeros and ones. These are usually based on non-standard logic styles, such as dual or dynamic logic, and require full custom design

4 Conclusion

In this paper, we provided an overview of physical hardware attacks, side-channel attacks on cryptographic coprocessors and associated hardware security features for state-of-the-art secure embedded devices. Both attacks and hardware countermeasures remain quite intuitive today, but Common Criteria evaluation labs work towards providing a more formal approach to security assurance. The overall hardware security of current embedded chips is rather satisfactory. Eventually, the amount of hardware security features being added on the chip is directly proportional to the value of the goods the embedded device should protect.

References

[AK97]   Anderson, R., Kuhn, M.: Low cost attacks on tamper resistant devices, In M. Loman et al. (eds.), Security Protocols, proceedings 5th International Workshop IWSP, volume 1361 of Lecture Notes in Computer Science, pp. 125-136, Springer-Verlag, 1997.

[FS90]   Fruhauf, S., Sourge, L.: Safety device against the unauthorized detection of protected data, U.S. patent number 5,404,402; April4, 1995.

[K96]   Kocher, P.: Timing attacks on implementations of Diffie-Hellman, RSA, DSS, and other sytems, In Advances in Cryptology -- CRYPTO'96, volume 1109 of Lecture Notes in Computer Science, pp. 103-113, Springer-Verlag, 1996.

[KJJ99]   Kocher, P., Jaffe, J., Jun, B.: Differential power analysis, In Advances in Cryptology -- CRYPTO'99, volume 1666 of Lecture Notes in Computer Science, pp. 388-397, Springer-Verlag, 1999.

[KK99]   Kommerling, O., Kuhn, M.: Design principles for tamper-resistant smartcard
            processors, In Proc. USENIX Workshop on Smartcard Technology (Smartcard
            99), pp. 9-20, 1999.

[MDS99]   Messergers, T.S., Dabbish, E.A., Sloan, R.H.: Power Analysis Attacks on Modu-
            lar Exponentiation in Smartcards, In Cryptographic Hardware and Embedded
            Systems: CHES 1999, volume 1717 of Lecture Notes in Computer Science, pp.
            144-157, Springer-Verlag, 1999.

[OGOP04]   Ors, S. B., Gurkaynak, F., Oswald, E., Preneel, B.: Power-Analysis Attack on an
            ASIC AES Implementation, In Proc. Int. Conference on Information Technology
            (ITCC), volume 2, pp. 546-552, April 2004.

[MPO05]   Mangard, S., Pramstaller, N., Oswald, E.,: Sucessfully Attacking Masked AES
            Hardware Implementation, In Cryptographic Hardware and Embedded Systems:
            CHES 2005, volume 3659 of Lecture Notes in Computer Science, pp. 157-171,
            Springer-Verlag, 2006.

[TKL05]   Trichina, E., Korkishko, T., Lee K.-H.: Small size, low power, side-channel im-
            mune AES co-processor: Design and synthesis results, In Proc. Of the Forth
            Conf. on the Advanced Encryption Standard (AES 2005), volume 3373 of Lec-
            ture Notes in Computer Science, pp. 113-127, Springer-Verlag, 2006.

Security in Next Generation Consumer Electronic Devices

Tom Kan · Tim Kerins · Klaus Kursawe

Information and System Security Group, Philips Research Europe,
Prof. Holstlaan 4, 5656 AA, Eindhoven, The Netherlands
{Tom.Kan | Tim.Kerins | Klaus.Kursawe}@philips.com

Abstract

In this paper we categorise the goals of attackers of consumer electronic devices and identify common attack vectors. The challenges of implementing a security solution on consumer electronic devices are discussed and a defence strategy against common current and future attacks is outlined.

1 Introduction

The nature of consumer electronic (CE) devices is changing. Previous generations of devices included TVs, DVD players and mobile phones with a large proportion of device control hard-wired at manufacture time. Nowadays, an increasing amount of device functionality runs in software for increased flexibility over dedicated hardware solutions. The next generation of CE devices will also include "intelligent" household appliances and mobile computing devices, all running software and all interconnected as part of a ubiquitous computing environment.

The increasing value of information stored on such devices, and also their increased functionality and user reliance make them an attractive target for attackers. Conversely, the tendency to open-up and interconnect such devices will make them increasingly more vulnerable to attacks. Although it is unlikely that for example, a coffee machine will contain any highly privileged information, it may offer a digital channel to more sensitive data. This may happen since intelligent devices will communicate with each other across multiple domains.

The aims of this paper are to discuss the motivation of potential attackers of intelligent CE devices, as well as to identify immediate threats and common attack vectors. In response to this a layered security approach is described to protect CE devices against some of the most dangerous common threats.

This paper is outlined as follows: Section 2.1 describes the possible motivations of attackers of CE devices, and Section 2.2 describes some common attack vectors. The challenges of security engineering for CE devices are described in Section 3.1 and the layered protection strategy is outlined in Section 3.2. In Section 4 the need for dedicated security technology for CE devices is discussed and the conclusions of the paper are in Section 5.

2 CE Devices Under Attack

Manufacturers and users of CE devices would like their devices to behave exactly as advertised. An attack on a CE device can be defined as any tampering with a device that changes its documented, manufacturer advertised and user expected behaviour.

S. Paulus, N. Pohlmann, H. Reimer (Editors): Securing Electronic Business Processes, Vieweg (2006), 45-53

2.1 Goals of Attackers

The goals of potential attackers of CE devices are varied, but can be broken down into a number of main categories:

- Attackers might try to use content, which is processed on such a device, in an unauthorised manner. The content provider generally governs access to premium content. Usually the digital content data is not allowed to go anywhere other than in encrypted form and a successful attack is any method that circumvents this.

- Attackers might attack a vulnerability in a device to steal the user's assets, e.g. a signature key, or the IMEI –code. This would lead to significant privacy problems for the user and may result in the theft of user identity.

- Attackers may attack a specific device vulnerability in a device to simply disrupt normal behaviour. Depending on where the device is used, the effects can reach from simple annoyance (e.g., in media players) to significant damage and life threatening situations (e.g., in industrial controllers).

- Some devices impose software restrictions, e.g. differently priced models sharing the same hardware or subsidised cell phones. An attacker may be able to circumvent this to obtain services he did not in fact pay for.

- Attackers may attempt to illegally copy or clone part or all of a CE device. A current example of this is the problem of attackers unlocking and cloning SIM cards in cell phones.

- There is also a significant percentage of attackers that will attack devices just "for the fun of it"

It is a misconception to assume that potential attackers will be hobbyists. Even "private" attackers without financial backing may have very high levels of expertise and they also may have access to very high quality equipment [Huan03]; professional attackers can be expected to have even better means available. Often only a small number of experienced attackers are required to launch a successful attack. This knowledge can then potentially be widely distributed and codified into easy to use tools. Thus enabling many more relatively unskilled attackers. For software attacks this is known as the "break-once-run-everywhere" (BORE) problem and is currently a significant problem in the PC domain where systems are generally open.

2.2 Attack Models and Protection Profile

In the past, CE systems used to be simple, mostly fixed purpose hardwired devices, so attackers had little opportunity to change the behaviour of the devices. Modern CE devices, such as a digital TV, are increasingly complex. As a result many CE devices are currently implemented on programmable and flexible platforms running software on their own operating systems (OSes). This flexibility also allows software attacks, launched either intentionally or without the user's knowledge.

These attacks are dangerous because often, once an attack is known, it is relatively cheap to implement. If care is not taken then a single attacker can threaten an entire platform series. Although a percentage of devices will continue to be attacked using hardware methods, it is expected that the most immediate threats will be from malicious software. See [DaKl05, Huan03, Mull05] for examples of recent successful software and hardware based attacks on CE devices.

It is often assumed – wrongly – that due to their relatively closed architecture, future CE devices will be secure against most of the troubles we know from the PC world. However, any unsecured device interface, e.g. Bluetooth, USB, Firewire, DVD Readers, debug ports etc, may be potentially used by an attacker to introduce unauthorized code. The difficulties of securing a device from physical access, however, are only the tip of the iceberg as the move towards a completely connected world continues. Here multiple "intelligent" devices will communicate with each other. The potential for virus and worm propagation is potentially much worse than what is currently seen in the PC world due to the pervasiveness of CE devices in our society.

Consider the potential scenario where the media player in a home entertainment centre downloads infected media content – the recently published WMF vulnerability in the Windows Metafile Format is only one example of a security exploit in media data [Vuln05]. A multi-platform virus could then propagate to the user's PDA, obtaining the user's credit card numbers and then mailing them to the attacker. Then it propagates itself to all the other people in the user's address book From the PDA it propagates itself back to media players – this could even be in the user's car where it gains control of the vehicles on-board computer. The consequences of such an attack can clearly be devastating. A large number of cell phone to cell phone viruses currently exist [McDo05] and cross platform viruses have already been reported [Szor05]. In principle, virus writers are well capable of engineering cross platform viruses for CE devices.

The protection profile of a particular device will depend on the specific device functionality and also what the designer considers most important to protect. For example in components in medical systems reliable functionality has highest priority, even above confidentiality of information, while in a device such as a PDA which stores sensitive user data it may be preferable to risk device failure rather than leak this information to unauthorised parties. In general however, there are three important items that will require security:

- The correct device functionality
- Any operational secrets (such as cryptographic keys) stored on the device
- Particular content or user data stored on the device

For example in a device implementing a conditional access scheme, a primary concern is the content keys and also the secure output of decrypted content. This situation is further complicated as in certain cases there are a number of different stakeholders with different security goals. In the case of cell phones, for example, the consumer, the device vendor and also the network provider all have their own views on correct device behaviour.

3 Protecting CE devices

In light of the threats mentioned previously increasingly security is becoming an important feature of CE devices.

3.1 Security Strategy for CE

Experience has shown that successful security solutions are generally built into systems from the very initial stages of design and that is the approach that should also be adopted here. See [Ande01] for a good overview of successful (and unsuccessful!) security engineering. A good security solution must be pervasive throughout the entire device. In the case of CE devices, however, it must exist in a highly constrained environment in terms of space, clock cycles, power, etc.

These constraints imply that many of the tried and trusted security solutions from the PC security community cannot be naively applied to CE devices. Although not fully open systems, as in the case of PCs, CE devices are however partially open for software upgrades, and often there is potentially relatively easy access to internal components, debug pins, etc. As a result, this implies that the closed device model that has been successfully applied to smart card protection is also not directly applicable here. One should keep in mind though that, in principle, CE devices are also potentially vulnerable to the same side channel attacks as those computing platforms [Bern05, KoJJ98]. It is sensible to consider defences against these types of attacks but only after the device has reached a reasonable level of security against easier to mount automated attacks, malware and software vulnerabilities. It is also important that a security solution must not detract from the internal timing, and that it does not interfere negatively with the end user experience.

Despite these difficulties the device manufacturer has a number of unique advantages that can be leveraged. There is a degree of control over the choices of internal device design and running software stacks and introduction of new software into the device. These can be leveraged to architect a good security solution. The overall aim of a security strategy for CE is for the manufacturer intended and user anticipated behaviour to persist in a device. An attacker should not have the ability to disrupt the end user experience.

3.2   A level of Protection in CE Devices

It is possible to significantly raise the security of a CE device by a number of simple mechanisms. Here we outline a multi-level approach designed to prevent the proliferation of software-based exploits on CE devices.

3.2.1   Eliminating Errors in Code

Software errors and particularly the buffer overflow are amongst the most common attack vectors for exploiting software and device functionality. Attack code is generally based on errors in the existing software base [HoMc04]. Eliminating errors in software is a difficult problem. The number of errors in a software system is strongly linked to the programming language used. A "safe language" can give very good results eliminating at least the basic errors like buffer overflows and stale pointers. In a safe language the language compiler and runtime together ascertain that these basic errors cannot occur. This is often achieved by interplay between the language features, such as not allowing the programmer to explicitly allocate and deallocate memory, and implicit runtime bounds checking. Examples of languages with these features are C# and Caml.

The number of errors in a piece of software is broadly speaking proportional to the amount of code. This implies that the smaller its code size, the more confident one can be that exploitable bugs have been eliminated. This is especially true for that part of the code in a system that must be trusted for reliable device operation. This is referred to as the Trusted Code Base (TCB).

The TCB is a useful concept to gauge the effectiveness of a security technology as the TCB forms the foundation for the software security measures in the system. The TCB itself should be verified at design time using, for example, code inspection and formal modeling. The smaller the TCB, the easier it is to verify, the more likely that it is possible to obtain an acceptable level of trustworthiness for it. This makes it attractive to reduce the size of the TCB as much as is reasonably possible.

3.2.2 Secure Boot

Once the effort has been spent on eliminating design- and implementation-time errors in the code, eventually the system will have to be started-up. However, in a CE device there may be a significant window of opportunity for an attacker to modify the code in a system before it actually does start-up. A secure boot process can be used to close this window of opportunity.

A secure boot process on CE devices is important to ensure that the device starts in a well-defined state that is known to be secure. This defends against attackers who wish to modify the system software before the device starts up, for example reprogramming flash memories on a CE device. It consists mainly of a hard-coded start-up routine for the CPU that crypto-graphically verifies the authenticity of subsequent core modules before handing control of the device over to the next stage in the boot process. For an example implementation of this methodology see [ArFS97].

It is possible to chain several stages in this manner, each verifying the authenticity of a subsequent code module before handing over control to it. This part of the process can be performed in conjunction with a lightweight security module, the Trusted Platform Module (TPM), as discussed in Section 4. However, it can also be used without a TPM if another method of secure storage of the verification signatures can be used.

The reason for doing this is that it is only possible to trust a system if it is known which code has previously run on it, from the moment the system was started. The aim is to have the system start in a known state, which is trusted. This idea is closely related to the concept of a "root-of-trust" on a device. This is some known information that is used to validate the integrity of a device.

3.2.3 Prevent Unauthorised Introduction of New Code

If an attacker is prevented from introducing new code into a device it is going to be much more difficult to attack it. Preventing the introduction of new code into a system can be achieved using different approaches depending on the source of the new code.

An obvious way to introduce alternative code in the system is to upload an alternative code image. Modern CE systems often have their code stored in flash memory so that updates in the field are possible. As previously discussed, if no measures are taken to prevent updating the flash with just any code presented to the device, then all other security measures become irrelevant. An attacker could just update the flash with a modified code image and that would give him full control over the system. The secure boot process described in Section 3.2.2 is a good method of preventing these types of code image replacement attacks.

The device should verify the authenticity of the code image before using it to update the flash content. The system should proceed with the update only if the code image has been signed by an authorized party. This does assume that the system is in control during the update process. So an additional requirement is that it must be difficult (or at least very hard, as in a hardware attack, soldering etc.) to update the flash content while the system is powered off.

A potential source of unauthorized code is attackers trying to use buffer overflows and similar mechanisms to inject new code into the system at runtime. One approach to prevent this from happening is making the data spaces in memory non-executable and code spaces non-writable (write xor execute). This can be achieved by dedicated hardware support causing the processor to trap if an attempt is made to modify code or execute data. The reason this works is that the code in a buffer overflow attack generally starts as data in the buffer that is overflowing.

If the hardware of the system would trap any attempt to execute that data, then the buffer overflow attack would not succeed.

An indirect approach works by scrambling all the authorized code with a device key before it is stored on the device at design and update time. When executing the code, instructions are de-scrambled on the fly by the processor. A direct result of scrambling the code is a certain level of added confidentiality for the authorized code in the system, although that is not the primary goal here.

An indirect result that any attack code that has not been scrambled with the device key, because the attacker does not know it will be garbled by the de-scrambling process on its way to the CPU. This is extremely unlikely to lead to valid machine code and it will therefore most likely cause a crash of the affected process instead of giving the attacker control of the system. Of course this method should only be used when it is important that arbitrary code is not run, possibly at the expense of a device crash. This may be a viable option in some conditional access schemes.

The amount of confidentiality added depends on the strength of the scrambling algorithm used. If code confidentiality is deemed important, then a strong encryption algorithm will have to be chosen, leading to high overhead costs for the decryption process. If only blocking the introduction of unauthorized code is important then the strength of the encryption algorithm is of no importance and a very basic, lightweight algorithm can be chosen.

This method can be used to bind code uniquely to a device if each device has its own unique key and that it is possible to scramble code before storage on a per-device basis. Binding code to a device in this manner will greatly reduce the potential for CE virus and worm propagation previously described. It may also help against cloning of some device components. As software would no longer easily run on cloned components cloning would no longer be financially attractive.

3.2.4 Isolation

Isolation is the general term used for enforcing separation between different software components in a device. In a security context it is actually used for two reasons:

- Damage Control: When software components are unable to influence each other because of the employed isolation technology then this limits the amount of damage caused by a compromise of one of the components.

- Reducing the TCB: Strategically isolating software components from each other makes it possible to effectively remove certain components from the TCB. This leads to a reduction of the size of the TCB making it easier to verify.

Generally only a relatively small amount of code is needed to enforce software isolation. Isolation is important in a multi-layer CE device security approach as it gives the capability to limit the effect of one component (or software stack) from the remainder of the device.

A method of achieving isolation between software components on CE devices is by virtualization of the underlying hardware. It is possible to create entire virtual machines (VMs), i.e. the appearance of multiple complete computer systems within one physical machine. In this case the applications, or even entire operating systems, are not aware that they are running on a virtual machine, possibly next to other different operating systems. In this case components and software stacks are isolated from each other as, from their perspective, they are the only software running in a VM, and their only interaction with the rest of the device is through the virtual hardware architecture.

A Virtual machine monitor (VMM) is the component that actually implements the virtualization and creates multiple instances of VMs on top of a physical machine. Typically it is a software abstraction of processor architecture, memory manager unit (MMU), instruction set architecture (ISA), peripherals and physical memory. When using virtualization for security purposes it is useful to use virtualization on top of bare hardware because this leads to the smallest TCB. In this case the TCB is the software for the VMM itself. The functionality of a VMM typically offers:

- Memory management
- Scheduling
- Device virtualization

For further information and a good overview of virtualization technologies see [FiDF05].

Micro-kernels are designed with the design philosophy that only the core kernel functionality runs at the highest privilege level. Other functions, such as device drivers or network protocol stacks are implemented as processes running independently of the kernel at a lower privilege level. Historically the design goals of micro kernels did not include virtualization. Only recently some parts of the micro kernel community are starting to incorporate this. Micro-kernel based approaches such as those described in [Lied95], with the correct design choices for isolation also provide potential for a level of security, which is stronger than many traditional OSes with monolithic kernels. These also have the advantage that the TCB is relatively small.

3.2.5 Obstructing Analysis

After care has been taken to eliminate software bugs, to prevent the introduction of new code into a device and to isolate software components from each other, the next step in increasing the difficulty of mounting a successful attack is preventing an attacker from monitoring the data interfaces on a device. Encrypting or sufficiently scrambling all of the device interfaces can achieve this. This will make analysis of the device behavior much more difficult. Of course debug ports should also be disabled or suitably encrypted.

In a similar manner internal data encryption, code obfuscation and white box cryptography also have potential here in hindering analysis even if an attacker somehow manages to extract some data from the device. These methods are useful, as part of a "defense-in depth" strategy where even if an attacker does manage to extract some data from the device, it is difficult to extract meaning from it and so has no real advantage in constructing an attack.

4 Security in Small Spaces

Cryptography is an important element as part of a security solution on a CE device and is useful as part of a secure boot process and for securing and verifying code. It is important for these algorithms to run as efficiently as possible and to ultimately remain invisible to the device end user. The fundamental problem here is that high performance primitives are typically expensive in gate count, code size and power consumption. This leads to an interesting trade-off between performance and size in algorithm implementations.

An increase of the order of thousands of gates on a chip may be considered unacceptable for certain applications. The current requirement of many private key primitives is of the order of thousands of gates, with public key primitives requiring somewhat more. The development of new protocols and primitives, and the adaptation of existing primitives are necessary for use in CE devices to match this particularly constrained environment.

Similar restrictions hold if the specifications for a TPM as defined by the Trusted Computing Group [TCG06,Mitc05] are to be applied to a CE context. Being originally designed for PC and server platforms; it is a rather challenging task to fit such modules into the price and resource constraints of a consumer device. One current approach is the development of a "light" version of a TPM; such a module would offer a similar API but with restricted functionality. It is for example not necessary to equip a TPM in a DVD player with user management and opt-out functionality. Also, some functionality could be replaced by more resource friendly alternatives, e.g. using AES instead of RSA encryption. A first approach to adapt the TCG specification is currently under development by the TCG subgroup for mobile devices, which may also be a base for TPMs in CE devices.

5 Conclusions

The potential for software attacks on future CE devices is large and can have devastating consequences for user privacy and safety. A number of relatively cheap and simple precautions used together, such as:

- Taking care the code is free of exploitable bugs
- Secure bootstrapping
- Disabling the execution of arbitrary code
- Binding code to a device
- Isolating software components
- Obscuring analysis

can greatly help to prevent to propagation of CE viruses and other malicious software.

The security strategies presented in this paper will considerably "raise the bar" for attackers of CE devices. If applied correctly the potential damage caused my malicious software on CE devices can be greatly decreased. However, in general, the adaptation of security methods specifically matching the requirements of CE devices is currently still an open research problem.

References

[Ande01]   Anderson R. Security Engineering: A Guide to Building Dependable Distributed Systems, Wiley, 2001

[ArFS97]   Arbaugh W. A. Farber D. J. Smith J. M. A secure and reliable bootstrap architecture, In IEEE Symposium on Security and Privacy, 1997, p. 65-2

[Bern05]   Bernstein D. J. Cache-timing attacks on AES 2005

[DaKl05]   Daniel C. Kleffel T. Hacking TomTomGo, In 22nd Chaos Communication Congress 2005

[FiDF05]   Figueiredo R. Dinda P. A. Fortes J. IEEE Computer Magazine: Virtualization Technologies, vol 38, no 5. May 2005

[HoMc04]   Hoglund G. McGraw G. Exploiting Software: How to Break Code, Addison-Wesley 2004

[Huan03]   Huang A. Hacking the Xbox: An Introduction to Reverse Engineering, No Starch Press 2003

[KoJJ98]   Kocher P. Jaffe J. Jun Introduction to Differential Power Analysis and Related
            Attacks, Cryptography Research Inc.White Paper 1998

[McDo05]   McAffee & NTT DoCoMo The Future of Mobile Security – Here Today 2005,
            p 3-4

[LTMP00]   Lie D. Thekkath C. Mitchell M. Lincon P. Boneh D. Mitchell J. Horowitz M.
            Architectural Support for Copy and Tamper Resistant Software. In 9th Interna-
            tional Conference on Architectural Support for Programming Languages and
            Operating Systems SAPLOS-IX, 2000, p.169-177

[Lied95]   Liedtke J. On Micro-Kernel Construction. In 15th ACM Symposium on Operat-
            ing System Principles, 1995, p. 237-250

[Mitc05]   Mitchell C. Trusted Computing IEE. Professional Applications of Computing
            Series 6, 2005

[Mull05]   Mulliner C. Exploiting Pocket PC, What the Hack! 2005

[Szor05]   Szor P. The Art of Computer Virus Research and Defence, Addison Wesley
            2005

[TCG06]   www.trustedcomputinggroup.org

[Vuln05]   Vulnerability Note VU#121038 Microsoft Windows Metafile handler
            SETABORTPROC GDI Escape Vulnerability 2005

Security Architecture for Device Encryption and VPN

Ammar Alkassar[1] · Michael Scheibel[1] · Christian Stüble[2]
Ahmad-Reza Sadeghi[3] · Marcel Winandy[3]

[1]Sirrix AG Security Technologies
{a.alkassar | m.scheibel}@sirrix.com

[2]Ruhr-University Bochum
stueble@acm.org

[3]Ruhr-University Bochum
{sadeghi | winandy}@crypto.rub.de

Abstract

Encryption systems are widely used to protect stored and communicated data from unauthorized access. Unfortunately, most software-based encryption products suffer from various vulnerabilities such as insecure storage and usage capabilities for security-critical cryptographic keys and operations. In this paper we present a security architecture that allows secure, reliable and user-friendly encryption of devices and of TCP/IP communication. The architecture is capable of using Trusted Computing functionalities and offers a security level which is comparable to a hardware based solution, but is far more cost-effective. We have already implemented a device encryption system and a VPN client. Moreover, the security architecture is an appropriate basis for many applications such as Enterprise Rights Management (ERM) and secure Online Banking.

1 Introduction

Encryption systems are widely used to protect stored and communicated data from unauthorized access. Application areas include device (e.g. hard disk) encryption as well as Virtual Private Networks (VPN).

Unfortunately, most software-based encryption products suffer from various vulnerabilities such as insecure storage and usage capabilities for security-critical cryptographic keys and operations. The underlying operating systems (OS) cannot prevent other (potentially malicious) applications from gaining access to the critical key data. The reasons lie in conceptual weaknesses of common computing platforms, in particular in insecure OS architectures. This is evident by the huge number of exploits and constant security updates.

S. Paulus, N. Pohlmann, H. Reimer (Editors): Securing Electronic Business Processes, Vieweg (2006), 54-63

We present a security architecture that allows secure, reliable and user-friendly encryption of devices and of TCP/IP communication. The security architecture strongly isolates the secret (key) information and all related security-critical operations from the operating system. A security software layer is installed between the hardware layer and the operating system layer to isolate the legacy operating system (including legacy applications) from security-critical applications. This is similar to a hardware based solution but far more cost-effective. Moreover, the architecture is capable of using Trusted Computing functionalities to protect the cryptographic keys and to assure software integrity during the booting process of the system.

2 Existing Solutions

Existing software device encryption systems [Micr05a, PGPC05, Safe05, Utim05] provide features such as strong symmetric encryption, a centralized user administration and policy enforcement, key recovery mechanisms, two-factor pre-boot authentication, and multi-user support. Some of these solutions integrate a Trusted Platform Module (TPM) [TCGW05] to bind encryption keys to hardware and/or software components and for secure random number generation.

To the best of our knowledge, none of these systems strongly isolate the encryption keys and operations from the operating system. Thus, if the operating system fails (maliciously or accidentially), the encryption system will fail, too. This pertains to commonly used VPN clients as well, e.g., [Cisc05].

Representative examples of commercial software encryption systems serving both application areas are described next.

2.1 Windows Vista BitLocker Drive Encryption

BitLocker Drive Encryption (formerly known as "Secure Startup - Full Volume Encryption") is a hard disk encryption system integrated into the upcoming client version release of Microsoft's Windows Operating System ("Windows Vista").

The feature optionally uses a TPM version 1.2 to ensure that system files have not been tampered with while the system was offline. This is achieved by the TPM's "sealing" functionality: A TPM-aware bootmanager[1] first measures the integrity of all OS components before passing control to them. These integrity values are compared to reference values stored inside the TPM before unrevealing the encryption key.

BitLocker is transparent to the user as it encrypts the entire Windows volume including all user and system files. For full user transparency, BitLocker does not use the TPM authentication mechanisms. The authorization secret of the TPM Storage Root Key (SRK) which is needed for the sealing functionality is set to a value of 20 bytes of zero [Micr05b]. Thus, applications (even if running on other operating systems) cannot use the full security functionality of the TPM.

---

[1] Interestingly, the boot partition containing the bootmanager should be as large as 50 MB [Micr05a]. Code of this size provides a large attack surface and is very difficult to verify.

BitLocker Drive Encryption/Secure Startup does explicitly not protect the cryptographic keys from malicious software:

"...a Trojan[2] can be downloaded when the administrative user is connected to the Internet, compromising the system security including Secure Startup. In this situation, the system could be compromised if it is lost or stolen." [Micr05a], p.8.

2.2 Cisco VPN Client

The Cisco VPN Client establishes IP security (IPSec) tunnels to remote sites [Cisc05]. It is available for Microsoft Windows, Mac OS, Solaris, and Linux operating systems. Pre-shared keys are stored in RAM; passwords are stored in plain text files [Cisc04]. As the above operating systems have full access to both RAM and files, malicious software, having once gained system privileges, can read out these authorization secrets. An attacker may then connect to the Virtual Private Network from another host.

3 The EMSCB Project

Our solution has been developed in the context of the European Multilaterally Secure Computing Base (EMSCB) project [Emsc06]. This project which is partly funded by the German Federal Ministry of Economics and Technology aims at developing a trustworthy computing platform, based on open standards and open source, that solves many security problems of conventional platforms. The EMSCB consortium includes several scientific and industrial partners. An implementation of the security architecture developed within the EMSCB project has recently been published under the name "Turaya" [Emsc06].

The Turaya computing platform builds on a hardware layer that is optionally enhanced by Trusted Computing (TC) technology, e.g., a TPM. A security kernel provides an abstract interface to these hardware resources and guarantees strong isolation of applications. When focussing encryption systems, the isolation feature of the security kernel can be used to prevent potentially malicious software from accessing cryptographic keys and operations. Additionally, the security kernel integrates security-critical services such as a secure user interface, persistent storage, and secure booting. On top of the Turaya security kernel existing operating systems are running in parallel to - but strongly isolated from - security-critical applications (Figure 1). The security kernel is capable of integrating virtualization software such as the Xen virtual machine monitor [Univ06], and is prepared to take use of emerging hardware virtualization technologies [Adva06,Inte06].

In the sense of multilateral security, the Turaya platform allows the enforcement of security policies of different parties, i.e., end-users as well as business companys. Consequently, the platform enables the realization of various innovative business models, particularly in the area of Digital Rights Management, while averting the potential risks of Trusted Computing platforms concerning privacy issues. The basic Turaya technology will be made available under an an open-source license.

---

[2] A computer program with an apparently or actually useful function that contains additional (hidden) functions that surreptitiously exploit the legitimate authorizations of the invoking process to the detriment of security. [USDe85]

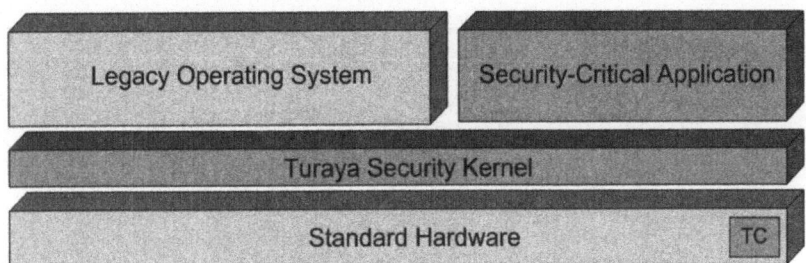

Figure 1: Turaya Architecture Overview

4 Turaya Security Kernel

The Turaya security kernel is a small security software layer which can be logically divided into a hypervisor layer and a trusted software layer (Figure 2).

The main task of the hypervisor layer is to provide an abstract interface of the underlying hardware resources like interrupts, memory and hardware devices[3]. Moreover, this layer allows to share these resources and realizes access control enforcement on the object types known to this layer. Currently we are using a microkernel[4] as the foundation of the hypervisor layer.

The trusted software layer builds on the hypervisor layer and offers a Trusted GUI, which controls the graphic adapter and the input devices, i.e., mouse and keyboard, to establish a trusted path between the user and an application. The Trusted GUI labels application windows with unique application names. Moreover, the Trusted GUI enforces a strong isolation between applications on the GUI level. Unauthorized applications cannot, for instance, access the graphical output of other applications or fake their interface to look like the usual password dialog

The Application Manager loads applications and measures the integrity of applications. These integrity measurements can then be reported to local applications as well as to remote applications. In cooperation with Trusted Computing hardware this functionality constitutes the basis for elaborate Digital Rights Management applications. The advantage of this approach in contrast to other integrity measurement architectures (e.g., [SZJv04]) lies in enhanced end-user privacy protection and improved manageability, e.g., of software updates.

The Storage Manager enables other applications to persistently store their local states. It preserves the integrity, confidentiality, and freshness of the managed data such that only the application or the user having produced the data may later re-access it.

---

[3] Device drivers that are able to directly access the main memory (DMA-enabled drivers) must be outsourced from the legacy operating system for security reasons.

[4] A microkernel is a minimalized operating system kernel that provides only essential services such as logical address spaces and inter-process communication (IPC). Processes on top of the microkernel run in their own address space and are therefore strongly isolated from each other.

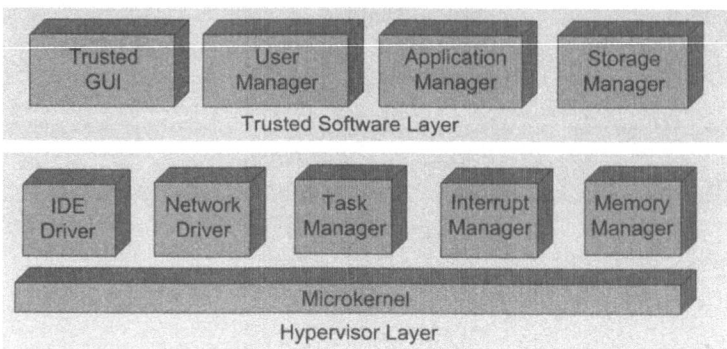

Figure 2: Turaya Security Kernel

Finally, the User Manager identifies and authenticates the users and assigns roles to the users. The user management is not part of the insecure operating system to prevent malicious software from "sniffing" user passwords or "stealing" the user identity.

The next two sections deal with the security-critical applications we have realized so far to run on top of the Turaya security kernel: a device encryption system and a VPN client.

5 Device Encryption

The device encryption system features user-transparent encryption of commonly used storage devices such as hard disks or USB memory sticks. In contrast to existing solutions, this encryption system is not vulnerable to worm/virus attacks on the legacy operating system (cf. Section 2).

Three operation modes have been implemented to fit various application scenarios:

- **Single-user mode with pre-boot authentication:**The user is asked to enter a password at boot time. The password is directly passed on to the encryption module before the legacy (untrusted) OS is booted.
  This operation mode is designed for road-warriors who usually need full, transparent encryption of a notebook's hard disk.

- **Single-user mode with just-in-time authentication (Trusted GUI support):** The user is asked to enter a password at time of resource access. The Trusted GUI strongly isolates the authentication dialog from the legacy OS which is running in a separate window.
  This operation mode has been developed for removable media (e.g., USB memory sticks, CD/DVD media).

- **Multi-user mode that enables centralized administration (Trusted GUI support):** Administrators are able to add/delete users or resources (i.e. physical storage devices). They grant or revoke access rights to resources and can change user passwords in case of a password loss.
  This operation mode is useful when multiple users share a workstation and its resources.

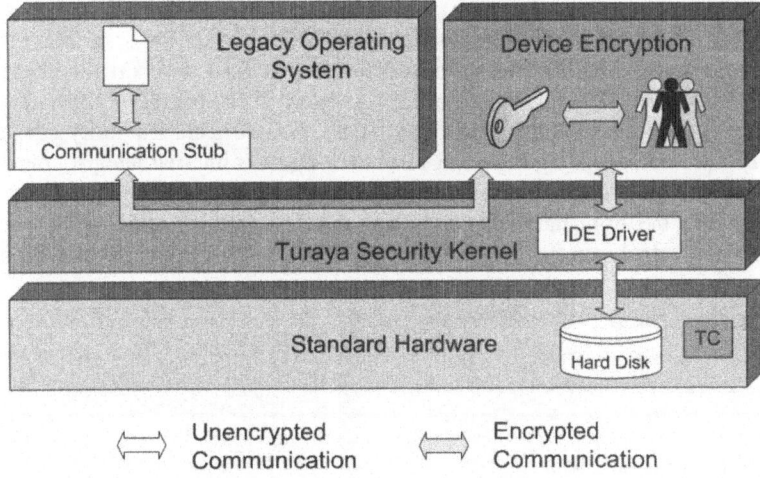

Figure 3: Device Encryption Architecture

Trusted Computing Support

The device encryption system uses a TPM to check the integrity of the Turaya security kernel. The Storage Manager as a component of the security kernel can only access security-critical data (in our case: cryptographic keys) if the integrity check succeeds. The integrity of the device encryption system which is not part of the security kernel is measured by the Application Manager. If this measurement has changed since the last storage of the cryptographic keys, the Storage Manager will refuse to provide the keys. To enable secure updates of software components digital signatures instead of hash values may be used as an integrity measure [MSMW03,MSWM03,MSW+04].

Note that the integrity of the legacy OS is irrelevant for the security of the storage and usage of the cryptographic keys.

6 VPN Client

Encryption of network packets is done by an isolated VPN client. The VPN client is interoperable with standard IPsec encryption protocols and fully transparent to the user. It integrates a firewalling component and network configuration via the Dynamic Host Configuration Protocol (DHCP). The security kernel enforces that the only communication path to the internet runs through the VPN client.

The network communication is encrypted with a secret key residing in the VPN component. As with the device encryption component this secret key is only accessible if the security kernel and the VPN client have not been tampered with while the system was offline. Online protection of the VPN client is enforced by the Turaya security kernel, more precisely by the hypervisor layer.

Trusted Computing Support

The Trusted Platform Module's attestation functionality is used to report the integrity of the security kernel and the VPN client to the VPN gateway. First, the TPM generates a signing key for external use (Attestation Identity Key, AIK). A Certificate Authority attests that this AIK is a TPM-protected signing key. The TPM then signs its internal integrity measurements (reflecting the integrity of the security kernel) and the integrity measurement of the VPN client as provided by the Application Manager with the AIK. The resulting certificate is sent to the VPN gateway which can then remotely verify that the VPN client has not been compromised.

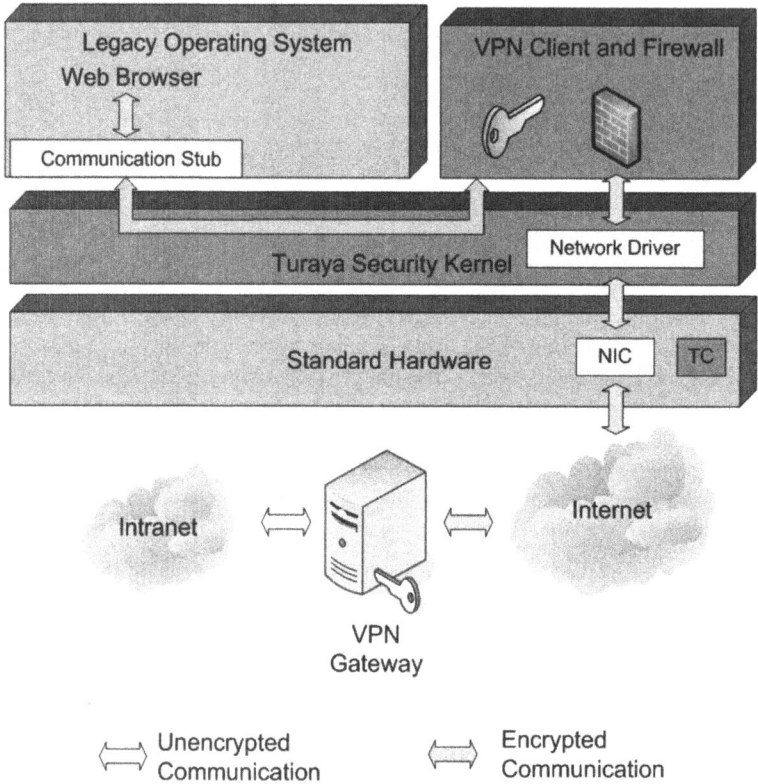

Figure 4: VPN Client Architecture

7 Implementation

Figure 5 shows a screenshot of the implementation, including the graphical user interface for the device encryption system as well as a web browser accessing a demonstration VPN server. Note that the encryption runs transparently both to the user and to the conventional operating system, Linux in this case. Common system benchmarks (e.g., compiling the Linux kernel) show a performance loss of about 12% compared to a Linux system running directly on the hardware.

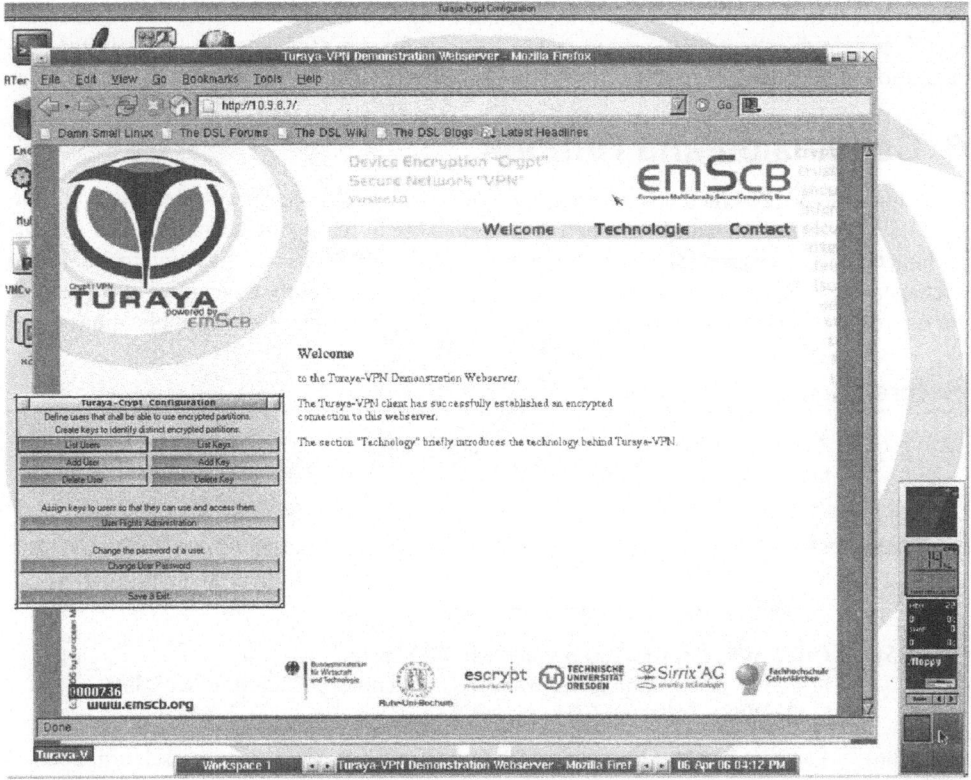

Figure 5: Screenshot of Implementation

Measurement of the integrity of boot stages and modules is done by a modified GRUB boot-loader called Trusted GRUB (tGRUB [SeSt06]).

We are constantly improving the security and reliability of the isolated encryption systems by means of code reviews and automatic testing. Besides, the code size is minimal (the device encryption system is about 8000 lines of code) compared to available software encryption systems which rely on a monolithic operating system kernel[5]. The small code base and a strong code modularization will ease a future security evaluation (e.g., under Common Criteria).

A crucial challenge will remain in dealing with the different configurations of both the Turaya security kernel and the security applications.The security kernel is not as complex as common operating system kernels and thus, the need for regular updates will be much less. However, finding an efficient way for managing these becomes essential in practical deployments.

We propose to digitally sign components of the security kernel and let the bootloader verify the signatures. Similarly, we let the application manager verify the signature of security-critical applications and report the signer identity instead of a binary hash as an integrity

---

[5] The Linux 2.6.12 kernel for example comprises 4.4 million lines of code including 2.2 million lines of driver code.

measurement to the VPN gateway. This approach requires a secure installation of public key certificates on the client platform but makes it easier for the VPN gateway to verify the configuration of the client.

8 Conclusion and Outlook

Both applications presented here serve as a proof-of-concept of the Turaya platform and show that solutions based on Turaya are perfectly applicable in real world scenarios. The security architecture is an appropriate basis for many other applications such as Enterprise Rights Management (ERM) and secure Online Banking. We are currently developing a framework for preventing identity theft attacks ("Phishing"-attacks) in Online Banking applications.

References

[Adva06]   Advanced Micro Devices, Inc.: Amd virtualization solutions.
            http://enterprise.amd.com/us-en/Solutions/Consolidation/virtualization.aspx,
            2006.

[Cisc04]   Cisco Systems, Inc: Cisco vpn client security policy, fips release 3.6.7.
            http://cco.cisco.com/en/US/products/sw/secursw/ps2308/prod_configuration
            _guide09186a00802218e3.html, 2004.

[Cisc05]   Cisco Systems, Inc: Cisco vpn client data sheet.
            http://cco.cisco.com/en/US/products/sw/secursw/ps2308/products_data
            _sheet0900aecd801a9de9.html, 2005.

[Emsc06]   EMSCB Project Consortium: The emscb project. http://www.emscb.org, 2006.

[Inte06]   Intel Corporation: Intel virtualization technology.
            http://www.intel.com/technology/computing/vptech/ , 2006.

[Micr05a]   Microsoft Corp.: Secure startup - full volume encryption: Technical overview.
            http://www.microsoft.com/whdc/system/platform/pcdesign
            /secure-start_tech.mspx, April 2005.

[Micr05b]   Microsoft Corp.: Trusted platform module services in windows
            vista.http://www.microsoft.com/whdc/system/platform/pcdesign
            /TPM_secure.mspx, April 2005.

[MSMW03]   Macdonald, R., Smith, S., Marchesini, J., and Wild, O.: Bear: An open-source
            virtual secure coprocessor based on tcpa. Technical report, Dartmouth College,
            2003.

[MSWM03]   Marchesini, J., Smith, S., Wild, O., and MacDonald, R.: Experimenting with
            tcpa/tcg hardware, or: How i learned to stop worrying and love the bear. Techni-
            cal report, Dartmouth College, December 2003.

[MSW+04]   Marchesini, J., Smith, S., Wild, O., Stabiner, J., and Barsamian, A.: Open-source
            applications of tcpa hardware. ACSA/ACM Annual Computer Security Applica-
            tions Conference, December 2004.

[PGPC05]   PGP Corporation: Pgp whole disk encryption for enterprises data sheet.
            http://www.pgp.com/products/wholediskencryption/pgp_whole_disk
            _enterprises.html, 2005.

[Safe05]   SafeBoot N.V.: Safeboot device encryption for pc.
            http://www.safeboot.com/products/device-encryption/pc , 2005.

[SeSt06]   Selhorst, M., and Stüble, C. : Trusted grub.
            http://www.prosec.rub.de/trusted_grub.html, 2006.

[SZJv04]   Sailer, R., Zhang, X., Jaeger, T., and van Doorn, L.: Design and implementation
            of a tcg-based integrity measurement architecture. 13th Usenix Security Sympo-
            sium, San Diego, California, August 2004.

[TCGW05]   TCG Work Group: TCG TPM Specification Version 1.2 Revision 85,   2005.

[Univ06]   University of Cambridge Computer Laboratory: Xen virtual machinemonitor.
            http://www.cl.cam.ac.uk/Research/SRG/netos/xen, 2006.

[USDe85]   US Department of Defense: Trusted computer system evaluation criteria (orange
            book). http://www.kernel.org/pub/linux/libs/security/Orange-Linux/refs/Orange
            /Orange0-5.html, December 1985.

[Utim05]   Utimaco Safeware: Security for mobile pcs and data media – safe guard easy
            whitepaper. http://www.utimaco.com/C12570CF0030C00A/vwContentByKey
            /W26L6EHK398CCHEEN , April 2005.

TPM Enterprise Key Management requires centralized Hardware-based Security

Bernhard Weiss

Utimaco Safeware AG
BU Transaction Security
bernhard.weiss@aachen.utimaco.de

Abstract

Finding a way in which to administrate the sensitive Trusted Platform Module (TPM) key information and benefit from the potential of TPM's is currently a major issue in most large companies. Enterprise customers are requesting centralized security management to guarantee reliable security. Thus security mechanisms whose use is controlled by the user do not provide companies with reliable security.

When compared to standard data backup utilities today's operating systems do not provide any backup and recovery procedures for TPM specific keys. Furthermore existing key recovery solutions tend to place the burden for backup and restore onto the individual user. By combing readily available technology a centralized backup, recovery and migration solution, based upon a hardware-security-module, is proposed which fulfills the requirements of enterprise customers.

1 Introduction

Seen as a strange 'Fritz chip' attracting negative attention in the past, the Trusted Platform Module (TPM) has now moved to an accepted standard (see Chapter 1.1). TPM's can now be found in an increasing number of devices, as shown in http://www.tonymcfadden.net/ tpmvendors.html. Furthermore it is expected that the market for TPM modules in Desktops and Notebooks will growth by the next years. It is assumed that nearly 100% of all Notebooks and around 90% of all Desktops shipped in 2010 will have a TPM embedded (see Chapter 1.2 for more details).

But what is provided by a TPM? The TPM is a microcontroller that stores keys, passwords and digital certificates securely. Furthermore it adds core security technologies that can generate keys for use in digital certificates, create digital signatures and provide encryption. Security operations are accessed and controlled through the secure subsystem using the defined interfaces. Applications like harddisk encryption, secure e-mail and identity/access management will benefit from the security functions provided by the TPM.

The question now is how to allow an IT organization to manage and control the sensitive TPM key information, rather than leaving it up to individual users.

Finding a way in which to administrate the sensitive TPM key information and benefit from the potential of Trusted-Platform-Modules is currently a major issue in most large companies. The areas of particular interest are the reduction of administration costs, the increase of interoperability between the different TPM implementations and the simplification of backup and restore of the sensitive key information needed to secure the associated information stored on the notebook or desktop.

S. Paulus, N. Pohlmann, H. Reimer (Editors): Securing Electronic Business Processes, Vieweg (2006), 64-71

The topic of key generation plays a significant role in the introduction of TPM's. When introducing TPM's, great care must be taken to set up appropriate procedures for powerful cryptography and effective key management.

The first part of this paper illustrates the challenges faced by the deployment of TPM's. The second part then details a concept, based on a centralized hardware security module (HSM), as a solution for TPM enterprise key management.

1.1 TPM background

The Trusted Platform Module (TPM) is a comprehensive approach to enterprise security. It is based upon an open specification for the modules building the TPM and its environment [Arch]. The specifications are led by the Trusted Computing Group (TCG) and include input from many sectors of the IT industry. Members and nonmembers of the TCG can use these specifications royalty free. A broad variety of products has already been released.

The range of specifications developed by the TCG include not only the TPM as microcontroller but also accompanying software, client PCs, storage devices, mobile phones, servers, secure network access and defines policies like backup and migration.

Today TPM's are mainly integrated into notebook and desktop computers sold to enterprises. Further implementations into servers, network devices, and secure mobile systems are in the works.

1.2 TPM market

It is assumed [Kay] that the TPM market will growth substantially as shown in Figure 1 over the next years.

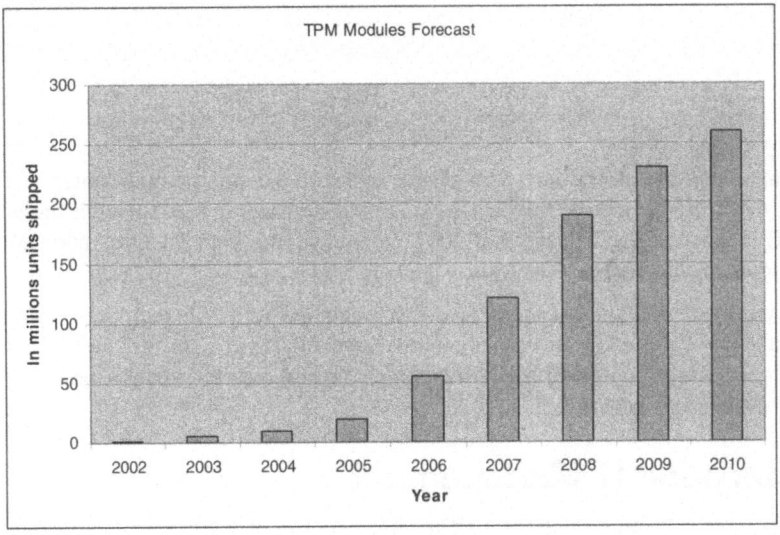

Figure 1: TPM Modules Forecast [Kay]

For the year 2006 50 million TPM units are expected. This will quadruple by 2010 exceeding 250 million units per year.

While Figure 1 shows the total number of TPM units shipped yearly it would be interesting to know how many Desktops respectively Notebooks are going to be equipped.

As shown in Figure 1 it is assumed that the number of TPM enabled Desktops will be significantly lower than the number of Notebooks in 2006. In 2006 a total of 40 million Notebooks with a TPM unit embedded will be shipped. It is estimated that the number of TPM's in Desktop will growth faster than the ones in Notebooks over the next years. By 2010 the number of TPM installed in Desktops will lead with aprox. 140 million units compared to aprox. 120 million TPM's in Notebooks.

By that time nearly 100% of Notebooks and around 90% of Desktops shipped yearly will carry a TPM.

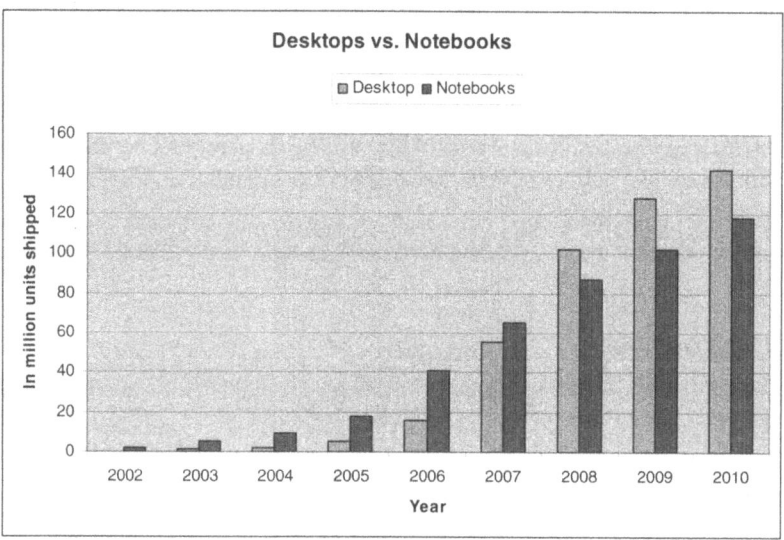

Figure 2: TPM units shipped in Desktops vs. Notebooks [Kay]

It is assumed that the rise of installed TPM's is due to the strong commitment of OEM's in 2005 for the TPM Version 1.2, here DELL should be named, together with the advance of Microsoft Windows Vista expected in 2007, in conjunction with the integration of the TPM into the South-Bridge by Intel® in 2008.

Furthermore Intel® already makes heavy use of an embedded TPM when using its security solution LaGrande Technology which is a highly versatile set of hardware extensions to Intel® processors and chips providing measured launch and protected execution based upon Intel® own virtualization technology.

2 Enterprise IT Management

Before discussing the current state of TPM enterprise key management it is necessary to reiterate the requirements enterprises have on IT and IT-Security administration.

Enterprise customers are requesting centralized security management to guarantee reliable security. Security mechanisms whose use is controlled by the user do not provide companies with reliable security. Even if users have been specially trained, you cannot rely on them to actually use the security mechanisms that are in place. They may decide not to do so, because the security mechanisms are inconvenient, or because they don't know enough about them, or even simply for malicious reasons. For this reason, in a corporate environment, the security software settings and rules must be defined and implemented centrally. Security administration staff is responsible for this. Their tasks include

- planning the security rules, defining the configuration settings and modifying security software to meet the organization's specific security requirements (customization),
- installing security software and distributing it to the clients,
- initial encryption,
- implementing security and monitoring the effectiveness of security mechanisms,
- maintenance – upgrading security software,
- backup and migration strategies and
- support for security software.

The ever present pressure on finances in a company environment requires IT departments to be extremely productive. Mobile members of staff work far away from their company's infrastructure and are therefore even more dependent on their "mobile office" functioning correctly. If problems happen it is vital that this "mobile office" can be returned to productive operation quickly and easily without the need for onsite support. Therefore helpdesk solutions with recovery options for security parameter like passwords or keys are required. These solutions might even allow the user to recover the necessary information online and independently from helpdesk staff.

Furthermore management solutions have to take into account the different IT administration roles already established in the enterprise sector such as:

- IT Administration,
- IT Security Administration and
- Identity Management.

IT Administration is responsible for helpdesk and hardware or software roll-out whereas Identity Management provides trustcenter services and IT Security Administration defines and monitors the security policies and the use of these rules.

Administrators must be able to integrate any protection system into the company's existing, and future, security infrastructure quickly and easily. The challenges this poses to the manufacturers of individual security management products primarily involve compliance with recognized standards, integration into existing organizational structures and processes and extensive compatibility tests.

Thus integration of TPM key management solutions will only be accepted by enterprise customer if the criteria listed above are met.

2.1 The current state of TPM enterprise key management

In principle the Trusted Platform Module (TPM) chip generates and stores cryptographic keys for use by secure applications. There are several different types of keys used in a TPM. Some are shown in the following table.

Table 1: Key types used by TPM

Type of key	Intended usage of the key	Examples	Migratable
Identity	Keys used to certify data	AIK	No
Signing	Keys used to sign data	EK	No
Storage	Keys used to protect sensitive data including key material	SRK	No
Binding	Keys used to bind and protect sensitive data	User specific	YES

Keys generated by the TPM which are allowed to be backed up are called migratable keys. Backup of non-migratable keys like identity attestation keys (AIK) or endorsement keys (EK) is not possible. This property is set by the application which initiates the key(s) to be created. Each storage key comes with two passwords - a usage password and a migration password. Whereas the usage password authorizes usage of the key the migration password authorizes the export a key. The migration types just described make up the key backup functionality in version 1.1 of the TPM.

In version 1.2 a new type – certifiable migration - was introduced meant to bridge the gap between the two methods. With certifiable-migration, users would have the ability to specify trusted third parties as migration authorities (MAs) and ensure that a certified-migratable-key (CMK) is not migrated to a particular destination without the permission of the MA. The destination key is picked either by the owner of the CMK or by the migration authority.

Furthermore a TPM does not store any additional key material internally besides its endorsement key (EK) and its own storage root key (SRK). Any key that is created or protected via the TPM is only wrapped with its SRK and usually stored persistently on the host machine. Keys of that type are referred to as 'Basic User Key' or 'Root Key'. All further keys created for a particular user are created as descendants of this basic or root key and are protected directly with this key. Generally, keys used to encrypt data are able to be migrated.

When the TPM is broken or the SRK has changed, all root keys that are directly wrapped by the TPM's SRK have to be restored and re-wrapped with the SRK of the new TPM or the changed SRK.

When compared to standard data backup utilities today's operating systems do not provide any backup and recovery procedures for TPM specific keys. Additionally available key management solutions are restricted to backup and restore scenarios as specified in [BaMS]. Thus enterprise requirements are not fully met.

But there might be more options available:

1. Wouldn't it make sense to give the customer the power to decide, whether they want to make key backups or not?

2. Wouldn't it make sense to give the customer the power to decide, where the keys are generated?

Up to now we did only discuss the scenario that a key pair is generated on the TPM via the published programming interfaces. This happens on each machine independently. Consequently the key backups need to be made on each machine independently – probably by the end user.

The question is, why not import an externally generated RSA key pair into the TPM.

3 Challenges faced by the different key management options

A user who doesn't want to be prepared for the scenario of a broken chip could simply look for another machine should the chip break and then reinstall the system newly and create another RSA key pair.

A user who wants to be prepared for this situation needs to have a backup of some sort: either may use the tools provided by manufacturer of the TPM or any other tool which backups and restores the RSA key pair.

Enterprises running a PKI might even already have machine key pairs or they might simply want to create them centrally. They could then also backup them up securely at a central point.

This would give a customer three different installation modes to choose from:

1. **No recovery solution**: TPM-generated, non-migratable RSA key pair. No key backups are made. If the TPM breaks, bad luck!

   a. Advantages: None

   b. Disadvantages: All sensitive data protected by TPM generated keys will be lost in the case of a disaster.

2. **Recovery via any backup and restore tool** handled by the individual user to use a TPM-generated, migratable RSA key pair. The end user must back up the RSA keys. Should the TPM break, then the end user would have to restore them by using another operating system.

   a. Advantages: Keys can be restored to allow recovery of sensitive data.

   b. Disadvantages:

      i. User is responsible for key backup.

      ii. User needs training to use the software.

      iii. Enterprise policy concerning key backup can not automatically be enforced.

      iv. Enterprise could be left without access to relevant data stored on the system if user intentionally destroys the key.

      v. Software roll-out and update processes must be established.

      vi. Onsite support for mobile workers is more likely to be required.

      vii. End user driven key backup is not compatible with organizational processes and roles already established.

3. **Centralized key creation**. The RSA keys are created centrally by a PKI and will be imported into the TPM later on. Whether they are migratable or not doesn't matter, because they can be recovered by the PKI anyway.

   a. Advantages:

      i. Full control over key generation and backup.

      ii. Solution is transparent to the user. No training is required.

      iii. Enterprise policy for key management can be enforced.

      iv.   Access to data even after user intentionally destroyed the keys.

      v.   Helpdesk processes can be optimized so that less onsite support is required.

      vi.   Reduced administration and helpdesk costs through centralized implementation.

      vii.   Key management functionality to support different vendor specific TPM's or new types of TPM's must only be adapted at the centralized solution to adapt to the new requirements.

      viii.   Integration into the established processes and roles.

      ix.   Combination with user controlled backup possible.

   b.   Disadvantages: None.

The security of the third option can be substantially enhanced by deploying a hardware security module at the centralized enterprise management interface.

3.1   TPM enterprise key management based on centralized Hardware Security Modules

Migration services, as described in [BaMS], are seen as a client initiated interaction with a service provider (SP). Nominally the SP is a Migration Authority (MA) where the keys are generated, or escrowed, in a secure location for use by a valid authenticated client. Once authenticated, the client may upload, download, or query the MA about Migration Packages (MPs). Additionally, it may be possible for the client to request deletion of a MP from a MA environment.

By implementing centralized HSM's, as shown in Figure 3, to generate and administrate TPM storage keys, it is possible to guarantee that

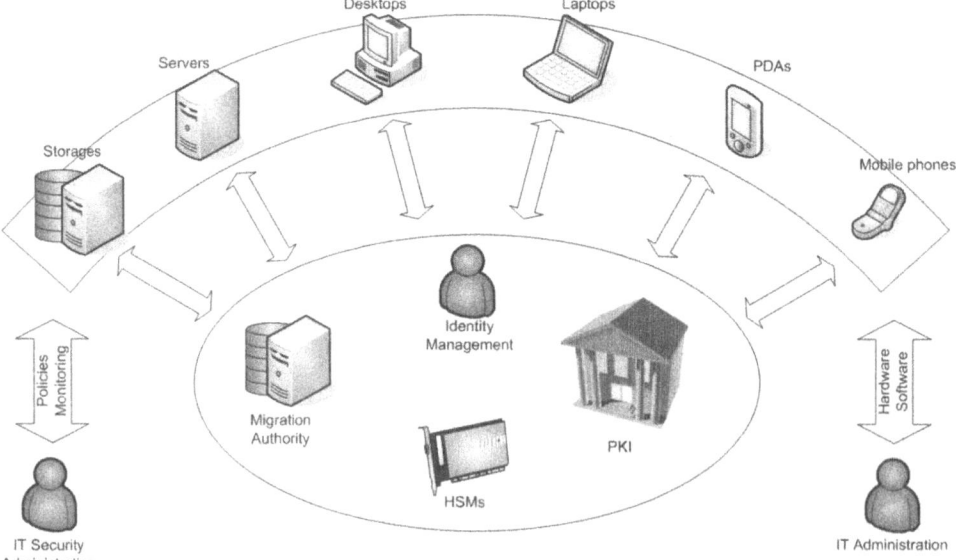

Figure 3: TPM key management based on centralized MA and HSMs

- key material for accessing business relevant data stored on laptops and desktops can be restored,
- access to the key material is limited to authorized and trained staff (IT-Security Administrators) and
- cryptographic keys can be managed at any time.

Furthermore secure recovery for mobile workers can be implemented and Identity Management, IT Administration and IT Security Administration can be effectively separated.

Like other businesses have long been aware of the need to generate and protect cryptographic keys in hardware security modules (HSMs) fully controllable by authorized administration staff. The use and administration of the security-relevant key information outside the TPM offers new possibilities to companies deploying TPM enabled devices.

4 Conclusion

Introduction of TPM enabled devices may issue a big impact on availability of data stored on devices in case of a disaster. However, by implementing a centralized key generation and administration unit based on hardware security modules, access to data secured by these keys can be assured. Additionally access to the key material can be limited to authorized persons only.

The shown concept also ensures that the requirements of enterprise customer regarding the integration of TPM key management solutions:

- centralized security management is provided,
- productivity of IT staff is not negatively effected and
- an integration into the established organizational processes and roles is possible

is met.

Only by using centralized hardware-based security is it possible to achieve a secure framework for the administration of all TPM key material used for data storage.

References

[Arch]   TCG; TCG Specification Architecture Overview; Revision 1.2, 28. April 2004; File: TCG_1_0_Architecture_Overview.pdf.

[BaMS]   TCG; Interoperability Specification for Backup and Migration Services; Revision 1.0, 30 June 2005; for TPM Family 1.1b Level 1; File: IWG_Backup_and_Migration_Services.pdf.

[Kay]   Kay, Roger L.; The Future of Trusted Computing, IDC, GovSec 2005.

[LaG]   Intel; LaGrande Technology, Preliminary Architecture Specification; May 2006; Link: http://www.intel.com/technology/security/.

Implementation of DRM Systems under the EU Legal Framework

Pius Alexander Benczek

BENCZEK Rechtsanwalt
Champ du Vert Chasseur 4, 1000 Bruxelles
abenczek@benczek.biz

Abstract

Digital Rights Management ("DRM") systems face the task of reflecting different, sometimes diverging interests, including those of authors and creators of works protected by copyrights, end users seeking access to such works and their own interests. While authors have an interest in establishing licensing policies and in tracking the use of their (licensed) works on the internet on the basis of DRM systems in order to ensure revenue streams in return for providing access and to prevent illegal copying of their works (including piracy), operators of DRM systems may have an interest to process data on usage pattern of customers for marketing purposes and to tie in customers into their own content distribution chains rather than providing for interoperability with other DRM system operators or content providers. By contrast, end users are concerned that DRM systems intrude into their privacy, that DRM may unduly restrict access to content where the provision of access is mandatory by law and that DRM systems are not interoperable. In a broad brush overview, it will be highlighted how provisions under EU laws reflect such different concerns and how those provisions determine the framework within which DRM systems must operate. In particular, the article highlights relevant provisions included in EU Directives on data protection as well as relevant provisions in EU copyright Directives addressing the protection of copyrighted works and of Rights Management Information against unauthorized access. The extent to which DRM must cater for access to content where copyright is limited by national laws of EU Member States will be discussed. The article will further highlight where and to which extent EU laws provide DRM operators with the freedom to take the initiative in shaping DRM systems further and where they leave open questions. Against the background of recent case law, it will further address whether EU competition laws can have an impact on enforcing interoperability. It will suggest practical approaches as to how DRM can provide viable solutions for copyright owners and DRM operators while catering for customer concerns. It will briefly point at the actual and potential impact that an increasing success of DRM will have on the position of Collective Rights Management Societies and on existing systems of copyright levies imposed on technical devices involved in the process of copying content.

1 Introduction

1.1 How does Digital Rights Management ("DRM") work?

A uniform or unified definition of DRM or its operational mode does not seem to exist[1]. However, a number of common features and aims of DRM systems crystallize. Hence, DRM

---

[1] Refer to Rump, Nils: Definition, Aspects and Overview in: Digital Rights Management – technological, Economic, Legal and Political Aspects in: Becker, Buhse Guennewig, Rump – Heidelberg (2003), pages 3 et seq.

can be broadly described as electronic security measures which serve to protect, to control access to, to enforce the conditions of use of copyrighted content in digital format and to prevent and to track illicit, unauthorized use of such content. To do so, the copyrighted works, right holders, the conditions of use and to some extent the identity of users are identified, and the authenticity of such information is protected. DRM systems extend to digital copies of works traded on CDs, DVDs and other carriers as well as to digital copies traded via the internet. They interact with software and hardware by means of which content can be accessed by the user. In brief, they serve to protect the interests of the owners of copyrights and ultimately to secure legitimate revenue streams resulting from the author's terms of use of copyrighted works.

A number of components used in different DRM systems can be highlighted as follows. While cryptographic algorithms[2] prevent unauthorized access, rights expression languages[3] define the conditions of use. Content identifiers can be combined with content description systems to identify content, its creator and descriptive metadata of all different types of media[4]. Cryptographic algorithms help to identify users or to authenticate devices while watermarking and fingerprinting technologies help to track infringements of copyrights (in addition to other functions). Event reports allow for the recording of content purchases. Electronic payment systems may be – and are on a regular basis - integrated in DRM systems, in particular where content is marketed via the internet.

As DRM systems are still in their infancy, technical and operational structures, payment systems and the extent to which data (particularly those on users and usage pattern and preferences) are collected differ significantly. Operators within the DRM value chain usually cooperate on the basis of contractual arrangement with one another, the most relevant of which can be highlighted as follows[5]:

- User Contracts regarding the purchase of individual content files between the user and the distributor (which may be the same entity as the music platform operator)
- "White-label-Shop" agreements between platform operators and distributors regarding the distribution terms;
- Cooperation and services agreement between platform host, software designer, providers of encoding solutions etc;
- Encoding agreement between platform operator and provider of encoding solutions;
- Web Hosting agreement with web hosting services provider
- Content licensing agreement between platform operator and owners of copyrights and owners of related rights (performing artists, producers of carriers) and / or labels and or collective right management societies.

---

[2] For example: "MMP", "Digital Multimedia Object", "DiGiBox", "DigiFile", "ebooks".

[3] For example: MPEG-21 REL (2003) with its Rights data dictionary MPEG-21 RDD.

[4] For example: ISWC, ISBN, ISRC, ISAN or DOI.

[5] For a more detailed overview on contractual arrangements refer to: Hoenike, Mark and Huelsdunk, Lutz, Leistungskomponenten und Vertragsbeziehungen bei kommerziellen Musik-Download-Plattformen im Internet, Multimedia und Recht, 2/2004, pages 59 et seq.

1.2 Interests in the DRM Value Chain

According to opinions given by various market participants as reflected in the final report of the "High Level Group"[6] on Digital Rights Management, there is wide spread consensus that although the legal basis for the introduction of Digital Rights Management system is established in the so called "InfoSoc Directive"[7], the success of any such system largely depends on its acceptance by users.

Users may in particular be concerned that their rights may be affected by DRM systems, including their rights to privacy and the right to free access to information. Where access to copyrighted content is privileged by law on the basis of public policy considerations (for example access for disabled people, for research purposes or "private copies"), users are likely to face tighter control in the "DRM world" than in the "analogue distribution world". Users might also face restrictions in accessing content where different proprietary DRM systems are competing on the basis of different standards which do not allow access to one another and which are potentially incompatible with the particular user's hardware and software devices.

By contrast, creators of works (Music, movies, literature) which are protected by Intellectual Property Rights (most notably copyrights) as inter alia addressed in the InfoSoc Directive have a vital interest to control the licensing of and the access to digitized formats of their works via DRM systems, in particular insofar as the use of the works on or via the internet is concerned. They are also interested in tracking usage pattern in order to fight the menace of "online piracy". Intermediaries in the value chain between owners of copyrights and the user may be interested to learn more about usage pattern of individual users for the purpose of focusing their marketing efforts.

2 DRM and Data Protection

2.1 What is the issue?

Owners of copyrights have an interest to collect as many transactional data as possible to track unauthorized reproduction and illegal file sharing of their works on digital platforms, in particular on the internet. This can be easiest achieved by identifying a purchaser of content, link him to the purchased item and track the use of the item he purchased. Indeed, an EC Commission working document recognizes the fact that "new technologies to identify and/or trace users are being established at the level of exchange of information as well as at platform level".[8] In other words, users are often requested to identify themselves prior to a transaction; subsequently, providers often use unique identifiers which enable tracking and profiling of users. To this end, DRM system operators offer the use of steganography tools, such as digital watermarks, encryption, electronic agents or "simply" the use of cookies or web bugs. The personal information can be included and hidden in the content primarily purchased by the user so that the usage of content on the web, for example on a file sharing system, can be

---

[6] Established by the EU Commission on 3 February 2004 – Final report March – July 2004 http://europa.eu.int/information_society/eeurope/2005/all_about_digital_rights_man/doc/040709_hlg_drm_2nd_meeting_final_pdf.

[7] Directive on the Harmonization of Copyright and related Rights in the Information Society (2001/29/EC). report

[8] http://europa.eu.int/comm/justice_home/fsi/privacy/docs/wpdocs/2005/wp104_en.pdf.

linked to a specific user by the company initially collecting the data.[9] In essence, all these tools collect data from the user which can be further processed. It may be unclear, to which extent those data are collected or processed and for which purpose. It is even possible that the initial purpose is changed and that data are sold or are being made accessible otherwise to third parties for purposes such as profiling of user preferences and subsequent marketing.

From a commercial perspective, the consumer take – up of DRM services is likely to be hindered if users sense intrusion into their privacy. Users may feel exposed and thereby inhibited to freely express their preferences. In particular in Europe, there is a legal tradition of protecting privacy related interests and informational self determination, thus enhancing mechanisms to maintain a pluralist society. Conversely, consumers in Europe appear to be more sensitive regarding the use and the protection of their personal data than it is the case in other parts of the world. Consequently, the InfoSoc Directive recognizes in general terms the importance of data protection legislation[10], and indeed, data protection legislation both at the EU and at the EU member state level heavily regulates the use of personal data.

2.2 Which Legislative Instruments are applicable at EU Level?

At EU level, two Directives are particularly relevant in the context of the protection of personal data.

The EC Directive on Data Protection[11] ("DDP") sets out general principles regarding the collection and the processing of personal data which are applicable across all industry sectors.

In addition, a sector specific EC Directive on privacy in electronic communications[12] ("DPEC") sets out more detailed, complementary and to some extent stricter rules, which apply to the collection and processing of personal data in the electronic communications sector. Although such rules primarily focus on communications services rather than on services for the provision of content, they potentially apply to some components of DRM services.

Effects of the above referenced Directives spill over to other jurisdictions outside of the EU as the transfer of personal data to jurisdictions outside of the EC is prohibited unless such jurisdictions provide an adequate level of data protection[13].

EU Member States had to effectively implement the above directives into their national laws.

---

[9] See for example "Palm e-book files" where the name credit card number used for the purchase is inserted in the purchased content and subsequently, files can only be accessed if the credit card number used for the purchase is entered. On other systems, individual user account numbers are created to identify the user if content is used on the internet.

[10] European Convention on Human rights (Article 8); Directive 95/46/EC; Directive 2002/58/EC.

[11] Directive 95/46/EC of the European Parliament and the Council of 24th October 1995 on the protection of individuals with regard to the processing of personal data and on the free movement of such data (OJ L 281, 23rd November 1995, 31 et seq.).

[12] Directive 2002?58/EC of the European Parliament and the Council of 12th July 2002 concerning the processing of personal data and the protection of privacy in the t electronic communications sector (OJ L 201, 31st July 2002, 37 et seq.).

[13] Article 25 (1) of the DDP.

2.3 What are Personal Data

The DDP broadly defines personal data is any information relating to an identified or identifiable natural person ("data subject"). An identifiable person is one who can be identified, directly or indirectly, in particular by reference to an identification number or to one or more factors specific to his physical, physiological, mental, economic, cultural or social identity"[14]. Direct, but more particularly indirect identifiablity (the latter for example by the use of additional, auxiliary data) can be assumed only if in the specific circumstances methods of identification are reasonably likely to be used[15]. Hence, there is no hard and fast rule to determine whether data are personal or not. A number of factors, including but not limited to the type of industry, its market conditions, operational habits and the type of transaction must be taken into account.

In addition, the DDP addresses information on "racial or ethnic origin, political opinions, religious or political belief, trade union membership and (...) health or sex life" as "sensitive data". The DDP and the DPEC provide an increased level of protection in relation to such data.

Obviously, names and contact details required to enter into a transaction on a DRM platform are personal data. Further, IP numbers, domain names and "clickstream data" may fall within the scope of the definition of personal data, depending on whether it is likely that under the specific circumstances methodology is used to link them to the identity of one specific individual. In this context, EU law[16] appears to acknowledge that cookies could be considered as (or could include) personal data. In considering the specific circumstances, the use of electronic agents[17] will also have to be taken into account. Although International Work Codes processed on DRM systems may also potentially include personal data of authors or creators of works, such data are less of concern in the context of addressing the extent to which privacy concerns of users may impact on the success of DRM – they are therefore not considered further in this article.

Whether or not certain data are sensitive personal data is difficult to determine in many circumstances. The collection of transaction data or browsing pattern on - for example - content on religious themes may reveal a person's personal religious belief or may just reveal a professional occupation with the subject matter of such content, even if transactions in relation to such content occur frequently. Entities involved in the DRM value chain as data controllers and processors appear to bear the risk of making the accurate assessment in each case, in particular when seeking to benchmark the purchase of any such content against the users' names - a challenge in the context of structuring DRM services.

---

[14] Article 2(a) of the DDP.

[15] Recital of the 26 DDP.

[16] Refer to Recital 25 of the DPEC.

[17] Electronic agents would for example be able to conduct automated researches on DRM systems and even have certain learning capabilities. For a more details analysis see Bygrave, L.A.: "Electronic Agents and Privacy: a cyberspace Odyssey" in: 9 International Journal of Law and Information Technology (2001), pages 275 – 294.

2.4 Responsibility for Compliance with Data Protection Rules

According to the DDP, the primary responsibility of complying with data protection rules is imposed on the "data controller", defined as the natural or legal person, public authority or agency or any other body which alone or jointly with others determines the purposes and means of the processing of personal data[18]. Data controlling refers to the factual organizational control rather than to the physical control over data. Therefore, data controllers do not need to collect or possess the personal data directly or personally with respect to which they assume organizational control. By contrast, data controllers ultimately carry the responsibility for data protection compliance of certain third parties, such as their data processors[19]. Conversely, not every entity which possesses data personally or directly is a data controller with respect to such data, such as in particular persons or organizations providing data transmission services in respect of data provided by third parties[20].

Data processors are defined as a person or organization engaged in the processing of personal data on behalf of the data controller[21]. Data processors also bear responsibilities as to the integrity of the personal data.

As data controllers and data processors can be a distinct entities or persons within a given DRM system or value chain, it is crucial

- To analyze clearly which of the different entities involved in a given DRM system carries the responsibilities of a data controller (as opposed to the data processor) on the basis of the factual allocation of tasks amongst such entities; and

- To agree amongst all entities involved in a given DRM system on
  o clear allocation of responsibilities in relation to data protection; and on
  o clear internal systems of liability and indemnity in case of non – compliance and related claims of affected individuals.

2.5 Which Principles Do In particular Impact on Data Processing?

Personal data must be processed fairly and lawfully[22]. These two overarching principles can be broken down into a number of basic legal conditions which must be met for the processing of personal data. Although the DDP breaks down such basic conditions even further into sub categories of detailed requirements, the discussion hereunder will be limited to such basic legal conditions, in particular to those which appear to be most relevant to the operation of DRM systems.

2.5.1 "Necessity of Processing" and Consent – Requirements

Processing of personal data is in particular permissible if one or more of the following conditions are satisfied:

---

[18] Article 2 lit. (d) of the DDP.

[19] Artilce 23 (1) of the DDP.

[20] Recital 47 of the DDP.

[21] Article 2 lit. (e) of the DDP.

[22] Article 6 (1) lit. (a) of the DDP.

- Processing is necessary
  - o for the purpose of electronic contracting, i.e. for the purpose buying copyright licenses on-line or for preparing such transaction (2.5.1.1 below); or
  - o to comply with legal obligations imposed on the data controller (2.5.1.2 below); or
  - o for the purpose of "pursuing legitimate interests" of the data processor that "override conflicting interests" of the consumer (2.5.1.3 below);
- The data subject (also referred to as the consumer or the customer) has given his "unambiguous consent" to the processing of his personal data (2.5.1.4).

The above listed conditions are highlighted in greater detail immediately below.

2.5.1.1 Contracting or Contract Performance

Data which are deemed necessary for the purpose of electronic contracting in relation to buying copyright licenses or the preparation or performance of same on a DRM system may be processed for that purpose[23].

In order to be deemed necessary, processing must be proportionate in the relation to the aim of the contract. Hence, the processing of contact data as well as contract related data should be permissible to the extent that they are required to ensure compliance with basic contract conditions (for example: expediting payment, pursuing infringements once that an infringement is established). Processing of personal customer data collected while the customer was browsing should only be permissible if browsing can be deemed as being already part of preparing a contract, hence if an active customer request for entering into a contract is imminent. However, there is considerable doubt that the processing of such data for the purpose of investigating into whether or not the customer complies with the licensing conditions is justified as being necessary for ensuring compliance with basic contract terms within the meaning of Article 7 lit. (b) of the DDP. This is in particular relevant for monitoring and tracking the usage of the purchased product on the internet.

2.5.1.2 Compliance with Legal Obligations Imposed on the Data Controller

Processing is further permissible to the extent to which it is necessary to comply with legal obligations imposed on the data controller[24].

Such obligations should mainly be those established under statutory laws. An example could be obligations to disclose certain data to public authorities or courts.

By contrast, obligations resulting from contracts concluded between operators within the value chain of a given DRM system should in general not be sufficient to justify the processing of personal customer data. If such contractual obligations generally served as a justification for data processing, the protection mechanisms of the DDP could be easily leveraged out and bypassed. However, this does not exclude that in specific, exceptional circumstances contractual obligations between entities within a DRM systems can be identified which would indeed justify data processing of personal customer data; nonetheless, it is difficult to imagine legitimate aims of a contract between entities in a DRM value chain in relation to which the processing of pure browser data or cookies could be proportionate and justified.

---

[23] Refer to Article 7 lit. (b) of the DDP.

[24] Refer to Article 7 lit (c) of the DDP.

2.5.1.3 Legitimate Interests Overriding the Interests of the Data Subject

The processing of personal data is also permissible if necessary to pursue the legitimate interests overriding conflicting interests of the data subject (i.e.: the consumer).

The DDP provides little guidance as to how the terms legitimate interest are to be construed and how conflicting interests should be balanced. Indeed, it largely leaves it up to the EU member States to provide such guidance in their national legal systems. Member States are for example, requested to determine conditions for the use of personal data in the context of the legitimate ordinary business activities of companies and other bodies[25].

As a general approach, it is suggested that legitimate interests include any interest of an idealistic or economic nature which is related to the operator's field of activity in compliance with the law. It exceeds the scope of purely legal interests. Ultimately, the processing of personal data processing may serve the purpose of pursuing legitimate business interests, depending how widely the legitimate interest can be defined under national laws.

The second test to be conducted is whether the processing of data would be necessary and proportionate in the light of the purpose pursued. Yet, if the processing is considered as being necessary, consumer interests relating to informational self determination may still outweigh the interest in processing personal data for legitimate interests.

By way of example, infringements of copyrights constitute criminal offences under certain conditions in most EU Member States. The EU commission has also taken an initiative with a view to harmonizing criminal sanctions of Intellectual property infringements. However, the EU data protection Directives themselves provide little guidance as to whether personal data collected in a transaction may be processed for the purpose of pursuing criminal copyright infringements and leave them, for example to private and public law enforcement bodies. In this respect, the DDP leaves to EU Member States the full discretion to implement such rules (thereby potentially derogating from the principles set out in the EU Data Protection Directives)[26]. It is therefore advocated that the enforcement of copyrights and the related tracking of usage of copyrighted works to prevent illicit use of copyrighted works on the internet, including internet piracy on behalf of copyright owners be accepted as a legitimate business interest of DRM operators and that such tracking is considered as necessary to pursue this aim. Under which scenarios legal interests of consumers and their right to informational self determination outweighs interests in tracking usage pattern of purchased content by individuals for the purpose of fighting illicit use of copyrighted works is an open question under EU laws. It is however suggested that the significant overall social and economic harm resulting from piracy be carefully taken into account in addition when making such an assessment.

Another example relates again to the storage and processing of browser data or cookies to the extent that such browser data are or include personal data[27]. Provisions under EU law have in general terms categorized cookies as legitimate and useful tools to enhance the provision of information society services[28]. Indeed, those operators of DRM systems who can be considered as being providers of information society services might benefit from the provisions of the DPEC. The DPEC has established a specific set of rules applicable to the setting of cook-

---

[25] Refer to Recital 30 of the DDP.

[26] Refer to Article 13 (1) lit. (d) of the DDP.

[27] Refer to number 2.3 above.

[28] Refer to recital 25 of the DPEC.

ies by providers of information society services. It allows for the setting of cookies on the user's computer for a legitimate purpose provided the user is notified and is given the opportunity to refuse the usage. Interestingly, the DPEC does not require an unambiguous consent of the user and it is silent as to when the user must be notified. Arguably, it is sufficient to notify the user further to the setting of the cookie and to impose the burden on the user of removing the cookies from his computer.

To the extent that the DPEC would not apply, it would be difficult to define a legitimate interest in relation to which the use of cookies would appear to be necessary and would ultimately not be outweigh by privacy interests of the consumer.

2.5.1.4   Consent

To the extent that the customer <u>unambiguously</u> consents to the processing of his personal data, any requirements and related concerns addressed above under number 2.5.1.1 – 2.5.1.3 would be of no relevance. Consent is defined as any freely given and <u>informed</u> indication of his wishes by which the data subject signifies his agreement to personal data relating to him being processed. It is not required that the consent be provided in writing, nor does it have to be explicit. The fact that the customer has approached the DRM operator to purchase content can in principle be understood as an implicit consent to process a certain amount of data necessary to conclude the transaction.

However, any passing on of personal data and the processing such data within the DRM value chain would already require the customer's consent (unless justified on grounds listed under number 2.5.1.1 – 2.5.1.3 above). Although no form requirements exist, operators are well advised to document the consent. Operators bear the onus of proof that that there was unambiguous consent. To this end, the implementation of specific procedures leading to the consent, potentially by dialogue boxes and confirmation of consent by "mouse click", may be helpful although in the extreme this might already lead to requesting and explicit consent which technically is not required by EU law.

The customer must be informed in detail about the purpose of processing and about the extent to which data are processed. Although the DDP is silent as to when the consent must be provided, it appears that the appropriate information must be provided to the customer before he gives his consent – he should know what he agrees to. Again, the use of dialogue boxes in which the customer is requested to actively "click" on boxes indicating his privacy preferences are helpful. In some online systems, even electronic time stamps are used to document when the user gave his consent.

The customer whose data are processed must be provided with the possibility to withdraw his consent at any time. He must also be informed about this right.

2.5.2 Sensitive Data

In general, the processing of sensitive data[29] is prohibited[30]. The DDP lists a number of exceptions to this rule of which three are relevant in the context of DRM:

- The data subject / customer has given his explicit consent[31]; or

---

[29] Refer to number 2.3 above.

[30] Article 8 of the DDP.

[31] Article 8 (2) lit. (a) of the DDP.

- The data subject has made the data manifestly public[32]; or
- The data are necessary for the establishment, exercise or defense of legal claims[33].

Consent must be explicit. In an online DRM system, it seems unavoidable to use active dialogue boxes in which the consumer can give his consent. All other consent requirement discussed above equally apply with regard to sensitive data (e.g. the data subject must be informed regarding the scope and purpose of data processing).

Insofar as the exception of manifest publicity is concerned, the data subject must have made such data available to the general public. Entering such data into a DRM system should not be sufficient. It is unlikely that the data are available to the public when entered into a DRM system, and the data subject would not assume they are.

The exception relating to the defense of legal claims should be limited to claims based on statutory laws (e.g.: the infringement of copyrights in both civil and criminal proceedings) and direct contractual claims against the data subject. Particularly strict criteria will apply in assessing whether or not it is necessary to process such data for the purpose of pursuing the claim.

2.5.3 Data Avoidance

Data avoidance is an overarching principle in data protection laws. It imposes the obligation to keep data in a form which permits identification of data subjects for no longer than it is necessary for the purposes for which the data were collected or for which they are further processed. The amount and quality of data must not be excessive, i.e: they must be limited to the absolute minimum necessary for the purpose pursued. In principle, a customer entering in an online transaction should have the possibility to stay as anonymous as if he completed the same transaction in a "real world" scenario, for example in a record shop. However, applying such a narrow view without limitation to DRM systems would not take due account of the fact that in the online world, the purpose and the necessity of data processing may have to be defined wider. The form of product delivery is different and conversely, the IP rights are protected in a different manner as compared to tangible media. On the other hand, users may be reluctant to use DRM systems on a broad scale if they cannot legally but anonymously purchase content. Although EU law does not directly resolve this dilemma, the DPEC appears to encourage (rather than to require) the development and the use of privacy enhancing technologies ("PETs"). Accordingly, "systems for the provision of electronic communications networks and services should be designed to limit the amount of personal data necessary to a strict minimum."[34]

2.5.4 Finality Principle

Data processors must explicitly specify a legitimate purpose for which the personal data are processed[35]. The purpose must be announced and notified to the data subject[36]. Data must not be processed in a way incompatible with the purpose specified. Processing must remain within the limits of what the user can reasonably expect behind the purpose specified.

---

[32] Article 8 (2) lit. (e) of the DDP.

[33] Article 8 (2) lit. (e) of the DDP.

[34] Refer to recital 30 of the DPEC.

[35] Article 6 (1) lit. (b) of the DDP.

[36] Article 10 and 11 of the DDP.

Although the legitimacy criterion should embrace a wider spectrum of permissible purposes than those immediately specified by law, legislation of many EU Member States require a connection between the data controller's or system operator's field of activity with the purpose for which the data are collected and thereby limit the legitimacy criterion. In practice, this should however, not be problematic for DRM systems.

A bigger issue may be whether it can be assumed that the use of personal data for tracking the use of the content on the internet for purposes of identifying illegitimate use falls within the scope of the user's reasonable expectation. It cannot be excluded that authorities or courts in EU Member states would at least require an explicit purpose specification to this end or even an informed consent of the user.

In the light of the requirement to process data in a way compatible with the purpose specified, it will be for example problematic to repurpose data collected for payment purposes for the use of marketing and advertising activities. An informed explicit and well documented consent from the user for such repurposing would be required, which can however be structured on line by the use of dialogue boxes.

2.6   Other relevant Principles

Other relevant provisions of data protection laws not specifically discussed hereunder include the following:

Data may only be disclosed to third parties with the data subject's consent or with legal justification[37]. Data must be accurate and complete[38] and must be protected from unauthorized access. The data subject must have the right to review the data and to correct them[39]. Further, rules on fully automated profiling[40] may impact on how DRM systems will be structured.

3   The Mechanisms of the "InfoSoc" Directive

3.1   Overview

The InfoSoc Directive mainly contains two elements to be considered in the context of DRM.

The so – called anti – circumvention provisions of the InfoSoc Directive prohibit

- the circumvention of "effective technical measures" against unauthorized use
- the marketing and trafficking of devices which enable the circumvention of such technical measures.

Those provisions also reflect certain public policy based limitations to copyrights which must be honored by DRM technology and determine the extent to which "effective technical measures" may limit access to content.

Provisions ensuring integrity of electronic rights management information ("RMI") by providing protection against

---

[37] Article 7 lit. (1) of the DDP.

[38] Article 6 (1) lit. (d) of the DDP.

[39] Articles 10 – 12 of the DDP.

[40] Article 15 of the DDP.

- the intentional and unauthorized alteration or removal of RMI; and
- the distribution of copyrighted works from which RMI has been removed or altered in the knowledge that such distribution infringes copyrights.

The relevant legal provision provisions relating to the above principles will be briefly highlighted.

3.2 DRM and the Rights of Beneficiaries of Public Policy Privileges (also: Private Copy)

3.2.1 Principles and Definitions

The InfoSoc Directive prohibits (i) the circumvention of effective technical measures implemented against unauthorized use of copyrighted works and (ii) the trafficking of devices to circumvent such measures.

Effective technical measures against unauthorized use are broadly defined to include "any technology (…) that in the normal course of its operation is designed prevent or restrict acts (…) which are not authorized by the rightholder of copyright"[41]. Hence they serve to restrict any act not tolerated by the copyright owner rather than just protecting the scope of copyright as such. Technical measures are deemed to be effective where the use of a protected work or other subject matter is controlled by the rightholder through application of access control or protection process such as encryption, scrambling or other transformation of the work or other subject matter or a copy control mechanism which achieves the protection objective[42]. In brief, effectiveness can be assumed if access control is applied, but technical measures are not limited to access control. Note should only be taken of the fact that a broad range of devices are covered, including but not limited to anti copy devices or copy limiting devices. In addition, and unlike in early drafts of the InfoSoc Directive, there are strong arguments in support of the view that also tracking and monitoring devices may be considered as effective technical measures[43], although the latter is being debated since they might only have deterrent effect rather than limiting the use as such[44]. In essence, authors and creators enjoy the possibility to technically lock up their copyrighted content, to impose any conditions of use and to track usage pattern. The discussion whether or not this mechanism provides a new right relating to copyright, a new "de facto right" or an rights enforcement mechanism in the hands of a private individual shall however, not be fuelled further at this point.

Unlike in pure trafficking cases as addressed below, personal liability in the case of circumventing activities shall only accrue if there was knowledge or reasonable ground to know that the objective of circumventing such technology is pursued.

The InfoSoc Directive further prohibits marketing and trafficking of devices which – as further outlined below - enable the circumvention of such technical measures.

---

[41] Article 6 (3) of the InfoSoc Directive.

[42] Refer to previous footnote.

[43] Dusollier, Severine, Tipping the Scale in Favor of the Rightholders: The European Anti – Circumvention Provisions in: Becker, Buhse Guennewig, Rump: Digital Rights Management – Technological, Economic, Legal and Political Aspects, Heidelberg (2003), pages 3 et seq.

[44] Refer to Bygrave, L.A., Digital Rights Management and Privacy – Legal Aspects in the European Union in: Becker, Buhse, Guennewig, Rump, Digital Rights Management, Heidelberg (2003), Pages 418 et seq.

The InfoSoc Directive specifies a list of trafficking and marketing activities which are prohibited[45]. Manufacture, import, distribution, sale rental, advertisement for sale or rental are included in the list and appear to be prohibited regardless of whether such activities are carried out for commercial or personal purposes. Further, the possession of such devices is prohibited, provided it is for commercial purposes. Member States have the discretion to also prohibit the possession for personal purposes.

The above prohibition relates to the following categories of products:

- devices promoted, advertised or marketed for the purpose of circumvention;
- devices which only have a commercially insignificant purpose or use other than to circumvent;
- devices which are primarily designed, produced, adapted or performed for the purpose of enabling or facilitating circumvention.

The InfoSoc Directive does not give further guidance which "multi-purpose" devices fall within the scope of the prohibition. An analysis on a case to case basis is therefore necessary.

Member States must provide the possibility for remedies, including injunctive relief, and the seizure of infringing materials and the claim for damages[46].

3.2.2　Limitations of Copyright

3.2.2.1　Introduction

EU laws addresses certain exceptions and limitations to copyrights which can be briefly highlighted as "fair use" or "public interest" copies (such as for example privileged access for the purposes of research, education, criticism, enhanced access for the disabled)[47] as well as and "private copy" regimes (including for example private back – up copies or private copies for close family members). The aim of such exceptions to copyright is to enable the use the copyrighted work by law under specific conditions. According to the InfoSoc Directive, most[48] of these exceptions are however, not mandatory; hence EU Member Sates are free to implement such exceptions or not. However, to the extent that Member States do indeed implement such exceptions to copyrights into their national laws, the InfoSoc Directive ultimately requires that mechanisms be implemented so that beneficiaries can make use of the respective exceptions under national law where content is protected by digital rights management systems[49]; however, the InfoSoc Directive limits this requirement to a number of exceptions with respect to which a particularly strong public interest is presumed[50].

---

[45] Article 6 (2) of the InfoSoc Directive.

[46] Article 8 of the InfoSoc Directive.

[47] Article 5 of the InfoSoc Directive.

[48] All limitations with the exception of the limitation included in Article 5 (1) of the InfoSoc Directive.

[49] Article 6 (4) of the InfoSoc Directive.

[50] Article 5 (2) a: Reproduction on paper or reprography; Article 5 (2) c: specific reproductions made by libraries, educational institutions, museums or archives; Article 5 (2) (d): ephemeral recordings of works made by broadcasting organizations; Article 5 (2) e: reproductions of broadcasts by social institutions for non – commercial purposes; Article 5 (3) a: teaching and scientific research; Article 5 (3) b: use for the benefit of disabled people; Article 5 (3) e: public security.

Although authors / creators must tolerate such limitations of copyrights imposed by law and must allow for such (privileged) use, EU law does not require that any such use be "for free" or free of charge. Indeed, copyright laws of many Member States pursue the aim of granting such privileged use free of charge only in cases of overwhelming or increased public interest (for example: public security), while in most other cases authors shall have the right to receive royalties in relation to such use. In particular, royalties for private copies and copies works which by their nature are susceptible of being copied from one carrier to another or of being reproduced[51] are often secured by a system of levies[52] imposed on the trade with devices that allow for or are designed for the copying and the reproduction of content. Those include without limitation different types of hardware (including PCs) as well as tapes, CD's and DVD's. DRM offers opportunities to provide alternative means to secure remuneration, as briefly addressed below.

3.2.2.2   Catering for the Limitation of Copyrights

The InfoSoc Directive addresses the issues how DRM systems must honor exceptions or limitations to copyrights and who is responsible for doing so.

It states that "in the absence of voluntary measures taken by rightholders, including agreements between rightholders and other parties concerned, Member States shall take appropriate measures to ensure that rightholders make available to the beneficiary of an exception or limitation the means of benefiting of such limitation or exception where that beneficiary has legal access to that work or subject matter."[53] Further, the Infosoc Directive stipulates that Member States may take such measures in relation to copyright exemptions relating to "private use"[54] "unless reproduction for private use has already been made possible by rightholders to the extent necessary to benefit from the exceptions concerned (...) and without preventing rightholders from adopting adequate measures regarding the number of copies" in accordance with provisions on "private use". It should be emphasized again that the number of exceptions with respect to which such means must be provided is limited and applies only insofar as Member States have opted to include such exceptions into their copyright laws.

Hence, EU law pursues an approach according to which effective technical measures or lock up mechanisms be engineered as such that the limitations and exceptions to copyrights can be lawfully exploited by legitimate beneficiaries. The user who benefits from an exception of copyright must be provided with the tools and the technical possibilities to do so. By contrast, in other jurisdictions, users who benefit from copyright exemptions must circumvent lock – up mechanisms and subsequently rely on legal justification on grounds of "fair use" for having circumvented the lock - up. EU law sought to avoid such an approach by imposing the burden of providing the appropriate access tools on the industry.

Primarily, EU law relies on industry led solutions to resolve the issue. Voluntary measures at industry level are not conclusively defined but may include technical solutions (serial copy management) as well as deposits of unlocked copies with trusted third parties from which us-

---

[51] Refer for example to subsections 53, 54 and 54 lit. (a) of the German Urheberrechtsgesetz.

[52] For a detailed overview refer to Ulmer-Eilfort, Constanze, Private Copying and Levies for Information- and Communication- Technologies and Storage Media in Europe in: Becker, Buhse Guennewig, Rump: Digital Rights Management – Technological, Economic, Legal and Political Aspects, Heidelberg (2003), pages 3 et seq.

[53] Article 6 (4) of the InfoSoc Directive.

[54] Article 5 (2) lit. (b) of the InfoSoc Directive

ers benefiting from copyright protection can request copies. Rightholders and DRM operators can develop alternative payment schemes taking into account a remuneration of copyright exemptions outside of the system of levies on reproduction devices addressed above. One of the difficulties that the industry faces is the fact that many of the public policy based exceptions are not mandatory – hence the level of copyright exceptions may vary from country to country. For example, unlike other jurisdictions, France does not have copyright limitations for scientific research purposes. DRM operators therefore have to take country specific approaches in determining to which extent they have to honor limitations of copyright in the jurisdictions to which they are accountable. Ironically, this may seem an easier task for operators who provide DRM as through e – commerce applications on the internet than for those distributing DRM on tangible media, such as CD's or DVD's. While providers of DRM systems acting through e-commerce cannels and deliver the digitally managed content on line are only subject to the laws of the EU Member State in which they operate, the distributor of DRM included in tangible media risks customer complaints if he imports DRM designed for jurisdictions which have little regard for copyright exceptions (and accordingly with little options for "privileged" use) into jurisdictions where copyright exceptions are broadly applied.

Member States must take (in the case of the private copy exception: may take) necessary measures only if industry fails to develop standards. The InfoSoc Directive does however, not specify any further conditions or requirements as to when such failure could be assumed and what might be considered as appropriate measures. In the absence of any guidance at EU level, there is a high risk of market disintegration. Conversely, it is exactly that risk which should be an incentive for DRM operators and right holders to develop appropriate standards prior to any possible state intervention.

The InfoSoc Directive confirms that any measures or standards developed by the industry or imposed by member states enjoy the protection against circumvention and against the trafficking of circumventing devices as outlined above under number

The InfoSoc Directive provides further in its Article 6 (4) that certain measures to ensure copyright exceptions shall not apply to works (...) made available to the public on agreed contractual terms in such a way that that members of the public may access them from a place and at a time individually chosen by them. Hence, it seems that on demand services could foreclose copyright exceptions.

Against the background highlighted above the main question appears to be whether the systems currently developed in the market are able to fully comply with legal requirements on copyright exemptions presentation. A number of examples should be considered[55]. With regard to CD's and DVDs, Serial Copying Management Systems and Copy Generation Management systems were introduced respectively. However, rights expression language will have to be increasingly complex when it comes to online licensing of content. While Adobe's and Microsoft's ebook reader can be referred to as examples for print works, FiarPlay (iTunes), Windows Media DRM and RealNetworks Helix DRM serve as examples for music downloads. All those systems have in common that they increasingly seek to express the preferences of both copyright owners and users, in particular in respect of private use provisions. However, at present, it seems impossible that any DRM system could comply with all requirements and preferences from either side under different legal systems. This factual con-

---

[55] For a detailed overview on DRM systems refer to P. Akester and R. Akester, Digital Rights Management in the 21st Century in: (2006) E.I.P.R., 159 et seq. (160 – 161).

straints have to be taken into account when national legislators consider whether or not it is appropriate and proportionate to impose standards for the purpose of safeguarding copyright exemptions under DRM systems.

3.2.3 Limits of the Protection of Anti – Circumvention Devices and "Fair Use"

As outlined above, "effective technological measures" are protected against circumvention. To the extent to which devices which track usage pattern are considered as "effective technological measures", their circumvention is equally prohibited. However, strong arguments have been discussed[56] which support the view that such monitoring and tracking devices might not be considered as being "effective technological measures" within the meaning of the InfoSoc Directive and that hence the disablement and circumvention of devices which track usage pattern of lawfully purchased copyrighted works would not constitute an infringement.

Similarly, it has been argued[57] that circumvention of technological measures or the dealing with circumvention devices could be justified to the extent that they serve to gain access to content insofar as rightholders and providers of DRM services do not provide the means to benefit from public policy based exemptions ("fair use") to copyrights. The European Convention of Human Rights (establishing a right of free speech and information) is quoted as legal justification. Indeed, such argumentation is likely to be valid as long as it can be established that owners of copyright receive revenues on the basis of levies charged on devices involved in the copying process. However, to the extent to which the scope of levies systems might be reduced if owners of copyrights implement on a large scale alternative payment schemes included in DRM systems for content subject to "copyright exemptions", such justification would ignore the fact that exemptions to copy rights do not provide "free of charge access" to content, and rightholders would be deprived of their remuneration if breaches were justified.

3.3 The Protection of Electronic Rights Management Information ("RMI") and its Limits

The InfoSoc provides protection against the removal or alteration of any electronic rights management information provided that such removal or alteration has been knowingly performed and without authority[58]. It equally prohibits "the distribution, importation for distribution, broadcasting, communication or making available to the public of works (...) from which electronic rights management information has been removed or altered without authority if such person knows or has reasonable ground to know that by doing so, he is inducing , enabling, facilitating or concealing and infringement of copyright or a related right (...)"[59]. According to the InfoSoc Directive[60], RMI is defined as any information provided by the rightholders which identifies the work or subject matter (...), the author or any other

---

[56] L.A. Bygrave, Digital Rights Management and Privacy – Legal Aspects in the European Union in: Becker, Buhse, Guennewig, Rump, Digital Rights Management, Heidelberg (2003), Pages 418 et seq.

[57] Refer to Akester and Akester (2006) above, page 162.

[58] Article 7 (1) of the InfoSoc Directive.

[59] Article 7 (1) of the InfoSoc Directive.

[60] Article 7 (2) of the InfoSoc Directive.

rightholder, information about the conditions of use (…), and any numbers and codes that represent such information." This shall apply "when any of these items of information is associated with the copy of or appears in connection with the communication to the public of, a work (…)".

The question whether information on personal data of the user and (the tracking of) usage pattern can be a considered as a component of and are (accordingly) protected as a part of RMI establishes a link with the above chapter on data protection.

Recital 57 of the DDP appears to construe the term RMI widely. RMI may include the processing "of personal data about the consumption patterns of protected subject matter by individuals and allow for tracing of online behavior". Although such information would not be provided by the rightholder directly as required by the definition included in Article 7, it is suggested that the conditions of Article 7 are met, since the rightholder has implemented tools to retrieve such information and thereby requests and collects directly it in an automated process.

Further, it appears that RMI, in particular personal data and usage pattern do not need to be or to remain embedded into or firmly attached to the work. Article 7 of the InfoSoc Directive seems to be sufficiently open ended to allow for an interpretation according to which it is sufficient that RMI shows a connection with the work which is not necessarily of a physical nature. Hence, also information which can "physically" be separated from the work, such as usage pattern related to a work, should fall within the scope of protection when they are retransmitted for tracking purposes to a server of a provider of DRM services.

The removal or the alteration of RMI is only illegal if performed "without authority". This also applies to personal data and usage pattern included in RMI. Individuals might try to seek legal justification to remove such information on grounds of data protection rules, in particular on grounds that the processing of such data might not be necessary in relation to the aim purpose pursued. However, the removal of such data can hardly be justified in the light of the interpretation of data protection provisions suggested above.

4 Interoperability vs. Exclusive Proprietary Systems

While some DRM systems aim at achieving interoperability (e.g. "CPRM – copy protection for recordable media" or Windows Media DRM), others (e.g. Apple iTunes FiarPlay DRM) try to defend their exclusively proprietary status by limiting the use to specific operating systems and by excluding others.

The InfoSoc Directive confirms[61] that "there is no obligation to design devices, products, components or services to correspond to technological measures, so long as such device, product, component or service does not otherwise fall under the prohibition" to circumvent effective technical measures. Hence, there are no specific requirements according to which equipment manufacturers would be explicitly obliged to include any specific DRM system into their products or to make their DRM products compatible with others. However, the EU Commission states in a communications to the Council[62] that interoperability is a prerequisite for a successful distribution of content under DRM systems. The Commission appears to sup-

---

[61] Recital 48 of the InfoSoc Directive.

[62] COM/2004/0261/final.

port the view of the High Level Group on Digital rights Management[63] that interoperable technologies should be developed by initiatives at industry level and should be industry led. Failing substantial progress in the field, the Commission would consider issuing a recommendation to reinforce the necessity of interoperability for DRM systems.

In the absence of any such sector specific regulation, unfair competition rules at both the EU and the national levels may become of particular importance, and indeed, iTunes FairPlay's proprietary standard was challenged in front of French competition authorities by VirgiMega on grounds of such rules. Related competition rules and the decision of the French Conseil de la Concurrence[64] will be briefly addressed as an example as to whether and to which extent mechanisms under competition rules may apply.

EU Competition rules [65] and national competition rules[66] prohibit – inter alia - the abuse of a dominant position. Therefore, companies having a dominant positions must supply their goods or services to competitors if refusal to supply would significantly impact competition. Beyond the scope of supplying goods or services, the prohibition to abuse a dominant position may turn into an obligation upon the dominant undertaking to provide competitors with access to its "essential facilities", although subject to a number of strict conditions which include the following:

- A dominant company must controls a so-called "essential facility';
- It refuses access to competitors without objective justification; or
- it grants access only on terms less favorable than those that it offers its own associates.

The existence of an essential facility is recognized only if

- access to such facility is indispensable for the entity requesting access to conduct its activity;
- denial of access is capable of eliminating competition on the relevant downstream market
- from a business perspective, no alternative exists; and
- denial of access is not objectively justified.

Hence, in its attempt to challenge iTunes Fairplay on grounds of competition rules, Virgin-Mega alleged an abuse of dominance and argued that

- Apple is a dominant player,
- FairPlay is a facility access which is indispensable to supply Virgin's customers with music services,
- alternative DRM standards do not constitute economically viable options, and
- Apple's interests in safeguarding capacity, security, technical standards and reasonable remuneration are satisfied.

However, the French Conseil de Concurrence rejected the request for access on grounds that FairPlay was not an essential facility for a number of reasons, including the following:

---

[63] Refer to Footnote 5 above.

[64] Decision No 04-D-54 of the French Conseil de la Concurrence, VirginMega / Apple Computer dated 9. November 2004.

[65] Articles 81 and 82 of the EC Treaty.

[66] Recent Case under French Competition Rules – ITunes.

- Only a minority played music on portable MP3/AAC players downloaded from the web (the majority burnt downloads on CD);
- Even in the absence of interoperability, there were possibilities to upload VirginMedia's music on iPods; and
- A sufficient degree of competition for iPod devices existed on the relevant market.

At EU level and at the level of other Member States, an equivalent assessment would seem likely at the moment. Therefore, competition rules are unlikely to serve as a tool in the near future for requesting access to a competitor's DRM system.

It appears that at present, there is no legal obligation on DRM operators to ensure interoperability, although it is addressed as being desirable at a political level.

5 Further Impact of DRM

Ultimately, an expected wide spread success of DRM is likely to have impact on fields related to copyrights in addition to those discussed above. By way of example, the impact on levy systems and on the conduct of collective rights management is briefly put into perspective.

5.1 Levy Systems

The system of levies has been briefly addressed above. Currently, owners of copyrights are entitled to receive revenues resulting from levies imposed on devices involved in the process of copying content. This applies to devices for both, digital and analogue copying. Equipment manufacturers, importers and dealers, (large) users and right holders are currently burdened with the task to collect, to withhold and to disburse to collective rights management societies levies on copying devices (including computer hardware). In its communication on the Management of Copyright and related Rights, the EU Commission has taken the view that that the success of DRM in generating fair compensation on the basis of alternative payment schemes might justify the phasing down of levy systems as currently enshrined in national laws of EU Member States. This may be the case to the extent that computer hardware is concerned and DRM provides tools to efficiently factor in and provide revenue streams for the use of copyrighted works privileged by public policy considerations. An open question is however, the extent to which levies can be reduced and how the level of appropriate charges on DRM systems could be determined.

5.2 Collective Rights Management Societies

Regarding collective rights management[67], the EU Commission has further adopted a recommendation on the collective cross border management of copyright and related rights for legitimate online music services[68] and a related Commission Staff Working Document[69]. In brief, the recommendation favors an approach where rightholders have the choice to appoint a collective rights manager for the online use of their musical works across the entire EU. The

---

[67] Regarding the position of Collective Rights Management Organizations, refer for an overview to Hoeren, Thomas, Welche Chancen hat das Urheberrecht im Internetzeitalter? In: Picot, Arnold, Digital Rights Management, Heidelberg (2003), pages 5 et seq. (58 et seq.).

[68] Commission recommendation 2005/737/EC dated 18.October 2005.

[69] SEC(2005) 1254

Commission has therefore recommended that territorial restrictions and customer allocation provisions in existing arrangements with collective rights management societies be abolished and that rightholders be offered the possibility to tender their repertoire for EU wide direct licensing. The recommendation also includes provisions on governance, transparency, dispute settlement and accountability of collective rights managers.

Prior to the adoption of the recommendation, EU Commission officials[70] have already expressed views on how EU competition rules might apply to Collective Rights Management Societies in the future insofar as digitally managed content in the online world is concerned. EC case law dating from the early 1970ies suggests that Collective Right Management Societies and enforcement Agencies have been subject to little restrictions under EU Competition Rules, in particular insofar as the structuring of 'one stop shopping' arrangements for creators are concerned (including territorial restrictions and customer allocations in one stop shopping agreements). However, this assessment was "subject to technological developments". It appears that more recently, the EU Commission, considers scrutinizing under EU competition rules any bundled rights management services offered by collective rights management societies with a view to ensuring the freedom of choice to combine collective rights management with individual rights management services, such as internet based DRM. More particularly, it was suggested that the following issues may be addressed under competition rules with a view to facilitating the co-existence of both, collective and individual rights management systems:

- Collecting societies should allow for freedom of choice for copyright owners regarding their collective rights manager;
- There should be an option to combine collective and individual rights management – No unnecessary bundling of management service by dominant players;
- Free choice for the user as to where to obtain necessary licenses;
- One stop shopping agreements (and related reciprocal agreements between Collective Rights Management Societies) are favourable, but monopoly structures must discontinue where no longer indispensable;
- Territorial restrictions and customer allocations are likely to be reassessed in view of facilitating emerging new regional and global one stop shopping arrangements.

It can be expected that the EU Commission details its policy based on and resorts to the application of competition rules if the above mentioned recommendation does not show the intended effects. Ultimately, the licensing of copyrights through Collective Rights Management Bodies should become easier and more flexible[71].

6 Conclusion

While a basic legal framework for DRM is in place at EU level and licensing across the EU should become easier, a number of legal uncertainties remain. Although the legal framework also addresses most of the potential customer concerns in the fields of privacy and privileged access to content in fair use, interoperability remains more of a desirable goal the attainment

---

[70] Herbert Ungerer, Application of Competition Law to Rights Management in the Music Market – Some Orientations. Speech held at the Independent Music Companies' Association on 11 June 2003.

[71] Regarding the current status of licensing in Germany, see Stefan Ventroni and Guenter Poll, Musiklizenzerwerb durch Online – Dienste, Multimedia und Recht 2002, pages 648 et seq.

of which is currently left to DRM operators. Industry initiatives and emerging technical solutions will be helpful to overcome uncertainties over time.

6.1 Protection of DRM Systems and Licensing

Although the licensing of rights across the EU through collective rights management bodies is likely to be facilitated on the basis of recent EU initiatives of the EC Commission, EU law provides only limited guidance to DRM operators as to how they can structure their DRM systems to implement individual licensing schemes for rightholders while at the same time reflecting customer concerns. A number of areas of uncertainty remain.

Insofar as the protection of copyright through DRM systems is concerned, one area of uncertainty relates to the tracking of usage pattern. Where tracking of usage pattern for the purpose of combating IP piracy crime is part of a DRM business model, DRM operators are well advised to carefully check which EU Member State provides for the most generous legal system; as EU law offers little explicit guidance as to the extent to which such tracking is permissible, a country specific approach will be necessary in many cases. To the extent that tracking of usage pattern is permissible, another uncertainty relates to the extent to which tracking devices can be considered as "effective technological means" which enjoy protection against circumvention. Although it seems that EU law intended to include tracking devices into the scope of technological means enjoying protection against circumvention, arguments contesting such assumption have been introduced into the discussion. Ultimately, national and EU courts will have to clarify the issue. However, data collected on usage pattern should enjoy protection against alteration or deletion to the extent they are considered as a necessary part of Rights Management Information.

Further, DRM operators face the task of implementing technologies to ensure access rights to content for users privileged on grounds of public policy ("fair use"). One particular challenge is that different legal standards in EU Member States must be reflected. A significant degree of uncertainty remains regarding the extent to which DRM are currently able at all to comply with fair use requirements. EU law only allows for intervention by EU Member States to impose standards as to how their (different) respective copyright exemptions are to be honored, if industry fails to develop standards. Industry should therefore have an interest in taking initiatives to develop rights expression languages reflecting both authors' rights and users' rights in order to avoid state intervention which might ultimately impose binding requirements that are not entirely feasible.

Further, it appears that EU law does not restrict DRM operators and owners of copyright to implement payment schemes for "fair use". Unless systems of levies on copying devices under national laws are modified, users might identify the risk to pay double for the privileged usage rights of works. DRM operators should lobby national legislators to implement flexible solutions which better reflect the possibility of individual payment schemes and which make levies partially redundant.

Interoperability between systems is not mandatory, but is has been declared as desirable. Industry might consider agreeing on a broader basis on interoperability standards in order to avoid regulatory intervention at EU level in the future, although such intervention might only come in the "soft" format of a recommendation.

6.2 Data Protection

In the absence of an informed consent by the customer as to which extent his data may be processed, EU law allows for the processing of certain personal customer data collected in the DRM usage process to the extent necessary for specifically defined purposes. Indeed, a certain amount of processing is permissible while on the other hand preserving consumer interests. As far as the processing of browser related data is concerned, EU law seems to be rather restrictive, unless the operator of DRM system in charge of controlling the data can at the same time be categorized as a provider of information society services and can therefore benefit from some privileges related to the setting of cookies as addressed under the DPEC. Indeed, lot of issues could be resolved if the customer was asked consent to the processing of his personal data. It may even be the case that customers accept DRM more easily and broadly if their privacy concerns are addressed openly or if they could be reassured that automated licensing of copyrighted works is intertwined with Privacy enhancing technologies. Indeed, some indicators exist that this view is shared by parts of the industry and that it has even found its way into policy papers[72].

Some uncertainties remain. For example, DRM operators would face the risk of assessing whether or not data collected on their systems are to be considered as "personal" under the specific circumstances and which of those data might even be sensitive.

DRM operators should in any event clearly structure the responsibilities within the DRM value chain in order to be able to determine responsibilities under data protection laws.

6.3 Technical Solutions and Trusted Platforms

The use of rather straight forward solutions to inform the customer about privacy issues and to receive his consent for the processing of his personal data where necessary and appropriate as well as the possible use of PET's have been addressed above.

The use of trusted third parties and platforms has been suggested[73] as being potentially helpful to resolve some of the legal issues.

For example, it should be considered whether the need to fight internet piracy and to combat copyright infringement could be reconciled with data protection issues and consumer concerns for privacy or even anonymity by a system where copies of works can be identified by individual codes without however, immediately connecting the purchaser identity to the copy. Only a trusted certification authority would hold the key to ultimately make such a connection. Only law enforcement would have access to such aggregated information. Nevertheless, the system would in itself have to comply with data protection requirements.

Trusted computing platforms from which content can be consumed but not copied might help to resolve to implement solutions to access "fair use" copies; such solutions may also help to address technical problems, such as the decoding of decryption keys and the reverse engineering of the decoding codes of players.

A close cooperation between engineers, DRM business managers, economists and lawyers, including the copyright enforcement community is required.

---

[72] www.bsa.org/usa/policyres/7_principles.pdf.

[73] Refer to Akester and Akester (2006) above.

References

Akester, P and Akester, R.   Digital Rights Management in the 21st Century in: (2006) E.I.P.R., 159 et seq. (160 – 161).

Bygrave, L.A Digital Rights Management and Privacy – Legal Aspects in the European Union in: Becker, Buhse, Guennewig, Rump, Digital Rights Management, Heidelberg (2003), Pages 418 et seq.

Bygrave, L.A.:   Electronic Agents and Privacy: a cyberspace Odyssey" in: 9 International Journal of Law and Information Technology (2001), pages 275 – 294

Dusollier, Severine   Tipping the Scale in Favor of the Rightholders: The European Anti – Circumvention Provisions in: Becker, Buhse Guennewig, Rump: Digital Rights Management – Technological, Economic, Legal and Political Aspects, Heidelberg (2003), pages 3 et seq.

Hoenike, Mark and Huelsdonk, Lutz Leistungskomponenten und Vertragsbeziehungen bei kommerziellen Musik-Download-Plattformen im Internet, Multimedia und Recht, 2/2004, pages 59 et seq.

Hoeren, Thomas   Welche Chancen hat das Urheberrecht im Internetzeitalter? In: Picot, Arnold, Digital Rights Management, Heidelberg (2003), pages 5 et seq.

Rump, Nils   Definition, Aspects and Overview in: Becker, Buhse Guennewig, Rump: Digital Rights Management – Technological, Economic, Legal and Political Aspects, Heidelberg (2003), pages 3 et seq.

Ulmer-Eilfort, Constanze   Private Copying and Levies for Information- and Communication- Technologies and Storage Media in Europe in: Becker, Buhse Guennewig, Rump: Digital Rights Management – Technological, Economic, Legal and Political Aspects, Heidelberg (2003), pages 3 et seq.

Ungerer, Herbert   Application of Competition Law to Rights Management in the Music Market – Some Orientations. Speech held at the Independent Music Companies' Association on 11 June 2003

Ventroni, Stefan and Poll, Guenter   Musiklizenzerwerb durch Online – Dienste in: Multimedia und Recht, 10/2002, pages 638 et seq.

IT-Grundschutz: Two-Tier Risk Assessment for a Higher Efficiency in IT Security Management

Angelika Jaschob · Lydia Tsintsifa

Bundesamt für Sicherheit in der Informationstechnik
{angelika.jaschob | lydia.tsintsifa}@bsi.bund.de

Abstract

Using the pragmatic two-tier risk assessment and management approach of IT-Grundschutz helps organisations to optimise the efforts for the IT security management process as well as to achieve the requirements of ISO/IEC 27001.

1 Need for an Information Security Management Method

Along with the increasing importance of compliance, the use and implementation of recognised and well-structured methods for IT security has now become more important than ever in business. The decision of ISO/IEC to develop an entire series of information security standards – the ISO/IEC 27000 family- reflects the increasing importance of information security. The ISO/IEC 27001 standard specifies requirements for the design and implementation of an appropriate Information Security Management System (ISMS) in an organisation, ensuring that adequate and proportionate controls are selected to protect information assets and to give confidence to interested parties.

Complementary to the controls defined in ISO/IEC 17799:2005, ISO/IEC 27001 gives the specification for the certification of an ISMS. However, both standards contain generic controls, described on a high abstraction level and do not include a specific method for risk assessment. The Federal Office for Information Security (Bundesamt für Sicherheit in der Informationstechnik, BSI) in Germany provides via IT-Grundschutz ([BSI1], [BSI2], [BSI3], [BSIC]) a method to implement these high level controls in a practical and efficient way. Furthermore, the IT-Grundschutz Methodology can be applied to establish, maintain and monitor an ISMS. Part of this is the performance of à risk analysis for the IT assets in focus.

2 Optimising resources

One of the primary objectives of IT-Grundschutz is to increase the efficiency within the IT security process. Examining the cost-benefit trade-off of IT security one conclusion is, that the higher the IT security level is, the more hard and expensive it becomes to increase it respectively. Figure 1 illustrates this effect and demonstrates why it is not possible to achieve perfect IT security.

S. Paulus, N. Pohlmann, H. Reimer (Editors): Securing Electronic Business Processes, Vieweg (2006), 95-101

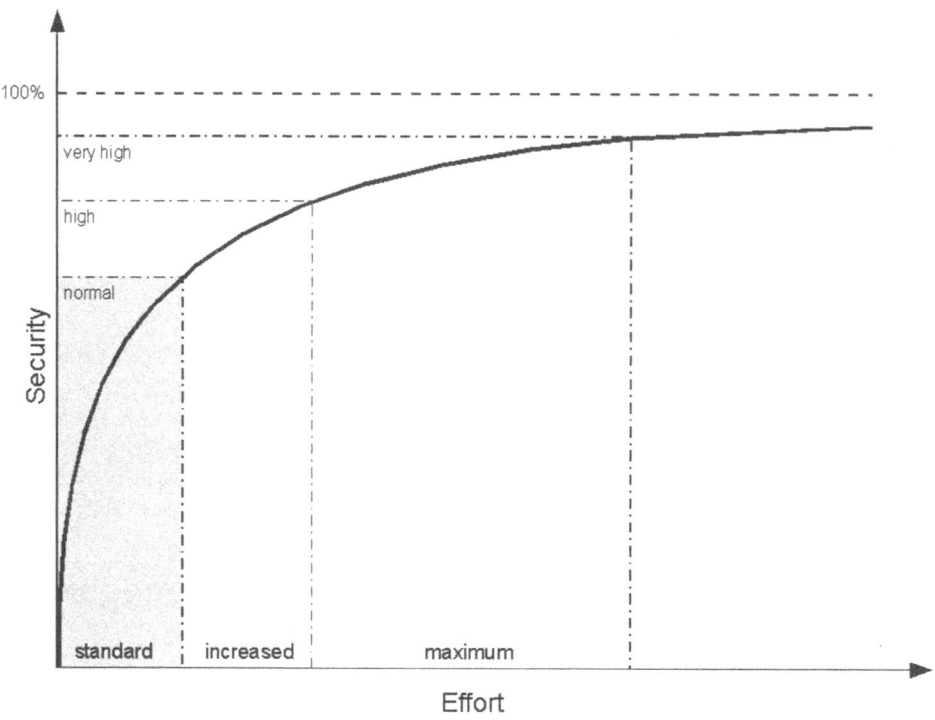

Figure 1: Cost-benefit trade-off for IT security

IT-Grundschutz takes into account this cost-benefit relation of IT security and first provides the means to reach a standard IT security level by using the framework concept.

2.1 The IT-Grundschutz concept

The main idea here of IT-Grundschutz is to break an information security management system down into reusable components, representing the basic elements in information security management. On this basis, an easily extensible standard system, that is adaptable to a particular case, can be created. The IT-Grundschutz Catalogues ([BSIC], [BSIM]) build thus a repository of characteristic threat scenarios and standard security measures for typical IT environments. Threats and countermeasures concerning one specific aspect of information security are grouped in "modules". Some IT-Grundschutz modules address higher level issues in information security, like "organisational aspects", "contingency planning" or "outsourcing" whereas other modules deal with technical topics like "Windows 2000 Server", "WWW-Server", "Mobile Telephones" or "Databases".

The modules also reflect typical areas in which IT assets are employed, for example client/server networks, buildings, communications and application components. Every module begins with a description of the typical threats which may be expected in the given area together with their assumed probability of occurrence.

The IT-Grundschutz modules build the fundament for developing an IT security concept based on the IT-Grundschutz methodology. They can be used in their original form or can be appropriately adapted. There is here some commonality between such a concept for IT security engineering and object orientation in software engineering, both arising from the need to handle the increasing complexity of IT environments.

After having applied the suitable modules of the framework, an additional risk analysis can be performed to reach a higher level of information security. IT-Grundschutz uses a two-tier risk assessment process, which considerably differs from the traditional risk assessment methods. The next section gives a short comparison of the two approaches.

2.2 Two-Tier Risk Assessment versus Traditional Risk Assessment

One way of creating a security concept is the "traditional" risk assessment. This entails ascertaining and examining the assets to be protected (IT systems, data, know-how etc.) to find out which threats they are exposed to. The next stage is to analyse the probability of a security incident and the likely extent of damage to assess the respective risks. Based on this risk assessment and considering the residual risks that remain after the IT security concept has been implemented, individual security safeguards for the particular IT environment are being devised.

Risk assessment following this approach provides valuable information. Nevertheless, it requires a high amount of resources, as it has to be carried out by experts. A quantitative risk assessment approach relies upon the use of input variables such as probability and extent of damage. Practical experience has proven that assessing the probability of IT security incidents is often difficult, not having a sufficient basis for reliable estimates. In addition, the interpretation of the probability is also frequently questionable.

Therefore, IT-Grundschutz uses a qualitative method for risk assessment and considers the probability of occurrence only implicitly as part of determining and assessing the threats. In addition, a central point of the IT-Grundschutz approach for risk assessment consists in the use of the IT-Grundschutz modules. In this way a quick identification of basic deficiencies in IT security management can be achieved.

During the first phase of the IT-Grundschutz risk analysis, only typical threats for standard IT assets are considered. In this context, "standard IT assets" represent typical parts of IT-environments, whereas not only the technical, but also organisational, infrastructural and personnel aspects are considered. "Typical threats" stands here for threats that could result in substantial damage and are realistic for the current application and area of use. Threats are also sorted into five threat catalogues: force majeure, organisational shortcomings, human failure, technical failure and deliberate acts. Each of them describes a "threat scenario" and provides the basis for the definition of specific security measures to counteract the respective threats in the context of the module considered.

Both threats and countermeasures are concretised in separate specification documents. Countermeasure specifications contain low level controls that can be understood and implemented without expert knowledge in information security. They are based on best practices, in order to achieve a reasonable level of security for the respective module using the latest available technology. The provided IT security measures can also be used to perform an actual versus target analysis between the measures already implemented and the recommended ones. The divergences must be analysed to find out whether a security deficiencies exist in the treated area.

This approach allows users to ensure a standard level of information security that is as fast and cost-efficient as possible.

In a second phase, an extensive risk analysis for selected components can be performed. IT-Grundschutz requires, that management has to examine the necessity of a supplementary risk analysis for those target objects (IT components or IT fields) which

- have high or very high security requirements in at least one of the three basic parameters of confidentiality, integrity or availability, or
- can not be adequately handled with the existing modules of IT-Grundschutz, or
- are operated in non-standard scenarios which are not covered by IT-Grundschutz, e.g. operation of IT in unprotected public environments.

Examples of applications or systems that should undergo a supplementary risk analysis include online banking services provided by a financial service provider and IT systems with special real-time operating systems.

A rationale for the decision in favour or against a supplementary risk analysis must be noted briefly in a management report for each target object that has one or more of the above characteristics. The final decision has to be approved and signed by management. The target objects that require a supplementary risk analysis are then to be consolidated into risk areas.

In order to perform a supplementary risk analysis for a single risk area, a "Risk Analysis based on IT-Grundschutz", described in the next section, can be applied.

2.3   Risk Analysis based on IT-Grundschutz

The following method is described extensively in [BSI3] and provides a simple procedure for carrying out a risk analysis as a supplement to an existing IT-Grundschutz security concept. It is recommended to apply it to those target objects, which were specified by the management to undergo a supplementary risk analysis. A benefit of this approach is that it takes into account the results of the first risk analysis phase. Another advantage is that the threats listed in the IT-Grundschutz Catalogues [BSIC] can be used for a further risk assessment. To perform a supplementary risk analysis based on IT-Grundschutz, the threats which were not considered or not handled sufficiently during the first phase have to be determined for each target object. This involves the following steps:

Step one: A summary of the threats already considered has to be prepared. The result is a table assigning to each target object all threats included in the relevant IT-Grundschutz modules. In order to facilitate the subsequent analysis, the protection requirements of each target object in respect of confidentiality, integrity and availability should also be listed in this table.

Step two: The additional threats, which have to be taken into account, have to be determined. For IT security the relevant threats are those, that:

- could produce substantial damage, and
- are realistic for the current application and area of use.

If a target object has a very high or high protection requirement in respect of confidentiality, integrity or availability, the threats affecting this aspect should be found first. If the target object has a normal security requirement in one of these aspects, then the threats considered in the IT-Grundschutz Catalogues are generally exhaustive.

The definition of additional relevant threats is particularly important if there is no appropriate module for the target object in the IT-Grundschutz Catalogues or if the target object is operated in a scenario (environment, application) which is not foreseen in the IT-Grundschutz Catalogues. For the determination of additional threats, considering the threat categories used in IT-Grundschutz can be useful. Also manufacturer product documentation, vulnerabilities published in internet and further threat sources specific to the business sector can provide relevant information.

To determine which additional threats will be added to the threat summary, a brainstorming session involving all the relevant employees and having clear objectives and limited time has proven effective. IT security officers, project managers, administrators and users of the target object under review as well as external experts, if appropriate, should be involved. An IT security expert should conduct the brainstorming session.

Step three: A threat assessment has to take place. During this step there has to be checked, whether the IT security measures already implemented or at least planned in the IT security concept provide adequate protection for each target object and threat. Thus, the following characteristics of the already implemented countermeasures have to be checked:

- Completeness: Do the standard security measures provide protection for all aspects of each threat? (Example: Was the back door to the building also considered?)
- Mechanism strength: Do the protection mechanisms recommended in the standard security measures counteract each threat adequately? (Example: Are the specifications for the minimum key length adequate?)
- Reliability: How difficult is it to circumvent the planned security mechanisms? (Example: How easy is it for users to gain entry to the server room and therefore circumvent the file access control?)

If the IT security measures implemented or envisaged in the IT security concept do not provide adequate protection against the respective threat and the threat is considered to be relevant for the current risk analysis, then the risk has to be treated in the next step.

Step four: The risks which are not adequately counteracted by the security measures already implemented or planned are now identified and a decision about their treatment has to be taken. In all cases management must be involved in this decision as there may be substantial risks or additional costs. Basically there are four options for risk treatment:

- Risks can be reduced via appropriate security measures.
- Risks can be avoided (e.g. by restructuring business processes or the IT assets).
- Risks can be transferred (e.g. by outsourcing or insurance policies).
- Risks can be accepted.

3 Consolidation of the IT Security Concept

At the end of this procedure a consolidation of the IT security concept is necessary to assure that the final set of safeguards will be:

- suitable to fend off the identified threats,
- interoperable with each other,
- user friendly, and
- adequate and appropriate for the targeted environment.

The following figure illustrates the process of creating an IT security concept with the help of IT-Grundschutz Methodology [BSI2], IT-Grundschutz Catalogues [BSIC] and Risk Analysis based on IT-Grundschutz [BSI3].

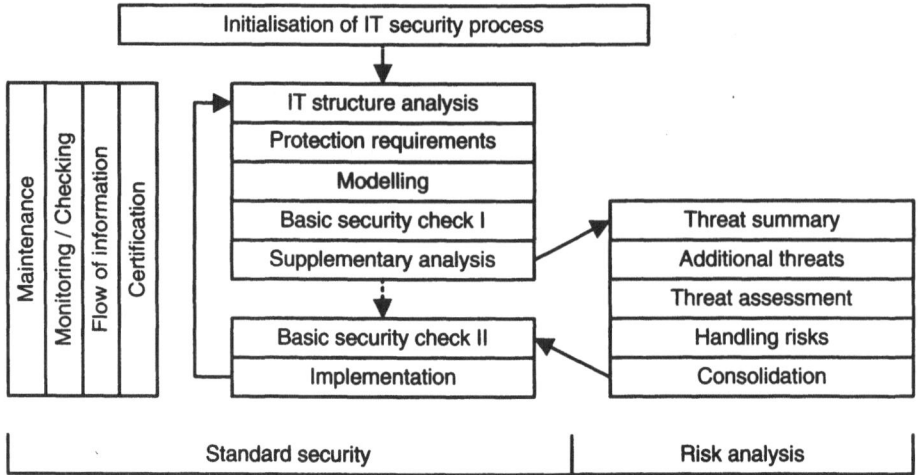

Figure 2: Using IT-Grundschutz for developing an IT security concept

The first phase of risk analysis is performed in the central part of the figure while the second phase is performed in the right part.

4 ISO 27001 Certification based on IT-Grundschutz

To allow organisations to demonstrate the successful implementation of the ISO 27001 requirements using the IT-Grundschutz framework, BSI has established a corresponding certification scheme for auditing both methods. The basis for issuing this certificate is an audit by an external auditor licensed by the BSI. The result of the audit is an audit report that is presented to the certification department, which decides on whether to issue the IT-Grundschutz Certificate. Within the scope of the audit report the auditor has also to examine whether a supplementary risk analysis has been performed in all required cases and whether this is complete.

The approach for checking the audit report and issuing the IT-Grundschutz Certificate is described in the Audit Scheme ([BSIZ], [CERT]). Criteria documents for this certification are, in addition to the ISO 27001 standard, the Audit Scheme as well as the IT-Grundschutz Methodology [BSI2] and the IT-Grundschutz Catalogues [BSIC].

5 Conclusion

The scope of IT-Grundschutz is to provide an efficient method for setting up a management system for information security (ISMS). To achieve this, IT-Grundschutz specifies an IT security process including assessing risks, implementing security measures and monitoring IT security.

The IT-Grundschutz Catalogues contain a framework of "modules", i.e. specific application areas of Information Technology that can be applied to accomplish a two-tier risk assessment. In the first phase, the typical threats included in the modules are assigned to the respective IT assets. In a second phase, a more thorough risk analysis has to be performed for selected IT assets, using the supplementary risk analysis procedure based on the IT-Grundschutz methodology.

Through the two-tier approach IT-Grundschutz enables a progressive accomplishment of the risk assessment task. An organisation can therefore ensure that elementary IT security measures will quickly get implemented while an elaborate risk management is being established.

The method also provides help for small and medium enterprises and organisations with limited resources for the risk management process, by providing a cost effective "standard" risk assessment.

References

[BSI1]   BSI Standard 100-1: "Information Security Management Systems",
           http://www.bsi.bund.de/english/publications/bsi_standards/index.htm

[BSI2]   BSI Standard 100-2: "IT-Grundschutz Methodology",
           http://www.bsi.bund.de/english/publications/bsi_standards/index.htm

[BSI3]   BSI-Standard 100-3: "Risikoanalyse auf der Basis von IT-Grundschutz",
           http://www.bsi.bund.de/gshb

[BSIC]   BSI, "IT-Grundschutz-Kataloge, Standardwerk zur IT-Sicherheit", Loseblatt-
           sammlung, Schriftenreihe zur IT-Sicherheit, Bundesanzeiger-Verlag,
           http://www.bsi.bund.de/gshb

[BSIM]   BSI, "IT-Grundschutz Manual 2004"
           http://www.bsi.bund.de/english/gshb/index.htm

[BSIZ]   BSI „Zertifizierung nach ISO 27001 auf der Basis von IT-Grundschutz"
           http://www.bsi.bund.de/gshb/zert/index.htm

[CERT]   BSI, "Certification conforming to ISO 27001 based on IT-Grundschutz" Scheme
           for ISO 27001 Audits

ISO/IEC 24727 – A Future Standard for Smart Card Middleware

Stephan Spitz · Jens Urmann · Gisela Meister

Giesecke & Devrient GmbH
{stephan.spitz | gisela.meister}@gi-de.com

Abstract

This paper describes the features of the future-oriented ISO/IEC 24727 smart card middleware standard for a broad audience; i.e., from a basic to a good technical understanding. Not only technical aspects are covered, but business and market aspects as well.

ISO/IEC 24727 contains a number of interesting differences in comparison with other existing middleware solutions (e.g., PC/SC). These differences are described in the following chapters.

This future standard contains various new features regarding smart card access. These also help to increase the convenience of smart card usage and integration in applications and in infrastructures.

1 Overview

The ISO/IEC SC17 WG4 standardization group has almost finalized the work on the main parts of the ISO/IEC 24727 standard. This standard describes a middleware concept for future-oriented smart card access.

This new middleware standard will be the choice for upcoming smart card infrastructures (e.g., based on the ECC [ECC_2] specification (European Citizen Card, CEN TC224 WG 15), the German ID Card (dPA, deutscher Personalausweis) or the eHC (German Health Card).

The main features which make this standard so interesting for future smart card based systems are:

- High-level, easy-to-use service access layer for application developers
- Optional calling interface via a network connection
- Unification mechanism for different smart card types
- Extendable and flexible framework architecture

In addition, ISO/IEC 24727 considers legacy aspects, and existing middleware technology can be encapsulated in an implementation of the ISO/IEC 24727 standard.

2 Market Impact of ISO/IEC 24727

The ISO/IEC 24727 standard will also have an impact on the business world of smart cards due to several of reasons:

- The usage of smart cards in different applications will increase in the future due to an easy-to-use and flexible interface in conjunction with the widely available e-ID and eHealth cards.
  Some functions of these smart card types will also be available for commercial applica-

S. Paulus, N. Pohlmann, H. Reimer (Editors): Securing Electronic Business Processes, Vieweg (2006), 102-107

tions besides their usage in eHealth or eGovernment infrastructures. Thus, the smart card is supported as it evolves to become a multi-user and multi-purpose security token.

- For the first time, the smart card can be accessed from other computers in a network. The smart card is no longer only available at the local host and is becoming established as a fully network-enabled device [HiSp06]. The ISO/IEC 24727 standard closes the gap between classical smart cards and future network cards.

- Smart card access in no longer bound to a specific programming language (e.g., C or Java) due to a neutral calling interface (currently an ASN.1 based calling interface is proposed in WG4). This is a major step to hide implementation details from the pure functionality offered by smart cards in an infrastructure. Nevertheless, Java Cards will still play an important role, but the RPC (Remote Procedure Call) interface is not bound to the Java language like RMI (Remote Method Invocation). This gives the flexibility in using different smart card operating systems all having the same calling interface.

- The smart card becomes independent of a host operating system due to a network connection and the WSDL interface [Spi02]. In association with the application independence, the smart card access also becomes independent of the host operating system, which offers further flexibility in smart card integration.

3 Parts of the ISO/IEC 24727 Standard

The future ISO/IEC 24727 standard consists of several parts:

Part 1 ([24727_1]) provides a general overview about the architectural design.

Part 2 ([24727_2]) defines the unification mechanism; i.e., the Generic Card Edge (GCE) for different smart card types. This part can be also replaced by a predefined smart card application structure which has the same behavior on different smart card operating systems. An example for such a structure is an application based on the ECC specification. In addition, the GCE can be implemented either on the smart card or as a software layer in a smart card terminal.

Part 3 ([24727_3]) specifies the Service Access Layer (SAL), which is the relevant part for the interaction with client applications. This SAL describes the interface between a client application and the middleware. Moreover, the SAL contains mechanisms to establish a secure channel between the middleware and the smart card based on differential-identities. Especially this document is considered in the system design of the dPA and the eHC.

Part 4 ([24727_4]) will cover all security aspects, especially transport security in association with the different layers of the middleware. Special attention is placed on the network transport layer security; i.e., the security between the network client- and the card application proxy. These security mechanisms are independent of the differential-identity of part 3.

Part 5 ([24727_5]) describes test appliance regarding the Generic Card Edge of part 2 and the Application Interface of part 3.

3.1 Encapsulation of Smart Card Access

One main idea behind the future ISO/IEC 24727 standard is to encapsulate the smart card access on a highly functional level using a Service Access Layer (SAL) as shown in Fig. 1. This figure also shows the unification of different smart card types via a Generic Card Edge (GCE).

The Service Access Layer translates requests from the client applications into calls to the Generic Card Edge. This is not necessary in the case of a predefined card structure based on predefined smart card applications. In this case, a specification of a certain application structure ensures interoperability between the smart cards of different vendors.

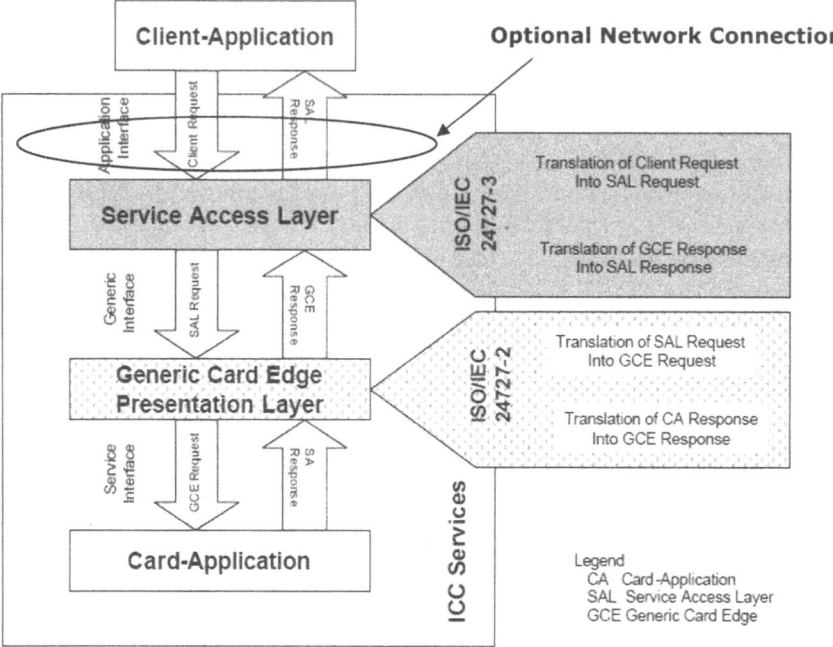

Fig. 1: Organization of the ISO/IEC 24727 framework with an optional network interface for client applications

3.2 The Service Access Layer

The main design goals of the SAL interface in part 3 are:

- A design in the style of topical software architecture; i.e., flexible framework architecture with the integration of extendable services
- A client-oriented approach which encapsulates the lower communication levels (e.g., APDUs). Other existing interfaces and middleware concepts (e.g., PC/SC or CT-API) are rather driven by a smart card view.
- Concurrent and remote access via a network connection on multiple smart cards

3.2.1 Default Services in the SAL Interface

The SAL offers the following basic services to the client application developer. These services encapsulate smart card functionality. In addition, the SAL is extendable, and other proprietary services which are beyond the scope of ISO/IEC 24727 can be subsequently added.

A **Connection Service** handles the initialization of the card connection from the client side to the smart card optionally via a network. In addition, the path to the smart card and the opening and closing of sessions is administrated using this service.

A **Card-Application Service** is responsible for deletion and creation of applications on the smart card.

A **NamedData Service** handles data storage operations on the smart card.

A **CryptographicService** offers encryption, decryption and digital signature creation and verification routines. Moreover, key generation on the smart card is supported.

An **Identity Service** helps to manage the different subjects (identities) which want to access objects (data and services) on smart cards.

An **Authorization Service** uses the subjects administrated by the Identity Service to enforce the access control on objects stored on the smart cards.

3.2.2 Model-based Architecture

The service-oriented architecture contains different model approaches which abstract the access to card applications.

The **Model of Computation** describes the different entities which are relevant for using card applications. The `Client Application` uses `Services` which contain several `Actions` (e.g., data access or usage of cryptographic operations).

To use this functionality, certain `Access Conditions` have to be fulfilled. The binding of `Access Conditions` to `Actions` is carried out via `Access Control Rules`. The Manager `Card-Application` controls this access using a `Differential Identity`, which is obtained after a successful authentication.

A special default service is the `Named Data Service`, which offers data access on smart cards via a handle which is well known from the access on file systems in other computing environments.

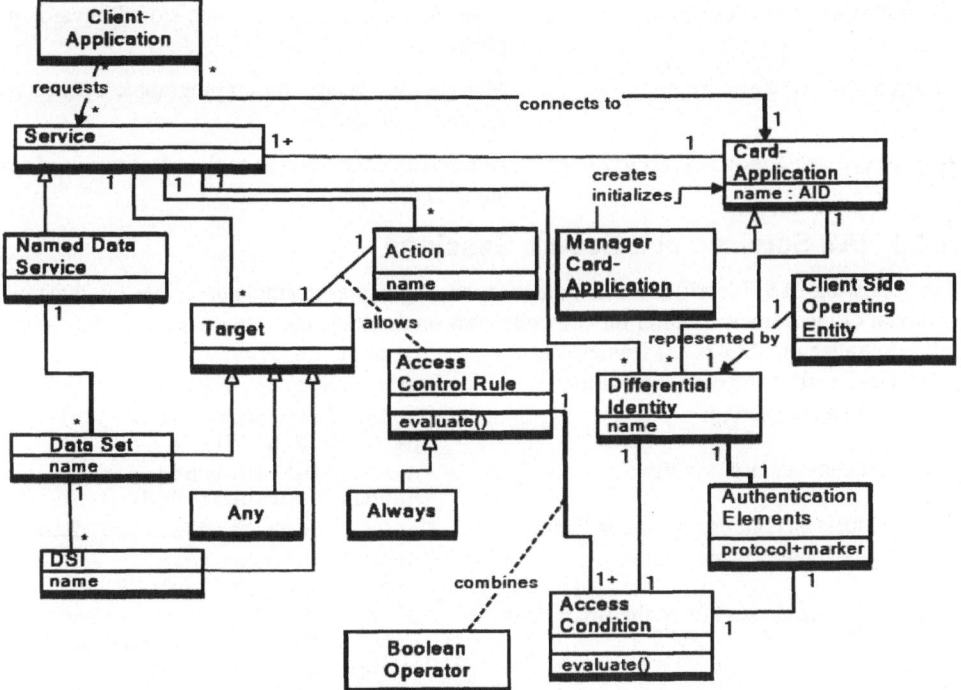

Fig. 2: UML description of the Model of Computation

The **Data Model** differentiates between data which is relevant for the administration of access rights (Identities, Access Control Rules and Access Control Rights, Service Application Descriptors, etc.) and data stored on the smart card (Named Data Service, Data Set, DSI).

The **Access Model** for access control on the framework is based on different types of ACLs (Access Control List). An ACL generally has the following structure.

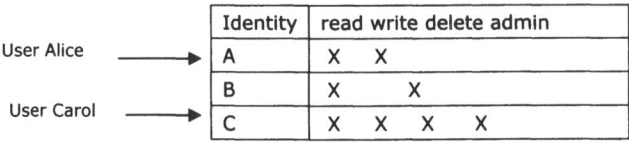

Identity	read	write	delete	admin
A	X	X		
B	X		X	
C	X	X	X	X

User Alice → A, B

User Carol → C

Fig. 3: Structure of an ACL

Different types of ACLs are responsible for granting access to the methods stored in services offered by the SAL:

ApplicationInterface-ACL	Gets access to the API.
ConnectionService-ACL	Stores the access conditions for opening a connection to a specific card application
Card-ApplicationService-ACL	Contains the access conditions for using the services and functions offered by specific card applications
NamedDataServiceControl ACL	Controls the access on the data stored in card applications
CryptographicServiceACL	Manages the access on cryptographic operations in card applications
DifferentialIdentityServiceACL	Administrates the access to the identities used for authorization purpose

3.2.3 IAS Services and Secure Sessions

The following IAS (Identification, Authentication, Signature) example describes the dynamic behavior of the framework after the previous view on the static data structure.

1. Initialize the ISO 24727 framework: Initialize()
2. Get a path to the card application: Path(myApp,path,0,path)
3. Open a connection: CardApplicationConnect (path,TRUE,handle)
4. Authenticate user via PIN: IdentityAuthenticate (handle,userIdent,PIN)
5. Request a challenge for second auth: GetChallenge(handle,userIdent)
6. Authenticate device with key: IdentityAuthenticate (handle, deviceIdent,CR)
7. Start a secure session to the smart card: CardApplicationStartSession (handle,"OIDTLS_ClientAuth" ,myAppIdent,myAppIdent,NULL)

After steps (1-7), a successful connection to the smart card is established, and the data exchange between client and smart card is transported via a TCP/IP-based and TLS-secured session.

The handling of a smart card session via a network interface is still not fully defined in ISO/IEC 24727, and specification work is still in progress.

References

[24727_1]   ISO/IEC 24727: FCD 2005, Identification cards – Integrated circuit cards programming interfaces – Part 1: Architecture

[24727_2]   ISO/IEC 24727: FCD 2005, Identification cards – Integrated circuit cards programming interfaces – Part 2: Generic card interface

[24727_3]   ISO/IEC 24727: CD 2005, Identification cards – Integrated circuit cards programming interfaces – Part 3: Application interface

[24727_4]   ISO/IEC 24727: WD 2006, Identification cards – Integrated circuit cards programming interfaces – Part 4: API Administration

[24727_5]   ISO/IEC 24727: WD 2006, Identification cards – Integrated circuit cards programming interfaces – Part 5: Testing procedures

[ECC_2]   CEN/TS 15480-2: Draft 2005, European Citizen Card - Part 2: Logical data structures and card services

[HiSp06]   Hinz, Walter; Spitz, Stephan: Zur Sicherheit von neuen Chipkarten-betriebssysteme: Herausgeber: P. Horster, D-A-CH Konferenzband, 2006

[Spi02]   Spitz, Stephan: Integration von Chipkarten in elektronische Geschäftsprozesse, Herausgeber: P. Horster Konferenzband Elektronische Geschäftsprozesse, 2002

Information Security Standardization – the ETSI Perspective

Charles Brookson[1] · Dionisio Zumerle[2]

[1]United Kingdom
Department of Trade and Industry
cbrookson@iee.org

[2]ETSI Secretariat
dionisio.zumerle@etsi.org

Abstract

The European Telecommunications Standards Institute (ETSI) has been involved in almost every aspect of information security standardization, from algorithms to smart cards, from fixed and mobile telecommunication infrastructures to electronic signatures, from lawful interception to broadcasting. As a result, with a unique expertise and a vision of security in ICT as a whole developed, the Institute is now attempting to face the next challenges.

This paper gives a comprehensive overview of the security-related activities that are taking place within the Institute, the major security standards that have been published and views on which are the major issues to be addressed in the future within ETSI, but also in collaboration with other standardization bodies and the Industry.

1 Introduction

As ICT becomes ever more essential for business, public administration, public safety and commercial needs, a vast number of new technologies are being developed. Security cannot be considered as an additional feature to be patched on if necessary after the adoption of a technology: it is a requirement that has to be taken into account since the design phase. Indeed, in many cases it results into a winning driver that enables the overall success of the technology.

Standardization of Information Security, sometimes in support of legislative actions, is essential to ensure interoperability between products of different vendors using the same security mechanisms, as well as to ensure an adequate level of security for these products.

ETSI's work is organised into Technical Committees (TCs) and Partnership Projects, responsible for producing and maintaining standards in specific technical areas. Some of the committees are closely related to security aspects; others have a much broader scope, but necessarily deal with security issues in the process of producing a complete set of standards for a technology. ETSI also works closely to develop standards in cooperation with other National, Industry and International groups. Some of the activities are driven by specific European requirements, for example Digital Signatures and Lawful Interception standardization.

The figure below illustrates the areas in which these committees operate.

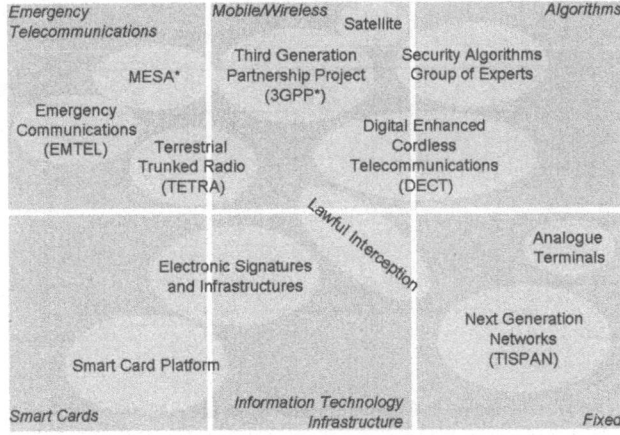

Figure 1: ETSI Committees per Security Areas

2 Mobile and Wireless Communications

The wireless infrastructure that terminals use to access the network makes these technologies very vulnerable to attack. Security mechanisms have been standardized for mobile telephony and mobile radio communications.

2.1 GSM and UMTS

Security has been a major driver for the success of GSM and UMTS. Specifications have been developed to prevent terminal equipment theft, to allow encryption and authentication, to control payment for copyright material downloading and to respond to many other security threats. The general description of the security architecture can be found in [1].

2.1.1 Anonymity

Anonymity consists in preventing the tracking of the location of the user or identifying calls made to or from the user by eavesdropping on the radio path. Anonymity in GSM and UMTS is provided by using temporary identifiers when the feature is activated by the operator, after a short period in which the real identity is used to issue the temporary identifier.

2.1.2 Authentication and Signalling Protection

Authentication is used to identify the user to the network operator and is based on encryption.

ETSI has developed three security algorithms for GSM: A3, A5 and A8. A3 and A8 are specific to the operator and are saved on the SIM card and in the authentication centre. A5 is saved in the mobile equipment and allows for data encryption and decryption over the air interface.

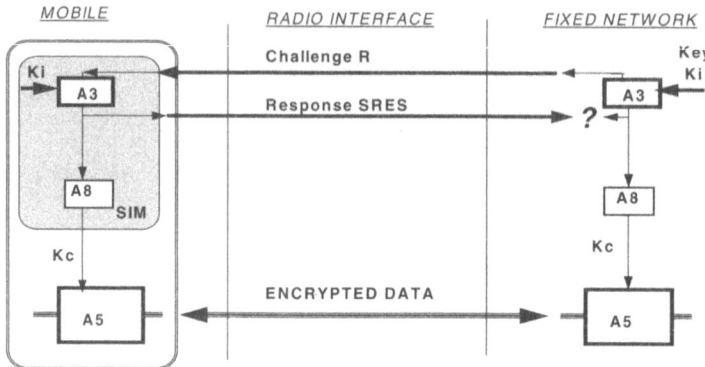

Figure 2: GSM Authentication mechanism

When authentication is performed a random challenge (R) is issued to the mobile, which encrypts it using A3 and the key (Ki) assigned to the mobile, and sends a response back (SRES). The network checks that the mobile has the Ki by performing the same process and comparing the responses with what it receives from the mobile. The response is then passed through A8 by both the mobile and the network to derive the key (Kc), used for encrypting the signalling and messages to provide privacy (A5 series algorithms). The process can be represented graphically as in Figure 2.

3GPP has adopted an innovative authentication and key agreement protocol for UMTS. The protocol retains the framework of the GSM authentication mechanism and provides mutual authentication, agreement on an integrity key between the user and the serving network, and freshness assurance of agreed cipher key and integrity key (see [2] and [15]).

2.1.3 IMEI

ETSI has created a set of GSM standards (see [3]) which define a system to prevent handset theft based on a handset identity number called the International Mobile Equipment Identity (IMEI). This is a unique number attributed during handset manufacturing, registered by the Mobile Network Operator (MNO) and implemented into the mobile terminal. Using the IMEI, mobile equipment declared as stolen can be blacklisted by the MNOs.

2.1.4 Fraud Information Gathering System

Fraud Information Gathering System (FIGS) is a method of monitoring a subscriber's activities to limit the accumulation of large unpaid bills whilst roaming. FIGS allows the network that roaming subscribers are entering to collect information about their activities. The network then sends this information back to the home network of the subscriber, which can then clear certain types of calls and prevent fraudulent use of the system.

2.1.5 Priority

GSM specifications include a public safety service called Priority. This allows users of the appropriate category (typically the emergency services, and government agencies) to obtain high priority access to network services in crisis conditions, when there is a danger of overloading a potentially impaired network.

2.1.6 Location

Concerning location services, several techniques have been specified to improve the accuracy of the positioning, from the simple retrieval of the radio cell where the mobile is located to the more advanced, assisted GPS positioning. There is also privacy protection for the users.

2.2 TETRA

ETSI specifications for TErrestrial Trunked RAdio (TETRA) define a mobile radio communications infrastructure targeted primarily at public safety groups (such as the police and fire departments). TETRA has been also widely deployed in other traditional private/professional mobile radio (PMR) markets, such as transportation, utilities, industrial and public access mobile radio (PAMR), as well as in the military sector for peacekeeping and other activities. The security-related functions of the standard comprise the features in the next clauses.

2.2.1 Mutual authentication

With mutual authentication over the air interface, a mobile station can check if a network can be trusted before entering, and the TETRA system can control the access of a mobile station. This mechanism offers guarantees against fraud, Denial of Service (DoS) and spoofing, while ensuring correct billing and access as well as a secure data distribution channel.

2.2.2 Encryption

As the air interface is vulnerable to eavesdropping, encryption is crucial. Air interface security is intended to secure the connection between mobile stations and the network. This interface is essential to provide certain security functions in a mobile network. Also, end-to-end security can be provided to offer a higher level of security. As TETRA is implemented by diverse user groups for many purposes, this last feature is essential.

2.2.3 Anonymity

Anonymity is achieved using temporary identities to identify the network nodes and encrypting these identities over the air interface. In addition, each time an identity is transmitted, it is encrypted in a different way, making it difficult to eavesdrop and identify active terminals.

3 Next Generation Networks

The new converged and access-independent network model of Next Generation Networks (NGN), is based on the use of a common IP-based platform, and is designed to accommodate the diversity of applications inherent in emerging broadband technologies. The Institute's work on NGN is being managed by its Technical Committee TISPAN (Telecommunications and Internet converged Services and Protocols for Advanced Networking). Security is one of its core concerns as the services will be delivered seamlessly over the most appropriate access network and will thus require a uniform baseline of security.

3.1 NGN Release 1

In its first version (NGN Release 1) TISPAN set the security requirements for the subsystems of Next Generation Networks ([4]), as well as conducting a risk and threat analysis and most of all defining an extensible NGN security architecture ([5]).

3.2 Security Design Guide

TC TISPAN is also producing a Security Design Guide which should be followed in the design of any new component of the network. This work references the guidelines on the use of the Common Criteria for the evaluation of IT security (see [6]), as a set of drivers to be used as the basis for the evaluation of security properties of IT products and systems. The Common Criteria primarily address the AIC triad (Availability, Integrity and Confidentiality).

The same set of TISPAN deliverables contains the guidelines for the preparation of Protection Profiles which define an implementation-independent set of security requirements for a category of communication equipment or system subject to evaluation under the Common Criteria.

4 Lawful Interception

Lawful interception (LI, the legally authorised act by which a network operator or service provider gives law enforcement officials content of the communications of private individuals or organizations), is ever more crucial to preserve national security, to combat terrorism and to investigate serious criminal activities.

ETSI, with active participation of the major telecom manufacturers, network operators and regulatory authorities of Europe and from around the world, is playing a leading role in this field.

4.1 Handover Interface

The ETSI LI specifications for the handover interface (see [7]) illustrate the flow that the intercepted data should follow in telecommunication networks or services. In this context, they specify the network or service protocols necessary to provide lawful interception, as well as the physical or logical point at which the interception has to take place (the handover interface) both for packet data and switched-circuit communications (see Figure 3).

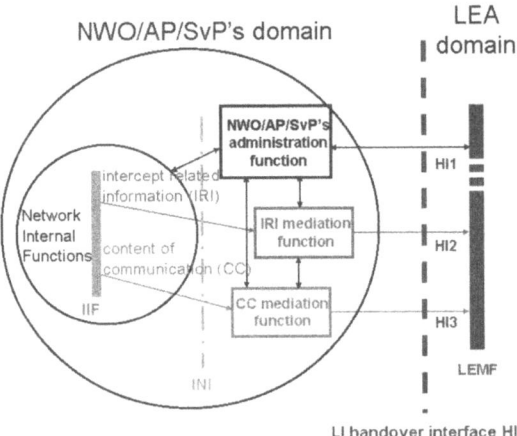

Figure 3: Handover Interface functional diagram

First adopted in 2003 by the Netherlands regulation authority, the LI handover specifications are widely used on a world-wide level.

4.2 IP interception and Service-specific details

The increasing trend in the use of packet-switched technologies has necessitated a standard for the delivery of IP-based interception: ETSI TS 102 232 ([8]) specifies the approach, the protocols and headers needed to perform lawful interception on an IP-based platform.

Lawful interception has to be possible on specific services that make use of the IP framework: TS 102 233 ([9]) covers the service-specific details for e-mail services, describing the hand-over to the law enforcement authorities, whilst TS 102 234 ([10]) covers the service-specific details for Internet access.

Publications include a specification on service-specific details for layer 2 lawful interception. This specification applies to access providers having access to information on layer 2 session information. The TS is particularly important when information on higher layers is either not accessible or not stored.

Also, the Internet access wireless LAN lawful interception specification has been produced (see [11]).

Currently, lawful interception handover and interception interface details specifications for multimedia services are being developed.

ETSI has also produced important specifications on lawful interception of TETRA, UMTS and other technologies.

5 Electronic Signatures

An electronic signature is data in electronic form, which, attached to or logically associated with other electronic data, serves as a means of authentication.

Standards to support the use of electronic signatures and public key certificates are a key driver in enabling electronic commerce. ETSI (and its sister organization CEN) standards for electronic signatures, in support of Directive 1999/93/EC on a Community framework for electronic signatures, focus on the area of electronic signatures and Public Key Infrastructure to support electronic commerce in open environments, establishing a legal and common European framework for the recognition of electronic signatures.

Concerning Electronic Signature Formats, specifications on Cryptographic Message Syntax and eXtended Markup Language formats for Advanced Electronic Signatures have been produced. These formats enable validity over long periods.

In addition, requirements and Profiles have been identified for Qualified Certificates issued by Certification Service Provides and for Time Stamp Tokens issued by Time Stamping Authorities.

A Trust-service Status Lists (TSLs) specification published enables interoperation of certificates among the European Union member states.

Concerning security mechanisms (and their parameters) for advanced electronic signatures, a set of algorithm papers for Advanced Electronic Signatures has been produced.

The following diagram summarises the entire work produced to date on electronic signatures and infrastructures.

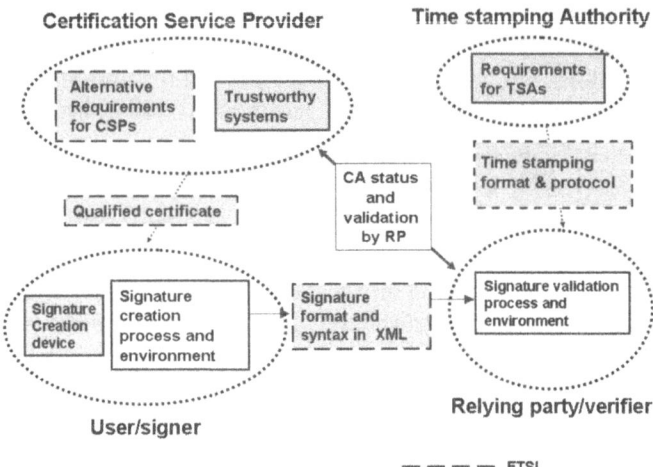

Figure 4: The Electronic Signatures EESSI framework

6 Smart Cards

A smart card is a credit card-sized token containing a micro-processor enabling it to process and store information, to support single or multiple applications and to operate both off-line and on-line.

Smart cards can be used to hold authentication information such as a user's private key, a PKI infrastructure scheme or a user's biometric template. The card may be activated by a user PIN or biometric sample, thus avoiding security issues associated with sending authentication credentials over computer networks. The potential attacker must thus have possession of the card to conduct an attack.

ETSI standardised the Subscriber Identity Module (SIM) card for GSM, one of the most widely deployed smart cards ever. The work produced in the GSM specifications has also been imported into the 3GPP specifications to create the USIM (Universal SIM) card used in UMTS. Work is also being done to introduce smart cards in TETRA.

Recent achievements see the implementation of the Extensible Authentication Protocol (EAP) in support to the Universal Integrated Circuit Card (UICC). The UICC security architecture is designed so as to be able to provide, if necessary, a multi-verification environment, i.e. an environment in which the card can have more than one first level application and may support separate user verification requirements for each application.

The main task of ETSI Technical Committee Card Platform (TC SCP) is to maintain and expand the smart card platform specifications for 2G and 3G mobile communication systems. After the important achievement of the completion of Release 6 of all specifications, current work aims to allow users access to global roaming, as well as to contribute to the growth of mobile commerce, by developing the standards for Integrated Circuit (IC) cards to secure financial transactions over mobile communications systems.

7 Algorithms

ETSI's Security Algorithms Group of Experts (SAGE) provides the Institute's standards makers with cryptographic algorithms and protocols specific to fraud prevention, unauthorised access to public and private telecommunications networks and user data privacy.

Among the algorithms produced are those for 3GPP, DECT, GSM, TETRA, audiovisual services, GPRS and Universal Personal Telecommunications.

Achievements include the design of encryption algorithms for GSM, EDGE and GPRS (A5/3 for GSM and EDGE and GEA3 for GPRS) which provide users of mobile phones with a higher level of protection against eavesdropping than previously available (the algorithms are being developed in collaboration with the 3GPP organisational partners).

The security algorithms for the UMTS radio interface (UTRA) – UEA1 and UIA1 –were also developed in collaboration with the 3GPP Organisational Partners. UEA1 is the standard encryption algorithm, and UIA1 is the standard integrity algorithm; both are based on the Kasumi block cipher. Also, the specification of the Milenage algorithm set, was developed for UMTS.

A second set of security algorithms for UTRA in addition to the Kasumi-based algorithms has been recently developed (UEA2 and UIA2 algorithms).

For an overview of the overall algorithm mechanisms in UMTS, see [12].

8 Future Challenges

The threat to the security of our ICT systems grows daily. Technology is constantly evolving and consequently criminals taking advantage of it become more powerful. Security standardization must evolve too to keep pace with the developing risks and threats.

The ETSI Future Security Workshop on the 16-17 January 2006 ([13]) attended by experts representing many organizations contributed to suggestions for future standardization. Furthermore, the European Commission Communication is urging for greater awareness of the importance of security in the IT sector (see [17]). ETSI as a European Standardization Organization (ESO) has the duty of serving the needs expressed by the EC; in addition, ETSI serves as a Global Standards Organization (GSO) delivering specifications that are used world-wide. The Institute is, consequently, planning further action in security, in collaboration with the Industry and other Standards Development Organizations to serve in its primary roles.

The Institute sees the following topics were identified as being of strategic importance:

8.1 Next Generation Networks

There are a great number of bodies active in this topic and co-ordination must be ensured. Also, there is a series of challenges that have to be addressed. First of all, legacy fixed and 2G/3G security is fundamentally different. Some of the assumptions of legacy fixed are not valid in 2G/3G (such as far-end NAT) and the other way round (such as explicit strong authentication of terminals through use of ISIM/USIM).

Co-ordination and attempt to align the technologies are the major challenges in this field.

8.2 Privacy

Definition of privacy and security levels for users needs to be further addressed, with guidelines for User Profile Management.

Security should be transparent; expert users should be able to reduce the security level, but a default level of high security should be guaranteed for users of equipment and terminals.

8.3 Product Proofing

Identifying and analyzing the threats for products and services to be the object of criminal activity is fundamental to reduce risk when designing products. The European Commission has mandated the ESOs to take action in defining guidelines to create products that are crime - proof (see [14]).

A lot of effort has already been made to achieve this throughout the years, with excellent results in some cases (e.g. IMEI, see section 2.1.2). These best practices must become the guidelines to take into account each time a new product or service is launched. A standard way to address this issue must be created. .

8.4 Data Rights Management

As triple play, and quadruple play more recently, is ever more considered a bundled solution increasing opportunity costs for customers and margins for providers, content becomes a key asset to be protected from unauthorized access. Numerous Digital Rights Management (DRM) schemes have been developed, with no single solution. The possibility of creating a single DRM specification should be explored.

The optimal layer (or layers) to take the security provisions has yet to be defined, as well as whether DRM has to be device specific. Online versus offline verification is another challenge. Also, one-time versus multi-shot verification, invocation limited access versus unlimited access and copy protection versus backup are issues that are still open.

8.5 Data Retention

Data Retention standardization is required to ensure that systems, networks and products conform. According to the relevant European Commission Directive [18], information on telephone calls and Internet use would be kept for six to twelve months.

ETSI TC LI has started to address the subject with a series of specifications that are being currently produced.

8.6 Mobile terminal security

Attacks on mobile data platforms from viruses have to be properly addressed. Especially for mobile devices used by enterprise employees, a series of threats such as viruses, trojans, rootkits and spyware can lead to considerable financial loss.

As done for laptops and desktop computers, similar security measures should be taken for mobile devices. Mobile terminal security (such as antivirus, firewall, intrusion detection) should define methods to disable a terminal that has been discovered to be under attack and to prevent DoS attacks .

In this perspective, false emergency calls are also an issue that the security standardization community must look into.

8.7 Banking security and eCommerce

Technologies for eCommerce and eBusiness currently are among the most important and profitable applications in ICT.

Electronic transactions require very high levels of security. Trusted computing and guaranteed levels of privacy are paramount to promote the use of electronic tools when dealing with money transfers and banking accounts.

The concept of a Service Oriented Architecture (SOA), enabling modular and scalable enterprise transactional architecture applications through web services is ever more adopted: there is not yet a guideline on how to provide embedded security in this environment.

Also, electronic signatures play a leading role in this field, applied in banking transactions, eInvoicing or Registered EMail (REM).

Banking, telecommunications and information technology organizations must seek close collaboration in this field.

8.8 RFID

Security in RFID technology can prevent illicit tracking and cloning of tags.

RFID tags present a low limit of computational resources within the tag, which makes the use of standard cryptographic techniques unfeasible. Implementation of lighter encryption algorithms must be considered for the RFID tags.

ETSI has recently established a Task Group (ERM TG34) to produce deliverables for future RFID technologies and products. Some specifications have already been published.

9 Conclusions

This paper has described the ways in which information security has been addressed by the Institute through its almost 20 years of history. Mobile communications, electronic signatures, smart cards, security algorithms, lawful interception are some of the technologies and aspects that ETSI has worked on.

The expertise that has been developed is now used to tackle the new issues that arise. An assessment of the most important areas has been given into this paper.

References

[1]   ETSI TS 133 102 Universal Mobile Telecommunications System (UMTS); 3G security; Security architecture (3GPP TS 33.102)

[2]   ETSI TS 143 020 Digital cellular telecommunications system (Phase 2+); Security-related network functions (3GPP TS 43.020)

[3]   ETSI TS 122 016 Technical Specification Group Services and System Aspects; International Mobile station Equipment Identities (IMEI) (3GPP TS 22.016)

[4]   ETSI TS 187 001; TISPAN NGN Security Requirements – NGN Release 1

[5]   ETSI TS 187 003; TISPAN NGN Security - Security Architecture – NGN Release 1

[6]   ISO/IEC 15408 Information technology Security techniques - Evaluation criteria for IT security

[7] ETSI ES 201 671 Lawful Interception (LI); Handover Interface for the Lawful Interception of Telecommunications Traffic

[8] ETSI TS 102 232 Lawful Interception (LI); Handover Specification for IP Delivery

[9] ETSI TS 102 233 Service-specific details for e-mail services

[10] ETSI TS 102 234 Lawful Interception (LI); Service-specific details for internet access services

[11] TR 102 519 Lawful Interception (LI); Lawful Interception of WLAN Internet Access

[12] ETSI TR 133 908 Universal Mobile Telecommunications System (UMTS); Security Algorithms Group of Experts (SAGE); General report on the design, specification and evaluation of 3GPP standard confidentiality and integrity algorithms (3GPP TR 33.908)

[13] ETSI Future Security Workshop: the threats, risks and opportunities, Output Report 2006 (http://portal.etsi.org/securityworkshop/)

[14] EC DG Justice M/355, "Elaboration of European Standards to identify and reduce crime risk in products and services"

[15] Charles Brookson, "GSM (and PCN) Security and encryption", 1994

[16] Charles Brookson, Dionisio Zumerle "Security for ICT – the work of ETSI", ETSI, 2006 - http://www.etsi.org/etsi_radar/whitepaper/wp_1.htm

[17] EC COM(2006) 251 A strategy for a Secure Information Society – "Dialogue, partnership and empowerment"

[18] 2006/24/EC Directive of the European Parliament and of the Council on the "retention of data generated or processed in connection with the provision of publicly available electronic communications services or of public communications networks and amending Directive 2002/58/EC"

Digital Signatures without the Headaches

Nick Pope[1] · Juan Carlos Cruellas[2]

[1]Security & Standards Associates
Grays, Essex, United Kingdom
nickpope@secstan.com

[2]Universitat Politècnica de Catalunya
Barcelona, Spain
cruellas@ac.upc.edu

Abstract

Deploying support for digital signatures can be a major headache for any organisation. In many cases signatures are created on behalf of an organisation but may be applied by a constantly changing authorised group of personnel. The need to manage the allocation and certification of the multitude of user keys can be particularly burdensome and difficult to secure. This paper presents an alternative approach to the digital signing, which significantly reduces these headaches, being supported by a number of companies and standardised by OASIS. The OASIS "Digital Signature Services" (DSS) standard specifies the use of a specialised server for the creation and verification of signatures under control of remote clients. Instead of keys having to be held and managed individually, OASIS DSS enables keys and other aspects of the signing service to be managed centrally on a networked server. The OASIS DSS protocol supports a range of signature formats including XML and CMS. It is designed around a basic "Core" set of elements and procedures which can be profiled to support specific uses such as time-stamping (including XML structured timestamps), corporate entity seals, electronic post marks and code signing.

1 Why OASIS DSS?

Electronic documents play a key role in today's modern business environment. No longer does paper form the basis for the day-to-day business. Information is prepared and stored electronically and exchanged on line through email and other online services. E-commerce and the electronic office is no longer just a buzz word but a reality. However, such key business information is generally stored and exchanged in unprotected form. Electronic documents can be readily changed and it can be difficult to prove its authenticity. Such information can be open to fraud and in modern regulatory environment where electronic documentation provides essential part of audit records and regulatory reporting. Organisations are leaving themselves vulnerable to attack and can also have difficulties in providing verifiable documentary evidence against claims of malpractice. The keeping of paper records for key business information is becoming less and less of a practical proposition.

A solution to ensuring authenticity of electronic documents has been available for many years – digital signatures. This enables the source of documentation to be quickly verified as coming from an authentic source and any document tampering is made immediately obvious. Furthermore, being based around public key techniques, digital signatures can be used at the global level. Given the appropriate public key infrastructure any party can readily verify a signed document's authenticity.

However, the widespread use of digital signatures has yet to be realised. Similar techniques have been generally accepted as the solution of securing web site using SSL. But, whilst use of digital signatures is gradually spreading, digital signatures have yet to obtain widespread adoption. The use of digital signatures is often seen as a major headache. The management of the keys necessary to produce digital signatures can be burdensome and often needs the use of special smart card devices to ensure the security of the keys. This can be particularly difficult in large organisations where there are large numbers of individuals who regularly need new keys because of change in roles as well as people joining and leaving the organisation. Furthermore, individuals often misplace or misuse the keys compromising their security adding the further burden of a major infrastructure for handling revocation.

The OASIS Digital Signature Services (DSS) standard provides a way of significantly reducing the headache of using digital signatures by controlling the application of signatures on an organisational basis through a network based server. Instead of each individual requiring to protect a document having to be allocate a key, with all the difficulties of managing and securing it, using DSS the signing keys are managed on a secure server with all the security controls necessary to minimise the risk of compromise. The creation of a DSS server based signature can be still under the control of an authorised individual but instead of needing specialised signing equipment for each user, the existing user authentication mechanisms (password, two factor, biometric ...whatever already is accepted by the organisation) can be used. A DSS signature can secure the organisation's documents, efficiently and effectively, whilst maintaining accountability down to the individual level. Furthermore, the security necessary to protect sensitive signing keys can be targeted at the signing server, for example through the use of tamperproof signing devices and placement in a secure room with controlled access, perhaps with dual control, thereby maximising security and yet reducing costs because the security can be highly localised. This is further enhanced by the ability to manage the auditing of signing events centrally.

The development of the OASIS DSS has involved the leaders in the digital security market including RSA, IBM, BEA Systems, Entrust, Surety, Cybertrust. Also, OASIS DSS has worked closely with the Universal Postal Union to facilitate the use of DSS within their Electronic Post Mark system [UPU EPM]. Several implementations exist and interoperability trials are being carried out to demonstrate the practicability of the standard. Much of the work of DSS has been aimed at building on the simplicity of time-stamping services to provide the full capabilities of digital signatures and support a range of signature forms.

This technique of network based signing is particularly appropriate where information is released on behalf of an organisation, for example with signing of code to indicate that the a program is created by a trusted corporation with the appropriate development and release organisational controls. By placing the organisational signature in shared server, the creation of the signature can be linked to the appropriate controls for proper authorisation and release of signed code. Similarly, DSS signatures can be used in electronic invoicing to sign electronic invoices where the appropriate release procedures have been met.

The use of DSS is not limited, however, to the signing of documents with corporate signatures. It can be used to provide general facilities to protect the integrity of key documents within any organisation by sealing or time-stamping data to ensure that it cannot be modified once protected. The approach of network based signing is also being recognised as form of proxy signing in legal environments such as court filing and notarial services.

2 What Does OASIS DSS Do?

The basic aim of the OASIS Digital Signature Service (DSS) draft standard is to define protocols for a networked web service to support digital signatures. It also supports a variety of variations on basic digital signature services such as time-stamping.

DSS is designed to support a range of signature formats. Not only does DSS support the World Wide Web consortium XML Signature [W3C XMLDSig], but also the widely used Cryptographic Message Syntax (CMS) binary signed data format [IETF CMS]. It can even be extended to support other forms of signature such as PGP. The protocol is also designed to be easily extensible to enable support of advanced forms of CMS and XML based electronic signatures such as defined by ETSI [ETSI TS 101 733] & [ETSI TS 101 903].

DSS supports two basic protocols one for the creation of digital signatures, the other for verification of signatures. The basic operation of a DSS sign and verify requests are illustrated below:

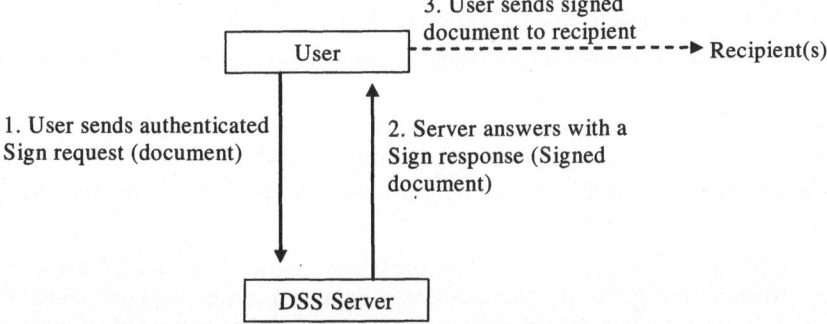

Fig 1: Illustration of DSS Sign Protocol (to be updated with prettified version)

1. The user sends the request for the document to be signed through a secure channel that authenticates the user (e.g. SSL with client authentication).

2. The server checks that the authenticated user is allowed to sign the document and if acceptable signs the document on behalf of the user with a corporate signing key or a key which the server holds on behalf of the user.

3. The signature is added to the document by the server and returned to the user back through the same secure channel.

Having obtained the signed document from the DSS server the user can then pass it on to one or more recipients who may verify the signature themselves or use the DSS verify protocol

The recipient may verify the signature himself or use the DSS verify protocol as indicated below:

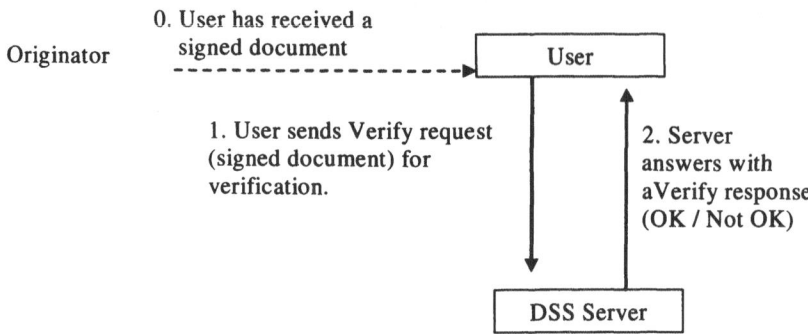

Fig 2: Illustration of DSS Verify Protocol

The user may be passed a signed document coming from a user with its own signing capability or one using the DSS Sign protocol as described above.

1. The user sends the request for the signed document to be verified through a secure channel (e.g. SSL).

2. The server verifies the validity of the signed document including checking the validity and revocation checks on any keys or certificates as necessary.

3. The results of this verification is returned back to the user through the same secure channel.

The DSS protocol removes from the user all the burdens normally associated with digital signatures. There is no need for the management of large numbers of keys distributed throughout the organisation, and no special cryptographic code or keys are needed on the client system. Where it is necessary to authenticate the client existing mechanisms can be used. All the problems of maintaining the security of the keys and cryptographic functions associated with digital signatures can be managed by the organisation through centralised controls.

DSS servers can be used to maintain an audit record to confirm that signatures are verifiable at the time of receipt, and through use of time-stamping ensure that the validity of archived signed documents can be assured long after the applicable keys have expired.

3 DSS specification set structure

The DSS specification set is formed by the so-called core document ("Digital Signature Service Core Protocols, Elements and Bindings") and a number of additional documents defining specific profiles of the aforementioned core protocols.

The core document defines the (XML-based) syntax and semantics for the basic services, namely: signature generation and signature verification. This includes:

*   Definition of four basic messages: SignRequest, SignResponse, VerifyRequest and VerifyResponse. They are defined to easily manage the most common signatures formats, ie, [XMLSig] and [CMS].

*   Definition of an extensibility mechanism that allows the clients to further qualify or even increase the extent of the requests through optional inputs. It also allows the servers to answer with extended responses through the corresponding optional outputs.

- Definition of a XML format for a time-stamp token, fully based on XML signatures as specified in [XMLSig].

- Definition of mechanisms for managing generation and verification of digital signatures carrying time-stamp tokens (both CMS-based as defined in [RFC 3161] and the XML-based specified in the core document itself) computed on the signatures themselves (signature time-stamps).

- Definition of bindings for transport and security. The first ones specify how DSS messages are encoded and carried over the most popular transport protocols (it defines bindings for HTTP –through HTTP POST exchanges- and SOAP 1.2). The security bindings establish rules for providing confidentiality, authentication and integrity to the transport binding; for example using the secure socket layer standard TLS or SSL. In this way clients may use wide-spread tools that do not jeopardize their implementation.

The profile documents further develop the basic messages so that they may be easily tailored to meet the requirements of a specific application or use case. Profiles may restrict the values ranges of certain message elements, or, if required, extend the basic core protocols defining new optional inputs, outputs and/or bindings.

The final result is not only a set of protocols targeting a number of relevant scenarios but also a set of generic protocols which may be easily further profiled as new uncovered use cases are identified.

4 Variations and Profiling DSS

The DSS protocol supports a number of variations in this protocol. For example, the signature may be passed back to the user on its own, detached from the document to which it applies, or placed within the document to which it applies. Another variation is that the document is reduced to a simple hash fingerprint for sending to the server instead of the document for either signing or verification, thereby reducing bandwidth requirements and reducing the opportunity for the confidentiality of the document to be compromised.

When signing a document the DSS server may add additional attributes or properties to the signature such as the claimed signing time or a time-stamp against the content applied immediately before signing.

Due to the number of variations a specific set of options can be selected in the DSS protocol to support a particular mode of operation or application requirement. This selection from the DSS protocol is defined in separate DSS profile specification. The DSS protocol is also designed to facilitate extensions and so DSS Profiles may also extend the protocol, as well as selecting specific options, defining its own profile specific input or outputs for profile specific attributes of a signature.

One of the simplest DSS profiles provides time-stamping equivalent to the existing time-stamping standard – RFC 3161, but incorporating the use of XML. In the DSS time-stamping profile selects from the core to provide simple time-stamping as follows:

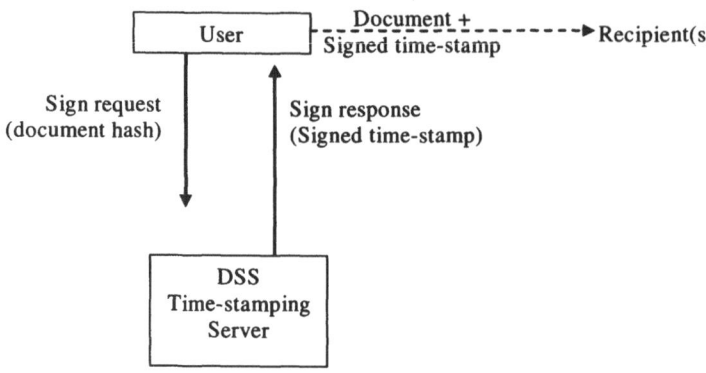

Fig 3: Illustration of DSS Time-stamp Profile

1. The user calculates the hash of the document to be time-stamped locally
2. This document hash is sent to the DSS time-stamping server.
3. The server creates a signed object containing the document hash and the signing time.
4. The signed time-stamp is returned to the user, and if the DSS server is not accessed through a secure channel the user may verify the signature as being valid and from a trusted server.

The user would pass the document and signed time-stamp on to one or more recipients. If required a profile of the DSS verify protocol may be used to verify the time-stamp at the recipient.

A number of profiles have been defined for DSS. This includes:

a. **Time-stamp profile**
   As described above, including support for XML format time-stamps.

b. **DSS Entity Seal Profile**
   This profile is a variation on a signed time-stamp, where the signed object includes not only the time but the identity of the authenticated user requesting the "entity seal". This provides further traceability and provides a form of "proxy" signature where the signature is produced on behalf of another identifiable party.

c. **Advanced Electronic Signature Profile**
   This profile produces signatures that have the attributes needed for legally qualified and long-term signatures

d. **Code signing Profile**
   This profile is designed to support the signing of code authorised for distribution with an organisational signature indicating its authenticity.

e. **Electronic Post Mark Profile**
   This profile is for providing an electronic post mark used confirm authenticity of email, as promoted by the Universal Postal Union (UPU).

f. **Signature Gateway Profile**
   This profile supports the creation of signatures at a gateway from a form only recognised internally to a standard form which can be recognised externally.

5 Technical Details

The DSS core document defines two protocols: one for signature generation (Sign) and one for signature verification (Verify). Each protocol defines two XML messages: one for requesting the provision of the service to the server (Request), and other for giving the result back to the client (Response).

5.1 Sign protocol

The `SignRequest` message has two different parts:

1. `InputDocuments`. This element contains information on the documents that must be signed. Binary documents are encoded in base-64 within `Base64Data`. XML documents may be escaped (`EscapedXML`), base-64 encoded (`Base64XML`) or without any previous processing (`InlineXML`). `InputDocuments` may also contain the digest of the documents (`DocumentHash`) or even a transformed version of the original document (`TransformedData`).

2. `OptionalInputs`. The core document defines some contents that may be useful to any profile. The core defines inputs for indicating the identity of the requester; for indicating the signing key to be used by the server; for requesting to the server the generation and incorporation of a time-stamp token on the signature; for requesting generation of multiple `ds:Reference` elements for a single `Document`, etc.

The core document specifies how the server must behave when receiving a `SignRequest` for generating the requested signature and building the corresponding `SignResponse`.

The `SignResponse` message has three relevant parts:

1. `Result`, with details of the result of the server's operation: a mandatory `ResultMajor`, notifying whether the server executed properly, an optional `ResultMinor` giving specific details, and an optional string (`ResultMessage`).

2. `SignatureObject`, which may enclose the signature created to be passed to the client. This may be a XML (`ds:Signature`) or a base-64 encoded CMS signature (`Base64Signature`). It may also contain a RFC 3161time-stamp or a XML based time-stamp as defined by the DSS core itself. Finaly, it may also contain a reference(`SignaturePtr`) to an enveloped XML signature within a document.

3. `OptionalOutputs`. An example is the one for including documents enveloping the signature requested.

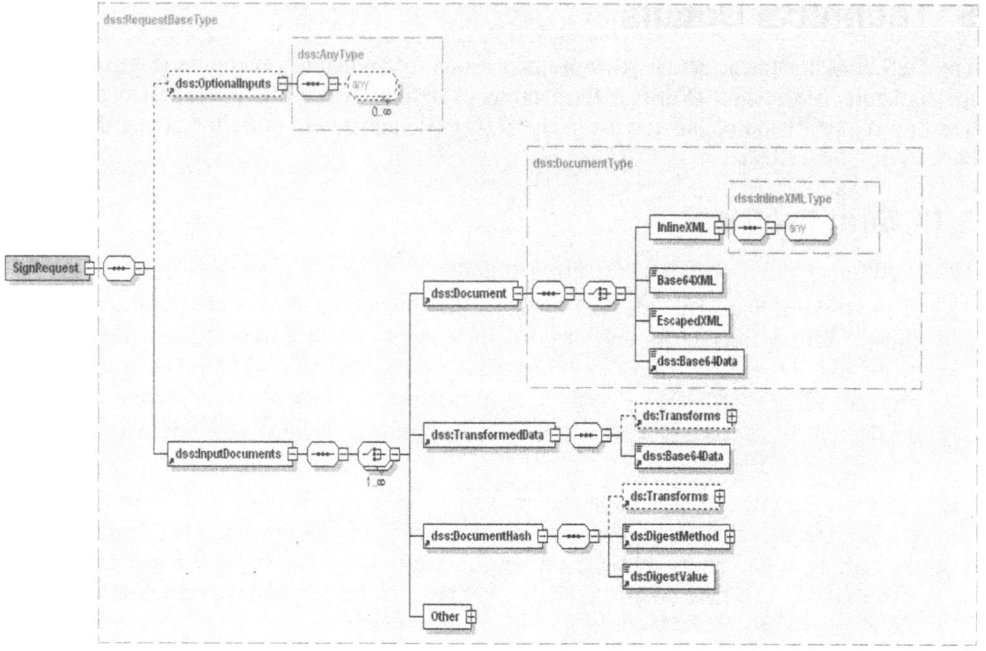

Fig 4: SignRequest message structure

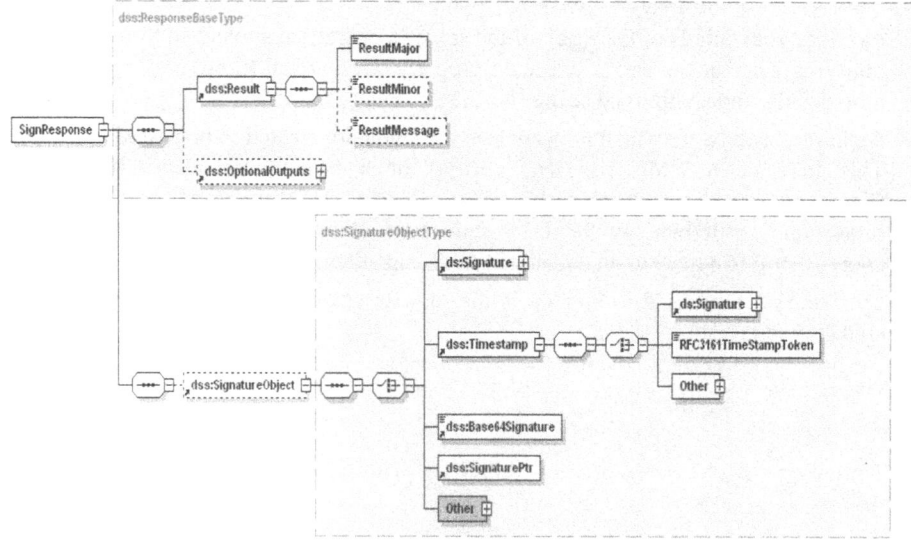

Fig 5: SignResponse message structure

5.2 Verify protocol

The VerifyRequest message has three main parts:

1. SignatureObject. This element is used for passing the signature to be verified to the server. Its structure is the same as the one present in SignResponse message.

2. InputDocuments. This element is used for passing the signed documents that the server must deal with while verifying the signature. They may even incorporate enveloped signatures.

3. OptionalInputs. The core defines inputs for instructing the server to verify any ds:Manifest element present in [XMLSig] signatures; for requesting to the return, of details on the verification process; for requesting the return of the signatory's identification, for requesting the incorporation of unauthenticated properties (cryptographic material used for verification, for instance) to the signature; and for requesting the generation and incorporation of a signature time-stamp as an unauthenticated property, among other purposes.

The VerifyResponse message shares its two elements with SignResponse:

1. Result gives details of the result of the server's operation.

2. OptionalOutputs. Generaly speaking, each optional input of VerifyRequest is related with thecorresponding optional output where the server passes to the client the result of the specific processing requested.

5.3 XML Time-stamp token

DSS core protocol also defines a format for XML time-stamps. A XML time-stamp is an XML Signature (as defined in [XMLSig]) that signs an ds:Object element enclosing the current time and related information in a TSTInfo element.

Contents of this TSTInfo element are equivalent to the fields defined in the binary timestamp structure defined in RFC3161. CreationTime contains the time when the token was issued; SerialNumber contains a unique serial number across all the tokens generated by a particular TSA. ErrorBound indicates the TSA's estimation of the maximum error in its local clock. Policy identifies the policy under which the token has been issued. Ordered indicates whether the time-stamps generated by a TSA are ordered according to the value of CreationTime. TSA contains TSA's name.

6 Conclusion

At the time of writing the DSS set of standards are currently in Committee Draft status and just about ready to be submitted for public comments. In parallel, certain members of the TC have started an interoperability initiative for assessing the protocols under a practical perspective, and suppliers are already working on bringing implementations to market. By implementing DSS, the power of digital signatures can be provided without the headaches of installing PKI capabilities at every user system and ensuring signing keys and devices are managed securely.

References

[OASIS DSS] OASIS Digital Signature Services Technical Committee
http://www.oasis-open.org/committees/tc_home.php?wg_abbrev=dss

[W3C XMLDSig]   XML-Signature Syntax and Processing – W3C Recommendation
12 february 2002, D Eastlake et al, http://www.w3.org/TR/xmldsig-core/

[IETF CMS]   IETF RFC 3852 Cryptographic Message Syntax (CMS), July 2004 R. Housley,
http://www.ietf.org/rfc/rfc3852.txt

[ETSI TS 101 733]   CMS Advanced Electronic Signatures (CAdES)
http://www.etsi.org/services_products/freestandard/home.htm

[ETSI TS 101 903]   XML Advanced Electronic Signatures (XAdES)
http://www.etsi.org/services_products/freestandard/home.htm

[UPU EPM]   Universal Postal Union – Electronic Post Mark
http://www.upu.int/news_centre/documents/en/brochure_the_electronic_
post_mark_en.pdf

Could Test Standards Help on the Way to Achieve Global e-Passport Interoperability?

Andreas M. Wolf

Cross Match Technologies GmbH
Unstrutweg 4
07743 Jena
Germany
Andreas.Wolf@CrossMatch.com

Abstract

Now the first e-passports issued by several countries are in the field, and the first real life experiences with them have been made. Will they be readable at all borders? Will the data stored on the chips be accessible, and can they be used to verify successfully the identity of the person carrying the document? These interoperability questions have several aspects that have to be discussed: Passport compliance, reader compliance, biometric data compliance, and biometric system performance. A status on standardization initiatives as well as on first experiences in e-border projects completes this paper.

1 Passport and Reader Compliance

Which equipment is necessary at the border crossing? Generally, in a scenario with staffed border control booths, e. g., at airports or street border crossings, the following equipment is necessary, even if each project requires specific adaptations. In this Section, the passport part of the equipment is analyzed; the biometrics part follows in the next Section.

First of all, reader equipment that allows automated and semi-automated checks of conventional and electronic passports is required. It has to be considered that most countries are just starting their e-passport programmes. In spring of 2006, ten countries began issuing electronic passports: Australia, Belgium, Denmark, Germany, Japan, New Zealand, Norway, Sweden, Thailand, and UK. The EU member states have to start the e-passport issuance by August 2006. For at least the next ten years we will see in the field a large number of conventional (i., e., without RFID chip) documents, even from these countries. These documents have to be inspected, too.

Additionally, many countries might decide not to issue electronic documents at all. Consider that we have had the ICAO requirement for machine readable zones (MRZ) in the e-passports for decades, but still today there are many passports without machine readable zone in the field. So the know-how on printed booklets and the inspection of their security features does not lose its importance. In many situations it will simply not be possible to read the chip, even if there is one in the passport. However, a visual inspection is possible everywhere and at any time.

The inspection process of the document itself should be designed in a way that is most comfortable for the inspector. He should only be required to open the passport, and to put it on the reader device. The inspector should be able to deal with the traveller instead of being concerned with the technical equipment. Therefore, ergonomic aspects are of great importance. In detail, if the inspector has to know where the chip is located in a certain passport, or if he has to ask the traveller which digital certificate has been used to sign the data in his passport, then the entire process slows down, loses security, and, at the end, is not feasible at all. One may assume that this is a matter of course, but at the recently held ICAO interoperability test in Berlin it was the case that reader manufacturers (= inspectors) asked the testers (= travellers) exactly these questions.

During the interoperability events another observation has been made: Especially in environments where a high throughput is required like at airport border crossings, any technology that forces the inspector to perform more than one activity with the passport will lead to suboptimal results. Swipe readers, where the passport has to be placed on an antenna after reading out the MRZ, have their application cases, however, for all high performance applications, full page readers that allow single step inspections should be the first choice. An example of this reader type is the AUTHENTICATOR 100 shown in the Figure below.

Figure 1: Full page reader example: Cross Match Technologies AUTHENTICATOR 100

Document readers shall ensure global interoperability. They must be able to read any ICAO compliant passport (even if there is no complete definition of what this means yet). A good indicator of the abilities of a chosen technology provider might be the participation of that company in the ICAO e-passport interoperability tests as well as the membership in the ISO and the national standardization bodies working groups.

The cross-over interoperability of passports and readers is currently tested in an ongoing series of interoperability test events of which the most recent ones took place in 2005 in Tsukuba (Japan) and Singapore, and in 2006 in Berlin. Here we have seen important improvements in terms of accessibility, readability and reading times. The values given in Table 1 have been measured with the Cross Match Technologies document reader AUTHENTICATOR 100/200.

Table 1: Results from the e-passport interoperability tests in Tsukuba, Singapore, and Berlin

Event/Passports	No. of Passports	Min. Read Time	Median Read Time	Max. Read Time
Tsukuba with BAC	45	2.0s	7.7s	31.1s
Tsukuba w/o BAC	54	1.6s	3.4s	18.7s
Singapore with BAC	74	1.1s	2.9s	23.5s
Singapore w/o BAC	17	0.4s	1.6s	6.1s
Berlin with BAC	86	0.2s	3.6s	16.0s
Berlin w/o BAC	4	0.3s	3.3s	4.6s

One can see that the duration of a passport reading process has dropped by 50% within the 7 months between Tsukuba and Singapore. Between Singapore and Berlin the time stayed relatively constant. Probably this indicates that the chip technology applied in the passports reached a certain maturity. On the other hand, in Berlin the certificate chain of the passive authentication (PA) has been checked for the first time, this might be the reason for the slightly higher time consumption in Berlin.

The following table gives a good impression of the fact that the goal of *RFID technical* interoperability is "almost" achieved. *Technical* means that a group of passport manufacturers is able to produce passports that can be read by almost all readers, and that there is a group of reader manufacturers whose readers read almost all existing passports.

Table 2: Results from the interoperability test in Singapore (Selection from [SDW06]). The total number of possible passports for testing was 95. If a passport was readable at a distance of 0 cm, 2cm or when the document was flipped over, it was counted as interoperable

Results from the Interfest ePassport Testing in Singapore (7-8 November 2005)			
Company Name	Number of Documents Tested	No of successful reads at 0 or 2 cm or flip	Percentage Interoperability
3M	82	81	98,78%
ASK	83	81	97,59%
Baltech 1	72	69	95,83%
Cross Match	85	85	100,00%
Desko	70	67	95,71%
EMSquares	80	74	92,50%
Gemplus	75	72	96,00%
ID3 Semiconductors	69	55	79,71%
Infineon Technologies	73	73	100,00%
Integrated Engineering 2	82	78	95,12%
IRIS Corp 2	68	68	100,00%
Oakwell Engineering 1	68	65	95,59%
Panasonic	72	62	86,11%
Rochford Thompson	73	72	98,63%
Rosan	75	73	97,33%
SCM Microsystems 3	79	73	92,41%
Sharp	80	75	93,75%
PCS Security 1	72	61	84,72%

Even from a single manufacturer's (Cross Match Technologies) point of view there was a big step between the events in Tsukuba and Singapore. In Tsukuba, we have been able to read all presented documents, at least on the last day of the test session. In Singapore, our developers did not change a single line of code. In Berlin, we did not even use a specially tuned application. The application that was used for the test was the usual demo application that is based on the available SDK. That is, the Berlin results reflect a system performance that might be reached similarly in a real world environment.

The following Figure 2 shows the stability and interoperability of the top 20 passport readers that participated in Berlin. Interoperability describes here the percentage of passports that can be read by a certain reader in at least one of a series of three trials, the stability value denotes the percentage of successful read attempts out of all trials.

Some other results of the Berlin test are very interesting, too. The numbers given in this paragraph are all results achieved with the AUTHENTICATOR 100 document reader. We have observed that the establishment of the Basic Access Control (BAC) for a reader session took between 26 and 818ms, with a median value of 143ms and an average value of 209ms. That is, BAC is not as time consuming as one was worrying about earlier. So we know that modifications of the BAC protocol that intend to save time are not necessary anymore. This might be the reason why we have seen in Berlin almost only BAC passports.

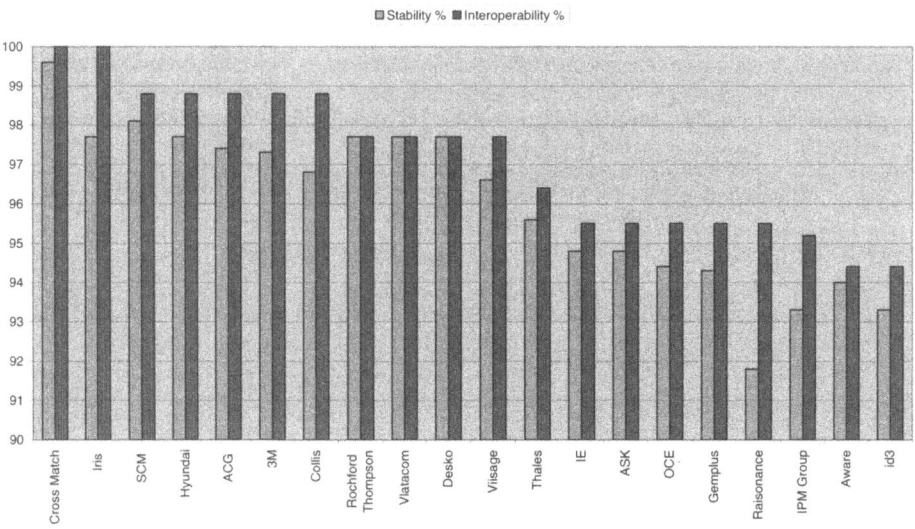

Figure 2: Interoperability and stability of the Top 20 readers in Berlin. An interoperability score of 95% means that this reader was able to read 19 out of 20 passports at least once. A stability score of 95% means that this reader was successful in 95 out of 100 trials to read a passport. In Berlin, 90 different passports were tested; each passport was placed on each reader 3 times, so there was a total of 270 trials for each reader. Exceptions are possible for some readers.

The time for Active Authentication (AA) establishment was between 25 and 719ms, with the median at 405 and the average value at 391ms. One third of the participating passports were AA passports.

In the past, the organizers measured the RFID read time. But RFID reading is only one subtask to be solved when inspecting e-passports. The MRZ must be read first of all, and optical security features of the printed document have to be inspected, too. Therefore in Berlin the total time from placing the document onto the reader until the moment the passport data have been displayed was measured. The pure RFID read time was between 172 and 15999ms with the median at 3606 and the average value at 4039ms. The total processing time, however, was between 2974 and 27489ms with the median at 6780 and the average value at 7758ms. All these values are given for BAC passports.

Last but not least there was another observation in Berlin. The size of the facial image stored in data group (DG) 2 on the chip was between 6512 and 35571byte, with the median at 18474 and the average size of 18336 bytes.

The next Figure 3 shows once again a visualization of the interoperability demonstrated in Berlin, this time combined with the average processing time of the readers. The table includes only those readers that have acquired the MRZ automatically. Otherwise the measurement of a processing time would not make much sense. The thick bars again denote the number of passports that have been readable, the thin ones the average time for successful read attempts. Dark thick bars denote that the manufacturers participated with their own reader software, light thick bars indicate that these manufacturers preferred to rely on the Golden Reader Tool (GRT) of the Essen Group.

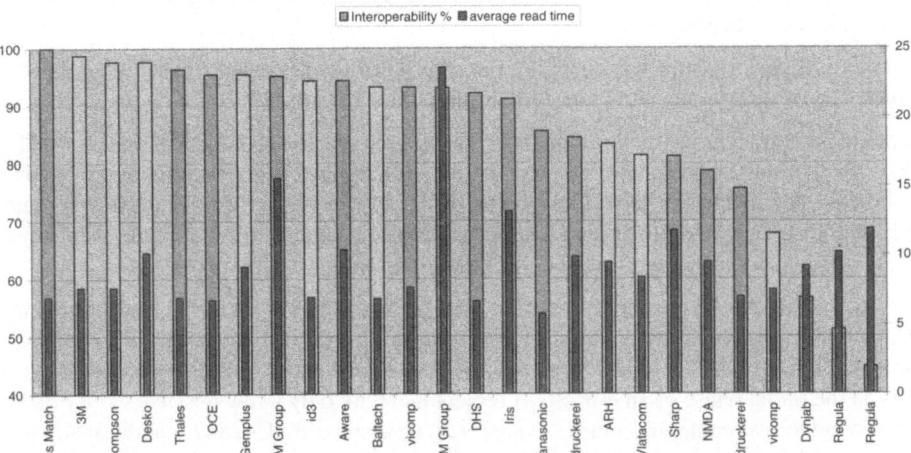

Figure 3: Interoperability and average read time for e-passport readers with automated MRZ acquisition. Dark interoperability bars denote that the reader used own software, light bars indicate that the Golden Reader Tool was used.

Even if test standards for e-passports and e-passport readers are not adopted so far: The ISO/IEC SC17 WG3 TF4 group is working very hard on preparing standards for testing both passports and readers. The number of reader manufacturers and of available passports increases. Performing a complete cross-over test will be impossible in the near future. Therefore, a systematic test approach is essential to ensure true interoperability. This is the reason why the ISO work is that important. Only if the test standards have been finalized, it can be defined what ICAO compliant passports and readers are.

The test standards for e-passports have made much progress in the past few months. One may assume that the standard suggestions will be forwarded to ICAO before the end of this year. But we have seen in Berlin that machine readable zones are not always machine readable. Therefore we need test standards for the MRZ of passports, too. Otherwise, the readability of BAC passports is endangered. For readers the situation is much more complicated. A test standard for readers must cover RFID reader components, swipe readers, full page readers, mobile devices, all based on a multitude of different scanning technologies. Here, we probably still need some time and some more experimental evaluations to check which tests are relevant, and, not to forget, feasible.

Especially for secondary inspections a border control station should have access to a few devices that can be used to capture images of a document at almost forensic quality level. It is probably sufficient to integrate some of the checks of highly sophisticated security features like kinegrams or identigrams into the "usual" document reader equipment. This is a minor, but nevertheless very important aspect of interoperability.

How can reading of e-passports be secured? Electronic passports make use of a contactless technology. That is, passports and readers are radio equipment. So eavesdropping on the communication is possible in general. It is possible to minimize this threat, but it cannot be completely eliminated. Metal housings of the document reader may minimize the radiation. But it can be ensured that even a recorded communication between passport and reader is useless for an eavesdropper.

First of all, ICAO recommends changing the chip ID of the passport chip for every boot procedure. That way, tracking of a chip using its chip ID is not possible.

Furthermore, the content of the chip may be secured by Basic Access Control. Applying BAC, a reader must prove that it has access to the lower line of the machine readable zone of the holder page of the passport. Only if the reader knows the passport number, the date of birth, and the expiration date of the passport, it is able to compute the communication key that is necessary to access the data on the chip. The communication itself is encrypted.

It is known that the contextual knowledge may help an attacker to guess the three numbers necessary to compute the BAC keys, e. g. if the day of birth can be estimated somehow, the document number follows some known rules, or the expiry date can be derived, because especially in the initial phase of an e-passport project there are only a few possible expiry dates. A workaround to overcome this attack is suggested, it is called BAC+, and it additionally uses a random number to be printed in the optional field of the machine readable zone for the computation of the communication keys.

Once again, only systematic and standardized tests may really ensure that all passports can be inspected by any reader. Cross-over tests are not able to guarantee this, at least not on a global scale. So the answer to the question in the title of this paper is clear: Yes, standards are essential. Without them we will never reach optimal results.

2 Biometric Data Compliance and Performance of Biometric Systems

The compliance of biometric data and verification systems is the second main aspect. Standards on biometric data formats exist. In addition to data formatting tasks, the biometric reference data to be stored in an e-passport has to meet certain quality standards, with respect to sensor and data quality. Which quality a scanner (face or fingerprint) must have in order to be applicable for e-passport enrolment applications? Which quality is necessary for border control verification? Can the scanner quality be measured in a standardized manner, even for different physical scanning principles? These questions are discussed mainly from the fingerprint perspective, but also address facial recognition aspects.

Border control solutions address one of the largest user groups of IT equipment: Virtually all human beings possessing a passport, all over the world. Therefore, global interoperability must be the most important design goal for all planned border control applications. Even if cheap solutions seem to be possible, the deployment of high quality equipment, possibly during a longer period of time if it is not feasible to deploy all devices at once, should be preferred. In principle, each passport shall be readable at any border control station, globally.

Therefore it is strongly required to follow the approved standards that are recommended by the ICAO in the current version of the Doc 9303 that cites the ISO 19794 standard family of ISO/IEC JTC1 SC37 with respect to the biometrics part as well as the standards and ICAO Technical Reports that have been provided by ISO/IEC JTC1 SC17 WG3 with respect to machine readable travel documents.

The results of the current tests of biometric technology are promising. The BioP II study [BSI05] has shown that a very low false acceptance rate – FAR (0/0.06%) and false rejection rate - FRR (4.73%/6.13%) are possible in real fingerprint and facial recognition applications, respectively. Even more promising, the FRR decreases significantly as soon as the travellers use the system more frequently. Frequent users reach at a system calibration of 0.1% FAR 4.77% FRR for facial recognition and 2.90% FRR for fingerprint on average. In this study the average time consumption for the verification of both biometric features has also been measured: 10s for fingerprint, and 5.9s for facial recognition.

In the future some improvements for the fingerprint part of border control solutions are imaginable (and desirable). One might want to use scanners for more than one finger like the L SCAN Guardian shown in the picture below. This device is able to capture the flat prints of four fingers in one step. This way it is possible to capture eight fingerprints in the same time that is necessary to capture two prints with single finger scanners. As soon as the storage capacity of RFID chips increases, we will probably see all ten fingers stored in the e-passports. Obviously more data of several fingers increase the recognition performance and the reliability of the system e-passport in general. For the Schengen visa system, ten flats are already planned today. Furthermore, misplacement of the fingers on a four finger scanner is more difficult than on single finger scanners, so even the aspect of ergonomics is addressed better by larger scanners.

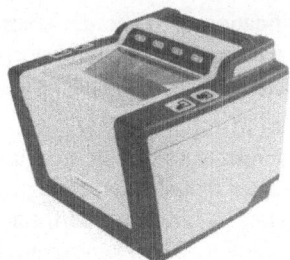

Figure 4: Fingerprint scanner for 10 flats: L SCAN Guardian

Even if large scale biometric applications seem to be quite new, it should not be forgotten that there is more than a decade of experience with fingerprint biometrics in automated fingerprint identification systems (AFIS) that are used by police organizations all over the world. Reusing the standards set for this domain, especially with respect to the quality of captured images, is a highly recommended approach and should be best practice. Even if fingerprints are only one of the secondary biometric factors defined by ICAO, this paper focuses more on this technology than on facial recognition due to our existing experiences especially in this domain.

The fingerprint scanners to be deployed at border control stations and especially in enrolment stations should be able to capture reliable and high quality images. It is a well known fact that due to the limited availability of memory space on the passport chips it is possible to store only a few images. Therefore the stored reference data must be of the highest available quality to ensure high recognition rates for all state-of-the-art comparison algorithms even after ten years. The requirements for border control scanners might be slightly more relaxed compared to the data enrolment equipment necessary for the passport application. However, reliable interoperability and optimal speed can be ensured only if equipment is used that follows standards, which have been developed to achieve interoperability like those standards that are known from the AFIS community.

Furthermore, high quality optical scanners typically have lower failure to acquire rates, that is, it is much easier to capture high quality fingerprint images with those scanners. It has to be taken into consideration that also disabled people must be able to provide their fingerprints, so it should be guaranteed that the scanner can be used accordingly. But this is more of an engineering problem. Summarized: To ensure biometrics interoperability, high quality scanners must be used, and quality assurance has to be performed on the captured images. Furthermore, the data has to be formatted in a standards compliant manner.

Images for facial recognition systems also must be of a certain quality. Before an image is presented to a comparison algorithm, its quality should be evaluated first to avoid unnecessary processing workload. The quality of facial recognition systems strongly depends on environmental conditions. The most important of them is the illumination. Good camera solutions should also be able to have a look ahead capturing feature that allows capturing facial images even if the person is still waiting in the queue in front of the inspection booth. This way, possible bottlenecks in the border control process can be avoided because only in a small number of cases additional photos have to be taken.

Similar to the discussion of the fingerprint topic, the quality of images to be stored in the chip is essential for the entire performance of the biometric system. Image quality that is lost in this step can never be recovered.

High quality images even for verification at the border control line ensure a good data basis for comparisons at this point and increase the chance that even the first photo taken is sufficient for acceptance. That way, image quality is a must for a high throughput even at the place of inspection.

Feature extraction systems for fingerprints and facial recognition are highly developed today. The data format that has to be used for the passport chip is standardized. Nevertheless, companies that have proven their abilities in biometric performance tests, many of them implemented by the NIST, might be preferable. The membership in the standardization organizations is another indication of a certain company striving for interoperability.

A good biometric system intended to be used over a long period of time and without possibilities to update the biometric reference data should also address the topics of biometrics fusion and template ageing: The system *electronic passport* may make use of three authentication factors: The printed document as something a person possesses (something *I have* following the well known distinction between authentication procedures) and the two biometric identifiers fingerprint and facial image as characteristics of a person (something *I am*). These three factors should be combined in an appropriate manner. Simple AND and OR combinations will not be enough. Solutions for biometrics fusion have to address this issue. Relevant results are available in the research area, e.g., [ViSc05]. The ISO has already prepared a framework for multi-biometric solutions [ISO05d].

The passports of many states are valid for up to ten years. It is known that all biometric features change in the course of time, and this fact, which is called template ageing, has to be considered for acceptance decisions. We still do not know enough about this ageing effect. Fortunately, the issue will become relevant within a few years from now, so it is possible understand the ageing effect and to find a solution until then. Current research results like [Wolf04] indicate that there is some ageing effect, and that the recognition performance might decrease by two to four percent per year. At least this is a result of a study on speaker recognition conducted by the author of this paper.

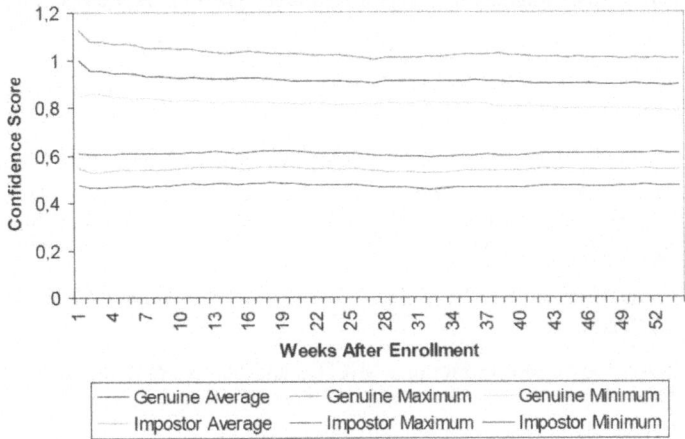

Figure 5: Speaker recognition template ageing within one year (Wolf, BCTP2004)

For automated border control solutions, additional fake detection mechanisms must be applied. These mechanisms might be supervision by inspectors (Even for fully automated solutions one might want to have some back-up or a means of secondary inspections) and technical means that detect masks, photos, or videos (facial recognition) and/or artificial fingerprints or cadaver fingers (This seems to be a quite difficult task. The industry still has some more work to do to achieve this goal reliably enough.).

3 Assessment

The technology for electronic passports has reached a level that makes this technology usable for global application. The e-passport interoperability tests have demonstrated that the readability of the electronic documents is already ensured today. Test standards for all relevant parts of the system e-passport (passport, reader, biometric system) are in place or under development. All involved technologies are addressed, like RFID, OCR, security features, biometric data, etc.

Of course, the introduction of new technologies is a field where new projects come along with new difficulties. But these difficulties can be addressed. Science and industry jointly will solve this task. We should consider the following: How do we want to get experience with huge scale biometric systems without having them in place?

References

[BSI04a]   Federal Office for Information Security (BSI). Studie: Evaluierung biometrischer Systeme Fingerabdrucktechnologien – BioFinger. Version 1.1, 2004.

[BSI04b]   Federal Office for Information Security (BSI). Studie: Untersuchung der Leistungsfähigkeit von Gesichtserkennungssystemen zum geplanten Einsatz in Lichtbilddokumenten – BioP I. Version 1.1, 2004.

[BSI05]   Federal Office for Information Security (BSI). Studie: BioP II - Untersuchung der Leistungsfähigkeit von biometrischen Verifikationssystemen – BioP II. Version 2.0, 2005.

[BSI06]   Federal Office for Information Security (BSI). Technical Report: Advanced Security Mechanisms for machine Readable Travel Documents. V. 1.0, 2006.

[EU05]   EU-Passport Specification. Working Document, 2005.

[EG06]   Results of the Berlin Interoperability Test 2006. http://www.essen-group.org/-berlin/download.html

[ICAO05]   ICAO Doc 9303. Machine Readable Travel Documents. Part 1 Volume 2. Machine Readable Passports. Specifications for discretionary expansion of Data Storage Capacity and Globally Interoperable Biometric Identification. Ninth Draft, 6th Ed., 2005.

[ICAO05a]   ICAO Machine Readable Travel Documents Supplement 9303. Version 2005-4 V3.0, 2005.

[ICAO05b]   ICAO Guide to Interfacing e-MRTDs and Inspection Systems. Version 1.0, 2005.

[ISO05a]   ISO/IEC JTC 1/SC37: ISO/IEC IS 19794-4. Information Technology - Biometric Data Interchange Formats – Part 4: Finger Image Data. 2005.

[ISO05b]   ISO/IEC JTC 1/SC37: ISO/IEC IS 19794-5. Information Technology - Biometric Data Interchange Formats – Part 5: Face Image Data. 2005.

[ISO05c]   ISO/IEC JTC 1/SC37: ISO/IEC IS 19794-6. Information Technology - Biometric Data Interchange Formats – Part 6: Iris Image Data. 2005.

[ISO05d]   ISO/IEC JTC 1/SC37: ISO/IEC WD2 24772 Working Draft Technical Report on Multi-Modal and Other Multi-Biometric Fusion. 2005.

[NMDA05]   New Media Development Association: ICAO Testing, Test Report. Tsukuba test session, March 08 thru March 10, 2005. Presentation of the organizer. Published via ISO.

[Sand04]   Sandström, Marie: Liveness Detection in Fingerprint Recognition Systems. Diploma thesis. http://www.ep.liu.se/exjobb/isy/2004/3557/ University Linköping, Sweden, 2004.

[SDW06]   Singapore passport interoperability results issued. Security Document World March 30th, 2006. http://www.securitydocumentworld.com/public/index.cfm?&m1=c_10&m2=c_4&m3=e_0&m4=e_0&subItemID=472

[SDW06a]   Raw data analysis from Berlin passport trials. Security Document World June 28th, 2006. http://www.securitydocumentworld.com/public/index.cfm?&m1=c_10&m2=c_4&m3=e_0&m4=e_0&subItemID=619

[ViSc05]   Vielhauer, Claus, and Scheidat, Tobias: Fusion von biometrischen Verfahren zur Benutzerauthentifikation. In: DACH Security 2005. Ed.: Patrick Horster, syssec, 2005, pp. 82-97.

[Wolf04]   Wolf, Andreas: Template Aging in Speech Biometrics. In: Proc. BCTP workshop of ICPR, 2004.

A New Standard Based Road to Interoperable Strong Authentication

Philip Hoyer

ActivIdentity (UK)
109 Borough High Street, London SE1 1NL
philip.hoyer@actividentity.com

Abstract

This paper analyses the new standards emerging to allow interoperability of systems that provide strong authentication. After a description of the entities that constitute a strong authentication eco-system, the paper provides a clear overview of existing and new standard drafts from the specific viewpoint of what kind of interoperability they allow between the different entities. It outlines what standards are available now and which ones are coming, detailing the interoperability now and in the future.

1 The strong authentication eco-system

1.1 Overview

This section will describe the fundamental entities of a strong authentication eco-system, it will lay the groundwork and vocabulary to put the standards work in the following sections in context.

1.2 Devices

Strong authentication is often achieved using 2 factors. The factors can vary but the most common variant is of 'something that you know (factor 1) and something that you have (factor 2). The proof of possession or the 'something that you have' is often solved using portable devices harbouring a cryptographic credential. Some popular form factors are smart cards (which can contain both asymmetric and symmetric credentials) or tokens capable of displaying a one time password, usually based on a symmetric credential. Devices can be categorized into two:

1. Unconnected devices, where the credential is put on the device at manufacturing or some proprietary connection
2. Connected devices, which are for usage connected to a workstation using standard interfaces (eg USB)

S. Paulus, N. Pohlmann, H. Reimer (Editors): Securing Electronic Business Processes, Vieweg (2006), 139-147

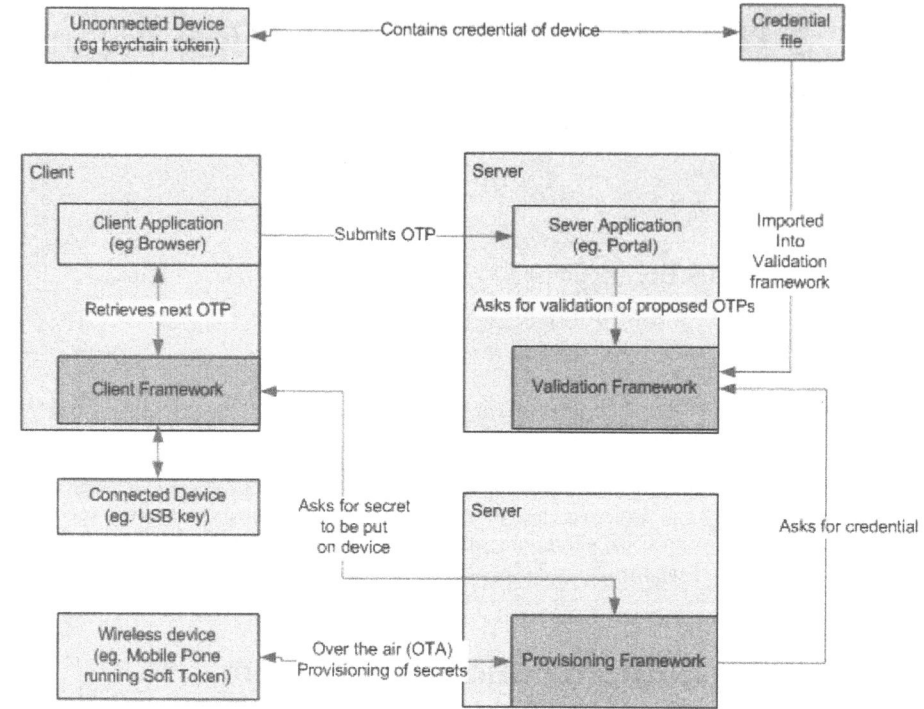

Fig 1: The strong authentication eco-system

1.3   The client framework

In case of connected devices an application wanting to make use of the strong authentication capabilities of a device needs to be able to communicate with it. Since these services are currently not part of an Operating System (although in the future they might well be) special device client software needs to be installed. Currently this client software is proprietary and shipped by the device vendor with a specific device. From the applications perspective consuming the services of the device this is undesirable and does not allow for interoperability between different devices. One area addressed by the new standards as we will see below.

1.4   Validation framework

The validation framework is that part of the eco system capable of providing digital identity assurance. It is normally a server capable of validating proposed responses from devices.

Currently the means of importing credentials into validation system are usually implanted with proprietary file formats. The means to provide a credential to be put on a system is provided through proprietary client-server protocols and the way for applications to validate proposed OTPs is handled via proprietary APIs.

This makes interoperability between devices and applications and a validation framework of a different vendor impossible, one of the main hurdles for adoption of strong authentication and addressed by the standards below.

1.5   Provisioning framework

The provisioning framework has the responsibility to manage the process of how the credentials will be getting onto devices.

It is important to distinguish between two very different models of provisioning:

1. Real-time provisioning to connected devices. This is an online mainly one-to-one model where the connected device (USB, Mobile Phone, Application on a PC, Smartcard, etc) receives the credential to be used for strong authentication directly from the framework. This case is more complicated because of the number of infrastructure components involved.

2. Bulk provisioning. This happens mostly off-line, where devices are manufactured and initialised with credentials and these are then in bulk imported into a validation system.

1.6   Applications

In the context of this paper applications are defined as those, which want to make use of the strong authentication infrastructure, are generally provided by a domain expert company and interface with the strong authentication components in two ways:

1. Client side applications requiring services from the device

2. Server side applications requesting validations of proposed credentials

2 The interoperability challenge

This section describes where the points of interoperability are and what the challenges are. It introduces the following section, which details the standards and how they will try to solve the challenges.

2.1   Interoperability between devices and validation systems

To achieve interoperability between devices and validation systems two fundamental pieces need to be in place:

1. The device and the validation system need to share a common cryptographic mechanism to be able to assert the proof of possession. Lets call this the algorithm.

2. It must be possible to import the credential on which the above algorithm is based. Either from the validation system to the device via a provisioning mechanism or from the device to the validation system.

2.2   Interoperability from an application view

From an application view it is important that the components of the strong authentication infrastructure can be changed, therefore the points of interoperability are the interfaces by which the application requests the services:

1. The client interface in case of connected devices

2. The interface to the validation framework

2.3   Provisioning Interoperability

Provisioning as mentioned above is the way credentials are managed onto devices or the mechanism by which the credential from the device arrives into the validation system. In case of connected devices these can be a complex server based infrastructure that is capable for an example to deliver over the air (OTA) a credential to a soft token running on a mobile phone. Interoperability here means the possibility to use devices from vendor A that receive credentials from a provisioning server from vendor B. In the offline and bulk provisioning case and referenced in Section 2.1 above it means the possibility to take unconnected devices from vendor A and import the bundled credential file into a validation system of vendor B.

3 Standards

3.1 Algorithms

This section describes the existing standards in the algorithm space and why they are important to allow true interoperability.

3.1.1 OATH – HOTP, RFC 4226 HMAC based one time password algorithm

The Initiative for open authentication (OATH) analysing the existing algorithms for one time passwords suitable for a strong authentication ecosystem realised that they were proprietary and from competing companies. So they endeavoured to create a royalty and patent free algorithm based on HMAC. This algorithm was submitted as a draft to IETF and has now become an RFC [RFC4226].

This algorithm being free and easily embeddable is seen as the first big step in terms of interoperability since sharing the cryptographic mean to assure a digital identity is the first step for interoperable strong authentication systems.

The uptake and interest in this algorithm bodes well for the success of having interoperable systems of different vendors. It is reasonably simple and easy to understand and implement.

3.1.2 OATH - Mutual OATH: HOTP Extensions for mutual authentication

Based on the work done for RFC4226 OATH realised that some applications do require an algorithm that is based on a challenge response mechanism. Additionally the RFC4226 allows authentication of one of the participants in a message exchange to the other but no a mutual authentication. To address these shortcoming a new draft has been submitted to the IETF [MOath05]. This draft allows a mutual two pass authentication using concepts of RFC4226 and uses a challenge response mechanism.

OATH hopes that building on the momentum of RFC4226 there will be many adopters of the new algorithm. Being royalty free and easily embeddable as HOTP bode well for wide adoption.

3.1.3 MasterCard EMV – Chip Authentication Program (CAP)

MasterCard EMV CAP is algorithm to generate one time passwords, challenge responses and simple transaction signatures using an application on an EMV smart card. This happens via a connected or more frequently through an unconnected reader with a PIN pad similar to a pocket calculator.

The MasterCard specification [Mas04] goes into detail not only about the algorithm itself but also about what the user interface should be. This algorithm and specification is interesting from a lot of viewpoints.

MasterCard is a company that knows how to solve interoperability problems, if not you credit card would not work abroad in the many ATMs or point of sale vending machines across almost the whole globe.

By making the interface to the device (EMV) interoperable, MasterCard allows different vendors of card readers to compete and it has experience in doing so (see point of sale devices).

MasterCard runs an accreditation program by which the validation services for CAP one time passwords are accredited to be compatible.

This means a true interoperability between devices (smart cards), readers and validation systems.

3.2 Device interface

This section describes existing standards to communicate to connected devices and their role to allow client framework interoperability

3.2.1 OTPS – PKCS #11 v2.20 Amendment 1: PKCS #11 mechanisms for One-Time Password Tokens

RSA Security, a long term player in the strong authentication space launched in 2005 the One Time Password Specifications (OTPS).

They will enable technology solutions vendors to more effectively integrate support for OTP technology and are intended to support a wide range of OTP approaches, including time synchronous, event synchronous and challenge-response methods

These proposed specifications will encourage maximum innovation in OTP methods and algorithms. They address critical components of OTP technology integration and management, including the provisioning, retrieval, transport and validation of OTPs.

One of the challenges of these specifications was to create a way to retrieve and validate OTPs from connected devices. The approach chosen was to extend an already existing and well known interface to communicate to connected security devices, PKCS#11, in a way to allow for specific OTP related methods.

This resulted into an amendment document to PKCS#11 [RSA05a].

The view here is that the application developer who needs to talk to a device will effectively integrate their application with the amended PKCS#11 interface. When a specific device is used the device manufacturer will provide the PKCS#11 amendment library implementation together with a profile. This will allow the application to function with the devices of that specific vendor without re-integration of a custom vendor specific API.

The slight drawback here is that devices from different vendors will have slightly different profiles (eg slightly different attributes in calls to the PKCS#11 interface) and if the application should function concurrently with devices from different vendors it is the applications responsibility to load different version of PKCS#11 implementations into memory and hold the mapping between a device and its specific library.

3.2.2 MasterCard EMV

MasterCard chose a proven interface to be able to retrieve an OTP from a connected device, the EMV (Europay – MasterCard – Visa) standard. This standard effectively defines the interface between the card and a card reader, detailing the commands and responses from the chip on the card.

This proven interface makes it possible for a credit card to be used in point of sales across the whole globe.

By defining the interoperability on this level a great level of interoperability is achieved. On the other hand, it is a very low level API and will not be able to be used directly by application developers. It is effectively the interface to the card itself.

This will mean that there is not an application level API defined by MasterCard.

Interestingly it would be possible and conceivable that the application level interface might be the exact OTPS PKCS#11 amendment detailed above.

3.3 Validation interface

This section describes the existing standards and drafts that exist around the interfaces used to validate proposed strong credentials and how they will allow interoperability

3.3.1 OTPS - OTP-WSS-Token: Web Services Security One-Time Password Token Profile

OTP-WSS-Token [RSA06a] defines means to integrate one-time password token-based authentication with Web Services Security, as defined in the OASIS Web Services Security:SOAP Message Security 1.0 specification.

Web Services are increasingly becoming a method of choice for application integration and having the ability to authenticate the sender of a message with One Time Password technology is an important point of interoperability between application developers and validation services.

This specification allows interoperability at the client (web services consumer).

3.3.2 OTPS- OTP Validation Service

OTP ValidationService [RSA06b] defines an XML request/response protocol ("OTP-ValidationService") intended for use by relying parties that receive one-time password (OTP) authentication data from claimants and make queries to validation services to determine whether the received data successfully demonstrates a claimant's authenticity.

This specification uses the OTP-WSS-Token as the container to transmit the proposed OTP.

The aim of this specification is to have a client use this interface to a validation service. If validation services from different vendors do adhere to this specification there should be a true interoperability between clients and validation services.

This specification based XML is a big step forward from custom APIs from different vendors and other authentication APIs that often are tied into a specific technology stack (such as the JAAS specification in the Java world).

3.4 Provisioning

This section describes the existing and drafts that exist around provisioning protocols and how these will allow interoperability

3.4.1 OATH - Portable Symmetric Key Container

After having defined a standard algorithm with RFC4226, the next step for OATH, especially in terms of first real interoperability between devices and validation systems, was to create a standard defining the exchange format of the cryptographic credential used within the algorithm.

Since most OTP algorithms use symmetric keys and after the analysis of other formats deemed them insufficient, OATH decided to create a new XML based exchange format called the Portable Symmetric Key Container [OPSKC06].

The specification has been submitted in February 2006 as a draft to IETF in view of it becoming an RFC in similar fashion to the HOTP algorithm itself (RFC4226).

The format allows conveying enough information to a validation system to be able to validate the OTPs generated from a device. It also includes the means to protect the cryptographic keys in transit.

This exchange format allows for the first time to have devices from vendor A to be used with validation systems from vendor B.

3.4.2 OATH - XKMS Provisioning of OATH Shared Secret Keys

In a more complex scenario when keys need to be injected into devices, these need to be requested from a credential provider. Whereas PSKC described above supplies the means to transport the key material it is not a protocol to request them. To be able to fill this gap OATH decided to extend the well known existing XKMS standard to be able to provisioning shared secret keys.

The specification [OXKMS06] describes means of provisioning OATH shared secret OTP parameters based on the XKMS protocol.

This will allow interoperability between systems injecting secrets into devices in bulk during manufacturing, online OTA (for example when registering a soft token of a mobile phone) and the system that provide the credentials.

3.4.3 OTPS – CT-KIP

The Cryptographic Token Key Initialization Protocol [RSA05b] describes a client-server protocol for initialization (and configuration) of cryptographic tokens, providing a secure method of initializing cryptographic tokens with secret keys without exposing generated, secret, material to any other entities than the server and the cryptographic token itself.

This protocol, primarily aimed at connected devices, allows for interoperability between the device itself and the service that will configure it (either a provisioning system or the validation system itself).

The strength of this specification is a clever mechanism by which the secret is effectively never transmitted on the connection between the device and the server, the secret is effectively generated at both ends. This is very powerful for compromised transmission channels or where device have limited capability to be able to protect the communication channel.

4 Interoperability

4.1 Now

The initiative for open authentication (OATH) has taken rapid steps to provide the two fundamental building blocks to security infrastructure product vendors to allow interoperability:

1. The device and the validation system need to share a common cryptographic mechanism to be able to assert the proof of possession. Lets call this the algorithm. In OATH this is HOTP algorithm as defined in RFC 4226 [RFC4226].

2. It must be possible to import the credential on which the above algorithm is based. Either from the validation system to the device via a provisioning mechanism or from the device to the validation system. In OATH this is the proposed draft of the Portable Symmetric Key Container [OPSKC06] and if the credentials need to be obtained via an online protocol the proposed draft of XKMS provisioning of OATH Shared Secret Keys [OXKMS06].

On the client side, the interoperable standard to communicate and request services from connected devices is OTPS – PKCS #11 v2.20 Amendment 1: PKCS #11 mechanisms for One-Time Password Tokens [RSA05a]. This has been adopted also by OATH.

On the server side the API to validate proposed OTPs has just been published as One-Time Password Validation Service [RSA06b], it is yet unclear if this will find widespread adoption.

As can be seen many interoperability points have been and are being addressed. The momentum of companies announcing products supporting these standards bodes well for the basic interoperability.

It means that now for the first time one can have strong authentication devices from one vendor and use a validation system and provisioning system of another.

4.2 The future

The amount of companies participating in the standard initiatives is growing. The need for stronger authentication beyond basic passwords is accelerating.

True interoperability bakeoffs are planned to produce credible documentation of how systems between different vendors can and are proven to interoperate.

The standards are maturing and the number if products implementing them increasing.

The future where the choice of device and the choice of infrastructure is not dictated by compatibility but interoperability is assumed like the assumption that with a browser you can connect to an SSL secured web site has just moved a lot closer.

5 Conclusion

There is momentum in the industry to agree and provide re-usable interoperable components. As experience in other sectors shows this can only be achieved by agreed standard interfaces and exchange formats. But true interoperability and success of a specification or standard comes through adoption. The onus here lays firstly with the providers of the security infrastructure, the software and hardware vendors that provide the pieces of the strong authentication eco system. Their products will need to provide the standard interfaces. Product features are driven by demand of the customers and they are increasingly demanding not to be locked into a costly custom solution. The first steps have been taken and as described above there are important emerging specifications in all interoperability touch points.

If you are an independent software vendor in this space, come and participate in the forums and implement the standards in your product, if you are a customer, know them to be able to demand them, freedom of choice knows little regrets.

References

[RFC4226] IETF, "HOTP: An HMAC-Based One-Time Password Algorithm",
           http://www.rfc-archive.org/getrfc.php?rfc=4226

[MOath05] IETF,"Mutual OATH: HOTP Extensions for mutual authentication",
           http://www.ietf.org/internet-drafts/draft-mraihi-mutual-oath-hotp-variants-02.txt

[Mas04]   MasterCard International Incorporated, "Chip Authentication Program - Func-
           tional Architecture", September 2004

[RSA05a]   RSA Laboratories, "PKCS #11 v2.20 Amendment 1: PKCS #11 mechanisms for
           One-Time Password Tokens", ftp://ftp.rsasecurity.com/pub/pkcs/pkcs-11/v2-
           20/pkcs-11v2-20a1.pdf

[RSA06a]   RSA Laboratories, "One-Time Password Validation Service",
           ftp://ftp.rsasecurity.com/pub/otps/vs/otp-validation-service-v1-0.pdf

[RSA06b]   RSA Laboratories, "One-Time Password Validation Service",
           ftp://ftp.rsasecurity.com/pub/otps/vs/otp-validation-service-v1-0.pdf

[OPSKC06] IETF,"Portable Symmetric Key Container", http://www.ietf.org/internet-
           drafts/draft-vassilev-portable-symmetric-key-container-00.txt

[OXKMS06]IETF," XKMS Provisioning of OATH Shared Secret Keys",
           http://www.ietf.org/internet-drafts/draft-hallambaker-oathxkms-00.txt

Identity Management
Biometrics
PKI-Solutions
Network Security

Identifying Patterns of Federation Adoption

Heather Hinton · Mark Vandenwauver

IBM Software Group
{hhinton | mvanden}@us.ibm.com

Abstract

"I don't see that [federation identity] happening this year, I don't see it happening next year or the year after that--that leaves 2009, and I'll leave that one open ... There are a lot of issues, but basically it boils down to trust and antitrust." [Penn06]. Despite this pessimism, federation technology and models are being deployed and are in production now, only not in those areas that they were originally expected. In this paper, we describe several adoption patterns that we have observed and the characteristics that have driven these deployments. Existing business relationships between companies are often strong enough to support federated relationships and are being used as the foundation of present-day federated identity deployments.

1 Introduction

Federation has typically been cast as the "next best thing" to happen to a user's online experience. For example, the much-hyped travel agency example has been used to illustrate the benefits of a federation relationship – when booking travel tickets with an online travel agency, John can seamlessly access the airline (to book seats and identify special requirements), the car rental agency and the hotel. Another equally well discussed example is based on the Internet Service Provider as *uber*-Identity Provider, allowing Jane to authenticate to her ISP and then engage in online shopping. These examples, while excellent for explaining some of the values of a federated single sign-on environment, do not yet have widespread adoption, leading many to question if, not even when, federation technology will be adopted.

What is interesting with these early examples of (hypothetical) federation adoption is that they all describe scenarios where federated technology is used to bootstrap a business relationship between companies. It helped, of course, that the average Internet user could immediately see the value of this type of environment. What hurt, however, is that it was not immediately obvious to the federation partners what value they would realize with this environment, if they acted in any role other than an Identity Provider. And given that they all act as Identity Providers right now, why would they willingly give that up? This leads to the conclusion that federation technology can not (and should not) be driving federation adoption in and of itself.

Our customer experience shows us that federation technology and models are being adopted right now though. Federated technology is being adopted in many environments between companies with **existing** business relationships. Adoption is taking place where there is a need for tighter integration achieved through the loose coupling offered by federation. The adoption/deployment of federated identity solutions that we have been involved with (to date), have all been based on scenarios where:

- Business agreements are already in place upon which a federation-driven trust relationship can be based, and,
- One of the participants is a clear "owner" of the user identities and is responsible for the identity lifecycle management

Federation solutions are being implemented today by companies that already have business agreements in place. It is not the case that trust must be established from the ground up as part of building these federations and hence trust is not an inhibitor for these deployments. Federation solutions are also being put in place in scenarios where one entity clearly owns a user's identity lifecycle. While other entities may need to own/manage user information specific to that user-entity relationship; these other entities have no business model that requires that they factually own the user's lifecycle management.

Over the past two years, we have been involved in many customer engagements regarding these types of federation adoption and deployment. Based on this, we are able to identify four patterns driving federation adoption. These patterns are characterized by business relationships and user lifecycle management characteristics. They can be classified as:

- Employer based federations
- Single Sign-On for companies/subsidiaries
- Specialized content provider federations
- Rich client based single sign-on,

In the remainder of this paper we will describe these patterns, the use cases driving them and the user lifecycle characteristics that drive the need for a federated identity solution. We will finish with our observations and conclusions.

2 Federation Adoption Patterns

In this section we provide an overview of the four patterns that we commonly see driving federation adoption. Each of these patterns has distinct characteristics that help define the pattern. The characteristics of each pattern that stand out as driving the type of federation adoption can be divided into pre-existing requirements (which can be viewed as pre-conditions to federation adoption) and business requirements that drive the need for a federated solution. These requirements are:

- Pre-conditions
  - Online presence
    Federation relationships are typically driven by the need to simplify a user's online experience, starting with the reduction in the number of authentication (or sign-on) steps that a user must undertake.
  - Existing Business Relationships
    Establishing the business and trust relationships over which federated functionality is to be leveraged is not simple. Starting from scratch with the establishment of these relationships to support a federation reduces the appeal of federations considerably. Leveraging existing relationships however makes a federation relationship easier to establish even if only from a process point of view.
- Business requirements
  - Identity Lifecycle Requirements
    Federation relationships allow one partner to off-load the majority of the user's life-

cycle management (account creation, management and deletion) to an authoritative source. Note that some business models dictate that a service provider does not wish to off-load this functionality; in these cases there is a much smaller incentive for federation.

Within these patterns, there are two types of federated single sign-on that may be adopted: *push based* (F-SSO request is pushed from Identity Provider to Service Provider) and *pull based* (F-SSO request is initiated from Service Provider to Identity Provider and then pushed from Identity Provider to Service Provider). Within either type of single sign-on, the user's accounts may be already *linked* (meaning that both parties already understand how to refer to the user) or *not linked* (meaning that each party has an independent means of referring to the user and no way to cross-reference or link these two).

In the remainder of this section we will briefly introduce each pattern example and then discuss the characteristics of this pattern that make it suitable for immediate adoption.

2.1 Employer Based Federations

Employer based federations are those where a company enters into a federation relationship as part of the provision of services to its employees. These services are typically employee-driven services, such as benefits (medical, dental, etc) and personnel (work-life balance resources, fitness plans, etc). This is in contrast to federations driven by the need to expand the company's business, such as supply chain management and customer relationship management.

Interestingly, we have found that employer based federations can be classified as *internal federations* and *external federations*. Internal federations are used to ensure single sign-on within an Enterprise. External federations are those federation relationships that are put in place between an Employer and its (external) third-party service providers.

2.1.1 Internal Federation

The first step in entering into an employer-based federation is for the "Enterprise-as-Employer" to put in place internal federation solutions to provide "Enterprise Single Sign-On". An internal federation solution is one that allows users (employees) to sign on to existing resources within the enterprise, typically from their employer portal. This approach to federation is most easily applied to Web based applications and access. It allows an enterprise to focus on getting their "internal house" in order before moving to an external federation, or employer-based Federated Single Sign-On (F-SSO), solution.

Benefits to an employer for implementing this type of Enterprise-based single sign-on solution include:

- Reduced in-house management costs
- Better user productivity
- Fewer lost passwords
- Easier access to resources required to complete daily tasks
- Preparation for Employer-based F-SSO relationships

Typically internal federation relies on push-based F-SSO and deals with linked users. That is, within an Employer's environment, even though a user may have multiple (seemingly) independent usernames, the Employer is able to establish a mapping or linking of all of these usernames, based on the Employer's ownership and control of the corporate directory.

2.1.2 External Federation

Once the internal house is in order, the enterprise is ready to move to external federation scenarios, exemplified by the "Enterprise-as-Employer" based federation. In this scenario, an
employer leverages third-party services providers to provide benefits (e.g., medical, dental,
retirement) and services (e.g., work-life balance, HR-related). Most enterprises already have
these types of relationships in place; most medium-large employers already "out-source" the
providing of these benefits to third-party providers; larger employers deal with tens or even
hundreds of third-party providers.

In this federation adoption pattern, the enterprise enters into Federated Single Sign-On (F-
SSO) arrangements with trusted third party partners. F-SSO to these third parties is typically
triggered from the employer portal, supporting a push-based F-SSO model, where single sign-
on information is pushed from the employer to the federation partner.

What makes these scenarios ripe for federated identity solutions?

- Pre-conditions:

   o Online presence:
      Both Employer and Third-party provider are making their services available through
      on-line techniques such as Web portals, meaning that these parties include password
      management and online account management services as part of their user lifecycle
      management functionality. As the employer adds *links* to third-party providers from
      the corporate portal, the completely independent nature of the two entities is exag-
      gerated.

   o Existing business relationships:
      The Employer and Third-party provider have already had to establish the business
      and trust relationships required to exchange and manage user information, including
      such sensitive/private information as Social Insurance Numbers, health care statis-
      tics, and so on.

- Business requirements

   o Eliminate duplicate identity lifecycle requirements:
      While the Employer is the authoritative source of an employer's lifecycle manage-
      ment (account creation, account deletion, and all activities in between), the third-
      party providers must also provide their own, in-house lifecycle management for
      these users so that the user can access third-party resources only when appropriate.
      Because users have access to the third-party provider's resources on the basis of
      their status as an employee, there is no advantage to the third-party provider to man-
      age the user's lifecycle – the third-party provider cannot typically make money by
      offering additional services to the user.

Typically external, or Employer-driven, federation relies on push-based F-SSO of linked users. The push-based F-SSO takes the employee from the Employer's site to the third-party
provider through a link on the Employer's corporate portal. The Employer is able to assert a
known, unique identifier to the service provider. In this scenario, it is possible that this value
is the user's Social Security Number, or some other value, such as an email address or an employee serial number. Because the users are participating in this federation on the basis of
their status as an employee, the employer has the ability to assert this type of personally identifiable information to the service provider.

In moving to a federated identity solution, the employer and the third-party service provider achieve multiple benefits, to both their user experience and to their "bottom line." For example, the employer can now provide seamless access to third-party providers based on federated identity driven single sign-on. This removes the need for the third-party provider to authenticate the employer's user, which in turn will reduce the help desk and user management costs for both companies. The third-party provider can also improve its integration and retention of customers (the employers whose users are now engaged in a federated single sign-on relationship with the provider). An important observation about this scenario is that the third-party provider does not have a business model that involves control of a user repository

Adoption of these federation scenarios is common across all sectors, with health and financial benefit providers being the initial targets for third-party benefit provider single sign-on.

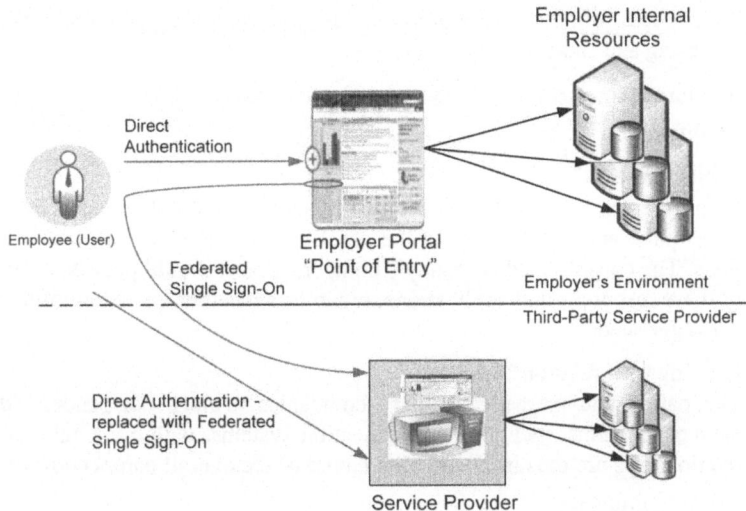

Figure 1: Employer Based Authentication & Single Sign-On

Despite this pattern being referred to as the "Employer Based Federation" pattern, we have found that to date, these employer-based, third-party federations have been driven by the third party providers, or service providers *and not the employers*. Service providers are driving this for several reasons, including reduced user management costs for users that are authoritatively managed by the employer and increased integration (lock-in) with these employers. The employer also stands to benefit from these relationships, namely in the form of reduced benefit provider costs. That is, as provider's costs go down, savings are likely to be passed to the employer.

2.2 Parent Company/Subsidiary; Mergers and Acquisitions

In this scenario, often referred to as a Mergers & Acquisitions (M&A) scenario, a company acquires a (new) company, with its own set of users. Federation provides a quick solution to allow these merged company's users to authenticate to the new parent company and continue to access resources of both the subsidiary and the new parent company. This M&A characterization of this scenario is simply one way of articulating a larger scenario, that of a large/multi-national company with multiple subsidiaries. Large companies often have a requirement for separate "islands" of identity management, perhaps driven by geographic requirements of subsidiaries (employees of a company in Europe often have different identity lifecycle management requirements, if only from a legal point of view, than those in North America), resulting in two separate identity management systems, including authentication requirements for users in those geographies. These subsidiaries are often independent, autonomous entities driven by different regulations and legislation based on their line-of-business and country of operation.

In this overall scenario, federated single sign-on solutions are used to emulate enterprise single sign-on in an environment made up of mutually independent domains. These mutually independent domains may be based on the newly merged/acquired companies or independent subsidiaries. In either case, the desire of the parent company is to provide all of its employees, regardless of location, access to resources, again, regardless of the where these resources are hosted. This example, while common across industry sectors, is especially prevalent in the retail, manufacturing and financial industries.

What makes these scenarios ripe for federated identity solutions?

- Pre-conditions:

  o Online presence:
    Employees and users of both the parent and subsidiary/merged companies need to have quick and easy access to the consolidated company's resources and applications. The consolidated company's company portal should provide easy access to all of these resources and applications, regardless whether the nature of the two entities is exaggerated.

  o Existing trust relationships:
    The parent and merged/subsidiary companies manage independent identity management systems, including authentication systems, within a single company; trust relationships are thus implicit in the nature of the overall parent company.

- Business requirements

  o Eliminate duplicate identity lifecycle requirements:
    While the parent company is the authoritative source of its employee's lifecycle management (account creation, account deletion, and all activities in between), this does not represent the complete set of *all* of the parent companies employees. The subsidiary/merged company is the authoritative source of its employee's lifecycle management. While there may be no long-term benefit for a merged company to continue to manage its employees, subsidiaries often require this separate of users from the parent company's user registry.
    Regardless of where the employees call *home*, however, they should be able to seamlessly access resources across the entire company, be these resources hosted by the parent, the subsidiary/merged company, or yet another subsidiary/merged company of the same parent company.

Typically parent company/subsidiary type federations must rely on both push-based and pull-based F-SSO of linked users. This allows a user to authenticate to their authoritative source (the parent or the subsidiary) regardless of which resource they request (a parent or subsidiary hosted resource), thus triggering the authentication requirement. The parent/subsidiary companies are able to assert a known value referring to the user (thus indicating a form of account linking) because the users are participating in this federation on the basis of their status as an employee of either the parent or the subsidiary.

In moving to a federated identity solution the users and employees of the parent/merged/subsidiary companies will be able to have the same online experience, including seamless access to required resources, even if they are hosted by a different entity within the overall parent company. Duplicate lifecycle management can be removed, as users are migrated from a merged company's system to the parent company. Independent lifecycle management can be tolerated for those subsidiary companies that must maintain a level of separation from the parent company.

The scenario is a specialized form of the employer-based federation, as described before. This pattern allows merged/subsidiary company employee to access both the parent company's resources and resources from other subsidiaries, as required. This pattern adds a layer of single sign-on, allowing two employer-based environments to single-sign-on to each other. Federated identity management and federated single sign-on provide employees of these entities access to world-wide resources, regardless of the *location* and *ownership* of these resources.

2.3 Specialized Content Providers

In the specialized content provider pattern, an identity provider leverages third-party service providers (or specialized content providers) to provide specific content. This allows companies to extend their reach by providing their customers with more, targeted services, which in turn increases customer loyalty. This scenario is largely seen within the financial and telecommunications industry, where customer retention is a key business driver. In this scenario, the driver of the federation is the specialized content provider as an identity provider (where in the previous patterns, the driver for the federation adoption was actually the service provider).

In this pattern, the specialized content provider (SCP) has a relationship with the user, typically as what the user would view as a content or service provider. However, this SCP is also able to act as an Identity Provider because it currently is able to authenticate the user (the first step in acting as an IdP) and because it typically is able to provide additional services to the user, where these services in turn may be provided by an independent service provider (SP).

Unlike the employer-based federation pattern, the user's relationship with these SPs is driven by the user, not the identity provider. That is, a user is able to select which SPs they wish to have a federation (and thus single sign-on) relationship with, within the broader context of their relationship with the SCP. The SCP allows the user to select and customize the set of federation partners from an SCP approved list.

- Pre-conditions
  - Online Presence
    More and more users/customers of a service provider are leveraging an online based approach to management, including such features as bill payment, service management and so on. Both the service provider and the specialized service provider typically provide these types of profile management services for their customers.
  - Business Relationships
    A service provider (possibly Internet based services but not required to be) provides additional third-party, specialized services to its users and thus has the ability to act as an identity provider. These specialized services may or may not be branded for the service provider.
- Business Requirements

- o Eliminate duplicate identity management requirements
  We have found that duplicate identity management costs are not a driver for this type of federation. In fact, this type of federation is not guaranteed to lower identity management costs. It is believed that this type of federation will increase customer retention due to a better overall user experience based on "one-stop-shopping" and seamless access to specialized content.

- o Increase market share/market uptake for services
  In many cases, a specialized content provider wishes to increase its market share for its services. It is able to do this in part by providing specialized services to a partner's customers.

Typically specialized content provider type federations must rely on both push-based and pull-based F-SSO of unlinked users. This allows a user to authenticate to their authoritative source (their "main" service provider acting as identity provider) regardless of which resource they request (a service provider resource or a specialized content provider resource) triggering the authentication requirement. The service provider and specialized content providers are not able to initially (first time) assert a pre-determined value representing the users, therefore requiring the users to go through a form of account linking to cause this value to be established. As part of establishing this account linking, both the service/identity provider and the specialized content provider may need to collect a "consent" to participate in the federated relationship from the user.

Both the service providers and the specialized content providers tend to be large entities with large customer databases. The specialized content providers that are adopting this type of federation scenario are not *boutique* type providers; as an example, these specialized content providers may include all of the subsidiaries of a media company, where the service provider that provides the entry portal to the federation is a service provider such as a broadband service provider, and the specialized content providers may include VOIP services, search portal services, and cable television services offered by a subsidiary of the broadband service provider.

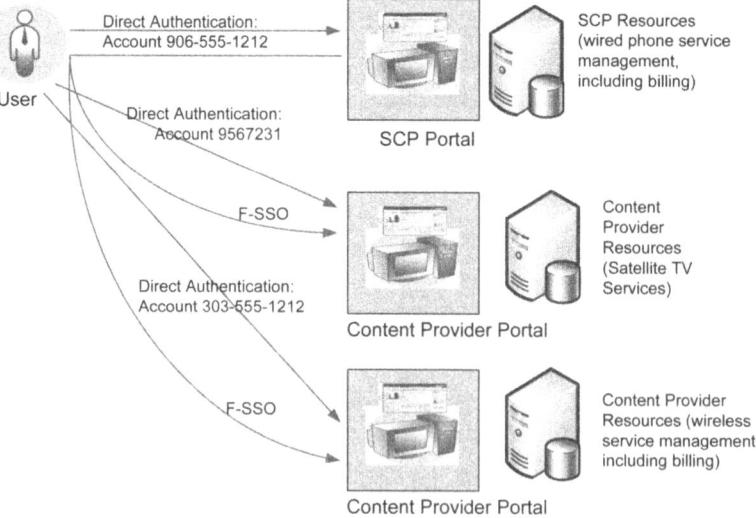

Figure 2: Specialized Content Providers: Federated SSO Replacing Direct Authentication

This federation pattern provides an improved user experience. Consider an SCP that is a (local) telephone provider – typically this provider has relationships with a (preferred) long distance provider, a broadband access provider, a television provider (cable or satellite) and so on. By allowing a customer to federate all of their individual accounts at these different service providers, the SCP is able to provide a tight coupling with the user. This in turn makes it less likely for the user to switch telephone providers, because of the ease of management of all of their related services that is obtained through the SCP-brokered federation.

Interestingly, we have found that this pattern does not always result in lowered user management costs. This is because in many scenarios, the SCP and federated SPs are required by law to allow and support the user to both federation to the SPs from the SCP and to directly authenticate to the SP. Thus the tight coupling of the user through improved user experience is the primary driver of this type of federation pattern.

2.4 Enabling Internal Users: Rich Client Adoption

With the *rich client* use case, web services based federation techniques are used to enable single sign-on from a desktop, to a desktop-based rich client, to the back end resources that provide the rich client services. While not a typical browser-based federation scenario, this type of active-client environment is commonly used in the financial and insurance sectors and can be the basis of federated single sign-on across trust domains.

This is a specialized case of the employer based federation, in that federation techniques are used to provide enterprise-based single sign-on (from a desktop to an enterprise's internal resources) and federated single sign-on to both enterprise-based back-end resources and third-party resource.

3 Observations

The key observation from our experience is that federated identity solutions are being adopted today, in a broad reach of environments and industries. The common, uniting characteristic of these adoptions is that they are all based on **existing** business relationships between partners. This allows the participants to bootstrap the federation process by leveraging these business relationships to define the federation relationship. So while *trust* between entities may be an issue, the nature of the business relationships provides the framework on which to build the federation relationship. That is, in every case where we have examined the nature of the trust relationship between partners, these partners have leveraged existing business relationships to scope/define this trust. This leads us to assert that while federation adoption may be hindered in some environments because of a lack of trust between participants, this lack of trust is a reflection of the lack of a business relationship between the participants.

Looking at this another way, in all of the scenarios we have seen where there is an existing business relationship between the partners, simplifying assumptions about the users participation in the federation have been made. These assumptions include:

- Typical F-SSO patterns are for push-based F-SSO
- Typically, partners can assert a pre-existing identifier that links the user's account at each partner
- Typically, partners do not need to collect *consent* from the user to participate in the federation, as the federation is based on a user's status as an employee of a company

The only exception to these assumptions is with the specialized content providers, where a more varied user experience must be accommodated (the user cannot be required to login to their health care benefits from their corporate portal). Even in this case, however, there is a strong business relationship between the participants in this service provider/specialized content provider federation that is helping to drive the federation adoption.

4 Conclusions

While federation adoption is in progress, it is definitely not as rapid as initially projected and tends to be more tightly focused on specific projects. Customers are opting for tightly-scoped adoption patterns that leverage existing business relationships to provide enhanced services to users. This approach is allowing the customer to cleanly determine the value and return on investment of the project. Thus, contrary to initial projections, **federation technology is not driving its own adoption**. Just like any technology, adoption of federation solutions is based on business requirements and business relationships. Instead, customers are basing their federation technology adoption on their business use cases.

References

[Penn06]   Penn, Jonathan: Principal Analyst for Security and Identity with Forrester Research, http://www.securityfocus.com/brief/141, 2006-02-16

Glossary

Identity Provider - An entity that is able to authenticate a user and assert the user's authenticated identity to its partners.

Service Provider – An entity that is not able to authenticate a user and must rely on the assertion of a user's identity from an identity provider partner. Note that in some cases a service provider may act as a "transitive" identity provider by providing a user's authenticated identity to another service provider based on the identity that was provided to it by its identity provider

Federation – A relationship between two entities that allows these entities to share information and provide access to services in each entity's domain. Typical functionality implemented with a federation relationship is federated single sign-on.

Federated Identity Management – Management of identities across federation partners. While this can include complete lifecycle management issues (account creation, management, deletion), this term is often used as slang for a federated single sign-on relationship.

Federated Single Sign On – Overall process by which a user may authenticate to one party (an Identity Provider) and have that party assert information to a second party (the Service Provider) where it is used to establish a local identity and a *session* for accessing the second party's resources without requiring direct authentication to the second party

Session – The time period bound by an authentication (or single sign-on) and a logout, during which access to resources, including protected resources, may be granted or denied

Fidelity: Federated Identity Management Security based on Liberty Alliance on European Ambit

Manel Medina[1] · Miquel Colomer[1]
Sandra García Polo[2] · Antoine de Poorter[3]

[1]esCERT-UPC – TB-Security C/Gran Capitán, 2,
08034 Barcelona, España
medina@escert.upc.edu, mcolomer@tb-security.com

[2]AMENA C/Avila n°45,
08005 Barcelona, España
sgarciap@amena.es

[3]ERICSSON España Av. Poblados, 13,
28033 Madrid, España
Antoine.de.Poorter@ericsson.com

Abstract

On the Federated Digital Identity ambit, the Fidelity project will put in practice a system defined by Liberty Alliance specifications into a pan-European context, focusing on solving the problems that can be found in an international environment, and that can be subject to regulation(s) addressing the user data confidentiality. Currently, user identification and authentication are the key enablers for Internet business but until now the user's personal information and authentication remain inside the organization's boundaries. To solve this problem, the Liberty Alliance Project (LAP) has defined a *Federated Identity Management* environment that allow independent service/attribute providers, to hold user attributes relevant to the service they provide, to the end-user meeting always the personal data protection legal requirements. LAP proposes the creation of Circles of Trust (CoT), which associate identity and service providers, through the adequate service agreements, allowing them to share user information. The Fidelity Project implements an interoperability proof of concept in a pan-European context of the Liberty Alliance protocols and framework by setting up 4 CoT in four different EU countries. Each CoT is led by a telecom operator and has access to all the users' attributes. This environment will allow testing the federation of identities and the sharing of the users' attributes by different services with different authentication levels.

This approach is opposite to the one proposed by other service providers that try to concentrate all the user information in a single server, which is not quite appropriate in Europe, where there will be thousands of potential service and identity providers, that should share user attributes, with explicit consent in some cases.

The members of the Fidelity Project have strong liaisons with Liberty Alliance Project members, to allow the incorporation of the Fidelity results into new versions of the LAP protocols and framework implementation guidelines.

The project will also define codes of practice for the security policies and service level agreements amongst the partners, as well as the testing methodology of the Liberty Alliance protocols implementations.

S. Paulus, N. Pohlmann, H. Reimer (Editors): Securing Electronic Business Processes, Vieweg (2006), 161-167

1 Liberty Alliance Federated Identity Management approach

One of the most interesting characteristics of LAP approach is that it solves the main concerns of users of web services:

- **Personal Data Protection**: Federated Identity Providers (IdP) guarantee that each Service Provider (SP) will get only the user attributes required to provide the service s/he is actually requesting, avoiding miss-use of personal data.

- **Identity federation and Single Sign On**: The user can federate (=connect) an already existing account at a service provider with the IdP account. Since a SP can request the IdP to authenticate the customer on its behalf, the user only needs one federated identity to access all SPs of the same CoT. In the case of integrated value added services, the LAP environment provides also Single Sign On (SSO) functionality, i.e. once the user has been authenticated by the IdP, any web service provider (WSP) accessed by the main SP to process requested specific user attributes, needed to provide the service actually requested by the user, will get the confirmation of user identity by the IdP, without disturbing the user with additional identification requests.

- **Roaming of web services**: Mobile users can access SPs belonging to a different CoT than his/her Home IdP while benefiting from all the advantages of Single Sign On and attribute sharing, since the Visited IdP (belonging to the CoT of the visited SP) will be able to request user identification by the Home IdP (where user has registered his/her credentials), so that users can use their "single" federated credentials, even when they visit other countries, or are connected through a roamed network, in general.

The proof of concept of the last of those characteristics is the main contribution of Fidelity Project, since all the pilot scenarios will involve several CoT managed by different Telecom Operators. These scenarios will cover a wide range of choices: multiplicity of services, mobile users accessing from fixed (Portable computers) or wireless (GSM terminals) networks, user identification based on traditional UId/password or e-signature (WPKI) credentials, specific treatment of personal data depending on its sensitivity and the service requested.

In the Liberty approach, each CoT guarantees mutual trust of different types of actors: IdP, SP, WSP, AP (attribute providers) and DS (discovery service). All of them should sign commercial, business and service agreements, through which they regulate their rights and duties to handle users attributes to provide tailored services to the users in the most transparent and user friendly way. The Attribute Providers (APs) allow their users to choose which SPs will have the right to "access" his/her personal data within the CoT. The Discovery Service provides all other services in the CoT: information about the AP or WSP, that holds the requested attribute type of one particular federated user.

The Personal Data Protection may be achieved through two strategies:

1. The trustworthiness of the involved actors, as has been already explained, preserved and guaranteed through contracts amongst them and with end users.

2. Providing the choice to identify users through pseudonyms, allowing users not fully trusting the system to hide their real identity. Those identifiers will distinguish a user amongst all the others, without revealing his/her real identity. Moreover, end users may choose to grant those identifiers validity for a single session, which provide them an effective anonymity, since they completely avoid the possibility to "trace" the services consumed by them on the system.

End users, not so concerned by their privacy, may also choose to allow the same pseudonym to be re-used in different sessions with the same service provider. In this case, the SP can keep record of the services provided to the user, and any relevant user attribute required to provide a tailored (personalised) service. Nevertheless, even the SP and WSP collaborating in the provision of the service, will not have the information about the real end user identity, and will not even know that it is the same physical user, since the pseudonyms generated by the IdP to identify one user, are different for each SP or WSP.

2 Liberty Alliance Protocols suit proof of concept

To understand the project, we have to mention the three sets of protocols issued by LAP:

1. Liberty Identity Federation framework (ID-FF): which defines the identity federation and management functionalities, like the Single Sign On, Global Sign-Out, and others addressed to the management of metadata (user certificates, service end points) by the Liberty entities.

2. Liberty Identity Web Services Framework (ID-WSF): which defines the framework needed to create, discover and consume services related with user identity functionalities, like: Attributes sharing under user permission, SOAP invocation environment, etc.

3. Liberty Identity Services Interfaces Specification (ID-SIS): is a set of specifications that allow the deployment of interoperable services, over ID-WSF. Those services include: contacts, calendar, localization, alerts, etc.

In all those sets, the specifications have been built by extension of existing standards, like: SAML, SOAP, WS-Security, XML, etc.

The standardisation process is almost finished, but there have been no report of full implementations of the LAP protocols in international production or evaluation environments, which is the objective of FIDELITY project, and makes it very advanced in this field.

In this project there are four main objectives:

- To show the technical feasibility of a **large scale implementation** based on the Liberty Alliance specifications. This is done by creating an **international and multi-vendor proof of concept** environment of the whole set of protocols and actors in 4 EU countries, involving Telecom Operators, as IdP,s, Industrial partners, SME,s and research institutes. The environment will consist of 4 CoT's (France Telecom/Orange, Telenor, TeliaSonera, Amena/Ericsson), which will incorporate multiple access networks, and where each CoT implements realistic and commercial user scenarios (Italtel, tb-security, Moviquity, Gemalto, Linus, Oslo Univ.College).

- We also show that seamless authentication and **attribute sharing across CoT boundaries** is possible, managing authentication methods of different trustability level, ranging from anonymous to full identification based on PKI and e-signature. The FIDELITY project will also exploit the capabilities of smart cards (e.g. SIM/USIM cards) and implement support for Authentication and personal profile/attributes on a smart card, which will act as Attribute Provider to all Services accessed by the user, in any CoT.

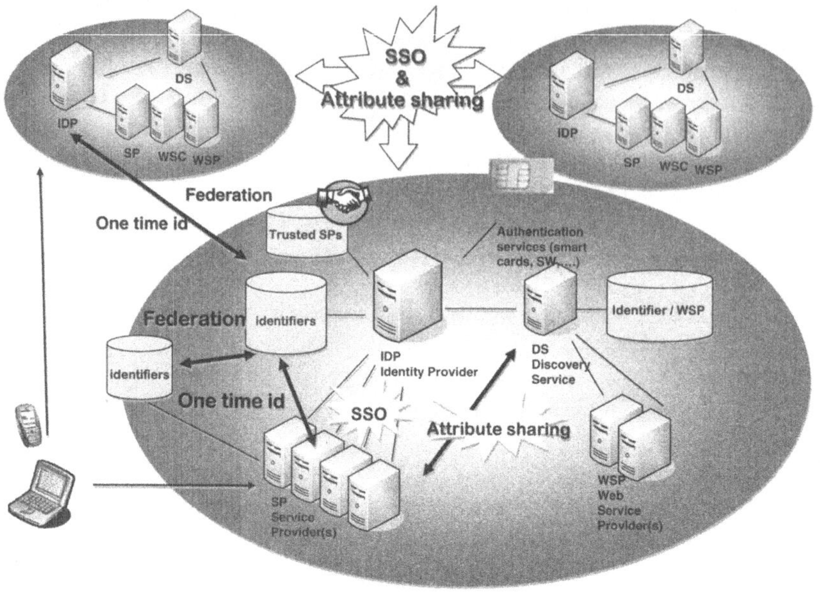

Fig. 1: Multi-national CoT architecture.

- To **explore the EU legislation** applicable on those environments and to produce recommendations for the technical mechanisms and legal agreements that will provide: control of the use of their personal attributes to end users, and control of their liability on the whole service provision to the rest of the actors.

- To produce best practices recommendations to guarantee the adequate security to end users, Telecom Operators and all the other Service Providers hosted by the same CoT, and which provide Identity and other services, mainly from personal data protection viewpoint.

3 Technical approaches

Several mechanisms, provided by the LAP, exist that allows us to fulfil the objective of providing secure user identification in a multi-CoT environment, with the adequate levels of privacy:

- **Single-Sign-on and Federation protocol**. This protocol assures that both the identity provider and the service provider have been federated. Once this is done, the Single Sign-On of the user is enabled so from the user's perspective, this SSO is realized when the users logs in to an identity provider and uses multiple affiliated service providers without having to sign on again. The mechanism also permits single log-out, and federation termination. The federation mechanism guarantees that service and identity providers will agree on the same levels of personal data protection.

- User attributes are federated within a CoT, and inter-CoT through its publication in a **Discovery service**.

- **Liberty Artifact Profile**: provides a mechanism to avoid replay of user identification queries. The use of secure communication protocols, which implement e-signature of involved entities, guarantee also integrity and confidentiality of transferred data.

- **Access control policy**: includes not only the above mentioned secure channel, but also the existence and content of Service level and business agreements, that will guarantee the adequate liability transfers between all the agents involved in the provision of one service, and that transferred data will be used for the intended purpose, during the required time-slot (no more, no less).

- Liberty-enabled implementations allow both service and identity providers to assign a meaningless identifier to a user, so that none of them may be able to associate this identifier to a physical person. Nevertheless those **pseudonyms** will persist beyond the notion of service provision, so that end-users will be able to get personalised services, based on previous service choices.

- To achieve **Anonymity**, users may request the non-persistency of the pseudonym. In this case, each new service provision will start from scratch, i.e. without history, and pseudonyms will be different each time, and even different for each WSP collaborating in the service provision, avoiding the traceability of users.

- Users also have to provide authorisation to **transfers of their personal attributes** between agents sharing them to in order to provide a service, either implicitly, just once at registration time, or explicitly each time a sensitive attribute value is requested by a SP.

- **Authentication mechanisms**: the different levels of trustworthiness of user identity offered to SP, and the pseudonimity levels offered to end users, are agreed in the authentication context and require the acceptance of several authentication mechanisms:

    o Strong: like **PKI** based user identification, which may be stored in **smart-cards**.

    o Moderated: like strong **password enforcement** or one-time-password solutions.

    o Basic: like conventional Uid/**Password**.

- Liberty also provides a **Proxy Identity providing** mechanism, to allow access of users through mobile telephones with WAP.

4 Security Aspects: Attacks and testing tools

The security of communications between the different CoTs, is guaranteed using LAP protocols. The testing strategies used are focused on demonstrating that installations of products based on those protocols have been made according to the security specifications and policies. We have identified the following potential threats:

- User **session hijacking**: obtaining the session access token or hijacking the connection between the user and a service of a CoT.

- User **identity theft**: getting Principal's username and password, or the credentials needed to validate his/her identity, using social engineering or malware tools in Principal's client or IdP database. Consequently attacker would be able to act on the Principal's behalf at any time.

- **Service** Provider **identity hijacking (phishing)**: to impersonate a Service Provider to obtain credentials of its users or interact with other members of the network as the original Service Provider.

- **Identity Provider identity hijacking** (more phishing): to impersonate a Identity Provider to get user's credentials or interact with other members of the network.

These threats have been analysed following the Common Criteria methodology, in order to make the results of the analysis more widely applicable. The threats have been simulated using the following specific testing tools:

- **Fake IdP**: to impersonate one of the main pieces of a CoT. A complete IdP implementation is needed. It is used to verify that certificates are validated by all the other actors. This tool may be used to lie a SP, or another IdP either a visited or a home one.

- **Fake DS**: to redirect WSC to fake WSP, to provide wrong attributes from users, in order to sabotage the service, or to impersonate WSC, to get user attributes without authorisation.

- **Fake SP** (WSP and WSC): to impersonate one or more of the Service Providers. It is used to verify that the certificates are validated, by other actors, like IdP, DS or SP.

Common security testing tools have also been used, like:

- **Sniffing** tools: to analyze the communications between two actors of the same or different CoTs.

- **Non-valid certificates**: issuer, to be used in the previous Fake services, which will be "fake" just because they identify themselves through non-valid certificates, certificates of non-trusted CA, revoked certificates, certificates of non-authorised users or actors.

- Other network tools: used to **replay** communication sessions and to send specific data to a SP. A good network Swiss knife is Netcat.

- A **web browser and web applications attack tool**: to simulate the access of a user to the different services of each CoT.

- DNS spoofing or DNS cache poisoning to implement a Pharming attack.

- Hacking tools to gain privileges in Service Providers or IdP.

- Password cracking, to complement social engineering attacks.

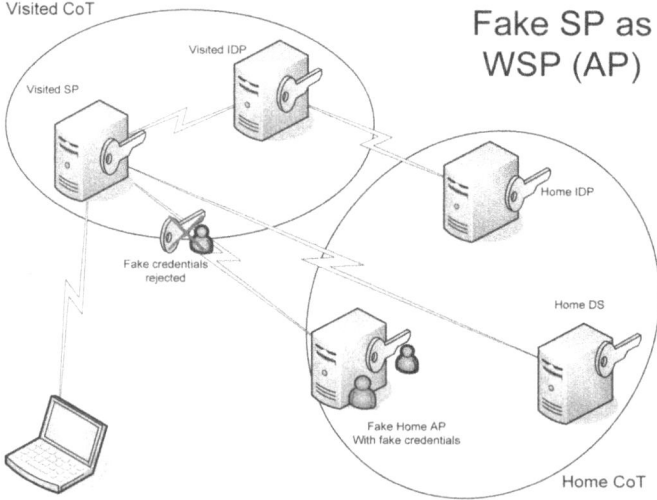

Fig 2: Testing scenario

5 Concluding remarks

This article describes the security issues related to implementations of Liberty Alliance (LAP) Protocols, from different viewpoints: legal, technical and economical.

We demonstrate that the approaches taken by the LAP, and used in the reference implementation environments set up within the FIDELITY project as proof of concepts follow all the security requirements, and consequently, are trustworthy to all the involved actors:

- End users accessing their home or roamed services, with different levels of anonymity, and guaranteed preservation of Personal data privacy.

- Service Providers joining the Circle of Trust (CoT) and sharing users' attributes, which will have non-repudiation proofs that the attribute providers are providing the right information about the end-user: no more, no less, updated, and with the adequate consent from the user. This will be achieved through the business agreements, authentication contexts and access control policy mechanisms.

- Telecom Operators providing Identity services, federated with other CoTs, since service level agreements signed with other IdP, will guarantee that their liability on user identification will be limited to the users they have registered, and not to those federated through other IdP. These liability transfers will be agreed through the authentication and Service Level agreements.

The project will also test innovative mobile user identification and attribute sharing solutions based on smart-cards, which will provide additional protection against user and Service identity theft.

The testing methodology has proven efficiency in checking the right installation choices from a security viewpoint, and the chosen approach is extensible to other user identification and authentication platforms, providing a good strategy to fight against current threats like phishing or pharming. The main points to be checked are: PKI authentication context initialisation and security Policy checking.

To finish, the presentation will address three topics related with LAP:

- Interoperability in a multi-vendor environment
- Privacy and Personal Data Protection in multi-national scenarios.
- Economical aspects, like: intra- and inter-CoTs service level and business agreements.

References

Circles of Trust: the implications of EU Data Protection and Privacy Law for establishing a legal framework for Identity Federation. February 23, 2005. editor Stephen Deadman

Privacy and Security Best Practices http://www.projectliberty.org/specs/final_privacy _security_best_practices.pdf Nov 2003. Christine Verney (Liberty alliance)

Liberty Technical Glossary http://www.projectliberty.org/specs/liberty-glossary-v1.4.pdf

Liberty ID-FF Bindings and Profiles Specification https://www.projectliberty.org/specs /draft-liberty-idff-bindings-profiles-1.2-errata-v2.0.pdf

Liberty ID-FF Architecture Overview https://www.projectliberty.org/specs /draft-liberty-idff-arch-overview-1.2-errata-v1.0.pdf

Liberty ID-WSF Security and Privacy Overview https://www.projectliberty.org/specs /liberty-idwsf-security-privacy-overview-v1.0.pdf

Liberty Technology Tutorial http://www.projectliberty.org/resources /LibertyTechnologyTutorial.pdf

Deflecting Active Directory Attacks

Jan De Clercq

Hewlett-Packard, HP Security Office,
Luchtschipstraat 1, B-1140 Evere, Belgium
Jan.DeClercq@HP.com

Abstract

Many of today's enterprises use Microsoft Active Directory (AD) either as their enterprise directory or as the network OS (NOS) directory for their Windows infrastructure. AD has become an important asset in most enterprises, and valuable things must be protected accordingly. This paper provides examples of attacks against Active Directory and shows how an enterprise directory can be protected against them. The attacks addressed in this paper include password cracking-, elevation of privilege- and denial-of-service-based attacks. The main goal of this paper is to show AD users the urgent need for taking a multi-pronged approach toward locking down and securing AD.

1 Introduction

Active Directory can be attacked from many directions— this paper looks at five common attacks and how to protect AD against them. The first three attacks can result in an elevation of the privileges of the attacker in AD. The last two attacks can affect the availability of the AD infrastructure. Unless stated otherwise, the information in this paper applies to both the Window Server 2003 and Windows 2000 Server versions of AD.

The main goal of this paper is to show AD administrators the urgent need for taking a multi-pronged approach toward locking down and securing AD.

2 Attack#1: Cracking Passwords Based on the LM Hash

Password cracking is the process of hashing a number of potential passwords by using the same hashing algorithms used by an OS, then comparing the results of the cracking operation to the password hashes stored by the OS. Password cracking can be time-consuming; password crackers typically have to try many (and sometimes, all) possible passwords. However, freeware tools such as John the Ripper and LCP can help automate password cracking. These tools can crack passwords particularly easily in AD environments that use the plain-vanilla NT LAN Manager (NTLM) authentication protocol.

NTLM is the default authentication protocol of Windows NT 4.0 and is still supported in Win2K and later OS versions for down-level compatibility reasons. NTLM is made up of two authentication protocols: LM and NTLM. The two protocol flavors use different hashing algorithms; these hashes are referred to as the LM and the NT, or Unicode, hashes, respectively.

The way Windows generates the LM hashes contains weaknesses that can significantly speed up the password cracking process. One weakness is that passwords can't be longer than 14 characters. LM also limits the character set by converting all password letters to uppercase

S. Paulus, N. Pohlmann, H. Reimer (Editors): Securing Electronic Business Processes, Vieweg (2006), 168-175

during the LM hash calculation. In addition, the LM hash doesn't actually use a hash function but rather a symmetric cipher to generate the hash.

2.1 Attack#1: Prevention

To mitigate the risks posed by LM password hashes, you can do the following: Get rid of the LM hashes in the AD database, ensure that your Windows users are using the stronger NTLMv2 authentication protocol, or ensure that your users honor specific password creation rules.

You can prevent the storage of the LM hashes in the AD on Windows 2003, Windows XP, and later platforms with the following Group Policy Object (GPO) or Local Policy setting: *Network security: Do not store LAN Manager hash value on next password change.* This setting doesn't remove LM hashes from AD or the SAM (the local security database); it ensures only that LM hashes aren't stored the next time users change their password. Thus, after you make this change, you should force all affected users to change their passwords. The *Network security: Do not store LAN Manager hash value on next password change* setting doesn't clear the LM hash history entries in a Win2K security database. They are cleared in Windows 2003 and XP.

On Windows 2003, XP, and Win2K Service Pack 2 (SP2) or later platforms, you can also edit the registry directly to prevent LM hash storage. To do so, set the HKEY_LOCAL_MACHINE \SYSTEM\CurrentControlSet\Control\Lsa\nolmhash registry subkey (REG_DWORD) to value 1.

If you make this change in a domain environment, you must be sure to make it on all domain controllers (DCs). You shouldn't make this change if you have an environment in which users are still using Windows 98 or Windows 95 clients that don't have the Directory Services client (explained below) installed. These clients can use only LM authentication.

To ensure that your users are using the stronger NTLMv2 authentication protocol, you must make the NTLMv2 software logic available to users that are running older Windows platforms. On Win98 and Win95 systems, install the Directory Services client, which you can download at [MS106]. The NTLMv2 logic is available on Windows 2003, XP, Win2K, or any NT machine running SP4 or later.

To force your clients to use NTLMv2 in a Windows 2003 or Win2K AD environment, you can set the Network Security: LAN Manager Authentication Level GPO setting to the value *Send NTLMv2 response only, refuse LM*. You can get the same effect by setting the corresponding registry subkey, HKEY_LOCAL_MACHINE\SYSTEM\CurrentControlSet\Control \Lsa\lmcompatibilitylevel (REG_DWORD), to value 4.

Finally, Windows won't generate an LM hash if users honor the following password rules:

- Use a password that's longer than 14 characters, or
- Use certain ALT characters in the password. These ALT characters can be entered by typing a four-digit numeric code while holding down the ALT key.

3 Attack#2: Cracking Passwords Based on Kerberos Pre-authentication Data

For a long time, we assumed that when we used the default Kerberos authentication provider on Windows 2003, XP, or Win2K machines to protect our passwords, brute-force password cracking attacks such as the ones outlined in the previous section couldn't be successful. But in late 2002—2 years after the release of Win2K—a tool named KerbCrack appeared on the Internet. KerbCrack—which is made up of two tools, kerbsniff and kerbcrack—can perform brute-force cracking attacks on Kerberos packets. Kerbsniff captures Kerberos packets from the network, and kerbcrack performs the actual brute-force cracking on the output of the first tool. Both tools can be downloaded from [NTSEC06].

Kerberos preauthentication is a feature that was introduced in Kerberos 5.0. A client uses pre-authentication data to prove the knowledge of its password to the Kerberos Key Distribution Center (KDC—the Kerberos service running on every Windows 2003 and Win2K DC) so that the client can be issued a Ticket Granting Ticket (TGT). Kerberos cracking attacks target the encrypted timestamp that's embedded in the Kerberos preauthentication data. The timestamp is encrypted by using the user's master key (i.e., a key that's based on the user's password).

3.1 Attack#2: Prevention

There are two ways to protect against Kerberos preauthentication attacks: Use Windows smart card logon, or encrypt the network traffic between the Kerberos client and the DC by using IPsec. Windows smart card logon uses a Kerberos extension called PKINIT, which doesn't encrypt the packet by using the user's master key but rather uses the user's private key. For more information about PKINIT, see [IETF03]. At the time of writing it is impossible to perform a brute-force attack on packets that are secured by using public-private key cryptography.

4 Attack#3: Privilege Elevation by Using SIDHistory

Microsoft added the SIDHistory attribute to AD user account objects in Win2K. SIDHistory facilitates resource access in interdomain account migration scenarios and intraforest account move scenarios. For example, when a user account is migrated from an NT 4.0 domain to a Win2K domain, Windows automatically populates the SIDHistory attribute of the newly created user account in the Win2K domain with the SID of the corresponding user account in the NT 4.0 domain. When at logon, the user's authorization data (group memberships and so on) is gathered in the Win2K domain, the DC adds the user's old SID from the SIDHistory attribute to the authorization data. The resources located in the old domain don't have to be re-permissioned (i.e., their ACLs don't need to be updated); users can continue to access them, even with a new account.

A malicious AD administrator could try to modify the SIDHistory attribute of a user account object to elevate its privileges. For example, in a domain trust relationship, the administrator of the trusted domain could try to add the SID of an administrator account in the trusting domain to the SIDHistory attribute of a user account in the trusted domain. If the administrator were successful, the user account of the trusted domain would get administrator access to the trusting domain.

In the first releases of Win2K, the DCs of the trusting domain don't check the authorization data included with resource access requests from the trusted domain. The trusting domain

DCs automatically assume that the requests contain only SIDs for which the DCs of the trusted domain are an authoritative source.

Although modifying the SIDHistory attribute of AD user accounts isn't easy (it can be done only when AD is in offline mode), it's possible. Tools are available that help malicious administrators populate the SIDHistory attribute. A good example is the SHEdit tool that can be downloaded from [TBIRO06].

This attack can be carried out in any kind of Windows domain trust setup: between the domains of a single forest or between domains that are linked by an external or forest trust relationship. In a single forest setup, for example, a rogue child-domain administrator or any rogue user with physical access to a DC could attempt to leverage the SIDHistory vulnerability to elevate themselves to the Enterprise Administrators group.

4.1 Attack#3: Prevention

To mitigate the risks related to the SIDHistory attribute, you must make sure that members of the Enterprise Administrators group and Domain Administrators group are very trusted individuals. You must also ensure a high level of physical security on your DCs to prevent rogue users from taking DCs offline and exploiting this vulnerability.

To prevent an administrator from changing the SIDHistory attribute, you can also use the SID filtering feature on trust relationships set up between domains in different forests. SID filtering allows administrators to quarantine domains. When SID filtering is enabled, the DCs of the trusting domain check whether the authorization data included with resource access requests from the trusted domain is related to the trusted domain. The DCs of the trusting domain automatically remove the SIDs that are not related to the trusted domain. Because this operation also removes SIDs that were added to the authorization data because of the SIDHistory attribute, SIDHistory and SID filtering are mutually exclusive features.

SID filtering is available in Win2K SP2 and later. You can turn it on or off by using the netdom.exe command-line utility; in Win2K, use the trust and /filtersids switches as described in [MS102]. In Windows 2003 use the trust and /quarantine switches. SID filtering is turned on by default for Windows 2003 external and forest trust relationships.

You shouldn't use SID filtering on trust relationships between domains in the same forest. Doing this breaks AD replication and transitive trust relationships. If you want to quarantine a domain, you should put it in a separate forest.

5 Attack#4: DoS Attack Based on Excessive AD Object Creations

Another way for users with administrator permissions to launch a Denial of Service (DoS) attack against AD is to flood it with new object creations. An authorized user can for example bring down an AD server by creating AD objects until the DC runs out of disk storage space. Another example is an authorized user adding many thousands of group members to a group by using one add command.

5.1 Attack#4: Prevention

To protect against this attack, you must again be extremely careful about whom you give AD object creation permissions to. Another feature you can use is the AD object quotas introduced in Windows 2003. A limited version of the object quota feature is also available in Win2K.

AD object quotas determine the number of objects that can be owned in an AD naming context (NC) or directory partition by a particular security principal. AD object quotas can be specified and administered separately for each AD NC and directory partition. However, you can't define them for the Schema NC. You can define a default quota for every AD NC and partition; if you don't explicitly set a default quota on a partition, the default quota for the partition is unlimited.

AD tombstone objects owned by a security principal are counted as part of the AD object quota consumption of the principal. Tombstone objects are temporary AD objects created when an AD object is deleted. AD uses them to keep deleted object data consistent across AD DCs. For each NC and partition, you can specify a tombstone quota factor that determines the weight given to a tombstone object in quota accounting. For example, if the tombstone quota factor for a given NC or partition is set to 25, then a tombstone object in the partition is counted as 0.25 of a normal AD object. The default tombstone quota factor for each partition is set to 100, so by default, a tombstone object has the same weight as a normal AD object.

You can assign quotas to every security principal, including the user, computer, group, and inetOrgPerson principals. A security principal can be covered by multiple quotas; for example, a user could be assigned an individual quota and also belong to a security group that has an assigned quota. In such a case, the quota that will be applied is the largest quota assigned to the security principal. Members of the Domain Administrators and Enterprise Administrators groups are exempt from AD object quotas.

AD object quotas are stored in the NTDS Quotas container of the AD NC or partition as objects of the msDS-QuotaControl class. To set an AD object quota of 10 for user Joe in the Accounting domain NC, you could type the following Dsadd command:

```
Dsadd quota
    part DC=Accounting,DC=COM
    -acct Accounting\Joe
    -qlimit 10
    -desc "Quota for Joe"
```

To change the tombstone quota factor for the Accounting domain NC to 25, you would type the following Dsmod command:

```
Dsmod
    partition DC=Accounting,DC=COM
    -qtmbstnwt 25
```

To change the default object quota setting to 0 for the Acounting domain NC, you would type the following Dsmod command:

```
Dsmod
    partition DC=Accounting,DC=COM
    -qdefault 0
```

Only DCs running Windows 2003 can enforce quotas. Quotas are enforced only on originating directory operations. They aren't enforced on replicated operations. To effectively use AD object quotas in an AD domain directory partition, all DCs in that domain must be running Windows 2003. To use AD object quotas in an AD configuration partition, all DCs in the forest must be running Windows 2003 (i.e., all domains and the forest must be at Windows 2003 functionality level 2). Realize that the availability of the AD object quota feature itself isn't related to any specific functionality level—it's available on any Windows 2003 DC. If a Windows 2003 domain that has quotas defined still has Win2K DCs, users can continue connecting to these DCs and work around the quota restrictions.

Win2K includes a very limited version of the Windows 2003 AD quota system. In Win2K, administrators can restrict how many computer accounts can be created by a particular user account. To do so, they must use the ms-DS-MachineAccountQuota attribute of the AD domain object. The restrictions don't apply to members of the Domain Administrators and Account Operators groups. The ms-DS-MachineAccountQuota attribute is supported in Windows 2003 (the default value is 10). To disable the addition of computer accounts, you can set this attribute to 0.

A similar effect can be obtained by taking away the *Add workstations to domain* user right from the Authenticated Users group. In both Windows 2003 and Win2K, this right is given by default to the Authenticated Users group.

6 Attack#5: DoS Attack Based on the MaxTokenSize Property

Microsoft extended the base Kerberos protocol to enable a Kerberos authentication ticket to include authorization data. A Windows Kerberos ticket and Ticket Granting Ticket (TGT) both contain a special field called the Privilege Attribute Certificate (PAC), which enables the Kerberos protocol to transport authorization data such as user group memberships and user rights in the Kerberos authentication tickets.

The Kerberos ticket has a fixed size, which indirectly also limits the PAC size. If a user is a member of a large number of groups (100 or more), this ticket size might be exceeded and Windows authentication and group policy processing might fail. Users that have the Active Directory (AD) permission to create and modify groups could exploit this weakness to mount a Denial of Service (DoS) attack against administrator accounts. Such an attack could prevent administrator accounts from logging on to the network.

6.1 Attack#5: Prevention

To prevent this attack, you must start by being extremely careful when delegating AD administrative permissions for group management. You must also restrict the permission to manage an administrator's account group membership. This restriction is difficult to achieve with the default permissions in AD because delegated administrators don't need any special rights to add any user account in the forest to the local and universal groups the administrators are allowed to manage. So, you must place Enterprise Administrators or Domain Administrators accounts in special organizational units (OUs) without read permissions for delegated administrators.

In addition, you can adjust the maximum size of a Kerberos ticket by using the HKEY_LOCAL_MACHINE\SYSTEM\CurrentControlSet\Control\Lsa\Kerberos\Parameters\ MaxTokenSize registry subkey.

The MaxTokenSize subkey (REG_DWORD) should be adjusted on all Windows machines from which users use Kerberos to log on to a domain. In Win2K, the default MaxTokenSize value is 8000 bytes. In Win2K SP2 and later and in Windows 2003, the default value is 12,000 bytes.

To reduce the PAC size, Microsoft also implemented a new method to store authorization data in the PAC in Win2K SP4. The new PAC authorization data storage method can be summarized as follows:

- If the groups are local or are from other domains, the entire SID of the group (e.g., S-1-5-21-1275210071-789336058-1957994488-3140) is stored in the PAC.

- If the global and universal groups a user belongs to are local to the domain the user is in, then only the Relative Identifier (RID) of the group (e.g., 3140) is stored.

Microsoft provides a special process on the client and server side to explode RIDs back to the SID format during the Windows authorization process. Note that even on platforms where this new PAC authorization data storage method is available, you might still need to adjust the MaxTokenSize or reduce the number of group memberships for a user.

To avoid wasting space in a Kerberos ticket's PAC field, you should remove the SIDHistory attribute from your AD accounts when your migration from the NT 4.0 domain to the Windows 2003 or Win2K domain is done by following the instructions in [MS104].

Microsoft released the Tokensz tool to troubleshoot problems related to the Kerberos token size. You can download the tool from [MS206]. The following Tokensz command lists the current system value for MaxTokenSize and the size of the current token:

> tokensz /compute_tokensize
>
> /package:negotiate
>
> /use_delegation
>
> /target_server:<MachineName>

7 Conclusion

The attacks outlined in this paper underline the importance of taking a multipronged approach to securing an AD infrastructure. In addition to technology-focused security solutions, you must also think about physical and organizational security measures. Physical security measures include securing physical access to Windows DCs, your network infrastructure, and your organization's buildings. Organizational security measures include the creation of security policies and operational procedures, regularly performing external security audits of the AD infrastructure, and continuously training administrators and users on security risks and best practices. Securing AD is a big task that should be a high priority for a team of people in your organization that focuses on the combination of technical, physical, and organizational security.

References

[MS106]   Microsoft download website, directory services client software: http://download.microsoft.com/download/0/0/a/00a7161e-8da8-4c44-b74e-469d769ce96e/dsclient9x.msi, 2006

[NTSEC06] NT Security website, kerbcrack tool: http://www.ntsecurity.nu/toolbox/kerbcrack, 2006

[IETF03]   IETF website, "Public Key Cryptography for Initial Authentication in Kerberos": http://www.ietf.org/proceedings/03mar/I-D/draft-ietf-cat-kerberos-pk-init-16.txt, 2003

[TBIRO06] Tbiro website, shedit tool: http://www.tbiro.com/projects/shedit/index.htm, 2006

[MS102]   Microsoft Knowledge Base website, article "MS02-001: Forged SID could result in elevated privileges in Windows 2000": http://support.microsoft.com/?kbid=2892432002, 2002

[MS104]   Microsoft Knowledge Base website, article "How To Use Visual Basic Script to Clear SidHistory": http://support.microsoft.com/?kbid=295758, 2004

[MS206]   Microsoft download website, tokensz tool: http://www.microsoft.com/downloads/details.aspx?familyid=4a303fa5-cf20-43fb-9483-0f0b0dae265c&displaylang=en, 2006

Implementing role based access control –
How we can do it better!

Marko Vogel

KPMG
Alfredstrasse 277
D-45133 Essen, Germany
mvogel@kpmg.com

Abstract

Protecting internal information is a critical factor for every organisation and moreover essential to meet regulatory requirements these days. Permissions within critical business applications and systems must be aligned with the business structure and processes. Furthermore the actual state of users and assigned access rights must meet the reality of people's authority for their actual position and function.

By strictly mapping business positions and functions to roles within IT systems it is easy for an organisation to prove that target state and actual state are aligned. RBAC – role based access control – is a standard that defines what a role is and what functionality a system implementing roles as an authorisation model should support. However, the standard does not define how role engineering can be done. This article describes the different approaches to role engineering, a proven methodology for role engineering in ERP systems and how this methodology can be adjusted to be used for organisation-wide multi-system role engineering.

1 Introduction

For a few years CIOs pay increased attention to compliance. This is due to the fact that the importance of external regulations and internal policies has generally increased. One corner stone of an organisations information security policy framework is an access control policy defining *who can access what*. However, there are different possibilities and models to restrict user access to resources according to the policy. The classic access control models are described in chapter 2.

Furthermore, it is important to know *why* a person has access to a resource. Only then an organisation - but also an independent third party - is in a position to decide whether that person needs the access furthermore or not.

Therefore it is necessary to consider the business context within the access control model. A model allowing this is the role based access control model as described in chapter 3.

The key questions of our clients facing the problem of defining roles are

- How should we do it?
- How can we do it in an efficient way?

Taking into consideration the experience in defining authorisation concepts for ERP environments for many years, this article will give some general guidance concerning these two questions.

S. Paulus, N. Pohlmann, H. Reimer (Editors): Securing Electronic Business Processes, Vieweg (2006), 176-185

2 Classic access control models

The classic access control models are DAC (Discretionary Access Control) and MAC (Mandatory Access Control). MAC is based on a classification of the resources in security levels (e.g. internal, secret, top secret). Depending on the trust level of the user, access to a resource can be granted. Due to the fact that every user has only one trust level, this model is not very flexible.

The DAC model is in some respects a contrary model. Access to a resource is granted individually to every user by the owner of the resource. This type of model is usually implemented by "access control lists" within the application. "Access control lists" include the user-id combined with the type of permission (e.g. read, write, print). This model allows a fine-grained authorisation concept but is limited due to the increasing administration effort for large numbers of users or resources.

3 Role Based Access Control (RBAC)

Vendors had started to implement role based access control features in their database management systems, security management and network operating system products without a general agreement on a definition of RBAC features.

In an effort to harmonize these activities the National Institute of Standards and Technology (NIST) has developed a standard on role based access control to provide a consistent and uniform definition of role based access control features. The ANSI INCITS 359-2004 standard was adopted in 2004 [ANIN04].

The RBAC standard defines a role as follows:

"A role is a job function within the context of an organisation with some associated semantics regarding the authority and responsibility conferred on the user assigned to the role."

With this definition the business context is addressed and the model can fulfil the requirements mentioned in the introduction.

The RBAC reference model consists of four model components: *Core RBAC, Hierarchical RBAC, Static Separation of Duty Relations* and *Dynamic Separation of Duty Relations (constrained RBAC)*.

However, an application or IT system does not have to support all of them.

Core RBAC model elements and relations are defined in Figure 1:

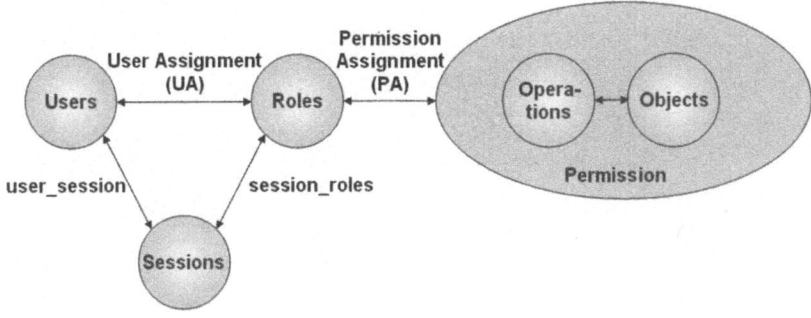

Figure 1: Core RBAC

The core functions of the RBAC model are assigning individual users to roles on the one hand and permissions to roles on the other hand. Like this, a role is a means for handling many-to-many relationships between individual users and permissions. In addition, the core RBAC model includes a set of sessions where each session is a mapping between a user and an activated subset of roles that are assigned to the user.

Hierarchical RBAC introduces role hierarchies as a natural means of structuring roles to reflect an organisation's lines of authority and responsibility. Role hierarchies define an inheritance relation among roles.

Constrained RBAC adds Separation of Duty relations to the RBAC model. Separation of duty relations are used to prevent that users have access rights to critical business functions that should be separated. Its purpose is to ensure that fraud within an organisation is caused only as a result of collusion among individuals. To minimize the likelihood of collusion, individuals of different skills or divergent interests are assigned to separate tasks required for a business function.

The RBAC standard allows for both *Static* (SSD) and *Dynamic Separation of Duty* (DSD).

SSD means that if a user is assigned to a role and within a conflict policy this role is defined as separated from a second role, the user is prohibited from being a member of the second role.

DSD allows defining constraints on the roles that can be activated within or across a user's sessions. DSD allows a user to be authorized for two or more roles that do not create a conflict of interest when acted in independently, but result in a policy conflict when activated simultaneously.

Furthermore, the RBAC standard defines system and administrative functions specifying the features that are required for an RBAC system. These features fall into the three categories "administrative operations", "administrative reviews" and "system level functionality".

The administrative operations define functions that provide the capability to create, delete and maintain RBAC elements and relations (e.g. to create and delete user role assignments). The administrative review features define functions that provide the capability to perform query operations on RBAC elements and relations. System level functionality defines features for the creation of user sessions to include role activation/deactivation, the enforcement of constraints on role activation, and for making an access decision.

Only core RBAC is mandatory for all packages of functional components. The other components can be selected optionally. Figure 2 gives an overview of the dependencies for defining the functional requirement package.

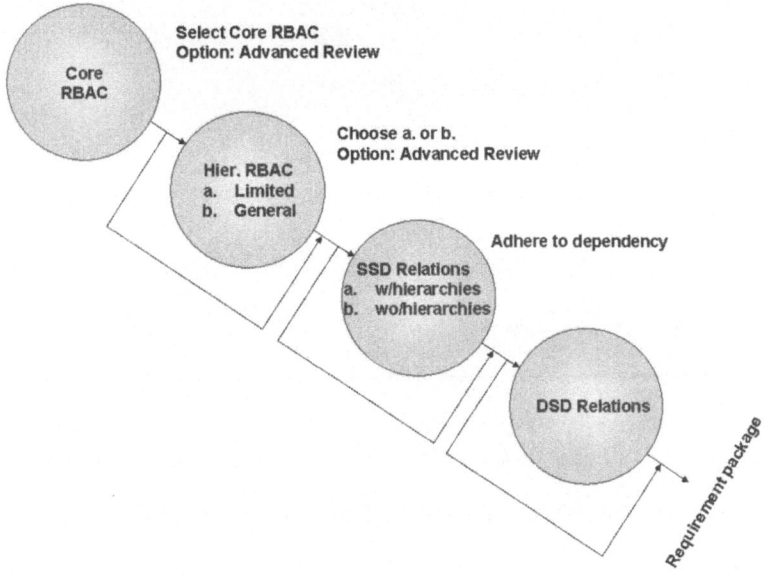

Figure 2: Dependencies of components

The introduction of the RBAC model at the beginning of the 90s and its enhancements later on shows that this model has the flexibility missing in the MAC model and that it allows a simplified administration. Since DAC and MAC are recognised as a special case of RBAC [OSM00], it is obvious that the advantage of a policy based on RBAC depends on the implementation of the role model.

Furthermore the model itself defines roles within a business context. But only the correct implementation of the model within the applications and IT systems of a company ensure the proof of compliance. Especially the consideration of separation of duties aspects can be achieved easier with the use of roles defined in a business context.

4 Role Engineering

As mentioned above the RBAC model of the standard is intended for a more technical use concerning roles within systems and applications. The standard does not define an approach on how to define a role in a business context and connect it with the right permissions (also referred to as role engineering).

For this reason, different approaches to role engineering have been proposed in [RSW00], [NeSt02] and [KKSM02]. They differ basically in the starting point of the approach (see also Figure 3).

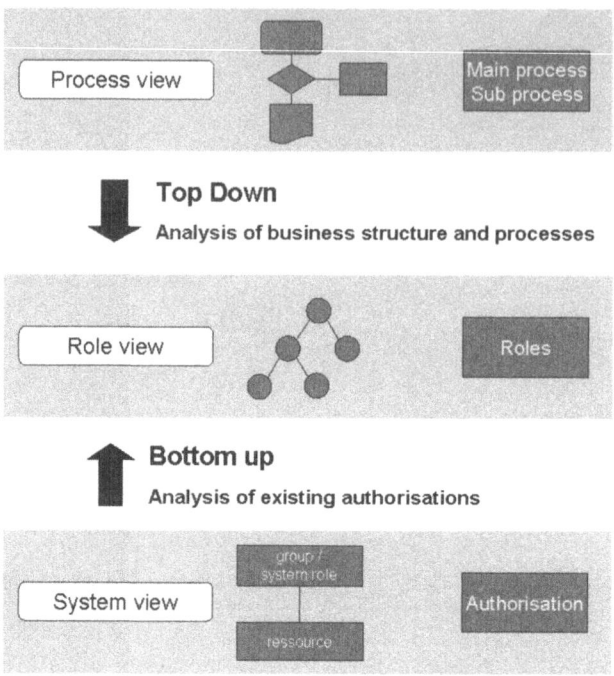

Figure 3: Approaches to role engineering

4.1 Top-down approach

Role engineering can be done top down starting from the business processes. The processes are described in detail and are combined with the necessary resources assigned to the roles included in the process. This approach has turned out to be very time consuming.

One of the problems is the different definition - or better: granularity - of process descriptions in terms of business or IT. The business units define the processes in process maps or process flows to visualize the process from the point of view of customers or employees (see Figure 4). In terms of IT a process model means a detailed description of activities on the level of data, information and functions. The consequence is a gap between business and IT in the top down approach which has to be closed manually.

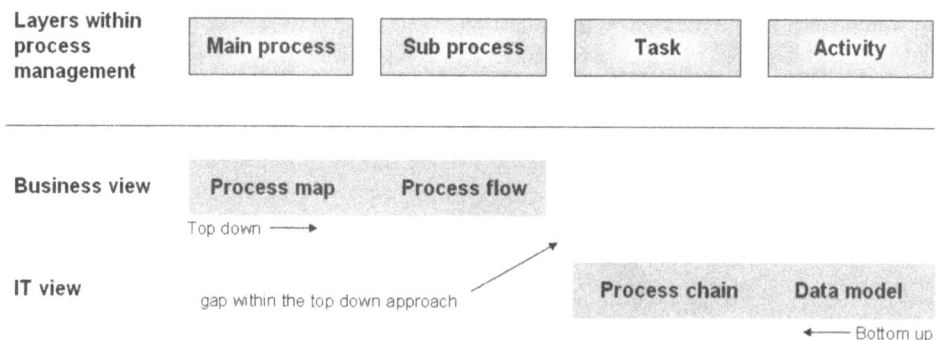

Figure 4: Problem of top down approach

In the top-down approach it is important to define the different criteria which are the origin of the role definition. Such criteria are for example organisation, location, function, position, etc. For the different criteria a list of possible values can be defined. In some cases, like "organisation" it is easy: the organisational structure defines the different values and also the hierarchy for the roles. But especially for the criteria "function" it is a time consuming work to define the functions and their corresponding permissions.

But with the documented chain "criteria – criteria value – role – permission" it is possible to easily answer the question why a user has an access right to a certain resource from a business perspective:

- Because he works in department "Finance" and all users of department "Finance" have that access right (role)

- Because he works in location "Berlin" and all users working in location "Berlin" have that access right (role)

- Because he has the function "bank teller" and all users with the function "bank teller" have that access right (role)

Another problem of the top-down approach is that the "paper results" from the top-down approach do not correspond with the reality of permissions within the different systems. Therefore it is necessary to do a gap analysis to find out whether the defined role does not have enough permissions or the user has more permissions than necessary.

4.2   Bottom-up approach

The bottom up approach assumes that a role structure exists within the current authorisations of different systems. These roles can be identified by clustering or data mining methods. Some vendors offer these kinds of tools as add-on for their user management tools. The procedure for the bottom-up approach is grouped in three phases:

1. Consolidation
2. Preparation and Correction
3. Analysis

In the first phase the authorisation data from the different systems and applications is collected. After that (phase 2), the different data is prepared, adjusted and - if necessary – corrected. After phase 2 the data is in a condition and format ready for analysis in phase 3. Within the analysis phase the tools search for clusters of identical authorisations for groups of users. It is also possible to use user attributes representing the organisational structure in addition to the authorisation data.

With this approach it seems to be possible to automate the role engineering process. But a discussion of the output with the data or process owner is also necessary. He has to analyse because of which criteria the user group has the authorisation. This is important to decide why a user (group) has an authorisation. The second aspect of the manual analysis is the examination whether the principle of least privilege is adhered to. Because of the manual maintenance of authorisations in applications and systems without the consideration of the business context in the authorisation models for years, in a lot of cases the authorisations are too comprehensive and user are assigned access rights they are not supposed to have.

If these cases of inaccuracy are not corrected, the new role based authorisation model is as weak as the old one.

If reduction of costs is the main reason for using a role based access control model the bottom-up approach can be used to identify quickly and partly automated potential roles. In contrast, if the reason for the introduction of the role based access control model is compliance, the top-down approach or a mixed approach is essential.

4.3 Role Engineering in ERP Environments

Most of the mentioned problems are also known within the context of role engineering for ERP systems. KPMG has a proven methodology for role engineering in ERP systems like SAP.

Key element of the approach is the workplace concept (see also Figure 5). The workplace bundles all the necessary permissions (read, write, etc.) in the context of the business object (what) and the business structure (where).

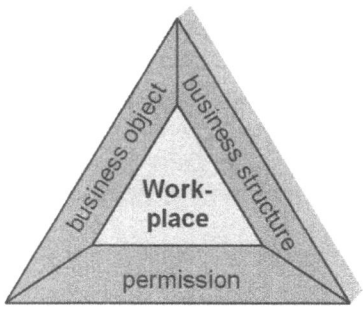

Figure 5: workplace

The comparison of the definition of a role within the RBAC standard with the definition of a workplace shows that every definition can easily be transformed to the other one. For that reason both terms can be used synonymously.

KPMG uses the structured project approach described in Figure 6 for defining workplaces. Using this approach KPMG has implemented authorisation concepts based on workplaces within ERP environments. This approach uses a top down approach as described in chapter 4.1.

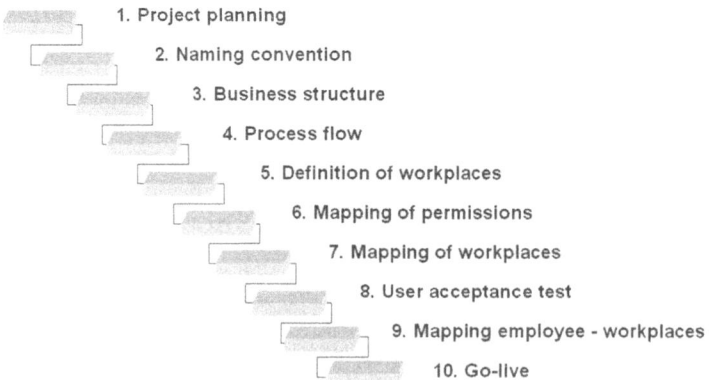

1. Project planning
2. Naming convention
3. Business structure
4. Process flow
5. Definition of workplaces
6. Mapping of permissions
7. Mapping of workplaces
8. User acceptance test
9. Mapping employee - workplaces
10. Go-live

Figure 6: KPMG project approach

The main phases for the definition of the authorisation model are described in the following:

Phase 1 – project planning
In this phase the different activities and following phases are scheduled and the programs and tools to be used are determined. Furthermore, the documentation structure is defined. The project objectives are communicated during a kick-off meeting.

Phase 2 – naming convention
The naming conventions for workplaces, authorisation, profiles, etc. within the ERP system are defined in this phase. Naming conventions are important for the transparency and ability to audit the authorisation concept. In this phase the approach for the use and maintenance of roles is worked out and documented.

Phase 3 – business structure
In this phase the needed business structure and the detailed characteristics are defined. It is helpful to use the pre-defined objects of the ERP system.

Phase 4 – process flow
In this phase the different functions and tasks are separated into the different modules and components of the ERP system. This is the basis for the definition of template roles as basic components of the new authorisations.

Phase 5 – definition of workplaces
The workplaces are defined together with the business owner and comprise the naming and the business and technical functions. They bundle functions according to the principle of least privilege.

Phase 6 – mapping of permissions
The template roles of phase 4 are specified and adjusted according to the results of phase 5.

Phase 7 – mapping of workplaces
By using and bundling the template roles the defined and documented workplaces from phase 5 are implemented within the ERP system.

This approach is especially designed for projects where compliance aspects come to the fore. It is mainly used in projects where new authorisation models are designed but it can also help to adjust an existing authorisation model.

The following chapter describes the advantages and restrictions in using this approach for a company-wide multi-system role model.

4.4 Company-wide multi-system role engineering

The implementation of a role model either for ERP systems or a multi-system landscape has to consider three dimensions:

- Organisational scope
  Which part of the organisation or processes has to be included?

- System scope
  Which applications and systems (and existing authorisation structures) have to be included?

- Authorisation scope
  Which level of detail concerning authorisations has to be included?

In two of the three dimensions there are no - or only minor - difference between role engineering for ERP systems or multiple systems. Concerning the organisational scope, an ERP implementation comprises most parts of the organisation and processes. Furthermore, the authorisation concept is implemented in detail in the ERP system so that the level of detail is often higher than in multi-system approaches.

Only the system scope is - by nature - not comparable even though most ERP systems are not one monolithic block but using a modular architecture with more or less independent modules.

But what are the consequences that more systems are involved?

Permissions are possibly created based on other criteria as described in chapter 4.1. For example the permissions are structured on a "project" base and therefore the roles can not be defined based on existing criteria.

In a multi-system role engineering project it is important to discuss some aspects during the planning phase:

- The motivation has to be discussed. If compliance is the main motivation, this can influence the scope, e.g. the systems in scope. Furthermore, the top-down or a mixed approach should be preferred because then the gap between target state and actual state can be analysed and the permissions can be corrected accordingly. Separation of duties can be defined according to the policies and considered within role definition. In case of process improvement being the motivation for role engineering the bottom-up approach can be more effective. In this case the roles with a low rate of changes within the permissions but a high rate of changes within assigned users are especially interesting. These roles can increase efficiency in administration.
- The different scopes have to be restricted. Otherwise the analysis phase lasts too long and no results are visible.
- The approach which will be used later on has to be defined.

Afterwards, the described methodology can easily be adapted. The business structure and processes are analysed and the naming convention is defined. After defining the roles within their business context they are mapped to the permissions within the systems and applications in scope.

The biggest challenge of role engineering is the cooperation between business units and IT to define a role model within a business context across system boundaries.

5 Conclusion

The existing standard for role based access control defines what a role is and what functionality a system implementing roles as authorisation model should support. The main extensions are the support for role hierarchies and separation of duties aspects.

But the existing standard does not define a process model for role engineering. Organisations which want to introduce a role model are confronted with that problem. To solve the problems it is necessary to analyse the requirements of the organisation to use the right approach and to find stable roles to minimize administration efforts.

The motivation for starting a role project influences the type of approach. On the one hand it can be done top-down by analysing the organisational structure, processes and tasks within their business context and the associated permissions within the different systems and applications. With this approach the target state is defined and can be compared with the actual state. Afterwards, the two states can be harmonised.

On the other hand role engineering can be done bottom-up by analysing the existing structure of permissions and finding "clusters" of permissions for groups of users. These clusters are used for defining roles. Roles with large groups of users and low changes within permissions are interesting in terms of reducing administration efforts. But the defined roles can only be as accurate as the old permissions have been. Therefore, it is often necessary to discuss the results with the process owner.

The definition of a good role model and the role engineering can be facilitated by a methodology considering the motivation and requirements for the project. The methodology for ERP environments – as shown above - covers already most of the aspects relevant for a role engineering project. Furthermore, it can easily be adapted for use in a multi-system landscape.

However, it is necessary to have a sound experience to customize the methodology for the requirements and needs of the organisation. The roles are as individual as every organisation is.

References

[ANIN04]   American National Standards Institute; InterNational Committee for Information Technology Standards: American National Standard for Information Technology – Role Based Access Control, ANSI INCITS 359-2004, New York, February 2004

[KKSM02]   Kern, Axel; Kuhlmann, Martin; Schaad, Andreas; Moffett, Jonathan: Observations on the Role Life-Cycle in the Context of Enterprise Security Management. In: Proceedings of 7th ACM Symposium on Access Control models and applications (SACMAT) 2002, Monterey (CA), p. 43-52.

[NeSt02]   Neumann, Gustaf; Strembeck, Mark: A scenario-driven Role Engineering Process for Functional RBAC Roles. In: Proceedings of 7th ACM Symposium on Access Control models and applications (SACMAT) 2002, Monterey (CA), p. 33-42.

[OSM00]   Osborn, S.; Sandhu, R.; Munawer Q.: Configuring Role-Based Access Control to Enforce Mandatory and Discretionary Access Control Policies. In: ACM Trans. On Information and System Security, Vol. 3, No. 2, Mai 2000, p. 85-106.

[RSW00]   Roeckle, H.; Schimpf, G.; Weidinger, R.: Process Oriented Approach for Role-Finding to Implement Role-Based Security Administration in a large Industrial Organisation. In: Proceedings of the 5th ACM Workshop on Role-Based Access Control, Berlin, 2000, p. 103-116.

Identity and Access Control – Demonstrating Compliance

Marc Sel · Bart Van Rompay

PricewaterhouseCoopers
{marc.sel | bart.van.rompay}@pwc.be

Abstract

Identity and particularly access control present various challenges, particularly for larger organisations. The combined complexity of users from various communities, accessing multiple systems and applications in the context of business processes can be significant. The US NIST proposed the Role-Based Access Control model in order to effectively and efficiently manage authorisations. While this model certainly also has its drawbacks, it gave rise to various interesting software solutions. One particularly relevant one is the Sage tool. This tool builds a model of the actual authorisations across platforms by consolidating and enriching them in its own database. Subsequently, the built-in pattern-matching engine can identify a number of less desirable patterns in the data and can recommend solutions, e.g., for role structuring (role-mining). Furthermore, business constraints can be expressed in so-called business process rules, which can, e.g., reflect segregation of duty requirements.

In the pilot project described here as case study, we combined both role-mining and compliance verification. The case study organisation is subject to both national competition regulation and the US Sarbanes-Oxley act. They employ approximately 25.000 employees. Analysing existing access controls through a unified approach and applying compliance rules to them has shown to be a quick and reliable way for them to demonstrate compliance (or identify actions where compliance was not yet achieved). The fact that the control library is available both at the level of principles and at the level of specific business process rules makes the approach transparent, repeatable and affordable. Furthermore a number of observations were made that allowed to remove undesired authorisations through data cleaning. As a result of the pilot project the client decided to implement BPR-based compliance verification for all applications that are subject to Sarbanes-Oxley.

1 The challenge of Identity and Access Control

1.1 Introduction

Most medium to large sized organisations today built up and manage what could be referred to as their 'authorisation space'. This space is essentially structured into three dimensions: the different user communities (subjects), the ICT services and applications (objects), and the processes allocating users authorisations onto these services.

This can be represented as:

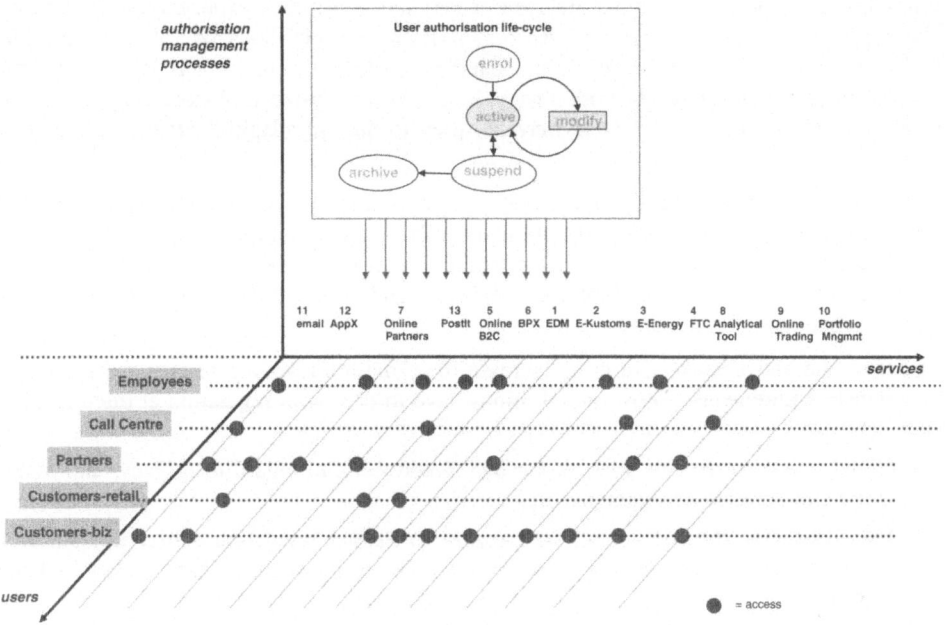

Figure 1: The three dimensional authorisation space

The user dimension (subjects) is structured into various types of user communities, ranging from employees to partners and customers, or the public at large. Nowadays, even some regulators are asking access, or are forcing companies to open systems to competitors in order to liberalise a particular market. The services dimension (objects, left-to-right axis) can be further decomposed into individual applications or transactions within these applications. Finally, the authorisation management dimension (vertical axis) is organised into sets of processes that support the user authorisation life-cycle ("from hiring to firing/retirement").

In the real-world, this space can be impressively large. For one particular company with 40.000 employees (and excluding the authorisations of customers on company systems) we estimated the total number of authorisations that were managed around 35 million. Since that organisation's authorisations were decided by a core team of 10 persons, this meant that on average, every authorisation manager was dealing with approximately 3,5 million authorisations. Most of these authorisations have been built up over the years, often surviving multiple rounds of business reorganisation.

1.2 IdM initiatives often fall short of meeting expectations

Many vendors tout Identity Management (IdM) systems as the overarching solution to the management of user identification and authorisation. Such systems are aiming essentially at quicker turnaround time for user-id and authorisation provisioning. These systems typically address the aspects of authentication, directories, provisioning and access control. While the actual success rate of such Identity Management projects varies, their approach with regard to access control is typically incomplete. High-level or coarse-grained access control can be managed, but more fine-grained or application-specific access control is often not addressed. Also, while web-based solutions are typically covered, legacy systems are often left out. For many organisations legacy systems will stay around for the near or not-so-near future.

In practise, such projects are often delayed or less successful than expected due to the over-whelming combinatory complexity. An organisation with ten-thousands of users and hun-dred-thousands of resources (applications, databases, files, …) quickly has multi-millions of authorisations to manage across both legacy, ERP and web systems. Automating the existing authorisations in a new IdM system may fall prey to the old adagio "garbage in – garbage out".

Furthermore, while we think that quicker turn-around time and improved user and authorisa-tion management are valid objectives, these are still missing an important point. Equal atten-tion should be paid to understanding the structure of the authorisation space in order to reduce and restructure it in order to facilitate more effective and efficient management processes over the authorisations.

Adding to the above, there is a clear increase in regulation resulting in ever more complex compliance requirements. Most organisations have to deal with regulation at three levels at least:

- Global – e.g., directives such as various directives with regard to privacy, anti-money laundering, electronic signatures etc;
- Industry-sector specific – e.g., with regard to market regulation and/or liberalisation. Examples include the US-originated Sarbanes-Oxley act or an EU national law on Com-petition;
- ICT specific – e.g., ISO/IEC 27001 or 17799 for information security.

So most organisations find themselves confronted with both a complex authorisation space to manage and the requirement to do this in a sufficiently transparent and understandable way. The onus of demonstrating this is imposed on the organisation.

2 The way forward

2.1 Increasing abstraction

In order to effectively and efficiently manage such a complex space, a high degree of abstrac-tion is mandatory. Traditional mechanisms such as Bell-Lapadula and the access control ma-trix have evolved into today's model of roles. Adequate access control management requires abstraction to make decisions, while the business processes demand sophisticated and often complex IT systems and infrastructures. These IT systems typically include authorisation mechanisms and repositories from many different backgrounds and technologies. However, good management (and extending it to governance and compliance) requires a unified ap-proach to address the many possible constraints that have to be taken into account, such as lo-cation-based limitations, confidentiality, segregation-of-duty, functional limitations etc. We are convinced that the most effective way forward is to increase the level of formalisation by modelling the complex multi-technology access space.

2.2 A possible way forward

We see the most realistic way forward as the combination of two key elements. On one hand: unifying technologies, and on the other hand, control libraries.

2.2.1 Unifying technologies

Mathematics came to the rescue by allowing us to formulate models such as RBAC – role based access control (which originated from the US NIST – [NIST2001]). This is an overarching model for authorisation management that is gradually gaining acceptance and standardisation.

The basic model is based on a "User-Role-Permission" paradigm. Since users typically access a system via (multiple) sessions, this is also reflected.

RBAC – Role Based Access Control

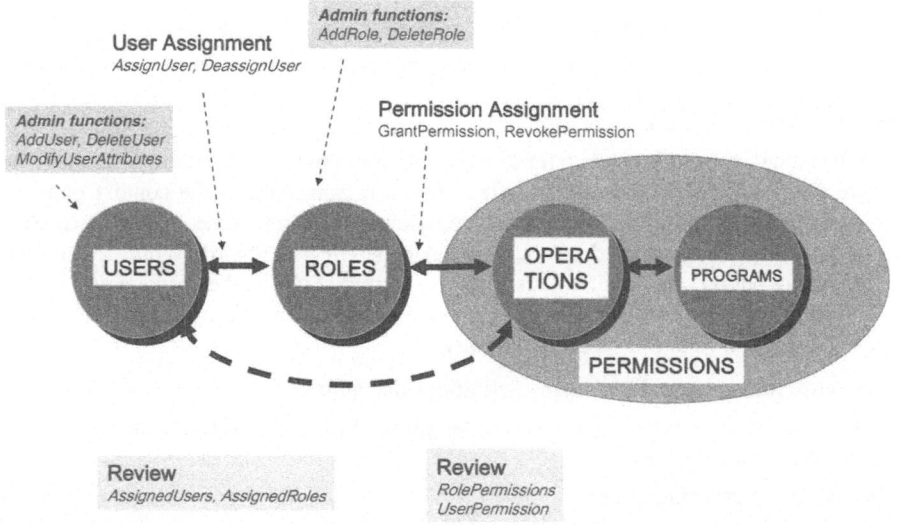

Figure 2: RBAC at a glance

The role model was widely accepted, and is currently still gaining popularity. It allows to model the diverse authorisations in an organisation quite well, striking a balance between effectiveness and efficiency. Nevertheless, we want to mention two areas where we think the model falls somewhat short for meeting the requirements of larger-scale commercial organisations:

- Within such organisations, there is often a natural grouping of users into user communities on one hand and permissions (or resources) into permission communities on the other hand. This leads to a four tier-model that is used in practice (user – user cluster – permission cluster – permissions). However, it is not easily modelled in RBAC. It can be argued that a role-hierarchy makes this possible, but this is rather theoretical in our opinion. Larger-scale commercial organisations often prefer to have more conceptual layers to model their authorisations than just three.

- Also, within such organisations, the organisational dimension itself is both very important and changing at a high pace (e.g. due to mergers and acquisitions). Larger-scale commercial organisations often have a need to model the organisation itself in their authorisations model.

RBAC's main competitor is probably the rule-based model, where access is dynamically cal-culated by rules that evaluate the values of attributes (e.g. LDAP attributes). We will not dis-cuss this rule-based access control model here.

Based on the role model, additional models and algorithms were introduced that are able to analyse the actual patterns exposed by the existing authorisation repositories. Pattern recog-nition algorithms can quickly sift through vast amounts of data and identify patterns that are out-of-sync with normal expectations, or can propose improved structures. Provisioning mis-takes (the account receivable clerk with system-level access) or redundant role definitions can be immediately identified (and rectified).

Furthermore additional formalisms can be defined that specify constraints (e.g. segregation-of-duty) on the data. Applying those formalised constraints allows testing for compliance.

2.2.2 Control library

We use the name control library to refer to a collection of control principles. By control prin-ciples we refer to the typical controls defined by an organisation in the context of internal control, or a preparation for Sarbanes-Oxley compliance, or comparable. The first COSO re-port can probably be considered as the seminal paper in this regard. While regulation or COSO typically outline the requirements for a. o. internal controls, they remain at a high and often abstract level. In practise, this abstract level is translated into more pragmatic sets of controls, that we will refer to as a control library.

Such a control library typically contains definitions that address:

- restriction on organisational scope (coarse grained/fine grained access, across organiza-tional and/or legal entities)
- access to critical transactions
- segregation of duty (SOD)
- orphans (i.e., entities such as users, roles or resources present in the system but not con-nected to another tier. As such they contribute to the complexity but not to the actual access control definitions)
- collectors (people or processes that accumulated a significant amount of authorisations, typically over a longer period of time and due to a lack of good management processes).

We propose a three-tier structure for a control library that is focused on identity and access management:

- tier #1: the control baselines;
- tier #2: controls related to organisational structure and processes;
- tier #3: controls related to time.

The control baselines (tier #1) specify commonly accepted principles with regard to identity and access management, such as

- Individual accountability – authorisations are granted to specific individual users (which can be physical persons or technical users such as daemons or address spaces). As a consequence, userids/accounts are not shared;
- Single user identification – a user should have a single identifier per platform. Situa-tions where users have different identifiers across platforms or multiple identifiers on the same platform should be avoided;

- Authorisations should be allocated through roles (or a similar grouping mechanism). Direct links between users and resources should be avoided;
- No single user should have all authorisations. If such users need to exist from a technical perspective, they should be blocked for daily operational activities;
- No users should accumulate so many authorisations that there can be reasonable suspicion that the risk for (un-)intentional misbehaviour increases. There should be a form of monitoring that users should not accumulate a set of authorisations that deviates significantly from their peers or comparable functions (unless justified).
- There should be no "orphans" in the identity and access management system, i.e., there should be no users without authorisations connected to them, there should be no roles without users and authorisations connected to them, and there should be no authorisations without users connected to them[1].

The controls related to organisational structure and processes (tier #2) should reflect that a user performs a function (role) within an organisation, typically in the context of one or more processes. This leads to the following principles:

- Authorisations should be limited to the appropriate functional organisational scope and processes. Where required this may lead to 'Chinese Walls (or the well-known Brewer-Nash model)';
- Authorisations should reflect a high-level segregation between production, acceptance/test and development environments;
- Authorisations should reflect the required segregation-of-duties (combinations of certain authorisations are to be forbidden);
- Specific functions within the organisation require specific authorisations. For example, auditors will have read authorisations only.

The controls related to time (tier #3) should reflect the fact that only active users and active authorisations need to be present in the system:

- Users that are no longer employed or servicing the organisation need to be blocked;
- Users that have not accessed the systems for the last 90 days need to be blocked

Please note that this is an example of a typical implementation of a control library for identity and access management. It should not be considered as automatically suitable for a particular environment, but rather it should be validated.

2.2.3 Combining unification and control libraries

Organisations rely on many applications across multiple platforms (SAP, Oracle, in-house developments, ...). There are many solutions available today that address the definition of controls as well as their enforcement and compliance. Most identity management solutions cover parts of this spectrum. Approva and Virsa focus specifically on the controls aspects. We used the Sage tool from Eurekify[2] in the case study. This tool allows unifying the authorisation data from the different platforms, and allows cleaning and optimising this authorisation data. For information on the mathematical foundation of the tool, refer to [Rymon93].

---

[1] Obviously the organisation may keep expired users and authorisations for historical reasons, these should however be separated from the active set.

[2] www.eurekify.com

Furthermore, it allows defining so-called Business Process Rules, which can be used to test for compliance.

3 Case study

3.1 The challenge

The case study organisation is a European company that is subject to both national competition regulation and the US Sarbanes-Oxley act. They employ approximately 25.000 employees. The company will be subject to Sarbanes-Oxley compliance audits as from January 2007.

They recognised the need to strictly manage authorisations, and initiated a company-wide identity management project. It is expected that this project will deliver what is required from an authorisation management perspective in due time. However, demonstrating regulatory compliance is not intended to be a direct outcome of the project. The primary challenge was to define compliance rules and to demonstrate that the actual authorisations across the various applications and systems comply with those. There were approximately 60 applications identified for which compliance needs to be periodically demonstrated. We will now discuss the case of one specific application, which we will call PICASSO.

3.2 The solution

A team from PwC was invited to create a solution. We based our solution on the application of our in-house developed control libraries on the PICASSO application, and on the Sage tool from the company Eurekify. We loaded the user and authorisation information, analysed the structure and contents of the authorisations and defined compliance rules. Analysing the structure and contents of the authorisations allowed us to recommend changes to the actual authorisations in place. Applying the compliance rules to the authorisation data allowed us to identify compliance violations (or through the lack of these, demonstrate compliance).

3.3 Role-mining the authorisation data

Initially we used the Sage product to identify potential improvements in the structure and contents of the authorisation data. This information was then fed back to the identity management project and the application owners.

The following tasks were performed. The authorisation files were extracted from the PICASSO application. This data was loaded into Sage via CSV[3] files, and enriched with user attributes from the HR database.

We then had the following basic authorisation data available:

---

[3] CSV: Comma Separated Values

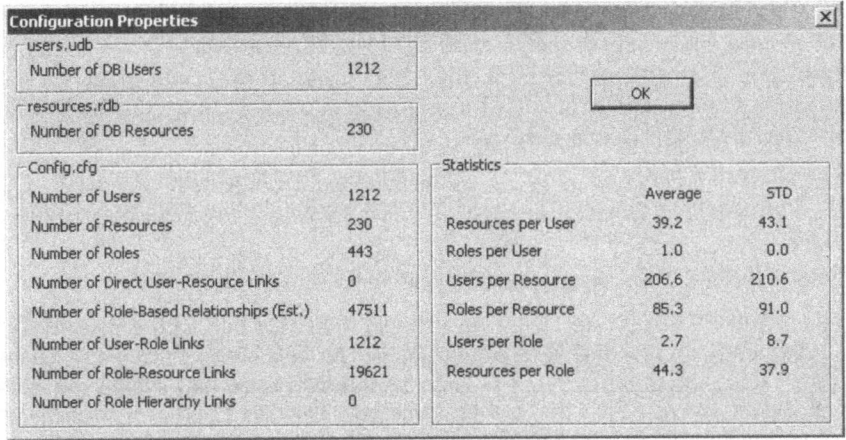

Figure 3: The dimensions of the actual PICASSO authorisations – Sage screen capture

As one can easily see, this configuration handled the authorisations of 1.212 users, via 443 roles onto 230 resources. There were no direct links from users to resources (as dictated by 'best-practice').

We made the following observations:

- 5 roles (32 users) have all resources – this is not in line with good practice;
- 22 users had no access to any resources at all – they were only present for historical reasons;
- 251 of 443 roles have no users at all (due to reorganizations – should be cleaned on a short term);
- 74 roles have only 1 user;
- Many sets of roles exist with the same (or almost the same) resources.

Furthermore, a significant number of users could not be related to the official HR database.

These observations were communicated to the Identity Management project which could take them into account when defining and simplifying their authorisation infrastructure.

However, it became quickly apparent that the compliance problem was even more important, due to the fact that a lack of compliance immediately results in business problems such as violating the US Sarbox policy, which has an immediate and significant impact (such as loosing the right to be quoted on a US stock exchange).

3.4 Defining and testing compliance via business rules

We implemented compliance rules via the business process rules of Eurekify's Sage tool. We will now discuss the consecutive steps performed and results obtained. These steps are: the definition of compliance drivers, the specification of business process rules, and the testing of the authorisation data according to those rules.

The first step consists in identifying the compliance drivers. We identified:

- The existing authorisations matrix, manually maintained in Excel;
- Restriction of a particular resource (PICASSO function) to specific employee classes - access to function F5909 restricted to billing employees (role R-HSE-BLL) and TNU disturbance analysts (role R-BPX089);
- Restriction of a particular function combination to a specific employee class - access to the combination of functions F5909-F5326 restricted to billing employees (role R-HSE-BLL);
- Users belonging to the 'retail' organisational unit may only have 'read' access.

Once all compliance drivers are identified, they are translated into BPR's (business process rules). These are XML files that specify constraints over the various elements of the authorisation data. The same authorisation data that were loaded for the role-mining can be reused. There are three types of BPR's that can be specified. They are referred to as business constraints, segregation of duty, and license.

The first type, business constraints, allow to express constraints on the following combinations:

- Role-Role – a restriction on the users in two sets of roles;
- Role-Resource – a restriction between the users in a set of roles and a set of resources;
- Resource-Resource – a restriction on the users in two sets of resources;
- User Attribute – Role – a restriction between users with a certain attribute value and a set of roles;
- User Attribute – Resource – a restriction between users with a certain attribute value and a set of resources.

The constraints that can actually be expressed are:

- Forbidden – Users in left side are not allowed to be on right side
- Must be – Users in left side must also be on right side
- Only allowed – Users in left side are only allowed to roles/resources on right side
- May be – Only users in left side (and not others) are allowed to roles/resources on right side

The second type, „segregation of duty" allows to express segregation of duty constraints either at the level of roles or at the level of resources. Finally, the third type is oriented towards license verification. As this was out of scope for the project we will not elaborate on it any further.

Let us now provide an example. The second compliance driver (access to function F5909 is restricted to billing employees (role R-HSE-BLL) and TNU disturbance analysts (role R-BPX089) is expressed as the following BPR-rule:

```
<BPR>
     <ENTRY TYPE="1201" ID="F5909" DESCRIPTION="Function 5909 should
     be restricted to billing functions and SNT disturbance ana-
     lysts">
          <LEFT F1="R-HSE-BLL"/>
          <LEFT F1="R-RPX069"/>
          <RIGHT F1="RELAY BDAF" F2="5909" F3="380"/>
     </ENTRY>
</BPR>
```

Obviously, the compliance analyst is not required to manually encode XML statements, the BPR definitions are created through a GUI.

Finally, testing the BPR's over the actual PICASSO authorisation data led to the following observations.

With regard to the first compliance driver (authorisations matrix), we identified six violations in the actual authorisation data. Both the second (functional restriction) and third (restriction on functional combination) compliance drivers resulted in six violations each. With regard to the fourth compliance driver (only 'read' access for members of the retail organisation) we found in total 151 violations. This included three persons that were within retail but simply had all possible authorisations.

4 Conclusion

Analysing existing access controls through a unified approach and applying compliance rules to them has shown to be a quick and reliable way for this particular organisation to demonstrate compliance (or identify actions where compliance was not yet achieved).

The fact that the control library is now available both at the level of principles (based on Sarbanes-Oxley and other regulations) and at the level of specific business process rules makes the approach both transparent and repeatable.

Furthermore, a number of observations were made that allowed to remove undesired authorisations through data cleaning.

As a result of the pilot the client decided to implement BPR-based compliance verification for all applications that are subject to Sarbanes-Oxley.

References

[Rymon93]   Rymon, Ron: An SE-tree based Characterization of the Induction Problem. In: Proceedings Machine Learning Conference, Amherst, MA, 1993.

[NIST2001] ACM Transactions on Information and System Security, Vol. 4, No. 3, August 2001, pages 224-274.

Robust and Secure Biometrics: Some Application Examples

T. Kevenaar · G.J. Schrijen · A. Akkermans · M. Damstra
P. Tuyls · M. van der Veen

Philips Research Europe
High Tech Campus 34 MS 61, 5656 AE, Eindhoven, the Netherlands
{tom.kevenaar | geert.jan.schrijen | ton.h.akkermans | marijn.damstra
pim.tuyls | michiel.van.der.veen}@philips.com

Abstract

In the past years there has been much theoretical interest in secure extraction of robust strings from noisy measurements. In particular this technique allows extracting robust cryptographic keys from noisy biometric data. This paper starts with an overview of the ideas behind robust and secure string extraction in terms of information reconciliation, privacy amplification and helper data. The main part of the paper gives three application examples explaining how these techniques are used to enhance the convenience and security of devices (e.g. tokens) while preserving also the privacy of the user because neither biometric information nor secret cryptographic keys need to be stored on applications. We discuss a server access token, a 3-way check for a biometric ePassport and a password vault.

1 Introduction

Biometrics have been studied for over 20 years but only recently we see an increase in the use of biometrics in ePassports, at airports, in cell phones, in PDAs, etc. Biometrics potentially offer more secure solutions because they are more tightly linked to an individual than, for example, a security badge or a password. They are also more convenient because unlike passwords and PIN codes they cannot be forgotten and are always at hand.

An inhibitor for the widespread use of biometrics is the privacy concern regarding storing personal biometric reference information in devices or databases. Even if legislation allows storing biometric information, public opinion still hinders the acceptance of biometric applications. Technological solutions that inherently protect the privacy of biometric information mitigate these concerns.

Recently techniques were developed to securely and privately extract robust keys from noisy data [MaWo99, BrSa93, GaMa94, LiTu03]. When these methods are combined with biometrics, they not only protect biometric information but they also enable new and more secure applications using biometrics. We give an overview of these techniques in Section 2 while Sections 3 to 5 give three application examples.

S. Paulus, N. Pohlmann, H. Reimer (Editors): Securing Electronic Business Processes, Vieweg (2006), 196-203

2 Key Extraction from Noisy Data

2.1 General Setting

In the past years there has been much interest in the secure extraction of robust strings from noisy data. A general setting (e.g. [MaWo99]) is given in Fig. 1 containing three parties traditionally called Alice, Bob and Eve. Alice and Bob communicate over a public, noisy communication channel and the adversary Eve eavesdrops this channel. The purpose of Alice and Bob is to derive, by communicating over their public channel, a common string about which Eve has only a negligible amount of information.

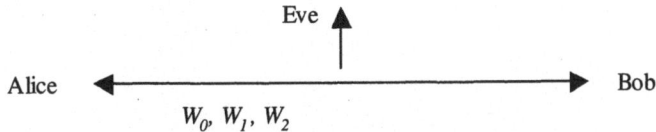

Fig. 1: General setting for secure extraction of robust strings from noisy data where W_0, W_1 and W_2 are the messages communicated between Alice and Bob.

Typically, Alice starts with a string X and Bob with a string X' correlated to X. Alice and Bob then go through the following steps.

- *Advantage Distillation* (e.g. [GaMa94]): by communicating W_0, Alice and Bob create a string X_1 (possibly with errors) about which Bob has more information than the attacker Eve and thus Alice and Bob have created an advantage over Eve.

- *Information reconciliation* (e.g. [BrSa93]): Alice and Bob exchange error information W_1 to correct errors in X_1 and arrive at a common string X_2.

- *Privacy Amplification* (e.g. [Shou05]): by communicating the information W_2 over their public channel, Alice and Bob compress the string X_2 to a string X_3 about which Eve has only a negligible amount of information.

In Section 2.2 we explain how to use this general setting in the context of biometrics.

2.2 Application to Biometrics

In order to use the general setting explained in Section 2.1 for biometrics, the roles of Eve, Alice, Bob and their public noisy communication channel are interpreted as follows: Alice is interpreted as the enrollment device, Bob is interpreted as the verification device, the communication channel is interpreted as storage in the biometric system and Eve is an attacker who has access to this storage. In this setting it is reasonable to assume that the enrollment device (Alice) and the verification device (Bob), that both have access to a biometric measurement of an individual, already have an advantage over an adversary who does not have access to the biometric measurement. Consequently, an Advantage Distillation step is not required. Thus, in order to extract secure and robust strings from biometrics, only two steps are required: Information Reconciliation and Privacy Amplification. A schematic representation of these steps based on so-called *helper data* [LiTu03, TuGo04] is given in Fig. 2.

For Information Reconciliation, during enrollment we have a biometric measurement X and a random string S generated by a Random Number Generator (RNG). From X and S, helper data W_1 is derived using a function $G(\cdot,\cdot)$ where W_1 is constructed such that

- it allows, during verification, reconstruction of S if a noisy version X' of X is available (using a function $F(\cdot,\cdot)$ in Fig. 2), and,

- it reveals little information about X and S [TuGo04].

A practical implementation of $G(\cdot,\cdot)$ and $F(\cdot,\cdot)$ [KSV+05] uses Error Correcting Codes, similar to the ones making Compact Discs insensitive to scratches and dirt. The information W_1 is stored in the biometric system.

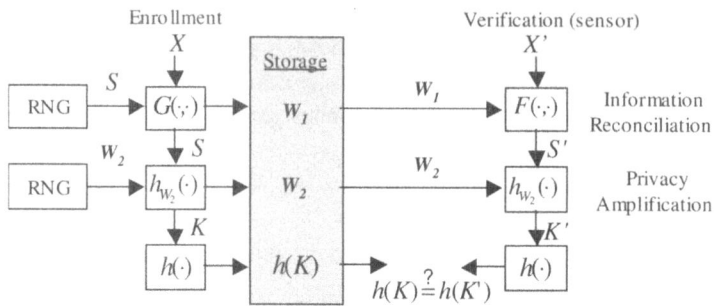

Fig. 2: The helper data architecture.

In some situations, the information that W_1 reveals about S is not small enough and Privacy Amplification is required which compresses S to a shorter, but highly secret string K. In order to obtain a highly secure key K, the compression function $h_{W_2}(\cdot)$ is chosen randomly from a family of compression functions and W_2 indicates the actual choice made during enrollment. Note that secrecy of K is retained even if W_2 is known [Shou05] such that W_2 can also be stored in the biometric system.

Summarizing we have that from an enrollment measurement X, helper data $W=(W_1,W_2)$ and a key K is derived such that W gives very little information on X and K and therefore W can be stored on an application. Then, given X or a noisy version X' of X it is possible, using W, to derive the key K. Depending on the application, the cryptographic hash value $h(K)$ of K can also be stored for reference because it is infeasible to find K from $h(K)$. The functionality explained in this section will be used in the following sections to describe three applications.

3 A Server Access Token

3.1 Introduction and Problem Definition

Corporate computing is becoming increasingly mobile as can be seen, for example, from an increase in the notebook to desktop shipment ratio of PCs [Kay05]. This means that an increasing number of employees connect to their corporate network from a remote location.

Traditionally, access to these corporate networks has been protected using a so-called server access token. These tokens, often implemented as a small key ring device, typically contain a secret key, an accurate time reference and a small LCD display. Based on the key and the time reference, some (cryptographic) function generates random access codes that appear in the display of the token. The corporate network also knows the secret key and using an accurate time reference it can verify if a proper token is used. In combination with a PIN code assigned to the owner of the token, access will be allowed to the corporate network.

In order to increase the convenience of using such a token, biometrics could be used rather than PIN codes. A preferred implementation would be to equip the token with a biometric sensor such that any PC could be used to log on to the corporate network.

A straightforward approach is to store biometric reference information in the token and if the offered biometric is close enough to the reference information, the token will send a random access code derived from the key and the time reference to the display. This approach has the drawback that biometric information and the secret key is stored in the token and both can be retrieved by reverse engineering. Another possibility is to attack the point where the decision on the similarity of the stored and measured biometric is made. The following section gives a solution for these problems using secure key extraction.

3.2 Deriving the Secret Key from the Biometric

In this section, we propose an architecture for securing the server access token using biometrics. The solution is such that neither biometric reference information nor the secret key is stored on the device.

In order to obtain a personalized server access token, an employee goes to the Corporate IT department where the following steps are performed (enrollment):

- A biometric (e.g. fingerprint) is measured several times resulting in a enrollment measurement X;
- Random values S and W_2 are chosen. From X and S the value W_1 is derived using $G(\cdot,\cdot)$ and $W=(W_1,W_2)$ is stored on the token;
- A secret key K is derived from S and W_2 as $K = h_{W_2}(S)$ and stored in the database of Corporate IT. The time reference of the token is synchronized with the reference of Corporate IT.

When the employee wants to log on to the corporate network, (s)he puts the proper finger on a sensor on the token and a measurement X' is obtained (see Fig. 3). The token computes K' using $W=(W_1,W_2)$ and combines this with a time reference to form a random access code ac_t which is shown on the display of the token.

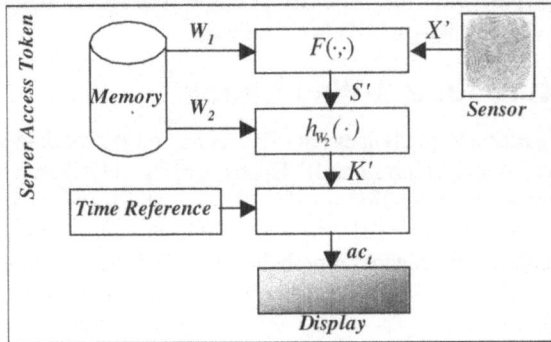

Fig. 3: Architecture for a secure server access token.

At the moment of logon, Corporate IT combines the stored value K with a local time reference giving an access code ac_c. If $X' \approx X$ we have $ac_t = ac_c$ and logon is allowed.

The proposed architecture enhances the security of the token because the secret key is not stored on the token but derived from a biometric thus thwarting a physical attack on the token. The architecture also does not compromise the privacy of the owner because no biometric information is stored.

4 3-Way Check for Biometric ePassport

4.1 Introduction and Problem Definition

The use of biometrics for identification or authentication of individuals implies that biometric reference information must be stored somewhere in a biometric system. Most commonly, this reference information is stored on a personal smartcard. An example is the Privium system [Priv] used for automatic border passage at Schiphol airport where reference information of an iris scan is stored on a personal Privium card.

However, many applications would benefit from storing biometric reference information on a central server or in a centralized database. One of the reasons is that this might lead to more secure applications because not all reference information is placed in the hands of possibly malicious individuals. The International Civil Aviation Organization (ICAO) [ICAO] recently proposed an optional 3-way check for the new biometric ePassport where a live biometric measurement is not only checked against the information on the passport but also against reference information stored in a database.

The main problems with the use of centralized databases are privacy concerns. In many countries legislation allows storing biometric information in centralized databases provided that (complicated) procedures are put in place regulating access to the stored information. However, public opinion and privacy interest groups still can delay or prevent the use of databases.

In the following section we propose an architecture for a 3-way check around the biometric ePassport where the reference information stored in a database contains no information on the biometric. Although the architecture will be explained for the ePassport, many other applications could benefit from this architecture. One could imagine an aircraft boarding system where the boarding card contains secure biometric information and where a 3-way check is performed against the passenger list. Another example is a soccer stadium entrance system where supporters are checked against a list of hooligans.

4.2 Architecture for a 3-Way Check

As can be seen from Section 2, the helper data W depends on the random values S and W_2 and different biometrics can result in the same W. Hence, storing only W in a biometric systems is insufficient for biometric authentication or identification and some representation of K must also be stored. We propose to store the cryptographic hash value $h(K)$ of K. The hash is required to prevent an attacker from generating helper data W for an arbitrary biometric X^* such that W and X^* together generate $h(K)$. It further prevents learning K (and X) from the stored information.

The architecture for the 3-way check we propose is given in Fig. 4 where Kiosk represents the location where a passport is checked. In order to explain the architecture we assume that when the passport is issued, secure biometric information of the form $(h(K_c), W)$ is stored in the passport and reference information of the form $h(K)$ is stored in a database. A 3-way check then proceeds as follows:

- The Kiosk reads $(h(K_c), W)$ from the passport and sends W to the Sensor;
- The Sensor performs a biometric measurement X' and combines this with W according to $S' = F(X', W_1)$ and $K_s = h_{W_2}(S')$ to generate a key K_s. The hash $h(K_s)$ is sent to the Kiosk.

- If $h(K_s) \neq h(K_c)$ authentication fails, otherwise the individual is considered to be the owner of the passport;

Next, the Kiosk verifies if $h(K_s)$ is in the database. Depending on the response, the Kiosk allows or denies the individual access.

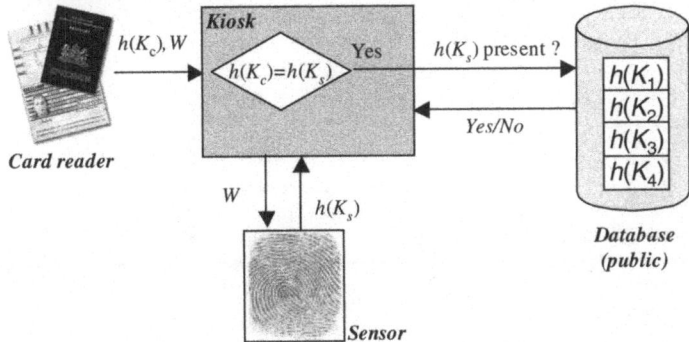

Fig. 4: Architecture for ePassport 3-way check.

Note that K is chosen independently from the biometric measurement X and thus $h(K)$ can reveal no information on X. Clearly, it is possible to add additional information, such as name and address, to a stored value $h(K_i)$ but for the biometric part of the system this is not required.

Summarizing we have presented a biometric system where biometric reference information can be stored in a central database without violating the privacy of individuals.

5 A Secure Password Vault

5.1 Introduction and Problem Definition

Nowadays people have to remember a large number of passwords and PIN codes. Besides PIN codes for bank accounts, the average computer user has to remember several different passwords for access to email, internet accounts, web services, etc. [Kay05]. Remembering all these passwords is inconvenient, especially when systems also require passwords to be changed frequently. Moreover, strong passwords are random sequences in which all allowed characters have an equal probability of being used. This, however, makes them inherently hard to remember for humans.

In order to make life easier, a user often chooses passwords that are easy to remember or writes passwords on a piece of paper that is kept close to the login terminal. Both methods are insecure: easy-to-remember passwords can be guessed without much effort and using a piece of paper allows a malicious individual to just read the passwords from the paper such that all the user's passwords are compromised at once.

We propose to solve these problems by introducing a Secure Password Vault (SPV) that uses biometrics and the techniques described in Section 2.

5.2 Architecture for a Secure Password Vault

The SPV is a small device that is easily carried by the user and consists of the following components: a biometric sensor (e.g. a fingerprint sensor), a small display for showing a password or PIN to the user, some memory for storing helperdata and a processing unit to process the biometric data that is read from the sensor. Optionally the SPV contains input means (e.g. a keyboard) allowing the user to choose a password and/or a random generator to generate random passwords. An example architecture of an SPV with keyboard and random generator is given in Fig. 5.

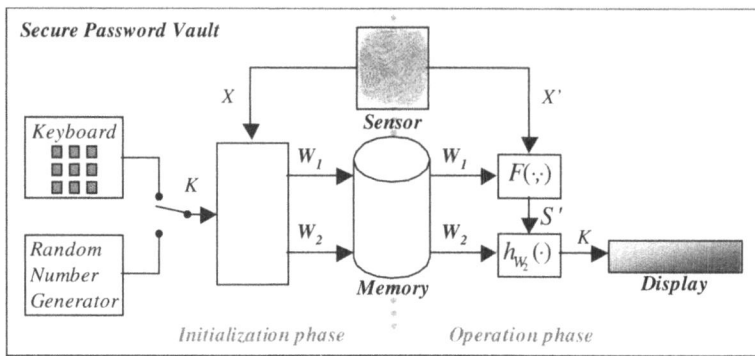

Fig. 5: Architecture for Secure Password Vault.

The basic idea behind the SPV is that it displays its user's password or PIN code whenever the user presents his biometric to the sensor. This is achieved by storing the appropriate helperdata $W=(W_1,W_2)$ in the memory of the SPV (see Section 2) during the initialization phase which contains the following steps:

- The user presents his biometric to the sensor (resulting in a measurement X) and enters the desired password K via the keyboard (alternatively, the SPV could use its Random Number Generator to generate a (strong) PIN or password K);

- Given X and K, the SPV generates helperdata W and stores it in memory (W is computed by choosing W_2 randomly and inverting $h_{W_2}(\cdot)$ and $G(X,\cdot)$);

Clearly, the SPV could also connect to an external device that enrolls the user, computes the appropriate helperdata W and stores it in the SPV's memory.

During operation, the user presents his biometric to the sensor and the SPV obtains measurement data X'. Subsequently, the SPV performs an Information Reconciliation step $S'=F(X',W_1)$ and a Privacy Amplification step $K'=h_{W_2}(S')$ using the stored helperdata W. This results in a reconstructed password or PIN code K' and finally K' is displayed on the display of the SPV such that the user can read the result.

Note that the actual password K is not stored in the memory of the SPV. In case the user loses his device, there is no risk of losing any private information. An attacker could read helperdata W from the memory, but this does not give him information about the password K or the user's biometric X.

Obviously, by storing multiple sets of helperdata in the SPV, multiple passwords can be retrieved for different applications and the user could select the required password by choosing the application. Finally, we note that the SPV could be built into another personal device such as a GSM phone or PDA.

6 Conclusion

In this paper we gave an overview of applications of secure and robust key extraction from noisy biometrics. The architectural design freedom provided by this functionality allows for a large number of applications in which biometrics can be used in a secure and private manner because neither biometric information nor secret cryptographic keys need to be stored on applications. The versatility of the approach was illustrated by describing three application examples based on secure and private biometrics.

References

[BrSa93]   Brassard, G, Salvail, L.: Secret-key reconciliation by Public Discussion, Advances in Cryptology, EUROCRYPT'93, Springer Verlag, LNCS 765, 1994, p.410-423.

[GaMa94]   Gander, M.J., Maurer, U.M.: On the secret-key rate of binary random variables. Proc.1994 IEEE International Symposium on Information Theory, p.351, 1994.

[ICAO]   http://www.icao.int/

[Kay05]   Roger L. Kay, "Protecting Mobility", IDC White paper, 2005
http://www.synaptics.com/support/Protecting_Mobility.pdf

[KSV+05]   Kevenaar, T.A.M, Schrijen, G.J., van der Veen, M., Akkermans, A.H.M. and Zuo, F.: Face Recognition with Renewable and Privacy Preserving Templates. Proc. 4th IEEE Workshop on Automatic Identification Advanced Technologies (AutoID 2005), Springer Verlag, LNCS 3546, 2005, p.21-25.

[LiTu03]   Linnartz, J.P and Tuyls P.: New shielding functions to enhance privacy and prevent misuse of biometric templates, Proc. 3rd Conf. Audio and Video Based Person Authentication (AVBPA 2003), Springer Verlag, LNCS 2688, 2003, p.238-250.

[MaWo99]   Maurer, U.M., Wolf, S.: Unconditional Secure Key Agreement and the Intrinsic Conditional Information, IEEE Trans. on Information Theory, Vol. 45, no. 2, 1999, p.499-514.

[TuGo04]   Tuyls P. and Goseling J.: Capacity and Examples of Template Protecting Biometric Authentication Systems, Proc. Biometric Authentication Workshop (BioAW, Prague 2004), Springer Verlag, LNCS 3087, 2004, p.158-170.

[Shou05]   V. Shoup, "A Computational Introduction to Number Theory and Algebra", Cambridge University Press 2005.

[Priv]   http://www.schiphol.nl/privium

Selecting the Optimal Biometric
2-factor Authentication Method –
a User's Viewpoint

Gunter Bitz

SAP AG
Dietmar Hopp Allee 16, 69190 Walldorf, Germany
gunter.bitz@sap.com

Abstract

We present the concept of a new biometric Smart Card based authentication method for our enterprise by discussing the motive, possible form factors and technological specialties such as using a TPM. Usability and user's feedback were determined through a pilot phase.

The business case is mostly determined by integration, thus rendering other existing authentication mechanisms and devices obsolete.

This paper discusses briefly conceptual advantages and disadvantages of 2-factor authentication methods and describes the decision making process we undertook in finding the optimal authentication method for our enterprise. We did a very thorough evaluation of an USB device containing a smart card and a biometric fingerprint reader. The pros and cons of this combination are discussed in detail and compared to other 2-factor authentication methods as well as to the old fashioned password (1-factor method).

1 Concept

We believe that single factor authentication methods such as passwords are no longer adequate to cover the information security risks a modern, multi national enterprise has to face. Passwords lack two important security criteria: They are not unique and they are not bound to a particular person. There are various ways to obtain a copy of a valid password: Shoulder surfing, malware and Trojan horses, key loggers and not to underestimate the intentional passing on of a password to a vacation stand-in or delegate. This is seen very often even if the company policy explicitly forbids employees to give their passwords to others – doing so is just more convenient than dealing with delegation rules.

To mitigate these risks to a certain degree you have to define measures such as increased password complexity (including numbers or special characters) and length, the need for changing it in regular intervals and of course defining unique passwords for different systems. We all know that this does not really work in practice: Firstly a huge number of different passwords will lead to the situation that employees keep on forgetting them and therefore creating help desk costs through password resets. Increased complexity and length, short change intervals have a similar or worse effect: it will lead to the situation that people simply write down passwords again. Remember, it took a long time and a lot of awareness campaigns to defeat the yellow post-it under the keyboard containing the list with all of the user's passwords.

S. Paulus, N. Pohlmann, H. Reimer (Editors): Securing Electronic Business Processes, Vieweg (2006), 204-210

Table 1: Comparison of different authentication technologies

	Password	**Wireless Token + PIN**	**Fingerprint Token**	**Cardio Token**
Use of duplicates	Possible, unde-tected	Not possible	Not possible	Not possible
Intentional propagation	Easy	Easy	difficult	Very difficult
Attack Vector	Guessing, brute force, shoulder surf-ing	Steal device & same as PW ap-ply	Steal device + obtain FP (cup, glass)	Steal device + obtain cardio-gram (very diffi-cult)
Support issues	High number of PW resets	Low number of PIN resets Lost & forgotten devices	Very low num-ber of Hardware failure Lost & forgotten devices	Very low num-ber of Hardware failure Lost & forgotten devices
User action	Regular pass-word change mandatory	Regular PIN change recom-mended	none	Re-enrolment (after years of use)
Privacy issues	none	none	None with "match on card" technology	None with "match on card" technology
Integration	none	Facility access, OTP possible	Facility access, OTP possible	Facility access, OTP possible
SSO	Via Password management tool	integrated	integrated	integrated
Investment	No direct costs loss of produc-tivity (pass-word reset)	> 150€ per seat high conven-ience	< 150€ per user high conven-ience	< 100€ per user high conven-ience

Therefore our favored concept uses smart cards, which offer a concealed storage for secrets. No one – not even the system administrator can copy a secret key from a smart card. In short: These devices can guarantee the uniqueness of the authentication device – it is impossible that two users can posses the same digital identity.

As second factor we use a biometric fingerprint reader [BSI04,Biot02] instead of the classical PIN to solve the problem of intentional passing on of credentials. The biometric unit is con-figured in such a way that fingerprints can be enrolled only once. A later re-enrollment can be initiated by an administrator but this will lock the smart card and requires erasing of all se-crets stored in it.

To ensure that the digital identity stored in the Smart Card matches the physical identity of the human being, the device is bound to the rightful owner by conducting the fingerprint en-rollment under the supervision of the local IT department. Ideally this is done when issuing the device to the end user. Even in case a user figures out how to reset the biometric unit and re-enrolls other fingerprints, still the smart card needs to be personalized again. This task must be initiated by the administrator, who would follow the process and erase the finger-prints again and repeat the enrollment process in full. So we have addressed the topic of passing on logon credentials successfully. By means of a technical impossibility employees now are forced to assign delegation rules, which will improve security significantly and reduce misuse of credentials.

Table 1 shows a technology benchmark which we used during our decision making process. We compared password, wireless solutions (very convenient but also very expensive), USB Tokens with fingerprint and USB Token with cardio biometry (see Chapter 5.2 for details).

We achieved a very good user experience, since remembering or changing of a password or PIN has become obsolete after implementing this solution. The Smart Card ensures that the device can not be duplicated, while the biometric part prevents misuse of the device by another user. Since the biometric data never leaves the device and there is no possibility to read the fingerprint data we also got a good rating in terms of privacy. This solution was accepted by all of our pilot users.

2 Integration

We put a very strong focus on integration. Access to all business relevant IT systems could be integrated by using a Smart Card based SSO solution. Furthermore the device supports our PKI rollout by acting as a personal certificate store, allowing E-mail encryption and Digital Signatures.

Other IT scenarios (e.g. remote access), which by company policy require the use of a 2-factor authentication method, were migrated to the new technology - making the existing authentication token obsolete. Also the wireless facility access card functionality and the wireless canteen payment system could be integrated into the new device by adding two transmitter chips to the device.

Combing the physical access control with IT access in a single device provides a huge security advantage since the employees are now required to take the authentication device with them when they leave the office, otherwise they can't get back in. This little trick solves a common issue of many 2-factor authentication methods. The hardware device is often left behind on the desk – or even worse the smart card or the USB Token will remain connected to the PC and therefore reducing the 2-factor authentication to effectively a single factor again. So in our case we really can achieve the goal that the authentication device is understood as a personal device.

It is very common that people don't behave in the same way as the security professional wants them to behave. If there is an easy way to get around it, the people will use the easier way. Typically they don't do that in purpose to defeat security controls they just take the path which creates less effort for them. So security should be designed in a way that the easy way is the most secure way or you have to make sure that there are no alternatives. We took this approach of eliminating alternatives by integrating the facility access into our authentication device.

Figure 1 shows all these components of our authentications device and supported applications as described above.

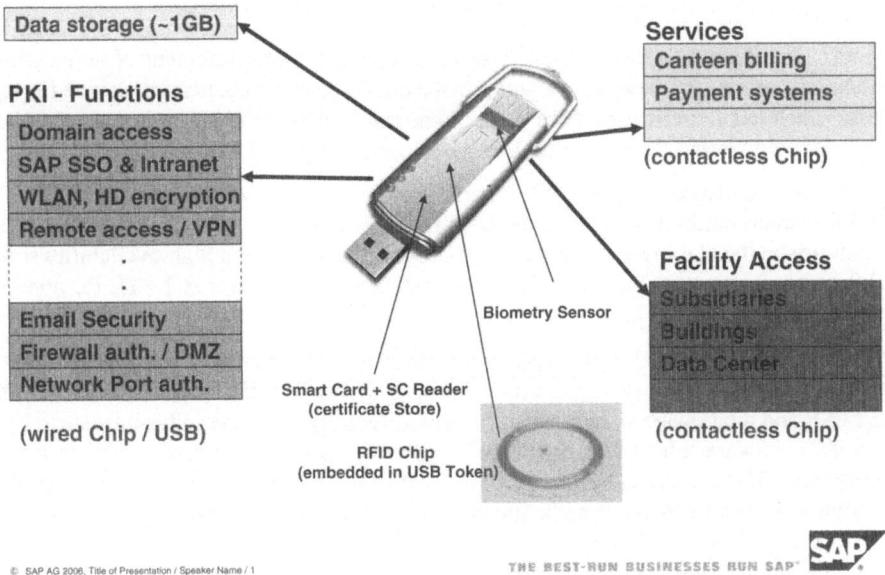

Figure 1: Components and Applications supported by the authentication device

3 Business Case

Obviously a successful consolidation of various authentication methods leads to a significant cost saving effect. Other contributions to a successful business case are savings through non-existent password resets and increased security. In our case we could save 2 FTEs in the help desk department dealing with password resets. In addition the employee efficiency will increase by avoiding calls to the help desk for the same reason. Roughly estimated the overall saved working time sums up to the same amount on the employee's side: about 2 FTE in our case.

Of course the password reset costs on the one side have to be compared to costs of lost or forgotten devices on the other side. While the costs of a replaced device are higher than a single password reset we expect an overall positive ROI since the number of lost devices is very small. It should be in the same range as lost car keys for example – how often did you loose your key recently? We expect initially a higher number of forgotten devices (e.g. employees forget them at home), which don't require a full replacement. Employees will bring back their device the next day. For these cases we will implement a cheap solution (most likely based on one-time passwords), which allows the employee to continue his or her daily work. But this "temporary access scenario" will not grant access to applications, which have a higher risk profile and therefore demand a secure user authentication – for example our HR system. This approach will not just save costs for replacement devices it will also induce a motivation element for the employee to remember carrying the authentication device to office as naturally as you take your door key when you leave home.

Our current access cards for the facility access can be replaced within minutes at the front desk. Since it is so easy there is little motivation for employees not to forget the card at home – which is proven by a large number of single-day replacement cards in relation to the number of employees. We expect this number to drop down to almost zero after the roll-out of the new device.

The next contribution to the business case is generated by a replacement of an existing authentication device. The new device will replace our 2-factor authentication device for remote access, which has a lifetime of three years. That means that the solution in place can be discontinued saving every 3 years the replacement costs of approx 2 Mio. €.

Our already established software PSE (single sign on) solution will be replaced by the hardware PSE (smart card). This adds to the savings as well. Since the certificates are now stored de-centrally on the employee's smart cards there is no demand for a high-availability software PSE Server infrastructure anymore. So server maintenance and approx 1 FTE for application maintenance can be saved here.

Increased security is actually the most important part of the business case but also the most difficult to measure. It is most important because the major difference between a software based PSE and a hardware based PSE is increased security. All other advantages can be realized with a software solution. A hardware based device and the biometrics adds to increased security only. The numerical approach to this part of the business case is by showing the risk reduction achieved by 2-factor authentication and by the strong binding to individuals. As a rough estimate the value of 76 € per user given by the CSI paper [CSI02] can be used. Nevertheless the risk reduction needs to be calculated for your enterprise individually. Helpful in this calculation are incident costs which lead back to weak user authentication. Good areas to search for these figures would be: Loss of intellectual property and monetary fraud. Of course the calculation of a risk reduction figure must be compliant to established risk management procedures in your enterprise; each business might have a different understanding of risk and also the risk acceptance level might be different.

Adding up all these factors together with the risk reduction of increased security leads to positive ROI in our case, if we assume a device lifetime of 5 years. Of course devices of employees leaving the company can be reused.

4 Form factor and user experience

The authentication device's form factor is very critical for achieving a positive user experience. It is discussed here which form factor (e.g. USB Token or "Bank" Card format) is the most convenient for the user. Roll-out issues and hardware cost have to be considered as well. The needs of mobile users differ from those of desktop users. While the first group dislikes additional devices, which have to be connected to the laptop every time (for a better convenience everything should be integrated), the latter group might find the combination of an authentication device with a mobile data storage device in the form factor of an USB thumb drive quite attractive.

Per definition a laptop computer is a mobile device. When considering a solution which attaches a new device to the computer, the mobility of the user should not be influenced in a negative way. Obviously it is for a mobile user more convenient to insert a smart card and use an integrated fingerprint reader rather than having an USB device attached to the computer by means of a cable.

Of course the integrated solution has other drawbacks. In particular you face the issue that hardware lifetime cycles are typically about three years. The investment to replace all end-user hardware at once is far too high. Furthermore all hardware vendors have to offer supported fingerprint readers otherwise the configuration and maintenance for different middleware to support all fingerprint devices might cause an additional cost factor. Integrated solutions are more convenient for the end user but create a significant challenge for the purchasing department. For desktop computers you need to roll-out additional fingerprint and smart card reader devices in order to be compatible with the laptop users.

These issues can be avoided by distributing the authentication device in the USB form factor to all end-users. The USB device contains all required components: Smart card, smart card reader, biometric fingerprint reader and in addition a flash memory (512MB up to 2GB) for data storage purposes. The hardware roll-out effort for desktops is limited to installing an USB extension cable with an integrated mount, which can be placed on the desk for better convenience. For laptops the roll-out costs are at the cost of an USB extension cable distributed with the token.

To increase the acceptance for mobile users we offer several methods of attaching the token to the laptop. When attached the mobility is good, the user is not hindered in his mobility by the device. When the employee leaves the laptop at his desk and walks away, the device can be detached from the laptop very easily.

We have conducted a large pilot to test the user acceptance of 2-factor authentication methods and biometrics in particular. The user feedback was good; most of the users do not have concerns with the fingerprint reading, since the biometric data is stored within their device only. In most cases the device authenticates the user with the first log-on attempt.

The log-on performance itself is also very good. Apart from the time needed to plug-in the USB Token a similar log-on time compared to traditional password log-on was be achieved. Unlocking the screen locked automatically by the screensaver is as fast as with passwords.

5 Alternative concepts:

5.1 The trusted platform module (TPM)

An alternative to Smart Cards could be given by using the TPM (trusted platform module) within the client PC instead. But doing so requires additional assumptions and a rigid use policy.

Using the TPM as storage location for secrets still fulfills one security requirement: the uniqueness. In this aspect there is no difference to smart cards. The TPM can be used as a certificate store and has the same ability of offering a storage location which is not accessible from the host. The private key stored inside the TPM cannot be copied; therefore the device is unique and can be used for authentication or signing purposes.

However there exists a significant and very obvious difference to smart cards. Since the TPM is part of the computer PCB ("main board") there is no possibility to remove it and use it as a personal authentication device. It is tied to the machine itself. From a security point of view a TPM offers a platform authentication rather than a user authentication. To achieve the same level of security as a personal device such as a smart card (regardless of the form factor as discussed above) the machine needs to be a personal machine used by a single employee only. The environment has to offer mechanisms to make sure that a potential attacker has no access to laptops of other employees. So either the company policy states that employees have to take home their laptop every evening (what we actually do in our subsidiaries in Asia – although just for theft reasons only) or every workspace needs to be equipped with some kind of locker which is big enough and secure to hold a laptop. Actually this is not a very cheap solution unless there is a need for lockers anyway to store confidential documents. And more importantly these policies have to be enforced – for example by guards, which could check for unsecured laptops in the offices every night.

Ignoring this will render the 2-factor "TPM" authentication method to a single factor authentication method effectively. Leaving a machine with a TPM containing log-on credentials in an unsecured environment is actually as problematic as not removing the authentication device from the machine as described earlier above.

5.2 Cardio sampling

Alternative biometric methods to fingerprint recognition are imaginable but most of them (face or voice recognition, palm geometry, iris scan) are too cost intensive or have high error rates, which would influence the user experience in a negative way.

However there is one method, which looks quite promising: cardio sampling. This method uses the electrical signal of the human heart beat as unique biometric feature.

The error rates are in the same range as for good fingerprint sensors, the signal recoding hardware is even much cheaper than a fingerprint sensor. Basically it requires two simple electrical contacts, which the user needs to touch with both hands for a period of 1-2 seconds. Personally I see a huge advantage over fingerprints simply by the fact that this biometric feature is not disseminated in the environment in the same way as fingerprints are. We leave our fingerprints on a lot of objects throughout the day. A skilled attacker could obtain these by picking them up from a glass or cup after the legitimate user left this object behind on the table. With cardio sampling this attack vector is not working anymore – an attacker would need to convince us to touch two contacts and allow him to sample the heart beat signal.

These new biometric solutions are close to market entry now and it might be a very good idea to have a closer look. At this point I did not have the chance for a deeper evaluation yet making it impossible for me to report any practical experiences.

6 Conclusion

We believe that we identified a very attractive authentication solution using a smart card based biometric authentication token with a very high degree of integration. Also analysts such as Gartner and Bill Gates itself predict that passwords are outdated soon (One year ago Gartner predicted the end of passwords by "End of 2006".). Therefore we should look for the ideal authentication technology, which fits our increased demand for security right now and get ready to implement it in 2007.

This publication will help in deciding if the 2-factor authentication approach using biometry as 2nd factor is feasible in your environment.

References

[BSI04]   Second BSI-Symposium on Biometrics 2004; Biometrics in the Reflection of Requirements; Bundesamt für Sicherheit in der Informationstechnik; SecuMedia Verlag, Ingelheim; ISBN 3-922746-55-1; 2004

[Biot02]   TeleTrusT Project BioTrusT; http://www.atbc.de/biotrust/

[CSI02]   CSI / FBI http://www.gocsi.com/press/20020407.jhtml

A Face Recognition System for Mobile Phones

Paolo Abeni · Madalina Baltatu · Rosalia D'Alessandro

Security Innovation, Telecom Italia
Via Reiss Romoli 274, 10148, Turin, Italy
{paolo.abeni | madalina.baltatu | rosalia.dalessandro}@telecomitalia.it

Abstract

The present paper proposes a biometrics-based authentication system for mobile devices running the Symbian Operating System. Mobile devices are becoming more and more similar to personal computers, hence they are also becoming repositories for sensitive information. In this context a more powerful authentication mechanism than simple passwords becomes essential. The paper describes a face recognition approach for mobile devices, discusses some important issues related to the practical implementation of the authentication scheme, and gives some preliminary results outlining the performances and the limits of proposed recognition system.

1 Introduction

The mobile industry continued to grow strongly throughout 2005 and this growth is expected to continue for several years to come. The number of mobile subscribers worldwide at the end of 2005 increased of 374 million and is expected to increase to approximately 3.964 billion by 2011 [Portio]. In the same time, the growth of the worldwide mobile phones penetration has shown no signs of abating. For example in Italy, Sweden and UK, penetration rose from 93%, 93% and 89%, respectively, in 2003 to 104%, 103% and 101% in 2004. This increase is explained by customers buying multiple phones and/or SIM cards, particularly in conjunction with the launch of 3G technology, and is expected to occur elsewhere, resulting in a penetration in excess of 100% for Western Europe as a whole by 2007.

However, in Western Europe mobile penetration is expected to near saturation, hence the operators are working at developing new mobile data services for sustaining and growing their revenues. Telecommunications operators are focusing their attention on content services, such as entertainment services, or more critical services, such as mobile banking, mobile commerce, mobile e-mail and so on. All these services are sensitive and involve considerable security threats. These threats will continue to raise with the increased sophistication of mobile devices, which are becoming more and more powerful. They offer more functionalities and to store and handle more data (e.g. sensitive personal or corporate data). Due to their incremented capabilities, though, mobile terminals are also becoming a more appealing target of attacks. Analysts said that from June 2004 till March 2005 at least six basic viruses had been detected for mobile phones, which had proliferated into some 30 variants as source code for them had been published on the Internet. In this context, the security threats for mobile devices cannot be neglected by Telecommunications operators. Some of the first security measures to be introduced are related to authentication.

S. Paulus, N. Pohlmann, H. Reimer (Editors): Securing Electronic Business Processes, Vieweg (2006), 211-217

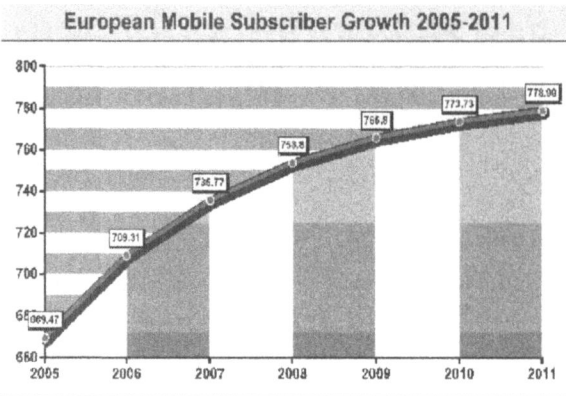

Figure 1. Foreseen European Mobile Subscribers Growth.

At the present moment, the most common authentication schemes used to protect mobile terminals are mainly based on passwords. It is commonly accepted that passwords represent a weak authentication method. Furthermore, in the current wireless world, the authentication credentials are generally easy to forge: they can be compromised through the interception of poorly protected wireless traffic. As a consequence, the need for stronger authentication mechanisms than simple passwords is fundamental.

More reliable authentication schemes may use biometrics in alternative to or combined with traditional mechanisms like tokens and passwords. Biometric techniques use a unique, physical or behavioral characteristic of an individual for automatically recognizing her/his identity [PaBoJa].

Since biometric identifiers are uniquely and permanently associated with their owners, they can efficiently prevent identity theft and un-authorized access to terminal resources and stored data. They cannot be lost or forgotten, they are rather difficult to forge, easier to use and they eliminate the need to carry tokens or remember secrets.

Currently, several mobile technology providers have announced the availability of biometrics-enabled mobile devices, in which biometrics is mainly deployed for terminal access protection. The main technologies used are face [TMCnet], voice [SKPHF], and fingerprint recognition [AuthenT].

In the present paper we discuss the potentialities of a novel biometric face recognition technique for mobile devices running the Symbian OS v8.0. In the following section we present the face recognition procedure. Afterwards, we describe some practical issues related to the implementation of the system. In the fourth section we provide some preliminary experimental results, outlining the performances currently achieved by the recognition engine on a Symbian OS v8.0 mobile phone. The paper ends with a conclusion section.

2 System description

The proposed face recognition algorithm is based on the one-class classification paradigm [DMJTax], which is a recently introduced approach to face recognition [BiGoTi]. Succinctly, one-class SVM is a kernel-based learning method able to learn unary classifiers only from positive examples of the user's class, thus avoiding the need to deal with the difficult task of creating an impostor training set.

The mathematical model we use was proposed by Scholkopf et al. in [SPSTS] for the estimation of the support of high-dimensional distributions. Basically, the algorithm returns a model f of the user's class that takes the value +1 in a small region containing most of the training vectors, and −1 elsewhere.

The system consists of two modules (as shown in Figure 2): the first for one-class SVM enrollment and the second for verification. The modules work on feature vectors extracted from live video sequences representing facial images. The operations performed in order to obtain the training and test vectors are:

- face detection based on the Viola et al. [JonVio] Haar detector and Ada Boosting for training;

- image normalization consisting in color conversion from RGB color space to gray levels, image scaling to a fixed size (e.g., 128 x 128 pixels) using bilinear interpolation, and image enhancement with the adaptive histogram equalization approach proposed in [JiSatSa] and the light direction compensation method proposed in [TanYes];

- features extraction by means of the bi-dimensional Fourier transform of the normalized gray levels face images and the selection of relevant Fourier coefficients from the resulting spectrum to form training or test feature vectors.

Face detection and image normalization are performed by the biometric sample acquisition module in Figure 2. The feature extraction is a separate module.

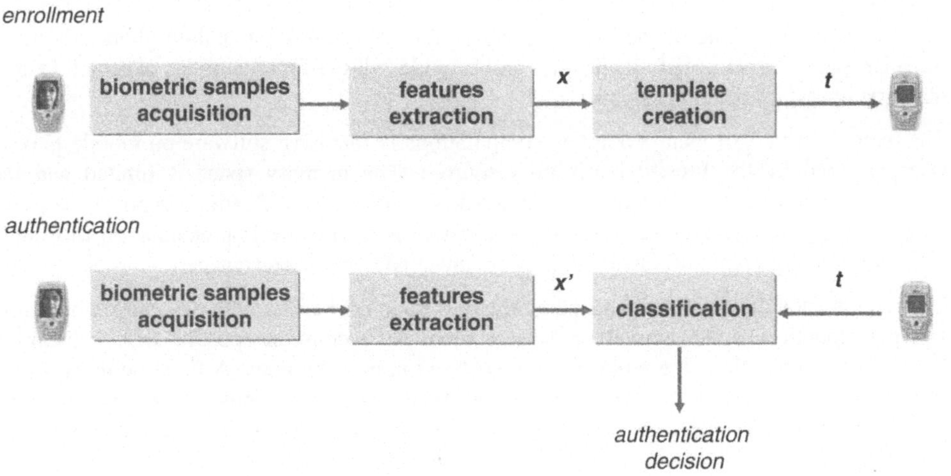

enrollment

authentication

Figure 2. The logical authentication system scheme.

If $L \times L$ is the dimension of the normalized image, and $f_{x,y}$ the gray value at position (x, y) in the image, then the bi-dimensional Fourier transform coefficient value $F_{u,v}$ at frequency location (u, v) depends on the entire image pixels and is given by:

$$F_{u,v} = \sum_{y=0}^{L-1} \sum_{x=0}^{L-1} f_{x,y}\, e^{-2\cdot\pi\cdot j\cdot\left(\frac{xu}{L}+\frac{yv}{L}\right)} \quad , \ j = \sqrt{-1}.$$

The Fourier spectrum of real face images is concentrated around the origin in a rhombus-like region. It can be demonstrated that almost all the information is contained near the centre, i.e., within the low frequencies. The low frequencies encode the most discriminant information about the user's face and, therefore, provide the best ground for the recognition system. Furthermore, because of the hermitian property of the bi-dimensional Fourier transform, it is sufficient to consider only the lower frequencies from two of the quadrants of the spectrum (e.g., the two upper quadrants). Actually, we determined empirically that a given number of coefficients of the upper quadrants are enough in order to obtain the maximum recognition rate. This number roughly corresponds to the upper quadrandts side equal to a quarter of the original Fourier matrix size ($L/4$).

During the enrollment phase, a one-class SVM is trained for each user using a training set of a configurable number of vectors (typically 15), extracted from live video sequences. These frames can be selected from the input sequence uniformly or so that no two equal images are chosen. At the end of the enrollment procedure, the user's model (the reference template t) is stored in her/his mobile phone.

During the verification phase, from each frame, a Fourier feature vector is obtained and processed using the OC-SVM corresponding to the subject. Thus, each feature vector produces a matching score, which represents the distance from the center of the user's class region. If the distance is below a given threshold, the subject's identity is confirmed. The final authentication decision is computed after all frames are processed using a simple majority voting scheme.

3 System implementation

The Symbian OS is one of the most popular operating systems for mobile phones. It has a modular micro-kernel based architecture and provides all the functionalities expected from a real time operating system [Digia].

The main drawback of using complex, computationally intensive software on mobile phones is represented by the limited hardware resources. The memory space is limited and the processors commonly used on mobile phones do not offer native floating support because of its complexity and hard power consumption. There is a software implementation of double precision floating point arithmetic but it offers un-satisfactory performances.

Our implementation is focused on finding the best trade-off between the recognition precision and the reduction of the overall processing time. As a consequence, the time consuming floating point operations are replaced by their fixed point analogous. A fixed point data type was implemented, which uses only native data types (integers), whose basic operations are directly supported by the ARM processor. The algorithm is faster but has lesser precision due to the quantization effects and to the fewer bits available for data representation.

The algorithms are mainly written in ANSI C using the POSIX standard as much as possible. Thus we take advantage of the existing prototype in C (for PCs) and of the ANSI/POSIX support offered by Symbian. The conversion from floating to fixed point concerns the image normalization algorithms, the features extraction and the classification modules.

The face detector is developed using the OpenCV library [OpCV], hence a part of the OpenCV library was modified and ported to Symbian. The Fourier transform was implemented "from scratch" using the Fast Fourier Transform (FFT) algorithm, while the OC-SVM classifier was implemented starting from the open source library LIBSVM [LSVM].

4 Experimental results

We tested both the floating and fixed point versions of the recognition algorithm on a general purpose PC and on a Symbian OS mobile phone. This permitted us to detect flaws and bottlenecks in the implementations and select the configuration with the best trade-off between the precision and execution speed.

We used a proprietary database built with respect to the guidelines suggested in [BiGoTi]. The database includes 40 subjects with 300 video frames for enrollment and 300 video frames for test. For each session, the video sequences were acquired in different days during one week, while the enrollment and test acquisition sessions were executed one week apart. The acquisition environment is not controlled, therefore the light conditions are different from one session to another.

In the best configuration, the normalized images size is 128 x 128 pixels and the Fourier upper quadrants size of 32 coefficients. The original input images for face detection are 320 x 240 pixels.

Table 1 presents the Equal Error Rates (EER) obtained by the original floating implementation and the fixed point implementation (both tested on an unconstrained PC environment). We note that the fixed point operations introduce a fixed error value of 0.81%, hence we can say that it does not have a dramatic impact on the accuracy of the recognition system.

Table 1. Equal error rates of the two implementations.

Implementation	EER [%]
Floating Point	5.14
Fixed Point	5.96

The same results are obtained running the algorithms on a mobile phone running Symbian OS v8.0, using the same video database. The execution time, though, is excessively long (mainly due to the face detection module), hence we were constrained to work with smaller 64 x 64 normalized face images and to limit the Fourier spectrum size. The original input images size for face detection is reduced to 160 x 120 pixels. With such a configuration though, the recognition rate decreases.

Note that, in this last case, the video sequences have been acquired with the mobile phone's video camera. As a consequence, the degradation of the error rate is also due to the reduced video camera capabilities, and the acquisition difficulties due to its intrinsic "mobility". For this reason, we also experienced some problems in the initial video acquisition phase of the verification process. In average, 5% of the subjects needed more than 40 seconds to correctly use the recognition system on the mobile phone, because the recognition phase will not start unless the face detection phase is successful. Practically, all the users needed a preliminary training session to be able to correctly handle the mobile device and the recognition software. To maintain a reasonable tread-off between the error rate and the execution time, we work with Fourier quadrants of size 12, obtaining an average execution time value of 1.4 seconds per frame, the bottleneck of the system being represented by the detection module, and an accuracy of the recognition of 90% at the EER = 10%. We estimated that a third of the deterioration of the recognition rate is actually due to the physical instability of the mobile environment.

The results presented up to now are computed considering a global decision threshold. If we work with individual thresholds (like suggested in [BiGoTi]), the recognition rate improves significantly. For the best trade-off configuration we obtain an average enhancement of 4% of the EER for the "mobile" database of video sequences (hence, with an Equal Error Rate of 6%).

5 Conclusions

This paper described the main issues related to the implementation and use of a face recognition system based on one-class Support Vector Machines for mobile phones running the Symbian OS.

From the implementation perspective, the difficulties encountered were the limited memory and processing power, and the lack of support for floating point arithmetic. The preliminary results show that in order to maintain a reasonable processing speed the algorithm has to be used in a configuration that yields high error rates with respect to the algorithm's potentiality. We noted that, globally, the conversion to fixed point arithmetic had less impact on the error than the low image resolution necessary to reduce the execution time of the face detection module.

From the deployment perspective, we can say that the current devices ergonomic can be improved in order to facilitate the use of the video camera, which should be centrally place on the device's front end. Even so, the users needed a period of preliminary training to get accustomed with the correct use of recognition software.

A future improvement is the development of the image processing functions in hardware, using the DSP capabilities of the latest Symbian mobile devices. The light normalization algorithms have to be improved to better adapt to the rapid light condition changes due to the intrinsic "mobility" of the recognition software.

References

[PaBoJa]   Pankanti, S., Bolle, R.M., Jain, A.K.: Biometrics: The Future of Identification. In: IEEE Computer, Vol. 21, No. 2, 2000.

[TMCnet]   TMCnet News: Oki Electric Releasess Image Processing Middleware that Supports Face Recognition for Use in Mobile Phones, http://news.tmcnet.com /news/2005/oct/1195024.htm, October 2005.

[SKPHF]   Saastamoinen, J., Karpov, W., Hautamäki, V, Fränti, P.: Accuracy of MFCC based speaker recognition in series 60 devices. In: EURASIP Journal on Applied Signal Processing, Issue 17, 2005, p. 2816-2827.

[AuthenT]   AuthenTec: The TruePrint® Technology for PDAs and mobile phones, http://www.authentec.com/technology.cfm.

[BiGoTi]   Bicego, M., Grosso, E., Tistarelli, M.: Face authentication using One-Class Support Vector Machines, In: International Workshop on Biometric Recognition Systems, 2005.

[DMJTax]   Tax, D.M.J.: One-class classification: Concept learning in the absence of counter examples, Ph.D. Thesis, University of Delft, 2001.

[SPSTS]   Scholkopf, B., Platt, J. C., Shawe-Taylor, J., Smola, A.J.: Estimating the Support of
            a high Dimensional Distribution. In: Neural Computation, MIT, No. 13, 2001, p.
            1443.

[JonVio]   Jones M., Viola, P.: Rapid Object Detection using a Boosted Cascade of Simple
            Features. In: IEEE Conference on Computer Vision and Pattern Recognition,
            Vol. 1 , 2001 pp. 511.

[JiSatSa]   Jin, L., Satoh, S., Sakauchi, M.: A Novel Adaptive Image Enhancement
            Algorithm for Face Detection. In: 17th International Conference on Pattern
            Recognition, 2004.

[TanYes]   Tankus, A., Yeshurun, Y.: Convexity-Based Visual Camouflage Breaking, In:
            Computer Vision and Image Understanding, Vol. 84, No.3, 2001, p. 234 – 778.

[OrlDb]   The ORL database of faces, http://www.uk.research.att.com/facedatabase.html.

[Digia]   Digia Inc.: Programming for the Series60 Platforms and Symbian OS, Editor:
            John Wiley&Sons, Chichester, UK, 2003.

[OpCV]   OpenCV, The Open Computer Vision Library, http://sourceforge.net/projects
            /opencvlibrary/.

[LSVM]   LIBSVM, A Library for Support Vector Machines, http://www.csie.ntu.edu.tw
            /~cjlin/libsvm/.

[Portio]   Portio Research, Mobile Factbook 2006, http://www.portioresearch.com.

Advanced certificate validation service for secure Service-Oriented Architectures

Antonio Ruiz-Martínez · Daniel Sánchez-Martínez
C. Inmaculada Marín-López · Antonio F. Gómez-Skarmeta

Department of Information and Communications Engineering
University of Murcia, Spain
{arm | dsm | inma | skarmeta}@dif.um.es

Abstract

One of the most important components in e-commerce systems is the validation of digital signatures, which implies the validation of certificates in order to check the validity status of the certificates used to create a signature. Nowadays, several mechanisms to accomplish this process exist, but there is no agreement with which particular mechanism should be used in each scenario. On the other hand, infra-structures based on web services are widely spread due to their several advantages, so it is necessary to adapt the existing services to the new frameworks. There already exists a proposal for a digital signature web service, but there is not any for certificate validation. In this paper we propose a validation service which considers the existing validation certificate mechanisms, that is, it is not restricted to use only a particular protocol, with the aim of satisfying different domains in a homogeneous way, keeping the validation process under client control.

1 Introduction

E-government platforms and e-commerce systems require the use of signature services so as to offer non-repudiation services. As an essential component of this kind of services, the certificate validation is one of the most important tasks that have to be performed by these systems. Thus, they are usually the responsible for checking certificates from different domains and through different validation protocols.

Nowadays, those infrastructures are based on web services and Service-Oriented Architectures (SOA). These architectures introduce some interesting advantages such as the use of XML for the message description and standard protocols, like SOAP or HTTP for message transport, high degree of compatibility between applications, the registration possibility through UDDI or the simple interoperability between web services, making the extensibility and the integration inside other distributed applications and services easier.

Up to now, although there is a proposal for an electronic signature service based on SOA, such as OASIS DSS [DreesS06], there is not any similar proposal for certificate validation services. However, these services become essential in any secure application and they should be invoked inside electronic signature verification and user authentication process. In this paper we are going to propose an advanced certificate validation service according to the OASIS DSS philosophy, offering important benefits such as flexibility and adaptability to different kinds of clients, different certificate validation mechanisms and different PKIs.

S. Paulus, N. Pohlmann, H. Reimer (Editors): Securing Electronic Business Processes, Vieweg (2006), 218-227

In section 2, we are going to describe some issues related to the validation of certificates, such as path construction and path validation. Then, we mention briefly the main mechanisms that are available to perform these tasks nowadays: Delegated Path Discovery [PH02], Delegated Path Validation [PH02], Data Validation and Certification Server [ASZ+01], Standard Certificate Validation Protocol [FHM+05] and SAVaCert [BL02]. Besides, we discuss why these multiple options could become a problem for signature services.

In section 3 a new validation architecture is proposed. We present its most important objectives and its main components (clients, PKIs and certificate validation service), trying to establish the relationships among all of them. At this point we analyze the different types of potential service clients (thin and thick), making especial emphasis on the simple requirements for using the service. Next, as an important part of the architecture, we explain, in a detailed way, the main characteristics of the service as well as its functionality.

In section 4 we introduce some possible application scenarios for this service, such as electronic government platforms, to verify identities and electronic signatures, third trusted parties offering add-value electronic commerce services in business processes, mobile environments with thin clients that need certificate validation support, and add-value services for a public key infrastructure based on service-oriented architectures.

Finally, in section 5, we point out the main conclusions and introduce some possible future work.

2 Certificate validation

In this section we analyze the process to be carried out in order to validate a certificate. We also review the main existing mechanisms that our certificate validation service has taken into account.

With the purpose of validating a certificate, the following steps must be executed:

1. Building one or more candidate certification paths between the certificate and an established point of trust. This is called *path construction* or *path discovery*.

2. Checking that each certificate in the paths is valid, that is, its structure is correct and honours certain constraints (such as path length constraints, name constraints or policy constraints), it is within its established validity period, it has not been revoked (the data inside the certificate are valid) and the issuer's signature over the certificate is valid. This step is called *path validation*.

The process consisting of these two steps is referred to as *certification path processing* [PKIF02]. The certification path processing is a complex process. With the aim of facilitating it, several mechanisms have appeared. These are in charge of performing all or part of the process on behalf of the relaying parties, providing them with valid results. These mechanisms are, apart from the typical validation ones, CRLs [HPF+02] for off-line validation and OCSP [MAM+05] for on-line validation, DPV [PH02], DPD [PH02], DVCS [ASZ+01] and SCVP [FHM+05], which are commented next:

- Delegated Path Discovery (DPD) is a set of requirements to be taken into account when we define protocols with delegated path discovery processing. With this kind of protocols, a client can gather at one time, by sending a unique request to a particular server, all the information that might be obtained using different protocols or by querying multiple servers, necessary to know the validity of a certificate in the current time, according to a concrete discovery policy.

- Delegated Path Validation (DPV) is a set of requirements to be taken into account when we define protocols with delegated path validation processing. Using this sort of protocols, a server can validate (validation on-line) public key certificates, performing path discovery optionally, on behalf of a client in a time (past or current) according to a concrete validation policy, thus reducing client complexity.

- A Data Validation and Certification Server (DVCS) is a trusted third party in charge of attesting the validity of some kind of elements, specifically, public key certificates. Assertions generated by this server are signed and are called Data Validation Certificates (DVC). Once a DVC is created, it is only necessary to validate it in order to determine the validity, in the time indicated, of the data to which the DVC is associated.

- The Standard Certificate Validation Protocol (SCVP) allows a client to delegate certificate path construction and/or certificate path validation to a server, according to a discovery policy and/or validation policy, respectively, with the goal of making it easier to deploy PKI-enabled applications. This protocol is compliant with DPD and DPV.

As we can see, there are many mechanisms to know a certificate revocation status and protocols that allow the interaction with servers which perform certification path discovery and/or certification path validation. This involves a problem when implementing a signature service, since it might be conscious of their existence and, therefore, support all of them, with unawareness of their particular details. This is due to the fact that every PKI can offer different mechanisms to make certification path processing. Therefore, this aspect makes the signature service development more difficult and complex. Besides, this service must be able to archive certificate status information in order to demonstrate, in a future, that a particular signature was valid in a past time.

There exists an interest in resolving this aforementioned problem and, as a consequence, an architecture for the delegated validation of certificates has been proposed. This architecture is called SAVaCert and is commented next.

2.1 SAVaCert

SAVaCert [BL02] is a Secure client-server Architecture for the Validation of X.509 Certificates where a client delegates only path discovery or both path discovery and path validation to a server. This architecture consists of some modules defined generically and allows developers to choose particular protocols, validation mechanisms and the underlying support, both on the client and server side.

SAVaCert supplies clients with the possibility of configuring some parameters in order to control the validation process. Such parameters are:

- Indication of what information used during path processing must be returned (Validation Parameters).

- Set of acceptable certificate policies for the CAs in a certification path (Certificate Policy Processing Parameters).

- Other parameters specific to the protocol between client and server (Validation Protocol Module Parameters).

The modules implied in the validation process, which are depicted in Figure 1 [BL02], are the following:

- Validation Module. The server validation module has these sub-modules:

  o Validation Protocol Module. It is in charge of managing requests and responses exchanged with client throw link L1.

  o Path Validation Module. It is responsible for obtaining the validation status of the requested certificate by accomplishing certification path validation.

  o Path Construction Module. It constructs certification paths for the requested certificate.

  o Certificate Status Module. It determines the revocation status of a certificate.

  o Policy Processing Module. It consists of two sub-modules: one for processing certificate policies and the other one for processing validation policies.

  o Time Module. It supplies an indication of time.

- Storage Module. It is appointed to store and/or retrieve certificates, certificate revocation data and policies.

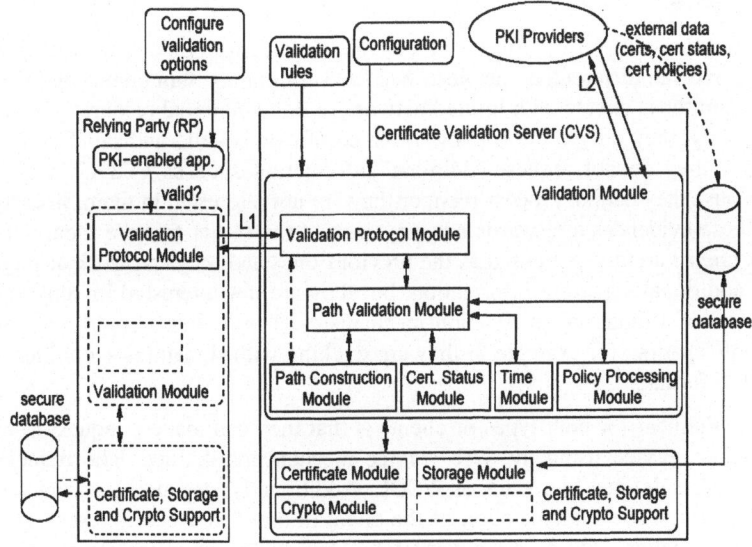

Figure 1: SAVaCert Modules

3 Validation architecture

3.1 Goals

Bearing in mind the problems previously mentioned, our proposal pursues as the main objective to design a certificate validation service which integrates the already existing validation mechanisms, as well as to support multi-PKI scenarios, to accept various kinds of certificates (not only Public Key Certificates but also Attribute Certificates and so on) and to provide and/or store validation evidences for future non-repudiation checking operations (CRLs, OCSP responses and so on).

To achieve this, we have taken into account the existence of two different types of clients, each of them determines a different service policy configuration. On the one hand, we consider clients that, due to either a lack of resources or ignorance in relation to security policies, need to trust a server which carries out the certification path processing on behalf of them. On the other hand, there exist clients that only need a server to evaluate the certificate policies and build certification paths or supply them with on-line responses (OCSP responses), so these clients can accomplish path validation by themselves. Besides, clients do not have to be aware of either existing validation mechanisms or the different services provided by each PKI.

3.2 Design

In the previous section we have commented the main requirements that we consider an advanced certificate validation architecture should satisfy. Next, in this section, we describe the different elements and components that should be part of the architecture and we define the relationships among them in order to satisfy the proposed goals. These components are: clients, PKIs and the certificate validation service. Now, we are going to comment the main features provided by each component.

3.2.1 Clients

Clients request the status of certificates in a concrete moment in time to the certificate validation service. We can differentiate between two kinds of clients: thin clients and thick clients. Thin clients are those clients with limited network or computational resources such as mobile devices. Usually, they only want to know if the certificate is valid and satisfies a determined policy. Thus, they do not request additional information such as CRLs, OCSP/SVCP responses because they cannot process them or they are not interested in them. In case these clients need these evidences afterwards on, they request the server to store them. On the other hand, thick clients are not as limited as the previous ones and they can work or might need to work with additional signature information, but they are not interested in supporting all the different kinds of validation certification mechanisms. These clients could make use of this additional information, for example, if they are working with signatures according to the XAdES [ETSI06] format.

The only requirement for both types of clients is that they can make a request to the Certificate Validation Service using the web service mechanisms defined. The requests and responses content is defined by means of WSDL. Additionally, depending on the scenario, the server could require the authentication of the client in order to access the service. The basic element in a validation request is the certificate. Optionally, the client can specify a time to validate the certificate at and a validation policy. If the time is not specified, the server validates the certificate at the reception moment. Similarly, if the policy is not specified, the server applies the default policy. Apart from requesting the status of a certificate in a concrete time, the client can specify the behaviour of the server in the process of validation by indicating, for example, the validation mechanisms or requesting additional validation information related to the validation process, such as answers and responses used, the path of the certificate up to a trusted point, a timestamp, and so on.

3.2.2 PKIs

In PKIs, the CA is the responsible for indicating the revocation status of a certificate. This status could be provided by means of different services such as CRLs, delta CRLs, OCSP, SVCP, proprietary mechanisms, and so on. For example, in the Spanish PKI (FNMT), the access to the CRLs or OCSP is a restricted feature that can only be granted to such entities that have paid for this service.

3.2.3 Certificate Validation Service

The description of the certificate validation service is carried out from two points of view. On the one hand, it is necessary to explain the architecture of the service. On the other hand, we describe the functionality and the protocol that the service follows.

As for the architecture of the service, we can say that it is based on SAVaCert. This architecture has been already commented in Section 2. Additionally to the components previously defined, our aim is to extend it with other new additional components such as: an authorisation module, an asynchronous request module and a service policy management module. These components are shown in Figure 2. The authorisation module is needed because the service could be offered by an entity that limits the access to the service to its own users, as it could occur in an enterprise that is paying for the services of a PKI. The asynchronous request module offers the client the possibility of requesting the validation of certificates in a subsequent moment, that is, it is not mandatory to answer in an on-line way a certificate validation request. Finally, the service policy management module allows the management of different policies and profiles in order to specify how the service has to work. The goal of this module is to simplify the operation of the service as well as the client's request to the service. Thus, we associate a set of parameters and a behaviour to a concrete profile, so the client only has to include this profile in the request instead of all the parameters.

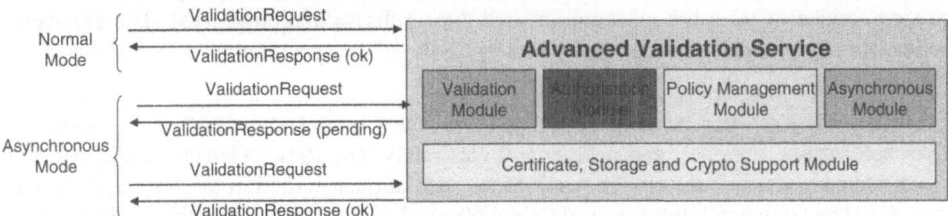

Figure 2: Advanced Certificate Validation Architecture

The service has a module for each validation mechanism mentioned in section 2. Besides, the service offers the possibility of supporting proprietary modules. Any of the mechanisms is referenced by means of the assignment of a URI. The client, in a request to the service, can specify the mechanisms to make the validation with. Moreover, the client can specify the whished priority for each mechanism. The service offers both certificate validation and path construction. The client can specify if he wants the service to make either tasks or only one of them. Additionally, the validation request allows the specification of parameters related to the validation task such as trust anchors to be used, parameters of a particular mechanism, data that the answer should contain according to the mechanism, and so on.

As for the functionality, the service is defined according to the design of a service-oriented architecture, that is, by a web service described in WSDL, whose methods use the document style. As it is depicted in Figure 2, the protocol is composed of three messages called *ValidationRequest*, *ValidationResponse* and *PendingRequest*. The *ValidationRequest* message is used to query and get information about the status of a (some) certificate(s). The *Validation-Response* message is the response to the *ValidationRequest* message. Finally, the *PendingRequest* message is part of a polling protocol used to check if a response is ready. Thus, we support an asynchronous mode in the protocol similar to the proposed one in DSS.

The *ValidationRequest* message is composed of three main components: *InputCertificates* (mandatory), *OptionalInputs* (optional) and a *Signature* (optional). The *InputCertificates* element contains a(some) certificate(s) that has(have) to be validated and through this, to get information about their status. The *OptionalInputs* element allows the specification of the rest of the parameters related to the validation and the information to be retrieved. We have defined some elements, which could be included in these ones, such as the exact time in which the certificate(s) has(have) to be validated (*ValidationTime*), the concrete protocols to make the validation (*ValidationProtocols*) with, the information to indicate that the service should make the complete path validation (*CertificationPathValidation*), and if the certification path should be returned in the response (*ReturnCertificatePath*). Besides, we have defined this message in such a way that the same verification mechanisms are applied and the same information is returned for all certificates indicated in the *InputCertificates* element. Thus, in the same request, it is not possible to validate a certificate in a different way, with different parameters. We made this decision in order to maintain the simplicity of the protocol and reduce the processing of complex structures on the server side. The access to the service could be authenticated by means of https or credentials such as SAML Assertions or Archifacts [CKPR05].

As a response to a request, the service could only send either a simple response indicating if the certificate is valid at the moment specified, or a more elaborated one with the complete path certificate chain, the answers returned by the mechanisms used, and so on. The service could also store the validation information provided that the client requested. This is useful when the resources of the client are limited or when we want a trusted party to offer us an archiving service to store the information used during the validation process. The parameters indicated in the request could be simplified by means of the specification of a policy and profile.

The *ValidationResponse* message is composed of three main elements: *Result* (mandatory), *OptionalOutputs* (optional) and a *Signature* (optional). The *Result* element is returned with every response and it indicates the result of the validation specified in the *ValidationRequest* message. The *OptionalOutputs* is used to include all the information asked in the request message. It is a similar approach to the *OptionalInputs*. Here, we have defined two elements: one to indicate the validity of the certificate and the information related to its validation (*CertificateValidity*) and another one to include the information about the path of each certificate (*CertificationPath*). Finally, the response message could be authenticated by means of a signature.

We have defined this service in such a way that it could be offered by a PKI as an additional component to allow interoperability or, it could be offered by an external entity, such as a trusted third party, or even it could be used inside an enterprise in order to avoid the complexity of the different validation mechanisms. In the following section we will comment some possible application scenarios.

4 Scenarios

The certificate validation service we propose has several application scenarios in different kinds of contexts. Next we are going to analyze some of them, making especial emphasis on the obtained benefits.

The first scenario in which this service could be applied is an electronic government platform that integrates the possibility of using certificates of different qualified certificate service providers (CSPs). These platforms are necessary in government context such as in the Spanish one. Besides, these platforms work with several CSP which generate different kinds of certificates and offer several certificate path processing mechanisms. This fact makes the process of validation difficult for the end clients because they have to support all of them. In this scenario, this type of platform makes use of certificates from different very simple CSPs, offering a central trusted point to electronic government services, and facilitating the incorporation of new CSPs certificates.

Another interesting scenario emerges in electronic commerce services. Small and medium businesses, which want to offer services to a large amount of potential clients, need to accept heterogeneous certificates in their commercial transactions. For the purpose of resolving this problem and trying to offer value added services to these businesses, new trusted third parties (TTPs) appear in this context. Some examples of these services are the parsing of different certificate fields, the transformation between several electronic signature standards or electronic billing formats, the time-stamping of electronic documents, and especially the validation of certificates against different CSPs. For these last value added services, our proposal is the best approach. And furthermore, it offers similar benefits than the previous scenario, highlighting the interoperability between certificates for this one.

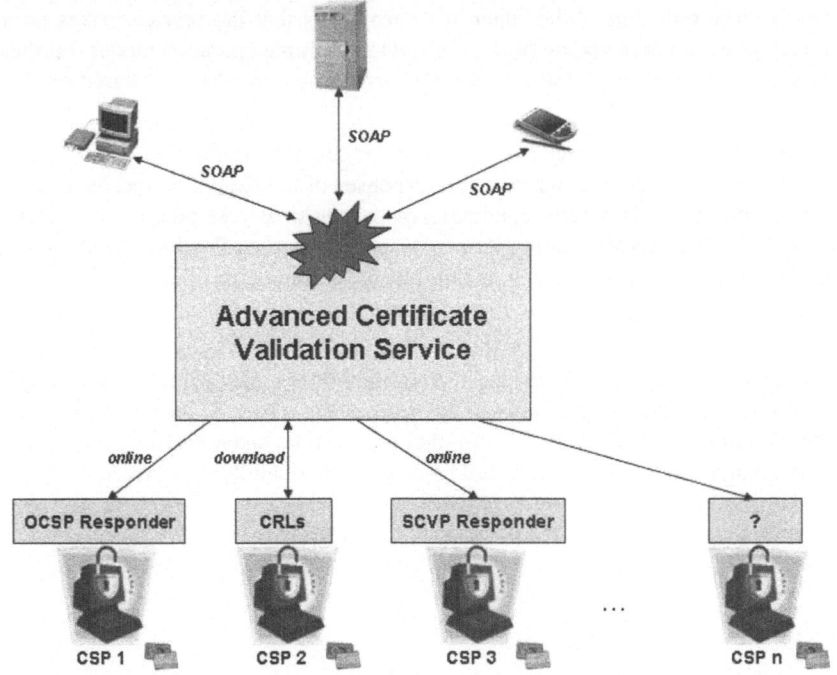

Figure 3: E-Government platform scenario

The third scenario is about thin clients. These clients have limited network or computational resources and are not able to support different mechanisms to check the certificate status. This context is usual in mobile devices, where clients only need to know if a certificate is valid to perform a transaction (for e-billing, e-commerce, e-government or whatever service that requires an electronic identity). For these devices, their network operator or some trusted partners could offer this centralized service as a value added service, making possible the incorporation of these phones and PDAs in electronic signature workflows.

Finally, we suggest another example of scenario for a PKI as a value added service. Usually, when a client needs to validate a certificate against a PKI, he has to analyze its certification practices document (CPD) to know the standards supported by that PKI, and finally he has to implement or install a proper client to work with the suitable protocol (CRLs, OCSP, SCVP...). Adding the proposed service as a new PKI one, different kinds of clients could validate certificates through a web service and a service-oriented architecture (SOA) with independence of validation protocols.

5 Conclusions and future work

As can be seen in the scenarios previously analyzed, the architecture and service we propose are designed taking into account some important characteristics. First, the service is a web-service offered over a SOAP transport protocol and therefore, it is possible to integrate it in a service-oriented architecture (SOA), getting important benefits in extensibility and interoperability with other distributed applications and services.

What is more, the architecture proposed supports different kinds of certificate status checking protocols and mechanisms that could be chosen by the clients. It also offers the possibility of checking certificates from multiple PKIs, facilitating a distributed environment with different certificate services providers. Other interesting feature is that the service makes possible a configuration based on policies and profiles, allowing multiple operation modes. Furthermore, through its authorization module the service can perform a control access based on the client credentials.

This service makes the retrieving and storing of additional information about a certificate validation process easy, such as answers and responses of the validation mechanisms. This is essential in scenarios in which non-repudiation evidences have to be present. Moreover, it can work asynchronously, making the request-response process more flexible. Finally, it is adaptable to different kinds of clients, such as thin clients, e-commerce clients, e-government clients, PKI clients...

As regards future work, we are considering the design of a whole long-term signature archiving architecture that includes this proposal as an important component. We should take into account the possible relationships between the service, the format of the information to be returned and the information to be stored. Another aspect to be taken into account is the trusted relationships that a validation service could have with other validation services.

References

[CKPR05]   Cantor, Scott; Kemp, John; Philpott, Rob and Maler, Eve: Assertions and Proto-
             cols for the OASIS Security Assertion Markup Language (SAML) V2.0. In:
             OASIS Security Services (SAML) TC, 2005.

[DreesS06]   Drees, Stefan: Digital Signature Service Core Protocols, Elements, and Bind-
             ings. In: OASIS DSS TC, 2006.

[ETSI06]   ETSI, XML Advanced Electronic Signatures (XAdES). ETSI TS 101 933.

[FHM+05]   Freeman, T.; Hously, R.; Malpani, A.; Cooper, D. and Polk, T.: "Simple Certifi-
             cate Validation Protocol (SCVP)", IETF RFC. 2005.

[MAM+05]   Meyers, M.; Ankney, R.; Malpani, A.; Galperin, S. and Adams: "X.509 Internet
             Public Key Infrastructure Online Certificate Status Protocol – OCSP", IETF
             RFC 2560, 1999.

[PKIF02]   PKI Forum, "Understanding Certification Path Construction", September 2002.

[HPF+02]   Housley, R., Polk, W., Ford, W., Solo, D., "Internet X.509 Public Key Infra-
             structure Certificate and Certificate Revocation List (CRL) Profile", IETF RFC
             3280, April 2002.

[ASZ+01]   Adams, C., Sylvester, P., Zolotarev, M., Zuccherato, R., "Internet X.509 Public
             Key Infrastructure Data Validation and Certification Server Protocol", IETF
             RFC 3029, February 2001.

[PH02]   Pinkas, D., Housley, R., "Delegated Path Validation and Delegated Path Discov-
             ery Protocol Requirements", IETF RFC 3379, September 2002.

[BL02]   Berbecaru, D., Lioy, A., "Towards Simplifying PKI Implementation: Client-
             Server based Validation of Public Key Certificates". 2002

An Introduction to Validation for Federated PKIs

Robert Dulude · David Engberg · Seth Hitchings

CoreStreet Ltd.
One Alewife Center
Cambridge MA, USA
bob@corestreet.com

Abstract

This paper investigates the security, performance and availability issues associated with establishing trusted identities for large populations spanning many different trust domains. A trusted path building approach is presented that scales to 100s millions of users with transaction response times of a few hundred milliseconds.

1 Introduction

Trusted identity is central to all security. This statement has never been more applicable than it is today. Electronic transactions over the Internet are now commonplace and no longer considered the wave of the future.

For government and industry, this brings the challenge of establishing trusted identities for large populations that are certified by many different trust domains. The use of public key technology and digital certificates has emerged as the preferred approach. Both commercial enterprises and government agencies are deploying Public Key Infrastructures (PKIs) to meet this challenge. The promise of PKI is that it can facilitate establishment of trusted identities for huge populations. This promise will only be realized if the building of trust paths between different trust domains can be automated in a scalable, affordable, and manageable way.

The initial focus of every enterprise rolling out a PKI is typically on the issuance of identity credentials. While the vetting of credential recipients and the secure issuance of these credentials is a formidable task, there are significant issues associated with the actual use of these credentials. Validation of these credentials in a timely manner for every transaction has proven to be a formidable challenge. Then, once an enterprise has successfully deployed a PKI for its own internal use, the inevitable question arises as to how to extend their PKI to include external partners, collaborators, supply chain vendors, sister agencies and foreign governments. The answer lies in setting up trust relationships among different trust domains in a manner that allows the verification of trust to be performed in a secure and timely manner. Inherent in this approach is trusting partners to authenticate their own users according to previously agreed upon vetting and credential issuance policies.

This paper explores the role of automated credential authentication and validation in achieving trust in a federated PKI environment. The key word here is "automated". The success or failure of a federated PKI, as with any PKI, lies in the end user's experience. If the deployed PKI is to be successful, users should not experience delay or difficulty in executing a secure transaction at the moment they wish to so. Critical to this success is the ability to scale the verification of trust relationships through automated credential validation.

2 Establishing Trust in a Hierarchical PKI

For the purposes of this discussion "trust" is defined in terms of the authenticity and validity of an identity credential, specifically a digital certificate:

- **Authenticity** – is the quality of being genuine. An authentic credential is one that has not been forged or tampered with.

- **Validity** – refers to the state of the credential. A valid credential is still in force, is legally binding and has not been revoked.

A trusted credential is therefore one that is both authentic and valid at the time of the transaction. Establishing that a credential can be trusted is a two step process.

In order to understand how trust is established in a federated environment it is essential to fully understand the basic mechanisms used in simple hierarchical PKIs. A typical hierarchical PKI is shown in Figure 1:

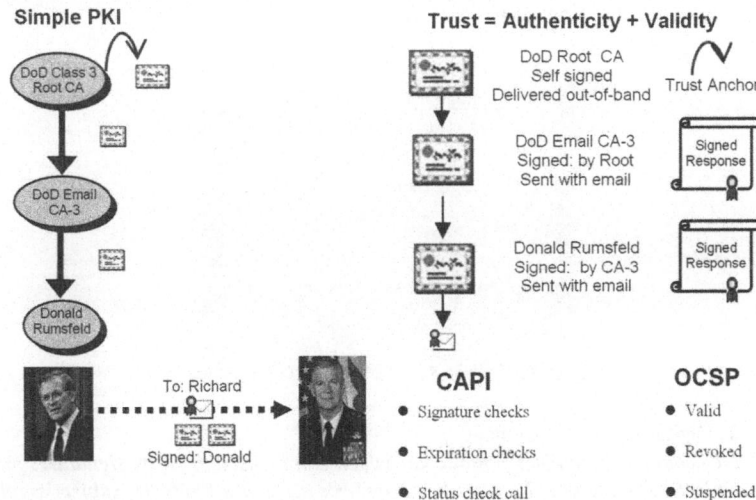

Figure 1: Simple PKI
Establishing trust for a secure email transaction in a simple hierarchical PKI. CAPI checks the authenticity of the certificate chain and checks the status of the certificates it receives as part of the transaction. Both the sender and receiver are members of the same PKI, in this case the US Dept. of Defense (DoD) PKI.

In this example we show a signed email transaction between two members of the same PKI. The PKI consists of a Root CA and a Subordinate CA. There are three digital certificates present, one from each CA plus the end user certificate which is used to establish identity. This is considered a "hierarchy" because each entity in the hierarchy certifies the entity below it. The Root CA is an exception in that it is self-certified. This means that the Root CA used its own private key to sign its certificate. The Root CA also certifies the CA below it in the hierarchy by signing the Subordinate CA's certificate. The Subordinate CA certifies the end user by signing the end user's certificate. In a typical deployment the Root certificate is delivered out-of-band (i.e., not as part of the transaction) in a trusted manner to all members of the trust domain served by the PKI. This is necessary because the integrity and authenticity of the Root certificate is not protected since it is self-signed.

As shown in Figure 1 the Subordinate CA certificate and the end user certificate were delivered to the relying party as part of the transaction (e.g., along with a digitally signed email). Before trusting the transaction the relying party client (i.e., the recipient of the signed email) must make several security checks, including checking that the certificates it received are both authentic and valid. We have assumed that the client is using Microsoft's Cryptographic API (CAPI) software to perform these checks. In this case CAPI explicitly trusts the Root certificate since it was registered as a trust anchor as part of the out-of-band delivery process. CAPI uses the public key from the Root certificate to verify that the Subordinate CA certificate is authentic (see Figure 2). In a similar manner CAPI verifies the authenticity of the end user's certificate by using the public key from the Subordinate CA's certificate. Finally the signature on the transaction itself is checked by using the public key from the end user's certificate. This completes the authenticity checking.

CAPI must still check that none of the certificates have been revoked (the Root certificate is assumed to be valid). This is done by retrieving either a Certificate Revocation List (CRL) or an Online Certificate Status Protocol (OCSP) response.[1] If all the certificates are valid and all signatures are authentic the transaction is considered trustworthy.[2]

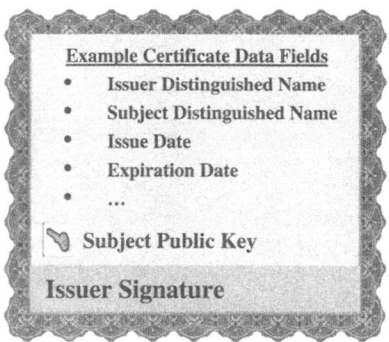

Figure 2: Digital Certificate Content
Certificates contain the subject's public key which can be used to verify signatures made by the subject's private key. The certificate issuer's signature binds the subject's public key to the subject identity and other data fields in the certificate such that they cannot be forged or altered. The certificate issuer's signature is checked using the issuer's public key.

---

[1] For a discussion of validation approaches see [D-OCSP].

[2] For completeness we note that the validation process includes several additional checks such as ensuring proper syntax, criticality, certificate expiration date, name chaining and that the intermediate certificates are CA certificates. These checks are not discussed here since they are unaffected by federated usage.

3 Establishing Trust in a Federated PKI

A federated PKI is by definition a collection of independent hierarchical PKIs, each serving separate trust domains, each with their own Root CA. The federated PKI is established when members of the federation agree on a common set of policies for the purpose of conducting secure transactions among them. Implementing trust across multiple domains is accomplished through the incorporation of a Bridge Certification Authority.[3] The primary function of a Bridge CA is to establish trust relationships among members of the bridged community. This is accomplished by setting the security policies and practices that are adhered to by all bridge members. Bridge CAs are also involved in the issuance of cross-certificates which are used in building trust paths of certificates from a trust anchor in one PKI to an end entity certificate issued by a different PKI. Several examples of PKI bridge communities exist today, including the European Union Bridge, the Pharmaceutical Bridge (SAFE – Secure Access For Everyone), the CertiPath Bridge (aerospace and defense agencies)[4], the US Federal Bridge, and the Higher Education Bridge (EDUCAUSE). Figure 3 depicts potential members of a generic bridge community.

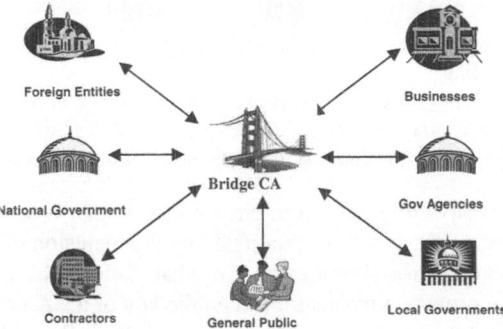

Figure 3: Bridge Community
A PKI bridge community is comprised of multiple trust domains served by independent hierarchical PKIs, each with their own Root CA.

To understand how a Bridge CA is used to provide trust paths within a federated PKI consider the following example. Figure 4 depicts a signed email transaction between members of two separate trust domains. In this example, Donald Rumsfeld, who is a member of the US DoD PKI, sends a signed email to Condoleezza Rice, who is a member of the US State Department PKI. (Condoleezza's trust anchor is the State Department Root. Explicit trust of this Root is achieved by registering the State Department Root certificate on her desktop.) Since she is not a member of the DoD PKI she does not explicitly trust the DoD Root certificate and therefore no complete path of trust exists for this transaction (i.e., there is no way to establish the authenticity of all the certificates in the chain). Consequently, when CAPI is presented with the

---

[3] While there are other trust models for establishing trust across multiple domains the Bridge CA approach has significant operational advantages making it the preferred choice. A comparison of different trust models is beyond the scope of this paper. For a broad discussion of trust models see [PKI-Imp].

[4] The Trans-Atlantic Secure Collaboration Program (TSCP) is actually extending the federation model a step further by establishing trust between different bridge communities.

task of checking the trustworthiness of this transaction the authentication check fails and the result is "not trustworthy".

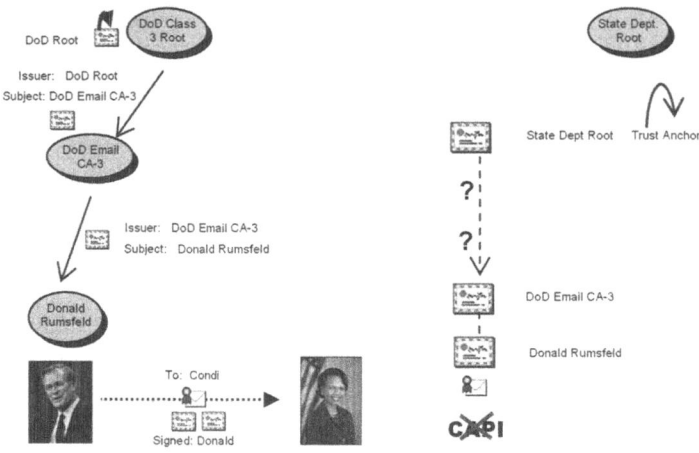

Figure 4: Trust Building
An example of establishing trust for a secure email transaction in a federated PKI. Here the sender and receiver are members of separate trust domains with different PKI trust anchors. Because the certificate chain is incomplete the authenticity check by CAPI fails.

The establishment of a trustworthy path from one PKI to another is accomplished through the use of a Bridge CA. Among the functions facilitated by the inclusion of a Bridge CA is that of providing cross-certificates. Cross-certificates are what "bridge the gap" between different PKIs. For example, they provide a means for the public key of a CA in one trust domain to be certified by a CA in another trust domain. There are no explicit flags identifying these certificates as cross-certificates. Cross-certificates are more likely to have extensions (e.g. policy mapping) that are uncommon in a hierarchical PKI but otherwise they are basically identical to subordinate CA certificates.[5] For example, in Figure 5 the US Federal Bridge CA (FBCA) has certified the DoD Root CA by using its private key to sign a cross-certificate containing the DoD Root public key. This has the effect of allowing the DoD chain of trust to extend through the FBCA rather than terminate on the DoD Root certificate.

The trust path to the State Department Root is completed using a cross-certificate issued by the State Department to the FBCA. This cross-certificate certifies the FBCA's public key and therefore any certificates issued by the FBCA will be accepted as authentic by anyone who uses the State Department Root as a trust anchor. The cross-certificate issued by the FBCA to the DoD can be checked for authenticity by using the FBCA's public key contained in the cross-certificate signed by the State Department. The entire chain of certificates can be processed in this manner and will now pass the authenticity checks. There is no change to the process of validating the status of these certificates.

---

[5] Cross-certificates do not need to be at the Root CA level. However for this discussion we will assume they are.

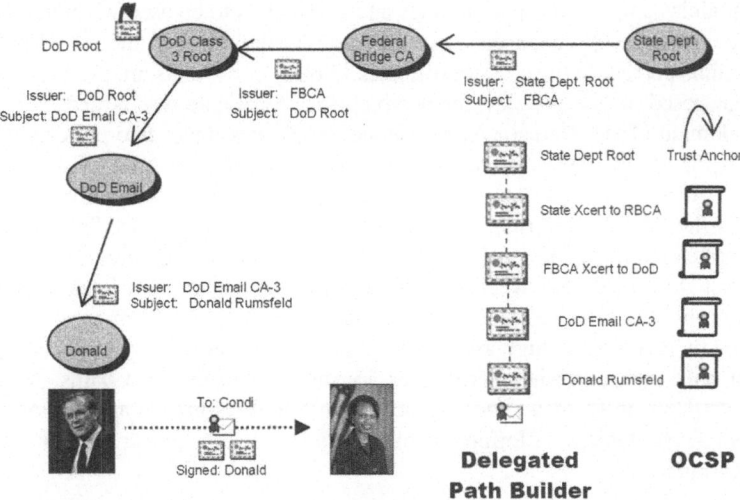

Figure 5: Bridging the "gap"
The certificate chain of trust is completed through the use of a Bridge CA. However non-CAPI software such as CoreStreet's Path Builder *is required to discover the complete trusted path.*

Even though a complete and trustworthy path now exists, there remains the issue of "discovering" the missing certificates. In general cross-certificates will not be included as part of the transaction or locally available for use by CAPI to perform full path validation. Consequently transactions of this type will always fail to be authenticated by CAPI. It is important to note that this failure of CAPI to authenticate transactions involving cross-certificates is not because there are any different or more complicated checks required to establish trustworthiness for federated PKIs. On the contrary, the required authentication and validation checks at the desktop are exactly the ones used for simple hierarchical PKIs. *The failure stems from the fact that CAPI does not possess the general capability to search external sources for the missing certificates in the chain.*[6] CAPI's shortcomings require an alternative solution to be deployed at the desktop in order to facilitate path discovery in federated environments.

4 Applying Validation Policies

One of the major advantages of using the bridge CA trust model is that it enables centralized management and automatic enforcement of validation policies. Cross-certification establishes a mechanism for building trust paths from one trust domain to another. Validation policies can be used to limit the scope of the trust relationships that are established through cross-certification. Enforcement of these policies at the time of the transaction, allows secure, trusted, business processes to be established among organizations participating in the federated community.

---

[6] CAPI does have the ability to discover paths if <u>all</u> the certificates in the chain have the AIA extension populated. However, this is not the general case. In addition, having each relying party application crawl all the way back to a trust anchor is not a scalable approach, a fact that has prompted the IETF to draft a new protocol as discussed in the *Building Trust Paths* section of this document.

Validation policies contain the specific rules and parameters to be used when validating a certificate. In the Bridge CA model these can be implemented through the use of policy and/or name constraints present in the cross-certificates.[7] Policy constraints are used to constrain certificate usage based on the policies under which that certificate was issued. For example, a given trust domain (Trust Domain A) may issue certificates under two policies which differ according to the level of identity assurance achieved through vetting of the individual to whom the certificate is issued. Low assurance certification may only require that the individual supply his/her identity information in an email. High assurance certification may require in-person application and a background check as part of the vetting process. Another bridge member, Trust Domain B, may want to limit the trust relationship with Trust Domain A to individuals for who this high assurance level of identity vetting has been applied. This can be accomplished by asserting a "high assurance" policy constraint in the cross-certificates which ensures that only high assurance certificates are included in the trust paths. A third bridge member, Trust Domain C, may choose to accept both high assurance and low assurance certificates from Trust Domain A. Enforcement of policy and name constraints can also be done at the application level.

Bridge community members may also want to limit the trust relationships with another member to specific sub-domains or to exclude specific sub-domains. This can be accomplished by listing the names (i.e., the X.500 distinguished names) from these sub-domains in the name constraint extension in the cross-certificates. The capability exists to either include or exclude specific names or subsets of names (e.g., everyone from abc.gov address) through this mechanism.

The major benefit of using the bridge CA approach for establishing trust relationships is that the process of building trust paths between the domains, including the enforcement of path constraints, can be automated. Once agreement is reached on which validation policies to implement, these policies are codified in the cross-certificate extensions. This facilitates automatic electronic validation processing for all subsequent transactions without the need to review the agreement terms for each transaction. Automated transaction processing is essential to making electronic commerce a reality for worldwide populations that are certified by many different trust domains.

5 Building Trust Paths

Building trust paths in a hierarchical PKI serving a single trust domain, as shown in Figure 1, is a simple process. Discovering trust paths which cross trust domains, as shown in Figures 4 and 5, is much more difficult. Fundamental to this issue is the problem of finding the correct repositories of the missing path links when cross-certification is used. The IETF has recognized that discovering the missing links and building appropriate trust paths is too difficult and time-consuming to rely on Public Key Enabled (PKE) applications to execute. This has led to the establishment of a new protocol called Server-based Certificate Validation Protocol (SCVP).[8]

---

[7] Part of the process of establishing trust relationships between members of a bridge community includes the agreement as to the security policies to be implemented by each participating PKI.

[8] At the time of this writing the proposed SCVP standard is a draft but is expected to be adopted shortly.

At the heart of SCVP is the concept of delegating the task of discovering the missing links and building appropriate trust paths. This is articulated in the SCVP Draft RFC:[9]

"The primary goals of SCVP are to make it easier to deploy PKI-enabled applications by delegating path discovery and/or validation processing to a server, and to allow central administration of validation policies within an organization."

As we have already noted the problem of path discovery is the fundamental issue. The required certificate authentication and validation checks made by the desktop application (i.e., by the client) are exactly the ones used for simple hierarchical PKIs.

The SCVP standard defines two approaches to delegating certificate path building. In the first approach, the client delegates the task of building a valid certification path to an SCVP server but not validation of the returned certification path. This approach is referred to as *delegated path discovery* (DPD). In the second approach, the client delegates both the task of building a valid certification path and the task of confirming that the public key contained in the end user certificate can be used for the intended purpose. This approach is referred to as *delegated path validation* (DPV). While both approaches unburden client applications of the difficult and time-consuming task of path building and provide for central administration of validation policies, the operational characteristics of the two approaches differ significantly[10]. Choosing between them is the subject of the next section.

6 Evaluating Validation Deployment Choices

The crucial factor in deploying any PKI is ensuring that the deployed validation architecture will meet the needs of the user population. As important as scalability is in simple hierarchical PKIs, [11] it becomes paramount to the successful deployment of federated PKIs where the number of trust domains can easily be in the hundreds and the number of certified identities in the hundreds of millions. It is readily apparent then that the number of PKE transactions will be orders of magnitude larger, in the hundreds of billions. Clearly the validation systems that build, authenticate and validate trust paths as part of validating each transaction must be automated in a scalable and secure fashion.

In choosing between delegated path discovery and delegated path validation architectures, it is important to compare the operational characteristics of each. The relevant criteria that must be met for certificate validation systems to be operationally successful are:

1. **High performance** – The system must provide fast responses to identity validation requests. Ideally the user should not be aware that validation is occurring.

2. **High availability** – The system must be available when the end user wants to use it.

3. **Scalable** – There should be no degradation in performance, availability or security as the system grows to meet the demands of an increasing number of users and trust domains.

---

[9] A copy of the draft RFC can be downloaded from [SCVPstd].

[10] These "unburdened clients" are often referred to as "thin-clients".

[11] For example, the US Department of Defense has deployed a simple hierarchical PKI consists of 34 certification authorities which have issued over 20 million certificates to 4.5 million users. The DoD found that scaling their validation system was one of their most difficult challenges. The solution was to deploy a distributed certificate validation system known as Distributed OCSP.

4. **Secure** – The system must ensure public trust in the security of information exchanged in any public key enabled electronic transaction.

5. **Interoperable** – The system must be based on open standards to ensure interoperability with all applications conforming to the standards. The use of open standards will also ensure that the system can interoperate with other PKIs in a bridged environment.

6. **Low risk** – The system must be based on technology that has been proven to work in realistic operational scenarios of equal or larger size.

6.1 Delegated Path Validation

Figure 6 shows a typical DPV deployment architecture. The SCVP server maintains the security sensitive validation data and performs the trusted operations of validating the certificate and digitally signing the DPV response. Typically the private key used in signing the response is housed in a Hardware Security Module (HSM) which also executes the signing operation.

The DPV SCVP server is a "trusted" server in that the client relies solely on the SCVP server's response as to whether or not the identity certificate in question is authentic, valid and can be used for the intended purpose. *Since the DPV SCVP server is commissioned as the ultimate authority for this determination of trust, much the same as a Root CA is the ultimate authority for the establishment of a trust path, it must be hosted and operated at the same security level as a Root CA.*[12] Unlike a Root CA however, the DPV server must remain online at all times, making it vulnerable to intrusion.

Performance of a DPV system is impacted by two factors: 1) it is inherently a centralized architecture and consequently impacted by network latency, and 2) every validation transaction must be digitally signed in real time.

The key to achieving high availability is to have multiple validation servers deployed in a manner that matches the geographical dispersion of the user population. This is difficult to achieve in a DPV system because of the security requirements associated with hosting and operating a DPV server.

Scaling of a DPV system is accomplished by replicating the trusted server. This has several drawbacks including the cost of the hardware and of securely housing and operating multiple trusted servers. It also complicates the key management plan for ensuring that clients can securely "fail-over" from one "trusted" DPV server to another (e.g., the transfer of the client's trust from one DPV server to another is dependent upon whether these servers all have the same signing key or separate signing keys.)[13]

The DPV approach contains several security vulnerabilities. As noted above, since the DPV server must remain accessible to all potential relying parties it is vulnerable to intrusion. Its highly centralized architecture makes it vulnerable to a denial-of-service attack and a potential single point of failure. In addition, the vulnerability to compromise of a "trusted" DPV server increases as the number of deployed DPV servers grows.

---

[12] Taken from [Chokhani].

[13] The DPV architecture is identical to that of Traditional (or first generation) OCSP. Consequently it has all the same security, performance, availability and scalability drawbacks. For a general discussion of the security issues associated with certificate validation see [Sec-Vul].

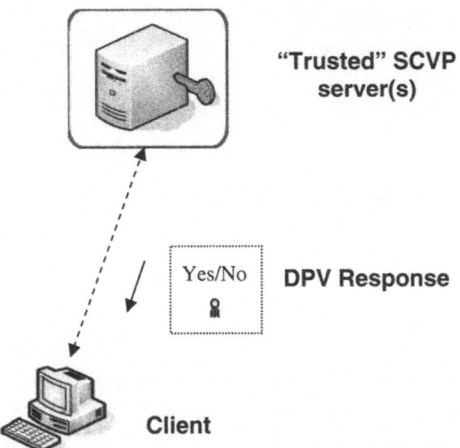

Figure 6: DPV System Architecture
In a DPV system a "trusted" SCVP server provides both path discovery and validation. The response returned to the client is a digitally signed Yes or No answer. In this system the client relies solely on the DPV server for validation which makes this server as security sensitive as a Root CA. It must therefore be secured and operated with the same level of security as a Root CA. Unlike a Root CA however, the DPV server must remain online with an "open port" to the outside world making it vulnerable to intrusion.

Deploying a Delegated Path Validation system may be appropriate for relatively small localized populations with good network connectivity to the DPV server. However, as we shall see in the next section, in most cases the Delegated Path Discovery approach is a better choice.

6.2 Delegated Path Discovery

Figure 7 depicts a SCVP validation system as could be deployed using the Delegated Path Discovery approach. In this architecture, a second tier of "untrusted" caching servers is inserted between the client and the trusted SCVP server. The trusted SCVP server is used to store all the security sensitive data and to execute all the security sensitive operations (e.g., signing of OCSP responses). While the trusted SCVP server must be housed and operated securely the "untrusted" keyless SCVP servers contain no security sensitive data and do not perform any security sensitive operations. Consequently they can be deployed anywhere. The data cached on these untrusted servers (i.e., the certificates that make up the trust path and their corresponding OCSP responses) are digitally signed and therefore may be transmitted and stored in the clear.

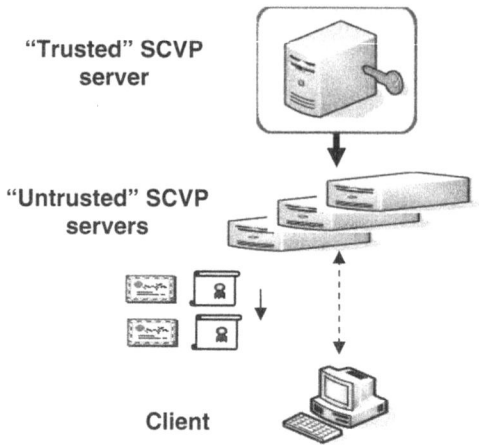

Figure 7: DPD System Architecture
In a DPD system a "trusted" SCVP server builds a trust path from the identity certificate in question to the client's trust anchor. The response returns the trust path and all associated OCSP certificate status responses. The client application then invokes the same authentication and validation checks as it would in a simple hierarchical PKI. While the "trusted" SCVP server must be housed and operated securely the "untrusted" keyless SCVP servers can be deployed anywhere. There are no security requirements for data protection at this lower tier since all data are digitally signed.

This approach greatly enhances the operational security and effectiveness of the system as a comparison with the previously defined success criteria clearly shows:

1. **High performance** – is achieved by providing the trust path and validation data on "untrusted" servers (called Responders) located close to the end users. This eliminates the need to digitally sign responses in real time and decreases the distance, and therefore the number of network hops, between the client and a Responder.[14]

2. **High availability** – is achieved by making a large number of Responders available to the end users. This ensures there is always a Responder available when needed. As these Responders are cheap to deploy (i.e., they require no special security hardware such as HSMs, can be located anywhere and do not require "cleared" personnel to operate) they can be freely replicated. Network load balancers can be used to route the users request to the closest available Responder.

3. **Scalable** – true scalability is achieved by separating the delivery process from the security sensitive operations associated with certificate validation. This fundamental design feature allows Responders to be freely added as the demand grows - ensuring high performance and high availability without incurring large costs, sacrificing security or degrading the end user experience.

---

[14] Response times observed by the US DoD in their global OCSP implementation using this architecture were typically a few hundred milliseconds.

4. **Secure** – the key security features of a distributed validation architecture include:

   o **Intrusion threat eliminated**: the distributed validation approach does not require nor allow any inbound communication to the "trusted" SCVP server (called the Authority) from the outside world. Certificate validation requests go only to Responders, not to the Authority. The Authority can literally be "off-line". This eliminates all threats of an outside attack on the security sensitive parts of the system.

   o **Denial of service threat mitigated:** the two major characteristics of a denial-of-service vulnerability are: i) highly centralized service, and ii) providing the requested service requires a relatively long computation. This threat is mitigated by deploying multiple, geographically dispersed Responders.[15] In addition, these Responders do not perform any long calculations since all validation and trust path data have been pre-signed and are ready for immediate release to the client.

   o **Eliminates single point of failure:** this approach also eliminates the single point of failure threat present in non-distributed validation systems. In fact, if a physical attack or natural disaster were to incapacitate the trusted SCVP server, service would continue uninterrupted via the untrusted Responders for a configurable period of time, allowing for a "recovery" period during which a backup trusted SCVP server can be brought on-line.

   o **Key compromise threat mitigated**: scaling a distributed validation system to serve increasingly larger user communities does not require distributing private keys or other security sensitive data to multiple locations. The Authority requires a single key housed in a hardware security module, regardless of the number of users, trust domains or Responders being supported. This greatly enhances the ability to securely manage the operation by minimizing the key management process.

5. **Interoperable** – this criterion is satisfied equally by either a DPV or DPD system.

6. **Low risk** –

   o Proven to work – a distributed validation architecture has been implemented by the US Department of Defense for its world-wide enterprise OCSP solution and by the US Intelligence Community because of the inherent security features of this infrastructure.

   o Proven to scale – the DoD OCSP deployment is currently servicing over 20 million certificates from 34 CAs with response times of a few hundred milliseconds

7 Conclusion

Today the Web is available worldwide and heavily used. By simply typing a URL into a browser, any user with access to the Internet can connect to servers anywhere in the world. The underlying infrastructure that makes this possible is both simple to use and efficient. For worldwide electronic commerce to become a reality it must have a simple and efficient underlying infrastructure. The core of this infrastructure must provide a secure and automated way of validating identity credentials from a worldwide population that are certified by many different trust domains. The DPD validation architecture is the best choice to meet these needs.

---

[15] On October 21, 2002 a "distributed denial of service" attack was launched against the 13 "root servers" that provide the primary roadmap for almost all Internet traffic. The attack, the largest such attack to date, failed because of the distributed nature of the Internet root server architecture.

References

[PKI-Imp]   Andrew Nash, William Duane, Celia Joseph and Derek Brink, *PKI Implement-
            ing and Managing E-Security*, Osborne/McGraw-Hill, Berkeley, California,
            2001.

[D-OCSP]   Distributed Certificate Validation, CoreStreet, 2003. Available from:
            http://www.corestreet.com

[SCVPstd]   Internet Engineering Task Force (IETF): Server-based Certificate Validation
            Protocol, Internet Draft, June 2006. Available from:
            http://tools.ietf.org/wg/pkix/draft-ietf-pkix-scvp/

[Sec-Vul]   Vulnerability Analysis of Certificate Validation Systems, CoreStreet, 2004.
            Available from: http://www.corestreet.com

[Chokhani] Chokhani, Santosh: Simple Certificate Validation Protocol (SCVP), presented at
            the DoD PKI Forum in Orlando, April 2005.

Acronyms

CA	Certification Authority
CAPI	Crypto Application Program Interface
CRL	Certificate Revocation List
DoD	Department of Defense (US)
DPD	Delegated Path Discovery
DPV	Delegated Path Validation
FBCA	Federal Bridge Certification Authority (US)
HSM	Hardware Security Module
IETF	Internet Engineering Task Force
OCSP	Online Certificate Status Protocol
PKE	Public Key Enabled
PKI	Public Key Infrastructure
PKITS	Public Key Infrastructure Test Suite
RFC	Request For Comment
SAFE	Secure Access For Everyone
SCVP	Server-based Certificate Validation Protocol

MADSig: Enhancing Digital Signature to Capture Secure Document Processing Requirements

Jean-Christophe Pazzaglia[1] · Stefano Crosta[2]

[1]SAP Labs France
805 Avenue du Dr Donat - BP 1216
06254 Mougins Cedex - France
Jean-Christophe.Pazzaglia@sap.com

[2]Institut Eurecom
2229 Route des Crêtes
BP 193 - 06904 Sophia Antipolis - France
Stefano.Crosta@eurecom.fr

Abstract

Businesses, government agencies, and educational institutions all share information electronically. While digital signature based on public key infrastructure is commonly accepted as the natural answer to secure data exchange, the actual digital signature formats largely fail to capture regulation and business level semantic. Indeed, electronic documents (business contracts, law texts, European directives, European arrest warrants...) can no longer be simply seen as their paper counterparts: the trust and the accuracy of the information carried by electronic documents are transitory; and they utterly depend on the instant and the perspective of the document consumer. For example, a contract signed by only one part may give a competitive negotiation advantage to the potential matching part. For that reason, we propose a technical solution which is aiming to mitigate the risks of discrepancy. Our solution is based on the paradigm of Business Process Modeling extended to provide security annotations and functionalities. Documents are perceived as business processes' artefacts and embed a subset of the process with associated security annotations. These descriptions combined with basic digital signature primitive and certified data make possible to verify the compliance of collaborative processes that may eventually span across borders. A practical example, the European Arrest Warrant is described to show the model's expressiveness to capture complex legal constraints.

1 Motivations

Businesses, government agencies, and educational institutions all share information electronically. Key documents are handled online, and this practice has become nearly universal, and in some cases mandatory by law[1]. Identity theft and online fraud impose two main challenges to enable sharing electronic documents: to insure the document's integrity and to reliably

---

[1]For example, the new public procurement Directives, regulating a key sector of the EU economy accounting for about 16% of GDP [8], aim to computerise traditional procedures for the award of contracts.

S. Paulus, N. Pohlmann, H. Reimer (Editors): Securing Electronic Business Processes, Vieweg (2006), 241-248

identify the document's author. Digital signature based on public key infrastructure (PKIX [13]) is commonly accepted as the natural answer to these issues. However, despite the soundness of their technical basis (cryptography) [15], the European regulatory effort [11] and the extensions to carry certified information (time, certificate ...)[9][19] the actual digital signature formats largely fail to capture regulation and business level semantic. Indeed, electronic documents (business contracts, law texts, European directives, European arrest warrants...) can no longer be simply seen as their paper counterparts: by essence they are highly dynamic, and carry additional challenges as a consequence of their flexibility. Moreover, they are the outcome of complex interactions involving different socio-economic actors. The trust and the accuracy of the information carried by electronic documents are therefore transitory; and they utterly depend on the instant and the perspective of the document consumer. For example, a contract signed by only one part may give a competitive negotiation advantage to the potential matching part. Similarly, a judicial procedure may be invalidated by a judge because the delays, the actors' qualifications or other constraints are not respected. Instruments should be provided by the system to allow an *a posteriori* validation.

In this paper, we propose a technical solution which is aiming to lower these risks of discrepancy. Our solution, which will be referred to as Multiple Advanced Digital Signature (MADSig), is based on the paradigms of Business Process Modelling (BPM) which we extended to provide security annotations and functionalities. It sees the documents as artefacts of business processes. For a given document, a subset of the process and associated annotations are bind to the document itself enabling to verify its compliance with the procedure. By allowing a verification of the correctness of the procedures at any point in time, this solution is an emblematic application of the *'beyond'* workflow security principle presented in [16].

This document is organized as follow: after describing the Digital Signature technical landscape and limitations, we present the details of the MADSig solution. A practical example, the European Arrest Warrant (EAW) [7][21], will then be described enabling to understand the model's expressiveness. This example was formulated during the analysis performed on judicial procedures for the eJustice project [4], and provides sound basis for the work in R4eGov project [14] under which our solution will be extended and applied.

2 Technical Landscape

XML Digital Signature Standard (DSig) [20] does provide a flexible structure to sign documents and particularly XML Documents. Its structure enables to define profiles suitable to digitally sign documents which may be used as legal evidences or contractual basis. These profiles enable to impose the inclusion of mandatory information of major importance in this perspective: the underlying semantic of the signature is therefore richer while still relying on a strong cryptographic proof. The ultimate goal of these profiles is to raise the level of trust of the digital signature to, at least, the level of the physical signature. Ensuring this level of trust is intrinsically more difficult since we need to provide a counterpart to the physical presence and face to face controls in the virtual world. These new issues should thus be addressed by extended signing mechanisms in different directions:

- the validity of the date, and possibly location, of the signature;
- the conformity of the credentials (Identity, roles, permissions...) exhibited by the actors to signature authorization requirements;
- the support for concurring multiple signatures to avoid to advantage one party and
- the guarantee of the what you see is what you sign principle.

The complexity and sometime proprietary nature of electronic documents formats and the use of a possible compromised viewer (software or hardware) make this guarantee particularly difficult to insure. Therefore, it is strongly advised not to sign documents described using a proprietary and undocumented format and to sign carefully complex document or, even worse, ones containing dynamic elements (e.g. linked to databases).

XAdES [19] extends the XML Digital Signature framework in order to provide other validation facets such as Time-Stamp (XAdES-T), complete validation data (XAdES-C) or archiving in a way that they are protected if the cryptographic data become weak (XAdES-A). However, XAdES and DSig are focusing on single signature constraints: they do not provide a framework to capture constraints related to multi-party workflow although they enable to add multiple signatures to a single document.

The following section will show how MADSig is addressing these limitations.

3 MADSig principles

MADSig can be described as a signature profile enabling to capture the information expressed by the mean of workflows annotations related to the document lifecycle. The idea is to carry, within the document itself, different constraints (called `multiSignatureConstraints`) describing the mandatory elements and relationships among the different elements of the signed document (signatures, certificates and attributes...). When the document is created or manipulated for the first time, the workflow runtime engine is responsible to create a composite document containing the document itself and a new instance of the `multiSignature-Constraints`. This constraints instance is itself signed by the workflow engine or by a trusted authority. In the same way that a document will be processed by standard workflow engine, the composite document follows the control flow and will be transformed during specific activities by the different actors [17] through the completion of the procedure. Unlike non secure workflow, at the end of each transformation, a blocking non-repudiable signature request is triggered by the workflow engine to the actor. Those transformations correspond to specific workflow operations, and correspond to business-process related modifications of the document (adding clauses, amendments, signatures...), and obviously, should not to be considered as a secure versioning. Consequently at any moment, an actor or an external auditor can control that the composite document followed a valid procedure and that it complies with the security properties defined in the annotations.

Initially, we envisaged to use generic purpose rule languages [1] and associated engines such as CliX [3] which enable to describe and validate generic constraints on XML documents. However they poorly support notions such as date/time and are not able to deal with cryptographic and digital signature related information. Consequently, to support this principle, we developed a specific XML based language to capture multi-signature constraints and associated tools [6]. This language enables to specify the sequence and ordering of signatures but also to describe the properties for each signature. More precisely, our schema enables to specify:

1. Multi-signature constraints:

    a. **signers:** the number of expected signatures ,

    b. **signature flow:** the signature order imposing strict ordering (sequence), partial ordering (all) and alternative (choice);

2. Single signature constraints (facet):

a. **document properties:** the type of document, usually a reference to an XML schema type, and the subset of the document which should be signed using the XML-Signature XPath Filter syntax[21],

b. **signer properties:** the type of certificate (X509 or EureCA), the credentials (represented by a set of attributes) or the identity that should be revealed by the signer,

c. **time properties:** the temporal ordering and fixed deadline that the signature should comply with (obviously the timestamp attached with a signature should be provided by a certified provider),

d. **cryptographic properties:** the algorithm and the minimum key strength that should be used to sign the document,

e. **digital signature profile:** the type of signature profile (DSig, XAdES-T...) that should be used.

Obviously, the validation mechanism of such signatures requires in addition to the standard XML DSig validation engine, the presence of a dedicated constraints validation engine. It should provide the support for the multi-signature constraints language against the XML data structure. The validation of the signatures is achieved in 3 steps:

1. Validation of the certificates (involving standard X509v3 and / or EuréCA validation mechanisms)

2. Validation of the DSig/XAdES compliance of the signatures (including canonicalization, transformation and cryptography)

3. Validation of the embedded constraints by our dedicated constraints validator.

It is important to notice that the use of extensible XML based certificates like EuréCA [16] and the introduction of attributes related to the procedure enable to capture task specific information in a uniformed way.

4 The European Arrest Warrant Example

The European Arrest Warrant[10] (EAW) is a judicial judgment by a court of the member state for the arrest or surrender of a requested person that is in another member state. This can only be for the purposes of conducting a criminal prosecution, carrying out a custodial sentence or detention order. The EAW is an attempt to increase the speed of extradition throughout EU countries, as well as change the mechanism from having a "political and administrative phase" into a system run by the judiciary. The basis of the EAW was agreed '*in principle*' by member states of the EU at the Laeken Summit in December 2001, and the framework was adopted on June 13, 2002 in directive 2002/584/JHA. The 'Date of entry into force' was August 7, 2003, with the deadline for final implementation by member states to be December 31, 2003. The legislation for the EAW came into force for 8 of the then 15 EU countries on January 1, 2004, with the remaining 7 countries missing the deadline.

The complexity of the procedure, the number of interactions, actors and transformations, and the strong security requirements qualify it as the perfect case study for an electronic transposition into a workflow system enhanced by our solution. The model describing the exhaustive European Arrest Warrant (EAW) procedure being rather complicated, we will highlight here a relevant part of the BPM.

The example is as follows: a European citizen was judged in absentia with respect to his co-ordination role in the bomb attack in London, he was convicted by the Magistrates Court and sentenced under the Terrorism Act to a 20-year imprisonment. Intelligence sources provided him with reliable information about the current localisation of that person in France. The Judge issues a European Arrest Warrant, however in order to inform the France executing judicial authority, he should provide the warrant in French.

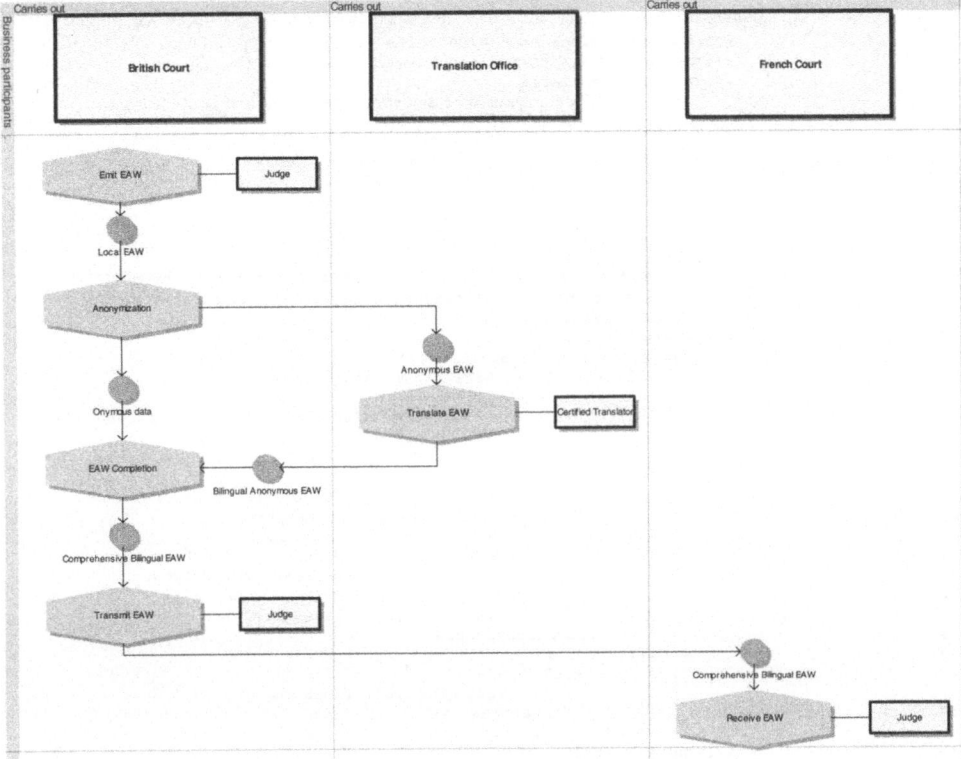

Figure 1: Extract of the EAW process

The translation of such document can be rather delicate since sensitive information is attached to the warrant and its disclosure to criminal organisations maybe damageable. Moreover, the Warrant should not be misinterpreted by the foreign court that could eventually refuse to transfer the suspect if the procedure is not respected. To mitigate these risks, the European Warrant Procedure imposes to contact a certified translator[2] . In addition, the period allowed to achieve the translation task is limited to 24 hours, and only a subset of the information, and anonymous version of the warrant, should be provided to the translator. Finally, after the translation, the judge should provide as soon as possible a comprehensive version of the warrant to the executing judicial authority that should arrest the suspect. A simplified version (an extract) of this procedure is shown in Figure 1.

To support this translation activity, we envisaged three versions of the EAW corresponding of the artefacts produced by the process described before:

---

[2] A recent European legislation also enables an intermediate language, therefore an alternative may require two certified translators and associated signatures, this can similarly be specified as MADSig constraints.

(w1).   an anonymous version of the warrant in English,

(w2).   a bilingual anonymous version of the warrant (English-French),

(w3).   a bilingual comprehensive version of the warrant.

```
1    <MultiSignatureTemplate name="ID00000">
2            <sequence>
3                    <SignatureTemplate name="ID00001">
4                    <SignatureType>XAdES-T</SignatureType>
5                    <CertificateTemplate>
6                            <CertificateType>AttributeCertificate</CertificateType>
7                                    <AttributesTemplates>
8                                            <AttributeTemplate>
9                                                    <Name>Role</Name>
10                                                   <Value>Judge</Value>
11                                           </AttributeTemplate>
12                                   </AttributesTemplates>
13                           </CertificateTemplate>
14                   <DocumentTemplate>
15                           <Schema>http://ejustice.eu/eaw#ANONYMOUS-EAW</Schema>
16                           <XPathSubstract>/*/*/*[position()>1]</XPathSubstract>
17                   </DocumentTemplate>
18                   </SignatureTemplate>
19                   <SignatureTemplate name="ID00002">
20                           <SignatureType>XAdES-T</SignatureType>
23                           <CertificateTemplate>
24                                   <CertificateType>AttributeCertificate</CertificateType>
25                                           <AttributesTemplates>
26                                                   <AttributeTemplate>
27                                                           <Name>Role</Name>
28                                                           <Value>Translator</Value>
29                                                   </AttributeTemplate>
30                                                   <AttributeTemplate>
31                                                           <Name>Certified Language</Name>
32                                                           <Value>EN FR</Value>
33                                                   </AttributeTemplate>
34                                           </AttributesTemplates>
35                           </CertificateTemplate>
36                           <TimeTemplate>
37                                   <isBefore>
38                                           <DateTmie ref="TimeStamp@ID00001" delta="+1d"/>
39                                   </isBefore>
40                           </TimeTemplate>
41                   </SignatureTemplate>
42                   <SignatureTemplate name="ID00003">
                             <!--Content deleted -->
65                   </SignatureTemplate>
66           </sequence>
67    </MultiSignatureTemplate>
```

Figure 2: Example of Multi-Signature Template

The associated MADSig constraints, details provided in Figure 2, are as follow:

(sig 1). w1: should be signed by a person which exhibits the role Judge (attribute of the certificate of the signer – line 9), w1 contains one anonymous section (specific schema type – line 15),

(sig 2). w2 (including w1) should be signed by a Translator certified from English to French (attributes of the certificate – line 26-30) within 24 hours since sig1 (line 16),

(sig 3). 3 should be sign by the same signer than sig1, w3 should include two anonymous sections as well as private details (specific schema type),

All signatures should use XAdES-T (lines 4 and 20) since the respective timestamps should be certified.

These signatures should refer precisely to specific section of the signed document to remain valid (line 16 for sig1), moreover we should also highlight that signatures are logically nested since they are sequential (line 2): these properties are merged and enforced by the tool within the signature by specifying an appropriate transform method (in the document instance).

It is also worth noting that, in case of constraints violation, the tool provides error messages explaining the cause of the error such as:

```
Signature error - Template ID00002: the value of the Cer-
tified Language is erroneous (EN DE instead of EN FR ex-
pected)
```

Perspectives and Conclusion

The current trend in enterprise software solution is to bypass the traditional database oriented vision of enterprise because it does not provide the right information at the right time for the right reason [18].This pitfall is commonly attributed to the insufficient infrastructure and due to the lack of process-orientation of the legacy tools. Indeed Business Process Modelling becomes the new focus of management and enterprise software development. Among other benefits, processes are becoming the common communication platform between business and IT and they may run across multiple administrative domains. Several eGovernment research projects (Athena, R4eGov ...) are exploring how to adapt these principles to enable trans-European government agencies interaction.

We decided to develop our own signature constraints language since we did not find any existing digital signature solution bridging the gap between procedures and their artefacts. Our initiative to move from a *paper-alike* signature to a *process-oriented* digital signature scheme is comparable with the BPM trend: MADSig enables to capture regulatory and procedure requirements and to enable their traceability. Obviously, a remaining problem is to understand the minimal and sufficient relevant constraints that should be extracted to insure compliance. Nevertheless, we believe that precise requirements in this respect can be imposed by the legislation.

The MADSig constraints language is, as shown in the previous section, rather straightforward and its recursive nature enables to define very complex signature constraints. If needed, new facets like location constraints may be relatively easy to add although it requires the modification of the schema and the validation engine. The real issue of adding new signature facets relates to the appropriate technical infrastructure to certify this information, for example geographical information may require to use a specific network protocol to measure the maximal distance to a known host [2]. A possible enhancement of our prototype is to extract automatically the signature constraints from the annotated process model, reciprocally the signature constraints may be used to generate a compliant process. Automated translation of the signature constraints and associated documentation may also participate in the correct information of the actor (for example citizen) to understand document processing.

Finally, since our scheme rely on existing standards (PKIX and DSig), it is compatible with legislative requirements. According that the holder's certificate is a qualified X509 certificate and that the key is stored in a SSCD, we believe that this profile is compatible with the notion of qualified signature without modification of the European directive [11].

Acknowledgment and Disclaimer

The authors wish to thank Thomas Van Cangh and Abdelkrim Boujraf from Unisys for their important contribution on modelling the European Arrest Warrant Procedure

This work has been initiated within the context of the EU FP6 project eJustice IST-2002-001567, the usage and integration of the library within our BPM toolkit is an on-going task in the R4eGov "Towards e-Administration in the large" (IST-2004-026650) project.

This paper represents the view of the authors only.

References

[1]   Business Rules and Web Architecture: W3C Creates Rule Interchange Format WG http://xml.coverpages.org/ni2005-11-09-a.html

[2] ˙ Bussard, Laurent;Bagga, Walid Distance-bounding proof of knowledge to avoid real-time attacks IFIP/SEC2005, 20th IFIP International Information Security Conference, May 30 - June 1, 2005, Makuhari-Messe, Chiba, Japan

[3]   CLiX – "Constraint Language in XML" http://www.clixml.org/

[4]   eJustice "Towards a global security and visibility framework for Justice in Europe (IST 001567)." http://www.ejustice.eu.com/

[5]   eJustice D6.6.2 - Rights Management and Multisignature requirements - 2005

[6]   eJustice D6.7.2 Prototype Library implementing Roles Management Framework API EuréCA/MADSig User guide version 2.0 - 2005

[7]   eJustice D8.3.x WP6-8 Case study scenario

[8]   Electronic Public Procurement - http://europa.eu.int/comm/internal_market/publicprocurement/e-procurement_en.htm

[9]   Electronic Signatures and Infrastructures (ESI); Policy requirements for time-stamping authorities, ETSI TS 102 023 V1.2.1 (2003-01).

[10]   European Arrest Warrant Project – http://www.eurowarrant.net/

[11]   European Directive 1999/93/EC, on a Community framework for electronic signatures, December 13, 1999.

[12]   European Directives 2002/58/EC on Privacy and Electronic communications (supersedes European Directive 1995/46/EC)

[13]   Public-Key Infrastructure (X.509) (pkix) http://www.ietf.org/html.charters/pkix-charter.html

[14]   R4eGov "Towards e-Administration in the large" (IST-2004-026650) http://www.r4egov.info/

[15]   RFC 2527 - Internet X.509 Public Key Infrastructure Certificate Policy and Certification Practices Framework: ftp://ftp.isi.edu/in-notes/rfc2527.txt

[16]   S. Crosta, J.-C. Pazzaglia, and H. Schottle, "Modelling and Securing European Justice Workflows," presented at ISSE, 2005.

[17]   Team-and-role-based organizational context and access control for cooperative hypermedia environments, Weigang Wang,Proceedings of the tenth ACM Conference on Hypertext and hypermedia, 1999.

[18]   W. Martin Team, "Analytics meets ESA, Enriching Business Processes by Analytics," 2005.

[19]   XML Advanced Electronic Signatures (XAdES) W3C Note 20 February 2003: http://www.w3.org/TR/XAdES/

[20]   XML-Signature Syntax and Processing, W3C Recommendation 12 February 2002, http://www.w3.org/TR/xmldsig-core/

[21]   XML-Signature XPath Filter 2.0 – http://www.w3.org/TR/xmldsig-filter2/

PKI Consolidation Project and Multiapplicative Smart Payment Cards

Milan Marković[1] · Miloš Kilibarda[1] · Aleksandar Milošević[2]

[1]Banca Intesa ad Beograd, Security Department
III Bulevar 1c, 11070 Belgrade, Serbia
{milan.markovic | milos.kilibarda}@bancaintesabeograd.com

[2]Pexim Solutions, Goce Delčeva 44,
11070 Belgrade, Serbia
aca@pexim.co.yu

Abstract

In this paper, main characteristics of the consolidated PKI system in Banca Intesa ad Beograd are described. This PKI system is used for electronic banking services for external users (home banking for physical persons and e-banking for legal persons), as well as a part of the identity management system (windows logon, single sign-on) and other security services for Bank's internal users (secure e-mail, SSL client authentication). One of the main features of this project is an introduction of the EMV DDA MasterCards in Banca Intesa ad Beograd. These are PKI Multos cards which will have three applications on them: M/Chip Select 4 and CAP payment applications, as well as PKI application. This way, our Maestro users could make payment through POS and ATMs by using the M/Chip payment applications, via Internet in unconnected mode by using external CAP reader and CAP application on the card and, in connected mode, via Bank's web portal by using the connected smart card reader and PKI application on the card with X.509 digital certificate issued by the consolidated PKI system of Banca Intesa ad Beograd. The PKI consolidated system of Banca Intesa ad Beograd is based on the fully customized domestic PKI solution.

1 Introduction

Banca Intesa ad Beograd has advanced security solutions applied in its banking operations. As many other commercial banks in Serbia (for a survey of a current status of PKI experiences in Serbia, see [Mark04]), Banca Intesa ad Beograd has electronic banking solution for legal persons based on PKI smart cards and digital certificates issued by an in-house PKI solution. By using these e-banking cards, companies could make payment directly online via Bank's web portal by using a secure web transaction system [SaMa03]. Besides, companies could prepare transactions offline via specialized offline application, sign and encrypt them by using the e-banking card and send them afterwards to specialized web service on the Bank's side.

Also, Banca Intesa ad Beograd has operated a secure home banking system for physical persons that is currently based on a specific PKI system and specialized mini CD for citizens that stores private asymmetrical key (in encrypted form) and digital certificate. This home banking system is currently based on the out-sourced PKI system. This way, citizens that have registered current account in the Bank, could use these CDs to make signed and encrypted payment transactions via Bank's web portal through the form of secure web transaction system.

S. Paulus, N. Pohlmann, H. Reimer (Editors): Securing Electronic Business Processes, Vieweg (2006), 249-258

Besides the mentioned PKI systems for external users, Banca Intesa ad Beograd has its own in-house PKI system for internal users (all employees in the Bank) based on smart card USB tokens that store private key and digital certificate. These certificates are integrated into the Windows Active Directory and employees' USB smart cards are used for Microsoft Windows Logon on the Bank's Intranet system, as well as for secure e-mail (based on S/MIME protocol) and SSL client authentication for specific web services which are need for some business operations.

Besides the mentioned e-banking solutions, Banca Intesa ad Beograd is also a leader in payment card operations in Serbia. In the year 2003, Banca Intesa ad Beograd (with a name "Delta banka" in that time) issued a first EMV Visa chip card in Balkan area. Very soon (these days), there will be also start of mass issuing of EMV MasterCard chip cards. These will be Multos 32 K cards with PKI capabilities that include three applications on it: EMV DDA MasterCard payment application, 3D Secure CAP application and PKI application with multiple asymmetrical keypair capabilities. Recently, Banca Intesa ad Beograd also started issuing Amex EMV cards. This way, Banca Intesa ad Beograd is currently 100% in EMV acquiring and issuing for all three brands: Amex (SDA), Visa (SDA) and MasterCard (DDA).

The paper is dedicated to a description of the PKI consolidation project in Banca Intesa ad Beograd which will consist of the unique Root CA and in-house intermediate CA systems for external and internal users. Namely, facing with various issues in dealing with two different PKI systems (current in-house and out-sourced PKI solutions) and introducing new multiapplicative MasterCard EMV DDA chip cards with PKI application and digital certificate on them, Banca Intesa ad Beograd decided to run a PKI consolidation project that will result in an establishment a consolidated and integrated unique in-house PKI solution for both internal and external users. This PKI system will be used also for issuing certificates for SSL servers, as well as for different devices (IPSec enabled routers, firewall, etc.). As a CA software/hardware solution for our PKI consolidated system, we have chosen a Digitrust PKI domestic solution ([Pexi05]) which satisfies all PKI and security international standards, as well as which could be fully customizable to our specific needs and requirements from banking business environment. For example, possible customizations could be related to optimal realization of RSA and standard symmetrical algorithms, according to the results presented in the papers: [UnMÐ01], [ÐoUM02], [MaÐU02a], [MaÐU02b], [MaÐU03], [MaÐo05], [MaÐo06a], [MaÐo06b].

The paper is organized as follows. The main characteristics of the PKI consolidation project in Banca Intesa ad Beograd is described in Chapter 2. Chapter 3 is dedicated to brief consideration about multiapplicative smart payment cards. Main characteristics of the implemented PKI solution are listed in Chapters 4-6 while conclusions are given in Chapter 7.

2 PKI consolidation Project of Banca Intesa ad Beograd

PKI consolidation Project in Banca Intesa ad Beograd was necessary from the following reasons:

- Establishment of unique in-house PKI solution for all external users – physical and legal persons (home banking and e-banking systems, as well as for some specialized applications like web loans, etc.).

- Using the multiapplicative Maestro EMV smart cards for secure electronic payment of physical persons based on PKI system and electronic signature.

- To decentralize issuance of digital certificates from central location of the Bank to branch offices.
- Preparation for issuing qualified certificates according to European Directive and Serbian Electronic Signature Law,
- Introduction of the qualified electronic signature based on smart cards.

In EU countries, Electronic signatures Laws are adopted much earlier and there exist considerable experiences in establishment of Certification Authorities (CAs or CSPs – Certification Service Providers) that issue qualified certificates according to the European Directive on Electronic Signatures. It is a world's trend that organizations that have wide network of external users doing some e-business with the organization, and that have also a big number of internal users using some forms of internal e-business activities, have the following combination of PKI systems:

- Microsoft PKI system – MS Enterprize Certificate Services, domain-integrated, which provides certificate generation on smart cards that enable users to log onto Windows operating system (Win logon), as well as for many other useful security functions that are based on domain integration (e.g. secure e-mail system or SSL client authentication) – for internal users.
- PKI system, proprietary developed, or purchased on the market, for purposes of issuing certificates (possibly qualified also) to external users (legal and physical persons) that do some specific e-business with this organization.

Namely, it seems to be that MS Certificate Services, integrated in Windows 2000 or 2003 server, are very much useful for internal users in Windows domain based organizations. On the other side, the most often case is that PKI products for external users have been chosen from the market which provides possibilities for issuing qualified certificates according to corresponding national signature law and corresponding European Directive. This combination is also a basis for the Project of PKI consolidation in Banca Intesa ad Beograd where the integral and consolidated PKI system consists of:

- Offline Root CA for internal and external users – a proprietary Root CA system (Digitrust PKI system),
- PKI system for internal users which already exists and is based on MS Enterprize subordinate CA which is fully domain integrated and
- Unique PKI system (based on Digitrust PKI system) as intermediate CA for external users, devices, SSL certificates, etc.

Thus, the PKI consolidation project of Banca Intesa ad Beograd is based on the following concept:

- There is one unique Root CA for Banca Intesa ad Beograd which is offline and which is not connected in LAN.
- Intermediate CA certificates for external and internal users are generated so that PKCS#10 certificate requests are generated on the intermediate servers and processed by the Root CA system resulting in corresponding certificates that are implemented back into intermediate CA online servers. In the near future, after the establishment of the Serbian Acrreditation and Supervision Body, and its corresponding Root CA system, some intermediate CA server of Banca Intesa ad Beograd will eventually apply to obtain the certificate from this National Body's CA for issuing qualified certificates for the Bank's external users.

- For external users, this system (the intermediate CA for external users) issues certificates on mini CD or Maestro PKI smart payment cards for physical persons, as well as on PKI smart cards (e-banking cards) for legal persons.

- External users, as well as special internal users from branch offices and from a central location, use WEB enroll CA server for realization the following functions:

- Requesting certificates,

- Renewing certificates and

- Revoking certificates.

- Both legal and physical users are registered for using the corresponding payment system (home banking or e-banking) in branch offices acting as RA (Registration Authority) locations. After registration, smart cards for legal and physical persons are given empty to the users (along with necessary smart card reader) and they will enroll for certificates either by themselves lately via Web enroll CA server with the proper and secure user authentication or with a help of the corresponding Bank's branch employee with corresponding RA administration role at the Bank's branch office location. Also, there are possibilities for complete personalization of the cards (e.g. e-banking cards for legal users) at the Bank's central location, if this is specified so in the corresponding certificate policies.

- In the consolidated PKI system, there will be also some administrative applications (RAO – RA Operator, and CAO – CA Operator) which are used from dedicated workstations from Bank's Intranet performing some necessary administrative functions (managing the whole PKI system, managing user certificate profiles, requesting, renewing and revoking certificates, unblocking smart cards, defining administrative users' roles, etc.) and from employees with special PKI administrative roles (security officers, as well as RA and CA administrators and operators).

- There will be separate Intermediate CAs issuing certificates for information resources (SSL, routers, servers, code signing, ...).

- Smart cards for both legal and physical persons could be enrolled for maximum 3 different certificates of maximum 2048 bits key length.

- This PKI system supports publication of CRL list, as well as different HSM (Hardware Security Module) devices, some brand name HSMs or some proprietary ones (e.g. like the one described in [MSON01]), for offine and online (intermediate) CAs. These devices could be classical HSMs, but currently they are smart cards that stores private keys of 2048 bit length for Root and Intermediate CAs since smart cards provide better cryprographic protection of the private key (when generated on the card itself and never leaves the card) compared to the some currently available HSMs.

The unique PKI system for external users of Banca Intesa ad Beograd could consist of three different intermediate/subordinate CA for e-banking users, home banking users, and information resources, respectively, which are hierarchically under one unique Root CA for external users. Or it could be one intermediate CA supporting several different certificate profiles. The simplified diagram of the solution is given on Fig. 1. We could see that the new PKI system's architecture is divided into components that are placed in different security zones (DMZ, internal zones, ...). Namely, WEB enroll CA server is in DMZ zone, the Application server is internal zone and Intermediate CA servers are also in internal zone but with higher security level. The Root CA server is completely separated and disconnected from any LAN network. All communication between main components of the system, WEB enroll CA server – Application server – Intermediate CA server, is secured by using the SSL protocol with client and server authentication. Namely, each windows service – web service communication between each of the two mentioned servers is secured by the SSL protocol including the SSL client authentication based on the certificate issued for the corresponding windows service on the given server.

Also, the PKI administrative applications (RAO and CAO) access through the internal network to the specialized web service on the application server through SSL with client authentication based on the certificate issued on the smart card of the corresponding administrator. In this case, there is an additional security measure. Namely, any RAO and CAO could access the PKI administrative applications based on his smart card only from one dedicated workstation where the tumbprint of his certificate is registered into the application. From any other workstations, their access will be denied.

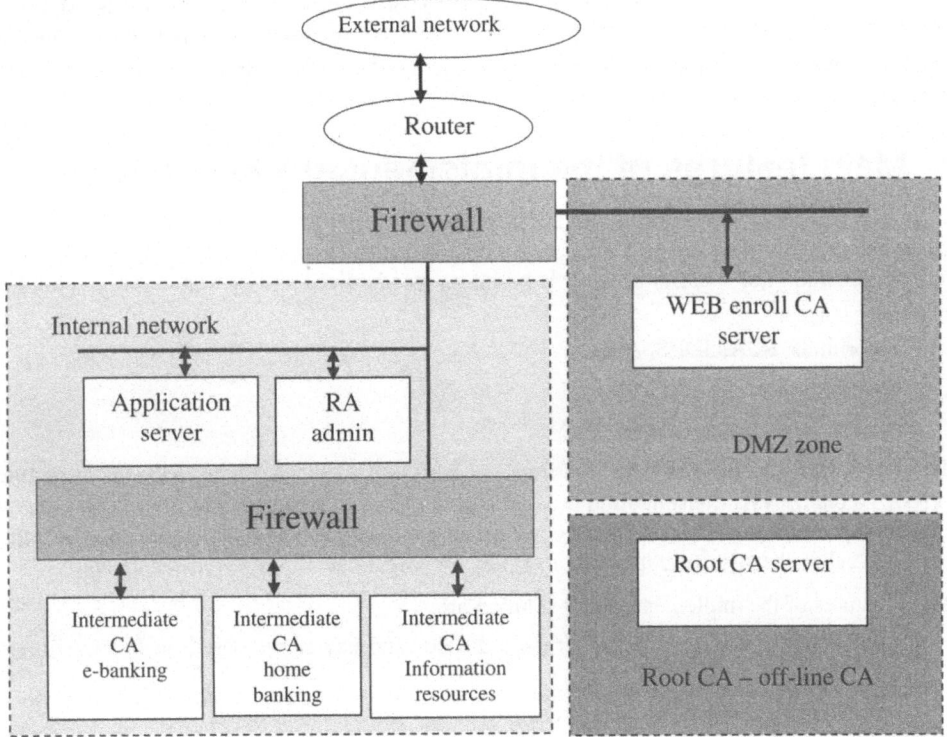

Figure 1: A simplified block diagram of the consolidated PKI system of Banca Intesa ad Beograd

3 Multiapplicative smart payment cards of Banca Intesa ad Beograd

The Banca Intesa ad Beograd's MasterCard EMV chip cards are multiapplicative smart payment cards for citizens that include the following applications:

- EMV DDA M/Chip Select 4 payment application,
- MasterCard SecureCode CAP payment application and
- PKI application that will enable multiple (three) keypairs (at least keypairs for digital signature and digital envelope) and electronic signature generation.

This way, citizens that have MasterCard chip cards from Banca Intesa ad Beograd could pay:

- through POS and ATM terminals on the basis on MC EMV DDA M/Chip Select 4 payment application,

- via Internet by using the MasterCard's SecureCode CAP application and corresponding CAP-enabled and certified OTP (One-Time Password) token – unconnected reader and

- through Banca Intesa ad Beograd's web site/portal (online.bancaintesabeograd.com) using the PKI authentication and digital signature exploiting the PKI application and corresponding keys implemented on Maestro cards via an appropriate PC/SC smart card reader. Also, these cards could be further enrolled for some e-government qualified certificates and used for creating qualified signatures.

These cards are Multos 4 with 32KB cards with PKI capabilities that include three applications on them. There will be issuing smart cards for different MasterCard products: Maestro, standard, business, gold and MC^2. These cards will be personalized either in an in-house small personalization center in Banca Intesa ad Beograd or out-sourced in some external personalization centers.

4 Main features of the implemented PKI solution

Today, security is a key word in internet business. The aspiration of free data exchange confronts the requirement to restrict data access only to authorized persons and applications. The newest generation of security systems is based on standardized and proven cryptographic solutions.

- algorithms: RSA, 3DES, AES,
- protocols: SSL, TLS, IPSec,
- devices: smart cards, tokens, HSMs.

The magic that ties all this solutions into a meaningful whole is Public Key Infrastructure (PKI). To realize PKI consolidation project, Banca Intesa ad Beograde has chosen an integral PKI software/hardware solution that comprises of applications that enable registration of subjects and subscribers, certification services, key and certificate life-cycle management.

Main features of the implemented PKI solution are:

- Support for a variety of cryptographic devices and key stores based on MS CAPI and PKCS#11,

- Variety of deployment options according to specific customer needs,

- Support for X.509v3 certificate profiles with different certificate extensions and policies,

- Extensibility options through special hardware based (HSM) and software based plugins for key storage, and cryptographic algorithms (ECDSA),

- Multi-tier architecture with option for high security mechanisms between tiers,

- Multiple authorization levels: MasterUser, CAAdministrator, SecurityOffices, RAOperator,

4.1 Interoperability

The implemented PKI solution is based on wide adopted international standards to ensure compatibility with other software solutions:

- X.500 directory distinguished names in registration database,

- X.509v3 certificate profiles,
- X.509v2 CRL profiles,
- PKCS#1 signing format,
- PKCS#5 password based encryption,
- PKCS#10 certificate requests,
- PKCS#11 cryptographic token interface,
- Microsoft CSP interface for access to cryptographic modules,
- SOAP, WSDL, HTTPS protocols between distributed elements of the architecture,
- Certificate extensions compatible with Microsoft® Outlook, Microsoft® Internet Explorer, Microsoft® Authenticode.

4.2 Architecture of the implemented PKI solution

The implemented PKI solution in Banca Intesa ad Beograd supports both online and offline deploying CA model, see Figure 2.

- In online model only Root CA is hosted on server disconnected from any LAN network, all other servers are in DMZ or internal zone.
- In offline model all machines (all can be in only one machine) are disconnected from any LAN network.

In the following text, main components of the realized PKI solution are described.

4.2.1 Certification Service

Certification service is a windows service responsible for storing and using CA private key. Certification service is configured to start automatically, but for the reasons of additional security, the configuration is loaded and the full operation mode is reached only after Master User enters his password, which could be also realized as an appropriate key sharing procedure. After the configuration is loaded, the Certification service uses CA private key for certificate and CRL signing. Certification service supports extension plug-ins that can provide additional mechanisms for storage and additional algorithms for usage of CA private keys. Certification service functionality is exposed through a corresponding CA Web service installed on the same machine. The CA Web service secures connection and approach to the CA windows service, through SSL with client authentication based on the certificate, and logs all actions in Registration Database or appropriate log files.

4.2.2 Registration Service

Registration service is a windows service responsible for complete evidence of the corresponding CA system. This includes data about one or more Certification services, data about users, organizations, organizational units and other entities (intermediate CA, WEB servers ...). Registration service is also responsible for Registration Database management. Registration service processes certificate request, forms „to be signed" certificates and CRLs and sends them to Certification Web service for signing. Registration service functionality is exposed through two Web services installed on the same machine. WebCAAdmin service exposes high priority functions to MasterUser and CAAdministrator roles through CA Administrator application. EnterpriseRA service exposes large set of methods for certificate enrollment, renewal and revoking (see Fig. 2).

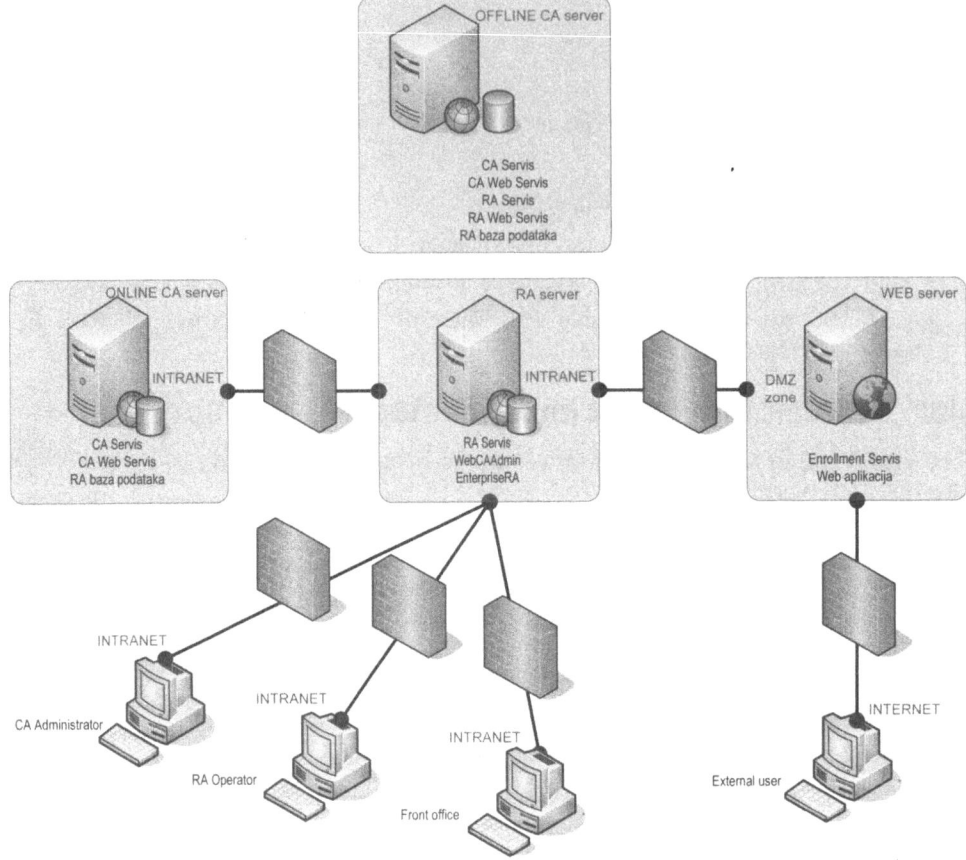

Figure 2: Functional architecture of the implemented PKI solution in
Banca Intesa ad Beograd

4.2.3 Enrolment Service

Enrolment Service delegates certificate requests to Registration Service. Entire communication with Registration service is secured through SSL client authentication (secure communication between enrolment service and EnterprizeRA Web service on the RA server) and with
appropriate authorization based on X509v3 certificate.

4.2.4 Web server application

Web server application of this PKI solution enables end users to enrol for certificate, as well
as for renewing or revoking a certificate. It is used also for publishing CA certificates, end entities' certificates and CRLs. This Web server application enables a use of corresponding
ActiveX control (for use in MS Internet Explorer) on the client side which is used for end
user certificate enrolment by using standard key stores (MS Crypto API) and different smart
cards or custom developed key stores for specific purposes (e.g. mini disks).

4.2.5 RA Operator application

RA Operator is a PKI application for enrolment of entities and certificate issuing. RAOperators through this application can enrol users, organizations, organizational units, other entities. RA Operator applications can attach additional plug-ins for smart card personalization, mini disk creating, CSP compatible certificate issuing and so on.

4.2.6 CA Administrator application

CA Administrator is a PKI administrative application for complete managing of the implemented PKI solution. Through this application, MasterUser, CAAdministrator or SecurityOfficer can enable use of CA keys, manage certificate profiles, manage administrative profiles, manage directory distinguished names, etc. The actual authorization level for performing different functions is determined by the certificate of the client who starts the application.

4.2.7 Application Programming Interface

A corresponding Application Programming Interface (API) is used in the realized PKI solutiuon. This API is set of both ActiveX controls and .Net controls developed for smart card access, key generation, cryptographic operations and certificate and store management. Main components of this API are:

- PexCryptoAPI – ActiveX that enables use of MS Crypto API and appropriate Cryptographic Service Providers,
- PKCS11API – ActiveX that enables use of PKCS#11 standard for cryptographic token interface,
- ManagedAPI - .Net support for RSA algorithm, hash algorithms, symmetric ciphers, prime numbers generation, certificate and store operations, Basic Encoding Rules, ...

The API also supports variety of custom cryptographic solutions developed on market.

5 Conclusion

Main characteristics of the PKI consolidation project in Banca Intesa ad Beograd are given in the paper. This PKI system is used for electronic banking services for external users (home banking for physical persons and e-banking for legal persons) and for Bank's internal users (Windows Logon, secure e-mail, SSL client authentication). One of the main driving force for this project is the introduction of the EMV DDA MasterCards in Banca Intesa ad Beograd. These are PKI Multos cards which will have three applications on them: M/Chip Select 4 and CAP payment applications, as well as PKI application. This way, Maestro users could pay through POS and ATMs by using the M/Chip payment applications, via Internet by using external CAP reader and CAP application on the card and via Bank's web portal by using the connected smart card reader and PKI application on the card with X.509 digital certificate issued by this consolidated PKI system. This PKI system is based on the fully customizable, and fully compliant with international standards, domestic PKI solution – Digitrust PKI system. This PKI system enables full integration in the existing banking environments, e.g. in the core banking applications in branch offices. The greater possibility of customization is one of the main advantages of the chosen PKI system compared to the other considered PKI solutions.

References

[Mark04]   Marković, M.: Recent PKI experiences in Serbia, "ISSE 2004 Securing Elec-
              tronic Business Processes" (Highlights of the Information Security Solutions
              Europe 2004 Conference), Eds.: Sachar Paulus, Norbert Pohlman, Helmut
              Reimer, Vieweg, ISBN 3-528-05910-9, pp. 321-332.

[SaMa03]   Savić, Z., Marković, M.: Development of Secure Web Financial Services in Ser-
              bia, in Proceedings of ISSE 2003, October 7-10, 2003.

[Pexi05]   www.pexim.net.: Digitrust PKI brochure,

[UnMĐ01[Unkašević, T., Marković, M., Djorđević, G.: Optimization of RSA algorithm
              implementation on TI TMS320C54x signal processors based on a modified Kar-
              atsuba-Offman's algorithm, in Proc. of ECMCS'2001, 11-13 September, Buda-
              pest, 2001.

[ĐoUM02]   Đorđević, G., Unkašević, T., Marković, M.: Optimization of modular reduction
              procedure in RSA algorithm implementation on assembler of TMS320C54x sig-
              nal processors, in Proc. of DSP 2002, July, Santorini, Greece.

[MaĐU02a]   Marković, M., Unkašević, T., Đorđević, G.: RSA algorithm optimization on as-
              sembler of TI TMS320C54x signal processors, in Proc. of EUSIPCO 2002, Tou-
              louse, France, Sept. 3-6, 2002.

[MaĐU02b]   Marković, M., Djorđević, G., Unkašević, T.: Influence of key length in possible
              optimization of RSA algorithm implementation on signal processor, in Proc. of
              ICEST 2002, Oct., 1-4, pp. 23-26, 2002.

[MaĐU03]   Marković, M., Đorđević, G., Unkašević, T.: On Optimizing RSA Algorithm Im-
              plementation on Signal Processor Regarding Asymmetric Private Key Length, in
              Proceedings of WISP 2003, Budapest, Sept. 2003, pp. 73-77, 2003.

[MaĐo05]   Marković, M., Đordjević, G.: On optimizing DSP implementation of standard
              symmetrical cryptographic algorithms, in Proc. Of EURASIP EC-SIP-M 2005,
              June 2005, Smolenice, Slovak Republic.

[MaĐo06a]   Marković, M., Đorđević, G.: On Optimizing Standard Cryptographic Algorithms
              on TI Fixed Point Signal Processors, In Proceedings of ICT 2006 Conference,
              Madeira, Portugal, May 9-12, 2006.

[MaĐo06b]   Marković, M., Đorđević, G.: On Implementation Aspects of Standard Asymmet-
              ric and Symmetric Cryptographic Algorithms on TI Signal Processors, in Pro-
              ceedings of the Second International Workshop on Security, Privacy and Trust
              in Pervasive and Ubiquitous Computing (SecPerU 2006), 29 June 2006, Lyon,
              France.

[MSON01]   Marković, M., Savić, Z., Obrenović, Ž., Nikolić, A.: A PC Cryptographic Co-
              processor Based on TI Signal Processor and Smart Card System, Communica-
              tions and Multimedia Security Issues of the New Century, R. Steinmetz, J. Ditt-
              man, M. Steinebach, Eds., Kluwer Academic Publishers, 2001, pp. 383-393.

Security Analysis and Configuration of Large Networks

Antonio Lioy

Politecnico di Torino
Dip. Automatica e Informatica
lioy@polito.it

Abstract

Providing and managing security for large networked systems is difficult because their size and complexity makes manual design and management nearly impossible. Current security management tools lack functionality and mostly work only in mono-vendor environments. The POSITIF project has developed an open framework (and related tools) to support the design and management of security architectures, based on formal methods to describe a network system and the security requirements. The framework is easily expandable and can interface with limited effort to several open-source or proprietary security technologies and tools.

1 Introduction

It's everybody experience that large networked information systems are increasingly difficult to manage. Their complexity is such that standard network and system management operations are nearly impossible to be performed manually and require dedicated management suites.

When it comes to security, problems are even bigger, less understood by the average system/network manager and less supported by management products. As a consequence, most managers will handle the problem by a "divide-and-conquer" approach, concentrating on a few different areas: typical examples are boundary defence (i.e. firewalls) and malware protection (i.e. antivirus products). While these areas might be supported by proper automatic management tools, there is virtually no tool able to handle the security design and management of large heterogeneous networked systems.

As a consequence, several key concepts of system protection remain just buzzwords and are rarely thoroughly applied. For example, let's consider the following two principles:

- "Defence in depth" would require setup of several levels of defence, but – due to the design and management complexity – a minimum set of protections is nearly always adopted;
- "Biological diversity" calls for the same function being implemented by different tools, to protect against failures due to bugs or errors, but usually mono-vendor solutions are adopted because management tools are often vendor-specific.

If we want to improve the security level of our networked systems, automatic tools are needed to design and manage the configuration of the protection elements. This was the main target of the POSITIF project [1], funded by the EC through contract IST-FP6-002314, and some of its main results are described here.

S. Paulus, N. Pohlmann, H. Reimer (Editors): Securing Electronic Business Processes, Vieweg (2006), 259-265

2 The POSITIF framework

The basic idea behind POSITIF is that security is going to be a pervasive requirement for every function and element of a networked information system. In other words, the good old days – when a firewall at the network border and anti-virus software on every node were sufficient to protect a network – are gone forever. In turn this requires the ability to design and manage very complex protection systems that integrate multi-vendor solutions and a mixture of commercial and free open-source software. We therefore designed a framework that can integrate several solutions and tools that support designers and managers in creating and running secure information systems.

2.1   Overview

Figure 1 depicts the overall schema of the POSITIF framework. For sake of generality, we have named "security block" any element that can perform a security-related action, such as filtering packets, encrypting data, or monitoring events. Therefore a security block can be a physical device, such as a router or a VPN concentrator, or a software module, such as a personal firewall or a SSL-enabled server.

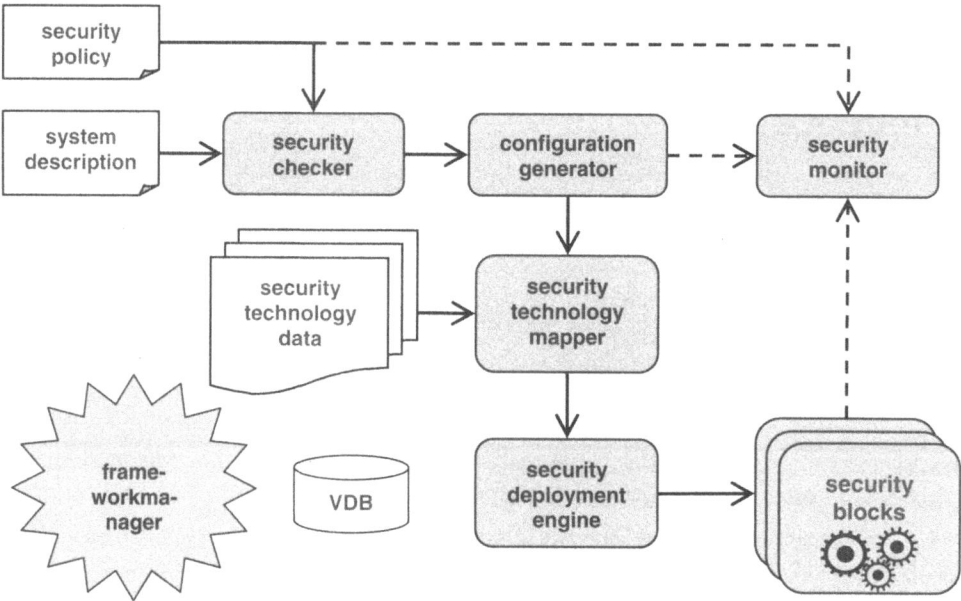

Figure 1: overall schema of the POSITIF framework.

Following a top-down approach from design to implementation and management, first of all the framework user must provide a formal description of both the target networked information system and the security policy (i.e. requirements) that must be satisfied.

In turn these data are processed by a tool that checks if the security requirements can be satisfied by the given architecture and provides a rough measure of the resulting security level. If this check fails, a proper explanation is given (e.g. "privacy required but no encryption capability available") to support the designer in fixing the problem. Since this analysis can be performed multiple times before a system is actually deployed, there is space to evaluate different alternatives in system architecture, service design and protection choices. This could include also a rough economic evaluation if meaningful costs are attached both to losses caused by attacks and security blocks.

Next, abstract configurations are generated to implement the security policy. They are abstract as they are block-independent and expressed in a generic configuration language. They are later translated to real element-specific commands by the security technology mapper that must be fed also with the command syntax of the real elements. The mapper has a modular architecture so that it can be easily extended by writing simple modules. This can be done by anybody (if the commands are well documented) or the designer of the target element, if this is a proprietary one.

Finally POSITIF offers also the option to automatically deploy the configuration through standard channels (e.g. SNMP, SSH) or plugins for proprietary solutions. It should be noted that configurations are generated and deployed not only for the policy enforcement elements (e.g. firewalls) but also for the monitoring ones (e.g. IDS).

Last but not least, a special security monitor tool has been developed: it goes beyond standard IDS functionality because – thanks to its knowledge of the security policy and the expected configurations – it can generate security alarms when an event that violates the policy is detected.

Although not directly linked to the flow, two other elements are very important. The framework manager handles the user interface, provides centralized storage (for descriptions, policies, and configurations) and manages all framework operations (such as deployment and alarms). VDB is the vulnerability database: it contains known vulnerabilities, both general (e.g. normal IP packets can be read and changed in transit) and product-specific (e.g. version X.Y of the HHR web server is vulnerable to URL overflow attacks).

Note that POSITIF is not a monolithic system: proper open public interfaces are defined between each module and XML-based data formats are used for data exchanged between the various modules. Standards have been used wherever available. This provides room for integration of external solutions addressing a specific area, as well as generates input that can be used by other tools.

2.2 P-SDL

P-SDL (POSITIF System Description Language). is the language used to describe the target system. This includes the real network topology (e.g. cables and ports), the virtual topology (i.e. VLANs), and the services offered (e.g. transport protocol, port, application protocol, software module offering the service). Moreover P-SDL offers support to describe the security capabilities of the various blocks, such as the IPsec stack of an operating system or the SSL support of an application.

P-SDL is based on XML and is defined as an extension of the CIM model [2] from DMTF that guarantees compatibility with several network management products. P-SDL is currently evolving to offer better support to describe services (through the BPEL and WS-CDL standards) and their security properties (via UML-sec). Additionally, it is being evaluated as a possible language to describe – with proper extensions – also some dependability-related issues, such as power supply, environmental support systems, and physical protection.

Note that, as a side advantage, P-SDL could be used also to exchange network descriptions in a vendor-neutral format, for several purposes. Besides the most obvious one (i.e. internal documentation), it could be the basis for external certification, law compliance evidence and benchmarking of different security tools (a thing that is dramatically missing in the security arena when compared to other engineering fields).

2.3 P-SPL

Besides describing the topology and functionality of the target system, the user must also formally describe her security requirements, via another CIM-based XML language: the P-SPL (POSITIF Security Policy Language).

Five categories of security requirements are currently supported by this language: network traffic filtering, agent authentication and authorization (with an agent being a human operator, an active network node, or software module), channel protection (from OSI layer 2 up to layer 7) and operational policies (with conditions such as "system down" or "traffic higher than X packets/second").

Requirements can be described at several levels, from high-level protection of services (confidentiality, integrity, availability) down to network level filters. While most security administrators are currently familiar with low level specification of requirements (e.g. "block all ICMP type 8 packets" or "permit TCP packets to port 80 of the node www.my.com"), the effort of POSITIF is towards high-level specifications, such as

> *permit access to the web-based database front-end to all my customers, with guarantee of privacy, authentication and integrity*

with the supplemental definition of the group "my customers" (e.g. identified by their IP address). In this way we hope to involve higher management people and application owners in the definition of the security policy and therefore avoid misalignment between the business-level expected behaviour and the actual security configuration. This would be beneficial also for all those SMEs that need security but don't have enough internal knowledge to manage it themselves or even just to clearly specify their requirements to an external consultant.

2.4 Checking security and generating configurations

Once the target system has been described and its security requirements formally specified, two modules operate on these data: the security checker (SEC) and the Configuration Generator (COG).

SEC uses graph-based algorithms to perform a security analysis, not an abstract but a specific one, targeted only to the services to be protected and to the specific requirements expressed by the user via P-SPL. By using knowledge of the general weaknesses (e.g. sniffing, hijacking) and the known vulnerabilities in the VDB, the tool provides two outputs: which attacks can be countered by the system and how it should be configured to achieve the desired protection level. This can also be read as a measure of the security of the system, that is the number of known attacks or vulnerabilities that can be countered by the system.

It should be noted that the SEC is not "yet another" security scanner or vulnerability analysis tool because it does not dynamically scan a real system and look for known vulnerabilities. Rather it performs a static analysis of an ICT system, looking for design weaknesses with respect to the services to be provided. In this sense SEC is complementary to common dynamic analysis tool as it is more oriented to static design validation. One important point to notice is that SEC is service-oriented and policy-driven: it considers the nodes, links and software components needed to provide a specific service to the end-user and looks for problems related to the security policy defined by the service manager. For example, in a public service (e.g. flight timetable) often privacy is not an issue and therefore the tool will not consider the related attacks. Moreover, since the service is provided through a specified set of elements (e.g. a router, a web server and a DBMS) only the weaknesses directly or indirectly related to these elements will be considered.

The configurations required to protect the system according to the user requirements are formally created by the COG that solves potential conflicts and creates generic configurations for the various blocks. The generic nature of these data is useful for two reasons. First, for defence-in-depth we can easily require that all elements with a certain capability do enforce the same protection rule. For example, we could filter unwanted traffic not only at the network border but in every element with a filtering capability, be it a router, a switch or a server. Additionally, the use of a generic configuration allows an optimal splitting between the block-independent and the block-specific parts.

2.5 Mapping to actual protection technology

The generic block configurations created by the COG must be translated to configurations for the actual blocks found in the live system. This requires knowledge of the configuration syntax for the real blocks but it is not a mere translation from one format to another. Actually a single simple abstract command (such as dropping all packets originating at a certain subnet) might require multiple commands to be issued for certain blocks (for example, the creation of a filter followed by its application to one or more interfaces).

Therefore for each block supported by POSITIF a set of Java functions must be provided to be called by the STM (Security Technology Mapper) to translate the generic commands. Although promising, other simpler approaches (such as those based on XSLT) have proved to be ineffective in that they cannot support all the kinds of translations to be performed.

2.6 Configuration deployment

Once the configuration for a specific block is available, it should be deployed to the actual node. The SDE (Security Deployment Engine) of POSITIF supports various technologies towards this goal.

Manual deployment is always possible (i.e. printing out the configuration for manual typing by a human operator) and might be the preferred choice while testing the system or to compare its results to those currently in place.

Automatic deployment may take place via standard protocols (such as SNMP or SSH) or by activating specific plugins if the target block can be managed only via a proprietary protocol.

2.7 Monitoring security

The POSITIF security monitor incorporates several technologies, some standard and some innovative. The principle behind its design was to have a proper mixture of reactive and proactive approaches, because it is common knowledge that there is not a single approach able to detect any kind of attack. Therefore, besides standard IDS technology based on SNORT, the monitor uses three other types of components: PCC, PVS, and SEM.

The PCC (Proactive Configuration Checker) periodically checks if the actual configuration running on a block is consistent with the last deployed one. This is useful to detect attacks that have modified the configuration as well as mistakes performed by support personnel that have operated directly on the block rather than through the framework.

The PVS (Policy Violation System) is a component that compares events against the policy. It has a modular architecture so that specific modules can be loaded corresponding to those features required by the specified security policy. As an example of a feature rarely found in other systems, a module has been developed to monitor several aspects of SSL channels, such as SSL version, acceptable certificate issuers, and negotiated cryptographic algorithms and parameters. Other modules monitor violations of the mail policy or of web-based applications.

Finally the SEM (Security Modules) are small footprint modules to be hosted by various network nodes for specific functions. For example, a very successful module is the one created by one POSITIF partner based on SOM (Self-Organizing Maps). It enhances the detection capabilities of SNORT because it is able to compare actual network traffic to the expected one (as specified by the policy) by looking only to the packet payload, irrespective of the packet headers [3]. It is therefore able to detect also forbidden traffic on non-standard ports or encapsulated inside other application protocols.

2.8 Supporting new blocks

POSITIF is a research project. Therefore it will design and test the framework, but will not create a full-fledged product. Rather, in the classical open-community spirit, it will provide its results mostly in open-source form but for some specific developments of an industrial partner. So community effort is required to support many security blocks. For supporting a new block of a known type (i.e. one of those corresponding to the policy categories) the following steps must be followed:

- create a template to simplify use of the block inside P-SDL, with all its configurable parameters and security capabilities;
- create the Java routines needed to translate from the generic configuration to its native configuration language;
- specify if the block supports network deployment and by which protocol (if a non-standard one is used, then provide also the plugin for the SDE).

The POSITIF web site will act as a repository for contributed work.

2.9 Managing the framework

The framework manager provides the support functions and coordinates the work of all the modules described above.

The system description, security policy and configurations are stored inside a native XML database (for faster access, as all the data formats are XML-based). A graphic user interface is provided for human operations but the framework manager offers also a rich set of webservices for automatic operations of the internal modules or for connecting to external tools. This greatly simplifies the development work because programmers don't need to learn the gory details of CIM and have direct access to high-level views of the system. For example, the SEC exploits a webservice that provides a graph-like view of the network, with native methods to identify the shortest path or the reachable nodes.

The manager handles also the registration and activation of specific sub-modules (such as those of the deployment engine or the monitor). Finally import-export filters are provided for easy backup and exchange of the system data.

2.10 The framework at work

The framework is currently in alpha-version and it is being tested in several different environments. PWR, the Wroclaw University, is testing the tools in a typical research setting, mostly with Unix-based open-source applications, with the need to balance protection and user access. Vodafone is running a test-bed to check the framework capabilities with respect to multi-vendor support and policy-based monitoring of network traffic. Finally the Italian Ministry of Justice is running tests to compare the configurations generated by POSITIF against those developed by skilled security administrators. All the tests are showing positive results and helped to identify problems and improvements.

Finally, as an example of a possible industrial application, BULL is integrating some of the POSITIF concepts and tools in its line of IPsec and SSL network security appliances, by providing specific plugin modules to generate and deploy the configurations through its management tool (TDM, Trustway Domain Manager).

2.11 For further information

Language manuals, examples and the framework tools are available at the project web site (http://www.positif.org).

3 Conclusion

While commercial suites exist to manage some aspects of the security of a system for some specific products, there is a lack of product independent security management tools. Moreover there is nearly no support to design the protection for a networked system and evaluate its effectiveness at the design stage. We think that the framework and tools developed in POSITIF provide a first viable approach to solve these problems and – thanks to their open-source nature – could hopefully provide the foundation for a community effort.

References

[1]   "POSITIF – Policy–based Security Tools and Framework", http://www.positif.org

[2]   Distributed Management Task Force (DMTF), "Common Information Model (CIM) standards", http://www.dmtf.org/standards/cim/

[3]   U. Payer, S. Kraxberger, "SOM-Based Lightweight Policy Verification", Terena Networking Conference, Catania (Italy), 15-18 May 2006

S-VPN Policy: Access List Conflict Automatic Analysis and Resolution

Simone Ferraresi[1,2] · Stefano Pesic[1] · Livia Trazza[1] · Andrea Baiocchi[2]

[1]Elsag S.p.A.
Via Naide, 43 - 00155 Rome, Italy
{simone.ferraresi | stefano.pesic | livia.trazza}@elsag.it

[2]INFOCOM Dept. - University of Rome "La Sapienza"
Via Eudossiana, 18 - 00184 Rome, Italy
{andrea.baiocchi | simone.ferraresi}@uniroma1.it

Abstract

S-VPN gateways are today core elements in network security infrastructure. As networks and services become more complex, managing IPSec access rules becomes an error-prone task. Conflicts in a policy can cause holes in security, and often they can be hard to find when performing only visual or manual inspection. We have defined firstly a methodology to systematically classify the severity of rule conflicts and secondly we have proposed two different solutions to automatically resolve conflicts in an access list, implementing and testing one of them.

1 Introduction

A key feature of secure systems, including network ones, is the management of security policies, from those at high level down to the platform specific implementation. Security policy defines constraints, limitations and authorisation on data handling and communications. In a network environment many problems may also arise due to the inconsistency of policies implemented by security gateways and firewalls interconnected over an insecure network. As distributed secure systems increase in complexity, policy configuration and maintenance tasks become increasingly prone to errors. These errors can give rise to holes in security in the entire system, that are difficult to detect before an attack is suffered. For this reason a verification phase should be performed when policy is defined and after any modification or integration.

We assume that policies are formally stated according to a well defined formal language, so that the access lists of a security gateway can be reduced to an ordered list of predicates of the form C → A, where C is a condition and A is an action. We refer to predicates implementing security policies as rules. For security gateway the condition of a filtering rule is composed of five selectors:

<protocol><src ip><src port><dst ip><dst port>

The action that could be performed on the packet is allow, deny or process, where process imply that the packet has to be submitted to the IPSec algorithm (ESP, AH). How to process that packet is described in a specific MAP which details how to apply the security mecha-

S. Paulus, N. Pohlmann, H. Reimer (Editors): Securing Electronic Business Processes, Vieweg (2006), 266-274

nism. Conditions are checked on each packet flowing through the device, applying it exclusively the action required by the first matching rule.

In general a conflict occurs when desired effects of a policy are ambiguous or not clear. In this paper we focus our attention on automatic conflict detection and resolution on a policy implemented in a single security gateway.

Policy consistency has been the subject of a lot of attention from the research community. The most significant contributions to this subject are [AlHa04] [AlHa05] [AlHa03] [AlHM05] [HaSP00]. In [HaSP00] the authors only attempt to detect if firewall rules are correlated to each other, while in [AlHa04] [AlHa05] [AlHa03] a set of techniques and algorithms are defined to discover all of the possible policy conflicts, with a particular focus on S-VPN policy described on [AlHM05]. However, none of these studies provided a resolution phase. Original contributions of our work are the definition of a general methodology for policy conflict classification and detection and exploitation of this methodology as a basis to define automatic conflict resolution algorithms. The output of such algorithms is a corrected policy file plus possibly feedback to the security manager to fix detected conflicts that cannot be decided automatically.

This work is organized as follows. In Section II we briefly present logical relationships between rules as in [AlHa04] [AlHM05]. In Section III we present our formalization of severity classification for conflicts. In Section IV two algorithms are defined for automatic conflict resolution. In Section V, we give a summary of the software implementation. Finally, in Section VI, we give our conclusions and plans for future work.

2 Modelling of Rules Relation

To be able to introduce S-VPN policy conflict analysis and resolution it is useful to define all the relations that may tie a couple of rules. These relations, as defined in [AlHa04][AlHM05], require a comparison between the network fields of filtering rules independently of the rule action. First we state formally what a rule is in our context.

Security gateway policies as well as firewall policies specify a filtering condition C and an action A. The condition C aims at selecting those IP packets that the corresponding action applies to. Packet filtering is based on the values of five header fields: IP destination and source addresses (dst ip, src ip), destination and source port numbers (dst port, src port) and the IP header protocol type (prot). For each of these selectors we need to specify a value or a range of values. To each predicate listed in the policy file we associate a rule R defined as a five-tuple of selector variables ranges:

$$R = \left\{ S_{prot}, S_{src\_ip}, S_{src\_port}, S_{dst\_ip}, S_{dst\_port} \right\}$$

where $S_{sel} = ANY$ or $S_{sel} = \left[sel_{\min}, sel_{\max} \right]$ for $sel \in \left\{ prot, src\_ip, src\_port, dst\_ip, dst\_port \right\}$,

ANY being a "don't care" flag; equivalently we could replace ANY by the entire possible range of the corresponding selector. In the following we refer to the five selector with an integer values variable $i = 1, \cdots, 5$; we denote the i-th selector range associated to a given rule R by $R[i]$. We also define a set operator as $\Diamond \in \{ \subset, \supset, = \}$; also $A \Diamond B$ means that the set A is not a superset nor a subset nor the same as the set B.

2.1 Rules Relations

We now state formally the basic relations among rules for the conflict analysis.

Definition 1: Rules R_x and R_y are Completely Disjoint if every field in R_x is not a subset of, nor a superset of, nor equal to the corresponding field in R_y. Formally,

$$R_x \mathfrak{R}_{CD} R_y \Leftrightarrow \forall i : R_x[i] \lozenge R_y[i]$$

where $\lozenge \in \{\subset, \supset, =\}$ and

$$i \in F = \{prot, src\_ip, src\_port, dst\_ip, dst\_port\}$$

Definition 2: Rules R_x and R_y are Exactly Matching if every field in R_x is equal to the corresponding field in R_y. Formally,

$$R_x \mathfrak{R}_{EM} R_y \Leftrightarrow \forall i : R_x[i] = R_y[i]$$

where $i \in F$

Definition 3: Rules R_x and R_y are Inclusively Matching if they do not exactly match and every field in R_x is a subset of or equal to the corresponding field in R_y. R_x is called the subset match, while R_y is called the superset match. Formally,

$$R_x \mathfrak{R}_{IM} R_y \Leftrightarrow \forall i : R_x[i] \subseteq R_y[i] \text{ and } \exists j : R_x[j] \subset R_y[j]$$

where $i, j \in F$

Definition 4: Rules R_x and R_y are Partially Matching if there is at least one field in R_x that is a subset of or a superset of or equal to the corresponding field in R_y and there is at least one field in R_x that is not a subset nor a superset, nor equal to the corresponding field in R_y. Formally,

$$R_x \mathfrak{R}_{PM} R_y \Leftrightarrow \exists i, j : R_x[i] \lozenge R_y[i] \text{ and } R_x[j] \lozenge R_y[j]$$

where $i, j \in F, i \neq j$

Definition 5: Rules R_x and R_y are Correlated if some fields in R_x are subsets of or equal to the corresponding fields in R_y and the rest of the fields in R_x are supersets of the corresponding fields in R_y. Formally,

$$R_x \mathfrak{R}_C R_y \Leftrightarrow \forall i : R_x[i] \lozenge R_y[i] \text{ and } \exists i, j : R_x[i] \subset R_y[i] \text{ and } R_x[j] \supset R_y[j]$$

where $i, j \in F, i \neq j$

3 Conflict Analysis

To deal with the resolution of S-VPN policy conflicts we have to elaborate a new classification of them which is more selective than the one presented in [AlHa04][AlHM05]. This has been done by introducing the concept of conflict severity.

Definition 6: The severity of a conflict is defined as the rank of correlation between the presence of the conflict in the policy and the erroneous behaviour of the respective device.

A device behaviour is considered erroneous when it does not correspond to the aim of the security manager. To univocally identify the aim of security manager it has been necessary to formulate a working hypothesis on his behaviour.

Working Hypothesis. The security manager inserts a rule in the policy because he wants to apply it to at least one packet.

S-VPN policies are formalized into rules and rules are listed in an ordered file; for each packet the list is scanned and the first matching rule is found (if any); the corresponding action is applied to the packet. Rules further down in the file are ignored for that packet. Let ω be a positive integer denoting the position of a rule in this list: lower values of ω mean higher priority. The position of rule R is denoted by $\omega(R)$.

3.1 Conflicts Classification

In this section we introduce the classification of conflicts according to severity levels:

Exact Match: A rule is in exact match with another one when the two rules are equal in all selectors independently of the value assumed in the action field. These two rules match the same traffic, on which, however, only the action of the rule with higher priority is performed. Formally,

$$R_y C_{EM} R_x \Leftrightarrow \omega(R_x) < \omega(R_y), \ R_x \Re_{EM} R_y$$

The Exact Match conflict is the most severe since it is impossible to understand which one of rules Rx and Ry the security manager wanted to be performed. This is a major problem both in case the actions of the two rules are different and in case they are the same, since the rules in between them might act on packets matched by the condition of rules R_x and R_y, so that it can make a critical difference to eliminate either R_x or R_y.

Shadowing: A rule is shadowed when a previous rule, with different action, matches all the packets that this rule matches so that the shadowed rule will never be activated. Formally,

$$R_y C_{SH} R_x \Leftrightarrow \omega(R_x) < \omega(R_y), R_y \Re_{IM} R_x, A[R_x] \neq A[R_y],$$

where $A[R]$ = Action corresponding to rule R.

This kind of conflict is very severe because the inactivity of the rule R_y represents a violation of the aim of the security manager, consequently performing an erroneous behaviour of the device.

Post Redundancy: A rule is in post redundancy when a previous rule, with same action, matches all the packets that this rule matches so that the redundant rule will never be activated. Formally,

$$R_y C_{PO} R_x \Leftrightarrow \omega(R_x) < \omega(R_y), R_y \Re_{IM} R_x, A[R_x] = A[R_y].$$

Since the actions are the same, an erroneous behavior of the device does not necessarily occur. Yet, this kind of conflict is severe because the inactivity of the rule R_y represents a violation of the aim of the security manager, according to our working hypothesis.

Correlation: Two rules are correlated if they have different filtering actions, and the first rule matches the same packets that the second rule matches and vice versa. Formally,

$$R_y C_{CO} R_x \Leftrightarrow R_y \Re_C R_x, A[R_x] \neq A[R_y].$$

In this situation a violation of the aim of the security manager does not occur because both the rules are active, but is not possible to decide if the behaviour of the device on the traffic matching both rules is erroneous or not, because it depends on the relative order of the two rules.

Pre Redundancy: A rule is in pre redundancy with a previous rule if these have the same actions and if the second rule can match all the packets that the first rule matches. Between the two rules there should not be rules that are in relation with the redundant rule. Formally,

$$R_y C_{PR} R_x \Leftrightarrow \begin{cases} \omega(R_x) < \omega(R_y), R_y \Re_{IM} R_y, A[R_x] = A[R_y] \\ \exists R_z : \omega(R_x) < \omega(R_z) < \omega(R_y) \\ R_x \{\Re_{IM}, \Re_C\} R_z, A[R_x] \neq A[R_z] \end{cases}$$

This kind of conflict can be seen just as an anomaly, not a severe conflict, because both rules will process some traffic.

Generalization: A rule is a generalization of a previous rule if these have different actions and if the second rule can match all the packets that the first rule matches. Formally,

$$R_y C_{GE} R_x \Leftrightarrow \omega(R_x) < \omega(R_y), R_y \Re_{IM} R_x, A[R_x] \neq A[R_y]$$

This kind of conflict is also not severe because both rules will process some traffic performing different actions. This case has to be labelled as a normal and desirable situation.

No Conflict: When two rules do not fall under any of the previous categories there is a state of No conflict.

To perform the comparison with the selectors of the rules necessary for the detection of conflicts the state diagram presented in [AlHa04] has been changed. The modified state machine transition diagram is shown in Fig. 1, with some simplification for space reasons.

4 Conflict Resolution

S-VPN policy has to be declared incorrect if a progressive rules analysis points out at least one of the severe conflicts as Exact Match, Shadowing and Post Redundancy. Therefore it can be judged correct if the analysis discovers that the policy does not have any severe conflicts.

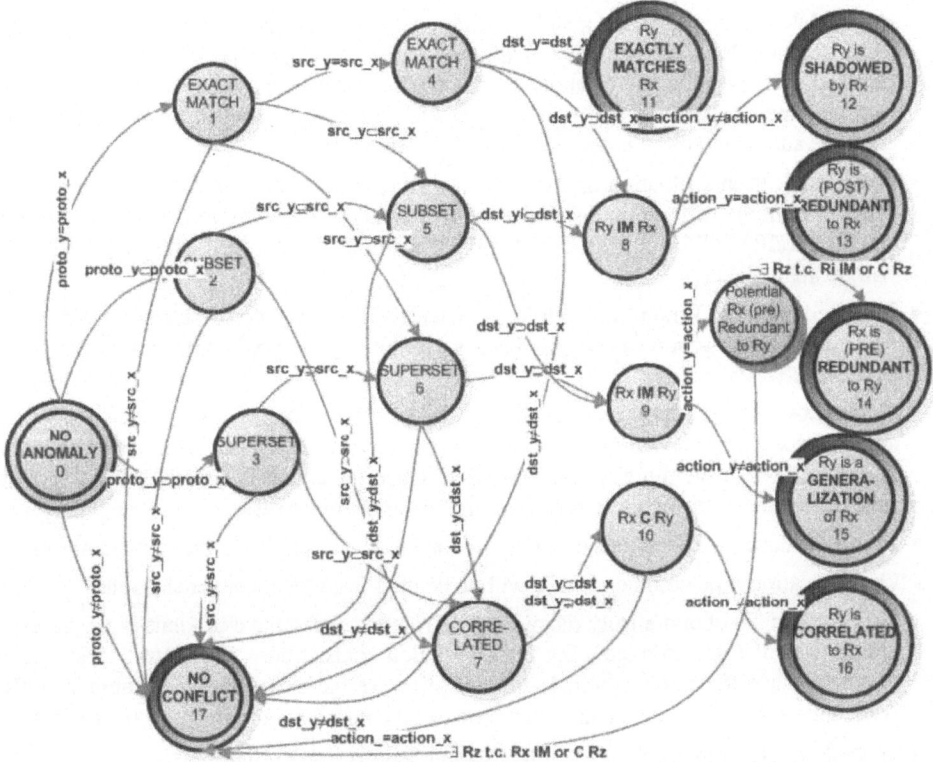

Fig. 1 - The modified state machine transition diagram

Conflict resolution makes changes in S-VPN policy so that it becomes free from the severe conflicts, without losing any of the security services required by security manager. Two resolution algorithms have been formalized.

4.1 All Disjoint Algorithm

The purpose of this algorithm is to obtain a policy without any conflicts, not even anomalies. This objective could be reached by implementing a series of changes to the set of rules according to the criteria specified below. The result of this process is a set of completely disjoint rules.

This method arises from the consideration that only one action can be performed on an incoming packet in the device. Priority is just an artificial concept elaborated to help the administrator during the writing of the policy and it is, in reality, the source of the conflicts we are analyzing.

The algorithm is composed of two phases. During the first phase the rules are modified. In the second phase there is post processing that eliminates all the rules with the same action as the device's default. Changes are performed when a conflict is detected between the analysed rule and another one previously inserted. Thus, when a new rule is inserted we are certain that the rules previously inserted are already disjoint and it does not present any conflict, not even anomaly.

Below we will illustrate the resolutions corresponding to each conflict category:

- Exact Match: When an exact match conflict occurs it is not possible to make an autonomous decision. We will then have to ask the security manager who will decide which action and priority he wants to apply on the traffic matched by the two rules. The other rule will then be deleted. In case of opposite actions, the conflict resolution process could be automated by selecting the most restrictive action.

- Shadowing: In this situation the two considered rules, despite being in the wrong order, bring to light the different aims of the security manager for the two flows of traffic.The common traffic will be deleted from the most general rule. Becoming disjoint, both rules will be maintained.

- Post Redundancy: When this conflict is detected it is possible to delete the redundant rule given that its action has already been performed by the implementation of the previous rule.

- Correlation: As with the exact match conflict, here it is not possible to decide what the aim of the security manager was about the common traffic. We can ask the user or maintain the rule with the more restrictive action. Once the action is chosen, the traffic flow matched by the corresponding rule is deleted from the other rule.

- Pre Redundancy: As in the case of Post Redundancy we can delete the redundant rule.

- Generalization: The common traffic will be deleted from the most general rule.

- No Conflict: To obtain a truly disjoint set of rules, we also have to identify the cases in which two rules are correlated but the correlation conflict does not occur because these two rules have the same action. In this situation we have to delete the common traffic from one of the two rules. In any other case of no conflict no action has to be performed.

The All Disjoint algorithm is the most effective in suppressing conflicts, as it removes any inter-dependence among all rules in the policy configuration file. However, in doing so it may split a single original rule into a large number of new rules, to separate different ranges of selector variables. This destroys completely the original file and can give rise to an impractical number of rules in the configuration file. For these reason we consider next a different algorithm that solves the most severe conflicts by reordering existing rules.

4.2 Inclusive Match Ordered Algorithm

This Inclusive Match Ordered (IMO) algorithm ensures that, through the elimination of some rules, and modifications of the priority value of the remaining rules, the list of all S-VPN policy converges to a final state without severe conflicts.

Let B be any set consisting of n distinct rules, subset of set A which includes all the rules. B's elements can be assumed distinct provided to have taken care of all the rules in Exact Match relation as described in the previous algorithm.

Any pair of rules arising a severe conflict other than Exact Match, i.e. Shadowing or Post Redundancy, are in $\Re_{IM}$ relation, so that the most specific rule has a higher priority than the other rule. Thus, the research of a severe-conflictfree policy list state can be reduced to a problem of partial ordering of the rules related by $\Re_{IM}$.

Algorithm description: The IMO algorithm is composed of four steps:

1. Delete Exact Match conflicts asking the user on the processing he wants to apply to the examined traffic (or by a conservative philosophy automatically deleting the less restrictive rule).

2. Scan the policy list and solve any found conflict $R_x C_{SH} R_y$ or $R_x C_{PO} R_y$ by moving R_y immediately before R_x which was hiding it.

3. Repeat step 2) until reaching the state of absence of Shadowing and PostRedundancy conflicts.

4. Compare the output of the previous two steps with the initial policy list and notify the security manager with the possible presence of Correlation conflicts so that the respective rule order is modified.

The existence of a conflict-free state and the convergence of the research algorithm on this final state within a finite number of steps, are both formally proved.

Incidentally, the last equality of the proof process poses an upper bound on the computational complexity of IMO algorithm which is,

$$\sum_{i=2}^{n}(i-1) = \frac{(n-1)\cdot n}{2} .$$

5 Software Implementation

Analysis and resolution methodologies have been implemented in a software tool developed in C#, the object oriented Microsoft programming language. The tool is named PETRA.

Development phase has been realized in the now freeware environment MS Visual Studio 2005 Express Edition based on the framework .NET 2.0.

The detection phase achieves the necessary comparisons using a tree data structure. This structure is built according to a recursive procedure. The policies are read from a SQL database that gives a general representation model of the network security policies. The database stores the configuration of all the network security devices; it can be populated either manually in a general case or by means of automated tools developed specifically for ELSAG networking products. The resolution phase is performed by the implementation of the algorithm Inclusive Match Ordered Resolution. The user can choose between using a completely automatic or an interactive conflict resolution. A testing phase has also been performed so that the component was put through a set of scenarios which allowed to verify the resolution action undertaken every time. In all scenarios the component performed the modifications as expected, by taking a negligible running time.

6 Conclusions and Future Works

One of the most critical aspects of security problems is the impossibility of accurately checking system real weaknesses.

In a complex and distributed environment this problem is greatly accentuated. During the process of configuration and implementation of the network security policies errors can occur, resulting in holes in security and, consequently, compromising the entire system functionality. These errors are often very hard to detect by performing a manual or visual inspection. For this reason, automatic management of this phase is required.

We define a framework and algorithms to alleviate this problem for a single S-VPN device, by means of automated policy conflict identification and resolution. In this way, the security manager is supplied with an automatic tool that can detect, locate and solve conflicts that may occur within a S-VPN policy file. Based on the previous literature on this subject we have formalized a new conflict classification founded on the severity concept. Moreover we have proposed two automatic resolution algorithms, and implemented one of them in a software tool. Our future research plans include extending the proposed anomaly resolution techniques to handle distributed firewall policies, S-VPN policies and their interaction.

References

[AlHa04]   E. Al Shaer and H. Hamed, "Modeling and Management of Firewall Policies", in IEEE eTransactions on Network and Service Management, Volume 1-1, April 2004.

[AlHa05]   E. Al Shaer, H. Hamed, R. Boutaba, M. Hasan, "Conflict Classification and Analysis of Distributed Firewall Policies", in IEEE Journal on Selected Areas in Communications,vol.23, no.10, October 2005.

[AlHa03]   E. Al Shaer and H. Hamed, "Firewall Policy Advisor for Anomaly Detection and Rule Editing", in Proceedings of IEEE/IFIP Integrated Management Conference (IM2003),March 2003.

[AlHM05]   E. Al Shaer, H. Hamed, W. Marrero "Modeling and Verification of IPSec and VPN Security Policies", Proceedings of IEEE ICNP'2005, November 2005.

[HaSP00]   HB. Hari, S. Suri and G. Parulkar, "Detecting and Resolving Packet Filter Conflicts", Proceedings of IEEE INFOCOM 2000, March 2000.

[GoLi04]   M. Gouda and X. Liu, "Firewall Design: Consistency, Completeness, and Compactness" Proceedings of the 24th IEEE International Conference on Distributed Computing Systems (ICDCS'04), March 2004.

[IKBS00]   S. Ioannidis, A. Keromytis, S. Bellovin and J. Smith, "Implementing a Distributed Firewall" Proceedings of 7th ACM Conference on Computer and Comminications Security (CCS'00), November 2000.

[ChBe95]   W. Cheswick and S. Bellovin, "Firewalls and Internet Security", Addison-Wesley, 1995

Lock-Keeper: A New Implementation of Physical Separation Technology

Feng Cheng · Christoph Meinel

Hasso-Plattner-Institute, University of Potsdam
Postbox 900460, D-14440 Potsdam, Germany
{feng.cheng | christoph.meinel}@hpi.uni-potsdam.de

Abstract

"Physical Separation" is a simple, but hard to be realized, security concept. The paper proposes a new implementation of this principle, named Lock-Keeper. By means of the SingleGate Lock-Keeper system, which is an initial realization of the Lock-Keeper technology, the possibility of direct network attacks to a protected network can be eliminated entirely and data can be exchanged between two networks through a completely secure and reliable way. The analysis on comparing the Lock-Keeper with other similar "Physical Separation" approaches shows that this new implementation has a lot of remarkable innovations. As an advanced implementation, the DualGate Lock-Keeper is proposed by including another new "gate" unit. Along with this development, the Lock-Keeper's performance on data transfer, especially the throughput, is improved significantly as well as some other new functional characteristics appear to make the Lock-Keeper technology more efficient, flexible and applicable. In addition, several application scenarios are revealed to explain how the Lock-Keeper can be integrated into complex structures and provide a higher level of security.

1 Introduction

More and more computers are now connected to open networks such as the Internet on a global basis. This is the result of an ever-growing need for information exchange for businesses, government offices, academic researchers and various other users. Correspondingly, plenty of important and confidential resources on the web become easily available to employees, partners, customers, contractors, or even everyone else. However, all these data flows over public networks have also created many dangerous opportunities for attacks. When data are transferred on the web, especially between a company's internal network and an outside source, there are multiple risks, for example viruses, worms, unauthorized accesses, etc. Thus, the task of securing private data and simultaneously permitting secure data exchange has become a primary problem [ChMe04].

To this effect, various defensive mechanisms, such as firewalls, anti-virus tools, or intrusion detection systems, have been developed and offered to protect internal data and networks from unauthorized access. Nevertheless, in spite of the ubiquity and constant development of such solutions, networks and their attached resources still remain quite delicate and vulnerable. Based on the simple principle that "the ultimate method to secure a network is to disconnect it" [ChBe+03], complete physical separation with the external world has been an important alternative for most high security organizations to protect their sensitive IT infrastructures, see Fig. 1. The idea of "Physical Separation" is to separate the private networks in any levels, not only logically but also physically, and permit secure data exchange with outside simultaneously.

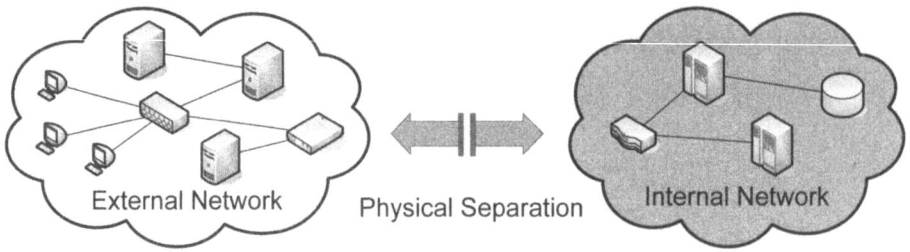

Fig. 1: "Physical Separation" Principle

This paper will introduce a new implementation of "Physical Separation" technology, named Lock-Keeper ([HEMe98], [ChMe04], [LWSI05] and [LWHP04]), and its up-to-date advancements in detail. The remainder of this paper is organized as follows. The next section generally explains the "Physical Separation" principle after a short illustration of the traditional firewall technology and its shortcomings. Detailed information about two realized systems, the SingleGate Lock-Keeper and DualGate Lock-Keeper, including the architecture, functionalities, characteristics and performance measurement, are introduced in the third and fifth section. A brief comparison with other similar implemented "Physical Separation" technologies is given in fourth section. The sixth section proposes some practical examples of the Lock-Keeper applications. In the last section, we summarize and add an outlook to further development of this security solution.

2 Physical Separation Principle

This section will briefly analyze firewall techniques and their shortcomings, and then explain the principle of the "Physical Separation" technology. The Lock-Keeper sluice idea is proposed as an implementing example of this simple concept.

2.1 Firewalls and their Drawbacks

Up to now, firewall technologies have established themselves as popular and crucial tools in providing protection for the computer systems and networks [ChBe+03]. A firewall may be a hardware device or a software program. Most firewalls are architected based on the packet filtering principle [Ziem+96]. It can analyze TCP/IP packets by verifying the sender and the receiver IP addresses and also can monitor the TCP ports to ensure that the selected service is authorized [Tane03]. However, any misconducts or carelessness cannot be controlled by firewalls. Policies involving the use and misuse of passwords and user accounts must be strictly enforced. These are management issues that should be raised during the planning of any security policy, but that cannot be solved with firewalls alone. A firewall should be able to divide requests into authorized and unauthorized. It must authorize the former and deny the latter. This conceptual weakness enable unauthorized attackers easily to obtain an internal IP address and then gain access to valuable internal data which has been thought to be protected safely behind the firewall. On the other hand, firewalls are mostly designed to allow a wide range of "acceptable" behaviours. This functional principle also poses an inherent security risk.

In addition, the operating system on which the firewall is based also provides lots of opportunities to attack and compromise the system. Moreover, caused by the complexity of firewalls and their security polices, firewalls are often expensive, hard to configure. In most cases, firewalls can only be comprehended by security experts. "Keep it easy, if it is complex, it's probably wrong". Drawback on this psychological factor also makes firewalls untrustworthy.

2.2 Concept of Physical Separation Principle

Unlike firewalls which separate the data transfer on the application or protocol level, the "Physical Separation" technology has a completely different aspect. It disconnects the communicating networks at all the network levels [MeSa04], including the physical level, see Fig. 2.

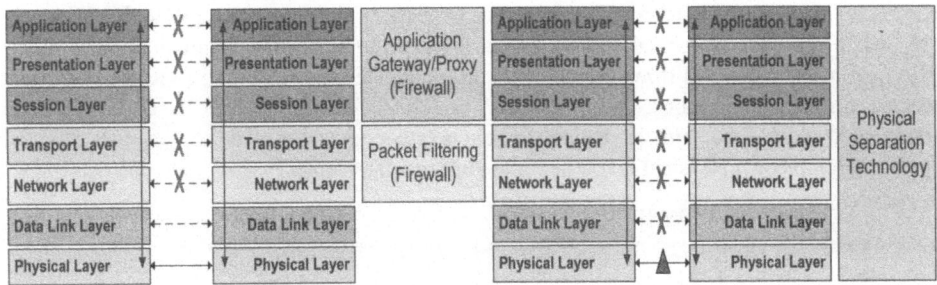

Fig. 2: Separation on OSI Levels of the Network Connection

The aim of "Physical Separation" is to find a way to transmit data between two different networks – usually classified as a high security internal network and a less secure external network - without having to establish a direct physical connection, no matter how short-lived such a connection would be. Compared with the complicated firewalls, the "Physical Separation" principle is simple, clear and easy to be understood. By reason of the psychological advantages, the proposal of the "Physical Separation" technology helps to change the saying from "Build it first, secure it later" to "Secure it first, build it later".

2.3 Lock-Keeper Sluice Technology

Based on the simple "Physical Separation" principle, the patented Lock-Keeper technology was proposed. It works like a sluice, as indicated in Fig. 3. Data are transferred through a gate without ever creating a direct connection between the internal and external network. In this way, it can be guaranteed that attackers and malign data have no opportunities to break into the internal network by any means of online attacks.

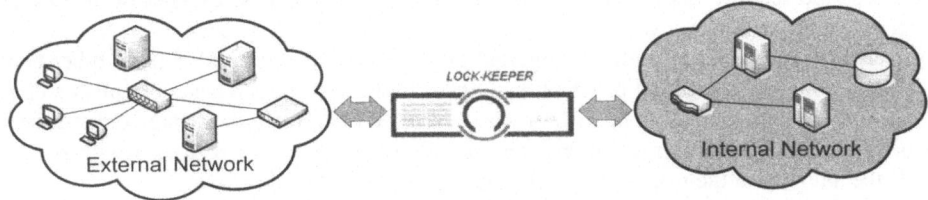

Fig. 3: Topology of the Lock-Keeper Sluice Technology

3 The Lock-Keeper System

As an implementation of the Lock-Keeper sluice technology, the SingleGate Lock-Keeper is described in detail in this section.

3.1 Architecture of the SingleGate Lock-Keeper

A SingleGate Lock-Keeper system consists of three active PC-based components, see Fig. 4. The innermost Lock-Keeper Computer is connected to the internal high security network, for example an intranet of a company. The Computer on the opposite side is connected to the less secure network, e.g., the Internet. The third Lock-Keeper Computer, also called GATE Computer, which provides the actual lock function, is set up to perform a detailed analysis of the traffic passing through. All three components are connected to a patented switching unit that restricts their communications. Only "INNER" and "GATE" or "OUTER" and "GATE" can be connected at any time. This is ensured by relays (switches) on a PCB[1] that enables and disables connections on a physical level, i.e., interrupt the data cables.

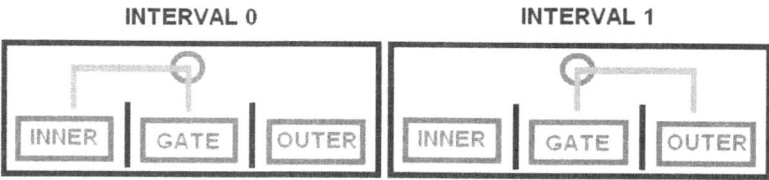

Fig. 4: The SingleGate Lock-Keeper Switch Status

As indicated in Fig. 4, the switch mechanism has two defined states. The function and timing of this unit is autonomous and can not be changed or disengaged by someone who has access to the rest of the system. Thus, neither external attackers nor insiders can change or bypass the state of the physical separation of the networks. Each Lock-Keeper Computer, realized by a SBC[2] respectively, has its own components (CPU, RAM, hard disk, network cards, etc). On each SBC, there is also an independent operating system and some other additional programs which help to transfer or verify data.

3.2 Functionalities

As discussed earlier, the lock mechanism of the Lock-Keeper separates the lower structures of networks physically, eliminating the online status. Thus, it is impossible, even for insiders, to get across the security barrier of the network hardware separations. Crashes or attacks can never create a scenario that will connect the two networks directly to each other, since the relays stay in a defined state (either an internal or an external connection). On the other hand, software, as well as accidental or intentional errors in the system, can never establish a direct connection through the lock, either. In a worst-case scenario, faulty software components or incorrect or insufficient configurations can only adversely affect the data exchange as such, while the integrity of the internal network is never endangered at any time.

---

[1] PCB: Printed Circuit Board

[2] SBC: Single Board Computers

In addition, it is worth to point out that the basic operating system on the GATE Computer makes it possible to integrate some general third-party security software into the Lock-Keeper system, which can check data traffics during they pass the GATE computer and provide more extensive protection to the data exchange. For example, we can install virus scanning software or mail analysis tools to check the data ([Sear05] and [Brun94]). It is also possible to install content filtering tools which can provide similar functionalities as traditional firewalls. Moreover, some accounting and statistics tools can also be done on the Lock-Keeper to monitor and record the system access and the network usage. With the help of these security measures, the Lock-Keeper system enhances the security level of the protected network.

3.3 Performance Analysis

As mentioned earlier, the physical disconnection of the networks makes the Lock-keeper system a complete security solution for data exchanges on the network. However, it also brings a lot of limitations and problems for either applications or extensions of Lock-Keeper. The data transfer through the SingleGate Lock-Keeper may not be rapid enough to provide network services that depend on a permanent online connection. In other words, a lot of intended network protocols can not be run directly through the Lock-Keeper system. For example, web browsing, which is currently the most popular use of networks, can not be easily protected by the SingleGate Lock-Keeper, since there is at least a two switch interval delay before the user receives a response. If we take "cycle" as the description of the time span for data transfers between two computers, the Lock-Keeper system needs two cycles, one to transfer data from the two external computers to GATE Computer and the second to deliver the data from the GATE Computer to the other external computer. The duration of one cycle is determined by the fixed physical connection interval, i.e., enforced by the PCB. On the other side, if the GATE does not happen to connect with the source external computer, data must wait there for the switch change. The maximum of overhead waiting time may be a switch interval. So it has become a big problem of a SingleGate Lock-Keeper that the latency imposed on the data transfer is quite high which limits its utilizations.

However, it has also provided great potentials for the Lock-Keeper improvement. The performance on the data transfer and the long latency has become key factors to extend usability of the Lock-Keeper system. On one hand, use of properly optimized core software to increase the capacity of data transferred in a single cycle is a solution to enhance the data transfer functionality of the Lock-Keeper system. On the other hand, Employment of adjusted hardware components to manage the data transfer with minimal overhead is another absolute necessity.

4 Comparison with other "Physical Separation" Implementations

Besides the Lock-Keeper, there are other similar approaches to realize the "Physical Separation" concept. In this section, a few of these implementations are described and compared with the proposed Lock-Keeper system.

Woodward [Wood79] and Denning [Denn84] use the SG[3] as a (hardware) link between a "low" (distrusted) and a "high" (trusted) computer. The SG provides "one way traffic" be-

---

[3] SG: Security Guard

tween two systems and a kind of "Human Review" is a central part of this structure. The most important difference between SG and the Lock-Keeper is the need of a special hardware to provide a very clear hardware security, whereas the Lock-Keeper does not need any unusual chips.

Myong H. Kang and Ira S. Moskowitz [KaMo93] proposed a communication model, named "Pump", which can push messages from a low- to a high-level system. Although it cannot really separate the two communicated sections in the physical layer because both the high (destination) and low (source) "processes" share a same "communication buffer", the "Pump" approach has realized more rapid, reliable and secure data transfers by the separation of MLS[4] systems.

Air-Gap from Whale Ltd. and the Reflective Net-Gap from former SpearHead Co. are two representative solutions recently appeared in the field of "Physical Separation" [ChMe04]. In despite of some nuances on the implement interface, the two solutions are basically built on the same idea, named by the term "Gap". The main components of the Gap technology include two independent computers, normally two SBCs, a connection switch and a "Memory Bank". The connection switch is the key part of this architecture which can ensure that the "Memory Bank" can only connect one SBC at a time. The "Physical Separation" between the two SBCs can be realized by such a switch mechanism and the two separated SBCs can also communicate through the "Memory Bank". Based on this module, many other research institutes and enterprises also proposed their own solutions and most of them have already been applied in the commercial arena of network security successfully. The difference between the Lock-Keeper with such solutions as Gap technology is that the Lock-Keeper uses another independent computer to replace the "Memory Bank". Compare to the "Memory Bank" which can only work passively with the control of CPUs on the external two SBCs, this new additional computer can process (receive, check and delete/send) the passing traffic on its own initiative. In addition, a lot of Third-party security products can be easily integrated on this central computer to scan and check the data separately. Some necessary operations, for example data deletion when a virus is found, can be executed quickly on the independent central computer.

5 Architecture Improvement: DualGate Lock-Keeper System

The requirements of secure data exchange on one side and comfortable services on the other lead to an incompatible conflict. The development of modern security architectures are always driven by the changing and growing demands for the data exchange. In this section, an advanced, flexible, and applicable Lock-Keeper system, the DualGate Lock-Keeper, will be introduced in detail.

5.1 Architecture of the DualGate Lock-Keeper

As indicated in Fig. 5, another GATE Computer is introduced into the SingleGate Lock-Keeper system. We call the Lock-Keeper system with two GATE Computers the DualGate Lock-Keeper.

---

[4] MLS: Multilevel Secure

With the addition of another GATE Computer, the PCB and its switch mechanism is modified accordingly. The new switch principle is to automatically establish two separate, disjoint connections at the same time. As indicated in Fig. 5, the switch mechanism has two defined states in that either GATE1 is connected to INNER and GATE2 to OUTER, or the other way around.

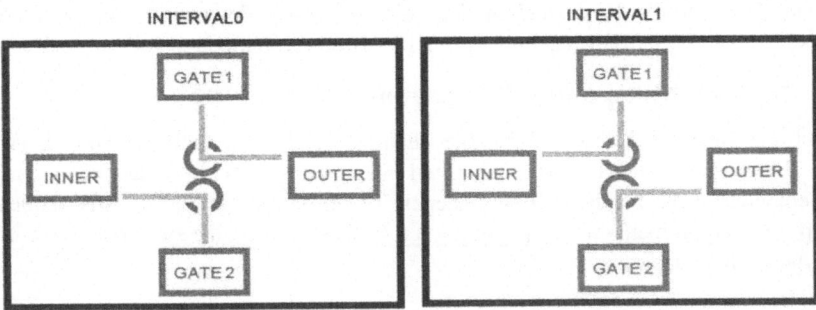

Fig. 5: The DualGate Lock-Keeper Switch States

Besides modifications of the Lock-Keeper hardware, updated core software had to be developed to control and harmonize data transfers through the two connections. A strict and proper file queuing algorithm which is responsible for generating two queues of files to be transferred on both external Computers ("INNER" and "OUTER") is also required. This is because, unlike the SingleGate Lock-Keeper which permits the unique GATE Computer to choose the files, the DualGate has to prepare files for two GATE Computers ("GATE1" and "GATE2") separately. The mechanism of the file queuing is flexible and can be determined optionally by different application requirements.

5.2 Functionalities and New Characteristics

By using two Lock-Keeper gates, we can transmit two files at the same time, even in two different directions simultaneously. In addition, in the new system every Computer will always have a communication partner ready to receive data. There will be no idle Computer during the whole process. In other words, by adding another GATE Computer, we can adequately use all the resources of the system. In addition, some new useful characteristics go perfectly with this development. Thus, compared to the SingleGate Lock-Keeper, the DualGate Lock-Keeper is more efficient. Improvements of the DualGate Lock-Keeper can be summarized in following:

5.2.1 Increasing the transmit capacity (TC)

By means of this modification, the Lock-Keeper file transfer speed can be improved twofold. In theory, the DualGate Lock-Keeper may be able to reach the same overall throughput between inner and outer as a direct and permanent Fast Ethernet connection which is important for extending the Lock-Keeper applications.

5.2.2 Reducing the minimum round trip time of small messages through the Lock-Keeper

Small messages which can be transmitted during one interval between two hosts can reach the target in a minimum time of two intervals. By the DualGate Lock-Keeper, the external computers are always connected with one of the two gates. Files can be transferred as soon as they arrive at the respective external computers without any other redundant waiting time. It is very important for achieving the optimal QoS[5].

5.2.3 Using the whole time for transferring files between connected hosts

A constant data flow can be created and kept as long as the file queue is not processed completely which is important for reaching optimal transmit throughput.

5.2.4 Implementing a few file queuing algorithms

As which has mentioned above, some file queuing algorithms, such as "First in First out" (FIFO), "Last in First out" (LIFO), "Weighted File Queuing" (WFQ) or any other criteria can be implemented in the DualGate Lock-Keeper. The flexibility of file transfer sequence can meet different requirements which are important for customizing the system and to enable different types of applications.

5.3 Experiments on Performance Measurement

Table 1: Performance comparison between the SingleGate and the DualGate Lock-Keeper

	Transfer Duration (s)	
Experiments	Experiment A (one file with 1GB)	Experiment B (several files with total size 1GB)
The SingleGate Lock-Keeper	694 (in the best case)	3306 (in the best case)
The DualGate Lock-Keeper	726 (Delay = 60s)	852 (Delay = 60s)

As shown in the table 1, in the experiment A, we use respectively both Lock-Keeper system to transfer a file with 1 GB. The results show that the two Lock-Keeper systems have nearly the same performance for transferring a single file. However, the experiment B, which transfers a queue of file with several files (e.g. 44 files for the shown experiment result), show that the speed of the data transfers is improved significantly.

5.4 Lock-Keeper Cluster

As shown previously, a DualGate Lock-Keeper system, both the architecture and the working process, is very similar to a cluster of two SingleGate Lock-Keepers, except for throwing off two unwanted external computers. Accordingly, two DualGate Lock-Keeper systems can also be integrated into a DualGate Lock-Keeper Cluster, as indicated in the Fig. 6. It can be anticipated optimistically that the DualGate Lock-Keeper Cluster would possess more powerful performance and advantageous characteristics.

As shown in Fig. 6, besides the two DualGate Lock-Keeper systems, there is an advanced PCB in this the Lock-Keeper Cluster which can help to harmonize working processes of two DualGate Lock-Keepers. The running of this PCB is automatic and can not be controlled by any other components either hardware or software of the system. According to the basic concept of the Lock-Keeper technology, any direct physical connections between two networks are all forbidden. Therefore, when the DualGate Lock-Keeper Cluster runs, there may be only four permitted states of connections between external computers and gate computers in the

---

[5] QoS: Quality of Service.

two DualGate Lock-Keepers, as shown in the Table 2. This switching mechanism is guaranteed by both the abovementioned advanced PCB outside of the DualGate Lock-Keeper system and two inside Lock-Keeper PCBs.

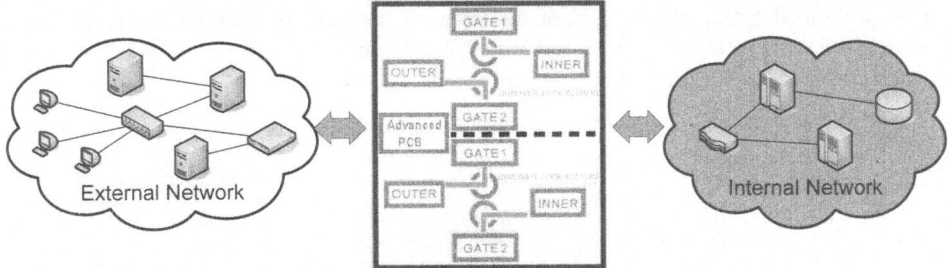

Fig. 6: The DualGate Lock-Keeper Cluster

In order to improve the efficiency of the file processing and optimize the data flows in the cluster system, a new file queue algorithm is appointed on the external computers of both the DualGate Lock-Keepers to help data choose the best and optimal transfer path. By the use of this DualGate Lock-Keeper Cluster, the minimum round trip time of a small message can be decreased to one Lock-Keeper switch interval. It is very useful for providing security protection for such network applications as Web Services by the Lock-Keeper technology. In addition, the reliability of the system can also be enhanced by using the DualGate Lock-Keeper Cluster. If one of the two DualGate Lock-Keepers is accidentally in failure, the other one could still be able to work normally. The method for searching the optimal path can help every file pass the Lock-Keeper as soon as possible. The waiting time either in the file queue or on the gate is shortened significantly.

Table 2: The change of connection state of the DualGate Lock-Keeper Cluster

	DualGate Lock-Keeper1		DualGate Lock-Keeper2	
Connection state	GATE1–OUTER GATE2– INNER	GATE1–INNER GATE2–OUTER	GATE1 – OUTER GATE2 – INNER	GATE1 – INNER GATE2 – OUTER
< t_0	... ...	... ...	... ...	... ...
T_0	√	×	√	×
T0 + T/2	√	×	×	√
T0 + T	×	√	×	√
T0 + 3T/2	×	√	√	×
> t0 + 2T	... ...	... ...	... ...	... ...

6 Lock-Keeper Applications

Thanks to "Physical Separation" concept, the Lock-Keeper provides higher levels of security and completely prevents specific intruder attacks. Following will propose some practical examples of the Lock-Keeper applications. The most frequently utilized service which can be protected by the Lock-Keeper system is the data exchange, either email or file exchanges, between internal networks and external networks. Besides, other new application modules, such as reliable database synchronizing and replicating, secure Web Services [BrCo+02] providing, and new VPN [FeHu98] implementing, are developed or being developed based on the Lock-Keeper system. Theoretically, the Lock-Keeper system can protect almost all network services, because it can provide a complete security protection for ordinary data exchanges.

6.1   Mail Transfer via Lock-Keeper

Electronic mail has now become the most frequently utilized Internet service. It also provides a classic practical example for a typical Lock-Keeper application, see Fig. 7. Mail exchange can be performed transparently in both directions if the mail is transferred via the Lock-Keeper in the same mode as proxies. The time delay doesn't really matter in this case since it is usually irrelevant whether mail arrives for example two minutes later.

Fig. 7: Practical Example: Email Exchange

6.2   File Transfer via Lock-Keeper

Similar to email transfer, file exchange can also be automatically transported offline via the Lock-Keeper, see Fig. 8. In this case, the data are, for example, copied into one file or several folders, from where they are transferred by the Lock-Keeper. On the GATE of the Lock-Keeper, the third party content scanning software can help to scan the data to prevent such offline attacks as virus which are targeted at the data content itself.

Fig. 8: Practical Example: File Exchange

6.3   Database Synchronization via Lock-Keeper

In this scenario, the Lock-Keeper is positioned between the actual database server of the company that contains all relevant (and possibly also very sensitive) data, see Fig. 9. The Lock-Keeper now offers the option to transfer data from the main database server (A) to the web server. This is done through a second database (B) that is connected to the web server online and that receives its data offline from main server A via the Lock-Keeper. Consequently, all relevant data is immediately available when a website is accessed. There is no delay. Meanwhile, web database (B) replicates and synchronizes its data with main database (A) in regular time intervals.

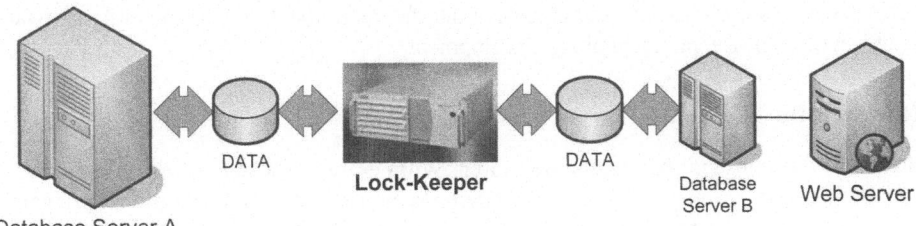

Fig. 9: Practical Example: Database Synchronization

6.4 Secure Web Services Provider

The Lock-Keeper based Web Services [BrCo+02] Provider, see Fig. 10, is proposed to meet the need of SOA[6]. The goal is to protect the source of the Web Services, which is normally located in the internal network. Through the Lock-Keeper, the standard SOAP messages, which include either Web Services requests or Web Services responses, can be transferred securely. On GATE, an independent SOAP verification module or authentication module can be deployed to guarantee the legal access to the specified Web Services.

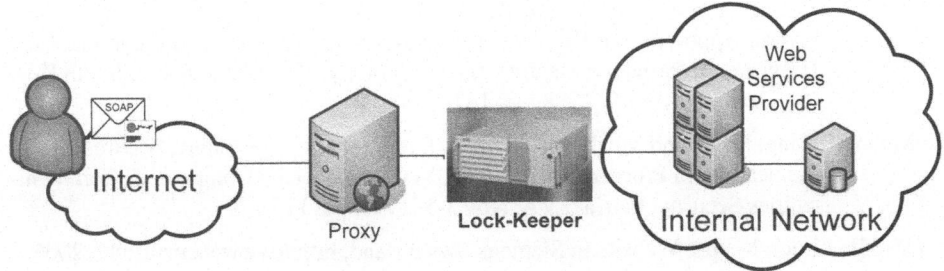

Fig. 10: Practical Example: Secure Web Services Provider

7 Conclusion

By the Lock-Keeper system, a complete security protection for data exchange can be achieved. The concept of "Physical Separation" technology breaks through the traditional mode of data transfer which is based on continuous connections and makes a thorough network security solution possible. Networks which employ such "Physical Separation" implementations as Lock-Keeper systems are immune to any online attacks. Instead, the Lock-Keeper system always stores any type of data transferred between two networks in an intermediate memory, thus preventing all direct attacks. However, the functionalities of the current Lock-Keeper system, even the DualGate Lock-Keeper system, can not satisfy the practical requirements. Data transfers offered by the Lock-Keeper system are not fast enough to accommodate all the web services, since the long latency is a big constraint. Moreover, how to combine Lock-Keeper systems with a suitable and powerful third-party security tool is also a crucial point for the extension of Lock-Keeper applications. A Lock-Keeper system with a

---

[6] SOA: Service Oriented Architecture.

short latency, fast data transfer and extensive interfacing to the third party security software is the object of Lock-Keeper technology development.

References

[Brun94]   Brunnstein, K.: Beastware (Viren, Würmer, trojanische Pferde): Paradigmen systemischer Unsicherheit, sichere Daten, sichere Kommunikation, Springer-Verlag, 1994.

[BrCo+02]   Brunner, R., Cochen, F., et al.: Java™ Web Services Unleashed, Sams Publishing, 2002.

[ChBe+03]   Cheswick, W., R., Bellovin, S. M., et. al.: Firewalls and Internet Security: Repelling the Wily Hacker, Addison-Wesley, 2003.

[ChMe04]   Cheng, F. and Meinel, Ch.: Research on the Lock-Keeper Technology: Architectures, Applications and Advancements, International Journal of Computer & Information Science, Vol. 5, No. 3, September 2004, pp. 236-245.

[FeHu98]   Ferguson, P. and Huston P.: White paper: "What is a VPN?", Revision 1, April 1998.

[HEMe98]   Haffner, Ernst-Georg, Engel, Th., and Meinel, Ch.: The Flood-Gate Principle - a Hybrid Approach to a High Security Solution, in Proc. of the International Conference on Information Security and Cryptology (ICISC'98), Seoul, South Korea, December 18-19, 1998, pp. 147-160.

[KaMo93]   Kang, M. H. and Moskowitz, I. S.: A Pump for Rapid, Reliable, Secure Communication, in Proceedings of 1st ACM Conference on Computer & Communications Security, Fairfax, VA, Nov 3-5, 1993, pp. 119-129.

[LWSI05]   Lock-Keeper Website in Siemens Switzerland, http://www.siemens.ch/, 2005.

[LWHP04]   Lock-Keeper Website in Hasso-Plattner-Institute at University of Potsdam, http://www.hpi.uni-potsdam.de/~meinel/projects/lock-keeper.html, 2004.

[MeSa04]   Meinel, Ch. and Sack, H.: WWW-Kommunikation, Internetworking, Web-Technologien, Springer-Verlag, Berlin, Heidelberg, New York, 2004.

[Sear05]   Sears, T.: Internet Access and Security Solutions: Description of Security Features and Benefits, Technical Report of Network Appliance, Inc., 2005.

[Tane03]   Tanenbaum, A. S.: Computer Networks, fourth edition, Prentice Hall, March, 2003.

[Wood79]   Woodward, J. P. L.: Applications for Multilevel Secure Operating Systems, proceedings of the NCC 48, 1979, pp. 319-328.

[Denn84]   Denning, D. E.: Cryptographic Checksums for Multilevel Database Security, in Proc. of the 1984 Symposium on Security and Privacy, Silver Spring 1984, pp. 52-61.

[Ziem+96]   Ziemba, G. P., et al.: Request for Comments: 1858, Security Considerations – IP Fragment Filtering, 1996.

SPEECH: Secure Personal End-to-End Communication with Handheld

A. Castiglione[1] · G. Cattaneo[1] · A. De Santis[1] · F. Petagna[1]
U. Ferraro Petrillo[2]

[1]Dipartimento di Informatica ed Applicazioni "R.M. Capocelli"
Università degli Studi di Salerno
Via Ponte don Melillo, I-84084 – Fisciano (SA)
{anicas | cattaneo | ads | fabpet}@dia.unisa.it

[2]Dipartimento di Statistica, Probabilità e Statistiche Applicate
Università degli Studi di Roma – "La Sapienza"
Piazzale Aldo Moro 5, I-00185 – Roma
Umberto.Ferraro@uniroma1.it

Abstract

Nowadays, there is a strong trend toward the integration of public communication networks. This is especially the case of the mobile phone networks and the Internet, which are becoming increasingly interconnected as to create a single unified network. One of the possible consequences of this integration is that the security issues, which already exist within each of these networks, become even more menacing in such an enlarged context. The possibility to operate voice calls is one of the most popular services that run on these networks. At the time of this writing, the user who calls another user by means of a mobile phone or a desktop computer equipped with Voice-over-IP software is subject to several threats. In this paper, we examine some of these threats and present SPEECH, a software system for making "secure" calls by using Windows Mobile 2003 powered handheld devices and a wireless data communication channel.

The notion of Security implemented by SPEECH is stronger than the one available in other secure conversation software, because it includes the mutual authentication of the endpoints of the conversation, the end-to-end digital encryption of the content of a conversation and the possibility to digitally sign the conversation content for non-repudiation purpose. SPEECH is able to operate on different types of networks and adapt its behaviour to the bandwidth of the underlying network while guaranteeing a minimal-acceptable quality of service (currently GSM and TCP/IP networks are supported). This has been achieved by adopting a very light communication protocol and by using a software codec explicitly optimized for the compression of voice data streams while retaining a good sampling quality. As a result, SPEECH is able to work in full-duplex mode, with just a slight delay in the conversation, even when using a 9600 bps communication channel, such as the one provided by GSM networks.

There are several application areas for SPEECH. For example, it can be used in an economic transaction conducted over a public phone line to verify the real identities of the parties who are participating to the transaction, to prevent the possibility for an eavesdropper to access the content of the conversation and to ensure that either party of the call could not deny the content of the conversation in a later moment.

S. Paulus, N. Pohlmann, H. Reimer (Editors): Securing Electronic Business Processes, Vieweg (2006), 287-297

1 Introduction

In these years we have been witnessing a significant growth of the telecommunication market. This growth can be temporally divided in two phases. In a first phase, the communication networks, such as the GSM mobile phone networks or the Internet, were growing autonomously and independently. A true interoperability between these networks was substantially absent, both because of technical and economical reasons. In a second phase, which is still in progress, several public communication networks are converging in a unified network which is accessible using the most disparate devices. Such a shift has been driven by the recent technological advancements and by the impressive push of the market. We cite, as example, the recent introduction of mobile terminals which can indifferently operate on a GSM network or on a Wi-Fi based network, or the availability of cheap flat rates for surfing the Internet through a mobile phone connection.

Even in this renewed scenario, one of the most popular applications remains the voice-based communication. A voice-based communication service is essentially a service where someone uses some sort of address (e.g., a mobile phone number, a nick name, an IP address) to contact and communicate, via voice, with a remote user by means of a communication network. There are essentially two types of security issues related to this service. The first type concerns with the problem of *trusting the other endpoint of the conversation* (e.g., is he really the one he claims to be?). The second type concerns with the problem of *trusting the communication network* (e.g., is someone eavesdropping my conversation?).

Mobile communication networks have historically suffered of several serious security weaknesses that were swept under the carpet by the telecom operators according to the principle of *security by obscurity* (i.e., a system is secure because only authorized people know how it works). Let us consider, as an example, the case of GSM based mobile phone networks. GSM networks are essentially organized in a hierarchical way (see [Rahn93]). The GSM enabled mobile equipments (i.e., the mobile phones) are connected to the network through a wireless link with the ground base stations (BS). The base stations are the endpoints of the physical GSM network and are, on their turn, connected to the local public switched telephony network (PSTN or ISDN).

The GSM standard uses three cryptographic algorithms to secure conversation: A5, A3 and A8 [BDG+04]. A5 is used to encrypt conversations, A3 is used for the authentication between the SIM card and the BS, and A8 is used to perform the key agreement between the SIM card and the BS. Unfortunately, the A5 algorithm, and some of its variants which are currently in use by most of the GSM networks, suffers of some serious security weaknesses, as described in the work of Golic [Goli97] and of Barkan *et al.* [BaBK03]. These weaknesses allow a determined user to eavesdrop and decrypt, at a relatively small cost, voice conversations on a public GSM communication channel. It should also be pointed out that the security mechanisms introduced by the GSM standard only apply to the communications occurring between a mobile equipment and the base station it is connected to, while no standard security mechanism is defined for the wired part of the communication.

The problem of avoiding the eavesdropping of a GSM conversation becomes even more dramatic with the progressive switch to the unified network because, in this case, a mobile conversation ending in a network other than the GSM will be subject to the security issues of all the communication networks it will traverse.

Another security problem that emerges from the interconnection of communication networks is the user authentication problem. This is both a problem of trusting the network and trusting the other endpoint of a conversation. In the traditional mobile phone networks, each user needs to be authenticated, through his SIM card, before accessing the network. By the same token, each mobile phone number can be related to a particular user. This implies that, given a mobile phone number, it is possible to determine the real identity of the user who owns that number. Such a scenario does not apply, for example, to users connected by the Internet. In this case, the only information we are supposed to know about a user is his IP address, which can be even masqueraded. It is relatively easy for a user connected to the Internet to call, by means of a Voice-over-IP software and a fake geographic number, a user of a mobile phone network while impersonating another user. The arising problem is, in this case, to be able to verify the real identity of the user we are going to talk to.

Finally, the last security issue we point out is the problem of non-repudiation of a conversation. The current communication technologies do not provide users with the ability to prove that the content of a past conversation has not been altered. Consider the case of a commercial transaction conducted during a phone conversation. After the conversation has ended, one of the two endpoints of the conversation could deny its content and refuse to go on with the transaction. Notice that, in these cases, even listening a recording of the conversation could not be enough to establish the truth because one of the two endpoints could claim the recording has been altered by the other endpoint. This is essentially a problem of trusting the other endpoint of a conversation. The aim here is to not allow a user to deny the content of a conversation he had in the past.

Starting from these considerations, we believe there is need of a strong formulation of the concept of secure conversation that should guarantee the following security properties:

- **Confidentiality.** The content of the conversation is encrypted. It should be unfeasible for a malicious user eavesdropping on the communication channel to determine the real content of the conversation.

- **Authentication.** Each of the endpoints of the conversation has a proof about the real identity of the other endpoint of the conversation.

- **Non-Repudiation.** It is not possible for the endpoints of a past conversation to deny its content.

2 Existing solutions

There are an increasing number of software and/or hardware solutions that a user can adopt in order to perform "secure" conversation using a mobile phone. We cite, as examples: Cripto-fonino [Casper], Cryptophone [Gesell], Sectèra [GeDyC4], VectroTEL X8 [Vectro], Snap-Soft-ZX2 [GTeckl] and SecureGSM [SeGSM]. All these products work by establishing an encrypted communication channel between the two endpoints of a conversation on the top of a standard GSM data call. Encryption is performed by using standard cryptographic algorithms such as AES [NIST01]. Moreover, special care is taken in using ad-hoc compression technologies which guarantee the possibility to transport the voice stream at an acceptable quality while using a low-bandwidth communication channel such as the one provided by the GSM standard.

In addition to these products, a new generation of voice communication software based on Wi-Fi networks is starting to appear. These software run on handheld devices connected to the Internet through a Wi-Fi connection and use cryptographic protocols like Blowfish to perform secure calls with remote peers connected to the Internet using an equivalent software. The most famous example of these applications is Skype [Skype].

It should be pointed out that all these solutions only provide support for the confidentiality of mobile conversations. They all assume that the other endpoint of a secure conversation is trusted. So, there is no explicit support for other security features such as user authentication or non-repudiation of conversations.

Finally, almost existing solutions are available as "closed-source" commercial products and there is a general lack of information about the way the security feature they claim are implemented.

3 SPEECH

SPEECH is a software system for making secure calls by using Windows Mobile 2003 powered handheld devices and a data communication channel. It works by digitizing the input voice, processing it using some cryptographic algorithm and, then, sending the outcoming data stream to the handheld device of the other endpoint of the conversation where it will be processed. Here, the stream of data will be processed in order to return the voice as it has been digitized at the start of the procedure. The whole process is organized in a way to guarantee the following properties for the conversation:

- Confidentiality;
- Authentication;
- Non-repudiation.

The confidentiality of conversation is obtained by encrypting the input voice stream using the AES256 symmetric cipher. The encryption of the communication is done according to the end-to-end paradigm: this means that the voice stream remains encrypted along all the communication channel joining the two endpoints of an ongoing conversation. Moreover, SPEECH supports the authentication of the peers of a conversation either by using X.509 digital certificates or passphrases. Finally, non-repudiation of conversations is implemented through a digital signature scheme.

One of the noteworthy features of SPEECH is the ability to operate on different types of communication networks (currently, GSM networks and generic IP-based networks). For this reason, SPEECH adapts the quality of the digitalized voice stream to the bandwidth of the underlying communication channel. The management of the voice stream is done using Speex [Vali06], an "open-source" audio codec which, together with a light communication protocol, allows to talk in full-duplex mode with good audio quality and short delay over a standard GSM data connection. Figure 1 and Figure 2 show some screenshots of SPEECH.

The SPEECH architecture, shown in Figure 3, is organized as a stack of five independent modules. During a conversation, the input voice is sampled by the audio module in a voice data stream and is sent down through the other modules of the architecture. These modules encode the voice data stream, compress it, encrypt it and, then, send it to the other endpoint of the conversation. The communication between modules is defined through a standard interface. The main advantage of this approach is that it keeps minimal the amount of changes needed to introduce new features in the system, such as the support for a new type of communication channel or the introduction of a new security feature.

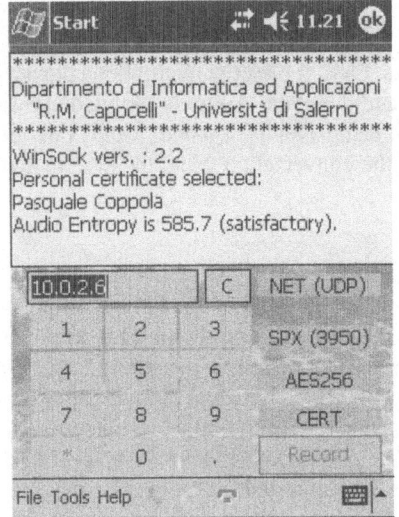

Figure 1: the SPEECH application.

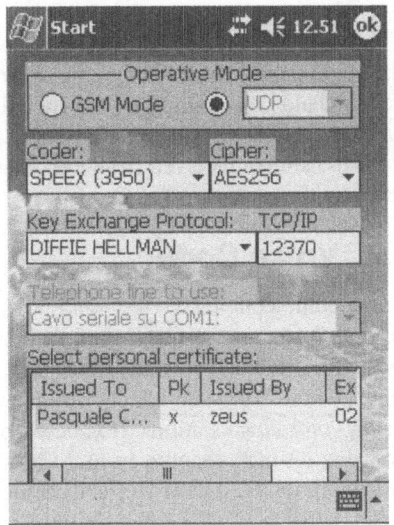

Figure 2: SPEECH options panel.

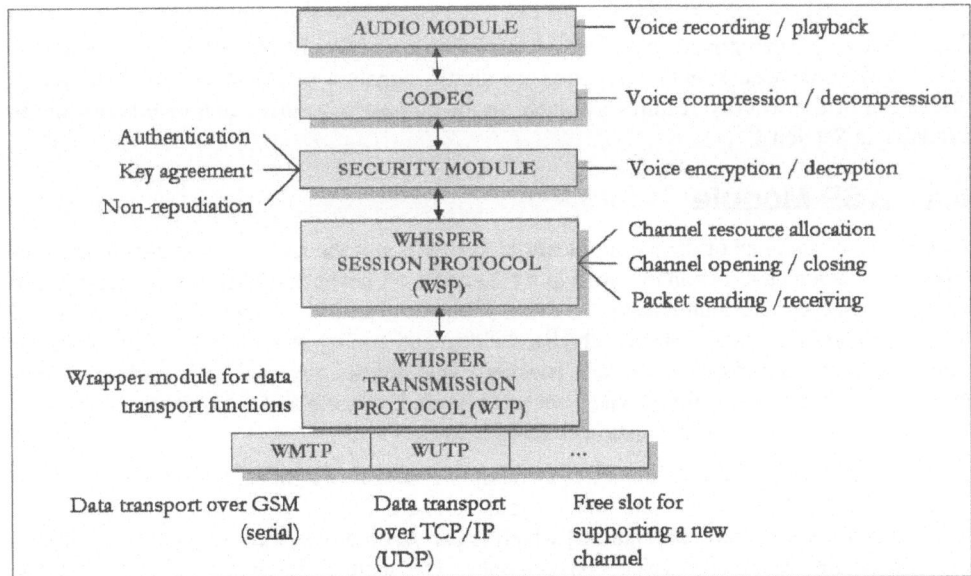

Figure 3: SPEECH architecture.

All the modules of SPEECH work in a multi-threaded architecture so they are able to process, at the same time, the voice stream going to the other endpoint of the conversation and the voice stream coming from it.

In the following sections we examine in details each module.

3.1 Audio Module

The audio module is in charge of performing two tasks. First, it uses the microphone device of the handheld it is running on for encoding the input audio stream. Audio is sampled at a frequency of 8000 Hz where each sample is represented using 16 bits. Second, it plays the output audio stream received from the other endpoint of the conversation using the system audio device at the same sample rate.

3.2 Voice Codec

This module compresses the input stream coming from the audio module and uncompresses the output stream coming from the other endpoint of the conversation through the lower levels of the stack. The compression and uncompression is done using the Speex codec, an "open-source" software which uses an efficient audio compression format optimized for processing voice conversations. It is based on the CELP codec [ShAt85] and is designed to operate using bit rates ranging from 2 kbps to 44 kbps. The compression factor is adapted to the bandwidth of the underlying communication channel. An important advantage of the Speex codec is that it is, at the best of our knowledge, the only "open-source" codec that has been explicitly optimized to run on devices not having a floating point processing unit (this is typically the case of handheld devices).

3.3 Security Module

The security module implements all the security features of SPEECH, such as peers authentication, key agreement, stream encryption ,or digital signature of conversations. A thorough discussion of the security features available in the current implementation of this module is available in Section 4.

3.4 WSP Module

As previously said, one of the requirements of SPEECH was the ability to operate on different types of communication channels such as GSM or Wi-Fi networks. This is an engaging task because each type of communication channel is characterized by its own performances (e.g., the *round-trip-time* of data packets, the bandwidth) and quality of service (the error rate, the support for retransmission of lost data packets). This implies the need for a communication protocol which is light, efficient and, wherever needed, reliable and which abstracts the details of the underlying communication channel in use.

The WSP module implements the *Whisper Session Protocol,* a light session-based communication protocol which can operate both on reliable and unreliable mode. It is an evolution of the Nautilus Session Protocol [NautSP] which is part of Nautilus, a generic software for performing secure half-duplex voice conversations. The main difference with respect to the original protocol is that the *Whisper Session Protocol* supports full-duplex data transmission. This required the introduction of several synchronization primitives and a multi-threaded architecture needed for handling, at the same time, the outgoing and the incoming voice streams.

Data packets exchanged by WSP are formed by a fixed length header and a variable length block of user data. The header is made of 2 bits used to specify the type of packet and 14 bits used to maintain a progressive sequence number used to detect gaps in the communication. The current version of WSP supports the following types of packets:

- **Reliable**. The receiver of this packet has to acknowledge to the sender its reception. Whenever a new reliable packet has to be sent, a new unique sequence number is generated and used to mark it. After the transmission, the sender waits from the receiver a packet of type "Acknowledge" carrying the same sequence number. If a sent packet is not acknowledged within a fixed interval of time, the packet is assumed to be lost and it is retransmitted.

- **Acknowledge**. This kind of packet is sent as an acknowledgement for a "Reliable" packet previously received. The sequence number field is the same of the packet to be acknowledged.

- **Unreliable**. The packet is sent without any acknowledgement.

3.5 WTP Module

The WTP module implements the *Whisper Transmission Protocol*, a low-level data transmission protocol which has been designed to abstract the primitives (e.g., establish a new session, send or receive data) needed to perform voice calls over different types of data communication channels. Currently, SPEECH offers two implementation of the WTP protocol which use, in turn, a GSM based and TCP/IP based communication channel.

In the GSM based WTP implementation, the user wishing to initiate a new conversation has to supply the mobile phone number of the other user he is interested to talk to. The WTP module will try to establish a serial communication channel with the destination of the call through a GSM data calls.

In the TCP/IP WTP implementation, the user wishing to initiate a new conversation has to supply the IP address of the other user he is interested to talk to. The WTP module will try to establish a connection with the remote user by means of UDP datagrams.

In both cases, once the connection has been established, the initialization of the conversation will be managed by the upper level (the WSP module) of the SPEECH architecture.

4 The SPEECH Security

In this section we introduce the security features available in SPEECH and the way they are implemented by the security module (see Section 3.3).

4.1 User Authentication and Key Agreement

Whenever two users try to initiate a new secure conversation, the two SPEECH installations running on their handhelds engage in a key agreement protocol. The purpose of this protocol is to agree on a common session key to be used for performing cryptographic operations on the voice data stream and, optionally, to verify the identity of the parties of the conversation. SPEECH supports three different types of user authentication and key agreement schemes, each with a different level of security. The output of these schemes is a shared random secret which is hashed in two keys, one for encryption and one for decryption, sized accordingly to the symmetric cipher currently in use.

Those three protocols run on the top of WSP and use only packets marked as "Reliable" (see Section 3.4).

- **Basic key agreement.** Whenever two users initiate a new conversation, the SPEECH installation running on their handhelds uses a vanilla implementation of the 4096 bit Diffie-Hellman key-exchange protocol [DiHe76] to agree on a common secret key. This form of agreement does not guarantee to each user the identity of the other endpoint of the conversation but it is enough when we are just interested in guaranteeing the confidentiality of the conversation.

- **Passphrase based key agreement.** Two users interested in having a secure conversation choose a common passphrase. Whenever a new secure conversation has to be initiated by these users, they will generate each a new session key starting from the shared passphrase. The session key is created using some random values that are generated by the two users and then exchanged after being encrypted. This guarantees the possibility to always reuse the shared passphrase without exposing it. This approach provides with a basic form of authentication since it is expected that the passphrases are known only by their legitimate owners.

- **Certificate based key agreement.** Two users initiating a new secure conversation own a legitimate X.509 digital certificate which has been previously loaded in their devices. Moreover, the two devices are supposed to be loaded with the certificate of the Root Certification Authority that issued the certificate of the user to be called. If these conditions are met, the two parties use the standard TLS 1.0 protocol [DiAl99] to perform the mutual authentication and key agreement. The caller plays the client role of the TLS protocol while the receiver of the call play the server role. According to the TLS specification, each client submits its X.509 certificate and provides its verification. Notice that this is the only user authentication scheme that makes possible to activate the non-repudiation feature of SPEECH.

4.1.1 Key escrowing

Providing end users with the ability of performing strongly encrypted phone calls arises once again, the problem about balancing the preservation of individuals' privacy and national security interests. For this reason, the system to design should support an "ethical" *key escrow* system allowing the decryption of a conversation if and only if a selected set of disjoint agencies have authorized it.

All the three key agreement protocols supported by SPEECH produce session keys in deterministic way starting from a larger non-deterministic common secret shared by the endpoints of a new conversation. The key escrowing algorithm used by SPEECH works as follows. Suppose there are n security agencies we want to involve in the key escrowing process and that each of these agencies has revealed its public key. At the beginning of a new conversation, the secret shared by the two users is split in n disjoint segments, where each segment is encrypted using the public key of the corresponding agency. Then, each segment is sent to the corresponding agency. If, in a later moment, there is need to escrow the key used to secure a past conversation, the agencies will decrypt their fragments and jointly assemble the whole original secret.

The problem that arises in this protocol concerns with the transmission of the fragments of the secret to all the agencies that participate to this process. As a matter of fact, it is not possible to always assume the possibility for a handheld device running SPEECH to establish several connections toward different destinations at the same time (e.g., a GSM based smartphone would only be able to make a GSM data call at time). For this reason, we decided to not deliver the encrypted secret fragments directly to each agency, but simply to put them on the communication channel before starting the conversation (i.e. sending them to the peers). In this way, all the agencies eavesdropping on the communication channel will get a copy of the encrypted secret fragments together with the whole conversation.

The key escrow process we developed is considered ethical because no agency can access private data without the agreement of all the others. Moreover, it is possible to extend this mechanism by using a different partitioning scheme, such as the one documented in [Sham79], so to allow a subset of all the agencies to rebuild the session key.

4.2 Confidentiality

All the conversations made with SPEECH are encrypted using the AES256 symmetric cipher with 128 bit block size and 256 bit key generated according to the common secret agreed using one of the approaches described Section 4.1. The cipher mode we use is *OutputFeedBack* (OFB). This mode works by repeatedly encrypting an initial vector and processing with the XOR operator the resulting 128 bit together with the original 128 bit data block. This is an operative mode suitable for our communication channel because when using a wireless communication channel like the one provided by GSM networks or by Wi-Fi networks, the number of data losses or communication errors is relatively high. By using the OFB mode, we are guaranteed that an error occurring in a data block will not propagate over the entire blocks chain.

4.3 Non-repudiation

Non-repudiation of a conversation is implemented in SPEECH by having each party of the conversation sign, with his private key, the hash of a recording of the whole conversation. The problem that arises is to make it possible for both parties to have, at the end of the communication, the same identical copy of the conversation. Such a task is not easy as it seems because both the underlying communication channel and the transport protocol may be unreliable and, so, voice packets can get damaged or lost. For this reason, SPEECH adds to each packet of the encrypted voice stream an integrity checksum and a sequence number. The first is used to verify if a received packet has been damaged by the transmission, the second is used to detect lost packets.

At the end of conversation, the total number of damaged and lost packets is evaluated. If a certain threshold is not exceeded, then the party will request to the other party a copy of all the packets to be recovered using a reliable protocol. Otherwise, the non-repudiation service becomes unavailable. The definition of the threshold is crucial because accepting a large number of contiguous errors may alter the real meaning of the conversation; in other words, peers could not be aware of what they are signing[1]. Another reason for bounding the number of packets to recover is that the resending of a large number of recovered packets may take a long time to finish. Finally, if the rebuilding process is successful, the parties use a reliable protocol to exchange the checksum of the whole conversation. Each user can later listen the conversation and decide to send or not the signature. The cryptographic part of this protocol has been implemented using the RSA algorithm and the SHA-1 hash function [NIST02].

5 Conclusions

In this paper we presented SPEECH, a software tool installable on modern handheld devices, which allows to converse in encrypted, authenticated and signed way using whatever commu-

---

[1] Adopting the same criteria introduced by current laws about digital signature, assuming that signer MUST visualize the document before signing it

nication channel which provides a bidirectional data communication, such as GSM networks and Internet.

The part of SPEECH concerning security is completely independent from the bearer service in use. It currently supports TLS 1.0 and Preshared Passphrase as authentication/key agreement protocols, Diffie-Hellman as key agreement protocol and channel encryption with AES256. The voice is encoded with the Speex codec which allows to converse in full-duplex mode still with 9600 bps of band usage as upper bound. The communication channels currently supported are GSM networks and TCP/IP networks.

With respect to normal GSM calls, connection and communications delays, introduced by SPEECH security features, remain under an acceptable threshold. The connection delay due to initiating a GSM based conversation is of about 7 seconds and mainly depend on the mobile phone operator. The time spent for Diffie-Hellman and Passphrase based key agreements is about 4 seconds while for Certificate based key agreement, which is the most complex, is about 12 seconds. These delays are much smaller when the communication channel is a TCP/IP network (i.e., Wi-Fi).

Communication delay is comparable to those of intercontinental calls, except for the case in which digital certificate are used. In this case, because of the integrity checksum processing needed for the tamper detection, the transmission is of about 2 seconds.

The security features offered by SPEECH, like non-repudiation and strong authentication, have never been employed into mobile voice communications. With them SPEECH overcomes the security limits of mobile communications allowing the users to accomplish critical transactions (such as m-commerce, trading online, phone banking, homeland security) using low cost handhelds, standard communication channels and without requiring additional dedicated hardware.

As future work, we are considering the possibility to make the SPEECH communication protocol in order to grant the interoperable with other protocols such as SIP/RTP [ScRo99] and SCIP [NatoC3]. Moreover, we are planning an extensive testing of SPEECH in order to provide a detailed characterization of its performance and of the quality of the resulting service according to the communication network being used.

References

[BaBK03]   E. Barkan, E. Biham, N. Keller: "Instant Ciphertext-Only Cryptanalysis of GSM Encrypted Communication". In Proceedings of *Advances in Cryptology – CRYPTO 2003*, 2003, LNCS 2729, pp. 600–616, Springer-Verlag.

[Casper]   Casper Technology. Available from: http://www.caspertech.com/

[Goli97]   J. D. Golic: "Cryptanalysis of alleged A5 stream cipher". In Proceedings of *Advances in Cryptology – EUROCRYPT'97: International Conference on Theory and Application of Cryptographic Techniques*, 1997, LNCS 1233, pp. 239–255, Springer-Verlag.

[Vali06]   J. M. Valin: Speex: Available from: http://people.xiph.org/~jm/papers/aes120_speex_vorbis.pdf

[Gesell]   Gesellschaft für Sichere Mobile Kommunikation mbH. Available from: http://www.cryptophone.de/

[ShAt85]   M. Schroeder, B. Atal: "Code-excited linear prediction (CELP): High-quality speech at very low bit rates". In: *Proceedings of the IEEE International Conference on Acoustics, Speech, and Signal Processing.* 1985, Vol. 3, pp. 937–940.

[GeDyC4]   General Dynamics C4 Systems. Available from: http://www.gdc4s.com/.

[Vectro]   VectroTEL. Available from: http://www.vectrotel.ch/

[GTeckl]   Global Teck. Available from: http://www.global-teck.com/

[SeGSM]   SecureGSM. Available from: http://www.securegsm.com/

[NautSP]   Nautilus Secure Phone. Available from: http://nautilus.berlios.de/

[Rahn93]   M. Rahnema: "Overview of the GSM System and Protocol Architecture". In: *IEEE Communications Magazine.* 1993, Vol. 31, pp. 92-100.

[Sham79]   Adi Shamir: "How to share a secret". In: *Communications of the ACM.* 1979, Vol. 22 no.1, pp. 612–613.

[Skype]   Skype. Available from: http://www.skype.com.

[BDG+04]   O. Benoit, N. Dabbous, L. Gauteron, P. Girard, H. Handschuh, D. Naccache, S. Socié, C. Whelan: Mobile terminal security. Available from "Cryptology ePrint Archive" as Report 2004/158 at: http://eprint.iacr.org/.

[NIST02]   National Institute of Standards and Technology (NIST), "The Secure Hash Signature Standard. (FIPS PUB 180-2)". August 2002. Available from: http://csrc.nist.gov/publications/fips/fips180-2/fips180-2withchangenotice.pdf.

[DiAl99]   T. Dierks, C. Allen: The TLS Protocol Version 1.0. IETF RFC 2246. 1999.

[NIST01]   National Institute of Standards and Technology (NIST), "Advanced Encryption Standard (AES) (FIPS PUB 197)". November 2001, Available from: http://csrc.nist.gov/publications/fips/fips197/fips-197.pdf

[DiHe76]   W. Diffie, M. Hellman: "New Directions In Cryptography". In: *IEEE Transactions on Information Theory.* 1976, vol. 22 no. 6, pp. 644-654.

[ScRo99]   H. Schulzrinne, J. Rosenberg: "Internet telephony: Architecture and protocols – an IETF perspective". In: *Journal of Computer Networks.* Elsevier Science B.V., 1999, vol. 31, no. 3, pp. 237–255.

[NatoC3]   NATO Consultation, Command and Control Agency (NC3A). "Secure Communication Interoperability Protocol (SCIP)". Available from: http://elayne.nc3a.nato.int/msec/scip/index.html.

Finding the Mobile Trusted Element

Fabio Ricciato · Maura Turolla · Antonio Varriale

Telecom Italia, Access and Mobile Terminals
{fabio.ricciato | maura.turolla | antonio.varriale}@telecomitalia.it

Abstract

Nowadays a number of services and applications delivered on mobile terminals need to be secured in order to guarantee the user privacy, the business stakeholders and the commercial and legal issues related to security threads.

Nevertheless, mobile terminals available on the market cannot be considered trusted in wide sense, since they do not meet the stringent security paradigms that, for instance, smart card based applications development and deployment require.

Locating key security elements inside mobile terminals becomes a most peculiar issue to deliver new applications which focus on the identification, authentication and protection of users and/or service delivery related to third parties information.

This paper highlights the security issues on mobile terminals, considering primarily Telecom Italia use cases and business experience, emphasizing the importance to identify the mobile trusted elements and stakeholders in the security management within mobile handsets.

1 Introduction

In the last years the role the mobile terminal has been playing in the ICT world is drastically changing.

While in the beginning its primary purpose was to set and receive voice calls, today it aims to video-calls, working and personal assistance, multimedia contents rendering, info services, remote controlling, games: in other words it has to encompass all the applications and services usually deployed on Personal Computers, limited only by screen size, battery life and computational power.

Moreover, new services rely not only on the mobile terminals; applications are more and more partitioned among mobile terminals and external appliances through the network connectivity and different communication channels (2G/3G, WIFI, Bluetooth, etc.). The services domain is extended to a wider environment which often is not reliable in terms of security.

In this scenario, one of the main issues in designing new services is to guarantee the security requirements, that become a key element in the definition of the service itself.

Whatever the technology or methodology adopted to implement security on mobile services, it is necessary to point out which the basic elements to build the secure service, their providers and the trust-model among system elements are.

The robustness of the secure service depends on different designing choices: symmetric and/or asymmetric cryptography algorithms, tens to hundreds of bytes long keys, certificates paradigms, enhanced techniques for session keys exchange and so on; however, the key strategic focal points for the success of the secure service is:

- where can primary secrets (e.g. private and/or symmetric keys) be stored and processed?

S. Paulus, N. Pohlmann, H. Reimer (Editors): Securing Electronic Business Processes, Vieweg (2006), 298-307

- who provides this secure operating area ?

And above all:

- who is responsible for the robustness of the service ?
- who do we actually trust in?

The answers to these questions lead to the choice of services implementations that have a deep impact not only from the technical security robustness point of view but especially from the commercial and legal ones. These are the questions we are trying to answer from the point of view of a telecommunication operator in this paper. In section 2 we are going to explain the concept of Mobile Trusted Elements as basic block for secure service definition, in section 3 the design of a secure service is analyzed versus different models and paradigms of interaction. In section 4 we describe a DVB-H secure service and finally we draw some conclusions.

2 Mobile Trusted Elements

The need for a secure environment is commonly considered to be univocally associated to an hardware and software fully closed system; this concept apparently seems to be in conflict with the need for an open mobile terminal, that would instead allow not only the mobile terminal manufacturer but also certified third parties service providers to develop and deliver applications having the full control of mobile terminal resources.

The Security-by-Obscurity concept is not able to guarantee by itself the mobile terminal secure usage [Kerc83]; an open mobile terminal can be trusted, instead, whether security infrastructure and a certified applications system management are available. For certain classes of services, especially when treating high commercial interest contents the security level becomes no longer acceptable whether content commercial and legal liability does not belong in full to the providers the user is trusting in.

Inside a security infrastructure we define Mobile Trusted Element (also referred as MTE)

- the operating area used to store secret information;
- the execution environment in which the security functional operations run.

The *trusted* attribute (more than "secure") characterizes the relation between the security provider and the security user. underling the key stakeholders of the security scheme.

The MTEs are mainly characterized by

- Form of implementation: obscured software, hardware elements (SIM, Smart cards, dongles), network elements, secure processors, secure OS;
- Provider: the stakeholder that provides the MTE;
- Responsible: the stakeholder responsible of the MTE and secure service (re)liability. It often defines also the security and service paradigm.

We can have different association and identification of *MTE provider*, *responsible* and secure service provider considering different MTE forms.

In section 4 the example of a service requiring particular attention in the choice of the MTE to use will be described.

The major challenge found in creating a shared MTE inside the mobile terminal is to make it trusted by any third parties might use it to build up its own secure service (assuming the mobile secure services market is open to all third parties).

Mobile terminals manufactures often adopt software MTEs, by placing security software routines within the operating system and by using undeclared memory areas to store keys and other secret data.

A practical example is the habitual implementation of the Digital Rights Management (DRM) agent to protect multimedia contents on mobile terminals according to the user rights.

In this case, primary information (private keys, etc.) is stored in memory areas not directly accessible from the application software layer. Some other implementations tends to have two or more separate operating systems having one dedicated to handle the MTE [Jalw06] [Kerc83].

Anyway in this solution the memory used, in details the internal flash memory, is physically shared with the applicative level.

In the application processor and chipset world for new generation mobile terminals in the last years the concept of MTE has been acquired and developed. A practical example of application processor level MTE is provided by *ARM TrustZone* architecture by means of which it becomes possible to implement security software platforms, such as *Trusted Logic* secure module [Truw06], that can be integrated into open operating systems like *Microsoft Windows Mobile* or *Symbian*.

In both cases, MTEs are developed and provided by third parties not necessarily involved in terms of legal liability in case the system get broken. In other words the secure service provider is trusting an MTE offered by the mobile terminal manufacturer, often even without being in relation with it from the technical, commercial or legal point of view. In this case the *responsible* role can change following different paradigms.

MTE as a property of the secure service provider, instead, is a widely spread concept in security scenarios beyond the mobile terminals world, where MTE is commonly identified as smart cards or secure tokens certified according to secure service specific criteria.

The mobile operator approach follows the philosophy of an external MTE, owned and managed by itself. In particular, MTE is represented by the SIM whereas the secure services it provides vary from network user authentication (billing, tracking, etc.) to entertainment services like subscription based Mobile TV (Pay Per View, Pay TV, etc).

We can identify three secure token classes.

- The first one includes plugged tokens. SIM is the plugged token for antonomasia in mobile phones. Designed for secure run timing and key handling, it offer high security and reliability and the trust chain is already in place. Some other examples are the external memory expansion cards that nowadays can be inserted in most of high tier phones: the most spread physical interfaces on the market are Secure Digital Cards (SD) and the Multi Media Cards (MMC). Both interfaces, in form factors often compatible, define a communication channel used not only to store data but also to send general commands to the cards. The communication protocol allows developing an SD or MMC based trusted device with smart card capabilities. In this way secure services providers can realize a new proprietary MTE.

- The second secure token class includes contact less devices, which are usually based on Bluetooth (BT) or Infrared (IR) wireless interface. The solution philosophy is the same as the previous one but, while the memory card market is still quite fragmented, the BT and IR tokens are the most spread wireless interface on new generation mobile terminals, making the solution really appealing from the interoperability point of view.. The only disadvantage is that the described MTE is an external unconnected dongle and it needs to be powered through batteries.

- The third class includes unconnected external devices directly synchronized to the secure service provider (e.g. by means of timers). They usually provide authentication features in order to simplify and strengthen password based services using techniques like the One Time Password. This kind of tokens is less flexible compared to the ones described so far. Nevertheless they belong to secure service providers and are independent of the mobile terminal used to access secure services.

3 Mobile Secure Services Design

In order to design secure services, we need to consider:

- Attributes
- Level of security
- Architecture types

Usually we need to target the *attributes* of **protection**, **integrity** and **authenticity.** These attributes can be related to the security stakeholders – users, providers, third party, institutional entities – and information – data (files, documents, contents, etc.), applications (programs, services).

The concept of protection implies that information has to be accessible only by authorized users, and protected during transfer as well as storage operations. Integrity refers to the fact that information has to be processed without any unauthorized tampering and changes. Finally, authenticity refers to all mechanisms which allow the unique association of information to its owner, i.e. to the (legal) entity that produced or subscribed it.

Depending on the service security requirements, the three security attributes previously described do not need to be all fulfilled and sometimes for a certain service we need to guarantee the different attributes in different point of time in service provisioning.

For instance, the basic phone calls and text messages service requirements history have targeted user authenticity, but neither information protection nor integrity: the authenticity is guaranteed by the authentication procedure the SIM (mobile operators MTE) activates at mobile phone startup. In more complex case live DRM application we need to guarantee integrity, authenticity and protection of information.

In secure services design it is also peculiar to identify the *security level* to be accomplished and its realization costs, what the most suitable technical solution is.

An effective way to define a solution security level is to start from the assumption that the solution can be broken and to estimate the legal/commercial issues the security system violation arises to the secure service players' chain.

Then, in mobile secure services design we can identify at least two distinct architectural service types: End-To-End and On-The-Terminal.

Secure services are usually built on the combination of the two architectures; nevertheless, the logical separation is useful to determine punctual sub-solutions (implemented according to the available MTE) and to evaluate any treats the system might be exposed to.

In the End-To-End architecture secure services do not fully reside on the mobile terminal but are distributed both on the terminal and on external systems connected through communication channels (usually wireless ones).

The diagram in Fig 1 shows the End-To-End architectural blocks in two possible system configurations.

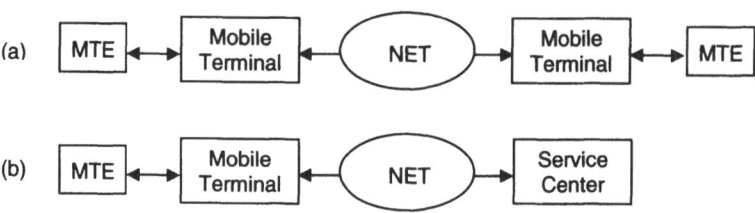

Fig. 1: End-To-End Architecture

In configuration (a) the secure service is distributed upon two mobile terminals usually symmetrically involved in the security mechanisms. In this case the system gets the attribute of *balanced*, and therefore we talk about *balanced secure services*.

A *balanced secure service* example is the encrypted call between two mobile terminals, where at least two security requirements are fulfilled: voice protection and mobile terminals authentication (in some cases it is possible to extend the authentication to the speakers by means of speech-recognition techniques).

At the implementation level the encrypted call uses first asymmetrical security algorithms for the mutual authentication between the two MTEs and then, after the session key negotiation, symmetrical security algorithms for data protection on a communication channel natively untrusted.

Ciphering algorithms and keys generation processes can be complex but the basic concept is that primary secrets and security operations must be confined within the MTE.

In configuration (b) the secure service is distributed between the user mobile terminal and an external service center, the latter being considered trusted, being a service provider property - i.e. the entity the user is trusting in.

In this case the system is *unbalanced*, hence *unbalanced secure services*.

An *unbalanced secure service* example is downloading on terminal a new version of a mobile operator certified software, for instance, referring to the previous case, the secure call application.

In this case two security requirements must be fulfilled: software upgrade integrity and the authentication of the mobile terminal having the relative rights.

At implementation level, authentication is performed by means of the previously described security algorithms, whereas software integrity is guaranteed using hashing and asymmetrical security functions based digital signature techniques. In this case of course authentication and digital signature validation operations have to be executed inside MTE.

The diagram in Fig 2 shows the On-The-Terminal architectural blocks, where secure services are distributed between the mobile terminal and the associated MTE.

Since in this configuration it is not always possible to concentrate all reserved data and functionalities inside the MTE, fulfilling the protection requirement (referred both for data and for applications) is challenging.

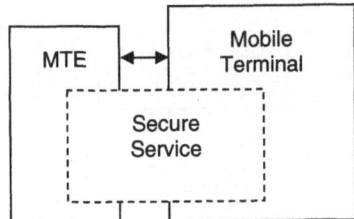

Fig. 2: On-The-Terminal Architecture

The DRM agent implementation is an example of such secure service for the mobile terminal multimedia contents protection.

From the security point of view the MTE is able to contain both the user rights database (for instance the multimedia contents licenses) and the rights validation procedure, according to the multimedia content to be accessed.

Nevertheless, sooner or later, the multimedia content will be uncrypted on the mobile terminal so that the audio/video codec is able to render it. In this context the MTE is therefore no longer able to guarantee the content protection but the security stands in the mobile terminal trusted structures: the secure service provider trusts the mobile terminal manufacturer.

As previously described, for any secure service implementations it is necessary to evaluate the information to protect, the agents who might cause a thread in the security system and the commercial/legal issues that would consequently arise.

In the DRM example the information to be protected is the multimedia content; users not having the rights to retrieve it must be prevented from accessing the content; liabilities existing towards audio/video content providers (e.g. Disney, Sony, Virgin, etc.). Hence it becomes clear that the key issue is to prevent the multimedia contents from being illegally distributed to unauthorized users.

On this purpose the MTE can be used to mark every multimedia contents by means of digital watermarking techniques in order to associate indissolubly contents to licensed users thus univocally identifying the user responsible for the illicit sharing.

The secure service application copyright is another example of common On-The-Terminal architecture inherent problems.

As shown in Fig 3 the secure service can be divided into several components: user front end (graphical user interface, keys interface, etc.), core function, libraries and internal data (images, database, configuration etc.). Each component can be designed to be stored/executed either on the mobile terminal or within MTE, according to the required information security level (both for data and functionalities).

This operation, usually known as *secure service partitioning*, forbids the integral copy of the secure service application since the piece of information inside the MTE is still not accessible.

In general, secure services often have functionalities that can be grouped into external common libraries to be executed in full security within MTE.

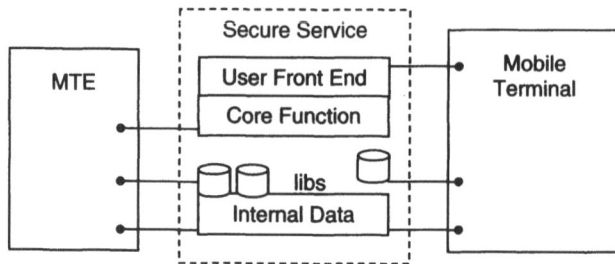

Fig. 3: Secure Service Partitioning

4 Use Case: DVB-H

In this section a recent Telecom Italia secure service use case, the Digital Video Broadcast-Handled (DVB-H) commercial launch, will be described. In particular, the security issues and the related implementation choices will be treated in details.

The DVB-H is a standard defined by the European industry consortium DVB [Dvbw03] and approved by the standardization organization ETSI (European Telecommunications Institute) [Etsw04] since 2004 with a high adoption rate worldwide. It specifies a terrestrial radio broadcasting technology designed to transmit TV, Radio and multimedia contents on handled devices (smartphones, PDAs, etc.).

The DVB-H originated from the DVB-T (Digital Video Broadcast-Terrestrial). It is a combination of digital video standards and Internet Protocol (IP). Contents are split into data packets to be transferred to the mobile terminal which performs the rendering operation to make them visible to the user. In this way data can be transferred whit high quality targets. The IP, moreover, allows simultaneous transmission of data packets (stream DVB) and control/application packets (IP Datacast) including news, financial information, multimedia contents, file transfers, and high speed Internet connection, using the mobile network return channel (SMS/2G/3G) for services interactivity.

The DVB-H allows transmitting data flows discriminating information which every user is able to access (free TV) from information that needs to be subscribed (PayTV, Pay Per View, etc.).

This operation is performed by the Conditional Access System (CAS), which scrambles the transmitted signal and makes it accessible to authorized users only.

CAS mainly provides two functions:

- Services scrambling. The digital broadcasting stream is scrambled by means of a cryptographic algorithm. The output of the scrambler is transmitted by the terrestrial broadcasting channel for delivery to end users;
- Keys encryption and decryption. The CAS generates the control word (CW) for the scrambler and encrypts special messages used in the MTE, according to the user subscription, to retrieve the CW for the stream descrambling.

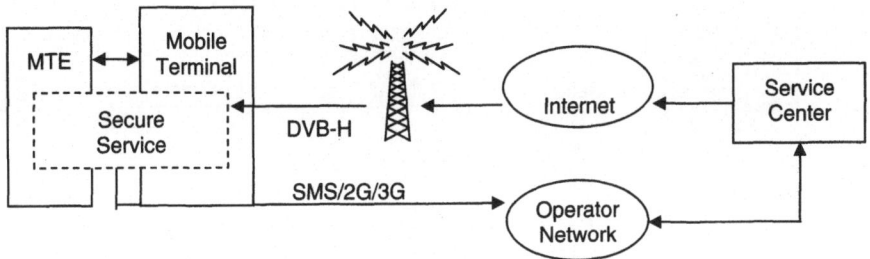

Fig. 4: DVB-H System Architecture

As shown in Fig 4 the DVB-H service is based on both the security architectures treated in section 3: End-To-End and On-The-Terminal.

The End-To-End topology, especially in configuration (b), provides a high level protection level. It is therefore used to guarantee the security of the following system elements

- CW flow, keys and messaging for the CW retrieving (DVB-H channel);
- Messaging flow for the new services subscriptions activation (DVB-H or SMS/2G/3G channel);
- Return channel messaging flow (SMS/2G/3G channel).

The On-The-Terminal topology instead is used for the implementation of the mobile terminal side secure service, which mainly performs the received multimedia contents rendering (as in the DRM example described in section 3).

As highlighted in section 1, the implementation choices in secure services are strictly based on considerations related not only to technical aspects but also to commercial and legal ones.

The main effect issued by a secure service threat resides in the distribution of DVB-H non-free contents to unauthorized users. The contents value determines relative legal and commercial issues burden the Secure Service provider has to face towards the Content Provider. At the same time the higher is the content value, the higher is the motivation/interest malicious users find in tampering the system.

In streaming services the contents value is time-dependent. For example an important event like the Fifa's World Cup final match has a greatest value while it is played (live content), destined to drop as soon as the match ends. Hence the secure service implementation has to guarantee a content protection adequate to the content importance, especially when they assume their maximum value.

On this purpose we chose a conditional access system in which CWs change about every ten seconds. In this way even if a malicious user sniffed the CWs, these keys would be able to descramble no more then ten seconds streaming e not the whole multimedia event. Using just a single CW for the whole event would instead expose the content to an undefined number of users not allowed to the vision, since the CW initially sniffed would decode the entire transmission.

The CAS may be implemented by means of an external MTE or a software one. As mentioned in section 2, the typical mobile operator approach is based on the use of the SIM as a proprietary MTE. In the DVB-H service, Telecom Italia opted for a SIM based implementation. Fig. 5 shows the SIM based DVB-H architectural scheme.

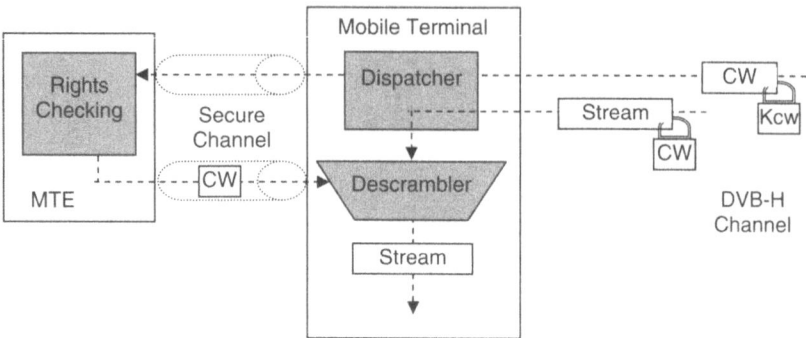

Fig. 5: External MTE Based CAS Scheme

The use of an external MTE versus a software terminal manufacturer provided MTE has some major benefits:

- The secure service can easily be partitioned, as pointed out in Fig. 3, to confine the most sensible functionalities (Rights Checking, CW generation, etc.) together with the service profile and the primary keys inside a Smartcard. The mobile terminal only performs the user interface/interaction operations and content rendering;

- The SIM is a mobile operator asset, thus completely managed and controlled through the network;

- The service is portable and mobile terminal independent (the user still benefits from his rights even moving his SIM to other terminals).

In both cases (External and Software MTEs) the content will sooner or later be descrambled on the mobile terminal; hence we are in the same case of the DRM agent dealt in section 3. In order to prevent the unauthorized distribution of live contents it is as well possible to add watermark technologies to identify the user who determined the system leakage.

The two protection approaches are also considered by standardization organisms in conditional access specifications. For instance, the DVB consortium defines both a terminal base approach (18C) and a SIM based one (Open Framework); as well the Open Mobile Alliance (OMA) [Omaw06] forum defines both a Terminal Based profile (BCAST) and a SIM based version (BCAST Smartcard profile).

The SIM based approach aims to centralize the security management into an operator proprietary module. Nevertheless this strategy move to the operator the liability the DVB-H service players are required to support towards the Content Provider.

In Fig 6 two simplified DVB-H service distribution chains are shown. In the first one (a) the mobile operator is both the service provider and the security manager, as sensible functions and data reside in its own MTE. The second chain (b), instead, includes a new player which is able to manage the security by means of its own CAS implementation. In this case the new player will verify possible system threads (security check/diagnosis) and t will assume legal responsibilities versus the Content Provider.

The Telecom Italia approach was to provide a proprietary MTE (the SIM) as trusted operating space where the CAS vendor implemented and put the conditional access system secure application.

This solution enables a high protection level (Smartcard based security), reducing mobile operator liabilities versus the Content Provider and provide a secure service portable on several mobile terminals by means of a unique user subscription.

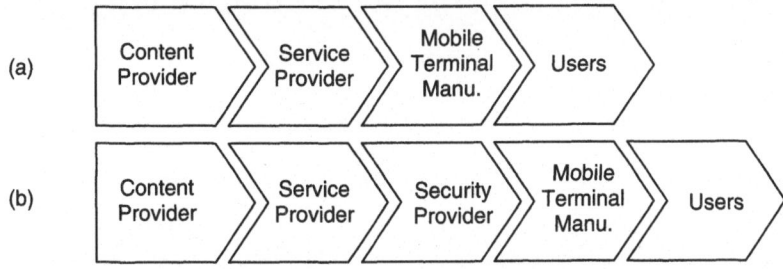

Fig. 6: Simplified DVB-H service distribution chains

5 Conclusions

The paper identified key points to design secure services in terms of attributes, stakeholders, level of security and liability defining the so-called MTE as primary secrets storage and processing area. The MTE and architecture implementation considerations are discussed highlighting that designing choices depend on security attributes to be targeted, the required level of security versus the legal and commercial risk as well as solution cost and the trust-in stakeholder.

The DVB-H use cases showed how a mobile operator identifies its MTE and architecture to deliver a protected broadcasting service.

References

[Kerc83]   Kerckhoffs, Auguste « La cryptographie militaire, Journal des sciences militaires », vol. IX, pp. 5–83, Jan. 1883, pp. 161–191, Feb. 1883.

[Armw05]   ARM Ltd web site; www.arm.com/trustzone, June 2005

[Truw06]   Trusted Logic web site; www.trusted-logic.com, June 2006

[Jalw06]   Jaluna web site; www.jaluna.com, June 2006

[Dvbw03]   DVB website; www.dvb.org, June 2003

[Etsw04]   ETSI web site; www.etsi.org, June 2004

[Omaw06]   OMA web site; www.openmobilealliance.com, June 2006

Security Management Applications

Centrally Administered COIs Using Cross-Organizational Trust

Kevin Foltz · Coimbatore Chandersekaran

Institute for Defense Analyses
Alexandria, VA, USA
{kfoltz | cchander}@ida.org

Abstract

We study collaboration among different organizations using the idea of a community of interest (COI). We consider not just sharing of data, but collaboration requiring tight integration of all elements of the collaborating organizations. Current models for COIs have shortcomings that limit their applicability to real-world situations. Our previous work addresses some of these shortcomings, but its restrictive architecture limits its applicability. All resources were required to collaborate within a single domain forest. In this work, we extend the prior model with new capabilities that allow collaboration across forests.

1 Introduction

Please note the following important formatting guidelines:

We study collaboration among different organizations using the idea of a community of interest (COI). We consider not just sharing of data, but collaboration requiring tight integration of all elements of the collaborating organizations. These collaborations may be long-term mergers, short-term goal-oriented tasks, or ongoing projects between different organizations. Rapid assembly of collaborating partners is required. However, they must still provide the proper functionality and security measures to ensure safe interaction and sharing of resources.

Ideas for COIs have been developed [Cent95][SJYS00][Khur02], but they all have shortcomings. We developed the Centrally Administered Community of Interest (CACOI)[FoCh05] to address these shortcomings. The centralized nature of the CACOI solved many problems, but its restrictive architecture limits its applicability.

Specifically, the requirement of importing all elements of the COI into a single domain or forest limits the way resources are shared and the way users can access the COI. Databases, for example, can be very large and cumbersome to import and export. Also, an organization unwilling to cede complete control of the resources it contributes would be unwilling to join such a CACOI. The CACOI structure simply does not provide flexibility in resource sharing. The resource is either in the CACOI or it is out, but there is nothing in between. This is a benefit for tightness of interaction and establishing a clear security boundary, but this is simply too restrictive for many types of collaboration. In addition, in a CACOI users must log in locally on a different account and different network. These issues limit the CACOI's applicability to real-world problems.

S. Paulus, N. Pohlmann, H. Reimer (Editors): Securing Electronic Business Processes, Vieweg (2006), 311-317

2 Cross-Forest Collaboration Goals

In this work we propose a new model, the Cross-Forest COI (CFCOI), which captures much of the transparency and distributed nature of the P2P approaches, improves resource management, and maintains the functional richness and administrative simplicity of the CACOI model. The main idea of the CFCOI is to allow collaborations to extend across multiple forests instead of being confined like the CACOI to a single domain or forest. To achieve this while maintaining functionality and security the CFCOI implementation has three main goals.

The first goal is authentication. In a CACOI authentication is done within the domain or forest. This is a built-in function of domains, and is easy to implement. Once implemented, the identity is secure, and authentication and authorization are done in a natural way within the domain. When creating COIs across forests, the notion of identity must change, since the identities within the domains will not carry across domains, leading to problems with authentication. There must be a new way to authenticate across forests to allow consistent treatment of users within the COI.

The second goal for the CFCOI we will call "credential shaping." In a CACOI authorization is based on the identity of the user within that domain or forest. When extending identities across domains a new issue arises. One user may be a member of multiple COIs with overlapping resource utilization in overlapping forests. A problem can arise when a user is a member of two COIs, one of which has access to a resource, and one of which is denied access. The problem is one of authorization. There is no clear-cut way to determine access to a user who is a member of both COIs. Credential shaping is a way to allow the user to specify which credentials to use for access.

The third goal is confinement. When users are distributed across different forests there is an increase in the risk of data being released without authorization from the COI. When files and users share physical hardware, the boundary between COI and non-COI is weaker than the CACOI, where the hardware and user identities are all contained within a single COI domain or forest. As a result, confinement must be managed at the level of individual resources, and not by the domain or forest.

3 Cross-Forest Collaboration Solutions

To address the three goals, we first establish the notion of identity across forests. This is done by credential providers (CPs). These CPs are located in each domain or forest, and they sign credentials for principles in their local domain or forest. The credentials include information such as Name, Group, Role, Domain, and COI. The principle requests the CP's signature for a certain combination of the indicated fields. If that combination is valid (i.e. if that principle has that name, is a member of that group, acts in the indicated role, and is a member of the indicated COI), then the CP signs such a credential. CPs in different forests establish agreements about COI membership rights and privileges. When these credentials are sent across forests, the local CP in the destination forest can verify the signature on the credential, based on the agreement between the forests that is established in advance, and verify the indicated principle's membership in the indicated COI. Thus, the identity is preserved across forests.

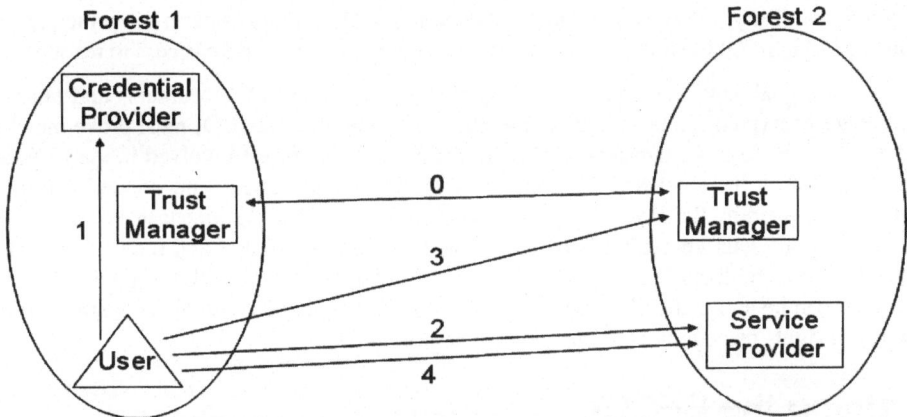

Figure 1: Cross-forest service access using WS-Trust. Step 0: TMs in the two forests establish rules and policies for cross-forest interactions. Step 1: A user first obtains a credential, indicating COI membership. Step 2: The user requests a service from Forest 2. Step 3: The user is referred to the TM in Forest 2 to verify the credential issued by Forest 1. Step 4: The TM in Forest 2 checks its policies, verifies the credential's validity, and refers the user back to the service provider with local authorization.

To address the first goal, cross-forest authentication, we make use of the Web Services Trust (WS-Trust) specification. This provides a standardized way to allow fine-granularity sharing of resources across different organizations. The specific implementation used for the CFCOI model is the Active Directory Federation Services (ADFS) add-on to Microsoft Server 2003. The organizations, modeled as domain forests, establish Trust Managers (TMs) that enforce sharing policies across the forests. When a principle from a CFCOI requests access to a CFCOI resource in another forest, the resource refers the principle to the TM in the resource's domain. This TM then checks its policies to determine local privileges and access rights to the resource. The trust relationships established in the TMs' policies allow a specified type of access to a specified resource to be granted to a specified principle in the CFCOI. If the principle is allowed access under the TMs' policies, the TM adds its own credential and refers the principle back to the resource, which then provides access to the principle. When modeling resources as web services, this transaction is very clean. The resource simply uses the http protocol to refer the principle to the TM, and the TM uses the same technique to refer the principle back to the resource, but with extra information that allows access. The net result is that resources in one forest can authorize principles in another forest with the help of the CPs and TMs. The basic idea is illustrated in Figure 1.

This approach is based on the industry practice of identity federation. In identity federation, different organizations agree to authenticate each others' users based on pre-negotiated trust policies. For the user, the net result is that logging into one domain allows access to the other domain's services transparently. Instead of requiring the user to authenticate in the second domain, the authentication is done automatically by previously established rules between the two domains. The Liberty Alliance and WS-Federation are two standards that address identity federation. Our implementation uses the WS-Federation approach, which fits cleanly with the CACOI domain concept.

To address the second goal, credential shaping, we use the CPs to provide the appropriate COI information for a user at a given time. The COI choice can be done at log-in, or it can be chosen dynamically, to allow switching between two COIs. In either case, the principle is in control of which COI is on the credential, thus allowing the appropriate access to resources.

For the third goal, confinement, we use digital rights management. Documents and other resources are encrypted. To access them, members of the appropriate COI must prove membership in the COI. Rights Managers (RMs) are present in each forest involved in the COI, and principles consult the local RM for access to COI documents. Documents created within the COI are encrypted by the RMs to prevent unauthorized use. The document itself contains information about what credential is required for the requested access, and indicates a RM or COI where this credential can be obtained. If a principle is acting within a given COI, this credential can be automatically granted based on the CP-signed credential. This allows transparency of rights management to the appropriate principles.

4 Using the CFCOI

In comparing the CFCOI to the CACOI, the main functional difference is that the CFCOI allows a COI to be established across multiple forests, whereas the CACOI requires the entire COI to exist within a single forest. The benefit of the CACOI design is that authentication, authorization, resource sharing, and confinement all come at relatively no cost. The domain and forest structure includes built-in mechanisms to implement all of these features. However, the cost of using a single forest is often too high for the parties involved, and an opportunity for collaboration is lost. The CFCOI provides more flexibility while preserving the benefits associated with the CACOI, thus allowing collaboration to take place where it otherwise would not be possible. Figures 2 and 3 show the CACOI and CFCOI model architectures.

A simple example showing the benefit of the CFCOI is the sharing of a large, complex, and proprietary database. A large company has a database of customers and account information, and they would like another small company to use its proprietary analysis techniques on parts of the data to determine if a long-term agreement would be worthwhile. The large company wishes to provide limited access to the database, and the small company wishes to interact directly with the database in a tight way. A COI is a good way to do this, since it is established quickly and involves a short-term, goal-oriented task with tight integration of resources. A CACOI would be good, except there are two problems. First, the database must be exported to a new domain. This would be very difficult and time- and resource-consuming. Second, employees of the small company would have full access to the database in the COI domain, since the database would be under the control of the COI, not the large company. This is not acceptable to the large company, since the database is too sensitive.

The CFCOI is a good solution to the situation. Both companies can agree on a level of access for the small company, and keep the database in the large company. TMs can be used to allow cross-forest access. The CFCOI avoids the costly import/export of the large database, and allows the large company to maintain control of the database while allowing limited access, as specified by the TM policies. The functionality and ease of use are preserved, since the database authentication and authorization are transparent to the users.

CACOI Structure

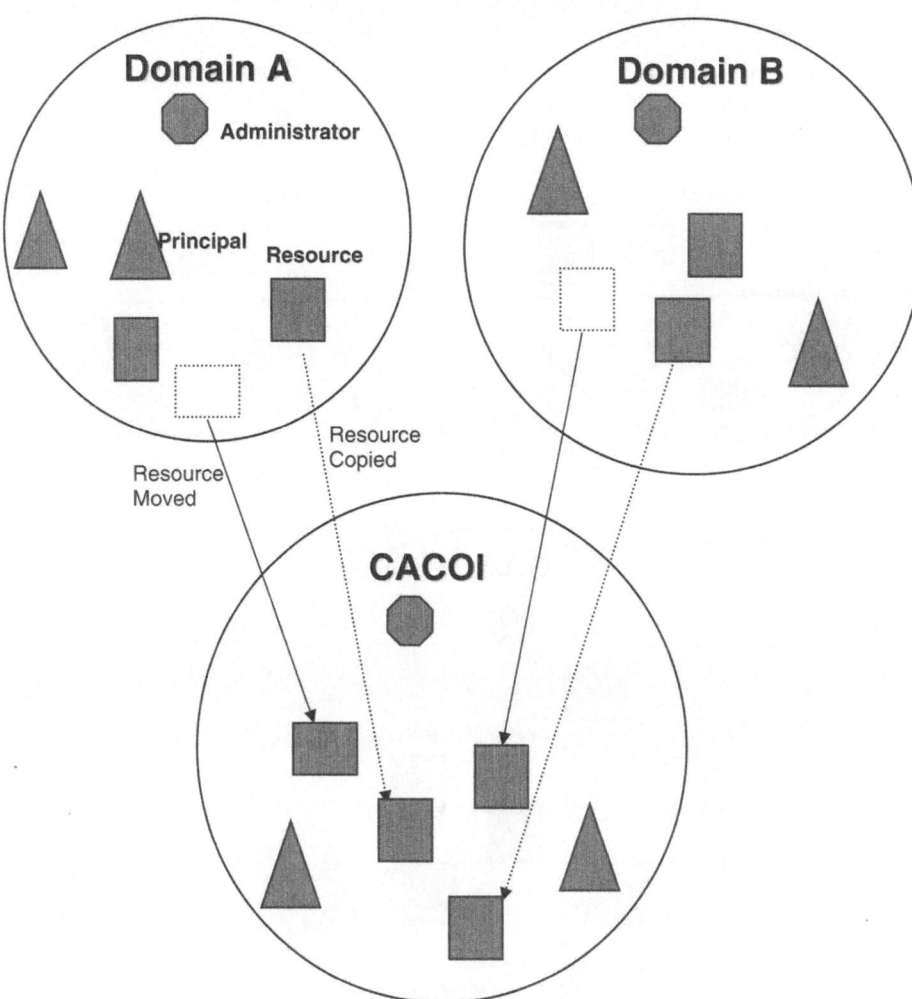

Figure 2: Structure of a CACOI. Domains A and B form a CACOI. All CACOI resources are either moved or copied into the community domain, and new principals are created in the CACOI. Once the CACOI domain is established, no outside communication is permitted. Users must log into the CACOI user account to function in the CACOI.

CFCOI Structure

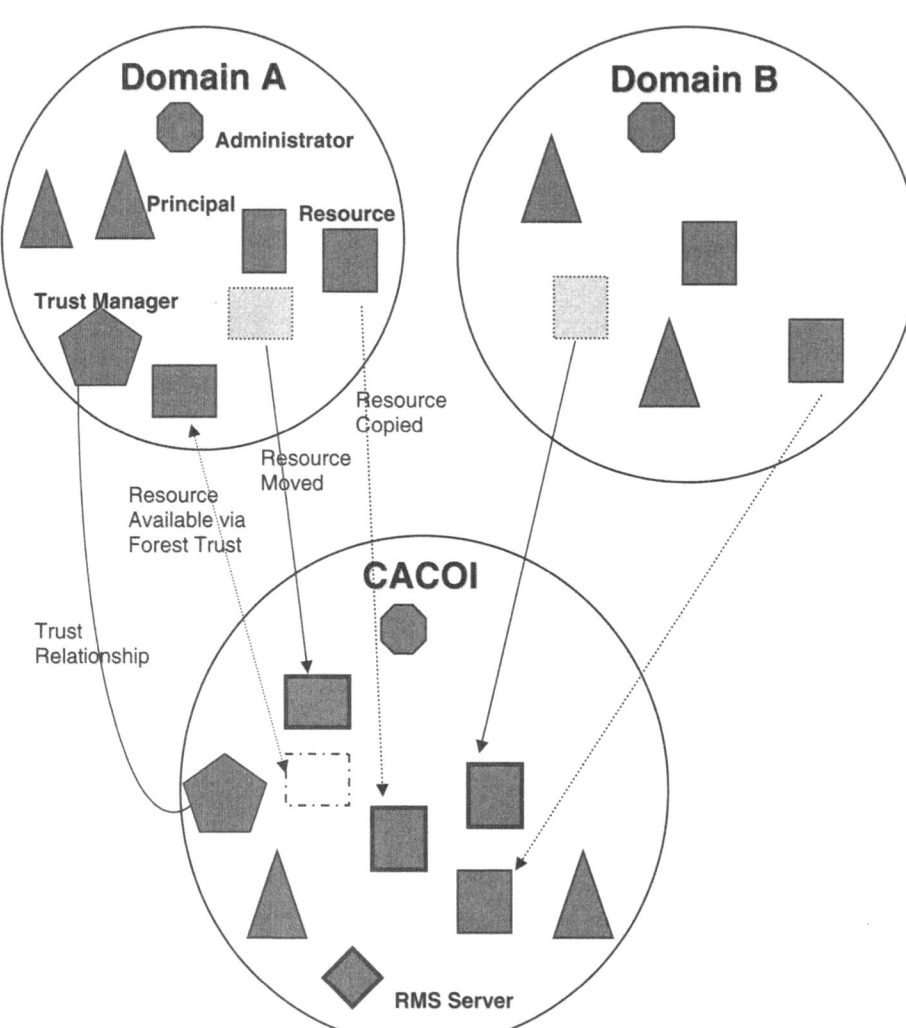

Figure 3: Structure of a CFCOI. Unlike the CACOI, some resources are made accessible to the community but remain in their original domains. Trust Relationships between Trust Managers allow secure sharing of resources. Resources with dark blocks are protected by Rights Management.

Another example, highlighting credential shaping, is work involving proprietary or otherwise restricted data. An individual may be assembling data to write a report on a topic, but the report must have only publicly available sources. The user in question might have access to many different COIs in different domains, allowing access not available to the public. In assembling the resources, the user specifies membership in no CFCOI when logging in. This prevents unintentional access to restricted data, and ensures that all work is releasable to the public. This could also be used when collaborating with an individual with no access privileges. Logging in without COI access ensures that all interaction with that individual is safe, in the sense that sensitive information will not be disclosed accidentally. This ability comes for free in the CACOI, since users in the CACOI forest are isolated. However, the point here is that even with the CFCOI, which has the benefit of cross-forest interactions, the "isolation" of the CACOI is still achievable when desired.

An example showing the benefits of data confinement is the case of someone working on the road, where only public Internet access is available. The individual copies working files to the local machine, works with them, and sends updated versions back to the COI. When the individual leaves the terminal, files are left behind (on the desktop, in the "Recycle Bin," or in hardware locations accessible with basic or more advanced extraction tools). In a CACOI this type of access is not permitted, since all principles, resources, and services must remain within the CACOI domain or forest, but if it was possible, there is the potential for data leakage. In a CFCOI, this type of access can be permitted, but after the individual logs out of the COI any remaining files are protected by encryption, and the RM in the CFCOI, which is needed for decryption, is not accessible to the public. Hence, the files left on the computer are no longer accessible, even though the full text of the encrypted files may be present.

5 Conclusion

The CFCOI builds on the CACOI model, which itself addressed many of the shortcomings of previous models of collaboration. Drawbacks of the CACOI's single domain/forest model are identified, and the requirement of keeping all resources in one forest is relaxed. This allows a more flexible COI model, capable of supporting a more diverse array of collaboration types. This flexibility presents new challenges in authentication, authorization, and confinement. To address these concerns, the idea of a cross-forest COI-based identity, enabled by local CPs and TMs, is established. This enables cross-forest trust relations, cross-forest authentication, and digital rights management. This is easy to implement using existing hardware, software, and protocols. The resulting CFCOI model preserves many of the features of the CACOI while removing the strict single-domain/forest structure. This makes the CFCOI model more suitable to real-world collaboration problems.

References

[Cent95]   Department of Defense (DoD) Goal Security Architecture (DGSA). Center for Information Systems Security (CISS), Defense Information System Security Program (DISSP), Version 3.0, 30 September 1995.

[SYJS00]   Shands, D.; Yee, R.; Jacobs, J.; Sebes, E. J.: Secure Virtual Enclaves: Supporting Coalition Use of Distributed Application Technologies. Proceedings of the Network and Distributed Systems Security Symposium, San Diego, February 2000.

[Khur02]   Khurana, H.: Negotiation and Management of Coalition Resources. Ph.D. Thesis, Department of Electrical and Computer Engineering, University of Maryland, College Park, MD, 2002.

[FoCh05]   Foltz, Kevin; Chandersekaran, Coimbatore: Sharing Resources through Dynamic Communities. Proceedings of ISSE 2005.

Improving Assurance of Information Security RoI

Michael D. Barwise

Integrated InfoSec
6 Maple Green, Hemel Hempstead, Hertfordshire HP1 3PY, UK
mbarwise@bcs.org.uk

Abstract

Changing business expectations of information infrastructures have imposed new demands on security architectures. Established technocentric perimeter-oriented security architectures are yielding ground to business-driven deperimeterised architectures that assume extensive information and resource sharing and global virtualisation. These changes provide the opportunity to take a new approach to security architecture specification, based at its highest level not on costing of reactive countermeasures to current technical threats, but on prioritising the allocation of resources to robustly and proactively protect business information assets against business-oriented exposures. This permits tighter specification of both requirements and budgeting with a concomitant improvement in RoI, but depends on a new approach to management described here.

1 Changing Security Architectures

Until quite recently, information security budgeting was a relatively simple affair. Perimeter-oriented security technologies and personnel awareness campaigns were the essence of the solution for the majority of businesses. The components, and thus the component costs, of such a security implementation were generally well-defined and their selection was driven almost exclusively by techno-centric architectural decisions. However, the resulting architectures (essentially an assemblage of secured cells each consisting of a hard shell surrounding a soft centre, coupled by hardened data corridors to similar cells) have never been optimum. They generally bear no close relationship to business structure, essentially echoing instead the geographical distribution of business premises, data centres and facilities, they suffer from single points of failure, and their greatest weakness has always been at the user interface endpoints.

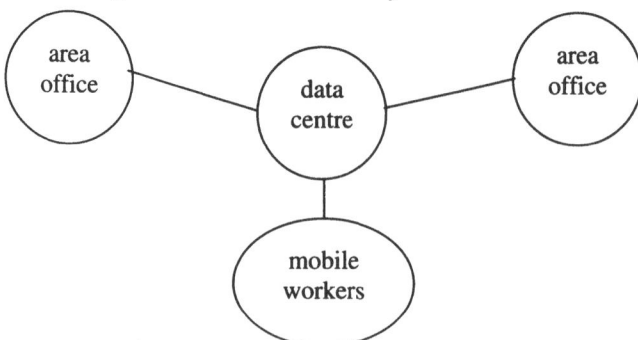

Figure 1: Traditional Perimeter-oriented Architecture

S. Paulus, N. Pohlmann, H. Reimer (Editors): Securing Electronic Business Processes, Vieweg (2006), 318-325

Such architectures also tend to reinforce a reactive approach to security, with the emphasis on countering technical threats from outside the perimeter as they emerge. The reactive stance makes the relationship between implemented security technologies and levels of protection achieved hard to demonstrate, and there is seldom any strong correlation between the value of the protected assets and the cost of protecting them. Uncertainty both in predicting the nature of emerging threats and in ensuring that reactions are appropriate and proportional both contribute to this. Typical of the problems faced are "zero-day exploits" (software vulnerabilities that are exploited by an attacker immediately they are publicised, prior to any remedy being developed). Such threats are extremely difficult to predict, and in the absence of proactive management for robustness can cause losses that are not only potentially large but also very difficult to quantify. Clearly, although the budgeting process is relatively simple to execute for traditional perimeter-oriented architectures, assurance of security and cost-effectiveness are both low, so poor RoI is to be expected.

1.1 New Demands

The expansion of technological facilities driving twenty-first century business has created new departures in infrastructure, not only in terms of scale but also in nature. The increasing ubiquity of web services, virtual networks and grids, distributed and shared data, mobile working and a host of other business demands that tend to destructure corporate network boundaries result in the requirement for tight integration of security solutions with business processes, rather than primarily with network physical infrastructures as in the past.

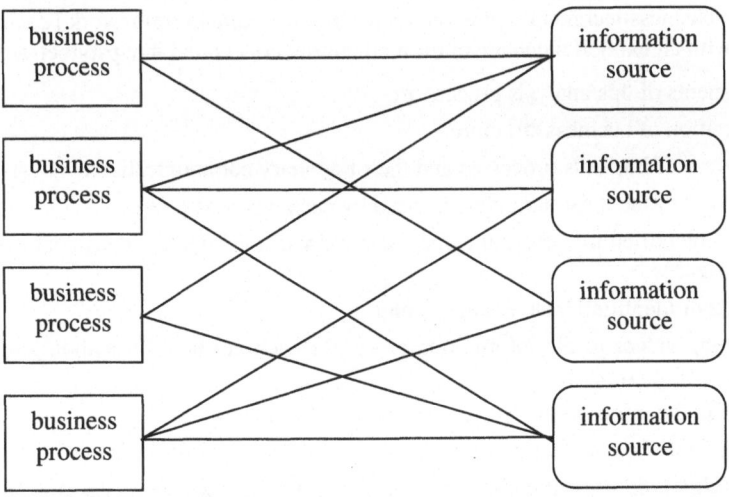

Figure 2: Business-oriented Architecture

Information security must become an intrinsic component of enterprise architecture. This need is driven by ever more complex mappings between data sources and users. Users may reside on partner networks over which data providers have little or no security authority, and business information is likely to be assembled from numerous data sources not necessarily under common control. These developments force us to take a more proactive approach to security architecture decision-making that is based on business structure and processes. Nevertheless, the ultimate security implementation remains a technical issue: the creation of a network of secure channels between segregated and secured assets and segregated and secured users that has no soft centre and has a much less well-defined corporate perimeter or, ultimately, even no perimeter. The change of emphasis provides an associated opportunity to improve the quality of the budgeting process and consequently both the cost-effectiveness and the assurance of security, but it requires a new management approach that encompasses both business expectations and technical solutions, and a rigorous methodology allowing business and technical personnel to collaborate effectively towards the common goal of security without loss of focus.

2 A New Approach

For the technical security architect, this blurring of boundaries has made the primary requirement one of understanding the assemblage of business processes and their associated information flows. For security management and budgeting personnel, the aim has becomes to prioritise the allocation of a security budget with reference to the business value of the various information assets to be protected, the first task being to place values on those assets in the context of the business processes they serve and the hazards to which they are potentially exposed. For both parties this must be in the first instance a business-centric matter, not a techno-centric one, so we must speak of information, not of data, must consider detriments in business rather than in solely technical terms, and must define hazards within a business, not a purely technical, frame of reference.

Whereas in the past techno-centric security architectures were generally derived from a single-stage technical requirements analysis, the need is now for a multi-stage analysis that bridges the business-technical divide on the lines of a Zachman framework [Zach99], but, and critically, with an explicit mechanism for maintaining conceptual integrity between layers.

The components of this analysis process are

1. recognition of business structure
2. discovery of business processes and their boundary communications
3. discovery of the information assets used by each business process
4. for the identified information assets, discovery of the business detriment caused by specific hazards
5. costing of identified business detriments
6. assigning values to the information assets for each attribute by mapping back from the discovered detriments
7. mapping the information assets to the physical infrastructure
8. aggregating the information asset values by attribute against the infrastructure
9. specifying proportional budgets for securing infrastructure components against breach of the attributes
10. delivery of technical solutions with reference to the required attributes and technical threats, and within the proportional budgets

Clearly this is a more complex specification process than has generally been deemed necessary in the past, but it must be recognised that it has to fulfil a much more sophisticated brief, not least in bridging the business/technical cultural divide to ensure that the necessarily complex business security vision is accurately reflected in the final technical implementation. It is also imperative to recognise that the way the process is performed will have an overriding influence on the quality of the results. Most extant security management and architecture development methodologies gloss over this distinction, but experience shows that it is absolutely critical to recognise it if consistency is desired. Uncertainty, and consequent variability in judgement quality, must be minimised as far as possible by some formalised process of debiasing [KaST99]. The key contributors to uncertainty in the current context are subjectivity and linguistic imprecision, which have been widely discussed in other spheres of risk judgement [MoHe90]. They will primarily affect components 3, and 4, 5 in cases where finite data are not available (for example when assessing regulatory liabilities), and possibly 2, depending on the complexity of the business process set. But these two causes of uncertainty can be minimised by making use of well-defined parameter sets, standard semantics and rigorously defined investigative methods.

2.1 Defining the Parameters

The precise definitions of business structure, processes and information assets will obviously be dependent on the nature of the enterprise. It is probable that existing business process management systems and tools can provide support here, remembering that for a complete security implementation any manual processes and information sources must also be included. However, the distinction between data and information is important. An information asset is defined jointly by the information used and the specific business process that uses it. The same actual information used by a different process constitutes a different information asset. This allows for the possibility of differing impact of a given breach depending on the nature of the business process that is affected.

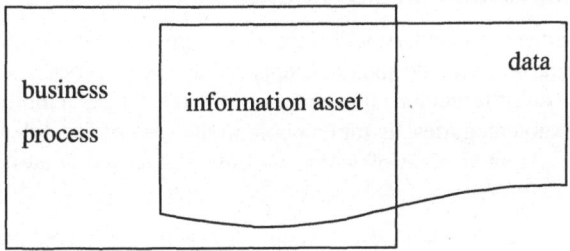

Figure 3: Venn Diagram of an Information Asset

2.2 Criteria for the Semantic Structure

To consistently assess information asset values, it is necessary to work within a well-defined semantic structure that expresses exposures and detriments unequivocally. Linguistic imprecision is one of the major contributors to inconsistency in risk decision-making, and much care must be exercised to minimise it. Any such structure must be transportable across the business-technical divide without ambiguity. Consequently it must be small in scale, and must exclusively make use of terminology that is simply expressed in both spheres. Considering first the exposure vocabulary, concepts such as "loss of reputation" from the business perspective, or "viruses" from the technical, are not useful as they are vague and their implications are subjective.

2.2.1 Information Attributes

The established information security trilogy of information attributes: "confidentiality", "integrity", "availability"; are a good starting point for an exposure structure. Each can be explained simply in terms of both business expectations and technical requirements. But this minimal vocabulary has to be extended to cover the range of current needs. A core vocabulary should include

- Confidentiality - only the right people accessing only the right information
- Integrity - freedom from corruption and unauthorised alteration of information
- Authenticity - assurance of authorised origin and validity of information
- Availability - assurance of authorised access to information when required
- Retention - fulfilment of both business and statutory archival requirements
- Ownership - control over the possession of supplied information
- Regulation - fulfilment of purely regulatory obligations for information management

2.2.2 Defining a Breach

The other crucial component of the exposure semantics is the definition of a breach. As we are not at this level of the framework addressing the incidence or likelihood of a breach (which is a technical consideration based on the driving events), we can usefully assume a Boolean operator: it either occurs or it does not occur. Thus any breach is deemed to be a total breach. This makes the process more manageable without losing any important detail. It also essentially ensures we work to worst-case scenarios in the first instance. The breach of an attribute in respect of a specific information asset is termed *exposure*.

2.2.3 Defining Business Detriments

The business detriment vocabulary will depend to a great extent on the nature of the enterprise, but core terms will include such concepts as "unable to process order", "delayed delivery", "customer lost", "fraudulent transaction enabled", "legal liability", and so on. There may of course be sub-categories, as for example in the case of fraudulent transactions and legal liabilities, the potential scale of which will depend on the context of specific business processes.

The key attributes of a well-defined detriment term will be its freedom from ambiguity and independence, i.e. its lack of intersection with other terms in the set. This is why terms such as "loss of reputation" are inadequate, as they are vague and puerly qualitative.

2.2.4 Costing Business Detriments

Having established a set of business detriments appropriate to the enterprise, costs can be placed globally on the detriments, based on recent business records for the enterprise in consultation with accounting, legal, audit and actuarial. It is strongly recommended that a minimum, median and maximum expected cost is calculated for each detriment, as the distribution may vary for different assets. In the case of simple detriments such as lost orders, accounts data for a suitable period can be analysed to directly establish values. Where the relationship between the detriment and the cost is less well-defined (for example contingent losses, legal costs) a formal enquiry method should be used as when identifying the detriments themselves. Time constraints such as process turn-round and throughput per time period must be determined and factored into the costings. In all cases adequate documentation must be preserved to show how the result was obtained.

2.3 The Process

Having established the semantic framework, how do we proceed? In the first stage, the information assets are unambiguously allocated identities that refer back to their data type and the business process they are derived from. This metadata is then carried forward to the business enquiry phase.

2.3.1 Business Enquiry Phase

Staff who operate the business process are asked to consider which of the defined detriments the process would suffer if each attribute of each information asset they make use of were breached. The output of this stage is a list of information assets by business process against which a detriment term is associated with each of the hazard terms. The list can be then merged with the established detriment cost data to yield values attached directly to the attributes of information assets. Where more than one possible detriment may derive from an information asset attribute breach, the costs of all should be aggregated with strict regard for the information attribute, although it may prove beneficial to keep a record of the breakdown as well. This aggregation is a useful simplification for the next (mapping) stage without loss of functionality. The metadata now consists of a list of information assets, each associated with a value for each attribute. At this stage, the value metadata can usefully be quantised in to a limited number of bands. Often, such quantisation is limited to three bands (high, medium and low priority) but experience has shown that the optimum is five bands (noted but not for action, low priority action, medium priority action, high priority action, immediate imperative).

2.3.2 Technical Mapping Phase

The attribute-costed information assets are next mapped back to the technical infrastructure as data in terms of storage and user nodes and transport pathways, not forgetting that manual processes are part of that infrastructure and manually handled information also constitutes information assets. This allows concentrations of exposure in the infrastructure to be identified in respect of each information attribute. It is here that the primary benefit of this approach becomes clear. Because the information attributes (until now considered only with reference to business expectations) have direct technical meaning in terms of generic security solutions, the transition across the business/technical divide is unambiguous. A technical architecture is automatically derivable, and budgets can be allocated to specific business/technical requirements with good assurance that the spend will be proportional to the value of the assets being protected and will be allocated to covering the real exposures of those assets.

3 Methods

It is important to use verifiably reliable methods when gathering the necessarily large and diverse body of metadata required for this process. A necessarily multi-stage process is open to considerable opportunities for error if inadequately robust methods are used at any stage, and the greater the number of stages the greater the cumulative potential for error.

The most significant characteristic of any method chosen to deliver this process is its ability to ensure consistency. Absolute (numerical) accuracy is much less important, as the primary contribution to the budgeting task made by this process is the optimisation of security spending priorities, i.e. the optimum distribution of the available budget. Therefore high confidence in relative measures is the essential goal.

3.1 Interviewing

The way enquiries and metadata gathering are conducted has been widely recognised in other fields of decision-making as having a strong influence on the reliability of results, although this is not yet common knowledge in the information security arena. Put simply, a major contribution to quality can be made by asking the right people the right questions in the right way. Although this seems obvious, it often overlooked. Security management committees still tend to look inwards for answers from their membership, and consultancy analyses still tend to concentrate their enquiries at senior management level. Experience suggests however that it is most effective to start asset and process analysis by interviewing the lowest echelon that handles any process or structure being investigated, the next tier above being resorted to if answers conflict or respondents are uncertain. The lowest echelon is most likely to be aware what is actually done, whereas higher echelons will generally be more guided in their responses by what is documented as the official procedure. In general, for best assurance, at least three individuals should be interviewed at any tier and the answers of each validated anonymously with the others (a simple variant of the Delphi method [Gord94]). In accord with the precepts of Delphi, standard question and answer sets must be carefully prepared both for consistency and to eliminate ambiguity. To this end, generic answers based on the detriment vocabulary are used to validate free-form answers from the interviewees in a two-stage process. The interviewee is first asked "what would happen if ..." and their answers are noted. When all questions have been answered, the interviewer returns to the start of the question set and agrees with the interviewee which of the standard answers best accords with their free-form answer. In general there should be good conformity, but significant discrepancies will indicate cases requiring further analysis. A Delphi approach should be applied in a similar manner to the detriment costing exercise wherever finite data are not available from which to draw an objective numerical response.

3.2 Metadata Management

Management of the necessarily large volume of metadata requires careful consideration. It is an extremely valuable resource for the business that can also be brought to bear on other areas of decision-making than security, but it needs to be carefully structured. Experience suggests that a good approach is a virtual tree of business processes with the root at the enterprise and the information assets forming the leaves, as this permits information assets to be uniquely identified by parsing the tree. However, metadata structural considerations will depend on local preferences, as often existing business management tools can be drawn on to support the process. It is indeed in many cases very possible than some of the business structure metadata is already available and will not need to be recreated. Common standards will eventually emerge, but as a minimum a consistent presentational standard should be provided throughout the enterprise. Collaboration from interested specialists would be welcomed.

The final important management consideration is the security requirement for the metadata set itself. It will be an extremely sensitive descriptor of the business as a whole, and therefore will quite possibly become the most highly costed information asset, particularly in respect of confidentiality.

4 Return on Investment

It must be asked whether implementing such a system compares favourably with extant security budgeting and specification methodologies from the perspective of RoI. RoI is recognised as notoriously difficult to determine in information security, so this is an extremely important question. There are several aspects to the response. First, the described approach improves quality of fit between business expectations and technical implementations. This must by definition lead to better allocation of resources to security implementations than blanket security applied across the board. Second, assurance of that fit is improved by the evidential support for decisions that is inherent in the methodology. Third, many extant methodologies are designed to be delivered as project-oriented consultancy, whereas the described method is intended to be implemented as an embedded component of ongoing business management on the lines of CMM. As when implementing any business management system, initial investment may be considerable, depending entirely on the maturity of business management currently in place and the extent of business process intelligence already available. In most cases, bulk metadata capture will be the most costly component of initiating the method. Once in place, the method should operate as a CMM level 5 self-sustaining business function with little further overhead except periodic updates when business changes occur.

5 Conclusion

A process has been described for proactively prioritising the allocation of information security budgets based on potential business losses resulting from detriments to defined business information attributes. It differs from previous approaches in that

- it makes used of a well-defined semantic structure to maintain conceptual integrity across the business/technical divide, thereby ensuring the correct problems are solved
- it is business-centric rather than techno-centric at the budgeting and architecture decision points

Its key advantages are that it promises to improve long-term RoI in information security management by optimising the fit between security requirements and solutions, that it offers improved assurance by relating security budget distribution directly to the value and distribution of protected assets, and that the process metadata provide an objective and auditable underpin for decision-making. The same metadata will also support additional purposes such as business continuity planning and process streamlining, further improving overall RoI.

References

[Zach99]   Zachman, JA: A Framework for Information Systems Architecture. In: IBM Systems Journal, IBM, 1999, p. 454-470.

[KaST99]   Kahneman, D Slovic, P Tversky, A: Judgement under Uncertainty: Heuristics and Biases. Cambridge University Press, 1999, p. 422-444.

[MoHe90]   Morgan, MG and Henrion M: Uncertainty. Cambridge University Press, 1990, p. 56-60.

[Gord94]   Gordon, TJ: The Delphi Method. Futures Group AC/UNU Millennium Project, 1994.

Modelling the Economics of Free and Open Source Software Security

Anas Tawileh · Jeremy Hilton · Steve McIntosh

School of Computer Science, Cardiff University
5 The Parade, Cardiff CF24 3AA, UK
{m.a.tawileh | jeremy.hilton | s.b.mcintosh}@cs.cardiff.ac.uk

Abstract

The increasing popularity and adoption of Free and Open Source Software (F/OSS) has fostered heated debates about the dependability of software developed in such an open, highly distributed context. Claims are made in favour of and against F/OSS as a viable alternative to proprietary software. Due to the complex nature of software security, and the large number of interacting factors involved, a wider systemic view is required to produce more defensible claims about the economics of F/OSS security. In this paper, we propose a quantitative approach based on system dynamics to validate stated claims about F/OSS security and its economic aspects. We sketch a first attempt towards a computer simulation model to test different hypotheses by using empirical data. The model applicability is demonstrated by an illustrative example; the preliminary results obtained are comparable to data reported in the literature. The example supports our belief in the validity of the system dynamics approach as a testing vehicle to explain observed phenomena and support or disprove argued hypotheses. The model is also useful for predicting future behaviour of F/OSS development projects and comparing F/OSS to other software development processes

1 Introduction

Growth levels of Free and Open Source Software (F/OSS) have been increasing at a substantial rate over the past few years [Whee05]. Users and decision makers are realizing the value of adopting F/OSS software and many organizations are seriously considering it as a viable alternative to proprietary, commercially distributed applications. While such growth and expansion could be attributed to multiple characteristics inherent in the F/OSS development products and process, security remains a critical aspect, and an area that needs further research and exploration if F/OSS is to make inroads into the business market.

The F/OSS development process is based on a set of rules and principles radically different from the traditions governing the organization of proprietary software development. Based on intense collaboration and communication, developers from all around the globe combine their efforts to produce high quality software. The final applications are built by incorporating the different contributions submitted by these developers. In order to cope with the complexity of managing and coordinating efforts on such a high scale, the community has invented novel mechanisms to maximize the efficiency of its development activities. For example, F/OSS development relies on frequent release of software versions and a transparent, open peer review process to discover software defects and enhance quality. These mechanisms have proved to be highly successful in enabling the inherently diverse F/OSS community to produce high quality software applications, which are currently considered to be a serious rival to the established proprietary software applications. This is clearly evident in the higher levels of

S. Paulus, N. Pohlmann, H. Reimer (Editors): Securing Electronic Business Processes, Vieweg (2006), 326-335

adoption of some F/OSS packages like the GNU/Linux operating system and the Apache web server.

Much effort has been invested in exploring and explaining the distinct characteristics of F/OSS and its open development process that enable it to compete against software which is developed in traditional commercial settings [MoFH02] [BLSN02]. The literature investigates many aspects of the F/OSS paradigm and how they compare against proprietary software development. Among these aspects, and an area that has attracted significant attention lately, is the dependability of F/OSS. Dependability is a broad term that covers many areas such as security, reliability and availability [LaJo02]. Also, the nature of dependability is perceived differently by different stakeholders [BLJM04]. Unfortunately, most of the work done so far has focused on specific issues. Although investigating these specific issues could generate a better understanding of the situation under observation, it tends to ignore the different factors affecting the situation and the complex interactions between them. This would result in explanations that are partial at best, and in some cases may lead to strange interpretations of the observed phenomena.

In this paper we propose a more elaborate, systems approach to the study of the economic aspect of F/OSS security and dependability. By taking a systems perspective, a richer understanding of the problematic situation can be achieved, taking into consideration all the different involved factors and their interactions. Such an understanding would facilitate the inquiry process and integrate the results reported in the literature to examine their validity and applicability when exercised in a complete, systemic setting; largely similar to the situation in the real world.

This paper provides some background information about software security in general and how it applies to F/OSS in particular. It reviews the relevant literature in order to lay the foundation for the progression of the discussion. Next, justification for the systems approach to investigate the problem is presented, along with our vision of the purpose of the dynamic model. Afterwards, model development is described and the resulting model sketched. Some preliminary analysis of the model behaviour is discussed as well. The model is then validated by using data sets from real world situations, and the results compared against values reported in the literature. The utility of the model and its applicability in practice are also described and demonstrated by an illustrative example. Finally, conclusions are drawn up and directions for future research are highlighted.

2 Software Dependability and F/OSS

With the increasing reliance on computers and software in almost every field of human activity, the need for more responsive, trustworthy and secure software has become a priority. Dependability of software systems has therefore gained substantial attention. In order to create more dependable software, a clear understanding of what dependability means in the context of software development, and a proper appreciation of its impact on the software development process is required.

Dependability is a broad term that covers different characteristics of the software artefacts, including, but not limited to, security, reliability, safety and availability [Lapr92]. Neumann [Neum02] suggests a practical definition for dependability: "Dependable systems are systems where trust can be justifiably placed in the service the system provides". Therefore, determining the dependability of a particular software artefact should consider the different elements that promote higher confidence in this artefact. The process and methods used to produce the software artefact also have major influences on its dependability characteristics, including user confidence in claimed dependability and consideration of the nature of the development process in the context of software dependability is of prime importance.

The distinct nature of the development processes within the F/OSS community has fostered heated debate about their ability to produce highly dependable software. Some might argue that exposing the source code would stimulate the exploitation of more vulnerabilities in the software and the introduction of backdoors, and therefore, would negatively affect security. Advocates of F/OSS, on the other hand, claim that by releasing source code and facilitating more intensive peer reviews, software defects will be discovered and fixed much faster, resulting in much higher levels of security [Payn02]. Eric Raymond describes this feature of the F/OSS development process as: "Given enough eyeballs, all bugs are shallow" [Raym02]. Another argument has been made about the honest motives of source code reviewers. The thread is that although availability of source code would enable more reviewers to check its integrity and security, doubts are often raised that people who possess the requisite knowledge to undertake such review do not always have entirely honest motives [Levy00].

These arguments illustrate the highly subjective nature of the claims made about the dependability of F/OSS. Both sides are using the same evidence to support their completely different thesis [ABGR02] [Payn02]. It is therefore very useful to investigate the different factors affecting the dependability of software in general, and F/OSS in particular, in order to clarify the different perspectives for or against F/OSS. This was described in a study about the issues of dependability of F/OSS [ABGR02]. The study stresses that due to the multiple facets of security, generalized claims such as "F/OSS is inherently more secure than proprietary software" are of little value. The study suggests that "there are different aspects of openness that may impact the dependability of software systems, aspects that may manifest themselves both in open source software and in non-open software projects" [ABGR02]. Littlewood and Strigini [LiSt00] confirm the need for an empirical method to clarify the advantages and disadvantages of the different aspects of the F/OSS development approach in influencing the dependability of resulting software.

Different studies concluded with fairly similar results [Payn02] [Levy00], suggesting that F/OSS is not inherently more secure or more dependable than proprietary software. However, there are different aspects of the F/OSS development process that would greatly affect its dependability. In an attempt to analyze the role of the development process in producing more secure software, Payne [Payn02] suggested a multilayered analysis model that incorporates different security and availability measures which are scored and averaged to form an overall indicator of the system's dependability. Another model was developed by Bosio el al [BLNS02] to determine the possible effects of certain factors on the dependability of F/OSS software. They propose a model to investigate and validate each claim made about F/OSS dependability based on empirical observations. The approach is fully described in [BLSN02].

3 A System Dynamics Approach

Given the complex interaction of the different factors affecting software security, approaching the problem with a narrow focus on specific issues yields limited results. In an attempt to clarify the mechanisms governing a complex, multi-faceted phenomenon such as software security, the full picture might be lost, and the interactions among the different factors may be unintentionally left out.

We propose a different approach to evaluate and test claims made about the security of F/OSS. Initially, we wanted to obtain further insight into the situation by taking a more elaborate, holistic perspective. System Dynamics, first introduced by Jay Forrester [Forr68], is a computer aided approach for analyzing and solving complex, systemic problems.

Human thinking is limited by nature, and can be rapidly overwhelmed by complex formulae and large interacting factors. System Dynamics' modelling provides a set of tools and techniques to aid human brains in focusing on the big picture of the problem under study, without losing the details. By making explicit the different factors and their interactions on an Influence Diagram, a richer understanding of the problem structure can be achieved, and behaviour patterns can be traced back to their real causes more easily. When supplemented by computer simulation, the model can be simulated to reproduce the behavioural patterns of the system in the real world. The simulation model can be used as a testing vehicle to analyze and interpret historical phenomena, and to predict future behaviour.

We aim to produce a System Dynamics model to represent the different aspects of software security. The developed model captures the multiple factors affecting security and provides a usable tool to test and validate different claims about F/OSS dependability. We can utilize the model to discover the specific effects of changes in the development environment that might have a visible impact on the security attributes of the developed software, particularly the economic aspects of security. This will make the validation of different hypotheses about software security and F/OSS much easier. Possible hypotheses to be tested may include: What feature of the F/OSS development process has the highest impact on the developed software dependability? Does a F/OSS application have fewer vulnerabilities than a comparable proprietary software product which has the same characteristics? To what extent are the development processes of F/OSS capable of producing more trustworthy software in a more economic way?

The first attempt to produce a system dynamics model of the F/OSS development process was done by Antioniades et al [ASAB03]. They aimed to model the different interactions within the whole F/OSS development community in order to predict future trends. We believe that the scope of the proposed model was very large. This has led the authors to make many predictions and estimations for different elements and parameters within the model. The model was validated using one case study of the Apache web server. Although the reported results were fairly satisfactory, little work has been reported since then to further confirm the model's general applicability. We suggest that by restricting the scope of our model to the economic aspects of software security and dependability, better clarity can be achieved in the model construction, and fewer assumptions would be required. The developed model, once validated well enough, can be extended to incorporate more aspects of the F/OSS development process.

4 Towards a Dynamic Model of Software Dependability

We have developed a preliminary model to illustrate the interrelations between different factors affecting software dependability. This model serves as the basis for further research and expansion to incorporate the effects of more factors that may influence dependability. The model can also be extended to demonstrate the economics of software dependability by incorporating mechanisms such as the iDave ROI model proposed by Boehm et al [BLJM04]. The current version of our model aims mainly to model the dynamics underpinning the security aspects of dependability, primarily the vulnerabilities that could negatively affect software dependability.

Software that has fewer residual vulnerabilities is considered to be more dependable from a security point of view. Understanding the mechanisms that affect the number of residual vulnerabilities is very important to clarify some aspects of software dependability. Vulnerabilities are a specific class of software defects [ScBL90]. During the development process, developers strive to discover and fix any defects in the code they are developing. However, because of the inherently complex nature of software applications, some defects will inevitably remain after the software is released. A subset of these defects is potential security vulnerabilities. Evidence in the literature indicates that a significant fraction of software vulnerabilities are discovered externally [AlMa05a].

Different attempts to model the software vulnerability discovery process have been developed [Fink98] [BLNS02] [AlMa05a] [ShDa05]. Most of these efforts use the same empirical techniques implemented in software reliability growth models to predict the potential residual defects or vulnerabilities. These approaches require statistical data about the defect detection behaviour in the specific development project in order to predict future trends. This requirement makes the validation of the proposed models fairly difficult in commercial proprietary software projects. Companies do not usually release data about the defects in their products, as a measure to protect reputation and to avoid negative publicity. In the F/OSS world, access to vulnerabilities reporting and removal data is much easier, as all the information relating to software defects and their fixes is left widely open in online repositories such as Bugzilla [Bugz06].

Another concern about the applicability of the current dependability models is the need for historical data about the project under consideration. This will lead to unstable estimations in the early stages of the project lifecycle where no sufficient information is available. A model was proposed [XiHW97] to rectify this issue by using historical data of similar projects to aid the prediction of residual defects and vulnerabilities. Our model can accommodate the different approaches for the estimation of software defects removal by enabling more flexible adjustment of the model's parameters.

The profile of vulnerabilities removal depends on many different factors. After the software is released, people start using it. Over time, defects and vulnerabilities in the software are discovered, reported, and eventually fixed. Therefore, the longer the software is used, the more defects will be detected and fixed, increasing the dependability of the software. In addition to usage time, the defect discovery rate will be influenced by the number of users of the software. More popular software will attract larger numbers of users, who will diversify the utilization profiles of the software, improving the odds of discovering defects. However, an important factor in relating user population to software dependability is the willingness of users to report the defects they encounter. It can be argued that expert users are more willing and likely to report vulnerabilities than normal users. Alhazmi and Malaiya [AlMa05] investigated these dynamics and proposed two models to assist vulnerability assessment of software: a time based model and an effort based model. Both models attempt to predict the discovery trend of software vulnerabilities in relation to the time the software has been tested or put into operation for, or the effort invested in discovering vulnerabilities (which is proportional to the users' base of the software). Usually, software popularity changes over time. The system dynamics approach we propose will facilitate more flexibility in testing wider ranges of scenarios and possibilities by incorporating simultaneously the dynamics of both time and effort.

Interactions among these different factors and their effect on the dependability of the produced software are illustrated in the influence diagram presented in Fig. 1. This list is by no means exhaustive of all possible influences related to software dependability. However, it provides the basis for further research and elaboration to incorporate more factors and dynamics. We assume that all the factors that are not included in this model (such as the link between dependability growth and user base size, the availability of formal requirements, changes of usage profiles over time, etc.) will be constant. This means that they will not have any negative or positive impact on software dependability.

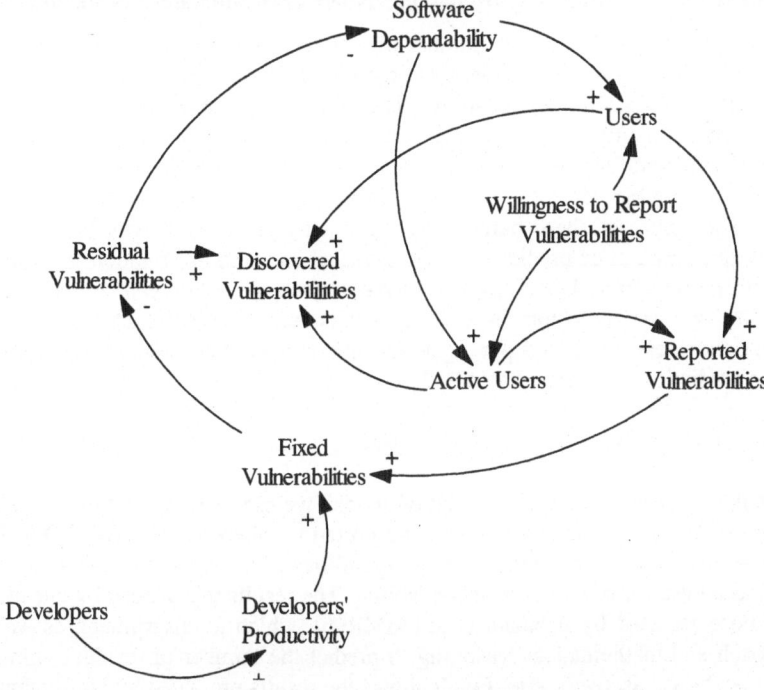

Fig. 1: Influence Diagram for Software Dependability

The influence diagram provides useful insights into the dynamics of vulnerability discovery and dependability of software development. Investigating the interactions between the model's elements explains different observable phenomena in software adoption and dependability growth. For instance, the influences in the model indicate that when the number of residual vulnerabilities in a given piece of software decreases, the software will be perceived as being more dependable. This will lead to an increase in the users' base. More users will encounter and report more vulnerabilities, and depending on the availability of qualified developers, the reported vulnerabilities will be fixed and the residual defects decreased. This is a reinforcing loop. The loop's growth is limited by the number of available developers and the willingness of users to report vulnerabilities. When the software project is perceived to have high dependability, it will attract more developers because of two reasons: firstly, developers are more likely to join a project with an established reputation for quality, and secondly, projects with higher popularity magnetize more developers. Clearly, this observation explains the failure of some F/OSS projects because they could not recruit the required number of qualified developers to fix the reported vulnerabilities. When considering the second limit to dependability growth in the model, it can be argued that projects with higher percentages of active users would benefit from the higher reporting rates. This explains the considerably higher dependability of server side F/OSS applications such as web servers (Apache) and database servers (MySQL) compared to desktop applications, because inherently, these projects command a population of more active (or expert) users.

However, the insights gained from analysing the influence diagram are mainly qualitative, in the sense that the model does not provide any measurable values of its elements. For the proposed model to become practically useful, more quantifiable data should be incorporated. A computer simulation version of the model was developed using the iThink™ simulation package to facilitate more empirical inquiry into the dynamics of software dependability.

Our main interest at this stage is the number of software vulnerabilities and how they can be affected by other factors in the development process. This will lead to better assessment of the economic impact of software dependability. The vulnerability discovery models described in the literature use probabilistic distributions to predict the number of residual vulnerabilities or defects and the vulnerability discovery rate. The first attempt to produce a comprehensive dynamic model of F/OSS projects by Antioniades et al also adopts the same approach [ASAB03]. The values of these parameters can not be precisely known before the project starts. However, they can be predicted using historical data and information from similar projects to start the simulation. Upon progress of the project, the values can be readjusted as real data about the specific development environment become available. This continuous readjustment of parameters (backward propagation) will enhance the results of the simulation and increase the predictions' accuracy [ASAB03].

5 Model Validation and Utilization

To validate the developed dynamic simulation model, we used vulnerability data collected for two versions of Red Hat Linux (6.2, 7.1) and reported in Alhazmi et al [AlMR05]. They propose vulnerability density (the number of vulnerabilities identified in the unit size of the software code) as a measure of software dependability. The results reproduced by our model were similar to those reported by Alhazmi et al [AlMR05], which is unsurprising as we used the same approach and mathematical reasoning to predict the number of residual vulnerabilities and the vulnerability discovery rate. Fig. 2 shows the results produced by our dynamic model compared to the real values reported by Alhazmi et al [AlMR05].

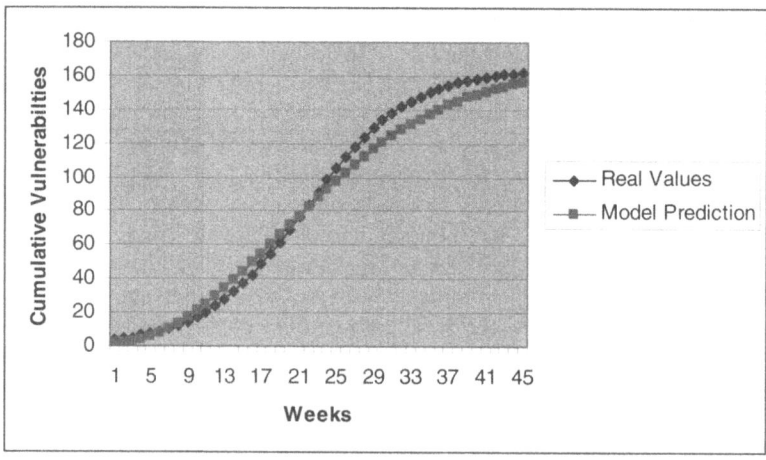

Fig. 2: Cumulative Vulnerabilities in Red Hat Linux 7.1

The model can be utilized by different stakeholders to achieve different goals. Maintainers of F/OSS projects may use the model to analyze the behaviour of their projects, and to identify the causes of possible trends or events. They can also apply it to determine the release date of their software when they are satisfied with the level of residual vulnerabilities. Users may exploit the model to evaluate the maturity and dependability levels of different F/OSS applications when they make their selection decisions. Also, they can evaluate different scenarios to assess the economic impact of different aspects of software quality. The model also can be utilized by researchers and practitioners alike to inquire into and explain observed trends in the evolution of F/OSS software, and to employ it as a test vehicle to validate different possible hypotheses about software development in general, and F/OSS processes in particular.

To illustrate the possibilities afforded by considering a systemic perception of the problem situation, aided by a computer based, quantitative dynamic model, we tested the behaviour in the model under different circumstances. We increased the value of the parameter incorporated to represent the market acceptance of the software, which also reflects its users' base. As shown in Fig. 3, the increase in market acceptance resulted in faster detection and reporting of vulnerabilities. This reinforces the stated claim about F/OSS development that by "releasing early, releasing often" [Raym00], software defects and vulnerabilities will be discovered and fixed earlier.

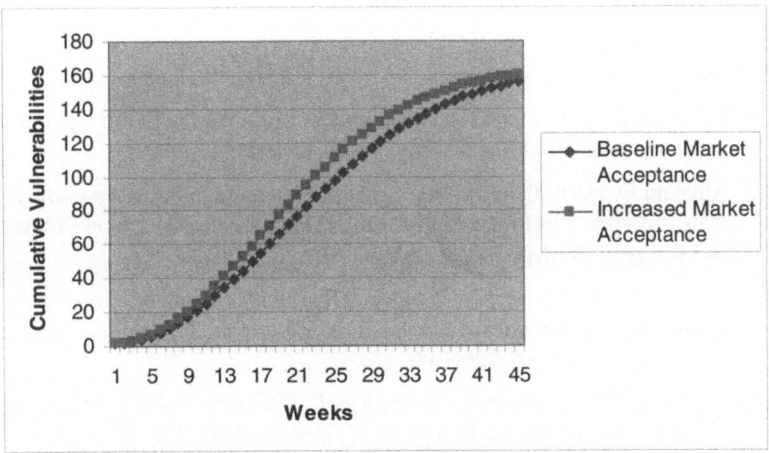

Fig. 3: Change in Cumulative Vulnerabilities Detected Due to Higher Market Acceptance for Red Hat Linux 7.1

6 Conclusions

Software dependability is becoming an increasingly important issue with the increase in reliance on computer systems and software in all sectors of human activity. Many claims are made about the dependability of F/OSS and how it compares against proprietary software, with very different, sometimes conflicting conclusions. In addition, dependability is perceived differently by different stakeholders. Subjectivity of interpretations remains a significant issue. Therefore, there is a need to establish a coherent tool to test and validate the different hypotheses with empirical evidence. We have proposed a wider, systemic approach to incorporate the many factors affecting software dependability and the interactions among these factors. We have suggested system dynamics as an appropriate tool because it provides more justifiable models and the ability to develop a computer simulation with which to interpret quantitative data and test the effects of changing selected parameters. We have described our first attempt to sketch a basic model to represent some essential factors affecting software dependability. This model, if validated using sufficient empirical data and other research, would serve as a basis for more elaborate, comprehensive models to accommodate and investigate other aspects of dependability thought to be relevant. The model was then investigated to derive qualitative explanations of observed phenomena in the F/OSS world. To facilitate the quantitative evaluation of our approach, we developed a computer simulation version of the model and validated its behaviour against work reported by other authors. Exploitation of the model was illustrated by testing the change of the model behaviour in response to adjustments in certain key factors. The results confirmed the expected utility of the model as a testing vehicle to validate different proposed hypotheses about dependability of F/OSS.

This model should only be considered as a first attempt to build a more comprehensive dynamic model for software dependability. Further research is required to validate the model using more extensive vulnerability data; this should include projects with different characteristics and development environments and processes. Moreover, work needs to be done to extend the model to include different aspects of software security and integrate the factors that affect them. The quantification of these factors and the relationships between them also requires further investigation. The model's utility and applicability will be enhanced by incorporating appropriate metrics that can be obtained reliably.

References

[ABGR02]   Arief, Bosio, Gacek and Rouncefield: Dependability Issues in Open Source Software. In DIRC Project Activity 5 Final Report, 2002.

[AlMa05]   Alhazmi O. H., Malaiya Y. K.: "Quantitative Vulnerability Assessment of Systems Software". In Proceedings of International Symposium on Product Quality and Integrity (RAMS 2005), January 2005, pp. 14D3.1-6.

[AlMa05a]   Alhazmi O. H., Malaiya Y. K.: "Modeling the Vulnerability Discovery Process". In 16th IEEE International Symposium on Software Reliability Engineering (ISSRE'05), 2005, pp. 129-138.

[AlMR05]   Alhazmi O. H., Malaiya Y. K. and Ray I.: "Security Vulnerabilities in Software Systems: A Quantitative Perspective". In Proc. Ann. IFIP WG11.3 Working Conference on Data and Information Security, Aug. 2005.

[ASAB03]   Antoniades I. P., Stamelos I., Angelis L., Bleris G. L.: A Novel Simulation Model for the Development Process of Open Source Software Projects. In International Journal of Software Process: Improvement and Practise (SPIP), special issue on Software Process Simulation and Modelling, 2003.

[BLJM04]   Boehm B., Huang L. G., Jain A., Madachy R.: "The ROI of Software Dependability: The iDAVE Model". In IEEE Software, vol. 21, no. 3, May/Jun, 2004, pp. 54-61.

[BLSN02]   Bosio D., Littlewood B., Strigini L. and Newby M. J.: "Advantages of Open Source Processes for Reliability: clarifying the issues". In Proceedings of the Open Source Software Development Workshop, Newcastle upon Tyne, UK; February 25-26, 2002, ed. C. Gacek and B. Ariel. pp. 30-46.

[Bugz06]   www.bugzilla.org , accessed 14 March 2006.

[Fink98]   Fink R. A.: "Reliability Modeling of Freely-Available Internet-Distributed
             Software". In metrics, Fifth International Symposium on Software Metrics
             (METRICS'98), 1998, pp. 101.

[Forr68]   Forrester J. W.: Principles of systems, Cambridge: Wright-Allen Press, 1968.

[LaJo02]   Lawrice Y. and Jones C.: "Goal-Diversity in the Design of Dependable Com-
             puter-Based Systems". In Proceedings of the Open Source Software Develop-
             ment Workshop, Newcastle upon Tyne, UK, February 25-26, 2002, ed. Gacek
             and B. Arief., 2002, pp. 130-154.

[Lapr92]   Laprie J. C. (Ed.): "Dependability: Basic Concepts and Terminology". In De-
             pendable Computing and Fault Tolerance – in English, French, German, Italian
             and Japanese, Vienna, Austria. Springer-Verlag, 1992.

[Levy00]   Levy E.: "Wide Open Source", http://www.securityfocus.com/news/19, 2002,
             accessed March 15, 2006.

[LiSt00]   Littlewood B. and Strigini. L.: "Software reliability and dependability: A road-
             map". In A. Finkelstein, editor, The Future of Software Engineering. ACM
             Press, New York, 2000.

[MoFH02]   Mockus A., Fielding R., Herbsleb J.: "Two case studies of open source software
             development: Apache and mozilla". ACM Transactions on Software Engineer-
             ing and Methodology 11 (3), 2002, pp. 1–38.

[Neum02]   Neumann P.:"Developing Open Source Systems: Principles for Composable Ar-
             chitectures" (keynote speech). In Proceedings of the Open Source Software De-
             velopment Workshop, Newcastle upon Tyne, UK, February 25-26, 2002, ed.
             Gacek and B. Arief. pp. 68-82.

[Payn02]   Payne C.: "On the Security of Open Source Software". Info Systems Journal,
             2002, pp. 61-68.

[Raym02]   Raymond E. S.: "The Cathedral and the Bazaar".
             http://www.catb.org/~esr/writings/cathedral-bazaar/cathedral-bazaar/, 2000, (ac-
             cessed September 4, 2005).

[ScBL90]   Schultz E. E. Jr., Brown D. S. and Longstaff T. A.: "Responding to Computer
             Security Incidents", Lawrence Livermore National Laboratory,
             ftp://ftp.cert.dfn.de/pub/docs/csir/ihg.ps.gz, July 23, 1990.

[Whee05]   Wheeler D. A.: "Why Open Source Software / Free Software (OSS/FS)? Look at
             the Numbers!", http://www.dwheeler.com/oss_fs_why.html, 2005, accessed
             March 15, 2006.

[XiHW97]   Xie M., Hong G.Y., and Wohlin C.: "A Practical Method for the Estimation of
             Software Reliability Growth in the Early Stage of Testing," In Proceedings of
             8th International Symposium on Software Reliability Engineering, Albu-
             queurque, NM, 1997, pp. 116–123.

[ZhDa05]   Zhou Y. and Davis J.: "Open source software reliability model: an empirical ap-
             proach". In Proceedings of the Fifth Workshop on Open Source Software Engi-
             neering (St. Louis, Missouri, May 17 - 17, 2005). 5-WOSSE. ACM Press, New
             York, NY, 2005.

Securing service-oriented applications

Anthony Nadalin[1] · Nataraj Nagaratnam[2] · Maryann Hondo[3]

[1]IBM Software Group, 11501 Burnet Road,
Austin TX 78758, USA

[2]IBM Software Group, 3901 S. Miami Blvd,
Durham NC 27703, USA

[3]IBM Software Group, One Rogers St,
Cambridge MA 02142, USA
{drsecure | natarajn | mhondo}@us.ibm.com

Abstract

Securing applications in a service-oriented architecture is challenging, because the loose coupling that characterizes a SOA can also expose existing security implementations' brittleness. Our solution includes well-defined trust models based on acceptable forms of proof, as well as reliance on policies, Web Services security, and security engineering best practices.

1 Introduction

Securing access to information is basic to any application. Security becomes even more critical for implementations structured according to Service Oriented Architecture (SOA) principles, due to their loose coupling of services and applications, and their operation across organizational boundaries. Such an environment often exposes the brittleness or limitations of existing security implementations.

Irrespective of the efficiencies brought by model-driven development and SOA-based service management, business applications must continue to secure information. Merely securing the perimeter (firewalls, routers, etc.) is not sufficient, since an on-demand business needs to be able to set up and tear down dynamic trust relationships over time as relationships among its partners, customers and employees evolve. Thus, a secure on-demand business needs a flexible, customizable infrastructure, so it can adapt to new requirements and regulations. To provide such flexibility, it should not hardwire policies into the infrastructure, but implement the requirements of the security model through a policy-driven infrastructure. This is no simple task.

This article will explain how business applications can leverage the security capabilities of an on-demand security infrastructure, and the design principles that give rise to a programming model for securing service-oriented applications.

Please note the following important formatting guidelines:

2 Business Applications and Security Infrastructure

Secure integration and access to business applications and information is typically achieved through authentication, authorization and accountability. How a business approaches the

S. Paulus, N. Pohlmann, H. Reimer (Editors): Securing Electronic Business Processes, Vieweg (2006), 336-343

management of authentication, authorization and accountability is dictated largely by its view of the trust relationships that exist among customers, employees and partners, these relationships' effects on the security of business applications, and the applications' relative importance and security.

When sensitive information is exchanged between business partners it must be secured. It may also need to be persisted in a secure manner. The integrity of the message origin needs to be guaranteed (e.g., through notary services) to enable validation, auditing and non-repudiation[1] when necessary. Sensitive information may need to be encrypted for confidentiality. It may also need to be digitally signed for integrity; digital signatures also play a role in non-repudiation. A complete SOA security design must address not only message- and transport-level security, but the need to secure persisted content to comply with government regulations and industry best practices.

Fundamentally, the trust relationships among a business and its employees, customers and partners govern the definition and enforcement of security policies, and what level of security is enforced. Relevant technologies such as certificates and cryptographic keys can be used to reflect and manage these trust relationships. Tools can be used to model and specify trust relationships between business partners, between consumers and the business, etc., and can translate trust definitions into technologies that are appropriate for the IT environment.

3 SOA Security Model

The SOA security model is based on a process in which a Web service can require that an incoming message prove a set of claims. Examples of claims include name, key, permission, capability, and so forth. Based on the proof provided, the appropriate trust models are applied between the requester, the service endpoint, and a set of possible intermediaries.

A message may traverse several intermediaries between a requester and a target service. The management of end-to-end security must take into account the trust models between the requester, the intermediary and the ultimate endpoint service (provider), illustrated in Figure 1.

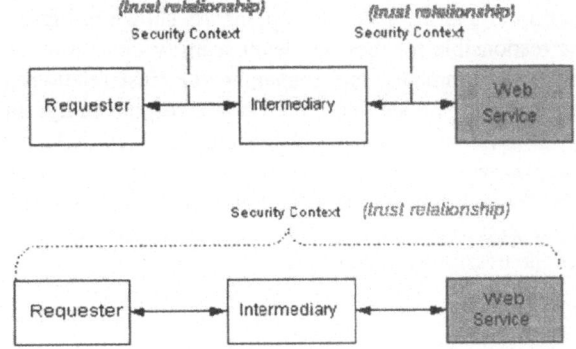

Figure 1: Trust Models from Requester to Provider via Intermediaries

---

[1] Non-repudiation is a procedure ensuring that a contract cannot later be denied by one of the parties involved. Here it refers to techniques that enable verification that the sender and recipient were, in fact, the parties who claimed to send or receive the message, respectively. In other words, non-repudiation of origin proves that data has been sent; non-repudiation of delivery proves it has been received.

Network and transport intermediaries (e.g., firewalls, routers, proxy servers, etc.) are generally not trusted with respect to message processing. All messages in transit should be protected from tampering by untrusted intermediaries.

The OASIS Web Services Security ("WSS") specification[2] provides protection for SOAP messages in transit. WSS can used to protect the authenticity, integrity and confidentiality of messages from untrusted network and transport intermediaries.

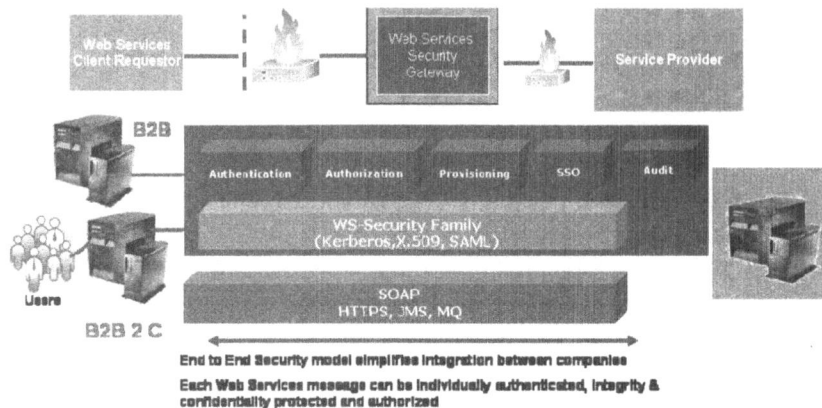

Figure 2: Message intermediary brokers trust relationship and federation

Not all intermediaries are untrusted. A Web services gateway and an enterprise service bus mediation service[3] are examples of message transformation intermediaries whose function in the SOA involves inspection and in some cases modification of message payloads. When designing your SOA security infrastructure, consider planning to allow certain trusted intermediaries.

Another trusted intermediary might be a message broker that handles trust relationships between requesters and an application service host. In this design, security responsibilities are divided between the broker and the service endpoint. As shown in Figure 2, the message intermediary would be responsible for message level security, federation of identities between requester and provider environments, and managing the trust relationship between the requester and service provider. The service would retain responsibility only for meeting service-specific security requirements, such as establishing (mapped, federated by the intermediary) identity to access the service, integrity and confidentiliaty of application-specific data in the message payloads. By factoring fragile or complex infrastructure code out of the business application and delegating it to the container, a SOA-based approach to security can improve flexibility and reduce the possibility of mishaps.

---

[2] OASIS Web Services Security: SOAP Security, http://www.oasis-open.org/committees/tc_home.php?wg_abbrev=wss

[3] "Introduction to the IBM Enterprise Service Bus," B.Hutchison, M.Schmidt, D.Wolfson, M.Stockton, http://www-128.ibm.com/developerworks/library/ws-soa-progmodel4/

4 Message security

The WSS specification also provides a set of basic message-level mechanisms for integrity, confidentiality, and authentication that can help Web service developers secure SOAP exchanges. These mechanisms can be combined in various ways to build a wide variety of security models, using a variety of encryption technologies.

WSS also provides an extensible mechanism for associating security tokens with messages that accommodates a variety of authentication and authorization formats and mechanisms. For example, a client might provide proof of identity and a signed claim that they have a particular business certification. A Web service receiving such a message could then determine if it trusts the claim, and to what extent.

Security token claims can be endorsed by an authority or left unendorsed. A set of endorsed claims is usually represented as a security token that is digitally signed or cryptographically protected by the authority. A familiar example of a signed security token is an X.509 certificate; it asserts a binding between one's identity and a public key. Security tokens can be "pushed" or carried in a message, or expressed by a reference so the receiver can "pull" the claim from the authority.

Because a security token is useful within a trust domain, there is a need for a way to articulate the scope of a trust domain. It can be articulated manually, by an agreement, or by implementing a set of rules enforcing the trust policy. An unendorsed claim can thus be trusted if there is any established trust relationship between the sender and the receiver. For example, the unendorsed claim that the sender is Bob is sufficient for a certain receiver to believe that the sender is in fact Bob, if the sender and the receiver use a trusted connection which they have set up through an out-of-band trust relationship. In this example, the existence of this trusted connection might be sufficient proof.

Protecting message content from illegal access (i.e., confidentiality) or illegal modification (i.e., integrity) are primary security concerns. The WSS specification provides a means to protect a message by encrypting and/or digitally signing a body, a header, an attachment, or any combination of them (or parts of them).

Authentication of requests is based on a combination of optional network and transport-provided security and information (claims) proven in the message, a technique better known as message origin authentication. Requesters can authenticate recipients using network and transport-provided security, claims proven in messages, and encryption of the request using a key known to the recipient.

5 Trust Model

One way to demonstrate authorized use of a security token is to include a digital signature using the associated secret key (from a proof-of-possession token). This allows a requester to prove a required set of claims by associating security tokens (e.g., PKIX, X.509 certificates) with the messages.

If the requester does not have the necessary token(s) to prove required claims to a service, it can contact appropriate authorities (which we refer to as security token services) and request the needed tokens with the proper claims. Security token services form the basis of trust by issuing a range of security tokens that can be used to broker trust relationships between different trust domains.

One mechanism would be the use of a challenge-response protocol as defined in WS-Trust[4]. This is used by a Web service for additional challenges to a requester to ensure message freshness and verification that the use of a security token is authorized. This model is illustrated in Figure 3, showing that any requester may also be a service, and that the requester and target service may have a trusted third party security token service that helps validate the security tokens that are required per the target service's policy.

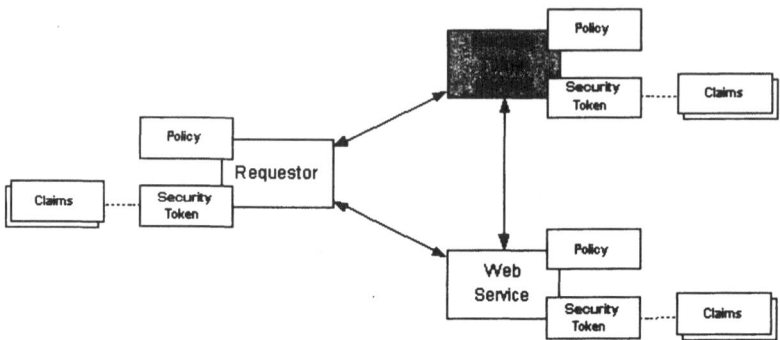

Figure 3: Security Token Service

This SOA security model – claims, policies, and security tokens – subsumes and supports several more specific models such as identity-based authorization, access control lists, and capabilities-based authorization. It allows use of existing technologies such as X.509 public-key certificates, XML-based tokens, Kerberos shared-secret tickets, and even password digests. The SOA security model, in combination with the Web Services Secure Conversation Language[5] (WSSC) and Web Services Policy Framework[6] primitives, is sufficient to construct higher-level key exchange, authentication, policy-based access control, auditing, and complex trust relationships.

A Web service has a policy applied to it, receives a message from a requester that possibly includes security tokens, and may have some protection applied to it using WSSC mechanisms. The following main steps are performed by the trust engine of a Web service:

- Verify that the claims in the token are sufficient to comply with the policy and that the message conforms to the policy.

- Verify that the attributes of the claimant are proven by the signatures. In brokered trust models, the signature may not verify the identity of the claimant: it may verify the identity of the intermediary, who may simply assert the identity of the claimant. The claims are either proven or not, based on policy.

- Verify that the issuers of the security tokens (including all related and issuing security tokens) are trusted to issue the claims they have made. The trust engine may need to externally verify or broker tokens (that is, send tokens to a security token service in order to exchange them for other security tokens that it can use directly in its evaluation).

---

[4] Web Services Trust Language, www-106.ibm.com/developerworks/library/ws-trust/

[5] Web Services Secure Conversation Language, www-106.ibm.com/developerworks/library/ws-secon/

[6] Web Services Policy Framework, www.ibm.com/developerworks/webservices/library/specification/ws-polfram/

If these conditions are met, and the requester is authorized to perform the operation, then the service can process the service request.

Network and transport protection mechanisms such as IP Security (IPSec) or Transport Layer Security/Secure Sockets Layer (TLS/SSL) can be used in conjunction with this SOA security model to support different security requirements and scenarios. As an added level of security, requesters should consider using a network or transport security mechanism, if available, to pre-authenticate the recipient when issuing, validating, or renewing security tokens.

6 Programming model - Design Principles

From a security perspective, the programming model includes decisions to be made about who is responsible for enforcing security policies (e.g., infrastructure or application) and what of this information needs to be made available to requesters. In addition to the operational aspects, some of the design-time policy (e.g., captured in J2EE deployment descriptors) can help manage the application. One of the key implementation decisions is whether the business needs will best be met by enabling the infrastructure to implement the security model or by codifying security enforcement into each application. Another dimension to consider is how variable is the service invocation: are service consumers given flexibility via choices they can customize during subscription? Lastly, when implementing any secure solutions, one should consider security engineering – an engineering methodology to build secure applications.

7 Infrastructure-managed vs. application-managed

Each organization typically gives certain people the responsibility for identifying and enforcing its security policies. In many cases this process is manual, causing the organization to devote significant resource to coordinating access across different entities and applications.

We recommend that complex organizations centralize, in the infrastructure, the enforcement of the security policies associated with a solution – i.e., validating the user challenge (e.g., userid/password), controlling access to applications (e.g., `reserve()` method on `travelService`), and delegating identity (e.g., `run-as travelAgency id`) to ensure a consistent approach. Initial application security policies can be defined in some deployment artifacts (e.g., deployment descriptors for J2EE applications). Then after development, when the application logic is largely known, the policy information can be made available to the deployment environment. Policy declarations can be abstracted into high-level policy requirements for later refinement, as implementation constraints are considered during the deployment phase.

The application design introduces decisions to be made about infrastructure- versus application-managed security. The security constraints and conditions are attached to the implementation artifacts. The time for deciding whether to let the infrastructure handle security, or codify security in the application, is during the implementation phase, when information about the application platform (e.g. J2EE, .NET) is usually available.

We recommend that applications focus on business logic, and defer securing the service access and the messages to the infrastructure (the runtime container hosting the application). In this infrastructure-managed approach, security policies attached to design artifacts are transformed into platform-specific policies (e.g., requirements expressed via a UML model are transformed into J2EE deployment descriptors).

In the application-managed approach, security enforcement is done in the application and the appropriate security callouts must be implemented. Even application-managed security has to translate its security callouts (e.g., `authenticate()`) into appropriate platform-specific functions (e.g., `loginContext.login()` using JAAS).

Authorization and access control can vary from coarse- to fine-grained. The choice of coarse-grained access (to the solution itself) versus fine-grained access (to one of its operations) is usually governed by business and technical considerations. Granularity is also influenced by factors including the instance of the information entity (e.g., credit account profile for a given traveler), in addition to contextual information such as user attributes (e.g., travel agent), temporal constraints (e.g., 9-5 pm), purpose of access (e.g., for purpose of making a travel reservation), access path (e.g., intranet vs. external request) and many others.

Authorization-related policy can be abstracted by defining application roles, where a role is a collection of permissions that allow certain actions on given application resources. For example, a travel application can declare that the `view()` or `change()` reservations methods on `ReservationBean` can be accessed by `TravelAgent` role. In other words, `TravelAgent` is an implementation-defined role that identifies *what* can be done by a "travel agent," in terms of a set of permissions to invoke specific methods on the respective EJBs. What is not likely defined during the implementation phase is *who* has the privileges of a `TravelAgent`. User-to-role assignments are typically initialized at deployment, and managed thereafter throughout the application's lifetime. Figure 4 shows an example of code defining some role-based method permissions.

```
<method-permission>
<role-name>TravelAgent</role-name>
<method>
   <ejb-name>ReservationBean</ejb-name>
<method-permission>
<role-name>TravelAgent</role-name>
<method>
   <ejb-name>ReservationBean</ejb-name>
   <method-name> view</method-name>
   <method-name> change</method-name>
</method>
</method-permission>
```

Figure 4: Defining some role-based method permissions

Applications that require authenticated identity information before performing some business logic must obtain to that information from the infrastructure. For instance, in a J2EE environment, the runtime establishes the user's identity after authentication; the application can retrieve this information with an API such as `getCallerPrincipal()`.

8 Flexibility of choice

Sometimes certain requirements or constraints on the access to the service itself – including authentication, integrity and confidentiality requirements -- are needed by a client runtime, and it may be desirable to support a wide variety of client runtimes (e.g., browser clients, non-browser clients, PDA thin clients, etc). To achieve this, you publish policies asserting that the client runtime must ensure message confidentiality and must provide evidence of the user's identity (i.e., userid/password or a certificate). The policy abstraction for authentication can list alternatives, such as the types of credentials that are acceptable or which credential-issuing authorities are trusted.

For instance, a `TravelService` web service can declare its intent to require certain security token types and confidentiality requirements. The implementation may support the declaration of intent via descriptors. Tools can, in turn, generate necessary machine-level details (e.g., a WS-SecurityPolicy expression), illustrated in Figure 5.

```
<wsp:Policy>
  <sp:SymmetricBinding>
    <wsp:Policy>
      <sp:ProtectionToken>
        <wsp:Policy>
          <sp:KerberosV5APREQToken

sp:IncludeToken="..../IncludeToken/Once" />
        </wsp:Policy>
      </sp:ProtectionToken>
      <sp:SignBeforeEncrypting />
      <sp:EncryptSignature />
    </wsp:Policy>
  </sp:SymmetricBinding>
  <sp:SignedParts>
    <sp:Body/>
    <sp:Header

Namespace="http://schemas.xmlsoap.org/ws/2004/08/
addressing"
    />
  </sp:SignedParts>
  <sp:EncryptedParts>
    <sp:Body/>
  </sp:EncryptedParts>
</wsp:Policy>
```

Figure 5: Example WS-SecurityPolicy Description

9 Security Engineering

In developing secure solutions, one of the best practices is "security engineering": you follow well-defined patterns so that your application, service or component will do exactly what its designers and users expect. You should assess the risk inherent in each implementation artifact, and designing and implementing it so as to avoid opening it up to vulnerabilities (e.g., efficient memory management, avoiding covert channels, etc.) Tools support and code reviews can also help minimize (or do no) harm to the environment in which your solution is deployed.

10 Conclusion

A SOA programming model must ensure that each service invocation adheres to security policies that are valid for both the requester and service end-point. The security infrastructure -- including the ability to authenticate requesters and authorize their access to services, propagate security context across Web service requests based on an underlying trust model, audit significant events, and effectively protect data and content -- forms a fabric of the SOA environment that helps secure components and services. At the core of all SOA security is a policy-based infrastructure and management of the policies. In the ideal case, the SOA application is centered on business logic, delegating the enforcement of security policies and the handling of trust relationships to the infrastructure. The Web services security model and approaches based on the Web services security specifications help meet the challenges of securing service-oriented applications.

A Service Oriented Trust Development Platform

Helena Rifà · Francisco Jordán

Safelayer Secure Communications, S.A.
{hrifa | jordan}@safelayer.com

Abstract

A Trust Development Platform that offers services for the generation and interpretation of trust based on the concept of ecosystem's federation is presented. Trust federation schemes allow to define bonds of confidence between systems managed under different domains and policies. Each ecosystem has a trusted service provider that will automatically deliver services for the local domain following its own security policies. Ecosystem's federation leads us to the federation of trusted services providers and therefore, to the development of federated trust systems. Unlike solutions based on global trust policies, the proposed architecture is easy to deploy and use, and conforms to the requirements for each environment. Moreover, an ecosystem's federation is also feasible because a common language is shared, XML, and a plethora of related standards are based on it. SOA and Web Services are intimately related to federation, so trust development is now something almost tangible.

1 Introduction

The evolution of Information Technology's application environments has suffered many revolutions over the past decade. We are currently immerse in a revolution in which applications are replaced by services based on open architectures named Service Oriented Architectures (SOA) [MLB+06]. They are specially designed to overcome the integration and automation processes. Service access is standardized by a common language based on XML [YCB+04]. That allows abstracting the offered functionality from the implementation details thus providing a reference for the integration of different environments within an ecosystem (intra), and also among them (inter).

Security in terms of trust is vital when talking about the global integration and automation of information systems that are managed by different domains and under different policies. Trust development must initially refer to authentication and identification of the parties. The most robust and popular authentication and identification mechanism is currently based on PKI (Public Key Infrastructure) technology and uses certificates and digital signature.

PKI trust development has been studied and analyzed from PKI origins. The most comfortable and simple way to manage trust is by means of a hierarchic structure that is headed by a root authority. However, the conclusion is that all this is only directly suitable within a single security domain, which is generally used by one or several ecosystems, but always within one unique administrative domain. There has been multiple efforts to try and take trust development to inter-domain level. Examples are the proposal to implant a global root authority (inappropriate for political reasons), and the use of intermediate or bridge authorities (complicated for both technical and political reasons).

S. Paulus, N. Pohlmann, H. Reimer (Editors): Securing Electronic Business Processes, Vieweg (2006), 344-355

We present a Trust Development Platform (TDP) that offers services for the generation and interpretation of trust, based on the concept of ecosystem's federation. Trust federation schemes allow us to define bonds of confidence between systems managed under different domains and policies. Each ecosystem has a trusted service provider that will automatically deliver services for the local domain following its own security policies. Ecosystem's federation leads us to the federation of trusted service providers and therefore, to the development of federated trust systems. Unlike solutions based on global trust policies, the proposed architecture is easy to deploy, viable and conforms to the requirements of each environment. Moreover, an ecosystem's federation is also feasible because a common language is shared, XML, and a plethora of standards based on it. SOA and Web Services are intimately related to federation, so trust development is now something almost tangible.

The rest of this papers is organized as follows: In section 2 we overview the architecture of the TDP. Section 3 describes the concept of ecosystem's federation, pointing out the benefits of identity and trust federation. Section 4 explains the TDP security policies. In section 5 we review the most popular PKI trust models and describe how to overcome its weaknesses using the proposed TDP model. Finally, section 6 concludes the paper.

2 Trust Development Platform Architecture

Trust is a key issue to develop business, both in a traditional or in an electronic environment. In order to take direct decisions with a minimum risk, trust management creates a unified framework for specifying and interpreting security policies, credentials and relationships. In a closed virtual organization trust is commonly established with the use of Trusted Third Parties (TTP), and propagated in a hierarchical model. However, this architecture is not appropriate for a global scenario formed of isles of TTP: trust management can quickly become extremely complex and tedious for people to maintain. The solution is a TDP that automates the trust management to make decisions about trust as users (Relying Parties) themselves would do (see figure 1).

The key principles of a TDP are the following:

- Hiding trust development complexity producing a final diagnosis of the trust level of a transaction, operation, document, etc. Trust evaluation is performed from all the security data involved within an operation (certificate chains, certificate revocation lists, time stamps, …) considering the trust offered by TTPs (CA, VA, TSA..) that issued them.

- Delegating security configuration in a centralized system based on policies releasing the consumers (users, applications or other web services) from its complexity.

- Easing the use, integration and interoperability of digital signatures and envelopes, encapsulating all the standard formats (PKCS#7, CMS, S/MIME, XML-DSig, XAdES, XML-Enc, pdf, etc.) and its processing complexity under a common service interface.

- Providing a centralized point of accounting and auditing, and even trust archiving, thus making it feasible to manage and develop trust material for long periods of time.

On the other hand, it is important that a TDP can be easily integrated with other services and accessible from any device. Our proposal is to deploy a TDP as web services (WS), offering an interface fully based on Extensible Markup Language (XML). XML currently is the universal format to represent structured documents and data on the Web. In the TDP it is used in services invocations as well as in configuration, personalization, monitoring, audit and access control. TDP transactions are wrapped with SOAP, which defines a standard framework for the composition of request/response messages to a service. WSDL provides an abstract definition of the service independent of the programming language used in its implementation, and UDDI is used for the publication and discovery of the services.

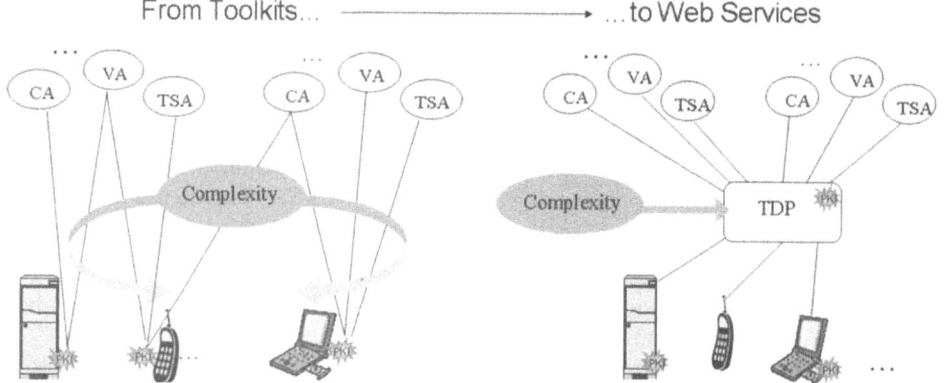

Figure 1: From Toolkits to Web Services

The proposed trust management framework is flexible and scalable and not only addressed to provide services for the internal security consumption. It can also be seen as a trusted platform that can be integrated in the enterprise workflows. The TDP provides business components with specialized trusted security services. The main TDP components are the following:

- An Authentication and Authorization service that includes different authentication mechanisms such as login/password, certificate-based (TLS/SSL, digital signature, etc.), etc.. This service also includes an open authentication extension mechanism (one-time password, tokens, kerberos, etc.) making possible the addition of new mechanisms. Access control is internally enforced and the Authorization service can be consumed through SAML protocol.

- An information management service which uses XML to provide uniform object and/or entity profiles: users, applications, web services, policies, certificates, logs/audit, etc.

- A digital signature service that allows to generate basic signatures in different well-known formats (PKCS#7/CMS, PDF, XMLDsig/XAdES and S/MIME).

- An advanced digital signature service that adds reliable time and revocation information to previously signed documents, as a base for long term signatures.

- A digital signature verification service (includes advanced or long term signatures) independent from the supplier, certificate verification mechanism (CRL, OCSP, etc.) and signature format.

- A digital signature custody service that enables to maintain the signature's validity for long periods of time by, therefore, implementing long term digital signatures by using XAdES ES-A standard.

- A document ciphering and deciphering service using PKCS#7/CMS and XML-Enc formats.

- A document ciphering key custody service that guarantees long term access to protected data.

- A key management service for key generation, registration, consultation, verification, etc., for instance, based on XKMS.

The access to the security services is performed with standardized WS protocols: Oasis DSS (Digital Signature Services), WSS (Integrity and confidentiality of SOAP messages) and SAML (Single-Sign On and Federation) are the basic standards.

Trust services are accessible for their composition, orchestration and consumption as any other business services from an SOA. The TDP facilitates to the rest of the business components a set of security specialized services that they can consume, such as:

- Authentication, authorization and unified access control
- Identity Federation
- Federation of attribute entity information
- Cryptographic key management, secure sessions, single sign-on, etc.
- Generation and validation of digital signatures
- Data protection
- Information notarization for non-repudiation using long-term digital signatures

3 Federation services

One of the outstanding characteristics of the proposed platform is that it offers federation services, both identity and trust federation.

3.1 Identity Federation

Identity federation can be defined as the agreements, standards and technologies that make identity and entitlements portable. Identity federation schemes allow decentralizing the user management thus distributing the identity data in partitioned repositories of different providers. They become a solution to increase sensible data protection and manage it uniformly in the most appropriate place.

In a federated environment, a user can log on through its identity provider and then use that authentication state to easily access resources in external domains. Since identity federation provides a mechanism to interchange sensible information regarding an individual to the service providers located in diverse security domains, users can ubiquily consume services catered to them without having to re-authenticate or re-establish their identity. Service providers can enforce access control using the applicant session token issued by federated providers and evaluating the security policies associated to the claimed identity.

Identity federation can help to enable Single Sign On (SSO), and provide users and customers with a more seamless and integrated experience. The benefits of successful federation projects include increasing security and control, cost reduction, simplification of the user experience and enabling the implementation of core business models.

But more importantly, identity federation enables the creation of a unique virtual identity that can be used to operate in any of the users services. That makes possible to achieve one of the principal goals of a TDP, the easiness of use.

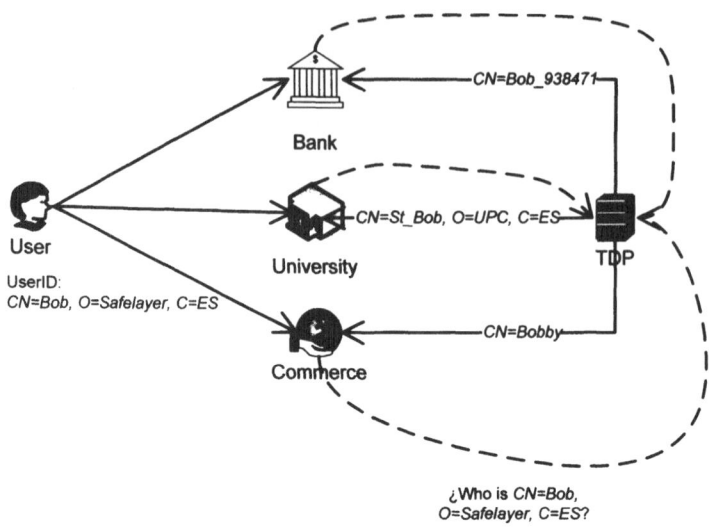

Figure 2: Identity Federation

3.2 Trust Federation

Trust federation allows defining trust bindings between different systems managed from different domains and policies. Nowadays, the most extended trust model is based on a public key infrastructure (PKI). Due to the lack of a global root certification authority (CA), the hierarchical model of the PKI has evolved into isolated and unconnected groups. Users that deal with security data generated in external domains have to manage by themselves a trust environment to handle these transactions, and this is complex and risky.

A federation scheme defines the trust rules between providers. These rules, expressed in XML, human readable and machine processable, allow to define with a great deal of granularity the trust placed in the security services offered by external providers. Therefore, for example, a TDP can accept the status result of a certificate whose chain is not registered in the system if it has a trust federation with another TDP that recognizes the named PKI and the security policies allow it.

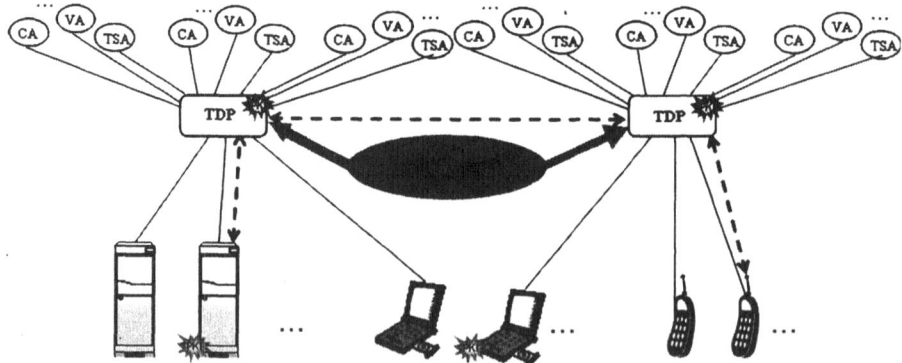

Figure 3: Federated trust management

A TDP offers security services that indicate the level of trust in the response information. The measure or trust classification is set considering all trust authorities involved in the process, i.e., Certification and Revocation Authorities (CA), Validation Authorities (VA), Time-Stamp Authorities (TSA), certification policies elements, etc. A TDP presents a clear and unique diagnosis result based on a centralized configuration (policy) that complies with some stipulated rules.

As well as Identity Federation, Trust Federation occurs in a bilateral way between Trusted Service Providers. Trust is developed more like Identity Federation in which a local name is mapped into another external name that becomes local for a remote provider. Thus, Trust Federation stands for the mapping of remote external security policies into local ones, by applying a set of rules defined in the local administrative domain.

One of the main contributions of a TDP is to uniform the trust domain management, that is, the enforcement of the system security policies.

4 Policies

The proposed TDP is a policy driven system. That means that the response of the system is based on a temporal context (running session) and the defined system policies. The establishment of policy based management solutions that cater for security has been impeded up to date because of the complexity to cope with heterogenous scenarios. It lacked some common language which could provide a unified approach to support the concepts of the policy models emerging from different research communities. Such a language has to fulfill the requirements of expressiveness, structure, composition, conflict resolution, extensibility and comprehensiveness, and XML does it. XML provides tools for designing textual descriptions of policies that are easy to generate and read by a computer, that are unambiguous, and that avoid common pitfalls, such as lack of support for internationalization/localization, and platform-dependency.

Security policies are the simplest solution to seamlessly deal with the growing complexity of secure and trust services. The TDP has tree types of security policies: authentication, authorization and service. The first two constitute the access control model. The service policies define the actions of the platform in front of a security service request, like the generation or verification of a digital signature. For example, in the case of a signature verification, the service policies would define the frame of trust with the external security providers, the security information details that have to be returned in a response, etc..

TDP manages the policies in a transactional cycle. When a service is requested, first of all, the authentication policy is applied. If successfully passed, an authorization policy is proposed and then evaluated upon the requested resource or service. If again passed, a service policy is proposed for the specific requested service. The latest policy is thus tailored for the service using information produced on the previous two phases. For instance, it is possible to restrict the algorithm of a digital signature generation service if the request comes from a particular IP address range, or during a time period (see figure 4).

Note that separating the management policy from the automated engines which interpret the policies facilitates the dynamic change of behaviour of a distributed TDP. This allows it to evolve adapting to system changes and new requirements. Changing the behaviour of the trusted platform can be achieved by changing the policy without having to re-implement nothing; this permits the use of the TDP in different environments.

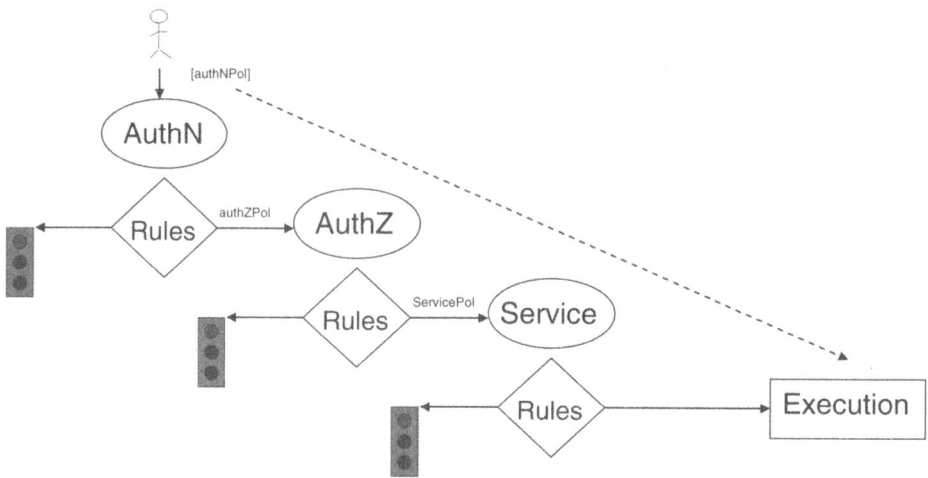

Figure 4: Dynamic Policy-based system

5 Trust Development Rationale

Our rationale for the proposed Trust Development model is a consequence of both i) several years of experience in PKI theory and real projects, and ii) the final conclusion that, everything that works on the Internet has been deployed in a bottom-up model, from a local to a wide domain, or deploy local and further interconnect with others.

Trust is a matter of locality and proximity. The furthest the party, the least it is trusted. This is the basic concept and the premise for our conclusion.

5.1 PKI Traditional Models

PKI trust development has been studied and analyzed from PKI origins. The most comfortable and simple way to manage trust is by means of a hierarchic structure that is managed by a root authority. Trust is established in a tree-like fashion and flows from top to bottom. In this model the path construction procedure is very simple, as a single path exists from any end entity up to the root CA. However, deploying a global unique root authority is inappropriate for political reasons. Thus the conclusion is that all this is only directly applicable within one domain, which is generally supported in one or several ecosystems generally forming different security domains, but always within one unique administrative domain.

There has been multiple efforts to try and take trust development to inter-domain levels. In the cross-certification model two CAs cross-certify each other if they agree to trust and rely on each other's public key certificates and keys as if they had issued them themselves. The Certification Authorities exchange cross-certificates and enable users from one Certification Authority to interact electronically and securely with users from the other. However, the number of cross-certificates tends to grow exponentially, policy (semantic) mappings are very complex and it is difficult to build certification paths between two generic end entities. Although some vendors have implemented cross-certification in their PKI management products and the IETF has included CA cross-certification in its Certificate Management Protocol, cross-certification is still not well supported by common general-purpose applications.

The Bridge CA (BCA) trust model is similar to the cross-certification one. The BCA acts as a facilitator to interconnect other CAs. Each relying party just trusts its own CA which in turn trusts the bridge that finally trusts the remote CA, so that each member needs only to maintain a single cross-certification with the BCA and then it is automatically able to build certification paths across all spokes. Although this model is quite simple from the end user perspective, in fact it presents technical difficulties because the path construction is intrinsically complex and several checks (e.g. policy and name constraints, certificate status, policy mappings) must be performed throughout the certificate chain.

The Bridge VA (BVA) trust model is a further step to the Bridge CA. It solves more of the technical complexities, for instance, when dealing with path construction, and offers to the relying end entities a more comfortable service. The Bridge VA concept is near to the Trust Development Service Provider concept, but more limited in scope since the BVA model only takes care of certificate chain construction and validation.

5.2 The Problem of PKI: Technology or Model?

The European Commission concludes in its "Report on the operation of Directive 1999/93/EC on a Community framework for electronic signatures" [Comm06] (we quote the first paragraphs of the "3.3.2 Technological Challenges" clause to consider it fully endorses our view):

> *There is no simple answer to why the market for electronic signatures has not developed faster, but the market is facing a number of technical challenges. One frequently highlighted problem that could contribute to the slow take up of advanced or qualified electronic signatures in Europe is the complexity of the PKI technology. The often stressed advantage of PKI is that this technology uses the system of the "trusted third party" which allows parties that have never met to trust each other on the internet. In many of the current applications there seems, however, to be little interest from the service providers, essentially for liability reasons, to allow their customers to use their authentication device for other services. This is probably why the use of different one-time passwords (OTPs) is still dominating the market and there is little indication of this changing in the near future.*

> *Other factors could explain this slow take up: the lack of provisions in the Directive on criteria for electronic signature verification services to be provided by the CSP to the end user and, the lack of provisions regarding the mutual recognition between CSPs. Depending of the countries, there are various solutions to validate a certificate such as the Root CA, the Bridge CA and the Trust Status List. In the framework of cross-border eGovernment transactions, in the IDA II Programme, action on Bridge/Gateway Certification Authority has resulted in a Bridge/Gateway CA Pilot project which has identified not only technological problems but also legal and organisational ones.*

> *The lack of technical interoperability at national and at cross-border level causes another obstacle for the market acceptance of e-signatures. It has resulted in many "isolated" islands of e-signature applications, where certificates can only be used for one single application. EESSI has worked on common interoperability standards but most of the Member states have specified national standards in order to promote interoperability.*

On the other hand, there are the USA Government E-Authentication [GoAc06], and the FBCA (Federal Bridge CA) [GoFB06] initiatives. Nowadays, the FBCA is trying to interconnect with other Bridge CAs, but it is reporting both technical and operational problems (see Top 10 issues from [Blan06]). We believe that in essence, these problems are inherent to the model of trying to globally interconnect PKI islands from the top.

In the paper entitled "PKI Interoperability by an Independent, Trusted Validation Authority" [Olne06], most of the shortcomings of traditional PKI models are cleverly described. A Bridge VA model is presented, however, we believe this is just part of the whole problem we are facing of.

Clearly, we also support the idea that the PKI concept has a problem, however, we disagree that it is technical, but we definitively believe that the problem is on how the PKI is organized, i.e. it is on the model.

5.3 Trust Service Provider Model

As clearly shown from the overviewed models, PKI interoperability issues are more related to political than technical problems. Setting up a global uniform network of trust is not viable because trust is not transitive. Every domain must be able to manage its trust regarding other entities, defining how, when and why these external entities can interoperate with the domain processes.

For instance, let us stop at the first of the Top 10 Issues in the FBCA [Blan06], "Policy Mapping". Policy mapping following a bottom-up or local-to-wide strategy becomes very complicated since we are trying to map hundreds or thousands of local existing practices into a very few global common set of policies. Definitively, it is almost impossible to summarize everyone's local particular semantics into a single common view (the one from the BCA), when at the top level, we have loosed the precision and richness of the bottom local policy. However, it is very easy to accommodate or map a very high policy into the best local practice. It is just a matter of a local decision, just because trust is a local matter.

Our proposed model deals with independent administrative domains that may include a set of PKIs. Rules governing the interconnection of PKIs are defined in the TDP and are particular of each domain. Thus the trust model can be seen as autonomous and overlapped sets of PKIs. Users belonging to an administrative domain can manage data generated to/from other domains under the security policies stated in their local TDP. TDP is responsible for the management of trusted entities, creating the trust path construction and validation, talking various protocols (e.g. OCSP, LDAP, SCVP) etc. so that the end user does not need to know how to manage all produced data.

Because at the end, users and entities (applications, web services, etc.) do not deal with certificates, but with authentication tokens, documents and data that contains digital signatures and encrypted information, what a TDP must provide is an integral solution to develop Trust given any form of secured piece of information. Certificates, CRLs and CAs are only part of the whole picture. The TDP must also deal with other third party trusted information, such as certificate status tokens and VAs, timestamp tokens and TSAs, authentication and authorization tokens and AAs (Assertion or Attribute Authorities), etc.

A TDP system may be compared to a firewall. We can figure out a TDP device in corporate networks just providing Trust Development services to the corporate users and applications. Configuration of Trust Development is done locally, i.e., there exists a corporate policy that dictates in what exactly the "corporation" trust, and what are the needed external-to-local policy mappings to developed such a trust. In doing that, there is no need for close collaboration, participation or interference from external entities, it is a local corporate decision. Global technical standards, operational guidance and common practices are what local corporations need to help them to accurately implement their local trust policies. Whether a corporation trusts a couple of end-entity issuing CAs only to develop its business, or it trusts a BCA that embraces several CAs and millions of users, is a matter of the local policy. However, the TDP system must allow the corporation to establish a local policy that limits the scope of what a BCA establishes. In other words, not everything that a BCA tells to be trusted in some degree is trusted by the corporation in the same degree.

The conclusion is that like in other activities and communities on the Internet, the global activity takes place thanks to a web of interconnected local systems in which end users actually rely on to provide the services. Trust Development may be one of such services.

5.4 Semantic Trust

Another important feature of a Trust Development service provider is that it provides to its users truthful Semantic Trust. A TDP system behaves as a translator of complex trust expressed as a collection of data tokens in different formats (certificates, CRLs, OCSP responses, timestamps, assertions, etc.) that are issued by Trusted Third Parties into a simple trust diagnostic expressed in an easy and well known format. Relying parties (users, applications, business processes, etc.) can not easily know about the degree of trust they can deposit on a signed document or transaction. Instead, they rely on a TDP to develop trust and produce a clear diagnostic.

The TDP evaluates the local established rules upon the protected data. The rules define all constrains and mappings the local policy mandates for a given set of trusted third parties linked to a given kind of secure token (e.g. digital signature, etc.). The final diagnostic is given to the relying party in the form of a unique Trust Level.

The Trust Level is a number of four possible values, namely:

- 0: low level of trust,
- 1: medium level of trust,
- 2: high level of trust, and
- 3: very high level of trust.

The final Trust Level is calculated as the lowest Trust Level assigned to each Trusted Third Party that participates with some trusted token (certificate, crl, ocsp response, timestamp, assertion, etc.) in the evaluation of the protected data (.e.g. a digitally signed document).

The Trust Level is always accompanied of the local policy identifier that has been applied to reach the conclusion. This policy identifier is perfectly understandable by the relying party since it is locally defined. However, the evaluated policy rules could assert (map) that this is equivalent to some external policy which indeed came in the protected data. Providing the external policy identifier to the relying party is worthless since, basically, it does not understand it.

Optionally, the TDP can provide information to the relying party about all trusted material used in the evaluation. In this case, the Trust Level is provided for each trusted token, and optionally, accompanied with a Trust Label for better identifying the context or semantic of trust assigned to the TTP that issued them.

In this scenario, it is easy for a relying party to make a decision taken into account a Trust Level number, and if requested more detail, a local understandable policy identifier.

6 Conclusion

We presented a PKI model based on Service Oriented TDPs. The TDP is a new PKI component that acts as the trust anchor for relaying parties. The suggested appoach addresses PKI interoperability, quality of service, easy of use and seamless integration into business processes.

The pillars of the TDP scheme are identity federation, trust federation, and policy oriented architecture.

Identity federation allows joining the sparce electronic identities of a person from diverse infrastructuctures in a single robust virtual identity. This makes it possible for users to obtain ubiquity services destined to them without having to re-establish their identity and thus simplifying the user experience and increasing security and control.

Trust federation enables the interconnection of PKI islands. Independent third parties are federated in an administrative domain with a specific level of trust for each security service they offer. Users are released from having to gather and interpret the required information (usually unreachable to them) to evaluate the certificates, evidences or secured documents they manage. The TDP computes the trustworthiness of signed documents on their behalf and communicate the resultant report to them.

On the other hand, the TDP is a policy driven system which permits to highly adapt the responses of the platform to the actual context of the client. The system can dynamically change its behavior based on the ambient conditions that embrace the request and its data. Moreover, as policies are expressed in XML, the configuration of the system is portable and simple.

Finally, it is worth noticing that all TDP interfaces are based on an SOA and Web Services so it is very easy to integrate the PKI services in the business workflow since there are a lot of tools to automate the development and deploying work.

TrustedX [Safe04] is an implementation of the presented TDP. More information can be found at http://www.trustedwebservices.org.

References

[ACPZ01] Adams, C., Cain, P., Pinkas, D., Zuccherato, R.: Internet X.509 Public Key Infrastructure Time Stamp Protocols, IETF RFC-3161, August 2001.

[AdFa99] Adams, C., Farrell, S.: Internet X.509 Public Key Infrastructure Certificate Mangement Protocols, IETF RFC-2510. March 1999.

[Blan06] Blanchard, D. (Cybertrust): I-CIDM Bridge to Bridge Interoperations. 5th Annual PKI R&D Workshop "Making PKI Easy to Use". April 2006. http://middleware.internet2.edu/pki06/proceedings/blanchard-bridge-bbwg.ppt

[Comm06] Commission of the European Communities: Report on the operation of Directive 1999/93/EC on a Community framework for electronic signatures. In: Report from the Commission to the European Parliament and the Council. Brussels, March 15, 2006.

[FHM+06] Freeman, T., Housley, R., Malpani, A., Cooper, D., Polk, T.: Server-based Certificate Validation Protocol (SCVP). IETF RFC Internet Draft. June 2006.

[GoAc06] US Government: E-Authentication Secure Government Access. http://www.cio.gov/eauthentication/

[GoFB06]   US Government: Federal Bridge Certification Authority (FBCA).
            http://www.cio.gov/fbca/

[HFPS99]   Housley, R., Ford, W., Polk, W., Solo, D.: Internet X.509 Public Key Infrastruc-
            ture Certificate and CRL Profile, IETF RFC-2459. January 1999.

[LMMP05]   Lioy, A., Marian, M., Moltchanova, N., Pala, M.: PKI past, present and future.
            Springer-Verlang 2005.

[MAA+99]   Myers,M., Ankney, R., Malpani, A., Galperin, S., Adams, C.: X.509 Internet
            Public Key Infrastructure Online Certificate Status Protocol – OCSP. IETF
            RFC-2560, June 1999.

[MLB+06]   Matthew, C., Laskey, K., McCabe, F., Brown, P., Metz, R.: Reference Model for
            Service Oriented Architecture 1.0, OASIS Technical Committee Specification,
            July 2006.

[Olne06]   Olnes, Jon (DNV Research): PKI Interoperability by an Independent, Trusted
            Validation Authority. In: Proceedings of 5th Annual PKI R&D Workshop
            "Making PKI Easy to Use". April 2006.

[Safe04]   TrustedX White Paper. Safelayer Secure Communications S.A., 2004-2006.
            http://www.trustedwebservices.org

[YCB+04]   Yergeau, F., Cowan, J., Bray, T., Paoli, J., Sperberg-McQueen, C.;., Maler, E.:
            Extensible Markup Language (XML) 1.1. W3C Recommendation, April 2004.
            http://www.w3.org/TR/2004/REC-xml11-20040204/

A Trust Label for Secure and Compliant e-ID Applications: The Belgian Experience

Geert Somers · Jos Dumortier

Lawfort
{geert.somers | jos.dumortier}@lawfort.be

Abstract

After a successful introduction and roll-out of the electronic identity card (e-ID) in Belgium, both private companies and governmental institutions show a pronounced interest in e-ID applications for authentication and transaction purposes. Both functions are incorporated in the Belgian e-ID card. Some first experiences exist but actual implementation of e-ID applications is still lacking behind. There appears to be a need to boost market confidence and consumer trust in the possibilities of e-ID applications for e-business and e-government.

Consumers are mainly concerned about what will happen to their personal data or fear abuse of the digital signature when using their card. Independent third parties can help countering such concerns and actually gaining consumer trust through the issuance of a trust label based on a professional standard. The recently founded Digital Identity Standards (DIS) Institute (www.disinstitute.be) developed such a standard and label to provide consumers with assurance about the security and trust level of e-ID applications. Clear guidelines also contribute to better quality management and common understanding of the technical, legal, design and policy aspects e-ID applications by the application owners. This paper will mainly highlight the legal aspects and the impact and value of the secure e-ID label.

1 Challenges of e-ID applications

1.1 Potential of e-ID applications

The roll-out of the Belgian e-ID has been very successful. A limited amount of cards was issued in 2003 and 2004. Large scale distribution started in 2005, with up to 1000 cards activated every day. By 2009, all Belgian citizens older than 12 years should be in the possession of an e-ID. The total number of users will thus amount to around 8 million.

The Belgian e-ID contains a microchip with two private keys protected by a pin code and two certificates, one for authentication and one for legal signatures. The microchip on the e-ID contains basic personal identification information, including a hash of the photograph, which can be retrieved upon mere insertion of the card in an e-ID reader.

The potential for e-ID applications is endless. By way of example, the card can already be used for registered electronic mail, for rights management of digital information, for remote access to company networks and for certain e-government applications, such as the online tax declaration. Apart from these early adopter projects from these early adopter projects, the e-ID offers many more possibilities for applications, which are currently not being used due to market concerns in relation to safety and security.

For children under 12 years of age, a special non-obligatory e-ID card has been developed as a means of identification and authentication when using online services such as chatting or offline services such as the library, swimming pool or sports club. This card does not contain a signature certificate because children younger than 12 years cannot place valid legal signatures.

1.2 Consumer concerns

Although the e-ID card in itself offers all guarantees requested by prevalent European norms and standards, users of the e-ID are concerned about the confidentiality and integrity of e-ID applications. Following increasing amounts of news items on stolen data, forgery of data, phishing, etc., they wonder what will happen to their personal information, including the national registry number. The latter is a unique identification number connected to each citizen and relates to administrative data (address, civil status, nationality, etc) but also to more sensitive data, such as one's judicial history.

The lack of user certainty with regard to the management and protection of personal data clearly slows down the development, implementation and actual use of e-ID applications.

In addition, users want to be sure that the electronic signature data will produce legal effects and will not be abused by anyone.

Finally, users will want some degree of certainty in relation to the availability of the e-ID application.

1.3 Countering consumer concerns

Consumer trust can be gained through good governance and legal compliance. Internal processes and systems must ensure security and protection of personal data in accordance with applicable legislation.

Legal compliance may also contribute to the reputation and credibility of the company and to better incident response in case of external attacks or abuse of the information system or the e-ID.

As we will see below, independent third parties may play a crucial role in countering such consumer concerns through the auditing and subsequent labelling of e-ID applications. Even for organisations that are fully compliant with legal provisions, a trust label provided by an external organisation will grant the application added value.

2 e-ID applications and legal compliance

2.1 Importance of legal compliance

Any e-ID application stands or falls with legal compliance. The processing of personal data is protected by data protection legislation and specific legislation relating to the use of the national registry number. Although it is possible to identify relevant applicable legislation in advance, actual compliance can only be assessed on a case-by-case basis. Every application is different and processes information in a different way.

Consequently, e-ID applications need to attach greatest importance to legal data protection aspects. This must be done in combination with design, policy and implementation aspects. By way of example, privacy legislation requires the adoption of adequate technical and organisational protection measures against accidental or unauthorised destruction, accidental loss or unauthorised processing. Compliance with such requirement can only be reached with an integrated, wide-box approach.

Transparency of legal compliance can best be reached by addressing the obligations from a front-office and back-office perspective. Front-office concerns the collection of data when interacting with the user of the e-ID application. All further processing of the data is part of the back-office systems. The importance of lawful back-office processing of personally identifiable information is of particular importance because users have absolutely no control at all over this phase.

2.2 Purposes of e-ID applications

Authentication and signature are the main purposes of e-ID applications. Moreover, they are the only possible uses in case of online use of the e-ID. As indicated above, authentication and signing can be done on the basis of the two private keys and certificates in the e-ID, in combination with the personal pin code.

- **Authentication**
  When used for authentication, the e-ID can be used for registration and access to a business or governmental platform. Access to a website usually does not require the placement of a signature.

- **Transaction**
  When used for transaction purposes, the e-ID may serve for the conclusion of contracts or the submission of documents to governmental authorities.

Travel booking is a typical e-business example where several e-ID applications may be involved. Below we will use this example when taking a closer look at the use of the e-ID for authentication and transaction purposes.

2.3 e-ID applications and authentication

From a front-office perspective, an e-ID application will need certain personal data to check whether the person using the e-ID is indeed the one he or she pretends to be. This is inherent to any process of authentication. Communication of the data enables the application to verify specific attributes of the user, such as age, gender or nationality.

Example: when booking a holiday through the e-ID application, consumers or travel agents may need to authenticate themselves to access certain websites with privileged information or offers. Depending on the information made available, such access can be given in a gradual way.

In the light of privacy legislation, it must be made sure that the processing of personal data is done fairly and lawfully. In particular, data collection must be limited to necessary and relevant data. This is important because the information on the e-ID is not in itself protected by the user's PIN code: once the e-ID is inserted in a smartcard reader, the application can potentially view or capture all the information on the card without the user's knowledge. The user could place a so-called sniffer between the computer and the e-ID reader to reveal the information viewed or captured from the card but average users will most likely not adopt similar measures.

Example: when accessing a website, it will probably not be necessary for the application to collect the user's birth date or picture, although such information may be interesting for marketing purposes or even for sale to third parties. Similarly, when the user of the e-ID application is a travel agent, the agent's private address will in principle not be relevant and should therefore not be collected.

From a back-office perspective, once personal data are collected from the user, any further processing must be in line with the principles of the law. This means for instance that the data may not be stored longer than necessary, that they must be adequately protected and that they may not be transferred to non-EU countries that do not offer an adequate level of protection. As is the case in an offline environment, lawful back-office processing of personal data is of particular importance to gain users' trust as they have no control over the processing in this stage.

Example: if a user registered to a travel booking website, the user's data should be deleted or anonymised in the absence of any activity during a longer time period after registration. Within the company, access to the data should be limited on a need-to-know basis.

A special legal regime applies to the national registry number. In Belgium this number may only be used by certain entities that qualify for and obtain the necessary authorisation. These restrictions should avoid or at least reduce the possibilities to misuse the national registry number as a tool for linking personal information from various sources. The national number is indeed used as a unique identifier in almost all of the government databases. The national register itself only contains elementary identification data such as name, age, sex, domicile, etc.

The restrictions for using the national registry number constitute a possible obstacle for applications based on the e-ID. To overcome this obstacle application developers are advised to use an irreversible hash of the national registry number combined with sufficient technical measures in order to prevent any form of linkability.

2.4 e-ID applications and transaction

When creating an electronic signature with the e-ID card, the user can express his or her consent with a transaction. As for authentication, information relating to the physical person contained in the card needs to be communicated to the e-ID application.

Any processing of personal data will again have to be in line with applicable legislation. In addition, users should be provided with proper advice on the application's signature process and its legal consequences and the user interface should be designed in such a way as to guarantee, to the extent possible, the user's intention to be bound by the signature.

Example: if a user needs to place a digital signature to book a flight through an online application, the application should be set-up in such a way as to obtain the user's informed consent with the transaction.

3 A standard and label for secure e-ID applications

3.1 Importance of an independent audit

As pointed out above, users have no control over the collection and management of their personal data when using e-ID applications. Consequently, the use of e-ID applications depends on the level of trust users have in the application. Evidently, some companies generate more trust than others. Nevertheless, even well-known companies will benefit from an audit of their application by an independent third party.

Especially in an online environment, where there is no direct interaction with users, the latter need to obtain certainty with regard to the technical safety and security of the application. An audit by an independent and objective third party can reassure the application owner that the application adequately covers legal, design, policy and implementation requirements and helps to make the application more reliable and trustworthy for the user when a positive audit results in a visible and verifiable label.

3.2 Development of a standard

An audit can only be performed on the basis of a previously developed standard, which sets control objectives and controls to be performed during the audit for all aspects involved with the safety and security of the application.

Legal compliance, as discussed above, is only one aspect of a safe e-ID application. A horizontal and integrated approach is needed to guarantee reliability and security of e-ID transactions. The currently developed standard for secure e-ID applications therefore reflects technological, legal, design and policy aspects. It is also in line with other information security standards.

The standard does not envisage legal requirements other than information security. Nevertheless, it draws the attention of the e-ID applications owner to compliance with legal requirements resulting from legislation on e-commerce, fair trade practices and consumer protection. Such requirements may relate to the formalities, information duties or certain prohibitions. It is important for a provider of e-ID applications to be aware of the legal framework applicable to the entire process in which the e-ID application is integrated.

As it is the case for other information security standards, the standard for secure e-ID applications will be made available for self-implementation by companies and governmental authorities. To ensure proper implementation of the standard and to help forward a positive audit, most companies and governmental authorities will call upon internal or external consultants to assist with the implementation.

3.3 Setting up and functioning of a standardisation organisation

The secure e-ID standard has been developed by the recently founded DIS Institute (www.disinstitute.be), which is the copyright holder of the standard. The main tasks of the DIS Institute are to control, maintain, safeguard and promote the secure e-ID standard as well as other information technology standards.

To this extent, the organisation set up an accreditation and certification scheme. The founding members are automatically accredited partners of the organisation. Other companies may apply for accreditation if they abide by the quality assurance requirements set forward by the organisation.

Through its accredited partners, the organisation will audit companies and governmental institutions for correct adoption of the secure e-ID application standard and possibly other standards.

3.4 Development and granting of a label

A catching and strong label will be made available for use on websites and in offline applications.

Organisations that correctly adopt the standard will receive a license to use the label in connection with their e-ID application for the time period during which the certificate of compliance with the standard is granted. This will in principle not be longer than three years. Depending on the purpose for which the e-ID application is used, companies will be able to choose between a basic and an advanced label, with a different audit level for each label.

Upon expiry of the compliance certificate, the company or governmental authority will only be able to extend the use of the label following a new and positive audit. Consumers will be able to click on the label to verify its validity at any time. Any possible abuses of the label will be communicated to users. In case of non-compliance with the requirements of the secure e-ID standard during the validity period of the certificate, the certificate and license to use the label will be revoked. Such revocation, if necessary, is important to support the long-term value and credibility of the label in the market.

In addition to the label proceedings foreseen by the DIS institute, the provider of the e-ID application may consider implementing procedures to effectively deal with consumer complaints. Such approach will be highly appreciated by consumers and will often be sufficient to solve problems in a satisfactory manner.

4 Protection of the standard and the label

The DIS institute developed the e-ID standard and is therefore copyright owner of the standard. This means that the standard may not be copied or distributed by third parties without its consent. The institute will also further maintain the standard in function of technological and legal developments.

In addition, the organisation is the rightholder of the trademark to the label. This means that the label may not be used by any third party, e.g. for posting on a website, without the organisation's consent. This is important to avoid abuse and confusion in relation to the value of the label. Consumers need to be sure that any use of the label is the result of a positive audit and verification process.

5 Official launch of the standard and the label

Before actually launching the standard and the label, the standard will be reviewed by independent information security experts and tested in some selected companies and public administrations. The organisation will only call upon true and widely known experts. This mechanism aims at ensuring the highest possible quality and practical value of the standard. Once the standard has been reviewed and finalised, it will be made available to the general public for consultation and implementation.

6 Promotion of the standard and label

6.1 Belgium

The official launch of the secure e-ID label will be given adequate publicity with the support of the federal government, so that consumers easily recognise the label and its trusted source, which in turn will boost the use of the e-ID for e-business and e-government. In the meantime, more and more Belgian citizens are in the possession of an e-ID.

6.2 Europe

Different EU member states engaged in the deployment of an e-ID. The Belgian experience with standardisation and labelling of secure e-ID applications may be very useful for other European countries and the standard is therefore open for adoption throughout Europe. It will be further developed for use in other EU countries that implement an e-ID. The pioneer position of Belgium in the adoption and roll-out of the e-ID and the development of e-ID applications will certainly be beneficial for the openness of other countries towards the standard.

The organisation behind the e-ID standard will play an active role in promoting the secure e-ID standard and other standards to be developed in the future throughout Europe. International positioning of the organisation behind the standard will be important for cross-border transactions based on the e-ID. The organisation will also make sure to closely follow and monitor all European framework initiatives and to keep the support of governments. This will increase visibility and credibility of the label and thus user value for consumers and commercial value for companies. Such increased value is in its turn crucial to boost faith in electronic commerce, a strong point of focus in the European Union.

7 Conclusion

The success of the e-ID for authentication and signature in e-business and e-government applications largely depends on the level of user trust in such applications. Due to the lack of interaction with the actual e-ID user and the general fear that data may be stolen or abused, users need confirmation from a trusted third party with regard to the security level and trustworthiness of e-ID applications. This can be assessed by an audit carried out by an independent third party on the basis of a previously developed and expert-reviewed security standard, which covers the necessary legal, design, policy and implementation requirements. Upon a positive audit, companies and governmental authorities can obtain the right to use a label in connection with their e-ID application. The company that owns the standard must make sure to further develop and maintain the standard in line with legal and technical developments, thus keeping the value of the correspondent label as high as possible.

It is to hope that the success of the e-ID standard and label and its positive impact on e-business and e-government applications may serve as an example for the development of other information technology and security standards by independent organisations in Europe and throughout the world.

Electronic signature in Italy after ten years of "running in"

Giovanni Manca

Via Isonzo 21/b – 00198 Roma (Italy)
Ufficio standard e tecnologie d'identificazione - CNIPA
manca@cnipa.it

Abstract

– achievements in Italy in the field of electronic documents
Electronic documents were introduced by a very slim paragraph that, after having been devised in 1996, was issued in year 1997 as art. 15(2) of Law 59. After ten years the whole spectrum of possible usage of the electronic document has now become real in Italy: from the, now nearly trivial, qualified electronic signature, to the long term electronic storage of any document, to the issuance and storage of signed electronic invoices, to a more and more widespread usage in the public health domain, to the Registered E-Mail that, by mimicking the registered ordinary mail, provides the users with the well known receipts, and more.
Exciting new usages are now moving to the front stage: electronic medical reports, electronic criminal court sentences, etc.
The previously hinted to slim paragraph of Law 59/97 was indeed, paraphrasing astronaut Neil Armstrong's most famous statement: "A small effort for a legislator, a giant leap for Italy".

1 The History

The history of electronic signature in Italy began one decade ago. Italy and Germany are still contending for its primogeniture: each of us rightfully believes their country was the first to issue an electronic signature related legislation. In fact both countries have issued their first law in 1997.

As far as Italy is concerned, on 15 March 1997 the Law No 59 was issued that stated at article 15(2) that "*Deeds, data and documents formed by the public administration and by the private citizens with electronic and telematic means, the contracts stipulated in the same ways, as well as their storage and transmission with electronic means, are valid and relevant to all legal effects.*".

Then came the Decree by the President of the Republic (DPR) No 513 of 10/11/1997, laying down the relevant legal provisions, but it was only on 8/2/1999 that the technical rules were also issued as a Decree by the President of the Council of Ministers – DPCM. It is to be acknowledged that these rules were so well crafted that, apart from some details, most of them withstood the passing of time and can still be found in the currently in force DPCM 13/1/2004.

On 13 December 1999 the EU Directive 1999/93/EC was issued, to be published in the EU Official Journal on 19 January 2000. The Italian implementations of this Directive are the Legislative Decree no 10 of 2002 and the DPR No 137 of 2003.

S. Paulus, N. Pohlmann, H. Reimer (Editors): Securing Electronic Business Processes, Vieweg (2006), 363-373

But the story continue, since in 2005 the Legislative Decree (Dlgs) No 82 of 07/03/2005, named "Code of the digital administration" or, shortly, the "Code", was issued and update most of the electronic document related provisions that were laid down in DPR 445/2000. This Code was further amended by another Legislative Decree: the Dlgs No 159 issued on 4/4/2006. The "Code" related technical aspects will likely be shortly issued to update the above mentioned DPCM 13/1/2004.

It is also to be taken into account what impact the legislation on electronic documents had on fiscally relevant documents, e.g. invoices (Decree by the Minister of Economy and Finance 23 January 2004, Legislative Decree No 52 of 20 February 2004), on long term documents storing (Centro Nazionale per l'Informatica nella Pubblica Amministrazione – CNIPA – Deliberation No 11 of 19 February 2004), on Registered E-Mail (Decree by the President of the Republic – DPR – No 68 of 11 February 2005, Decree by the Minister of Innovation and Technology of 2 November 2005), on the electronic public administrations log-book (Decree by the President of the Council of Ministers – DPCM – 31 October 2000).

As of today we can state that we have in Italy a consistent set of legislative instruments that cover all the characteristics of the digital documents' life: from their birth, by giving them legal value with an electronic signature, through their outgoing from/incoming into a Public Administration, their shipment via a legally valid e-mail and, eventually, their storage, not to mention the requirements to ensure them fiscal value.

In order to complete the list of the relevant normative documents, it is to be said that the Centro Nazionale per l'Informatica nella Pubblica Amministrazione (National Centre for IT in Public Administration) – CNIPA, as well as the Tax Authority, are the relevant bodies to issue additional detailed technical and operational piece of legislation named "circular letters".

2 The Present

In the years the spectrum of electronic document related applications has widened in Italy, and now it is possible to say that the electronic documents are creeping in nearly all possible fields, even in the criminal court sentences.

As of now, the legislative status covers all aspects as described in the following sub-clauses.

2.1 Electronic document

After ten years of seasoning the pieces of legislation currently in force for supporting the electronic document with electronic signatures are:

1. the "Code" (Dlgs 82/2005 as amended by Dlgs 159/2006) that lays down the electronic signature legal provisions;
2. the DPCM of 13/1/2004 that provides the technical and security requirements, such to ensure reliability and trust to the certification service providers, to the secure signature creation devices and, eventually, to the signatures themselves;
3. the CNIPA Deliberation 4/2005 that defines the interoperability rules regarding certificates and their revocation information, signature formats, time stamp tokens, verification applications.

Circular letters by CNIPA indicate the rules the certification service providers have to abide when applying for accreditations, etc. They are not mentioned here, being they not strictly related to the electronic documents legal validity.

2.2 Electronic log-book

1. The DPR 445/2000 (better: what still survives of this decree after many its articles have been repealed and replaced by the "Code") specifies the basic rules on the log-book enforcement, on its organisational requirements, on what and how it is to record in order to ensure a secure long term reference to the incoming / outgoing documents, and the requirements for its reliable seamless operations.

2. The DPCM 31/10/2000 details the technical and organisational requirements to be met by the log book implementers and by the governmental body in charge of centrally manage the single public administrations as far as their log book is required.

3. A CNIPA circular letter (n. 28 issued on 7 May 2001) goes into the smallest details of how the log book is to be implemented.

2.3 Registered E-Mail

1. The DPR 68/2005 is based on the provision, lately stated in "Code" art. 45: "The electronic document sent electronically is to be intended as sent by the sender if it is sent to their provider, and is to be intended as delivered to the recipient if made available at the recipient's electronic address, as declared by the recipient, in the electronic mailbox provided to the recipient by the relevant provider"; this DPR lays down the rules to endow an e-mail with legally erga omnes validity. This ensures that the moment a Registered E-Mail is sent, the moment it was delivered into the recipient's mailbox, and, where the sender selects the appropriate receipt type, the content of the delivered mail, have legal value and are admissible as evidence in legal proceedings.

2. The Decree by the Minister of Infrastructures and Technologies of 2 November 2005 gives the required technical provisions for REM providers, and its Annex details to the lowest possible level all the technical requirements to ensure interoperability, at least in Italy.

2.4 Electronic Substitutional Storage

The electronic substitutional storage legislative basis resides on what is now "Code" art. 23, that is useless to quote.

About the electronic substitutional storage is useful to mention that paper documents can be disposed of (well, not all of them: ancient texts will never be destroyed), provided one abides by the organisational rules laid down in CNIPA Deliberation No 11 of 19 February 2004. Yes, "Organisational rules", not "technical" because, maybe surprisingly, no very detailed technical provision is given on this subject.

In few words this Deliberation says: any organisation that wants to get rid of paper documents is free to do it, provided it ensures that these documents can be exhibited whenever necessary. Something that can be named "mandatory guidance" is specified, to help these organisations in suitably structuring themselves, but no technical specifications is given on the type of storage media, on how the disaster recovery plan is to address this issue, on how and where the backup copies are to be produced and kept, etc.

Needless to say, should such organisations fail exhibiting one specific document when required to do so, even after many years or even decades, they will have no excuse like, for example, saying that the media would not be read with the then current programs, or that they had a system malfunction that destroyed the media content. If they cannot produce, say, a fiscal document, they will endure the applicable consequences.

In principle, in my opinion, this is a correct approach: why getting entangled with technical details that, as it occurs in everyday's life, at times may become obsolete even before the ink they are printed with gets dry? The, in my opinion, correct assumption is that if one organisation wants to implement such technical solution, they must reach the specific goals.

2.5 Electronic fiscally relevant documentation

The governing rules are:

1. The DPR No 633 of 26 October 1972, providing rules addressing mostly the VAT, that was many times updated in the past years and, lately, but presumably not finally, by the Legislative Decree No 52 of 20 February 2004;
2. The Decree by the Minister of Economy and Finance (DMEF) 23 January 2004;
3. The Tax Agency Circular letter No 45/E of 19 October 2005.

It is interesting to remark that, regarding electronically signed fiscally relevant documents, Qualified Electronic Signatures are required, and that the CNIPA Deliberation No 11/2004 is used as a basis for the long term conservation of such documents, but with a correct amendment and a significant technical simplifying specification.

3 The state of the art

3.1 Electronic signature

As already said the Italian legislation addresses a number of facets of the electronic document: its content and presentation, the various signature types that can be employed, who and how can revoke a certificate, how to take into account the time to help assess whether a certain signature was valid, even after the corresponding certificate was revoked.

Let's go through all these aspects.

3.1.1 Electronic Document Content and Format

It's surprising to realize how many persons are not aware of what trivial tricks can be enacted to cheat people with a cleverly crafted document.

To better explain this concept the following very simple example may be useful, so simple that any layperson can create it.

In one Excel cell your may insert a very simple formula stating: if the current date (or time, or whatever external event can be perceived from inside the Excel sheet) has a certain value, then a certain value pops up. This value cannot be seen when signing, or when first verifying the document signature simply because that external event has not yet occurred. Furthermore, in order to make the formula invisible it is enough to define the cell holding it as "hidden" and then to protect the entire sheet. No-one would wonder that this Excel sheet is protected: it's absolutely logic to protect the "integrity" of an invoice. The signer, or a certain verifier, would not be able to read that formula. When that external event occurs the invoice value changes, yet the signature is perfectly valid: the bit content of the Excel file has not changed, because what has changed is something external to the Excel sheet, so the document digest is unchanged as well.

This has been taken into account by the Italian legislators since ten years ago. The Italian legislation states, in few words, that a signed document containing such "dirty tricks", suitable to modify the document presentation, has no legal validity. It is interesting to have a look at how this is handled in the different pieces of legislations above mentioned. In particular, while the DMEF 23/1/2004 on electronic fiscal documents repeats, more or less, this concept, the Dlgs 52/2004 that, mind, has a higher rank and therefore prevails on the DMEF, is adamant: an electronic invoice must not have whatsoever hidden code.

Of course this doesn't mean that are usable only the "static document formats" but that you must be aware that code and macros are not able to modify acts and declarations contained in the document.

3.1.2 Signature formats

When the first Italian technical rules were drafted, neither *.pdf nor XML signature had achieved the status of standards, so the only choice was between the enveloping and the detached signatures. Given the risk of losing the detached signature, thus depriving a signed document of any legal value, it was inevitable to choose the enveloping signature (the *.p7m, to be clear).

Now that both RFC 3778 on PDF signatures and W3C standards are available, CNIPA, having the right to stipulate this kind of agreements, agreed with Adobe an arrangement that ensures any user the availability of free readers capable to verify PDF signatures and any developer the availability of the specifications necessary to create similar signature verifications and creation applications. A similar arrangement is in progress for XML signatures.

Hence came an ever growing usage of the signed documents: with a PDF signature, gone is the hassle of having to verify a p7m "blob" before being able to look into it (think of the impacts on indexed searches): the PDF document is perfectly legible and machine readable even before verifying its signature.

3.1.3 Signature types

CNIPA Deliberation 4/2005 gives the technical details for single and multiple signatures, the latter one of two types: parallel and countersignature.

With the adoption of the PDF and XML formats these signature types are widened since a signature can refer only to a part of the document.

But there are other, more important signature types, that were defined in the Directive 1999/93/EC: "simple", so to say, advanced and qualified.

In Italy we have two different set of signatures.

The _"simple" electronic signature_ has the same validity defined in the above Directive at art. 5(2): it has no absolute legal validity per se, but it can be used in court, on the basis of its objective security measures, and, obviously, if the parties had previously agreed on using it.

The _qualified electronic signature_ – QES – is "**the**" signature: it has full legal validity unless formally challenged with a legal action. The legal definition of the QES contains the advanced electronic signature definition in compliance with the art. 2(2) of the Directive. It is to be noticed that no one should undertake this action light minded, because, in case the court decides that it has no basis, the plaintiff will not get out unscathed.

The relevance of the QES is such that all Public Administrations _shall_ have to equip themselves by 1/1/2008 with software applications suitable to verify these signatures. Another remarkable issue is specified in Code Art. 3: "_Citizens and companies have the right to request and obtain the usage of telematic technologies in their communications with the public administrations and with the public services providers, within the limits of the present code provisions_".

This provision is, however, watered down by the subsequent subparagraphs that subordinate this accomplishment to the single administration's actual technological and organisational resources, but it is a real milestone, that reverses the centuries old relationship between the Italian citizen, that was likened to a passive subject, and the public administration.

3.1.4 Time Referencing

The purpose of time referencing is to place in the right time one binary object, including, obviously, signed documents and files. This may serve either administrative purposes, for example testifying that one object was created before some deadline, or, and mainly, technical purposes, like ascertaining if a signature had been issued before or after the related certificate revocation time.

The time acknowledged as trusted by the Italian law, in relation to technical means is the time registered in the:

1. log-file records (for public administrations only),
2. registered E-Mail receipts,
3. time stamp tokens – TST – issued by a Time Stamping Authority – TSA.
4. substitutional documents conservation

It is to be remarked that the certification service providers accredited as per Directive 1999/93/EC art. 3.2 are requested to have in place a Time Stamping System compliant with specifics detailed in DPCM 13/1/2004. A consequence is that every certificate holder does have a trustable TSA of choice: the CA that issued their certificate, but they are however free to buy Time stamping services from any other accredited certification service provider.

But let's go back to technical issues.

A TST is a signed object, so its certificate as well may be revoked and, in any case, will expire. Let me remind that, as per ISO 9594.8:2001, certification service providers are free to remove from their revocation lists – CRLs – the references to expired revoked certificates, provided that their revocation has been published at least once in the CRL. Due to this provision, after the certificate has expired it is not possible to know whether it was revoked when alive.

The technical means to ensure that all the information necessary to verify a signature after its certificate issuance are:

1. to keep in a secure way the information proving that at signing time all certificates in the certification path was valid
2. to apply a TST chain to the signed object, to prevent that expiration of one TST related certificate voids the entire process.

To avoid both these hassles, at least as far as TSTs certificates are concerned, the Italian regulations require that the TSAs securely store all TSTs they issue for at least five years, and even more upon the user's request, and these stored TSTs have legal values.

But it is not to be forgotten that organisational means, such as depositing signed objects at a trusted party's, like a notary or a governmental agency, can avoid to make use of these technical mechanisms. In particular, as we will see in section 3.5 e-Invoicing, a timestamped signature applied to a set of fiscally relevant documents must be entrusted to the Tax Agency. This accomplishment relieves the taxable person from the above described hassles since it per se ensures long term validity to these documents.

3.1.5 Revocation

The revocation principle is very well known by all persons involved in electronic signature. The thorny point is not on how to trigger the revocation, but on how to handle this critical problem.

We have two issues here. One can be synthesised in another paraphrase: "to OCSP or not to OCSP?"

The other, and main, issue is: how can we verify long after a document was signed if any of its supporting certificates in its certification path was revoked at the signing time?

OCSP – OCSP can be a nice and agile mechanism, but it is to be carefully weighted against the actual signature usage.

Its main advantages are:

1. no need to download all the entire CRL set, that in the years can become bulky, every time a new CRL is issued or upon need: with OCSP a simple request is submitted when necessary to the OCSP responder that will send back its sentence on the specific certificate: "valid", "not valid since xx/yy/zzzz", "I do not know";

2. an OSCP response might provide a "just in time" information regarding one certificate revocation: no need to wait for the next CRL to be published when assessing a recently issued signature validity.

But let's look at the other side of these two issues.

1. If the signature verification is intensively performed by many agents within a single organisation, the bandwidth consumed by asking an external OCSP responder all these requests may remarkably grow; in such cases it should be considered whether it is more convenient to set up an OCSP responder inside that organisation that collects the revocation information from *all* the possibly involved certification service providers; in this case downloading the CRLs once and for all on one single organisation-internal server, to be accessed by the users soon after that download in their "private store", could be a functionally equivalent solution. It is useful to remind, to this regard, that a new PKIX RFC is being worked on by the relevant IETF Work Group, aiming to speed up the OCSP request – response process.

2. The "just in time" certificate status information might be achieved only if each involved certification service provider has a direct and secured channel with this OCSP responder, along which channel every single revocation information can be sent to the responder as soon as the single certification service provider itself enacts it, even before next CRL issuance time. This would work when the number of the referenced certification service providers is not too wide and if they all agree on setting up this secured connection.

Summing up: before implementing the OCSP solution, for it to be really effective, these issues should be carefully evaluated. Most likely, a trade off might be necessary.

While the current DPCM 13/1/2004 mandates the CRL usage, it by no means "outlaws" a complementary usage of OCSP, for which in fact the CNIPA Deliberation 4/2005 provides interoperability specifications.

As a matter of fact this issue is still being debated and chances are that a new technical decree updating DPCM 13/1/2004, that after over two years needs to be updated, might propose a feasible solution.

Long term verification of a signature – this is, most likely, the thorniest issue in the electronic signature field. At least two solutions have already hinted to:

1. making use of one trusted body that, years and even decades after the signing time, can vouch for the signature validity, based on its own internal trustable structure and nature;

2. timely collecting all necessary certificate status related information (the signer's certificate revocation information, as well as that of every certificate in the certification path, and, where required, of the time stamping authority's entire certification path) and securely storing all of them.

For the moment no useful indication can be found in the relevant all-encompassing Italian legislation. As specified above, the only help in slimming down a bit this potentially colossal set of data is given by the rules on Time Stamping Authorities that must keep in a secure and untamperable way all TSTs issued for at least five years, period that can be extended upon user's request.

In addition, the storage of all the certification path in Italy is simplified: as back as in 1999 Italy developed and implemented the embryo of what was later on developed by the ETSI ESI as the TSL – Trust-services Status List. This list is issued, in Italy, by CNIPA that also signs it. CNIPA is also planning to move from the current "TSL embryo" to the full TSL. Both this ETSI ESI TSL and its Italian embryo contain not only the accredited certification service providers current status, but also their story, so, it is enough to keep just the signing certificates' revocation status, timely fetched, because the certification service provider's status will always be present in the CNIPA TSL.

3.2 Electronic Log Book

This particular log book type was to be implemented by all public administrations by 1/1/2004, but they could not be forced in doing so, therefore only just over the 50% has such system up and running.

Where it was implemented, a significant improvement was registered: especially public administrations who have used the CNIPA developed ASP application implementing electronic log book, workflow and documents management functions have had great benefits in terms of saving, transparency and efficiency

CNIPA developed the above mentioned ASP service for all Public Administrations, in order to facilitate its implementation.

3.3 Registered e-Mail – REM (In Italian: Posta Elettronica Certificata – PEC)

Italy is the first country where this kind of solution has been devised and implemented and is effective, in particular since 2/11/2005. The Universal Postal Union has developed a standard for what is called "Electronic Post Mark", but the purposes of these two solutions somewhat differ.

1. The UPU provides verification of electronic signatures, time-stamping and maintains logs as necessary to support "non-repudiation" services. It includes optional services for data encryption. It includes optional facilities for end user signing but is more focused at providing services to enhance the electronic signature to provide "non-repudiation" of Origin, Submission, Delivery, Receipt, Knowledge.

2. The Registered E-Mail – Posta Elettronica Certificata purpose is to "mimic" the current ordinary registered e-mail with proof of delivery.

REM – PEC is in fact based on trusted providers that give the sender and the provider, respectively, signed objects proving:

* when an e-mail was sent;
* from which presumed (should not be used strong authentication) mailbox it was sent;
* when it was deposited at the recipient's mail box and what was its content (or, where required by the sender, a simple digest of the sent data).

No info on content knowledge is envisaged, since it would be legally disputable to say that, simply because one e-mail was opened by the recipient, the latter is fully aware of its content: what if, soon after the "opening acknowledge" reply was sent back, the recipient's system crashes in a way that this specific e-mail cannot be recovered?

This REM – PEC simple and agile, yet secure, mechanism does not get mingled in whether the sent data were originally signed: this is left to the specific user, as well as encrypting it. What really matters is the capability for the parties to exhibit, when necessary, a legally valid proof of sending and receipt of delivery issued by a trusted body of the above.

Simple, but effective and easily understandable by the users.

Furthermore, some specific requirements by the fiscal relevant legislation provide that, effective 1/9/2006, all communications between the Tax Agencies and the financial organisations regarding taxpayers' financial data are to be sent via PEC.

3.4 Substitutional Documents Conservation

The substitutional documents conservation received scarce, if any, attention when its first rules were issued, in 1998: it was, yes, very secure, but also too complex and, consequently, costly to be widely implemented. Only with the second version (AIPA Deliberation 42/2001) and, even more, with its latest version (11/2004) it began being broadly deployed, despite some technical "flaw", namely regarding the time referencing.

Just a simple qualified electronic signature is in fact required by the person in charge of the storage, or by a public officer only where unique analog documents are involved (e.g. documents for which no other document is to be legally kept that may provide the same information).

A similar requirement is to be implemented when the storage period or media is to be "closed".

No requirement is placed on the media type: the storing organisation shall implement suitable operational measures, a list of which is indicated in the CNIPA Deliberation 11/2004, such that their implementation helps ensuring the basic requirement: any document must be exhibited whenever necessary.

As above highlighted the storing body has a wide freedom in choosing the organisational mechanisms: what matters is achieving the purpose. The facts demonstrate that it works.

3.5 e-Invoicing

Without go in detail on a few issues that are still debated, such as:

1. which conditions are to be abided by to dispose of received paper invoices by keeping them in electronic format according to CNIPA Deliberation 11/2004?
2. how is EDI invoice transmission to be implemented?

Regarding issue No 1, that although clear and apparently ultimate specifications exist in the "Code", this possibility is not yet widely accepted: you know, in the fiscal world it is wiser to wait for clear statements by the relevant bodies.

About issue No 2., EDI, the Circular letter 45 specifies it can be used, under the requirement that "the electronic document [*transmitted via EDI*] authenticity and integrity must be guaranteed consistently with" Recommendation 94/820/EC. Now this Recommendation, no doubt, gives a number of indications, but it also states in Art. 6.2 of Annex 2: "*Parties are, however, strongly recommended to agree, where required, on additional security measures, the degree of which will no doubt depend on the value and importance of the subject-matter of the messages and the possible liability in the event of an unsuccessful exchange of messages.*" So: what are in each specific case the "additional security measures" that "guarantee" the required integrity and authenticity? Once again: Italian tax payers are very careful before undertaking pure electronic invoice transmission via EDI.

How can these issues be solved? The surest way is provided by the current fiscal regulations: the Tax Payer can submit the Tax Agency what is called "Interpello" (Interpellation) where they describe the solution they want to implement and they ask for the Tax Agency's opinion that would be undisputable thence on.

As a consequence, e-Invoicing is currently receiving real interest only by very large organisations, like utilities, large manufacturers, etc.

4 A few numbers

4.1 Qualified electronic Signatures

Qualified Electronic signature received a great support by an Italian law issued in year 2000, that mandated, effective few years ago, all company books to be deposited at the respective Chamber of Commerce only in digital format and signed with a qualified electronic signature. As a consequence all involved company executives were forced to accordingly equip themselves with a qualified certificate and a secure signature-creation device.

This paved the way to several other applications among which the "MarketPlace": a Ministry of Finance owned company – CONSIP – implemented a market place where, on the basis of agreed prices for a very large number of goods and services, Public Administrations can issue digital orders, to be digitally accepted by the suppliers. This is having emulators in other European Union Member States.

Independently from this "civil world" application it is very interesting to mention that in some Italian Criminal Court judges are starting to use the PDF signature, due to its simplicity and the above hinted to wide range of possibilities.

Accredited Certificate service providers

Certificate service providers: **18**
Qualified Certificates issued: **2.700.000 (about)**
Implementations: Chambers of commerce, MarketPlace, e-health Regione Lombardia, e-procurement, electronic payments.

Registered e-mail

Authorized providers for registered e-mail: **12**
Mail box provided: **700.000 (about)**

Substitutional conservation

Data supplied from central Public Administrations:

1. On april 2005 23% of documents subjected to conservation
2. It is evaluated to reach the 37 % in June 2006.

Electronic log book

Referencing the data available in Central Public Administration:

1. As of April 2005 40% of documents registered into electronic log book
2. It is evaluated to reach the 58 % in June 2006.

e-Invoicing

Nowadays approximately ten companies have implemented e-invoicing. The forecasts for the next future are really interesting. We can foresee a notable increase in the next 12 months.

5 Conclusion

Availability of useful instruments to the technological innovation have simplified and saved great amounts of money in documents flow, thus making relationships with public administrations faster, more efficient and transparent.

The introduction of the electronic log book is giving a greater efficiency in managing administrative procedures; the availability of e-invoicing has allowed to diminish drastically the time required by the public administrations to perform the due payments.

Substitutive documents conservation allows to free buildings space, nowadays used to keep tons of paper.

We find ourselves in a moment in which the instruments for the innovation of our country are really available and they start to be profitably used, but they still require some effort in order to be broadly used, thus allowing each of us to take advantage at least from some of the enormous deriving benefits.

As an example, the Italian postal service has estimated of being able to save approximately 2 billion euros each year by applying substitutional documents conservation to the approximately 600 million bulletins it deals with every year in Italy.

References

All the active (not repealed) laws referenced in the text are available (italian language) at

http://www.cnipa.gov.it/site/it-IT/Normativa/Leggi,_Decreti_e_Direttive/

http://www.cnipa.gov.it/site/it-IT/Normativa/Circolari_e_Deliberazioni/

Awareness Raising
Compliance
Data Protection
Cyberspace Regulation

Internet Early Warning System: The Global View

Norbert Pohlmann · Marcus Proest

Institute for Internet Security
University of Applied Sciences Gelsenkirchen
Neidenburger Str. 43, D-45877 Gelsenkirchen
{norbert.pohlmann | marcus.proest}@internet-sicherheit.de

Abstract

The constantly growing importance of the Internet for our knowledge and information society makes it necessary to analyze and be acquainted with its status beyond the limits of the individual network operators. Only precise knowledge of the normal status makes it possible to detect anomalies which influence the functionality of the Internet.

With the help of the probe-based Internet Analysis System, which is currently being implemented as a research and development project of the Institute for Internet Security at the University of Applied Sciences in Gelsenkirchen in collaboration with the German Federal Office for Information Security (BSI), it is intended to create and analyze local and above all global perspectives in order to make the generation of early warnings possible.

Particular focal points of the project are the collection of information in compliance with data protection regulations and optimization of the amount of information, so as to be able to store information in the long term and therefore allow the analysis of trends and developments over long periods.

1 Introduction

We have all experienced the situation: you are sitting in a traffic jam and all you can see is a long line of cars in front of and behind you. In this situation, without any assistance, you do not have an overview of the problem. There is no direct information concerning why the traffic jam has come about, how long it is, at what point of the traffic jam you are located or - the most important information - when the traffic jam will be over. As this is a problem faced on a day-to-day basis by thousands of motorists, solutions have been developed to overcome the lack of information. In Germany there is a close network of traffic counter loops which record the traffic volume and situation on the motorways/freeways. Important information about traffic jams is provided by means of radio announcements, SMS, telephone and the Internet, while modern navigation systems process the information directly when planning the route to be taken. Through the use of these resources, motorists are "liberated" from their constricted local view of the situation and can take decisions in good time on the basis of the global information available, e.g. leaving by the next exit and using an alternative route.

This situation can also be applied to the perspective that the network operators have today of the Internet. As a rule they have only a local perspective, i.e. an overview of their own network segments and the communication data that are transferred. If problems occur here and are detected, they can be rectified quickly and systematically. However, if it becomes apparent that a problem has occurred that is not within their own domain of action, or if the required perspective is lacking, the situation is more difficult. It is often not clear where the problem comes from, and for the correction of the problem we are reliant on third parties.

The global view required in order to detect the problem and select the correct solutions is missing. Such a global perception is difficult to achieve on the Internet as people like to play their cards close to their chest. The precise internal network structure, communication connections and topologies are often treated confidentially by the network operators.

Furthermore, in order to achieve a global perspective, there are a few challenges that have to be solved: communication data are relevant in principle to data protection, the quantities of data are enormous, the data rates are sometimes so large that they cannot always be analyzed "live", while long-term storage of the communication data in order to observe long-term developments appears to be impossible. Moreover, the question also arises of who feels responsible for creating a global perspective?

Nevertheless, the Internet has developed into an omnipresent medium over the past few years, without which very large areas of the economy, research and private life would be unimaginable today. For this reason the analysis and knowledge of the medium known as the Internet in its totality is of particular significance in order to be able to assess its development and guarantee the future functioning of all the services it provides.

2 Aims and Task of the Internet Analysis System

The task of the Internet Analysis System on the one hand is to analyze local communication data in defined subnetworks of the Internet, and on the other to create a global perspective of the Internet by bringing together the large number of local perspectives.

The functions of the Internet Analysis System can be divided up into the four subsegments of pattern formation, description of the actual status, alarm signaling and forecasting.

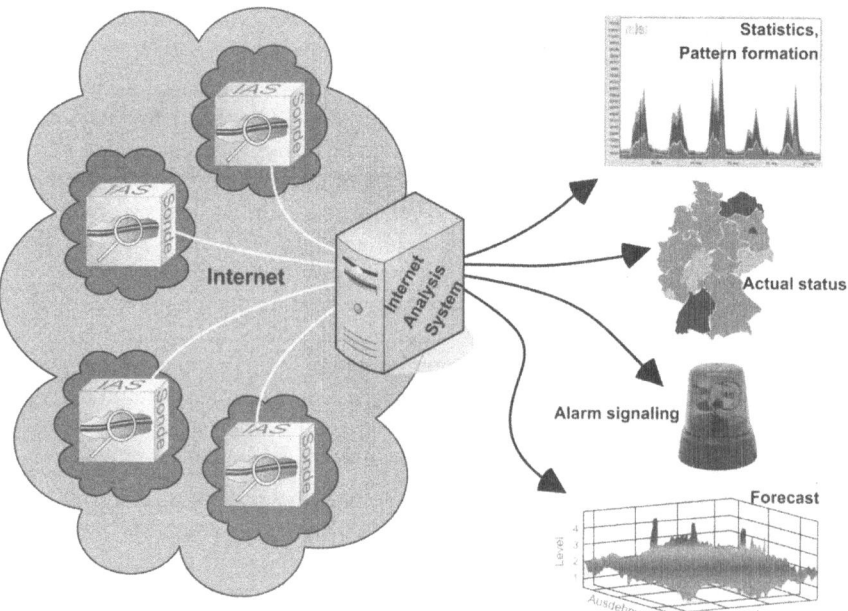

Figure 1: Tasks of the Internet Analysis System

The main task of pattern formation is a comprehensive analysis and interpretation of the communication parameters of Internet traffic, with the aim of detecting technology trends, interrelationships and patterns which represent the various statuses and perspectives of the Internet. On the basis of this knowledge a search is carried out for anomalies among the current measured values and the causes of status changes analyzed and interpreted. Here it is important to find out whether the status anomalies have a natural origin, for example as a result of a technological change, or whether they are attributable to a wanton attack. .

With knowledge of the current status of a communication line and the use of historical - i.e. previously collected - information (knowledge base) it is possible in the case of significant changes to traffic volumes or communication data to concentrate on analyzing these anomalies on the basis of which measures can be initiated to protect and maintain the correct functioning of the Internet.

A further important function is the visual depiction of the Internet status similar to a weather or traffic jam map. Here intuitive depictions are being developed with which the most important parameters are discernible at first glance.

Through the examination and analysis of the extrapolated profiles, technology trends, interrelationships and patterns it will be possible by means of an evolutionary process of the acquired results to make forecasts of Internet status changes. In this manner it is possible to detect indications of attacks and important changes at an early stage and forecast the effects of the damage [Pohlmann2005].

3 Mode of Operation of the Internet Analysis System

The Internet Analysis System consists of probes which passively access the network traffic of the communication lines of various networks and count communication parameters at various communication levels. In an evaluation system the communication parameters are evaluated from various aspects and displayed in a clear manner. Illustration 2 shows the interrelationships between the components involved in the Internet Analysis System.

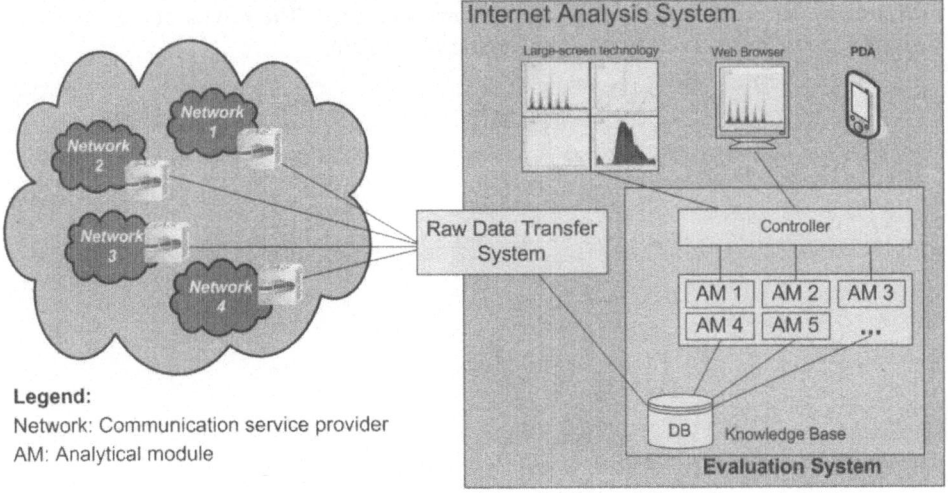

Figure 2: Components of the Internet Analysis System

In order for the Internet Analysis System to be able to supply meaningful results it requires as great a quantity of raw data as possible, i.e. very many counters of various communication parameters at all communication levels over time. All the analyses performed by the evaluation system are based on these raw data. They consist of aggregated counter readings with which the system is provided by various networks. The left-hand side of illustration 2 depicts the Internet, which consists of a combination of numerous networks. In each of these networks telecommunication service providers (ISPs, companies, universities ...) assume the tasks, for example, of providing Internet access to end-users, content or other services. The Internet Analysis System acquires its raw data from probes implemented and operated by the network operators. The raw data are transmitted via the Secure Raw Data Transfer Protocol (RDTPs) specified for this purpose.

The probes can send the raw data to one or more evaluation systems. Each network is able to perform its own analyses with its evaluation system. In order to achieve a global and representative perspective of the Internet, probes have to be operated in various types of networks, such as the Global Tier One Provider, Transit Provider, Eyeball Internet Service Provider, Content Provider and Business Networks, as well as various regions (see also in Internet Germany [Dierichs2005]).

4 Tasks and Mode of Operation of the Probes

It is the task of the probes to extract information from a communication data stream which provides details of the status and use of the communication line and the network or networks behind them. Here all information should be retained which is required to detect misuse, a misconfiguration, trend developments or an attack situation. At the same time, however, the quantity of information should be restricted to the minimum required so that the information can also be considered and analyzed retrospectively over long periods. A further important point for the operation of the probes is that the information extracted by the probes, the so-called raw data, does not contain any information relevant to German data protection law.

Technically the network connection is accessed passively and the communication parameters of the various protocols at the communication levels counted. The results of the counts are transferred at defined intervals to the raw data transfer system.

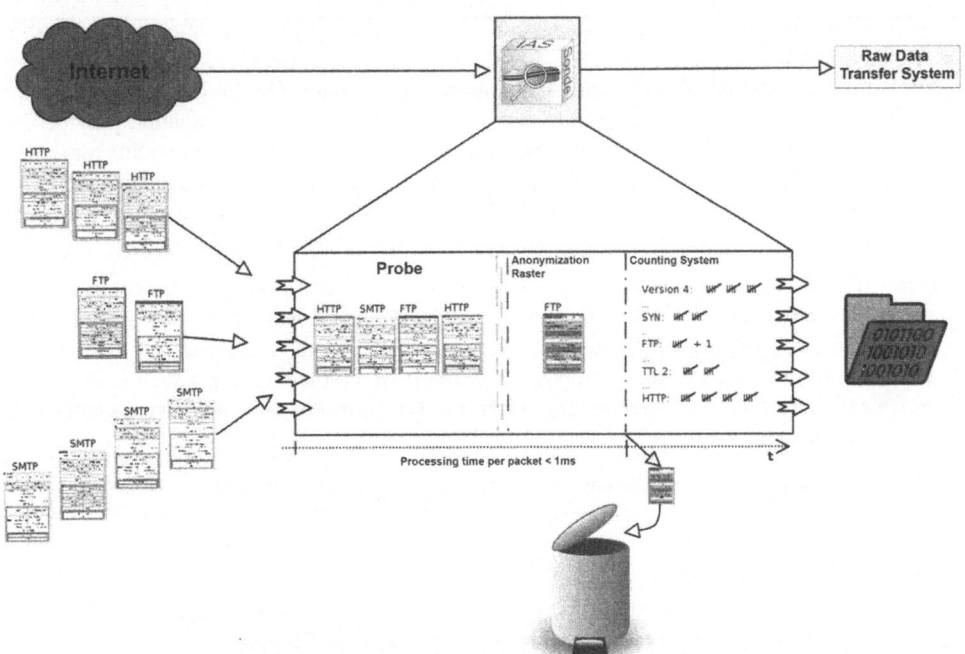

Figure 3: Principle of raw data collection

Illustration 3 shows the principle of raw data collection by the probes. This is divided up into three sections. The Internet is represented on the left. Packets of three different application sessions are shown: related HTTP packets, an FTP session and an SMTP session. The probe is located in the middle of illustration 3. The packets of the three applications are accessed passively by the probe one after the other in their random order and evaluated. The packet that is accessed is channeled through several analysis categories, each of which is responsible for a certain protocol. These evaluate strictly defined communication parameters in the protocol header at the various communication levels which are not relevant to data protection law. The counters allocated in the counting system are incremented according to how the header information of the packet is filled out. The frequency of certain header information is recorded in the same way as on a tally sheet. For example, in illustration 3 the accessing of the FTP packet is recorded by incrementing the FTP counter by 1. The raw data are therefore aggregates of counters, i.e. counters of communication parameters that have appeared at the various communication levels over a defined period. The packet - in illustration 3 an FTP packet - is immediately deleted physically, i.e. irreversibly and without trace, by the probe [Proest2005].

ID	Description	Count
131134	IP (Protocol Number 6)	: 18.854.151
131145	IP (Protocol Number 17)	: 1.123.149
327708	TCP (Flags: SYN)	: 334.435
327723	TCP (Flags: FIN/ACK)	: 480.697
327724	TCP (Flags: SYN/ACK)	: 275.779
545857	HTTP (Request Method POST)	: 2.026
545861	HTTP (Request Method GET)	: 293.616
545863	HTTP (Request Method HEAD)	: 18.992

Figure 4: Counting system in the probe

Reconstitution of the context of a packet or only a communication parameter is not possible or necessary. At definable intervals the counter readings (raw data) of the probes can be transmitted to the raw data transfer system. All of this information is completely anonymous, as shown in Illustration 4. On the right after the colon are the counter readings for the header information specified on the left. Each line stands for a counter. On the left-hand side of the colon is the count-if function (appearance of the corresponding communication parameters) and on the right the number of packets which contained the communication parameter during the defined measurement period. For example, line 2 of the raw data shown indicates that 1,123,149 packets with the IP protocol number 17 (UDP) appeared in the prescribed time. The count-if functions and their codings are specified in a versioned XML file.

The raw data transfer system functions as a server to which the probes can connect in order to transmit their raw data for a defined period. This is a unidirectional connection, meaning that a connection can only be established from the probe side. A probe can transmit the raw data to one or more raw data transfer systems. An example of a typical configuration is that every 5 minutes the raw data, for example 20 kilobytes in size, are sent to its own and a central raw data transfer system.

As the raw data are only a statistical formulation of the actual communication data, it would also be sufficient if not every packet were considered, but for example only every 10th packet. This aspect can be a pragmatic solution in the case of very high communication data rates, without producing a different result from a statistical point of view.

6 Evaluation of the Collective Raw Data

The actual evaluation and processing of the collected information takes place in various analytical modules (AM) of the evaluation system. In Illustration 2 these are designated "AM1" - "AM5". The modules procure the information exclusively from the knowledge base (raw data and evaluation results). The aim of the various modules is the compilation of profiles, statistics and interrelationships, as well as the detection of where threshold values are exceeded and the graphic processing of the raw data and evaluation results.

As the raw data consist of completely anonymous information, they could also be exchanged between various network operators or collected at a central point in order to be used as the basis for a global perspective and analyses of an IT early warning system.

7 User Interface of the Internet Analysis System

There are many conceivable methods of displaying the results of the Internet Analysis System. Illustration 2 contains examples of the following: large-screen technology, a Web Client and a PDA. The large screen technology serves the purpose of continually updating the display of certain statistics, profiles and current statuses. By means of an intelligent client, more extensive analyses can be carried out with the evaluation system and the results recorded. Additionally, warning messages from the system can be received in mobile form, for example by a PDA, so that an initial overview of the hazard situation can be obtained. Currently the Internet Analysis System uses a stand-alone client as a front-end. Through this client all counter readings can be displayed for freely selectable periods. It is possible to include further functions by means of a plug-in system.

8 Results of the Internet Analysis Systems

For the purposes of illustration some results are presented in this section in order to provide an idea of the possibilities of the current status of the Internet Analysis System. At present there are approximately 300,000 different counters of communication parameters incorporated for the various communication levels. This large number clearly shows how complex the results can be.

8.1 Transport Protocol Distribution

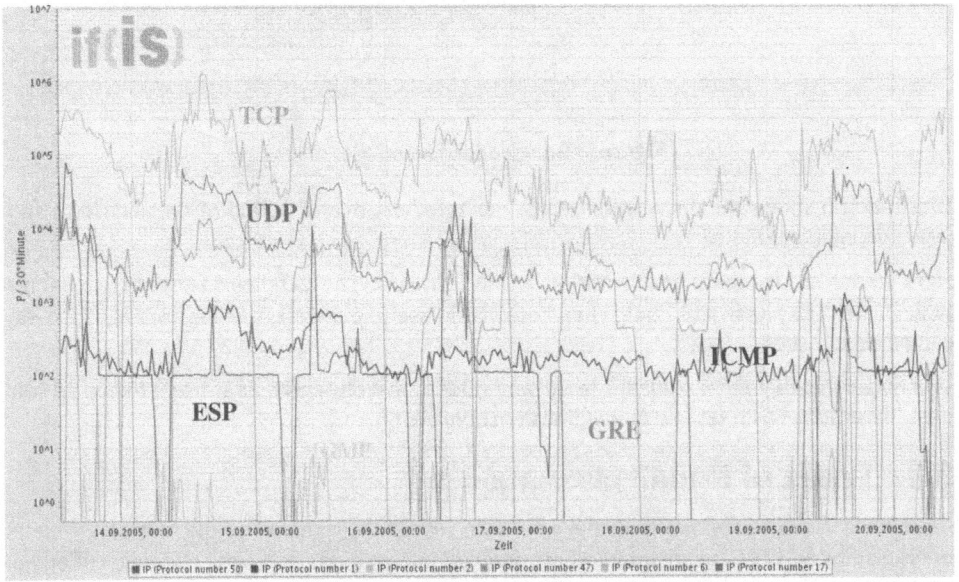

Figure 5: Protocols of the transport layer

Illustration 5 shows the distribution of the protocols of the transport layer used over a period of several days for a specific communication line. From the past the Internet Analysis System knows the profile, the standard deviation and from this can display an indication of untypical behavior. Additionally, the use of certain protocols can be determined, enabling capacity planning for the use of Virtual Private Networks (ESP protocol), for example. Protocol dependencies can also be detected: UDP appears to be proportional to TCP, which can be attributed to the dependencies of HTTP and DNS.

8.2   Browser Distribution (Technology Trend)

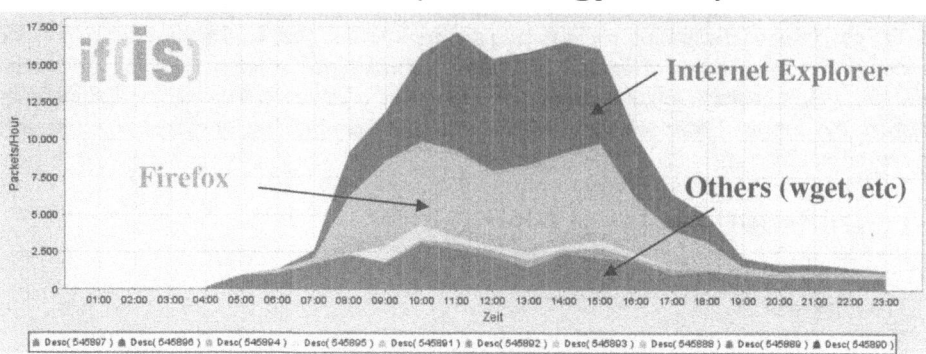

Figure 6: Browser distribution over time

Illustration 6 shows the distribution of various browsers over a period of one day for a specific communication line.

Here we can see the daily profile of the various browsers. The difference between manual use (e.g. Internet Explorer and Firefox) and automatic use (e.g. wget) over the course of the day can be clearly seen.

It is noticeable that these statistics in no way refer to a Web server, as is usual today. In contrast, these statistics refer to a communication connection.

8.3   Types of E-mail Messages

Illustration 7 shows the ability of the system to record the statistics of the headers of the e-mails sent by SMTP. The distribution can provide information on general communication behavior, as well as deviations from it. Illustration 7 shows an example of normal behavior in which the total number of messages without attachments represents 60% of all messages. These e-mails include messages with the text/plain, text/html and multipart/alternative content types. As a rule, e-mails with attachments are provided with the multipart/mixed content type. A mixed form is e-mails with the multipart/related content type. Here, for example, images are integrated directly into the text. If these e-mails are included in the e-mails with an attachment, approximately 36% of all e-mails are sent with an attachment. The remaining 4% essentially consist of confirmations of reading with the multipart/report content type. An abrupt change to these values in particular may indicate a wave of spam affecting a company from the outside, or indicate that a computer is sending spam from within the company.

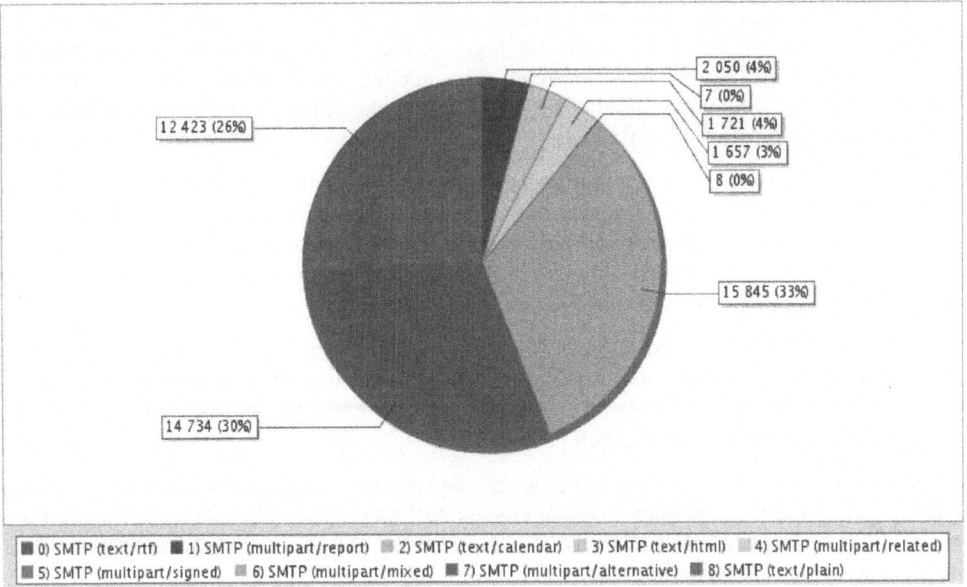

Figure 7: Distribution of e-mail "Content Types"

9 Uses of the Internet Analysis System

Special operators with their own evaluation system are informed by the system when problems occur and can use the wide-ranging resources offered by the system in the analysis of the problems. A clear representation of the current status of their own system and an informative reporting system represent the basis for reliable network operation.

If their own system forms part of a central evaluation system, information on problems with a participant is passed on in good time, so that countermeasures can be taken at an early stage by all.

10 Conclusion

With the help of the probe-based Internet Analysis System it is possible to continuously acquire raw data which provide a statistical reflection of Internet traffic. Through the evaluation of the raw data at the various communication levels, such as the network layer, transport layer and application layer, it is possible to derive very detailed information.

By analyzing the results of various probes it is possible to depict a global perspective of the Internet and define warning levels in the case of problems, such as infrastructure failures or attacks. Further analyses of the raw data allow the forecasting of trends in the use of protocols, network services and attacks.

A further important process is the exact analysis of the raw data in order to correlate the results with information from other network analysis tools. With the interrelationships that are created it is possible to detect patterns and thereby compile results in the form of statistics, patterns, attack scenarios and, as a subject of research at the moment, forecasts. In turn, these results can be incorporated into the review and evaluation process in order to acquire ever more accurate results at an increasingly earlier stage. Here the extent of the raw data pool is of crucial importance: the more raw data that can be analyzed - with respect not only to the number of various probes and their positioning, but also the time period of the information - the more accurate results are to be expected. This applies in particular to the forecast analyses, as algorithms which are suitable for carrying out the corresponding analyses require a particularly large quantity of initial data.

The Institute for Internet Security has successfully completed the second development phase in collaboration with the BSI. The system has proved its worth during operation. Partners are now being sought to join the network and operate further probes and evaluation systems. Organizations who wish to operate only one probe will receive an informative report about their network traffic once a month from the central evaluation system.

In addition to operation of the Internet Analysis System, the project will also be moved forward to a third development and research phase. In order to obtain additional information, further protocols will be implemented and existing ones extended. Furthermore, the evaluation modules and attack detection will be expanded.

In the field of research, statistical methods and data mining algorithms will be used to design intelligent processes intended to accelerate the evaluation process. The quality of the results is steadily improving as a result of the continuous analysis and the incorporation of the experience gained of the analytical process.

By its very nature the Internet is extremely flexible and complex and subject to daily changes. In order to be able to provide statistics on the Internet and for any future technologies, the Internet Analysis System also has to be extremely flexible in its basic form.

For an extensive IT early warning system the Internet Analysis System can, for example, be expanded by an availability system and log data evaluation system.

It is therefore important that this system is used both flexibly and globally in order to allow - just as in the traffic jam on the motorway/freeway - a global perspective of the structures and dangers.

Further information

Institute for Internet Security, https://www.internet-sicherheit.de

Federal Office for Information Security (BSI), http://www.bsi.de/english/index.htm

References

[Dierichs2005] Dierichs, Stefan; Pohlmann, Norbert: "Netz-Deutschland", iX - Magazin für professionelle Informationstechnik, Heise-Verlag, 12/2005

[Pohlmann2005] Pohlmann, Norbert: "Internetstatistik", Proceedings of CIP Europe 2005, publisher: B.M. Hämmerli, S.D. Wolthusen; Gesellschaft für Informatik, Bonn 2005

[Proest2005] Proest, Marcus: "Internet-Analyse - Ein Blick in die Dunkelheit", conference: Internet security 2005; http://www.internet-sicherheit.de/center-berichte.html

IT Security Vulnerability and Incident Response Management

Wim Hafkamp

Rabobank Nederland / University of Twente The Netherlands
w.h.m.hafkamp@rn.rabobank.nl

Abstract

This paper summarises the results of a Dutch PhD research project on IT security vulnerability and incident response management, which is supervised by the University of Twente in the Netherlands and which is currently in its final stage. Vulnerabilities are 'failures or weaknesses in computer (application) system design, implementation or operation which can be exploited to violate the security policy defined for that system'. Incidents are defined as 'events that have actual or potentially adverse effects on computer or network operations resulting in fraud, waste or abuse, compromise of information or loss or damage of property of information'. Hacking, denial-of-service attacks and computer viruses are examples of such events. The research project identifies a number of shortcomings in IT service management processes which affect the speed and quality of IT security vulnerability and incident response processes in enterprises. To shorten the lifecycle of vulnerabilities organizations should implement three basic process elements: (1) filtering and analyzing of vulnerability announcements and alerts, (2) prioritizing of vulnerability response activities and (3) scanning of infrastructure components. Each of these steps can be related to specific IT service management processes and to IT security incident management in particular. Using checklists, procedures and dedicated response capabilities, IT organizations are able to faster detect and respond to incidents.

1 Context

In a few years time, the amount of time available to fix known security vulnerabilities in software[1] has decreased tremendously. Time-to-patch is critical because programs that take opportunity of software vulnerabilities, the so-called exploits, are nowadays available for download from the Internet within a few days after such vulnerabilities are discovered[2]. Security experts have already warned for the appearance of so-called zero day exploits; these are exploits for which for which the IT branch of trade does not yet have patches available.

---

[1] Also known as 'security patching'.

[2] According to Symantec's Internet Security Threat Report, Trends for July 05 – December 05, volume IX (March 2006), the average time between the announcement of a vulnerability and the appearance of exploit code is merely 6.9 days.

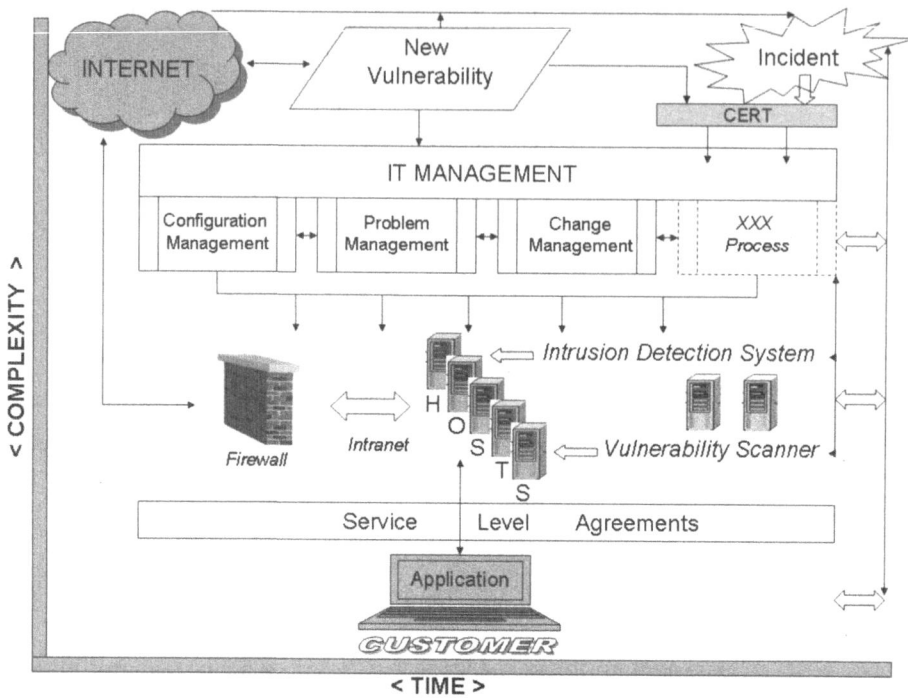

Fig. 1: IT service management processes related to vulnerabilities and incidents

The time-to-patch issue is of major significance to IT security vulnerability and incident management, the aim of which is to counter newly discovered vulnerabilities and associated exploits in a time efficient manner. Nonetheless, enterprises with complex IT infrastructures have usually organised IT service management according to an integrated process approach, which is often based on standards such as ISO/IEC 20000 (Information technology – Service management). In such organisations, it is well understood that solid IT change management procedures are essential for complying with contractual service level agreements. However, enforcing solid IT change management procedures could stand in the way of providing the quick responses that are required for effective IT security vulnerability and incident management.

2 State-of-the-Practise

2.1 IT Management

By the end of the 1990's enterprises in the Netherlands and in other European countries began organizing their IT management processes according to the principles defined by the IT Infrastructure Library (ITIL). As the abbreviation implies, ITIL is a library of best practices ('standards') describing knowledge and experience accumulated over many years with various aspects of development, maintenance and management of IT processes. The first set of ITIL books only described the IT viewpoint. From 2000 on, a 'Business Perspective Set' was developed to narrow the gap between business and IT, addressing subjects such as outsourcing and Business Continuity Management (BCM). The core of ITIL consists of two sets of books named 'Service Delivery Set [BART01] and 'Service Support Set'[BERK00].

Table 1: Examples of ITIL processes

What is needed to deliver IT services to customers (Service Delivery)	Access to IT services and to IT service providers (Service Support)
Examples:	Examples:
Customer Relationship Management	Incident Management
Service Level Management	Problem Management
Availability Management	Configuration Management
IT Service Continuity Management	Change Management

IT Security Vulnerability and Incident Response activities are related to several of these standardized IT service management processes. Take for example the ITIL Change Management process. This process aims at effective and efficient handling and execution of IT related changes[3], in such a way that the impact to the quality of service is minimized. IT organizations often appoint two authorities: the Change Manager who orders for a Request-For-Change (RFC) and a Change Advisory Board (CAB) which approves submitted RFCs. In many organizations the CAB is composed of IT management and business representatives and usually meets once or twice a week. According to ITIL, an RFC should contain at a minimum: details about the (specific) configuration items involved, the description of the proposed change, the foreseen impact on IT services, a fallback scenario and the proposed implementation date and time.

Within the change process three basic steps can be recognized. The first step is preparation. During this step an RFC has been initialized and drawn up and the impact for the IT organization, e.g. needed resources, and the urgency of the request has been determined and approved by the CAB. The second step is the testing and implementation of the change. After testing, the change is implemented in the IT production environment. Because IT service delivery cannot always be guaranteed during implementation of a change, organizations sometimes use a maintenance window for this purpose[4]. During the third and last step the implementation of the change is finally accepted by the IT manager. Important questions here are 'does the change work?' and 'are there any problems left?'. A back-out plan is needed in case problems do occur that are related to the implementation of the change.

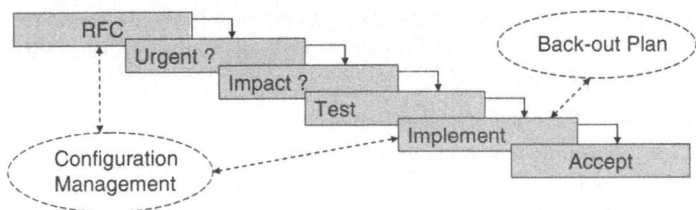

Fig. 2: a standardized change management process

2.2 Computer Emergency Response Teams

A major virus incident on the Internet in 1988, the outbreak of the Morris worm, has lead to the foundation of the first Internet related Computer Security Incident Response Team

---

[3] E.g. a new software release or a program temporary fix (patch) provided by a vendor.

[4] Non (or restricted) service hours used for testing and/or maintenance purposes; maintenance windows are often scheduled during weekends.

(CSIRT): CERT/CC[5]. Later on, many organizations, including universities, military and commercial product and service providers, etc. founded their own incident response teams. CSIRTs vary in size and often handle a variety of mission statements and operational frameworks. The main reason for differences between CSIRTs is that they work for different user groups (called 'constituencies'). What binds them is the type of services they provide, such as artifact analysis, computer security incident response, vulnerability analysis, announcement services, educational services, etc. [WESK03]. Forums like Terena's TF-CSIRT and FIRST offer CSIRT teams a platform for sharing knowledge and experiences about the services they deliver. One of the issues that CSIRTs[6] have to deal with nowadays is the so-called 'vulnerability disclosure problem' [OUUN03]. After having received information about a newly discovered IT security vulnerability, a CSIRT has to decide the time and level of detail of the announcements to their constituency. This is of particular importance when there is no strong solution, such as a security patch, available for solving the problem at the time of announcement.

2.3 Technology push

2.3.1 Intrusion detection systems

Some fifteen years ago, many organizations realized that firewall protection alone was not sufficient to mitigate the risks associated with external connections. One of the reasons for this is that firewalls do neither provide protection against system administration errors nor against insider attacks. For this reason, IT network departments began implementing real-time intrusion detection systems.

Intrusion Detection Systems (IDS) are either network based or host based and designed for anomaly detection or misuse detection.

The difference between anomaly and misuse detection is the way in which the IDS system interprets potential intrusions. An anomaly detection based IDS identifies (statistical) deviations from 'normal use' of a guarded system or network [Denn87]. An IDS system based on misuse detection compares data in system logs or data packets transported over the network with known attack signatures stored in a database. The outcome of the IDS analysis processes may lead to an 'active' or a 'passive' response. An example of a passive response would be sending alerts to a system console. Rebecca Gurley Base [Base00] distinguishes three forms of active responses:

1. searching for and creating extra information;
2. changing the environment, e.g. changing parameters;
3. generating automatic counteractions, e.g. back tracing the attack and denial-of-service an external IP address.

Dealing with false positives, wrongly automated responses and lack of generally accepted best practices are currently major challenges for organizations that want to implement intrusion detection systems [CMUS00].

---

[5] Computer Emergency Response Team Co-ordination Center, Software Engineering Institute of Carnegie Mellon University, Pittsburgh U.S.A.

[6] In particular CSIRTs working for IT software vendors.

2.4 Vulnerability Scanning

Vulnerability scanning is a structured way to find known vulnerabilities, such as misconfiguration and missing patches, in software components of the IT infrastructure. A variety of scanners is used today. Vendors offer specific (web) application scanners but also generic IT system scanners. Freeware scanners are available for download on the Internet [7].

Most scanners work with databases which contain 'fingerprints' of known vulnerabilities. This database should be updated on a regular basis to account for recently detected vulnerabilities.

A local scanner is implemented on a particular system and which is activated by an administrator. A remote scanner scans systems which belong to a defined range of network addresses. The remote scanner software and the remote scan results are often stored on a dedicated scan server. Remote scanning needs some fine tuning. Firstly, the effects of scanning on network and system performance needs to be addressed. Secondly, firewalls in the (internal) network may block the scanner's network packets and therefore, the firewall rules must be extended to allow specific network traffic from the remote scan server. Thirdly, one of the preconditions of remote vulnerability scanning is that all systems to be scanned should be online during the actual scan. For example, organizations where a large numbers of laptops is deployed face the risk that many of these laptops will not be scanned on a regular basis.

Although vulnerability scanning is usually associated with IT operations, more and more software developers use scanning tools to be able to discover security vulnerabilities during various stages of software development [Nico03].

3 Case studies

The research project started by the end of 2002. The research covers the three topics mentioned above and relates them to each other. In 2003 and 2004, three case studies were executed in the Netherlands:

1. a global study on IT security incident and vulnerability response management processes implemented by ten banks;
2. a study about the organization and operational framework of three CSIRTs;
3. a study about IT forensic methods used by the Dutch National Police.

Key findings in the case studies are described below.

3.1 ITIL

ITIL is a de facto IT management standard within the financial sector in the Netherlands. Every bank has implemented ITIL Service Support oriented processes like Incident Management and Change Management. Most of the IT organizations of the visited banks use service level agreements to formalize IT services provided to the business, including the performance and availability of systems and/or applications. The banks have a reserved attitude towards software patching. During interviews we often heard that software patching is considered a time consuming issue, due to formal test procedures and fixed maintenance windows. The

---

[7] NESSUS is a well known IT infrastructure vulnerability scanner; until recently it could be freely downloaded from the Internet.

case study uncovered that none of the banks had developed a specific security patch policy as part of an overall change management system. Some banks indicated the existence of emergency change procedures for urgent changes but use of these specific procedures was often quite intuitive. A lot of 'security media attention' stimulates the decision process for such changes but the IT Change Advisory Board and business representatives still decide on the implementation of urgent changes in much the same way as for normal changes.

3.2 IT security incidents

Crime related IT security incidents are in most cases difficult to handle. During one of the case studies an insider attack was analysed by interviewing and studying the victim organization and by interviewing the police investigators. The results show a poor recognition of incidents that are difficult (or impossible) to detect by automated scanners, segregation of incident response capabilities within large organizations and utmost emphasis on maintaining a 'chain-of-evidence' by using specific forensic procedures and tools.

3.3 Computer Security Incident Response Teams

Computer Security Incident Response Teams (CSIRTs) are common in the Dutch university IT environment. Surfnet-CERT is one of the oldest incident response teams worldwide. The members of Surfnet-CERT are computer specialists with a strong Unix, NT or computer networking background. The Surfnet CSIRT acts as a coordinating CSIRT [Kill03] for many other research or university related CSIRTs. The three visited CSIRTs vary in size and services offered. Incident response handling and communication of vulnerability announcements constitutes their major activity. Most CSIRTs operate conform an operational framework which prioritizes the handling of certain types of incidents, formulates a code of conduct for CSIRT employees and gives rules on how to register incidents. Surfnet-CERT is a member of the Forum of Incident Response and Security Teams (FIRST) and the TERENA Taskforce CSIRT (TF-CSIRT). Due to its connection to the worldwide network of specialists Surfnet-CERT often receives incident and information about newly discovered vulnerabilities in a (very) early stage. The external network also provides opportunities to discuss incident handling activities.

4 Conclusions & Recommendations
4.1 Conclusions

Generally speaking, the conclusion is that the effectiveness of IT security vulnerability and incident response of enterprises with complex IT infrastructures nowadays is rather poor. IT security patch implementation periods of two or more weeks are not exceptional. Furthermore, forensic evidence is sometimes destroyed or neglected due to shortcomings in the incident response process.

4.2 Recommendations
4.2.1 Vulnerability lifecycle management

The handling of unstructured vulnerability announcements which are received from various information sources is the first challenge of every managed vulnerability response process. Therefore, the process should start with the selection of appropriate vulnerability announcement sources. In the scheme below, four types of sources are included.

Having established that the information originates from a reliable source, it should be subjected to some level of quality control before being further analyzed. Structured layout, detailed impact and complexity level descriptions, CVE (Common Vulnerabilities and Exposures) number[8] and references to available fixes are minimum requirements. For further handling, the receiver of the information, which is often the IT security manager, should ticket a new vulnerability in the incident registration database (with the CVE number), to ensure handling of the information obtained according to the established processes.

Having completed the registration, the organization must determine the importance (relevance) of the newly discovered vulnerability. Two important questions are to be answered: (1) is a vulnerable component present within the IT infrastructure and if so, (2) how important is that component for the organisation? To answer these questions the ITIL configuration management process can be of help. The first question can be answered by checking the Configuration Management Database System (CMDS) that contains all IT configuration items of the infrastructure. The incident ticket can be closed, if the answer is to the second question is a simple 'not important' but in general, this question is a bit more difficult to answer. Some organizations record a criticality code for every configuration item in the CMDS and this will provide the answer. If this is not the case, a criticality classification of the infrastructure is advised, e.g. determination of the criticality of application servers, infrastructure components and workstations.

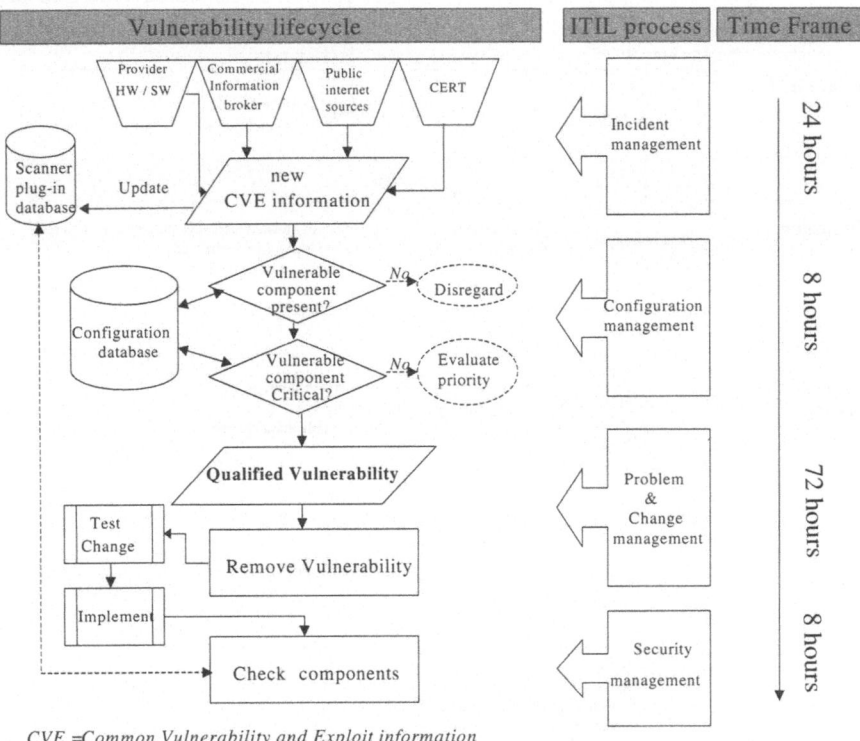

CVE =Common Vulnerability and Exploit information

Fig. 3: Vulnerability lifecycle

---

[8] See http://cve.mitre.org.

After having answered both questions, the organization knows whether or not it should trigger a (prioritized) change process. The change process will often take some time. I have averaged this towards 72 hours for 'qualified' urgent changes. During this time fixes or workarounds that are available have to be downloaded and tested and an implementation plan has to be set-up. The existence of a standardized infrastructure and patch management tools will of course accelerate the process.

Finally, IT security management should check within 8 hours after the implementation of the prioritized security change whether the vulnerability has been removed by scanning (parts of) the application systems or infrastructure.

In the model I have indicated a controlled vulnerability lifecycle management of less than five days for qualified vulnerabilities by using implemented ITIL oriented IT service management processes.

4.2.2 IT security incident responses

The second recommendation is about the handling of IT security incidents. As stated before, recognition of IT security incidents which are not automatically detected by tools[9] is a main problem. ITIL oriented organizations often deploy a structured incident management process which defines several support and escalation levels. An indicator checklist can help the IT organizations first level support to determine whether or whether not additional IT security support and/or escalation levels have to be involved once an incident has been reported.

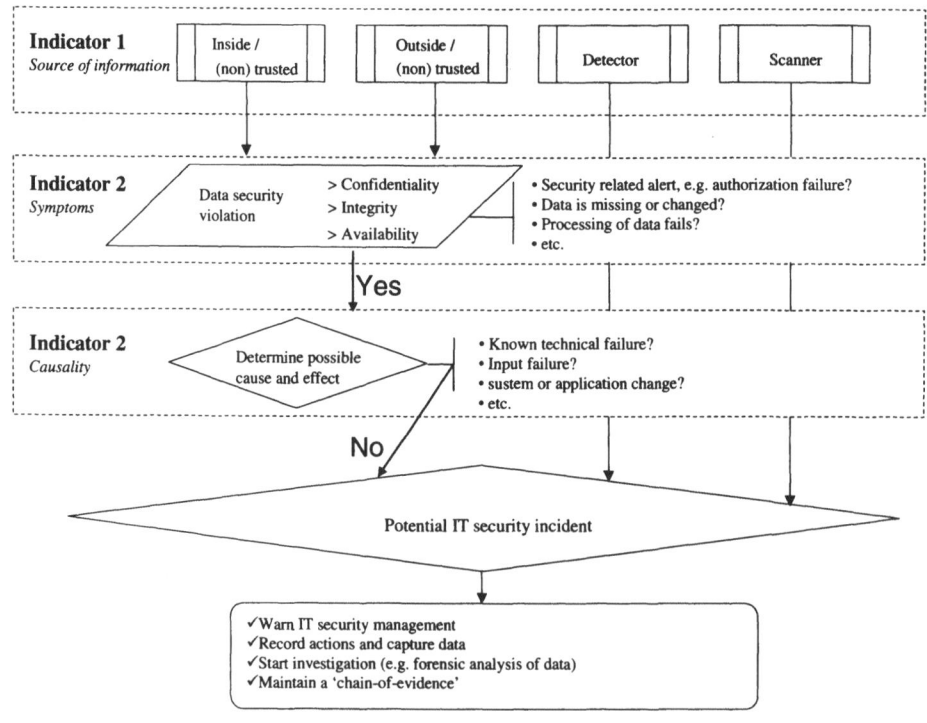

Fig. 4: IT security indicator checklist

---

[9] E.g. virus scanners or intrusion detection systems.

The checklist contains three indicators. The first indicator is about the information source. Scanner or detector alerts for instance should not be analyzed by IT first level support but should be directly forwarded to the department that bears the responsibility for these tools. Secondly, first level support should analyse the symptoms of the reported incidents to determine whether confidentiality, integrity or availability of information is affected [MAPR01]. The third and last step is about causality. By correlating the incident with other known issues, like a recently implemented change, technical system problems, etc. a possible cause can be determined. After the last step first level support may ticket the incident with a label 'possible IT security incident' and inform IT security management for further instructions.

IT security management should proceed according to a procedure which defines what actions have to be taken in case a potential IT security incident is detected. If the organization has a CSIRT in place, it is advised that in this stage the CSIRT takes over, investigates the incident and advises IT problem management which measures should be taken to start an investigation and to maintain a 'chain-of-evidence' [ADKR04]. Status reports should be send to the IT problem manager involved. This manager is also accountable for the implementation of any preventive measures that would be deemed necessary after having carried out the investigation.

References

[ADKR04] Alberts C. et al., *Defining Incident Management Processes for CSIRTs : A Work in Progress*, Carnegy Mellon University / Software Engineering Institute, Pittburgh U.S.A., 2004

[BART01] Bartlett J. et al, *Best Practice for Service Delivery*, The Stationary Office, Norwich U.K., 2001

[Base00] Bace R., *Intrusion Detection*, MacMillan Technical Publishing, Indianapolis U.S.A., 2000

[BERK00] Berkhout M. et al, *Best Practise for Service Support*, The Stationary Office, Norwich U.K., 2000

[CMUS00] Allen J. et al., *State of the Practise of Intrusion Detection Technologies*, Technical Report, Carnegy Mellon University / Software Engineering Institute, Pittsburgh U.S.A., 2000

[Denn87] Denning D., An *Intrusion-Detection Model*, IEEE Transactions on Software Engineering, Vol. SE-13, No. 2, February 1987

[Kill03] Killcrece G. et al., *Organizational models for Computer Security Incident Teams*, Carnegie Mellon Sofware Engineering Institute, Pittsburgh U.S.A., 2003

[MAPR01] Mandia K. & Prosise C., *Incident Response, investigating computer crime*, McGraw-Hill, U.S.A., 2001

[Nico03] Nicolett M., *Vulnerability Management Defined*, Gartner research note, available at www.gartner.com, September 2003

[OUUN03] Oulu University Secure Programming Group, *Communication in the Software Vulnerability Reporting Process*, available at www.ee.oulu.fi/research/ouspg, 2003

[WESK03] West-Brown M.J. et al, *Handbook for Computer Security Incident Response Teams, Second Edition*, Carnegie Mellon University / Software Engineering Institute, Pittsburgh U.S.A, 2003

Blending Corporate Governance with Information Security

Yves Le Roux

CA
25 Quai Paul Doumer
F-92408 COURBEVOIE CEDEX
Yves.leroux@ca.com

Abstract

Information security requires CEO attention in their individual companies and as business leaders seeking collectively to promote the development of standards for secure technology.

Furthermore, Boards of directors should consider information security an essential element of corporate governance and a top priority for board review.

In establishing this approach, there are five principles that will help guide executive thinking:

1. The first principle is that the CEO must get involved in the understanding of the security program, the measurement of that program and the relation that program has to business operations.
2. The second principle is that the organization itself has to understand that information assets must be thought of as being as measurable and as tangible as buildings and plants and other valuable business infrastructure
3. The third principle is that we must follow the information and not the system.
4. The fourth principle is that we evaluate the information security services that have been implemented and find a way to validate that they are working.
5. The fifth principle, every bit as important as the others, is that it is vital for organizations to analyze where they stand in their information security governance efforts compared to others in their industry.

To implement these principles, information security stakeholders need to make significant shifts in their perspective. Such shifts allow them to ask the right questions, make better decisions, and select actions appropriate to the effective governance of enterprise security. We will explain these shifts.

The next point is to divide the work across five areas of responsibility.

According to our principles, we will describe a framework addressing all components of the enterprise security program not just the technical components

1 How to define "Corporate Governance"

Governance has proved an issue since people began to organise themselves for a common purpose. How to ensure the power of organisation is harnessed for the agreed purpose, rather than diverted to some other purpose, is a constant theme.

The institutions of governance provide a framework within which the social and economic life of countries is conducted. Corporate governance concerns the exercise of power in corporate entities. The OECD provides the most authoritative functional definition of corporate governance [OECD]:

> *"Corporate governance is the system by which business corporations are directed and controlled. The corporate governance structure specifies the distribution of*

S. Paulus, N. Pohlmann, H. Reimer (Editors): Securing Electronic Business Processes, Vieweg (2006), 396-404

rights and responsibilities among different participants in the corporation, such as the board, managers, shareholders and other stakeholders, and spells out the rules and procedures for making decisions on corporate affairs. By doing this, it also provides the structure through which the company objectives are set, and the means of attaining those objectives and monitoring performance. "

However, corporate governance has wider implications and is critical to economic and social well being, firstly in providing the incentives and performance measures to achieve business success, and secondly in providing the accountability and transparency to ensure the equitable distribution of the resulting wealth. The significance of corporate governance for the stability and equity of society is captured in the broader definition of the concept offered by the World Bank:

"Corporate governance is concerned with holding the balance between economic and social goals and between individual and communal goals. The governance framework is there to encourage the efficient use of resources and equally to require accountability for the stewardship of those resources. The aim is to align as nearly as possible the interests of individuals, corporations and society. "

On 21 May 2003, the Commission adopted an Action Plan announcing measures to modernise company law and enhance corporate governance in the European Union. [CEC]

In the Action Plan, the Commission announced that it would confirm the collective responsibility of board members for financial statements and key non-financial information, increase transparency in intra group relations and transactions with related parties and improve disclosure about corporate governance practices.

With regard to the responsibility of board members, the prevailing principle in Europe is - in contrast to the US - collective responsibility for the financial statements. As can be seen from the Action Plan on Company Law and Corporate Governance, the Commission intends to clarify the application of this principle and to extend it to key non-financial information. Further corporate scandals have confirmed a need to clarify that all board members are collectively responsible for financial statements and key non-financial information and that all board members have to be held accountable for their actions and proper conduct of their responsibilities. This is a main difference with Sarbanes Oxley Act where CEO and CFO are personally responsible. On this point, we must notice that in Germany, half of the supervisory board seats of large companies (more then 2,000 employees) are filled by labor representatives. This gives labor control rights over corporate decisions and leads to a kind of negotiated management where labor has voice as an alternative to exit.

Many companies are organised in group structures. However, intra group transactions and the group's transactions with related parties often lack transparency seen from the perspective of investors, shareholders and other stakeholders. This can make it difficult for them to assess the true risks of investing in the companies.

In relation to transactions within a group and with related parties, the Commission will consider how further improvements can be made in line with International Financial Reporting Standards.

Corporate governance practices used differ across Member States. Enhanced disclosure about these practices could provide a useful insight into what happens in practice and to promote best practices. In its Action Plan, the Commission therefore proposed that listed companies should publish an annual corporate governance statement. The main objective would be to collect all relevant information concerning corporate governance elements and practices in listed companies in one single place. This should allow shareholders, investors and other stakeholders to assess whether the company pursues good corporate governance.

A recent Business Roundtable report, *Securing Cyberspace: Business Roundtable's Framework for the Future* asserted that

- "Information security requires CEO attention in their individual companies and as business leaders seeking collectively to promote the development of standards for secure technology.
- Boards of directors should consider information security an essential element of corporate governance and a top priority for board review."

2 Principles

Information security is an important part of the overall business risk and the external business environment that must be intimately understood by the stewards of the business. In establishing this approach, there are five principles that will help guide executive thinking.

2.1 CEO Involvement

The first principle is that the CEO must get involved in the understanding of the security program, the measurement of that program and the relation that program has to business operations. The CEO must take the lead in requiring regular reporting, evaluation and review of information security strategies and execution. He or she must engage with management teams throughout the enterprise to discuss what the security results look like, how security might impact the business, and how risk might be created or alleviated. He or she must then provide an overall assessment of the organization's security performance, including what is being done well, and what is being done to correct previously identified deficiencies. This assessment must be communicated to the board as well as to shareholders, stakeholders and employees.

2.2 Organizational Understanding of Information Assets

The second principle is that the organization itself has to understand that information assets must be thought of as being as measurable and as tangible as buildings and plants and other valuable business infrastructure. Day-to-day policies and procedures need to reflect the fact that it is up to the organization to protect these assets in the same way.

The policies and the procedures that the company creates have to be well thought out, so the culture is built with the understanding that there is some level of risk involved with the normal day-to-day business use of information assets. These assets need to be cared for and protected accordingly. Appropriate individuals within a security management infrastructure must be given both authority and accountability; one without the other is not sufficient.

Today, the majority of information security officers are often given authority without accountability. For corporate security to be a serious endeavor, these managers must be empowered. Moreover, organizational cultural politics must be overcome so that the newly empowered security executives can engage with business leaders. The IT group can't fix information security alone; modeling risk enterprise requires a broad mandate and cooperation between groups inside the organization who may not have traditionally worked together.

Policies and procedures must make it plain that everyone who has any interaction with the corporate data assets has specific responsibilities, as well as the authority and the authorization, to proceed to protect those assets and to manage the risk inherent in using them.

2.3 Integrating Data Storage with the System Lifecycle

People would traditionally say, "That's the financial management system", or "That's the HR system", and then create lifecycle management around those applications without necessarily thinking about the individual data assets that reside on that system. We must begin to follow the information and not the system. If this were better understood, the process of information security would likely be different.

Information management and information security must become better aligned and integrated into the way the organization develops, installs, deploys, uses, maintains, monitors and validates the systems that house them.

2.4 Systems Must Be Tested

The concept of governance demands that we evaluate the information security services that have been implemented and find a way to validate that they are working. Testing needs to be done periodically and, as a formal way of responding to defects — breaches and violations — needs to be established. There also needs to be a way to evaluate and correct deficiencies, as well as a mechanism to communicate the fact that re-mediation has taken place. Just as you cannot secure what you don't know, you can't establish confidence that information security services are functioning without testing and reporting.

Also important is the speed in which a deficiency is remediated and effectively addressed. Information security governance suggests that the company must have a security knowledge management capability not only to understand IT risk, but also to be able to test readiness.

Security knowledge management is the ability to transform raw data into information, and information to knowledge.

Information security governance suggests that organizations must establish an incident response capability to deal with crisis. This crisis center operates in a continuous mode just like the commander's central command center in a field of battle. Once this knowledge is obtained, then it is possible to translate that into remedial action to deal with the deficiencies and the information security challenges. Then, just like a field commander who might continually exercise troop readiness, company executives can continuously evaluate enterprise response capability by launching exercises to validate information security readiness.

2.5 Comparative Analysis

The fifth principle, every bit as important as the others, is that it is vital for organizations to analyze where they stand in their information security governance efforts compared to others in their industry.

The strategy is to have the ability to make informed, strategic decisions as to the company's place in the pack by knowing what others in the industry and the marketplace are doing with respect to securing their information and by studying standards and "best guidance." This enables the organization to decide what its investment and commitment to information security should be, above and beyond any established mandatory minimums, based on a risk analysis.

One might look at maximums instead, choosing to be ahead of the pack and using information security governance superiority as a competitive advantage. This idea of leveraging information security as a competitive advantage is a valid strategy for some companies. Alternatively, the company might make an informed decision to be a laggard in this area, establishing the bare minimum and using the capital instead to seek competitive advantage in other areas. Anyhow, this is clearly a business decision to be taken at the highest level in the company

3 Shifts in Information Security Perspective

To implement these principles, information security stakeholders need to make significant shifts in their perspective. Such shifts allow them to ask the right questions, make better decisions, and select actions appropriate to the effective governance of enterprise security. These shifts are summarized below:

From "Security is a technical problem":

- Technical network (hardware, software, infrastructure)
- Technical requirements (protect the perimeter)
- Technical assets (desktops, laptops, servers, databases)
- Technical specialty (in the realm of IT and system administrators)

To "Security is an enterprise-wide problem":

- Enterprise network (people, processes, business units)
- Enterprise requirements (privacy, asset protection)
- Enterprise assets (customer data, employee data, communication)
- Enterprise core competency

From "Security has a technical owner":

- IT is the driver, owner, and primary benefactor.
- Technical personnel are assigned to security.
- The CSO (Chief Security Officer) is considered a technical advisor

To "Security is owned by the business":

- The enterprise is the driver, owner, and primary benefactor.
- Business personnel understand security and have security responsibilities.
- The CSO is considered an advisor to the business.

From "There is an explicit focus on security":

- Security is sporadically singled out for attention, investment, and justification.
- Risk assessment is applied to security as a special case.
- Security is on the agenda to comply with regulatory requirements.

To "Security is transparent":

- Security is a requirement of conducting business, considered in normal planning and business conduct cycles.
- A more secure state results from effective risk management capabilities.
- Existing security controls meet compliance requirements.

From "Security is an expense":

- The benefit of security is not measured or is hard to measure.
- Return on security investments is not required or quantifiable

To "Security is an investment":

- The benefit of security is measurable, measured, and regularly reported.
- Return on security investment is required and quantifiable in business terms

From "The goal is security":

- The focus of security efforts is on threat, vulnerability, and protection.
- There is no articulated, desired security state.
- There is a potentially excessive deployment of security technologies undertaken in a piecemeal approach.

To "The goal is business continuity and ultimately resiliency":

- The focus of security efforts is on impact, organizational continuity, and preserving trust.
- Adequate security that meets business objectives is the desired state.
- Security costs and risks are in business objectives is the desired state.
- Security costs and risks are in balance.

4 The fives areas of responsibility

An organization that will be successful in implementing an information security governance program needs to divide the work across five areas:

4.1 The Board of Directors.

The program must be very clear about the board's responsibilities. It will assign strategic oversight to the board, and ensure that the strategic oversight is aligned with the actions taken by the executive management team.

4.2 The CEO.

CEO responsibilities will be clearly defined in regard to accountability and authority. The CEO is the top executive and the only one in a position to oversee compliance. It is the CEO's role to assign the responsibility to make sure that accountability and authority are in place. The CEO is also there to set the tone and drive the culture of information security.

4.3 Executive Committee.

The executive committee will be responsible for ensuring that the security programs being put in place are actually aligned with operational and business goal risks. Not too much, and not too little. They must make certain that money is not being wasted on unneeded security and that security is not placing an undue burden on the organization and adversely affecting operations and business objectives.

4.4 Senior Managers.

Senior management will have responsibility for day-to-day monitoring of risks within their area of responsibility. They're accountable for the mechanisms implementing the policies coming out of the security program and for ensuring that operations are secure.

4.5 Employees.

Each individual employee must be aware of the challenges of information security. Ultimately, security is a very personal matter, so each member of the enterprise should have an understanding of information security and why it's important. They should know their individual roles, so they can report accurately through channels. Just as we are trained to ask an un-badged person we see walking through our building, so too should we, as individuals, be taught to challenge information security deficiencies that we encounter.

5 The Security Governance Framework & Architecture

Today's organizations still need, and expect security to continue to innovate to support the achievement of the business's tactical and strategic objectives. They need to ensure the safety, reliability, efficiency and availability of the services they're delivering. To succeed, organizations must have a more holistic and pragmatic approach to managing the enterprise. The following diagram presents conceptually the interaction of objectives and security activities from a Corporate Governance perspective

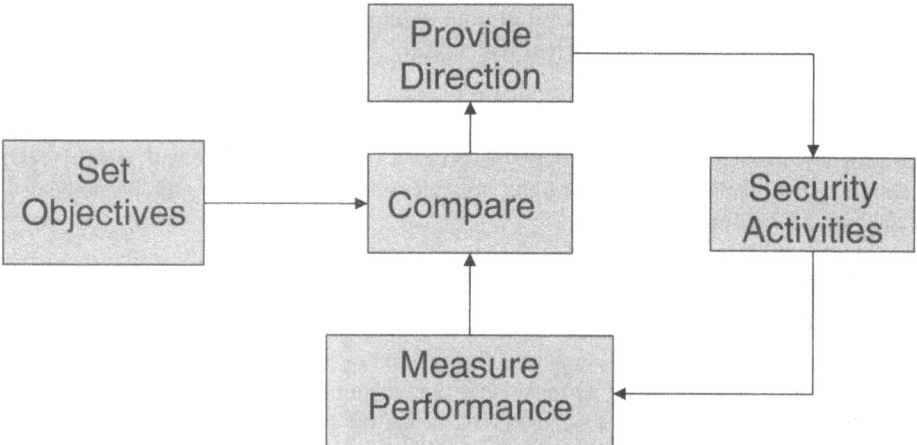

The governance process starts with setting objectives for the Information Security. The main objectives are

- To be aligned with the business
- To be a business "enabler" and not a "road blocker"
- To maximizes benefits
- To manage the risks appropriately

The architecture should be an obvious progression from the business requirements and justifiable as such. It should not be based on the current "wants" that is more typical with technology selection but on the business reason "why".

Starting with these objectives, a current status of the enterprise approach to Information assets risk will provide the "Information Security Culture" to gauge what the architecture has to be to be effective and how it will be received. Some important points to study are:

- How ready is the organization to adapt to change?
- Is the architecture going to be a significant change from where they are today?
- How much has the corporate approach to Information Security been considered?
- What are the business issues, and strategies that are defined that require an organized approach to security?
- Is there legislation or regulations that are pushing the organization in a certain direction?

The next step will be to provide direction for the security activities. The security activities will have four main objectives:

- **Manage Risk.** Control who has access to corporate assets, systems and information, and provide a comprehensive approach for information backup, recovery and failover. Enable compliance with consistently repeatable process automation and an audit trail of system actions to enable governance of the environment.
- **Improve Service.** Enable service level management to match the demands of the business to the delivery of the IT services that support them, ensuring that the needs of the business are met and the greatest value is delivered to the business. Manage the availability and security of services based on business priorities. Set IT management policies based on real-time business priorities.
- **Manage Cost.** Apply automation to decrease the labor costs required to maintain IT operations, thus freeing resources for strategic projects and new development to grow the business. Leverage the knowledge of the IT assets you own, what business services they support, and how much they are used to control capital expenses and optimize the financial value from the infrastructure.
- **Align Security Investments with Business.** Make more informed investment decisions. When you know how much it costs to support the business you can apply rigorous management techniques to ensure all of your resources, both people and technology, are being more effectively targeted and utilized.

In order to show the security effectiveness, the next step will be to measure performance.

Theses measurements must focus on a few critical objective indicators that truly enhance visibility and have a direct relationship with the defined objectives. It is important to work in good relationship with the internal audit. It seems also very important to communicate not only the successes but also the failures. Executives do not like "surprises". In order to improve the "customer" satisfaction, it seems important to sign with them a Service Level Agreement (SLA) and to monitor the key performance Indicators included in these SLAs.

These measurements have to be scheduled and a reporting made to the Executive Management and to the board in order to provide direction for the next period. This may be done through a balanced scorecard system.

We may represent the in more details the framework as follows.

A set of four linked models (or "reference architectures") are created, covering business requirements and the resulting requirements for data and information, applications, and infrastructure. Impact analysis is performed to ensure the models are appropriate for the environment.

A series of linkages are established to ensure that the plan is delivering on the initial requirements and metrics.

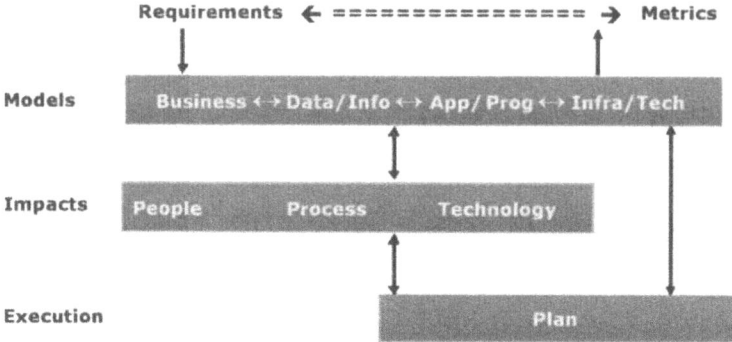

6 Conclusion

Information security is not a technical issue, but rather a corporate governance responsibility that involves risk management, reporting on controls, testing, training and executive accountability.

Without the active engagement of business unit leaders, executive management teams and boards of directors, a sustainable information security program cannot exist. This is no longer a technical problem relegated to the bowels of the enterprise. This is a challenge that requires a coherent information security management framework that aligns with the set of policies and internal controls used by enterprises to establish a culture of compliance and that will support the implementation of information security programs across all industries.

The time to embrace information security governance is now. Integration of information security into the core of enterprise management and governance must come about. And, focusing on security experience management will allow us to begin to manage security from a business perspective.

References

[BR]   Business Roundtable Report, Securing Cyberspace: Business Roundtable's Framework for the Future April 2004

[CEC]   Commission Communication (COM(2003)284) of 21 May 2003 modernising Company Law and enhancing Corporate Governance in the EU.

[OECD] OECD Principles of Corporate Governance: 2004

On Privacy-aware Information Lifecycle Management in Enterprises: Setting the Context

Marco Casassa Mont

Hewlett-Packard Laboratories
Trusted Systems Lab, Bristol, UK
marco.casassa-mont@hp.com

Abstract

This paper aims at setting the context for privacy-aware information lifecycle management within enterprises, i.e. the process of handling the lifecycle of personal and confidential information in a way that is compliant with privacy laws and people's expectations (including data retention, deletion, notifications, data transformation, etc.). Despite the fact that enterprises are already using Information Lifecycle Management (ILM) and Identity Management (IDM) solutions to store and manage various types of data, in terms of "privacy-aware" lifecycle management of information much is still done by means of manual processes that are complex and hard to monitor. This is a green field, open to innovation. We argue that automation can be introduced to address this aspect by leveraging, among other things, existing enterprise ILM and IDM solutions.

In this context, we investigate and analyse core privacy requirements and issues that need to be addressed by enterprises along with their implications and impact on existing ILM and IDM solutions. The goal is to create awareness and suggest potential ways to move towards their automation and simplification. We provide an overview of research and work done by HP Labs to develop approaches and technologies that can help enterprises to implement and automate aspects of privacy-aware information lifecycle management.

1 Introduction

Enterprises collect large amounts of *information* to enable their business processes and interactions. The term *"Information Lifecycle Management"* refers to the processes, mechanisms and solutions that are put in place by enterprises to handle the lifecycle of this information, including its storage, retrieval, usage, prioritization, update, transformation and deletion. Managed information consists of documents, files, records, etc. Enterprises have been investing in *Information Lifecycle Management* solutions to address the above aspects.

Enterprises also collect, store and process *personal information* and *digital identities* to allow them to authorise business transactions and interactions and provide users with more customised and effective services. In this context, enterprises have been investing in *"Identity Management"* solutions to: deal with user provisioning and account management; store and retrieve personal identity information; handle secure access to data and systems/services within their IT infrastructure; use digital identities and profiles for authentication and authorization purposes within an enterprise boundary or across multiple organisations. These solutions provide basic information lifecycle management functionalities – focused on managed digital identities and user profiles.

S. Paulus, N. Pohlmann, H. Reimer (Editors): Securing Electronic Business Processes, Vieweg (2006), 405-414

There is currently a "dichotomy" between *Identity Management* solutions and *Information Lifecycle Management* solutions due to: (a) the different nature of the managed information (identity information vs. more traditional documents/files/records); (b) different business requirements; (c) different information usage patterns (intensive operational usage vs. prioritised storage, off-line retrieval and consultation usage).

Both types of solutions handle *digital material* that might contain personal information. As such, this information must be managed according to privacy laws (e.g. HIPPA, COPPA, SOX, EU Data Protection Law, etc.) [Laur04], privacy guidelines [OECD80] and data subjects' preferences. This requires keeping into account *privacy rights and permissions* (e.g. privacy-aware access to data based on consent and purpose) and *privacy obligations* (e.g. data retention, data deletion, data transformation and notifications). In particular the lifecycle of this information needs to be managed in a privacy-aware way, according to stated obligations and other privacy constraints. Enterprises need to address all these aspects for regulatory compliance, to satisfy customers' expectations and to retain good reputation and brand. The increasing number of incidents - including identity thefts, misuses of personal data, data leakages, etc. - shows how complex and hard is to manage confidential documents and personal information in a privacy-compliant way: this involves knowledge of regulation, definition of privacy policies, implementation of good practices and processes, the deployment and usage of technologies to manage and enforce these policies and monitor/audit for their compliance.

In this context, enterprises need to enforce *privacy-aware access control* on stored personal and confidential information: data should be accessed or disclosed based on the enforcement of stated privacy policies. Progress has already been made in this space, as described in [IBM04a, IBM04b, CATB05]. In addition, *privacy-aware information lifecycle management* processes must be put in place by enterprises to effectively manage the lifecycle of personal and confidential information according to privacy requirements - over time and across various contexts and solutions. As anticipated, this includes dealing with data retention, data deletion, satisfying notice requirements, supporting data transformations and management of complex workflows.

This requires a *well-planned*, *systemic* and *ongoing* effort, because: privacy policies and personal preferences can change over time; data and confidential documents can be subject to different privacy and data protection laws depending on geographical and organisational boundaries; data needs to be disposed or transformed over time. The lifecycle of the involved privacy policies must be managed as well.

This paper focuses on the *privacy-aware information lifecycle management* aspect, as it is important for privacy management and still a green field. The dichotomy between "traditional" *Information Lifecycle Management* (ILM) solutions and *Identity Management* (IDM) solutions does not really help enterprises to address, in an integrated and common way, the lifecycle management of information driven by privacy policies. Today most of privacy management work involves human processes that are duplicated, prone to mistakes and subject to high operational costs.

This paper aims at setting the context for *privacy-aware information lifecycle management* within enterprises. It provides an overview of current enterprises' *ILM* and *IDM* solutions and their limitations. It investigates and analyses core requirements and issues that need to be addressed by enterprises along with properties and features that should be provided by *privacy-aware information lifecycle management* solutions. Related implications for ILM and IDM solutions are discussed. This paper also describes research and work done by HP Labs to develop approaches and technologies that can help enterprises to implement and automate aspects of *Privacy-aware Information Lifecycle Management.*

2 Overview of ILM and IDM Solutions

2.1 Information Lifecycle Management Solutions

Information Lifecycle Management (ILM) is a comprehensive approach to manage the flow of an information system's data and associated *"metadata"* from creation and initial storage to the time when it becomes obsolete and is deleted [PETR06]. ILM involves various aspects of dealing with data, starting with user practices, rather than just automating storage procedures, as for example, done by hierarchical storage management (HSM) systems. ILM enables basic criteria for storage management based on data age and frequency of access and includes policy-driven management of data, e.g. [BDJK05]. At the very base, ILM solutions automate the processes of: (1) Organizing data into separate tiers according to specified policies; (2) Data migration from one tier to another based on those criteria.

Newer data, and frequently accessed data, is stored on faster, but more expensive storage media, while less critical data is stored on cheaper, but slower media. ILM solutions provide degrees of support for the following information/data management phases:

- Assessment: this is about understanding what data resides on the storage assets in an enterprise environment;
- Data Analysis: based on the outcome of the assessment phase, this phase is about analysing and explaining the breakdown of storage asset utilization, data usage patterns and the costs involved;
- Classification: depending on how data is used and how critical it is to the business, data is prioritised based on business requirements (mission critical, business sensitive, etc.) and its value determined. This defines where data should be stored through its lifecycle and assist in creating policies to migrate data to the proper storage "class" over time. These classes might keep into account different data properties, such as: type, organisation, value and age;
- Automation: once data has been classified, policies must be established to determine on which storage resources data should be located. Tools can automate the migration of data from one storage class to another based on these policies and deal with aspects such as replication, mirroring and back-ups. Disaster recovery and business continuance criteria are also considered in this context to ensure that mission-critical data is always available;
- Review: this consists on an ongoing activity of continuously reviewing the usage patterns of storage resources and ensure adherence to policies and procedures.

Privacy-aware information and data management have become increasingly important as businesses face regulatory compliance issues in the wake of privacy legislation. So far, only few privacy aspects (such as data retention/deletion) have been taken into account by ILM solutions. A more comprehensive list of requirements that need to be fulfilled by enterprises is described in the *"Requirements and Open Issues"* section.

2.2 Identity Management Solutions

Enterprise Identity Management (IDM) solutions deal with the management of digital identities, user accounts and user profiles and provide services to enterprise applications and services [CaBP03,DeRo04]. Specifically, they support functionalities such as authentication, SSO, authorization, auditing, user provisioning, data storage, link to legacy systems and data consolidation. They target different types of users and contexts including e-commerce, service providers, enterprises and government institutions.

The main components and functionalities provided by current identity management products and solutions include [DeRo04]:

- **Directory services, meta-directories, virtual directories and databases** deal with the representation, storage and management of identity and profiling information and provide standard APIs and protocols for their access.

- **Authentication, authorization and auditing** functionalities. Authentication ranges from local authentication on a system to complex distributed authentication, including single-sign-on (SSO) within and across organizational boundaries. Authorization can include simple access control management at the OS level, more sophisticated role-based access control - RBAC - up to flexible, distributed, policy-driven authorization, at the application and service levels.

- **Provisioning** components are used by enterprises, organizations and e-commerce sites to deal with the lifecycle management of identities, including the enrolment, customization, modification and destruction of accounts associated to users, employees and customers along with associated identity information (including rights, permissions and access control information). Related functionalities deal with the issuance, certification, management and revocation of digital entitlements and credentials in a secure and trusted way;

- **Self-Registration, Personalization** components provide core functionalities to end-users (i.e. data subjects) in terms of self-registration and management of their personal information and identities.

In particular, the *Provisioning* component, that handles lifecycle management aspects of digital identities and personal information, is usually not integrated with ILM solutions.

3 Privacy-Aware Information Lifecycle Management

Privacy-aware Information Lifecycle Management is the process of ensuring that personal and confidential data - stored and used by enterprises - are managed according to stated privacy policies, people's preferences and enterprise privacy guidelines. This section describes requirements and open issues; highlights core properties and features that should be provided by *Privacy-aware Information Lifecycle Management solutions*; describes our current work in this space and next steps.

3.1 Requirements and Open Issues

Privacy laws, such as HIPPA, COPPA, EU Data Protection Directives [Laur04] and privacy guidelines, such as OECD [OECD80], dictate key privacy requirements for enterprises that have direct implications for *Privacy-aware Information Lifecycle Management* processes:

- Enterprises should clearly state the purposes for which they collect personal data and should take into account the consent (or lack of consent) given by data subjects (people) to use their data for these purposes;

- People should be enabled to express their privacy preferences on how their personal data should be handled (e.g. consent, retention, notifications) and change them afterwards;

- People should be notified of changes affecting the management of their personal data and they should retain a degree of control over it;

- Personal data should be deleted once its retention is not required anymore;

- Openness and transparency over how data is processed, manipulated and disclosed to third parties are also key requirements;

- Compliance to all these aspects must be monitored and any violation promptly reported and addressed.

As anticipated in the introduction, privacy policies are commonly used to represent and describe these privacy laws and guidelines, in terms of *rights* of data subjects, *permissions* over usage of personal data and *obligations* to be fulfilled. In particular *obligations* [Casa04a,Casa04b] describe expectations and duties on how to handle personal data. They might dictate deletion/data retention constraints, notification requirements, data transformation criteria (encryption, minimisation, etc.) and complex workflow that need to be executed on this data, involving human and computer-based interactions. *Obligations* have direct implications on the "*lifecycle management*" of personal data within enterprises.

As a consequence, the constraints and conditions dictated by obligations (on how to manage personal data) must be kept into account by ILM and IDM solutions, to really enable enterprise-wide *privacy-aware information lifecycle management*.

In this context, *privacy policies*, inclusive of *privacy obligations*, need to be managed as well. Related requirements follow:

- **Lifecycle management of privacy policies:** Privacy policies must be understood, refined and authored by enterprises. Their lifecycle has to be managed;

- **Deployment and enforcement of privacy policies:** privacy policies need to be deployed within enterprises data management processes and IT infrastructures and enforced;

- Privacy policies need to be audited and monitored for compliance.

Enterprises that span across different geographical and organisational boundaries might be subject to different privacy laws and privacy policies.

There are a few important, open issues that need to be addressed to enable effective *privacy-aware lifecycle management* of personal and sensitive information within enterprises:

1. **Lack of Automation**: current enterprise's privacy management practices are mainly based on manual processes, good behaviours and common sense. Not only are human processes prone to failure but the scale of the problem highlights the desire for additional technology to be part of the solution. The trend towards complexity and dynamism in system configurations heightens this need for automation to ensure that privacy and security properties are maintained as changes occur, and in addition to check that privacy is delivered as expected;

2. **Lack of Integration:** the duplication of data management efforts and capabilities – such as the ones provided by ILM and Identity Management solutions - do not help enterprises to deal with privacy matters. Even if in the short/medium term it is hard to envisage a convergence of these solutions into an integrated approach, progress should be made at least to avoid duplications of efforts in the management of privacy. Solutions that enable centralized management of privacy policies and *privacy-aware information lifecycle management* should be leveraged and integrated with both ILM and IDM solutions.

Next sections describe in more details core properties that should be provided by *privacy-aware information lifecycle management* solutions and introduce our R&D work done in this area.

3.2 Core Properties and Functionalities

Our analysis of requirements and open issues has identified a few core properties and functionalities that a *privacy-aware information lifecycle management solution* should provide:

- **Explicit modelling of personal and confidential data**: this solution should specify and use a model of stored personal and confidential data. This model, at least, should describe where this data is stored (database, LDAP repository, etc.), should provide data schema details, properties of data attributes, unique data identifiers, etc.;

- **Explicit definition of privacy policies, in particular obligations**: this solution should explicitly support the representation and authoring of privacy policies, in particular privacy obligations. A format to represent these policies should be defined and used;

- **Integrated lifecycle management of these policies**: this solution should support the overall lifecycle management (i.e. creation, authoring, versioning and disposal) of privacy policies, in particular of privacy obligations;

- **Deployment and enforcement of these policies, potentially by leveraging ILM and IDM infrastructures**: this solution should explicitly deploy privacy policies within relevant enterprise IT systems and enforce them. Part of the enforcement process can be delegated to ILM and IDM solutions (when feasible) to enable an integrated enforcement approach;

- **Integrated Monitoring and checking for compliance to these policies**: this solution should check that privacy policies are fulfilled over time and report any violation.

Current ILM and IDM solutions do not provide most of these functionalities: they basically support data deletion and aspects of data transformation. A *privacy-aware lifecycle management* solution must provide this core set of functionalities and be integrated with relevant enterprise systems/solution that already handle personal and confidential data, including ILM and IDM solutions.

Given the current dichotomy of IDM and ILM solutions, we believe that this *privacy-aware lifecycle management* solution must retain a key role in representing, authoring, managing, deploying and monitoring privacy policies, in particular privacy obligations. Another important role of this solution is also dealing with the lifecycle management of these policies.

3.3 Our Approach

HP Labs have been researching and workings in the space of *privacy-aware information lifecycle management* for the last two years. In this context, our work addresses the problem of automating the management and enforcement of privacy obligations in enterprises and enable *privacy-aware lifecycle management* of personal and confidential data.

Privacy obligations [Casa04a,Casa04b] dictate expectations and duties on how to handle personal and confidential data and deal with its lifecycle management, including: dealing with data deletion, data transformation (e.g. encryption), sending notifications, executing complex workflows, etc.

In our vision, at the core of *privacy-aware information lifecycle management* solutions there is an *Obligation Management Framework* to centralise (within enterprises) the representation and management of privacy obligations and orchestrate their overall enforcement and monitoring by leveraging and extending current enterprises IT solutions – specifically ILM and IDM solutions. This section describes our current approach, results and next steps.

An explicit model of privacy obligations is introduced along with mechanisms to handle privacy obligations and describe the affected data. In our work, we defined an *obligation management model* [Casa04a,Casa04b], where privacy obligations are "first class" entities, i.e. they are explicit entities that are represented and managed. In this model, a privacy obligation is an "object" that includes (at least) the following aspects [Casa04a,Casa04b]: *Obligation Identifier*; *Targeted Personal Data*; *Triggering Events* (e.g. time-based events); *Actions* (e.g. data deletion, sending notifications). Different categories of privacy obligation [Casa04a] need to be managed and enforced by enterprises: *transactional obligations*; *data retention and handling obligations*; *other types of event-driven obligations*. A complementary classification of our managed privacy obligations is based on their activation timeframe and period of validity: *short-term obligations*; *long-term obligations*; *ongoing obligations* [Casa04a].

A related *obligation management framework* [Casa04a,Casa04b] is also introduced to deal with the management of privacy obligations. In this framework data subjects (people, users) can explicitly define privacy preferences (e.g. on data deletion, notifications, etc.) on their personal data at the disclosure time (e.g. during a self-registration process) or at any subsequent time. These preferences are automatically turned into privacy obligations. Enterprise privacy administrators can further define other privacy obligations, for example dictated by laws or internal guidelines. This *obligation management framework* provides the following core functionalities (based on the properties and requirements previously described):

- **Scheduling the enforcement of privacy obligations**: it schedules which obligations need to be fulfilled and under which circumstances (events);

- **Enforcing privacy obligations**: it enforces privacy obligations once they are triggered. Enforcement may range from execution of simple actions (e.g. notifications, deletions) to complex workflows involving human intervention;

- **Monitoring fulfilment of privacy obligations**: it monitors and audits enforced obligations, at least for a predefined period of time, to ensure that the desired status of data is not changed and to report anomalies.

An *Obligation Management System* [Casa04a,Casa04b,CTCB05] has been derived from our privacy obligation model and obligation management framework. A working prototype has been fully implemented in the context of the EU PRIME project [PRIM06], as a proof of concept, providing the specified core functionalities: scheduling, enforcement and monitoring of privacy obligations.

The *Obligation Management System* can be leveraged to enable *privacy-aware information lifecycle management* within enterprises, by:

1. Providing centralized capabilities for representing, authoring, managing and monitoring privacy obligations;

2. Providing centralised modelling and abstraction of managed data;

3. Integrating the deployment, enforcement and monitoring (for compliance checking) of these obligations by interacting with existing IDM and ILM solutions.

Figure 1 illustrates the high-level architecture of this integrated solution.

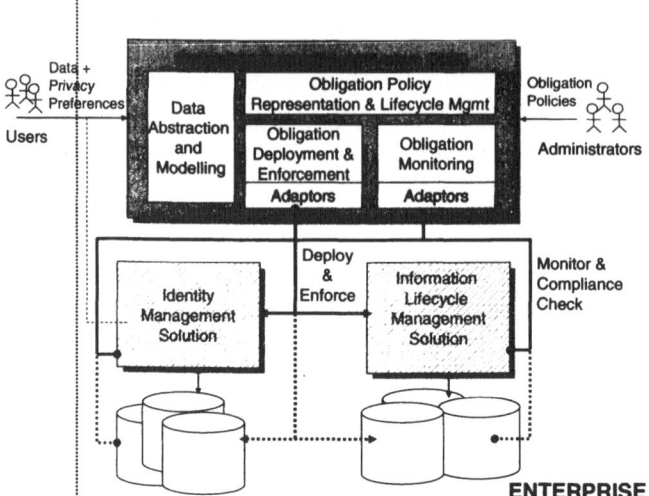

Figure 1: High Level Architecture

The *Provisioning* and *Self-Registration* capabilities of current IDM solutions can be used to collect people's privacy preferences on how their personal data should be managed. These privacy preferences can be automatically translated by IDM *add-ons* into privacy obligations and managed by our *Obligation Management System* (OMS). Similarly, privacy administrators within the enterprise can define additional privacy obligations related to personal and confidential information stored and managed by ILM solutions (or any other solutions).

In this context the OMS becomes the *central point of control and orchestration* of *privacy-aware information lifecycle management* in enterprises. Thanks to software adaptors and the usage of various APIs, the OMS can configure IDM and ILM solutions to deal with the constraints dictated by privacy obligations (e.g. deletion preferences, etc.) and enforce them. If the IDM and ILM solutions provide no support for this, the OMS will directly enforce these privacy obligations by directly interacting with the data repositories.

To demonstrate the feasibility of our vision and how this can be achieved in a practical way, we have already integrated the prototype of our OMS system with a state-of-the-art enterprise Identity Management solution [HP05a] specialized in user provisioning and account management capabilities. More details about current results are available in [CTCB05]. We are also exploring integration of this prototype OMS system with a state-of-the-art ILM solution [HP05b] as another proof-of-concept activity. We can anticipate that this is feasible and we are currently working on the implementation details. Results will be published once a first related prototype is implemented.

We believe that an approach based on a centralised management of privacy obligations and its integration with current ILM and IDM solutions (and potentially other solutions handling sensitive data) constitutes a suitable reference model to enable *privacy-aware information lifecycle management* within enterprises. It can be deployed in a variety of contexts, including on enterprise systems with a highly distributed topology. Part of our coming work consists of making experiments that leverage and use a heterogeneous set of IDM and ILM solutions. We are keen in getting feedback and engaging with "lighthouse customers" for technological trials.

4 Important Issues and Next Steps

This paper focuses on privacy and *privacy-aware information lifecycle management* within enterprises. The main goal is to create awareness of these topics and related requirements: little has been done so far in this space, despite an increasing need for better management and control of the lifecycle of personal data.

Usually security aspects are kept into account when dealing with the lifecycle management of information (mainly to protect the storage and transmission of personal data) whilst privacy aspects are not. A holistic approach to information lifecycle management within enterprises should encompass both privacy and security aspects i.e. how data should be stored, accessed, transmitted and disclosed in a secure and confidential way.

The paradigm of using obligation policies to explicitly describe expectations and duties on how to handle data in a privacy-aware way could also (potentially) be leveraged to deal with security expectations. For example obligations, in addition to describing data transformation and deletion requirements (dictated by privacy constraints), might also specify the desired security status of this data along with information protection requirements and how to handle violations. Ideally this integrated set of security and privacy obligations could also be used as a centralised "knowledge base" for decision support systems, for making informed business decisions in cases where the legal situation is ambiguous.

These important aspects need further research and investigation: despite the fact that it makes sense in theory, in practice handling both security and privacy aspects - in an integrated way - in the context of information lifecycle management is complex and has strong implications on the underlying IT frameworks and their various enforcement and management mechanisms. Our findings and results in this space will be published and discussed in coming papers along with our proof-of-concepts.

5 Conclusions

This paper sets the context for *privacy-aware information lifecycle management* within enterprises. Core privacy requirements and issues that must be addressed by enterprises have been analysed along with their implications and impact on existing ILM and IDM solutions. Key properties and functionalities of *privacy-aware information lifecycle management solutions* have been introduced.

Research and work done by HP Labs to develop approaches and technologies to automate aspects of *privacy-aware information lifecycle management* have been discussed. In this context, we described our current work on an *Obligation Management System* – a central point of control to author and manage privacy obligations, trigger their enforcement and check for their compliance – and how it can be leveraged and integrated with current ILM and IDM solutions. Further research and work is going to be done to refine our concepts and make experiments, both in the context of HP Labs and the EU PRIME project.

References

[BDJK05]   Beigi, M., Devarakonda, M., Jain, R., Kaplan, M., Pease, D., Rubas, J., Sharma, U., Verma, A.: Policy-based information lifecycle management in a large-scale file system. Policies for Distributed Systems and Networks, 2005, Sixth IEEE International Workshop on, 6-8 June 2005, 2005

[CaBP03]   Casassa Mont, M. Bramhall, P., Pato, J.: On Adaptive Identity Management: The Next Generation of Identity Management Technologies. HP Labs Technical Report, HPL-2003-149, 2003

[Casa04a]   Casassa Mont, M.: Dealing with Privacy Obligations in Enterprises. HP Labs Technical Report, HPL-2004-109, 2004

[Casa04b]   Casassa Mont, M.: Dealing with Privacy Obligations: Important Aspects and Technical Approaches. TrustBus 2004, 2004

[CaTB05]   Casassa Mont, M., Thyne, R., Bramhall, P.: Privacy Enforcement with HP Select Access for Regulatory Compliance. HP Labs Technical Report, HPL-2005-10, 2005

[CTCB05]   Casassa Mont, M., Thyne, R., Chan, K., Bramhall, P.: Extending HP Identity Management Solutions to Enforce Privacy Policies and Obligations for Regulatory Compliance by Enterprises. HP Labs Technical Report, HPL-2005-110, 2005

[DeRo04]   De Clercq, J., Rouault, J.: An Introduction to Identity Management. HP Reports, http://devresource.hp.com/drc/resources/idmgt_intro/idmgt_intro.pdf, 2004

[HP05a]   Hewlett-Packard (HP): HP OpenView Select Identity: Overview and Features. http://www.openview.hp.com/products/slctid/index.html, 2005

[HP05b]   Hewlett-Packard (HP): RISS Software Development Kit. http://h18006.www1.hp.com/products/storageworks/riss/sdk.html, 2005

[IBM04a]   IBM: The Enterprise Privacy Authorization Language (EPAL). EPAL 1.2 specification, http://www.zurich.ibm.com/security/enterprise-privacy/epal/, 2004

[IBM04b]   IBM Tivoli Privacy Manager: Privacy manager main web page, http://www-306.ibm.com/software/tivoli/products/privacy-mgr-e-bus/, 2005

[Laur04]   Laurant, C.: Privacy International: Privacy and Human Rights 2004: an International Survey of Privacy Laws and Developments. Electronic Privacy Information Center (EPIC), Privacy International, http://www.privacyinternational.org/survey/phr2004/, 2004

[OECD80]   OECD: OECD Guidelines on the Protection of Privacy and Transborder Flows of Personal Data. http://www1.oecd.org/publications/e-book/9302011E.PDF, 1980

[PRIM06]   PRIME Project: Privacy and Identity Management for Europe. European RTD Integrated Project under the FP6/IST Programme, http://www.prime-project.eu/, 2006

[PETR06]   Petrocelli, T.: Data Protection and Information Lifecycle Management. Prentice Hall, Chapter 8, 2006

Regulation of State Surveillance of the Internet

Murdoch Watney

University of Johannesburg, PO Box 524,
Auckland Park, Johannesburg, 2006, South Africa
mmw@regte.rau.ac.za

Abstract

The purpose of this paper is to investigate the legal justifiability of measures contained in state surveillance laws pertaining to the Internet.

The commercialisation of the Internet brought about many advantages but at the same time unlocked several challenges unknown to the physical world. Internet-connected countries battle to maintain control over information flowing across borders for the purposes of national security and law enforcement. State surveillance of the Internet may be utilised in addressing the abuse of the Internet, such as organised crime and terrorism.

The 9/11 terrorist attacks coupled with the effect of globalisation reinforced and accelerated the use of technology-based surveillance and that includes state surveillance of electronic communications in the USA. Many countries have since followed suit and introduced legislation providing for state surveillance of the Internet.

The western world has always jealously guarded the protection of human rights, yet new technological and political developments often challenge the human rights culture. The exploitation of the Internet for the commission of serious crimes challenges countries to find ways of controlling cyberspace, whilst at the same time encouraging the continuous growth of the Internet, stimulating technological innovation and enjoying the benefits brought by the Internet.

1 Introduction

Prior to the historical watershed terrorist attacks on the United States of America on 11 September 2001, the U.S. already grappled with challenges from Internet abuse. After 9/11 the following defining statement was made in respect of the Internet:

> 'On 10 September 2001, the Internet was still a place of hopes and dreams that was going to give everyone access to impartial information and undermine dictatorships. A few days later, it had become a lawless place where Al-Qaeda had managed to plan and coordinate its attacks. The Internet began to frighten people. 10 September was the last day of a golden age of free online expression. Since then, Big Brother has loomed ever closer.'[Bowr05]

One of the proposed solutions to address Internet abuse is state surveillance of Internet communications by means of technology. Whereas state surveillance previously posed challenges of its own, 9/11 seemed to have provided justification for a more focused surveillance programme.

In surveillance studies reference is often made to George Orwell's 1948 novel entitled *1984*. Orwell feared the coming into existence of 'Big Brother', a state-organised central surveillance system [Lyon03]. This paper focuses on two questions, namely:

1. has state surveillance of Internet communications for purposes of law enforcement developed into Orwell's much feared 'Big Brother'; and

2. is state surveillance an inevitable consequence of globalisation and a reflection of a changing world?

These questions can only be answered after the following issues have been considered:

1. the global impact of the development and implementation of information and communication technology pertaining to the Internet;

2. the effect of the terrorist attacks on the U.S. on 11 September 2001;

3. a general overview of the European Union (EU), U.S. and South African state surveillance laws regarding Internet communications for law enforcement and national security purposes with specific emphasis on the surveillance method, traffic data retention versus traffic data preservation; and

4. an evaluation of the justifiability of state surveillance of the Internet.

It should be borne in mind that the concept 'state surveillance' is not only an issue of information and communication technology and law, but surveillance also has political, economical, ethical, philosophical and sociological dimensions. These aspects are reflected in the implementation and use of state surveillance technology and legislation. In this paper the questions in respect of state surveillance of Internet communications will be discussed from a legal perspective.

2 Impact of the Internet

Although the development and implementation of information and communication technology and specifically the Internet brought about countless advantages, it also unlocked many challenges inherent to the characteristics of information and communication technology. The Internet is characterised by faceless, borderless, many-to-many 24 hours 7 days a week exchange and transmission of information worldwide. The Internet consisting of an interconnected system of networks that connect computers worldwide, introduced an information age and contributed to globalisation. The influence of the Internet on globalisation must not be underestimated, especially in view of the fact that the Internet severely affects governmental control. Several countries that previously exercised control over the lives of their citizens within the national borders, now battle to monitor and control information from across borders as the Internet serves as an excellent conduit for the commission of crime, such as online child pornography, the launching of computer viruses and distribution of copyright infringing material [Lyon03; Watn06]. Furthermore, countries have no control over the nature and content of communication between Internet users from different parts in the world.

Various countries realized that the characteristics of the Internet, which poses challenges on various levels, called for attention. As a necessary point of departure it should be borne in mind that the Internet as an international tool was not created with security as a primary consideration, but as a communication and information tool. Most countries recognise that the remedy for challenges posed by the Internet as well as its globalising effect has to be technology based, but at the same time laws have to regulate technology [Lyon94]. Surveillance technology is so invasive and extensive that it can easily be abused and therefore, legal regulation of surveillance technology must provide parameters and safeguards to the development and use of surveillance technology [Watn03]. Regarding state surveillance legislation, the focus is not on the applicable surveillance technology but on what the state (law enforcement and intelligence agency) is allowed to do and whether the state stays within the ambit of its authority bearing in mind that Internet surveillance legislation are technology based.

Global networks created by the Internet are perceived as a 'new form of power'. Central to the Internet is legal 'governance' of these networks. No central entity governs the Internet as a whole. Instead, Internet Service Providers (ISPs) administer small parts of the networks. If consideration is given to the legal position regarding the use of technology such as peer-to-peer file sharing, copyright, privacy regulations (such as the EU Data Protection Directives) and state surveillance in the format of traffic data retention and data preservation, it becomes clear that there are 'powers' that have a very direct influence on the legal development and use of technology and the use of the Internet [Bowr05].

3 Impact on State Surveillance by 9/11 U.S. attacks

A discussion of surveillance must be conducted against the background of the terrorist attacks on the U.S. on 11 September 2001 as this event was a watershed between the past and future of surveillance [EdHo03]. Although surveillance had existed prior to 9/11, a consequence of the U.S. terrorist attacks was the intensifying and reinforcement of surveillance by means of the use of technology.

The 9/11 U.S. terrorist attacks was not only a world event but also a globalised event that catalyzed change and set in motion various processes. Bearing in mind that the U.S. is a dominant globalising force, 9/11 triggered renewed attention worldwide regarding the combat of terrorism. A few days after the attacks, on 28 September 2001, the UN Security Council adopted Resolution 1373 that obliges member States to take all kinds of measures aimed at the prevention of terrorist acts and at the bringing to justice of those who participated in the financing, planning, preparation or perpetration of such acts or in supporting them.

Involved in the U.S. terrorist attacks had been air traffic, foreign nationals and networked messages and therefore airline passenger data, immigration records, telephone and e-mail logs became the focus of surveillance. The U.S. attack was not only organised from within the U.S. national border but it soon became known that the attacks had been prepared in part in Western Europe, particularly in Germany [FiWN04]. 9/11 highlighted the issue of security in a digitised world.

Subsequent to the 9/11 attacks, there have been bombings in Madrid in 2004 and the UK bombings in 2005. It is today a given that terrorism is not confined to a specific country but that it is an international issue. International cooperation is essential in the combat of terrorism. The two dominant international forces in this particular sphere of cooperation are the U.S. and the EU. The EU has strongly supported and extended cooperation to the U.S. in its initial reaction to 9/11. It is also interesting to note that the events of 9/11 provided an incentive to the EU to have a more unified approach to international terrorism and for the EU and U.S. to overcome the obstacles regarding international criminal law experienced prior to 9/11.

4 Overview of State Surveillance laws regarding Internet communications

4.1 Introduction

It is important to establish the relationship between security and surveillance. Surveillance at its broadest means 'to watch over' [Lyon03]. Surveillance is an umbrella concept that encompasses various categories of surveillance of which state surveillance is but one. State surveillance of the Internet may be achieved through various technological methods, such as monitoring, interception, data retention or data preservation and decryption of communications.

Surveillance within the ambit of state surveillance of the Internet means the gathering of information regarding unlawful activity or intelligence gathering. This contribution is aimed at the justifiability of laws that govern state surveillance of the Internet by means of the implementation and use of technology and does not focus on the surveillance methods *per se*.

As indicated, state surveillance must be seen against the background of the effect of globalisation on a country's internal control and sovereignty as well as the commission of international crime. Although much has been made of the threat of international terrorism, serious organised crime is increasingly committed by means of the Internet. Non-European countries such as South Africa need Europe as well as the U.S. as online trading partners and therefore legal developments in the EU as well as the U.S. are closely monitored. It is also for this reason that South Africa was a signatory to the first and only international convention on cybercrime, namely the Convention on Cybercrime of 2001, which was signed by 30 countries in 2001. The 30 countries includes the U.S. and South Africa and a further 2 non-European states.

The aim is to provide a brief overview of the impact of 9/11 on surveillance laws in respect of Internet communications with reference to the two most dominant Western 'powers' at present and the effect of EU and U.S. policies on South Africa.

4.2 Council of Europe Convention on Cybercrime

The Council of Europe is an international organisation that plays an important role in shaping the criminal policy of EU member states and in strengthening international cooperation against crime. The Convention on Cybercrime of the Council of Europe is the only international treaty regarding cyber crime. The Convention recognises that the investigation methods applicable to a physical crime cannot effectively be applied to cyber crime and outlines procedural methods specifically aimed at the collection of evidence for the detection and investigation of cyber crime. The Convention provides for surveillance methods such as interception and preservation (not retention) of data.

The Convention on Cybercrime requires that countries have an ability to implement interception of data either with the assistance of ISPs or in circumstances where there is no service provider or where the service provider is unable to provide assistance, to be able to exercise these powers themselves. The Council of Europe accedes that the meaning of 'interception' is problematic. The Council suggests that the procedure of interception be distinguished from the procedure of search by looking at the state of the information, namely whether the information is in transit or inert. Interception would be applicable to data moving between computers or storage files whereas the search procedure would be applicable to static information stored in one machine or one file store [Carr03].

The Convention provides for the request of preservation and disclosure of stored data and provides for data preservation for a maximum period of up to 90 days. The Convention contains no mandatory data retention obligation, but it provides for data preservation. It is important to distinguish between data retention and data preservation. Data retention would require providers to collect and keep all or a large portion of its traffic as a routine matter. Preservation requirements would on the other hand, during the course of a criminal investigation, enable law enforcement authorities to instruct a service provider to set aside specified data that is already in the service provider's possession until the necessary authorisation for disclosure had been obtained. The ISP is only obligated to preserve data in current storage if requested to do so by a law enforcement agency in respect of specified data in a particular case.

4.3 European Union (EU)

On 14 December 2005 the EU adopted the Data Retention Directive that provides for mandatory data retention of Internet communications between 6 to 24 months although provision is made for EU member states to extend the retention period. EU member states have 18 months to implement the mandatory data retention provisions into its legal system. The Directive does not limit retention to data pertaining to terrorism and organised crime, but includes all serious crimes as defined by each individual member state. It covers what is known as 'traffic data' and not 'content data'.

The mandatory data retention as a method of surveillance must be seen against the background of the:

1. Convention of Human Rights and Fundamental Freedoms of 1950 (hereafter referred to as ECHR);
2. Council of Europe Convention on Cybercrime of 2001;
3. Data Protection Directive 95/48 EC regarding the protection of personal data in general;
4. Privacy and Electronic Communications Directive 2002/58 EC in respect of processing of personal data within the ambit of an electronic medium; and
5. Declaration in Combating Terrorism adopted in 2004.

EU directives must be adopted in the EU member states as national law taking into account the circumstances, culture and history of the member state. The adoption of the mandatory Data Retention directives may be tested in the respective national constitutional courts if it is alleged to contain any human rights violations. In the case of the EU, it can also be taken to the European Court of Human Rights (ECtHR).

According to the general Directive 95/46/EC and the specific requirements of Directive 2002/58/EC for the processing of personal data and the protection of privacy in an electronic communication medium, 'traffic data' must be erased or made anonymous when it is not needed for transmission or billing purposes. The primary purpose of processing traffic data is to technically enable users, who are at a physical distance from each other, to communicate [Wald03; GoDu03]. Prior to the Data Retention Directive, article 15 of Directive 2002/58/EC provided EU member states with an optional data retention measure for a limited period of time if it proved to be a 'necessary, appropriate and proportionate measure within a democratic society to safeguard national security, defence, public security, the prevention, investigation, detection and prosecution of criminal offences or of unauthorised use of the electronic communication system.' Article 15 of the EU Directive 2002/58/EC has now been amended to provide for compulsory data retention of all traffic data.

The retention of data must be in accordance with the European Convention on Human Rights and Fundamental Freedoms as interpreted by the rulings of the European Court of Human Rights. Article 8(1) of the ECHR provides: 'Everyone has the right to respect for his private and family life, his home and his correspondence.' Article 8(1) is subject to article 8(2) of the ECHR that states: 'There shall be no interference by a public authority with the exercise of this right except such as is in accordance with the law and is necessary in a democratic society in the interests of national security, public safety or the economic well-being of the country, for the prevention of disorder or crime, for the protection of health or morals or for the protection of the rights and freedoms of others.' It is inferred that the EU considers the retention of traffic data necessary for law enforcement and security purposes and therefore the data retention obligation may be seen as an exception to the right to privacy.

4.4 USA

After 9/11, the Uniting and Strengthening of America by Providing Appropriate Tools Required to Intercept and Obstruct Terrorism Act of 2001 (USA Patriot Act) was implemented. The USA Patriot Act provides in title 11 for enhanced surveillance procedures that expand intelligence and law enforcement capability to identify and investigate terrorist activities and includes provision that among other things enhance law enforcement surveillance abilities [RaTy].

The EU has always had a very strict approach to privacy, which is also constitutionally protected. It appears that in the U.S. Internet privacy does not derive from the Constitution but legislation. The courts have held that an individual has no reasonable expectation of privacy in information revealed to third parties, for example, an Internet user cannot enjoy a reasonable expectation of privacy in non-content information sent to an ISP because the user has disclosed the information to the ISP. The U.S. courts have held that in general the Internet user has a reasonable expectation of privacy in content information that is sealed away from the network provider but does not retain such protection in information disclosed or openly visible to the provider. Where the contents of Internet communications are mixed together with envelope information (traffic data) and disclosed to the ISP, it is at least possible that courts will find that Internet users cannot have a reasonable expectation of privacy in Internet content information much like postcards and cordless phone calls [Kerr].

Although the U.S. signed the Convention on Cybercrime, it has not ratified the Convention. Furthermore, the U.S. legislation provides for data preservation and not data retention.

4.5 South Africa

South Africa has not ratified the Convention but gave effect to the Convention on Cybercrime by means of legislation such as the Regulation of Interception of Communications and Provision of Communication-related Information Act 70 of 2002 (hereafter referred to as the South African surveillance legislation), which came into operation on 30 September 2005. The South African surveillance legislation regarding state surveillance of the Internet pertains to law enforcement and national security purposes such as crime prevention, detection, investigation and prosecution.

The South African surveillance legislation provides for the surveillance methods such as interception, monitoring, decryption and data retention [Buys06]. It is interesting to note that the surveillance legislation and specifically the data retention provision of the traffic data of all Internet users for a period of 3 years was implemented prior to the EU Mandatory Data Retention Directive. Unlike the EU mandatory Data Retention Directive, the South African surveillance legislation defines serious crimes and it includes terrorism, organised crime, sabotage.

State surveillance in terms of the South African surveillance legislation cannot be seen in isolation but must be seen against the background of the South African Constitution 108 of 1996, which protects human rights such as the right to privacy and the right to freedom of expression as well as the government's duty to ensure state security.

5 Evaluation of the justifiability of State Surveillance regulation of Internet communications

5.1 Introduction

After 9/11, the debate has focused on the extent to which freedom of expression as well as privacy and especially freedom from surveillance may be compromised in the interest of detection, prevention and investigation of serious crimes and especially terrorism.

In paragraph 4 above the international as well as South African surveillance laws were briefly discussed. It is however important to scrutinise the justifiability of state surveillance laws. As indicated, the Internet is a global information and communication medium and national legislation should therefore be harmonised with international legislation to ensure effective legal regulation of the Internet.

5.2 Considerations

The following should be considered regarding the justifiability of legislation pertaining to state surveillance technology of Internet communications:

1. It would be erroneous to regard state surveillance as only a technical and legal issue without giving due consideration to the political, sociological, economical and ethical implications of this concept. A multi-disciplinary approach to state surveillance should be advanced. It has been alleged that state surveillance may result in a categorisation between different classes of people, ultimately ethnic or racial discrimination and that racial profiling might be easily accomplished with algorithmic surveillance; furthermore that there is a lack of accountability of these surveillance systems [Lyon03]. Surveillance laws clearly reflect the political climate in which they are passed, e.g. the USA Patriot Act and the EU mandatory Data Retention Directive were formulated in response to the threat of international terrorism.

2. State surveillance laws reflect the changing role of the ISP. Regarding state surveillance laws, most legislation provides for indirect state surveillance, meaning that the ISP must assist in the surveillance on behalf of intelligence agencies and law enforcement agencies. An ISP may experience this legal burden as cumbersome, especially in light of the fact that this has nothing to do with its main function, namely as a conduit of information.

3. The concept of data retention has evoked a lot of discussion and will continue to do so. Most countries are in the process of implementing data retention legislation. In the U.S. only a preservation order is applicable but following the EU approach, many countries will implement mandatory data retention of all Internet users. The EU (as well as South Africa) has deviated in this regard from the Convention on Cybercrime that proposed only the preservation of specific data in respect of an identified perpetrator regarding certain crimes. The reason may be that since cybercrime is not easily detected, the data of specific perpetrators cannot always be identified prior to retention. The following aspects regarding the practical application of mandatory data retention legislation should be taken into consideration:

    a. The mandatory retention of traffic data for a fixed period of time imposes huge and even unattainable obligations on the ISP [GoDu03]. This criticism is especially valid as these measures would generate considerable costs regarding the storing, preservation, retrieving and securing of such data in compliance with data protection regulations. It has been said that the EU does not understand the Internet and created an act that will be expensive to apply.

b.   The period of data retention vary between countries. In South Africa it is 3 years whereas the EU has proposed a maximum period of 2 years, although member states may extend the period. The Internet is however under constant change and it is an open question whether the data will still be relevant after for example 2 years, taking into account that the Internet changes a lot and websites as well as IP address may be obsolete after a period of time.

c.   Although the EU Data Retention Directive states the type of data that may be retained, namely traffic data, law enforcement interest may rather lie with content data [GoDu03]. From a technical perspective it might not be easy to distinguish between traffic data and content data. In practice, content and traffic data are often generated simultaneously resulting not only in revealing data which is necessary for the conveyance of an electronic communication (namely traffic data) but which also shows elements of the content indicating the interests of the user [Gros]. The overall purpose of the distinction between traffic data and other data is to set up separate legal regimes for transmission (traffic data) and content (content data).

d.   Various debatable questions may be raised such as why the traffic data of all Internet users, irrespective of whether they are suspected of committing a crime, need to be stored as it may result in the infringement of human rights, such as the right to privacy and freedom of expression [GoDu03]. It has to be considered whether the benefits derived from security attained by means of state surveillance really outweigh the freedoms lost? Can the human rights violation be justified vis-a-vis the possible positive effect of combating terrorism and preventing the commission of serious crimes?

e.   The question is often posed why traffic data is needed for law enforcement or security intelligence purposes? Traffic data may provide the only clues to the identity of the perpetrator, although nearly all forms of traffic data may be altered or masked by sophisticated criminals. Every piece of traffic data may be described as a piece of jigsaw puzzle and the more data there are to cross-check, the more difficult it will be to derail the investigations by law enforcement agencies. In opposing data retention laws, it has been argued that criminals can make use of methods to avoid having their communications recorded. The UK Home Office Voluntary Code of Practice of Data Retention admits that there are some Internet protocols that cannot be effectively monitored. It would for example be possible for criminals to avoid being monitored by using peer-to-peer file-sharing technology, Internet cafes, anonymous proxies or several other methods. The latter may be true and although it has been said that the police forces of the European Union are skeptical about the value of data retention, retention simplifies criminal investigations and may serve as a deterrent to the commission of cybercrime.

f.   It is also alleged that state surveillance laws such as the Data Retention Directive will result in more invasive legislation and that it will not prove to be the ultimate solution against serious crime. It is argued that once a surveillance regime commences, it achieves a taken-for-granted status and might be very difficult to dismantle [McGr04]. The mere existence of data might lead to increased demands for access and use by industry, law enforcement authorities and intelligence services. Even if access to data was limited by the EU parliament to a list of serious crimes, nothing prevents the expansion of this list. There may be calls for more draconian measures, such as the prior identification of all those who communicate, thus requiring ID cards at cybercafes, public telephone booths, wireless hotspots and identification of all pre-paid clients, in other words the end of anonymity; as well as the banning of all international communication services such as webmail and blocking the use of non-EU Internet service providers and advanced corporate services.

g.   Criticism has been leveled at the EU Data Retention Directive on the basis that it reverses the aim of the EU data protection which limit the collection, processing, retention and accessing of personal information. The aim of data protection was to prevent surveillance and it is alleged that the EU is currently leading the world in introducing mass surveillance of all Internet communications.

h.   Data retention laws are pro-active policing. This means that it aims at addressing the security risk or the crime commission risk before it is actually committed. This is commendable as policing is normally reactive. The question remains whether intelligence and law enforcement agencies will be able to identity a threat before its actual execution.

4. Growing resistance against state surveillance is on the increase [Kerr03]. One of the points of criticism leveled against the USA Patriot Act is that it infringes the right to privacy [Cass03] and the right to freedom of expression without increasing security. Has state surveillance with the aim of security not resulted in state control and in some instances, excessive state control?

5. Other considerations are that surveillance of Internet communications and specifically data retention, threatens consumer confidence as Internet users may avoid participating in Internet communications for fear that this will be logged for years. However, since the Internet has become such an integral part of society, I doubt if it will prevent consumers from using the Internet. It may be that consumers will feel more secure using the Internet knowing that surveillance may assist in crime prevention and detection, such as identity theft, which is a huge problem worldwide.

6. Anonymity as part of the right to privacy as well as freedom of expression regarding the use of the Internet, is also at stake in respect of law enforcement surveillance. Anonymity on the Internet may from a law enforcement perspective, be perceived as a tool for facilitating on-line criminal activity and as an explanation for the increase in cyber crime over the last few years. Cyber criminals can misuse online anonymity in order to avoid accountability for their acts [GoDu03]. As a result online anonymity may ultimately be banned.

7. It has been said that to effectively combat crime in a technoelectric age requires a proactive, comprehensive and visionary approach to criminal justice [Zaga04]. Could an integrated state surveillance system contribute in this regard?

8. George Orwell feared an integrated central state surveillance. State surveillance of the Internet today is much wider than Orwell's feared central state surveillance. Central state surveillance has progressed to a globlised surveillance network, which converges and integrates various surveillance systems in a country as well as extending surveillance to include co-operation between countries [Lyon03].

9. One should also distinguish between state surveillance and censorship as practiced by China. Censorship is an example of ultra-regulation and unlike state surveillance of the Internet, affects the free flow of information.

10. The final word on surveillance laws has not yet been spoken. Surveillance laws may still be challenged in national constitutional courts and regarding EU member states, it may also be challenged in the European Court of Human rights.

6 Conclusion

It is not surprising that state surveillance is often referred to as a pandora's box, since it is a complex topic that involves many inter-related issues. It is also clear that governments walk a tightrope in balancing the aims of state surveillance of the Internet with justifying human rights violations. Citizens will have to debate the use of surveillance technology and laws to prevent a country moving from a surveillance state to a police state. It should be borne in mind that technology is constantly changing and may render surveillance technology so extensive that it would be difficult for legislation to keep up with ensuring protection of the human rights of its citizens.

The development and implementation of state surveillance must be seen within the context of a changing society: globalisation, information and communication technology and free trade facilitate borderless transnational criminal operations. As transnational crime and especially terrorism increases and transnational criminal groups proliferate, national governments are challenged to prevent and combat criminals who operate in a borderless digitised world. National governments need international co-operation to be effective. Against this background the ultimate question is whether state surveillance of Internet communications is inevitable resulting in a global integrated surveillance information society and if affirmative, whether society should accept surveillance as a consequence of a changing world.

State surveillance of Internet communications cannot be seen as isolated from the issue of legal Internet 'governance'. South Africa's policies regarding the Internet and data protection is influenced by policy determination in the EU and the U.S. The U.S. has declared a 'war' against terrorism and is being backed by the EU and therefore South Africa has little choice but to adhere to the policy implementation in the EU and the U.S.

Although harmonisation of laws may be the solution to dealing with security issues resulting from the use of information and communication systems, it is undeniable that each country guards its sovereignty and has its own protected values, such as freedom of expression, privacy or in some instances even a national interest to control information flow. The importance of each of these values differs vastly from one country to another, for example censorship in China compared to freedom of expression in the U.S. The debate regarding data retention between European member states illustrate the conflict of values and sovereignty of each country. It all relates to which 'powers' will be the dominant force in the shaping of the laws that govern the Internet.

> *'Technology, it has often been said, is a two-edged sword. When it is applied for its intended useful services it is very good. But when it is misused it can be very bad. This is one of the major problems we face today as the refining of electronic surveillance devises and systems march on.' [Tayl87]*

Regulation of state surveillance of the Internet and especially the surveillance methods used will continue to be an issue of debate, but it is clear that the challenges of globalisation and the use of the Internet in the commission of serious cyber crimes have to be addressed. Whether Internet surveillance as an e-security method will provide the solution, only time will tell.

References

[Bowr05]   Bowrey, Kathy: Law and Internet Cultures. Cambridge University Press, 2005, p.196.

[Buys06]   Buys, Reinhardt: Newsletter, 2006. http://www.reinhardt@buys.co.za.

[Carr03]   Carr, Indira: Anonimity, the Internet and Criminal Law Issues. In: Nicoll, C;
              Prins, J E J and Van Dellen, M J M: Digital Anonymity and the Law: Tensions
              and Dimensions. TMC Asser Press, The Hague, 2003, p.199.

[Cass03]   Cassel, D: International Human Rights and the United States Response to 11
              September. In: Nicoll, C; Prins, J E J and Van Dellen, M J M: Digital Anonym-
              ity and the Law: Tensions and Dimensions. TMC Asser Press, The Hague, 2003,
              p.293-295.

[EdHo03]   Edwards, Lilian and Howells, Geriant: Anonymity, consumers and the Internet:
              where everyone knows you're a dog. In: Nicoll, C; Prins, J E J and Van Dellen,
              M J M: Digital Anonymity and the Law: Tensions and Dimensions. TMC Asser
              Press, The Hague, 2003, p.237.

[FiWn04]   Fijnaut, Cyrille; Wouters, Jan and Naert, Frederik: Legal Instruments in the
              Fight against International Terrorism: a Transatlantic Dialogue. Martinus Ni-
              jhoff Publishers, Leiden, 2004, p. 199.

[GoDu03]   Goemans, Caroline and Dumortier, Jos: Enforcement Issues- mandatory reten-
              tion of traffic data in the EU: possible impact on privacy and on-line anonymity.
              In: Nicoll, C; Prins, J E J and Van Dellen, M J M: Digital Anonymity and the
              Law: Tensions and Dimensions. TMC Asser Press, The Hague, 2003, p.169-172.

[Gros]   Grossman, Wendy: Will logging your email combat terrorism in Europe?
              http://technology.guardian.co.uk/weekly/story/0,16376,1683944,00.html.

[Kerr03]   Kerr, Orin: Internet Surveillance law after the USA Patriot Act: the big brother
              that isn't. Northwestern University Law Review, 2003. p. 627-630.

[Lyon94]   Lyon, David: The Electronic Eye: The Rise of Surveillance Society. Polity
              Press, Cambridge, 1994, p.162-163.

[Lyon03]   Lyon, David: Surveillance after September 11. Polity Press, Cambridge, 1994, p.
              5-57.

[RaTy]   Raul, Charles and Tyler, Amanda: The USA Patriot Act of 2001: Electronic
              Surveillance and Privacy. http://www.sidley.com/cyberlaw/features/patrot.asp
              ?print=yes.

[Tayl87]   Taylor, LB: Electronic Surveillance, Franklin Watts, New York, 1987, p.86.

[Wald03]   Walden, Ian: Anonymising personal data under European law. In: Nicoll, C;
              Prins, J E J and Van Dellen, M J M: Digital Anonymity and the Law: Tensions
              and Dimensions. TMC Asser Press, The Hague, 2003, p.152.

[Watn03]   Watney, Murdoch: Criminal and procedural measures regarding the prevention
              of cyber crime (part 1) Journal of South African Law, JUTA, South Africa,
              2003, p.58.

[Watn06]   Watney, Murdoch: Regulation of Internet pornography in South Africa (part 1).
              Tydskrif vir Hedendaagse Romeins-Hollandse Reg, Butterworths, South Africa,
              2006, p.227.

[Zaga04]   Zagaris, B: International Judicial Co-operation and Counterterrorism. In: Fi-
              jnaut, C; Wouters, J and Naert, F: Legal Instruments in the Fight against Interna-
              tional Terrorism: a Transatlantic Dialogue, Martinus Nijhoff Publishers, Leiden,
              2004, p.96.

How Can NRA Contribute to the Improvement of IT Security?

Rytis Rainys

Communications Regulatory Authority of the Republic of Lithuania
Address: Algirdo Str. 27, LT-03219 Vilnius, Lithuania
rrainys@rrt.lt

Abstract

The survey aiming to identify the main problems of the Internet security in Lithuania demonstrated that almost 80% of home users and enterprises and 100% of ISPs[1] faced computer viruses and spam. Despite the fact that a number of safeguarding tools against security incidents were used, 27% of home users, 25% of enterprises and even 68% of ISPs suffered damage from security incidents. In this situation, NRA[2], as a national regulator, should take its role in the execution of CERT[3] functions mostly in the ISP area, reducing negative impact of security incidents and enhancing legal and standardization measures. On the other hand, informing is even more important and is implemented through consumer awareness rising projects. Cooperation with non-governmental institutions may give excellent results in achieving those goals if private sector is involved in the process. Lithuanian NRA's key to success is to work by drawing on the principles of private and public partnership.

1 Introduction

In 2005 the number of Lithuania's households owning computers reached 29%, and by 2006 the number of regular Internet users reached 1.4 million, the reason for that being high competition in the market and one of the lowest Internet connection prices in the EU. Statistical comparison allows witnessing a 2.5 times annual increase in the Internet usage in the country. Unfortunately, criminal activities, just like social relations, have also moved to the virtual space, and more and more of our citizens face security problems.

1.1 The investigation of security incidents

General analysis of various security incidents, which spread over the Internet, and studies on the state security affairs in Lithuania show rather a threatening picture of network and information security. At the end of 2005, the survey carried out by the Lithuanian Communications Regulatory Authority, aiming to identify the main problems of security in Lithuania, demonstrated that almost 80% of home users and enterprises and 100% of ISPs faced computer viruses and spam. These results are not surprising as during 20 years of computer viruses existence approximately 150.000 viruses have been created and at present spam reaches

---

[1] ISP – Internet Service Provider.

[2] NRA – National Regulatory Authority.

[3] CERT – Computer Emergency Responce Team.

S. Paulus, N. Pohlmann, H. Reimer (Editors): Securing Electronic Business Processes, Vieweg (2006), 426-432

80% of the global volume of e-mail. Attacks against ISPs' servers and computers (44% Denial of Service attacks) potentially bring greater destructive effect than other incidents.

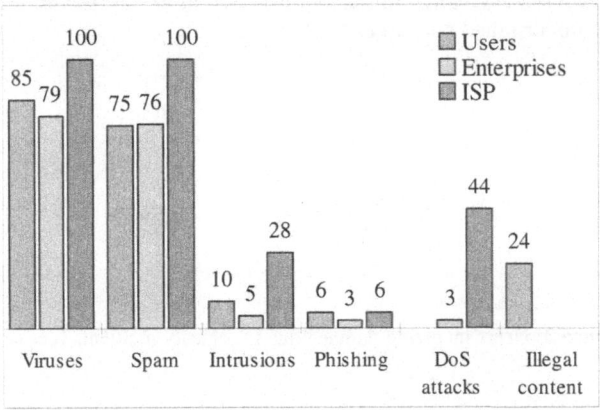

Figure 1: The security incidents, faced by the users (per cent)

The tool, most frequently used by the Internet users to protect from security incidents, is an anti-virus program. The study showed that ISPs also use other security tools, for instance, anti-spam, anti-spyware, firewalls and intrusion detection systems (IDS) quite actively. This could be explained by the fact that as the entire Internet traffic passes via the systems of ISPs, they are frequently attacked too; therefore, it is quite natural that ISPs are very active users of security tools. Attention should be also drawn to the fact that home users and enterprises upgrade their operational systems (further referred to as OS) too rarely, which is the critical factor for ensuring security, since OS security gaps are most often exploited to cause security incidents (viruses, spyware, etc.).

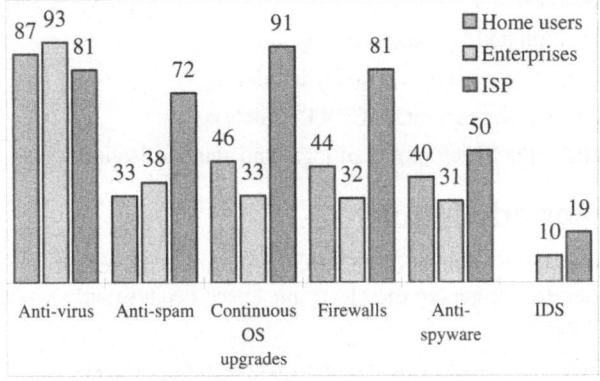

Figure 2: Usage of security tools (per cent)

Despite the fact that a number of safeguarding tools against security incidents were used, 27% of home users, 25% of enterprises and even 68% of ISPs suffered damage from security incidents. Security incidents disrupted normal organizational activities in approximately half of enterprises and ISPs.

The study of the situation in Lithuania illustrates that Internet/electronic communications users are subject to a large number of security incidents, incur damage and insufficiently use security tools. The survey indicates that the principal targets of criminal activity are ISPs because the entire Internet traffic goes over ISPs networks and, quite naturally, they incur a lot of damage due to security incidents. In our opinion, the most severe damage caused by security incidents is the undermined consumer trust.

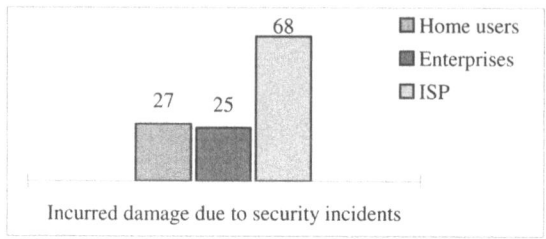

Figure 3: Users incurring damage due to security incidents (per cent)

2 NRA response

Taking into account network and information security, the national regulatory authority (NRA) should be able to adequately respond to security challenges because it is the NRA which is responsible for the customers' access to high quality and secure electronic communications services.

Generally, the NRA's activities in the field of security could be subdivided into two main areas, the first being regulation and the second being informing. Even though regulation of electronic communications is the main function of the NRA, it would be hardly possible to consider it as a priority in terms of security. Quite often different countries have their own priorities. The Lithuanian NRA has been working in the area of network and information security for slightly more than a year, but to the develop secure information society it is already working in the following areas:

- Consumer education and awareness rising;
- Reduction of negative impact of security incidents;
- Management of security incidents (CERT[4] functions);
- Encouragement of the development of legal and standardisation tools.

2.1 Consumer education

Due to a rapid-growth in the number of new Internet users in the recent years, it becomes vital to inform them about the dangers in the electronic space because only aware users are able to meet security challenges.

Up to now, there was no website in Lithuania, where Internet users could find relevant and topical information on electronic security. The NRA took the initiative and on February 7, 2006 commemorating the Safer Internet Day with the whole Europe, launched a new comprehensive website www.esaugumas.lt ("e-security").

---

[4] CERT – Computer Emergency Responce Team

At present the website seeks to provide information on electronic security in the language, manner and style acceptable to different user groups. The website aims to inform about security problems in electronic medium as well as to make recommendations and provide security raising instruments, which, if used and implemented, could increase security level of equipment and information of home users, small, medium and large corporations and institutions. The website presents information which meets any visitor's requirements as it includes sections for home users, organizations, public institutions and a separate section for CERT' activities.

Interactive and regularly updated, the website also provides information on different surveys in the field of network and information security, various inquiries and relevant forums. The NRA and its partners are putting much effort to make this portal number one in Lithuania for all interested parties, seeking to provide ICT users from private, business and public sectors with relevant information on network and information security.

It is not only in the electronic space that the work proceeds. Considering a growing number of phishing attacks in Lithuania, the NRA, in co-operation with commercial banks of Lithuania, promptly published 200.000 leaflets which explain phishing methods, the ways of how not to take frauds' baits and as well as actions to be taken in the worst cases. The leaflets were distributed throughout the branches of all commercial banks in Lithuania.

2.2 Reduction of negative impact of security incidents

Lithuania does not lack various public information campaigns organized by the NRA and other institutions that focus on security threats in the virtual space. However, how many users actually take any action to protect their computer and information contained in it? Obviously, not enough as problems in this area are not still decreasing. To protect from network and information security incidents, the NRA took the initiative of providing the Internet users with particular tools t that would be easily applied to user's computer software and would let considerably increase of the security level.

As both private and public sectors seek to develop network and information security culture, a special project was organized to reduce negative impact of incidents. Organised in cooperation with 16 partners from public, private and civil society sectors, the project was exclusively funded by a private sector.

During a special campaign in June 2006, 100.000 CDs containing security software packages were distributed in all regions of Lithuania, including rural areas. The virtual version of the CD is available on the website www.esaugumas.lt.

The CD contains not only easily installable software (such as anti-virus, anti-spyware, etc.; some programs operate free of charge for 6 months and some are absolutely free of charge), but also several pieces of advice and suggestions that help to ensure s computer and information contained in it safety on the Internet as much as possible.

The project showed that only on common attempts by state, private sector and civil society as well as by multilateral collaboration it is possible to implement initiatives, which render actual aid to the consumer.

2.3 Managing security incidents (CERT functions)

Organisation of separate campaigns for the consumers does not suffice to guarantee security at a national level; therefore, it is imperative to take systematic action to manage network and information security situation.

Drawing on other countries' experience (such as Finland), by the end of 2006 the Lithuanian NRA seeks to establish a network and information security management unit which will essentially be based on a widely applied CERT model.

A survey, carried out in 2005, showed that only 17% of ISPs have implemented units in their networks resembling CERT, even though a large part of ISPs (49%) are carrying out actual security incidents management, i.e. tackle the incidents when they occur. However, the remaining part of the ISPs (34%) is not ready to solve security incidents. This means that different Internet networks in Lithuania have different security levels, which negatively affects the overall situation of network and information security. Therefore, a decision was taken to set up a CERT service the activities of which would cover ISP networks as a critical sector, seeking an effective management of security incidents.

It is foreseen that the main functions of the CERT established by the NRA will be as follows:

- investigation of security incidents and response coordination;
- security threats and warning signals;
- prevention and awareness raising;
- encouragement of establishment of CERT centres;
- technology monitoring.

CERT service should also play an important role in the area of prevention of security incidents. Technical analysis of security incidents and organisation of response carried out by CERT are not sufficient. National Unit of Investigation of Cyber Crimes (NUCC) working in Lithuania under the Department of Police ensures prosecution of persons related with security incidents. However, not all security incidents reach NUCC. Moreover, NUCC is unable to process all information related to security incidents, therefore, NRA CERT would have to play an important role in collecting information on security incidents in IPT networks and processing them up to the level that would best guarantee successful investigation of such incidents at police.

However, such actions are not enough to properly manage security incidents at a national level. Individual CERT services need a coordination centre that should be an official contact point when solving international, inter-network incidents and would coordinate joint actions when ensuring network and information security. A hierarchical structure of CERT services should be introduced in Lithuania, as shown in Figure 4.

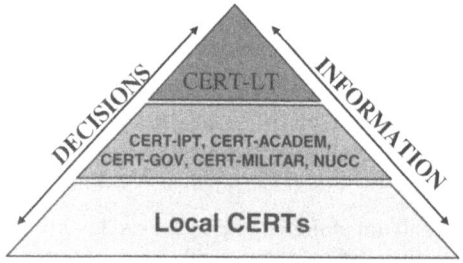

Figure 4: CERT architecture in Lithuania

2.4 Draft Law on Network and Information Security

Draft Law on Network and Information Security (hereinafter referred to as the draft Law) is a new policy making challenge in the field of network and information security. It should be a piece of a comprehensive primary legislation that systematically covers the most important network and information security issues and defines institutional structure in Lithuania.

The main national preconditions for the assumptions of the draft Law are as follows: there is no exhaustive regulation in the area of network and information security, therefore, there is an obvious demand of comprehensive and systematic regulation of the most important questions in the field of network and information security today.

The new regulation of network and information security will be based on the principles of co-operation between institutions, technological neutrality, functional equivalence, proportionality, minimal necessary regulation, legal certainty in a dynamic market, consumer rights protection, objectivity of regulatory criteria, conditions and procedures, transparency and non-discrimination. The draft Law will establish new definitions that have not yet been used in the national law. The main objective of the draft Law is to promote users' confidence in information society and encourage the development of secure information society.

It should be noted that this draft Law has the objective of regulating activities of the providers of public communications networks, publicly available electronic communications services, providers of information society services or providers of information society intermediary services. The act will define institutional structure, the role of other public institutions, preconditions for the formulation of policy and strategy on network and information security and rules of supervision of these activities. These institutions are the Government or an institution authorized by the Government (Ministry of Home Affairs and Ministry of Transport and Communications), Communications Regulatory Authority, The State Data Protection Inspectorate, Police Department and State Security Department. The above-mentioned state institutions will also have a possibility to cooperate with EU institutions and institutions of the EU Member States.

The draft Law will set the main requirements of network and information security. To ensure network and information security, offences relating to these activities will be prohibited. The draft Law will also establish detailed rights and obligations for undertakings. The main rights relating to network and information security are conferred to the Communications Regulatory Authority (RRT) - RRT will gain power to issue secondary legislation, detailing requirements for network and information security. This will empower RRT to control how undertakings implement the main requirements of network and information security. The national CERT will be also established.

The observance of voluntary declared conformity of networks and services with the main network and information security requirements is also encouraged. The draft Law will establish the basis for network and information security system of state and municipal institutions that will allow ensuring higher degree of network and information security in these institutions.

The draft Law will define conditions and procedure of the audit of network and information security. The basic requirements for network and information security auditors will also be established to create reliable security assessment system.

It seems that the first step in terms of comprehensive legislation in promoting safer use of information services has been made and users will benefit from it by receiving safe information services. It is also possible that RRT will be one of the first in the EU Member States passing primary legislation specifically in the field of network and information security.

3 Public and private partnership

The Lithuanian NRA seeks that its activities in the area of network and information security would not be restricted to institutional activities only but would rather be based on the principle of mutual cooperation between NRA and business sector, which has been detailed in the examples above. Public and private partnership has been recently consolidated by a joint *Memorandum on the Progress in the Area of Network and Information Security* signed between NRA, Association of the Lithuanian Banks and Infobalt, an association uniting IT companies. The document serves as a basis for the development and building a public culture in the area of network and information security in Lithuania. Public education, training, information, encouragement of the use of security tools, investigation and prevention of security incidents, co-operation to improve legal framework are the key priorities that the signatory parties of the memorandum will implement.

The Memorandum Implementation Committee, consisting of the representatives of the signatory parties, is operating at present. The Committee is planning and jointly implementing particular projects in the area of network and information security; the best example of its activities is a recently implemented CD project.

4 Conclusions

Being aware of the scope of the ICTs spread, their future development perspectives and each inhabitant's need to actively participate in the electronic environment, it is obvious that the need to safely disseminate and receive information and use electronic services in the electronic environment without fear will become increasingly important. As a growing IT use causes larger threats, it is crucial to draw attention to a rising number of the incidents in the virtual space and expertise of the criminals.

NRA should pay a particular attention to the education of users in the area of network and information security, as it is only an aware user who can counter security challenges.

First of all, incident management activities carried out by the NRA will comprise Internet service providers as a critical sector. Securing an effective incident management in the ISPs sector, it will no more be necessary to solve a good many of the problems for the consumers. It is essential to develop security incidents management via special CERT services in the future.

The success of NRA's activities can be ensured by a close and continuous cooperation between public and private sectors.

Information Security Regulation: Tomorrow Never Dies?

Andreas Mitrakas

European Network and Information Security Agency (ENISA)
andreas.mitrakas@enisa.europa.eu

Abstract

The widespread use of information technology in daily transactions has exacerbated the role of information security to protect information assets. The potential vulnerabilities that have been typically associated with transactions in public administration and private enterprise often pose challenges that governments, private organizations and individuals are compelled to respond to by adopting security measures. The setting up of a dedicated EU Agency on network and information security marks a turning point tin EU policy in this area. The recent decision of the European Court of Justice regarding the ENISA case sheds new light in the interpretation of article 95 of the Treaty and it provides new input with regard to the regulation of network and information security. This paper provides a snapshot on EU regulation regarding network and information security and reports on relevant recent work.

1 Introduction

The widespread use of information technology in daily transactions has exacerbated the role of information security to protect information assets. The potential vulnerabilities that have been typically associated with transactions in the Public Administration and private enterprise often pose challenges that governments, private organizations and individuals are compelled to respond to by adopting security measures. Information security is the response to such requirements as confidentiality, integrity and availability of resources. Beyond organisational responsiveness there is an emerging legal framework that has been promulgated at the EU and Member State levels. The recent set up of a dedicated EU Agency to address selected network and information security matters marks a turning point in EU policy. The European Network and Information Security Agency (ENISA) has emerged as a new element in supporting the approximation of laws in the Member States in the framework of EU First Pillar policy regarding the EU Internal market. The recent decision of the European Court of Justice has confirmed this view and it has outlined the extensive involvement of the EU in the regulation of network and information security. This paper addresses some areas of information security in a regulatory perspective.

2 Information security and the law

Electronic transactions typically require a high level of assurance with respect to content, authentication of the transacting partners etc. Security threats may lead to liability exposure for parties who fail to mitigate security risks appropriately. Liability might emanate from general legal requirements or as it has become increasingly more apparent in recent years, through specific legislation that addresses security requirements in various application areas. Information security measures in law are closely linked to evidence introduced in a trial for, example. The evidential value of electronic documents, for example, can be put in question as long as documents and their authors cannot be sufficiently ascertained. Sometimes certainty must be provided also through electronic means. Typical threats with potential legal consequences for transacting parties can be split in discreet categories such as the following:

- Natural threats which are described by terms such as Acts of God, sometimes also described as force majeur, like for example unforeseen events like a flood or an earthquake.
- Accidental threats caused by the actors involved like for example missing out in a plan or a security procedure.
- Intentional threats by actors directly or indirectly involved, like for example the deletion of organisational data.

The fundamental legal basis for the requirement to take information security measures from a legal viewpoint is the legal duty of care that transacting parties must show in their daily or business dealings. This duty of care is amplified in cases where a certain party acts under a specific role or in a trade, such as an attorney, as personal data controller etc. There are situations, however, whereby specific information security measures are mandated by law in order to protect against information threats, like for example in the case of processing personal data.

Information security is also an enabler to ensure specific basic rights like confidentiality for example. Within information society information security is gradually becoming a lynchpin to hinge upon basic rights in a way that allows them being exercised by members of the society. Information security as such is not a stand alone right. As information security is an instrument to exercise other basic rights it should be encouraged in a meaningful way. A challenge to overcome is to ensure that legitimate users have sufficient access to information security resources and that they are not unnecessarily limited in their choice of information security resources.

The commercial use of public networks has resulted in a surge of regulation concerning issues that touch upon or rely on information security. It is important to underline that the goals of legal framework on information security include:

- Addressing risks associated with attackers carrying out illegal acts, such as hacking or spreading viruses.
- Setting out the requirements for parties under attack to adopt appropriate measures by mitigating risk.
- Creating a set of security requirements to facilitate application areas.
- Supporting forensic studies in a variety of areas.

The principles of proportionality and reasonableness have been reflected in EU legislation and have been enshrined in the EU Directive 95/46/EC on the protection of individuals with regard to the processing of personal data and on the free movement of such data. The legal protection of databases raises the additional issue of observing privacy in databases that hold private data. Privacy protection requires the set up of discreet environments for treating data in a way that leaking such data to another environment is kept under control. An example includes the use social security numbers for example as a business identifier or as reliable input in building identification profiles that are merged into comprehensive databases. The duty to maintain the confidentiality of data that is stored within or exchanged between information systems is another necessary condition that concerns service providers and users of data alike because failure to protect might have consequences for the parties implicated.

An emerging legal framework that derives from the role that information plays in modern day transactions is setting up the pace for developments in business and government. Organizations that implement appropriate security measures mandated by industry regulations or legislation expect to benefit from the mitigation of potential liability of shareholders, employees, customers, trading partners or other third parties involved in a transaction. Additionally they can be more confident when responding to mandatory requirements emanating from the legal framework.

3 Sampling law

Taking a step back and looking at the policy situation that has been emerging in Europe the set up of a dedicated EU Agency to tackle selected network and information security issues is a remarkable development. ENISA aims at contributing to the better functioning of the internal market. ENISA assists the Commission, the Member States and, consequently, the business community in meeting the requirements of network and information security. As ENISA does not assume any operational tasks and its role is limited in advising the Commission and Member States on the areas of its competence, additional attention can be given to those areas that remain beyond the Agency's tasks and represent matters that are typically addressed by Member States themselves.

While ENISA is not the first measure that EU adopts towards network and information security, a long standing record in legislating with information security in mind can be demonstrated. The EU legal framework on information security also includes Directive 2002/21/EC of the European Parliament and of the Council of 7 March 2002 on a common regulatory framework for electronic communications networks and services (hereinafter, the Framework Directive) that lays down the tasks of national regulatory authorities that include a duty to cooperate with each other and the Commission to ensure the development of consistent regulatory practices, contributing to ensuring a high level of protection of personal data and privacy and ensuring that the integrity and security of public communications networks are ensured. Directive 2002/20/EC entitles Member States to attach to the general authorisation, additional conditions with reference to the security of public networks against unauthorised access in accordance with Directive 97/66/EC.

Protection of privacy is a key policy objective in the European Union. It was recognised as a basic right under Article 8 of the European Convention on Human Rights. Articles 7 and 8 of the Charter of Fundamental Rights of the European Union stipulate the right to respect family and private life communications and personal data. Striking a balance between law enforcement and privacy protection is delicate due to the new risks to which personal data is exposed to that must be appropriately managed to enhance trust and confidence. While identity theft for example has emerged in alarming figures law enforcement agencies have been afforded greater investigative powers to cope with it. The Commission also works together with the data protection authorities from the Member States (Article 29 Working Party) established through the general data protection directive 95/46/EC that sets out a clear obligation for the data controller to adopt security measures in order to protect personal data.

To counterbalance risks emanating from electronic communications the European Commission has taken action by adopting Directive 02/58/EC of 12 July 2002, on Privacy and Electronic Communications. This Directive has established an "opt in" regime that checks unsolicited communications and aims at a pan-European "ban on spam" to individuals. Stipulating a limited exception that addresses existing customer relationships, e-mail marketing is permitted subject to prior consent of the end user (Article 13). While consent can be given by purchasing similar products and services as those originally bought by the customer defining this term has not been addressed in the Directive. This provision includes two additional safeguards, namely that the data may only be used by the same company that has established the relationship with the customer and that each message includes an opt-out option.

As a security measure electronic signatures safeguard transactions against such risks as unauthorised access, repudiation etc. Through Directive 99/93/EC on electronic signatures a legal meaning has been sought for electronic signatures. The provisions of this Directive have impacted eGovernment applications, including eInvoicing, eProcurement, public identity etc.

The EU legal framework on information security might further require additional attention with regard to accommodating forthcoming applications as well as ensuring compliance with pertaining legal rules. Obviously any consideration of potential regulatory areas requires careful discussion and planning by the legislators in the Member States and possibly at the EU level. Areas of additional interest on a non-exclusive basis include aspects such as the following:

- Data protection legislation may further be expanded to include the duty of data controller to report breaches of personal data to data subjects directly. Such legislation has already become available in such jurisdictions as California.

- The limits for the potential liability of information society service providers may be further adapted in a way to allow them gain greater control over the trafficking of unsolicited commercial communications. Technical means can be implemented in a way that constrains service providers in the EU to take appropriate measures that counter spam.

- Filtering is an appropriate measure to sort spam from legitimate email that the end users do want to receive. The rules regarding filtering are not necessarily clear yet. While some Member States have already started introducing spam filtering rules, others lag behind creating a multiple speed situation for consumers and businesses. The result is prevailing confusion of service providers who are unable to determine the appropriateness of filtering with regard to their duty to attend to the requirements of the freedom of communication. If filtering is an appropriate mechanism to contain spam then the way that is put in place by service providers can be better specified or standardised in order to stop being just another service to the end user and become a recognised instrument against spam.

- Possible updates might be required in electronic signature legislation with regard to the legal validity of electronic signatures in specific transaction environments such as the ones over mobile networks.

3.1 Case Law

The ENISA case (C-217/04), UK v. EP & Council presents an example of challenging the legal basis of EU Agency based on article 95 of the Treat on the EU Internal Market. Regulation (EC) No 460/2004 of the European Parliament and of the Council of 10 March 2004 establishing the European Network and Information Security Agency (hereinafter, ENISA Regulation) has been recently challenged before the European Court of Justice (hereinafter, ECJ). ENISA was established to service EU Internal Market purposes on the basis of article 95 of the Treaty, that reads: "The Council shall, acting in accordance with the procedure referred to in Article 251 and after consulting the Economic and Social Committee, adopt the measures for the approximation of the provisions laid down by law, regulation or administrative action in Member States which have as their object the establishment and functioning of the internal market." As measures it is understood that are those that may be adopted for the approximation of legal provisions in Member States to achieve a functioning Internal Market. Measures aim at improving the conditions in the internal market and not necessarily set up bodies. In the area of Internal Market no general regulatory powers are conferred to the Community.

In the ENISA case the plaintiff being the UK claimed that ECJ should deem the ENISA Regulation invalid because it addresses institution building matters rather than providing measures for the approximation of legislation of the Member States in the internal market. Retorting the Parliament and the Council contend that the Court should dismiss the UK application as unfounded or if the ENISA Regulation were to be annulled, its effects should be maintained. The Advocate General was of the opinion that while the purpose that ENISA serves has been accepted by all MS except of UK ENISA is not a measure for the approximation of laws *per se*. It was widely held, however that although the UK challenges the ENISA Regulation it still considers desirable the setting up of ENISA. In any case measures in the meaning of article 95 must be directed towards MS laws and ENISA. It was argued that ENISA:

- Is but an intermediate step for the approximation of laws
- Cannot adopt any provisions on the approximation of laws
- Cannot take part in procedures for the adoption of such provisions

The Institutions and Finland, that actually intervened as the Member State that holds the Chairmanship at the ENISA Management Board, claimed that the contribution of ENISA to the approximation of laws consists of:

- Collecting and distributing information
- Striving for the cooperation of the private sector within the Internal Market
- Advising the Commission and the Member States
- Becoming a competence centre

Eventually the Council claimed that the approximation of Member States administrative provisions results in the approximation of laws. At the pre ruling stage the potential contribution of ENISA to the approximation of laws had not been sufficiently apparent because it was not predictable if and in what form ENISA would contribute to the approximation of laws in the EU Member States.

ENISA is a means to acquire the corresponding knowledge which runs counter to article 95, which stipulates that measures may only lead to the approximation of laws. The risk is that it might otherwise run counter to article 5 regarding the individual empowerment of EU institutions. No new legal forms of article 95 are permitted when they take effect alongside Member States laws.

In the end the ECJ ruled that the ENISA Regulation was yet another measure in a broader EU framework regarding network and information security. Being far from the only measure regarding the approximation of laws, as it had been claimed, the ENISA Regulation was part of a broader set of regulatory measures composed by the framework Directive and including specific directives that address various aspects of the EU Internal Market in the area of electronic communications. The Court went in great length to describe other regulatory measures that have been taken over time that all compose the EU information security regulatory framework. The decision highlighted the potential divergence in Member State laws that could emanate from the transposition of the Directives in this area. The ECJ has confirmed that ENISA is a measure that leads to the approximation of laws in the Member States. ENISA has been introduced as a measure to reduce such uncertainty when transposing Directives in Member State Law. The ECJ ruling also removed uncertainty by linking article 3 of the ENISA Regulation (EC) 460/2004 with the objectives of the framework Directive as well as of specific Directives in the area of network and information security.

The immediate consequence of the ECJ decision is that having ENISA executing its work plan does not appear as an open issue for the EU any more. Perhaps an additional message of the ECJ ruling on the ENISA case was addressed to the Member States that in a way have demonstrated their concern regarding the exercising of the principle of subsidiarity on network and information security. In this sense the existing regulatory output of the EU has already set the stage to address such matters at the EU level. Within the First Pillar EU cooperation on network and information security has already taken various forms and addressed several areas. ENISA is an instrument to manage some facets of this existing cooperation in the EU.

4 Relevant activities

Although it had not been explicitly foreseen in previous versions of its work program, ENISA has planned an additional working group activity in the area of regulatory aspects. In 2006 ENISA scheduled a new ad hoc Working Group on Regulatory Aspects of network information security (WG-RANIS). This working group aims at providing an overview of current EU legislation as it has become available in the area of network and information security. This working group addresses various regulatory actions at the EU level. Obviously the target is to compile a list of activities in an effort of presenting the current state-of-art. Any other activity is beyond the scope of this working group. The key objective is to adopt an inventory-centric approach that addresses legal actions on issues relevant to network and information security. An additional point of consideration for this working group might include the potential role of existing standards in EU regulation. As an example, the co-regulation approach that has been adopted in the area of electronic signatures gives sufficient assurance that standards are indeed significant from a legal viewpoint.

This working group addresses EU legislation as it has become available and remains within the scope of technical and organisational measures associated with electronic transactions in the Internal Market. This working group will deliver its reports that will be discussed internally, while additional external input might also be sought. Input through experts and background research is likely to be supported by a survey, if deemed necessary by the working group. The working group will additionally focus on an exchange of views in appropriate *fora* and seek to disseminate and test its own views in public events.

5 Conclusions

This paper briefly overviews information security related regulation in the European Union and it outlines the role that information security regulation has played in shaping the way that we transact in electronic communications. This paper also singles out some areas of potential future regulation from an EU perspective in a non exclusive manner. This paper reports on recent developments like the ENISA Case at the European Court of Justice that *inter alia* confirms the role of an Agency as an instrument in the approximation of Laws in the EU Internal Market. In this perspective the outlook for further cooperation at the EU level within the First Pillar of network and information security looks more promising than ever.

Note: The author acknowledges that this article reflects personal opinion and it does not in any way represent the opinion of ENISA or any other person or an ENISA body in any way whatsoever.

Introducing Regulatory Compliance Requirements Engineering

Shahbaz Ali[1] · Jon Hall[2]

[1]Tarmin Technologies Ltd
Shahbaz.ali@tarmin.com

[2]Centre for Research in Computing
The Open University
J.G.Hall@open.ac.uk

Abstract

A recent study by the University of California at Berkeley [Ucla03] has observed that information in e-mails and other electronic records is growing at a rate of 30% per year. Secure, efficient information asset usage lends increasing importance to the integration, protection, analysis, and storage in organisational systems. Information assets are valuable, not least to the individual, and the introduction of legislative and regulatory frameworks, such as the Data Protection Act acknowledges this; it is the duty of organisations to exercise Regulatory Compliance [Idc04, Fisma03, Sox02, Isgi06, and Grsm06], largely understood to be a component of the organisation's information security contexts and Information Lifecycle Management (ILM).

Despite the increasing number of publications in security requirements engineering (RE), little or no research has so far taken place in order to address requirements for software systems to which Regulatory Compliance applies. Although a number of security RE approaches appear to offer potential for a solution, we argue that current approaches to security requirements are inadequate when it comes to addressing the issues of organisations as they face the changing legislation and regulation.

This position paper also argues the need for a flexible and responsive approach to system RE that properly distinguishes between security and compliance requirements and facilitates the understanding of the overall role of compliance requirements in RE. It calls attention to the potential benefits to be had from the unification of the views of compliance requirements analysis from the standpoints of software RE and of organisational systems. Using Problem Frames, our research is exploring the use of conceptual tools as a foundation to model the impact of compliance requirements, and will lead to a stronger compliance RE framework that allows an organisation to engineer changes to their existing socio-technical systems and to do so in a non-disruptive manner.

1 Introduction

Software engineering (SE) consists of various activities and procedures for creating software systems. Requirements engineering (RE) is an early lifecycle activity related to the elicitation and analysis of requirements for software systems. SE, especially RE, is increasingly relevant for the class of systems that consist of both technological and social sub-systems that maintain and sustain organisational activities, also known as socio-technical systems. Flynn defines a socio-technical system as "any unit in the organisation composed of a technological and a social sub-system having a common goal or task to accomplish" [Flyn98]. The social subsystem comprises people interacting with other people and with technology in order to accomplish such tasks. Here, as well as software design, system engineering issues include the

S. Paulus, N. Pohlmann, H. Reimer (Editors): Securing Electronic Business Processes, Vieweg (2006), 439-447

development of employee and group training and education materials, and the partitioning of system functionality over social and technical subsystems.

Due to the rapid acceptance of business over the Internet, an organisation's socio-technical systems face new challenges: socio-technical systems can now typically be accessed by different stakeholders from remote geographic locations over wide area networks, and this outward facing role leaves the organisation susceptible to the difficult problem of compliance. The introduction of legislation and regulation has significantly increased the importance of integrating, accessing, analysing, and storing information in socio-technical systems. Examples include the Sarbanes-Oxley Act of 2002 (SOX), the Health Insurance Portability and Accountability Act (HIPAA), SEC 17-4A, UK Data Protection Act, UK Freedom of Information Act (FOIA), European E-SIGN Directives, US FISMA [Fisma03] which, due to their high impact on information flow and their content within socio-technical systems, are also known as Information Intensive Regulation [Idc04].

Government and legislators legally define the procedures and rules involved in regulation and legislation but these can be and are *interpreted* differently, depending on the context and viewpoint of those in the organisation responsible for implementing them. Regulatory Compliance can be defined as the organisational management function that respects and abides by all relevant legislative regulation and legislation. At its most basic, compliance is a mandate for a specific set of businesses to meet a specified set of objectives with the intent of protecting or enhancing the public good.

Legislation and regulation aimed at organisations by implication directly or otherwise constrain the behaviours and structures of an organisation's socio-technical systems. Preserving value and sustainability whilst satisfying regulation and legislation is sometimes a difficult trade-off. Examples of questions that must be answered for each organisation are, for instance:

- Which legislation and regulation applies to the organisation?
- To what extent must relevant legislation and regulation be followed?
- What are the valid interpretations of relevant legislation and regulation?
- Which areas (including geographic) of the organisation are covered by legislation and regulation?
- What are the changes that are required to satisfy legislation and regulation?

The challenge of redesigning the organisation is a matter of answering these, and other, questions. Most, although not all, organisations would wish to find the most cost-effective solution. "How far can current RE techniques help?" is, therefore, a timely question that we feel is worthy of further investigation.

2 Background

2.1 Compliance and Security

Due to their regulatory nature, rules and policy based contexts, compliance initiatives can often be seen as part of the Information Security domain [Cald03, Mass05, Isgi06, and Grsm06]. Indeed, a review of the major information-intensive regulation shows that they address some of the requirements for information security and process integrity. Examples include:

- Implementing airtight processes that support control over information processing, thereby ensuring its integrity [Ander02, Boza99, Schn96];

- Controlling and managing access to, or use of, specified information, along with the tools needed to audit use over time [Ander02];

- Information retention with content security: Managing the indexing, secure retrieval, and storage of information retained for long periods of time [Ander02, Irvi03];

- Trust Management and Policy Management [Blaz96, Blaz99, Blaz00].

Traditionally, security researchers and cryptographers have focused on threat analysis [Ander01], crypto-analysis, Trust Management and Algorithm Analysis [Boza99, Schn99]. For the analysis and design of secure systems, Security Requirements Engineering (SRE) has been identified as a separate area of research. There are a variety of SRE approaches and frameworks that appear to offer potential for their application in compliance initiatives. Examples include the Problem Frames approach (to which we return in the next section) [Jack00] and its extensions to security [Nuse03], goal oriented requirements engineering [Kava02, Lams01, Lams00, Sind03], Abuse case [McDe99], Misuse cases [Alex02], KAOS – Anti Goals [Lams01, Lams04], with UMLSec [Jurj01] as well as others. At a high level of abstraction, all of these techniques rely on similar information from stakeholders to capture requirements (e.g., through goals, domains or use cases), but differ in method, perspective and emphasis. However, although related, there are additional factors that make requirements stemming from compliance different from those stemming from security:

Firstly, RE and SRE generally focus on the needs of interested stakeholders, whether they be the customers, employees and users of the organisation's products and services, or hackers wanting to compromise security. Hence, much work in RE and SRE focuses on the elicitation of interested stakeholders' needs, dealing with the complexity of their expression – conflicts, ambiguities, etc – and establishing developer workable descriptions of their requirements. Compliance requirements, on the other hand, are not derived from the needs of any particular stakeholder group: legislators define entities such as the Security Exchange Commission Auditors, Data Registrars, and Compliance Officers who have responsibilities to ensure that organisations are compliant. In most cases, these entities have no detailed knowledge of the organisation and/or the organisational system's functional and non-functional requirements.

Secondly, compliance initiatives are associated with both intra and inter-organisation activities. Due to high impact of regulations on an organisation's operational procedures, financial policies and information workflow [Rules04], compliance requirements are constraints not only on system functions, but also the organisation's non-system functions such as organisational policies and day-to-day operations, including those of other organisations in the organisation's context.

As an example of what we mean consider the following example, from an Email Messaging and Archiving based workflow, in which an email is usually sent with a footer that contains the socio-technical information disclaimer statement (in order to comply with Freedom of Information Act as well as UK Data Protection Act) and a mandate of the organisational security and/or compliance policy. In this context this mandate is consent from the organisation on behalf of the sender. This type of interaction between stakeholders is part of a socio-technical system and requires a compliance policy. An example footer statement in a form of a legal disclaimer from, say, the ABC Corporation can be seen below:

DISCLAIMER

This message and any information contained within it, including but not limited to subject matter, addressees and their e-mail addresses and attachments hereto are intended only for the personal and confidential use of the designated recipients named herein. Internet communications may not be secure and may be intercepted, redirected or spoofed and therefore ABC inc. does not accept legal responsibility for the contents of this message unless independently verified in writing or digitally certified. Any views or options presented are solely those of the author and do not necessarily represent those of ABC Inc. unless otherwise specifically stated. You are hereby notified that if you have received this message in error any review, dissemination, distribution or copying of this message is unlawful and strictly prohibited, and you should, with normal business courtesy, immediately notify the sender of the incident and then destroy this message by deletion and removal from your Deleted Items folder. Any opinions, explicit or implied, are solely those of the author and do not necessarily represent those of ABC group of companies

This is a simple case but the net effects of these socio-technological cultural changes on employees, customers, other stake holders as well as online IT systems form an important part of the issues that compliance requirements engineering should address, for, in effect, ensuring that email communications comply has lead ABC Inc. to extend the boundaries of their policies to those outside of their organisation, in particular, to all those who intentionally or accidentally receive email from ABC Inc. Such culture has a high impact on the operating context of the affected socio-technical system, and so can complicate the implementation of requirements.

Finally, and as pointed out by Moffett and Nuseibeh [Nuse03], "... there is no satisfactory integration of security requirements engineering into requirements engineering as a whole". This makes it extremely difficult for requirement engineers to select and apply the appropriate security RE techniques to regulatory requirements. Moreover, Compliance RE should operate in the wider context of socio-technical systems. There is, therefore, an urgent need for conceptual tools that can aid in applying RE techniques to compliance requirements. This is the gap our research addresses.

2.2 Problem Frames

The Problem Frames Approach (PF) [Jack00] is an approach to software requirements analysis. PF is a set of concepts to be used when gathering requirements and creating specifications for computer software. Its basic philosophy is strikingly different from other software requirements methods in insisting that:

- Gaining a good understanding of the problem is an important step towards producing a fit-for-purpose solution.

- The best way to approach requirements analysis is through a process of parallel — not hierarchical — decomposition of user requirements.

- User requirements are about relationships in the real world; not about functions that the software system must perform.

One of the aims of the Problem Frames approach is to identify basic classes of problem that recur throughout software development. A recent extension [Brie06] considers the uses of problem frames in changing organisational contexts by capturing repeating responses to organisational change as *change frames*. Each class is characterised by a problem template that includes:

- The topology of the change problem – i.e., the relationship of the organisation to its environment and the information and other flows between;

- The characteristics of the domains involved – i.e., whether they are environmental or organisational, and which are their behaviours;

- The characteristics of the drivers, enablers, levers and foundations for change – i.e., what are the reasons for change, why is the change occurring, what are the mechanisms by which it can come about, and where will it be done;

- A way of building and discharging arguments that argue that the organisation's response is adequate.

When an organisation faces a particular change for which a change frame exists, i.e., for which the topology, domains involved, and driver, enablers, levers and foundations match, a change frame suggests responses that have proved adequate elsewhere, and provides the structure of arguments that can be used to justify the fitness for purpose of the suggestions in the new context. Brier's *et als*' view is relevant to compliance requirements engineering since change through compliance is typically of ongoing relevance for an organisation.

Of course, most real problems are too complex to fit single change frames and require, rather, the restructuring of the problem as a collection of (interacting) sub-problems, each of which is smaller and simpler than the original. Problem decomposition is the PF process through which this is achieved. Moreover, standard decompositions – called AFrames – can be used to guide problem decomposition. AFrames is short for Architectural Frames, [Rapa04], in which known effective solution structures – solution architectures – are linked to the expression of a problem.

2.3 Abuse and Misuse Cases

McDermott and Fox coined the term 'Abuse Case' [McDe99] as a way of eliciting security requirements; an abuse case "defines an interaction between an actor and a system that results in harm to a resource associated with one of the actors, one of the stakeholders, or the system itself". Abuse case may also be regarded as a synonym for misuse case [Alex02].

Abuse/Misuse Cases appear to offer potential to cover Non-Functional Requirements (NFRs) such as for safety and security. Problem description, such as those resulting from PF elicitation analysis, need to withstand security threats. Once problems are clear and have gone through elicitation stage, Abuse cases can be used to model security threats. In this context, our approach combines Use and Misuse Cases and is applied at any level from whole systems down through subsystems to individual elements and components. This approach is inherently stepwise, so it can be combined easily with step-wise problem decompositions.

Our research aim is to see regulatory compliance requirements engineering as the parametrisation of the problem frames framework for the satisfaction of compliance problems. This has three parts:

- Identifying languages and techniques that are able to record the detail of compliance problems;

- The building of frames suitable for capturing repeated responses to compliance problems; and

- The development of standard decomposition guides – compliance AFrames – for problem decomposition.

Based on Brier's Change Frames approaches, we propose to introduce a conceptual modeling tool, Compliance Frames, to model repeated problem structures found in compliance requirements engineering. Because of the importance of various stakeholders attached to these requirements (e.g. thought leadership of organisation, compliance attorneys, auditors and registrars and other unknown stakeholders), compliance frames will also use the Abuse Case approach to ensure that compliance procedures can withstand security threats covering interaction with internal policies as well as system boundaries.

3 Compliance Frames – A Data Protection Example

Email is easily the most widely used way to exchange and record information. The information exchanged can be sensitive and may have monetary value associated with it. Email is therefore subject to legislation and regulation in many ways, including Data Protection. In this section we present a simple case of Email compliance to make sure that email policies are activated.

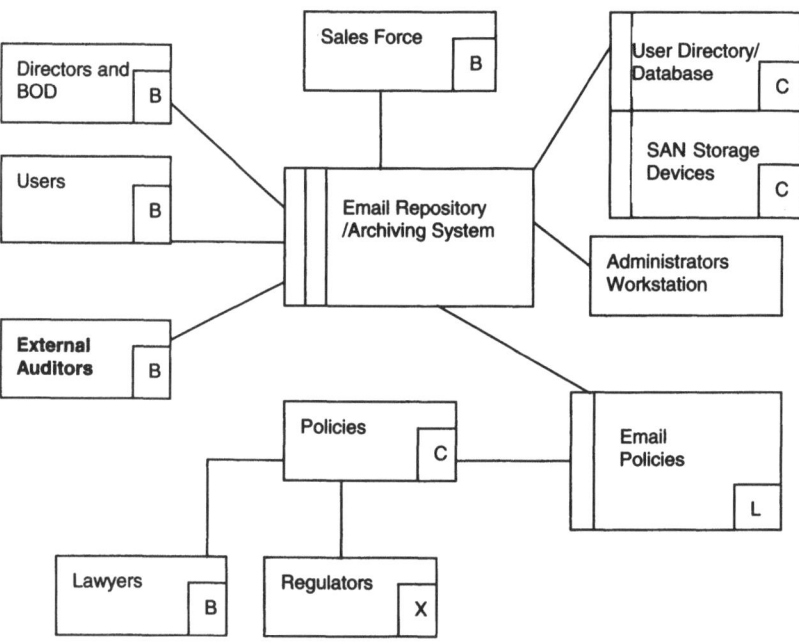

Figure 1: Compliance Frame Example for ABC Inc's Email Compliance
High Level Problem Context Diagram for Email Compliance with Data Protection Initiatives

Let use suppose that ABC Inc's existing Email system is based on a commodity messaging platform such as Microsoft Exchange or Lotus Domino and is linked with SAN based devices for efficient storage. The system uses LDAP (Lightweight Directory Access Protocol) for users to have access to user directory. Each of these entities is represented in the problem context diagram of Figure 1.

Now, consider the following scenario: ABC Inc needs to provide access to External Auditors for compliance with Data Protection. (This could be various regulations but for the purpose of this example we focus on Data Protection).

The regulation involves regulators, lawyers and the IT department to introduce the Email Policy domain in which is recorded the policies governing Email. This is necessary as this step simplifies *what* precisely may be required in order to implement the compliance.

We use biddable domains highlighted with a small square 'B' to model the social domains within this socio-technical system. The importance of each biddable domain depends on the regulation implemented. For example, in this context diagram, Sales Force deals and negotiated contracts with customers, partners or potential external 3rd parties to generate revenue. This information regarding customers, etc., needs to be protected.

To ensure that this particular elicitation approach can withstand the security attacks, we apply the Misuse Case approach (Figure 2)

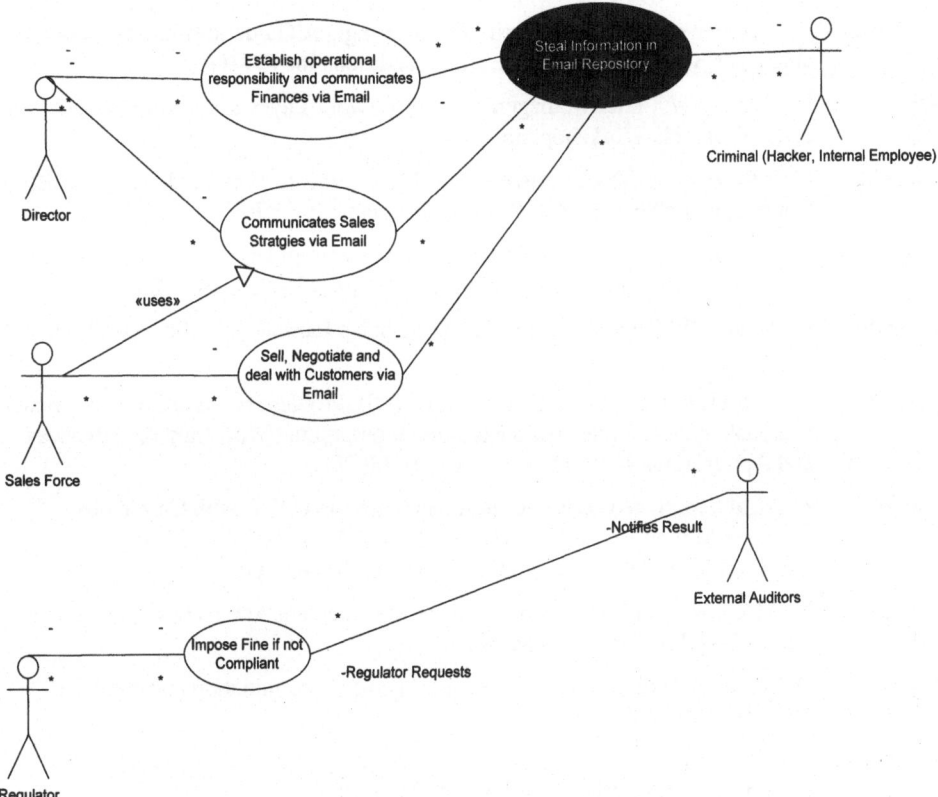

Figure 2: Misuse Case Modeling for ABC Inc's Email Compliance

These threats can be categorized on interactive *biddable domains* which can be modeled as *Actors*. Through the analysis (not presented) we are able to deduce those email activities that need to be safe guarded. This information can help in implementation of policies where rules can be defined to ensure that system deals with these threats.

4 Conclusion

Problem Frames capture important information about the problem context in the real world. *Compliance Frames* are based on Problem Frames and their application is highly appropriate on identifying well-understood problems from other domains such as those mentioned above (which are typically associated with social subsystem) and on offering the possibility of an appropriate well-understood solutions. Based on this understanding, we take the viewpoint that *Compliance Frames* can be applied to create these policies and procedures on well defined *compliance context requirements*.

References

[Alex02]   I. Alexander, "Misuse Cases," Proceedings of International Requirements Engineering Conference (RE'02), 2002.

[Ander01] Ross Anderson (2001), "Why Information Security is Hard – An Economic Perspective" University of Cambridge, Computer Labs 30th January 2001

[Ander02] Ross Anderson (2002), "Security Engineering", A Guide to Building Dependable Distributed Systems, John Willey and Sons Inc (2001)

[Blaz99]   M. Blaze *et el*, "Trust Management and Network Layer Security Protocols," Security Protocols Workshop, pp. 103-118, 1999.

[Blaz96]   Matt Blaze *et el*, "Decentralized Trust Management," presented at Proc. IEEE Conference on Security and Privacy, Oakland CA, 1996

[Blaz00]   Matt Blaze *et el*, "The Role of Trust Management in Distributed Systems Security," Secure Internet Programming, vol. 20, pp. 185-210, 1999-2000.

[Boza99]   E. Bozaki, "IP Security Protocols," Dr. Dobb's Journal, vol. 306, pp. 42-55, 1999.

[Brier06] John Brier, Lucia Rapanotti, and Jon G. Hall. Problem based analysis of organisational change: a real-world example, International Workshop on Advances and Applications of Problem Frames. ACM, 2006

[Cald03]   Jose Caldera, Survivability Requirements for the U.S. Health Care Industry, Carnegie Mellon University, Masters Thesis (May 2003) - pp37-45 http://www.cert.org/archive/pdf/surv-us-health-thesis.pdf

[Fisma03] FISMA – Federal Information Security Management Act. National Institute of Technology http://csrc.nist.gov/sec-cert/

[Flyn98]   D. Flynn. Information Systems Requirements: Determination and Analysis. McGraw-Hill, 2nd edition, 1998.

[Grsm06]   http://www.govtech.net/magazine/channel_story.php?channel=6&id=92578 Government Regulations and Security Management Survey

[Idc04]   Regulatory Compliance: What Role Will Technology Play? IDC #31213, April 2004.

[Irvi03]   C. E. Irvine, "Cybersecurity Considerations for Information Systems," Center for Information Systems Security Studies and Research, Department of Computer Science, Naval Postgraduate School, Monterey, California 93943, 2003.

[Isgi06]   Information Security Governance: Information Systems Audit and Controls Association. http://www.isaca.org/Template.cfm?Section=Research2&Template= /TaggedPage/TaggedPageDisplay.cfm&TPLID=14&ContentID=7396

[Jack00]   M. Jackson, "Problem Frames: Analysing and Structuring Software Development Problems", Addison Wesley. ISBN 020159627X

[Jurj01]   J. Jurjens, "Developing Secure Systems with UMLsec From Business Processes to Implementation," Paper at VIS'2001, Computing Laboratory, University of Oxford, GB, 2001.

[Kava02]   Evangelia Kavakli, Goal Oriented Requirements Engineering: A Unifying Framework, Department of Cultural Technology and Communication, University of the Aegean.

[Lams01]   A. van Lamsweerde et el, "Goal-oriented Elaboration of Security Requirements," Louvain-la-Neuve, Annee academique 2000-2001, 2001

[Lams00]   A. van Lamsweerde and E. Letier, "Handling Obstacles in Goal-oriented Requirements Engineering," IEEE Transactions on Software Engineering, 26(10). 2000. 2000.

[Lams04]   A. van Lamsweerde et el, "Elaborating Security Requirements by Construction of Intentional Anti-Models", Louvain-la-Neuve, Annee academique 2003-2004, 2004

[McDe99]   McDermott, J. & Fox, C. "Using Abuse Case Models for Security Requirements Analysis," 55-64. Proceedings 15th Annual Computer Security Applications Conference. Scottsdale, AZ, Dec. 6-10, 1999. Los Alamitos, CA: IEEE Computer Society Press, 1999.

[Mass05]   Fabio Massacci and Marco Prest and Nicola Zannone, "Using a Security Requirements Engineering Methodology in Practice: The compliance with the Italian Data Protection Legislation" CSI, 2005

[Nuse03]   B. A. Nuseibeh and Jonathan D. Moffett, "A Framework for Security Requirements Engineering," Open University Security Requirements Group, 2003.

[Rapa04]   Lucia Rapanotti, Jon G. Hall, Michael Jackson, and Bashar Nuseibeh. Architecture-driven problem decomposition. In 12th IEEE International Conference on Requirements Engineering (RE 2004), pages 80–89. IEEE Computer Society, 2004

[Rules04]   Rules Rules Rules –http://www.informationweek.com/story/showArticle.jhtml ?article-ID=20301021&pgno=1

[Schn96]   B. Schneier, Applied Cryptography, Second Edition: Protocols, Algorithms, and Source Code in C: Wiley Computer

[Schn99]   B. Schneier, "Attack Trees: Modeling Security Threats", Dr. Dobb's Journal, December 1999.

[Sind03]   D. G. F. Guttorm Sindre, Andreas L. Opdahl, "A Reuse-Based Approach to Determining Security Requirements," 2003.

[Sox02]   Sarbanes-Oxley Act of 2002 - http://www.sec.gov/divisions/corpfin/faqs/soxact2002.htm

[Ucla03]   How much information? University of California at Berkeley, 2003 http://www.sims.berkeley.edu/research/projects/how-much-info-2003/

Legal Issues in Secure Grid Computing Environments

Irene Kafeza[1] · Eleanna Kafeza[2] · Felix Wai-Hon Chan[3]

[1]Attorney at law
kafeza.e@dsa.gr

[2]Athens University of Economics and Business,
Department of Marketing and Communication
kafeza@aueb.gr

[3]The University of Hong Kong, Faculty of Law
fwhchan@hku.hk

Abstract

The Grid environment is rapidly emerging as the dominant paradigm for wide area distributed application systems. The world wide business demand for intense problem solving capabilities and grid computing makes it possible to share computing resources on an unprecedented scale among geographically distributed participants. In a grid environment virtual organisations are formulated and managed from a computing resource point of view. The grid provider allows for the dynamic discovery of computing resources, the immediate allocation and provision of the resources, the management and provision of secure access. Although the security problem in grid environment is being addressed from the technological point of view, there is no work to identify the myriad legal issues that are arising in grid business transactions.

1 Introduction

The new generation of advanced grid technologies enabled the use of pervasively networked and interoperable computing resources as a technological infrastructure for easier access to processing, reproduction and transmission of data. The shared access to widely distributed computing resources promises to greatly lower the time and costs of accessing and using data for a number of purposes. The placement of such powerful dynamically shaped technology into the mainstream comes with some complications. The danger this development brings with it is that what is gained in efficiency may be lost in privacy; thus, new ways of dealing with security are needed. Although the grid's unsuitability to regulation seems simply a fact , the structure of intellectual property rights could force technological gatekeepers to block unauthorised uses of data and allow only authorized data flows.

The Grid computing environment is a collection of heterogeneous computing resources that are shared by many individuals and organizations. These resources are collaborating to offer more effective solutions to a variety of business problems. A successful grid business model requires a secure platform that will enable safe and stable collaboration of various resource owners and service users. This requirement is twofold: on one hand a secure technical infrastructure has to be in place and on the other hand a legal framework has to be introduced to increase confidentiality and enable predictability of commercial transactions on the grid.

S. Paulus, N. Pohlmann, H. Reimer (Editors): Securing Electronic Business Processes, Vieweg (2006), 448-454

Regarding security, in the globus case the Grid Security Infrastructure (GSI) uses PKI and X.509 certificates. The system identifies every user/service on the grid by a standard X.509 certificate that contains information about the user/service signed by a third party CA to certify it. GSI uses the secure socket layers/transport layer security (SSL/TSL) authentication. The two parties exchange their certificates and when each verifies that a trusted CA signed the other/s certificate, they establish an authenticated session [F-98]. But from the legal point of view several issues have to be addressed in order to create a trusted grid environment for business transactions [K-05, KTB-05].

Applying the arguments of [Z-06] about the generative internet to the grid environment, the grid technology expands the boundaries of leverage, adaptability and accessibility for information technology. Hundreds and thousands of machines can be connected, convey and change information, deploy programmes, in seconds thus exposed to instantaneous change. In such an environment publishers are vulnerable to latest tools of IP infringement and information is available for installation within moments. Grid participants might have concerns about computer virus that can exploit their ignorance and be sceptical when allowing code to run on their machine. Cyber law has to deal effectively with these vulnerabilities without at the same time compromise the "generativity" property of the grid.

A legal framework is necessary that will allow safe transactions among the organisations and /or individuals that dynamically form the grid. The way contracts can be created and managed in a grid environment is of paramount importance for planning and implementing grids. In most cases grids operate in a globalized environment and the parties have to establish contractual relationships. A master agreement is formed among the parties for the sharing of the resources. At run time, the grid broker acts as an agent of the grid provider and dynamically discovers the appropriate resources that can execute the job and negotiates the contract with them.

Privacy and intellectual property requirements are magnified in the globalized grid environment due to the distributed nature of the data and computing resources. In our work we identify a set of intellectual property issues that need to be addressed in the grid environment. The grid provider transfers the data from the user to the grid resources. In some cases the data is cached and in other cases duplication of data is necessary in order to achieve better performance and minimize transfer times. During this process the data is copied hence potentially exposed to unauthorised use. In our work we discuss data access and use policies that have to be in place to protect the grid provider from copyright infringement.

2 Contracts in the Grid Environment

2.1 Licensing in the Grid

Copyright Law protection has proved to be ineffective in protecting the vendor software in grid environment therefore software license agreements are utilizing contractual provisions that are more restrictive than copyright law, to protect software usage. There are two major issues that concern the grid community regarding grid licensing. The first issue stems from the fact that most of the software modules that implement grid computing are open source and the second issue is that grid software provided by vendors executes in several nodes and traditional licensing schemes are ineffective.

Most grid software and middleware is developed by academic projects and is released under open source licenses. Globus Toolkit is an open source project and the most common component incorporated into a large number of grid packages therefore vendors that implement grid software based on Globus are concerned about licensing.

One of the most commonly used free software license is GPL. Software licensed under GPL is provided at no cost or at very low cost to cover the expenses of the transfer. GPL requires that any distributed modification must be licensed under the GPL. According to [Ca-05] in GPL the licensees are restricted from using GPL-covered code in proprietary derivatives in order to preserve access to the software for all users. In this sense grid software licensed under GPL discourages its commercialization because it is difficult for vendors to produce propriety software. Liability issues arise in enterprises when open source software is mixed with non-open source software in the production environment.

According to Ian Foster [F-05], Globus is using BSD licenses that allow individuals or organizations to make modification or enhancements to the code without contributing that code back to the open source community. He argues that such license encourages a vibrant commercial support industry. It seems that licensing for open source grid software and middleware is using an open source licensing model but other licensing issues are arising in commercial grid products.

The vendors that develop grid software and middleware utilize private contracts to control liability and separate the rights granted with the transfer of software from the rights excluded. The current software licenses work per processor, per device or per user. The essence of Grid computing is to provide efficient resource on demand and it is differentiated from conventional distributed computing by permitting large scale resource sharing. Grid accounting and grid economics is a problem of major concern and unless it is efficiently addressed it is likely to damage the grid market. Grid technology has started to move into mainstream enterprise but software vendors cannot license their software to satisfy the needs of an on-demand computation model. Currently many companies sell grid software "per processor" that makes grid solutions not affordable since grid computing is based on a dynamic resource allocation. A problem can be solved in 4 machines for 30 days or use partially up to 2000 machines in one day, in the latter case the enterprise should buy beforehand software licenses for 2000 machines. The issues arise because the grid user is paying full price for software that is not fully exploiting the machine that is shared in a virtual environment.

Users need dynamic pricing that will reflect their actual grid usage that might be a fraction of the maximum computing cycles they consume at peak times. Finding the pricing unit for the grid is a problem to be solved. Issues like network cost, on-demand availability, CPU time, disk space are to be considered. These issues should be addressed by new licensing schemes. There are some thorny issues to be addressed when considering new licensing schemes and their enforceability. According to [N-05] all agreed restrictions or conditions of use should be enforceable unless contradicting contract law doctrines. In the grid environment it is better for the market to tailor licensing in grid transactions to fit it actual needs rather than to use legislative or regulatory groups to impose the rules of copyright law.

Another issue that needs to be clarified when dealing with the enforceability of licenses is whether there exist proper offer and acceptance [M-03]. The internet as a place metaphor [M-03] seems to fail in the case of grid environment. Wrongful access to a computer does not have a clear boundary since it might concern the information stored on the client PC, the use of the processor, the use of storage, the computation cycles, and the consumed bandwidth. As new pricing and accounting models are being developed in the grid community and while most of them are results of academic research and not widely adopted in the market, it is essential for every new licensing mechanism to be well understood and accepted by both parties.

2.2 Contracting a node to the Grid

Grid technology separates applications and information from the infrastructure they run thus adjusting infrastructure to business demands. Any resources available within an organisation can participate in solving a grid problem including computing power, data, hardware, software, applications, networking services. At run time, the grid broker acts as an agent of the grid provider and dynamically discovers the appropriate resources owned by an organisation that can execute the job. A master agreement has to be formed among the parties for the sharing of the resources and there are several issues concerning the resource allocation.

The grid environment challenges basic assumptions of ownership, access, usage and assets. The existing metaphor that assumes an internet location as a place and the PC connected to the Internet as property of one owner seems inadequate in the grid environment. The master agreement between the grid broker and the resource owner concerns CPU cycles, deployment of software, temporal constraints, ownership, access rights to the data that is stored on user resource, access and ownership of the programs running on the resource. Applying [N-05] in grid, contracts are not property rights but creations of exchanges made in a marketplace and they should be enforced independent of issues about the proper scope of property rights.

Having in mind that the grid provider is also subject to Service Level Agreements with his/her client, Quality of Service has to be guaranteed. In this sense the contract between the broker and the resource owner should guarantee a certain degree of security regarding the availability of the resource and adequate pricing techniques should be in place. At the same time the resource owner is at risk when accepting third party software to use the resource because of viruses and other malicious code. The software might fail to work, acquire control of the host system without user authorisation and perform malicious actions, use memory that otherwise would be used by the owners programs thus slowing down their operation.

In more dynamic grid environments intelligent agents are employed by the grid to dynamically discover resources and negotiate the contract of their participation in the grid automatically (using web services technology). In these case issues that pertain to intelligent agent contracting should be carefully examined [KKC-05].

Therefore, contracts between grid providers and resource owners should clearly define who should bear the risk. This may vary depending on the nature of the relationship, and sometimes should be considered in case by case basis.

A central issue in grid computing is whether it is considered to be a lease agreement by the client or a service agreement by the grid provider. Several issues can arise based on the adopted view. For example in the leasing case the owner of the results of the grid processing is the client, while in the service case the service provider gives a license to the client to use the results. In a grid environment the grid provider is entering to a contract agreement (e.g. clickwrap) with all participating virtual organisations and independent grid node providers. Before entering into the agreement the grid provider has to verify that the virtual organisation has the right to provide the resource to the grid environment. It also has to specify service level agreements that will restrict the organisation. Due to the dynamic nature of the grid environment, it is very important that the participating nodes remain consistent to their commitment of availability of the resource. This will enable the grid broker to make an efficient scheduling of the resources and finish the data processing in time.

3 Privacy in the grid environment

The grid environment coordinates resource sharing in dynamic and multi institutional virtual organizations. Grid interactions are interactions among users and services that act on behalf of the user. Data privacy issues are becoming critical as more and more industry and academic organizations are connecting their resources implementing cross organizational computing infrastructures. Grids are capable of processing huge amount of data using new expanded possibilities of storing, comparing, linking, selecting and accessing personal data that can be placed simultaneously at the disposal of thousands of geographically dispersed users. In a commercialized grid environment clients should be able to share personal information as well as to place limitations on the current and future use of their personal information.

Data and data processing is protected by data protection laws [EC -02] thus exposing the grid provider and the grid participants to liability issues. At the same time, the use of data in heterogeneous distributed and dynamic environments (like the grid) increases concern of the clients regarding the misuse of their information. According to data protection principles [L-00] data held for any purpose or purposes shall not be used or disclosed in any manner incompatible with that purpose or those purposes. As mentioned in [EPPS-05] statistical disclosure is a major risk in grid environments. When data are given to the grid provider through the client or an intermediary, the provider partitions and replicates data in the grid infrastructure. This replication offers fault tolerance and improved performance. Can the client claim that the data is not used for the purpose collected? How can the provider guarantee that each participating node will use the data only for the specified purposes?

In the grid environment there is a need to balance competing interests of privacy. The user (the grid client) is entitled to access his/her data held by the grid broker and where appropriate to have such data corrected or erased. A controversial point concerning the grid broker's operation is that, while the user can request and obtain access to his/her data from the grid broker, it is not clear whether this access includes revealing information regarding where the data reside and other information regarding the grid nodes that store and process the data. The advanced ability of the grid agents to collect information could be considered as an invasion in individual's privacy and personal space. In service grids, resource owners might provide their resources but be unwilling to expose information regarding the characteristics of their resources and even the fact that they participate in the grid.

 In the case of the grid environment the data circulation is dynamic. The transfer of data is decided based on the availability of nodes that can execute the task at the specific point in time and the replication optimizing the performance of the grid at the specific point in time. These are real time decisions that can not be pre-defined. Moreover the rules that govern such decisions are part of the logic of the software of the grid broker and many times not publicly available. In discussing invasions of privacy, courts use the concept of reasonable expectation of privacy in the sense that data protection legislation protects information as to which the individual has exhibited a subjective expectation of privacy as long as the expectation is one that society recognizes as reasonable. The grid user reasonably expects in good faith that the grid provider will make sure that the circulation of data is done for their efficient processing and for no other reason than that.

A well drafted contract between the grid provider and the resource owner could ensure efficient and balanced protection. The contract should facilitate the lawful and fairly circulation of data within the grid environment and specify the obligations of the grid provider and the grid node. As noted in [GSW-04] in data grids users usually do not object to have the grid provider collect and publish cumulative statistics provided that the data can not be manipulated to obtain information about a specific record or a specific data source. In cases where data mining algorithms are allowed to execute in the data they should guarantee that the algorithm produces statistics that guarantee privacy.

We believe that appropriate software should be provided (by the grid provider to the user) to allow the user to view and update the application data as well as his/her personal data. The software should be able to inform the user regarding the number of nodes that execute his/her application, the number of partitions made of the application data and the number of replicas of the data at the moment of request.

4 Intellectual Property in the grid environment

In grid environment the grid broker distributes software and data that allow grid nodes to execute the specific jobs assigned to them. Although the grid network objective is to share digital files and programs in a collaborative environment, the capabilities and connectivity that exists in the grid environments allow recipients to easily distribute copyrighted material without authorization. As part of their services, grid providers transfer data and software files that may be accessed and by necessity copied in the grid nodes. Issues arise when the grid nodes abuse this privilege and copy and/or post material that violates copyright law [EC -00].

The software application provider (ASP) provides the software to be deployed to the grid nodes for the data processing. The software application provider can be the client himself or another organisation or several other organisations or an intermediary. Several issues arise regarding this software:

1. The grid provider usually has direct access to this software. This software is transmitted through the grid network, giving to third parties opportunity to copy and/or modify it. Therefore the grid provider is responsible to provide a grid infrastructure that guarantees secure transfer of information. The grid computing data exchange must be protected using secure communication channels (SSL/TLS) in combination with secure message exchange mechanisms (WS-security, GSI).

2. In cases where the client requests from the grid provider the use of processing software of a third party without a valid licence or outside the scope of the licence, the grid provider and the software provider may be found liable for intellectual property infringement.

3. If the grid provider modifies the software or the results of the software for their own purposes then the client is entitled to copyright protection.

Software licences used in a grid environment should constraint the grid provider and the grid nodes to only make authorised use of the software. The software provider (that might be the client, the grid broker, a member of the grid virtual organisation or an intermediary) should be liable if it fails to obtain appropriate rights. The contract should restrict software modifications. At the same time it should also clarify that the necessary exchange of data within the grid environment for efficient computing is not misuse of data under applicable data protection laws.

Another approach is that because the grid environment is an open, large scale, globally shared environment, when infringement occurs it may be difficult to enforce rights in the protected work effectively against the direct infringers. Therefore it seems that the only practical alternative might be to go after the grid provider.

5 Discussion

It is clear that several legal issues arise in grid environments and several steps need to be taken in order to regulate the smooth execution of grid transactions. In this work we identified issues we are expecting to arise in court cases in the near future. Although well drafted contracts may reduce the risks, they do not always provide a solution and clients should be aware that not all risks can be contracted away. In addition we believe that middleware should be developed that will allow for the efficient monitoring of the grid procedures by the grid broker. As the grid technology is being commercialised a legal framework is necessary that will deal with the described issues. As a first step it is necessary for the legal and the industrial community to identify the problems and look for efficient solutions.

In our future work we are looking into the problem of designing grid middleware that will provide adequate accounting and monitoring mechanisms. We are also looking into the legal problems that are arising in a grid pervasive computing environment.

References

[EC -00]   Directive 2000/31/EC on Electronic Commerce.

[EC -02]   Directive 2002/58/EC on Privacy and Electronic Communications.

[EPPS-05]   Elliot M., Pickles S., Purdam K., Smith D., Disclosure Risk and Grid Computing, Fifth All Hands Meeting, 18th - 21st September 2006 Nottingham.

[F-05]   Foster I., License to Grid, The Globus Consortium Journal, 7/2005.

[F-98]   Foster I., Kesselman C., Tsudik G., Tuecke S., A Security Architecture for Computational Grids. Proc. 5th ACM Conference on Computer and Communications Security Conference, pg. 83-92, 1998.

[Ga-05]   Carver B., Share and Ahare Alike: Understanding and Enforcing Open Source and Free Software Licenses, Berkley Technology Law Journal, 20 Berkley Tech. L.J. 443, 2005.

[GSW-04]   Giburd B, Schuster A, Wolff R, K-TTP: A new privacy model for large scale distributed environments, KDD 2004, August 2004, Suattle, USA.

[K-05]   Kesler J. C, Contractual and Regulatory Compliance Challenges in Grid Computing Environments, Proceedings of the 2005 IEEE International Conference on Services Computing , 2005.

[KTB-05]   Kanaskar N, Topaloglu U., Bayrak C, Globus Security Model for Grid Environment, ACM SIGSOFT Software Engineering Notes, November 2005, 30, 6.

[L-00]   Lloyd. J. Ian. Information Technology Law, Butterworths, 2000.

[M-03]   Madison M., Rights and the Shape of the Internet, Boston College Law School, 44 B.C.L. Rev 433, 2003.

[N-05]   Nimmer R., Introduction: Issues in licensing an introduction, Houston Law Review, 42 Hous. L. Rev. 941, 2005.

[Z-06]   Zittrain J., The Generative Internet, The Harvard Law Review Association, 119 Harv. L. Rev. 1974, 2006.

[KKC-05]   I.Kafeza, E.Kafeza, D.K.Chiu, Legal Aspects of Security in e-contracting with Electronic Agents, Sachar, P., Pohlmann, N., and Reimer, H. 2005 ISSE 2005 Securing Electronic Business Processes: Highlights of the Information Security Solutions Europe 2005 Conference. GWV-Vieweg.

The Impact of Monitoring Technology on the Law

Pieter Kleve · Richard De Mulder · Kees van Noortwijk

Erasmus University Rotterdam
Centre for Computers and Law
{kleve | demulder | vannoortwijk}@law.eur.nl

Abstract

This article first provides an overview of technology for monitoring and surveillance. From this overview it will become clear that the use of this type of technology is growing fast. At the same time, questions arise regarding its permissibility, in the light of legal and constitutions rights, such as the right to privacy. These questions are addressed here in the context of wider social developments. A conclusion that is reached is that with the increasing importance and use of surveillance technology, 'monitoring the surveillors' will become essential as well.

1 Introduction

Technology for surveillance and monitoring has, in today's society, become commonplace. In the Netherlands, for example, certain so-called 'sniffing poles' have been installed. These measure the level of air pollution and when a certain limit is reached a warnings system is activated. As a consequence of the disastrous tsunami in December 2004, a tsunami warning system has been installed in the Indian Ocean. Hospitals use technology to monitor the state of the human body and our financial obligations are monitored by computers that send us reminders and final demands if the payment has not been made on time.

Monitoring technology is used to supervise both social and physical processes, and to monitor individual behaviour. This technology is constantly being refined. For example, speeding, as an offence that forms a risk to public health, has for some time been dealt with by technology. The standard approach has been to have a camera that takes a photograph of the car once a certain maximum speed has been exceeded. Having established the level of the speeding, a fine is then sent to the car owner. However, in this set up the camera can only register the offence if it takes place where the camera is located; speeding either before or after the location of the camera cannot be registered. To remedy that deficiency, a new form of surveillance has made its appearance: it is now possible to follow the car along a section of the road. A camera located at one place on the road registers the speed of the car at that point and a camera placed a number of miles farther down the road registers the speed there. A computer then calculates the average speed of the car along that stretch of road between the two cameras. If the average speed is too high, a fine will be sent. For the road user, this development means that it is pointless just to slow down at the location of the first camera; speed must be kept down for the whole stretch of road between the two cameras.[1]

---

[1] It should perhaps be pointed out that this technology will not catch the driver who only speeds for a very short time on that section of road.

S. Paulus, N. Pohlmann, H. Reimer (Editors): Securing Electronic Business Processes, Vieweg (2006), 455-466

In the above example, there are legitimate legal grounds for the use of surveillance technology; the law has already laid down what constitutes the maximum speed and the carrying out of the procedure is the responsibility of the state. This surveillance technology has led to a certain conditioning of driving behaviour. However, even though we have become familiar with the use of road cameras, that does not mean that their existence is accepted by all road users. It could be that we consider that driving above the speed limit on that particular road, or section of the road, is not dangerous, or that we have a good excuse for speeding. When the check-points were manned by police officers, a sympathetic officer might have been prepared to accept a good story; a camera is not.

Road cameras have stimulated some drivers to find means of evasion. One such technique is the radar detection device, which warns of the vicinity of radar controlled speed measurement equipment. That has led some authorities to demand that such detection devices be made illegal (and consequently some manufacturers have developed detection devices that do not fall within the category of 'illegal radar detection devices'). What this shows is that a rule of law does not, of itself, produce compliancy. Individuals will act in their own self-interest, as they see it. [2] This action/ reaction phenomenon draws attention to the relationship between a rule of law and the enforcement of that rule of law. The enforcement of a rule of law is of great importance. The use of technology may promote compliance with the law, although that is not always necessarily the case.

Surveillance by camera is, of course, not confined to traffic situations. The use of camera surveillance is common in shopping centres, petrol stations and industrial areas, to name just a few examples. Moreover, camera surveillance is on the increase. If you wish to visit a company, instead of signing in using the traditional guest register, visitors may have to be prepared to undergo a video registration by complying with the friendly request to look in the camera and give their name.

Although camera surveillance is an obvious example of making people feel that they are 'being watched', it is by no means the only form of surveillance. It is already the case that foreigners who wish to enter the USA must provide fingerprints of both index fingers and a passport photograph. The charter company provides other personal data. Nor is Internet as anonymous as its users have long presumed. Surfing on the net leaves countless tracks, which can be picked up by businesses that chart users' Internet behaviour. Given the state's monopoly on coercion, it is not difficult for the state to obtain access to these 'tracks'. There was considerable consternation when the press revealed the existence of the Echelon program of the American National Security Agency (NSA). This controversial program could monitor (or tap) data exchange on the Internet, and thus in effect worldwide. However, the question must also be raised as to whether the consternation would have been greater if it had appeared that the NSA did not carry out such monitoring.[3]

A relatively new phenomenon is the use of mobile phone traffic data to find out where people are. In the Netherlands, this has recently been used in the following way. After a football match in Rotterdam, serious rioting occurred. To find witnesses of what exactly had happened, approximately 17,000 mobile phone users who, according to the transmitter data of the telephone provider, had been in the vicinity of the football stadium in Rotterdam on the day of the riots were sent an SMS message by the Rotterdam police force. In this message, all those

---

[2] C.f. [JeMe94].

[3] C.f. [Kerr03].

with any knowledge of the riots were urged to come forward and help the police with their inquiries. Such use of technology as an instrument of surveillance has not been without criticism, in particular with respect to infringing the right to personal privacy and creating a 'big brother' atmosphere.[4]

2 Surveillance with the help of technological means

From the above examples, it is clear that technology plays an important, and in some cases even an essential, role in surveillance. For that reason, attention will now be paid to a number of possibilities for surveillance that can be realized by using technology. Surveillance is not exclusively aimed at conformity with certain legal requirements. Surveillance by the authorities is often the starting point of a process that leads to tracking down offenders and prosecution. IT (information technology) has become a major means for implementing all the stages in that process.

2.1 Camera surveillance in public and non-public places

The use of audio-visual equipment (cameras) is closely connected to surveillance. Cameras allow real time surveillance as well as retroactive surveillance. It has been argued recently that it is the real time surveillance that makes cameras in public places particularly effective, as action can be taken directly once a situation appears on camera.

The traditional way of looking at the images allows the supervisor to call upon the signals from various cameras or to project the images from those cameras next to each other on a screen. Digital image processing, however, is now also a possibility, allowing the computer to analysis and process the material at various levels. The following examples illustrate this technique (ranked, more or less, according to the complexity of the operations).

- Motion detection: only store images in which something happens.
- Quality enhancement: increasing the sharpness and contrast of a recording, so that it is possible to zoom in on details (a number plate, a person's face).
- Facial recognition: identifying a person by recording that person's face.
- Where cameras are positioned at more than one location, it becomes possible to track and trace people for a certain distance and over a certain period of time on the basis of facial recognition.
- Object pattern analysis: this system makes it possible to look at images where something out of the ordinary is considered to be taking place.
- The use of images from special satellites, which have advanced cameras and sensory equipment.

2.2 Surveillance of telecommunication

As well as extensive camera surveillance, the monitoring of all forms of telecommunication has also become large-scale. That monitoring applies not just to telephone and fax messages, but also, and increasingly, to data traffic on the Internet.

---

[4] C.f .[Solo01].

From a technical viewpoint, in most cases it no longer matters what sort of communication is involved; even speech can often be directly digitalized and then transmitted. This is, for example, the case with respect to mobile telecommunication via GSM (mobile phones) and via VOIP, 'Voice Over IP'. This implies that there is little point in monitoring or tapping data on the basis of which type of communication is going to be the subject of the surveillance. It is usually not possible to distinguish these types before the data has been received and decoded. The decoding establishes, inter alia, what type of data is involved (digitalized speech or computer data etc). However, it is also quite likely that the sender of the data has sent them in an encrypted form. This is, in principle, very easy where digital data are involved. Trying to decrypt without the right key can be extremely difficult and time consuming, in particular when a so-called strong form of encryption has been used. Even the use of technology does not mean this problem can be easily solved. This is why authorities have considered placing encryption under legal regulation. In the Netherlands, an attempt was made to make the users of encryption provide the data for decryption where a criminal investigation was concerned. This provision never became law. Nor did the rule that encryption keys had to be deposited with 'Trusted Third Parties' (TTPs).

A specific form of surveillance, entailing the surveillance of people rather than of telephone or data traffic, allows people to be located, based on their mobile phone data. This information can be derived from one or more transmitters for mobile phones. It makes it possible to determine who was where (in the vicinity of one of these transmitters) at a certain time, at least if the mobile phone was on. This technique is now used regularly to follow a suspect. However, the use made of this data by the Rotterdam police to sent SMS messages to all those who had been in the vicinity of the football stadium at a certain time, was new, at least for the Netherlands. Of interest here is that the data of bystanders was used for the purposes of a criminal investigation, not just the data of those suspected of a criminal offence.

For this sort of location data, as well as data traffic itself, it is obvious that the registration and storage of such data can be of great important for retrospective monitoring. European law has already been introduced to make this possible. Nonetheless, its introduction has met resistance from providers and Internet user organisations, such as 'Bits of Freedom'.

2.3 Entry control; identification of persons and goods

The time that entry would be granted to a person based on no more than an identification card, specifying the carrier's name and photograph, is drawing to an end. The traditional identification papers are simply too easy to copy. It is, therefore, not surprising that measures have been taken to make passports, driving licences and similar forms of identification more difficult to forge. The newest weapon against forgery is the use of digitalized biometric information as a means of identification.

Biometrics (literally 'measuring life') has quite a long history. The use of the finger and handprint for identification was known in China in the 14th century. In Europe, fingerprints have been used as a means of identification since the end of the 19th century, based on a system developed by Richard Edward Henry of Scotland Yard.[5] Fingers are not the only parts of the body, however, that can be used for identification purposes: hands, eyes (the iris and retina), the face, the voice and the DNA itself can be used. However, they all require specific technology. The certainty of identification they provide may vary. DNA is generally regarded

---

[5] See [JHPB97].

as being the most accurate and reliable biometrical method. The disadvantage of using DNA for identification is that the process requires considerable time and cost, whereas an iris scan, a face scan or a fingerprint can be carried out quickly and cheaply. It is for these reasons, that the latter techniques are the ones used at entry points.

IT plays an important role in biometric techniques. For example, the characteristics of a fingerprint are normally stored in the form of a so-called template. The accuracy with which that process takes place determines the dimensions of the template and also its reliability. The template can be stored in a memory chip which, for example, can be used in an identity card.

Not only persons, but also goods can be identified and traced. One traditional form is the traditional metal detector, for example a screening doorway at airports, which makes use of a magnetic field. Other techniques that are increasingly being used include MRI scans, microwave radar registration and microwave dielectrometrics, each of which are capable of detecting specific types of objects, for example in baggage.

All these techniques have in common that they make use of the existing characteristics of persons or goods. It is, however, possible to track a person or goods by means of a tagging system. With respect to goods, a good example of this form of tagging is the security barcode label that is now found on many products, which triggers an alarm once the exit has been passed. A similar application can be found in cars and scooters, enabling stolen items to be returned to their rightful owners. One technique that is of much interest at the moment is RFID, 'Radio Frequency Identification'. It functions in the same way as the security bar code, but it is so cheap and so small that it can be inserted during the manufacturing process of virtually any product. This technique could replace the barcodes as an effective means of preventing shoplifting. The privacy aspect of this development, as it is possible to collect information unobtrusively about what products a person has, has led to much discussion. [6]

Finally, mention must be made of the GPS, the 'Global Positioning System'. Apart from being used for navigational purposes, this system can also detect the precise location of persons or goods. If this information is then passed on to the police, for example via a GSM connection, it makes it much simpler to track down stolen goods. When this system is applied to persons in the form of an ankle tag, new possibilities for electronic house arrest arise.

2.4 Detection and prosecution of crimes

Many of the techniques described above are suitable not just for the purposes of crime prevention, but also for detection and prosecution when a crime has been committed. For example, cameras can be used for face recognition, data from data exchanges and location data can be stored by computer and biometric methods can be used. Such techniques affect criminal procedure; evidence obtained through the use of highly advanced technology[7] must comply to the same standards of validity and reliability as evidence obtained in a more traditional way, for example by witness statements. The use of new technology can cause problems for judges, whose lack of familiarity with the technology involved means they have to rely heavily upon the expert opinions of those behind the technology. It is of great importance to deal with this problem because the probability is that the use of evidence obtained by technology will increase rather than decrease.

---

[6] [AGAO05].

[7] For background information on the use of DNA profiles, see for instance [BCCM00].

2.5 Conclusions regarding surveillance technology

In the future, surveillance technology will make use of various techniques. Information in a digital form makes it possible to use techniques that were unknown only a short time ago. Equipment can be used not only for (passive) registration, but also for analysis and interpretation. One example of the combination of techniques can already be found in American airports: video cameras utilising image recognition software used in combination with pre-existing information. This method is also used to deal with hooligans at football matches, rather than checking their individual club cards. Surveillance technology also includes fingerprint and DNA techniques. These methods are not only used for active control, for example to gain access to restricted areas, but also retroactively to reconstruct a given situation. Digital technology is also responsible for the increasing use of biometric techniques.

Surveillance technology has, without doubt, made an impact on society. *Technological advances*, in general, have been considerable over the last 150 years. It is a period that has seen the Industrial Revolution superseded by the Information Revolution. Technological applications are numerous and various, and have become integral to the society we know today. That technology should be used for surveillance is, in this context, not extraordinary. Indeed, its application is rather obvious given that the techniques are easily applied to surveillance and that society as a whole has acquired a more technically orientated character.

What perhaps is less obvious, is that technology offers diverse possibilities with respect to complex relations. *Management* is of vital importance in carrying out tasks, whether those tasks are related to business or public sector organisations. Technology can assist in planning, control and communication.

3 Legal considerations

This article will focus on five problem areas with respect to monitoring and surveillance technology. These areas include the invasion of personal privacy, the use of surveillance technology by the authorities in the enforcement of criminal law, surveillance technology as a means of social control, whether surveillance technology leads to a better use of resources, and the principles of proportionality and subsidiarity.

3.1 Privacy versus safety?

One opinion that is often voiced is that people find it unpleasant to be spied on and to know that their movements can be checked out later. However, when members of the public are asked if they would like to see more uniformed policemen on the street, the vast majority answer in the affirmative; most people apparently find a police presence on the streets reassuring. Is it, then, a question of finding the right balance: yes to surveillance in itself but no to surveillance in an extreme form? If that is the case, it implies a remarkable conclusion; that we actually *want* a certain level of uncertainty. Research has shown that the public judges risk not just in terms of the chance of something happening or the effect of that something happening. That other considerations play a role comes to the fore where behaviour in traffic or smoking habits are concerned.

With respect to the relationship between privacy and safety, the question seems to be how much of our privacy we are prepared to surrender in order to increase our safety. These two basic rights, the right to privacy and the right to protection, seem to be uneasy partners. However, the question itself is not as straightforward as it may seem. Why is it that most of us are perfectly prepared to have our baggage examined in airports but resent our past being looked into? Privacy is not a clear concept; the term includes various aspects of private life. It may encompass various dimensions, such as the spatial dimension. This spatial dimension is concerned with our freedom of movement: if there were no controls at airports would we feel freer or less free to go as we pleased? And if our past is looked into, would the examination of our baggage no longer be necessary? Privacy and safety do not have to be opposites, but the one can affect the other. It would be hard to think of something that is a greater infringement of a person's privacy than becoming the victim of violence or of damage of personal belongings, or to live under the continuous threat that these events may occur.

Constitutional rights have a special place in the relationship between the authorities and members of the public. Rights and freedoms are formulated intended to protect citizens against the arbitrary use of power by the authorities. In the course of time, the concept of the horizontal working of constitutional rights has developed. The right to respect for personal privacy is not just between the authorities and the public, but also between members of the public themselves. In former times, it was necessary to protect citizens from the arbitrary behaviour of the authorities (or the monarch). Today, in the developed democratic states of the West, it would seem that the 'danger' emanates not so much from the authorities, which are open to public review, but from those who reject authority. Fear restricts the movements of citizens, either because they are not sure if it is safe to take an airplane or the local metro, or to voice a possibly controversial opinion. It would now appear that it is the authorities that have become the champion of constitutional rights, rather than the body that could be guilty of flouting them. The question now before us is which aspects of privacy must weigh heavier in a given situation? The means used will depend upon how that question is answered.

Another question that comes to the fore in determining whether someone's privacy has been infringed, is what criteria should be used. Where there is a choice or where there is an advantage to the person concerned, it is less likely that an infringement of privacy will be considered as unacceptable. In order to respect personal privacy it would seem more important to formulate these criteria rather than paying attention to actual forms of behaviour, as this does not sufficiently take into account the personal character of privacy.

However, the choice for applying surveillance technology, or being placed under such surveillance, is often not one made at an individual level. This runs counter to the present day tendency whereby the individual plays a central role. That is because the protection of privacy is not just an issue for individuals; it must also take collective needs into account. Paradoxically, it would seem that the 'protection' of constitutional rights justifies a certain selective infringement of those rights. This can be explained in terms of the relative utility of the application. To the extent that it affects individuals, legislators must be careful not to make unwarranted generalizations, as this could result in the public rejecting the use of technology. This would be a pity as research into such matters as the registration of DNA and the use of extensive databanks holding sensitive information, has shown that many people attach more importance to safety than to privacy.

3.2 Suspects and non-suspects

When it is contended that surveillance technology infringes personal privacy, one aspect that is brought to the fore is that surveillance technology does not differentiate between people; the surveillance entails the monitoring of both suspects and non-suspects. This infringes the legal principle that coercive measures should only be used against those for whom there are reasonable grounds to suspect them of criminal activity.

Modern technology means that an innocent person's privacy can be infringed as a side effect of tracking a suspected person's movements. It is this, rather than the use of technology against the suspects themselves, that causes problems; those who are not considered to be suspects must also accept that they too are subjected to the coercive measures made possible by the application of this technology. This would seem contrary to the usual principle of criminal procedure that a person's status as 'suspect' must first be established (for example, that reasons for suspicion are first presented to a judge in order to obtain a search warrant before the premises of a suspect may be searched).

In the first place, it is not the case that the authorities, incl. police and the judiciary, may only do what has been laid down in detail. To a certain extent they may, just like ordinary citizens, ask people questions, telephone people and send sms messages. These activities cannot be categorized as coercive measures, for citizens are free in deciding whether to answer or not, nor are such activities limited to 'suspects'. That people do not like to be spoken to by the police, that they could feel intimidated, means that the police must be careful in the way they approach the public, but there is no reason, and indeed it would not be desirable, to fetter their capacity to ask questions. This applies even where if a person refuses to answer the question, he could become a suspect, and as such the subject of coercive measures.

Nor does receiving SMS messages from the police mean that recipients must be considered to be suspects. During an investigation, the police needs to contact people as potential witnesses. In the case of the football riots SMS messages, these messages were sent to ask whether anyone had seen anything of interest to the investigation. The police could have achieved the same result by carrying out a house to house check or asking questions to all those attending the next football match in Rotterdam. The choice to send an SMS message would seem more attractive: only those people who were in the vicinity of the football stadium at the time of the riots were 'bothered' by the police, it is much less labour intensive to send a message than to send out police officers, a message saves time and the costs of it are relatively low. An SMS message is also probably less intimidating than a personal encounter with the police.

Nor is it the case that the authorities may only exercise coercion against someone who is suspected of an offence. In many cases, the law lays down a general competence for a certain activity. For example, returning an income tax form is compulsory and surveillance cameras may be used to detect speeding. Checking that drivers do not exceed the maximum speed limit does not make all road users 'suspect'. And a possible automation of the surveillance of income tax forms, which could include coupling this with data from other sources, is, in principle, not an extension of tax control. Making data available – coupling files – should take place in accordance with existing legal regulations. However, because computers have made it easier to compare data, this area might be subject to further legal regulation.

3.3 Technology and social control

The use of surveillance technology, as illustrated by the above example of tax supervision, does not always entail an extension of an existing competence. It is more often a means by which that existing competence becomes more effective and efficient. The simple fact that something is useful, or more useful than it used to be, leads in itself to a certain shift in norms. It is, however, important that it is borne in mind that technology itself is primarily a 'means'; it is a means to make possible those things people find useful. Surveillance technology is, in this sense, a tool to enforce norms, in the same way as the law itself is a tool to enforce norms.

When people go on holiday, they often ask their neighbours to keep an eye on the house. If someone hangs around the deserted house, the neighbours might ask whether they can 'be of help'. That a police car would drive past the house more often while they were gone would also be welcome. In former times, it was far more common for people to keep an eye on the behaviour of others. There are various reasons why that is less the case today. One reason is the tendency noted above for increased mobility and individualization. People are also aware that an intervention may not be without risk.

The social control and cohesion typical of society several decades ago no longer exist, at least not in that form. It is generally recognized that social control and social cohesion have a useful function. The gap left by the lack of social control can be filled by the use of technology; it can give social control and social cohesion form once again. In any evaluation of surveillance technology, factors to be taken into account are not only the costs and disadvantages, but also what it contributes and its social advantages.

3.4 Technology and solidarity

Whether a decision is made to use surveillance technology seems to be largely a matter of efficiency. Efficiency is a norm more often associated with the private sector, yet this consideration is relevant with respect to the public sector as well. Although it would seem that efficiency as a norm has achieved greater acceptance in the private sector than the public sector, it is not the case that the aim of efficiency is without criticism in the private sector, for example with respect to commercial profit at the cost of service. When this criticism is analysed, it would appear that the services sacrificed are those that were not sufficiently profitable or provided at a loss. What the private and public sectors share is that those individuals who are affected want a result that suits them, even if it is disadvantageous for others, although they are not personally willing to contribute more. This leads to a conservative approach. Efficiency as a criterion is nevertheless an important guarantee of solidarity. The use of technology can promote efficiency.

An important question is to what extent people will be prepared to contribute financially to an expensive system of redistribution, in which not all those who are intended to benefit from the redistribution do so, and some of those who do benefit were not intended to do so. Many of the organizations charged with the task of redistribution are founded on the principle of solidarity. This solidarity could be in the form of unemployment benefits, insurance, housing or social security benefits, contribution to church funds, or charitable organizations. An important factor here is the tendency pointed out above; the increasing complexity of society, increased mobility and individualization. As a consequence, it has become more difficult to reach those who have the right to such assistance, and more difficult to prevent fraud by those who do not have this right. This puts solidarity under pressure and makes it crumble away. Surveillance and control could be made more efficient by using technology, for example to prevent the fraudulent use of social security systems, and indeed its use could be demanded.

In practice, it is no longer possible to implement complex legal projects without the use of technology. Technology has, in turn, influenced the content of these legal rules, as the automation process itself may impose certain requirements and restrictions. Creating and keeping consensus depends on correct implementation, certainly in the long term. Using technology as a means of control or as a means to support the enforcement of control, could give those involved a greater feeling of certainty. It is because we have computers that we can refine general rules, so that relevant individual circumstances can be taken into account. It is this very ability to distinguish between cases that makes it possible to uphold the principle of equality. In this way, technology could contribute to a feeling of solidarity.

3.5 Subsidiarity and proportionality

The use of surveillance technology cannot, in general, be seen as irreconcilable with the right to the protection of personal privacy. Safety is not in opposition to privacy, but an aspect of it. Furthermore, it could be argued that the right to personal privacy is not an absolute right; other factors can, and sometimes must, be taken into account. Thirdly, it has already been pointed out that the scope of the concept of privacy, and its interpretation, must be seen against a background of technical and social developments.

Similarly, it has been argued that a general application of surveillance technology does not have to be contrary to the principle of criminal procedure that there should be reasonable grounds to see the subject as a suspect. That is because surveillance technology is not in itself a coercive measure. Surveillance technology is a means that is not confined to use for the purposes of criminal procedure. A person may cooperate, for example at a check-point, without having first to be identified as a suspect. There are also positive effects, such as the use of technology to increase the usefulness of services to the public and to respect the enforcement of basic rights.

It is often not necessary to change the law in order to implement surveillance technology. Technology can already be implemented within the existing legal context. However, the use of technology, either in general or for particular forms of surveillance, can lead to shifts in norms. With respect to surveillance technology, just as with other means, attention should be paid to the legal issues that may arise from one situation to another. The boundaries for legal application are usually determined by the principles of subsidiarity and proportionality. In the example of the sms messages sent by the Rotterdam police, it can be argued, without trivializing the potential threat this could form, that this application stayed within accepted limits. Another example is the experiment with camera surveillance last year in the centre of Groningen, a city in the north of the Netherlands. These cameras did not operate continuously, but were triggered when the microphones that were attached to the cameras picked up sound. Although it could be said that the surveillance was continual, nonetheless the system was only activated if there was a reason: the sound registered by the microphones. This is a good example of proportionality; modern technology has made it possible to limit the infringement of privacy.

In setting down legal conditions for use, it should be realized that a too conservative approach could unfairly favour criminals. While acknowledging that there should be reasonable grounds before someone is considered to be a suspect, it should also be borne in mind that it is increasingly the case that the threat could come from an unknown source, as is often the case with terrorist threats. What should be taken into account is that surveillance technology does not only have to be seen as a means of repression: it is also a means of prevention. It gives a high quality service and is cost effective (for consumer and tax payer). It is possible to organise the surveillance in such a way that not all the information need be made known. It is sometimes sufficient that it can be made known. To use the example of the Rotterdam police once again, it would seem that no names or addresses were made available but only the telephone numbers. Much work is taking place in the field of so-called privacy enhancing technology (PET) and techniques to ensure anonymity. It is, of course, necessary to consider safety precautions, any loss of data and possible claims by those affected by a loss of data, misuse of data or use that causes damage. In general, it would seem wise to make the legal framework known on the introduction of the technology.

4 Conclusions

In part, the objections to surveillance technology arise when people are the objects of that surveillance: we do not mind if others are subject to surveillance, but we do not want to be the subject of that surveillance ourselves. If we see ourselves as honourable citizens, for whom surveillance is an unnecessary restriction on our privacy, there is indeed room for indignation. Not only is such surveillance unnecessary, it is straightforwardly insulting, as it implies we too are suspected of criminal behaviour. Nonetheless, the public appears to benefit from surveillance by the authorities. Most of the criticism emanates from lawyers and institutions, such as Data Protection Authorities, Amnesty International, Liberty, socialist political parties and law faculties. Given the rational model of man, it is quite easy to explain why the objections come from this direction: it is in the self-interest of these groups to protest.

Furthermore, it would seem that resistance is a characteristic of the assimilation process of new technology. It is resistance to technology and resistance to change. Not knowing whether there is surveillance, what the scope of that surveillance is, who is carrying out the surveillance and what will be done with the data can make people feel uncomfortable. It is rather like the situation of 'I can't see you, but you can see me'. Without transparency with respect to these issues, it is quite possible that people feel more vulnerable rather than less. That would inhibit the assimilation process, which would be a pity given how important it is that the usefulness of this technology is acknowledged; one conclusion that is rarely seen in legal literature is that technology, also surveillance technology, actually makes it easier to respect and protect basic rights.

A good example of how the authorities can use new technology is the questioning of potential witnesses on the basis of their locations revealed by their mobile phones. Another example of how authorities can use technology to deal with new, and partly unknown, threats is to keep data from networks for a certain period with the help of internet or telephone providers. These examples show how new technology can be used for the more effective enforcement of existing norms. However, there is a clear possibility of the infringement of rights such as the right to privacy. That the norms will adjust is a logical consequence of the technological developments. An important criterion is whether it works; the effectiveness must be tested.

Five points to be taken into account were presented above. The points were 'privacy and safety', the importance of the presence of a 'suspect', 'technology and social control', 'technology and solidarity' and 'cost effectiveness'. The conclusion has to be that surveillance technology leads to a new consideration of values and interests.

The right to privacy – and other rights that have arisen from technological and social developments, like copyright – are ripe for review. The automatic reaction of support for these rights is no longer adequate. The right to privacy is no longer just under pressure with respect to the concerns for safety, but also in its relationship with other rights, such as the freedom of information and there are even conflicts within the right to privacy itself. Often the privacy of one person means the infringement of the privacy of another person.

There is a steady, and growing, market for gossip publications; apparently people are quite happy to read privacy sensitive stories about others. Perhaps an even more important consideration than the dichotomy privacy/safety is that between privacy and the right to information. Where more weight is given to privacy than the right to information, the current trend for weblogs could be made impossible. A redirection concerning privacy is also in order for claims to privacy regarding a change of gender and age, for example. Limiting constitutional rights, or reassessing them, means that it is desirable to put into place an effective control on the power of the authorities. Those who object to surveillance technology not only point out the dangers to individual rights and the costs, but in particular the danger of misuse by the authorities.

Technology not only makes surveillance a more practical matter; in a more complex way it leads to a new organization of state power. This is possibly the most important point of discussion with respect to legal and social change as a response to technological progress. De Mulder[8] argues that a new fourth power is inevitable; just as the appearance of an executive power was inevitable once the law could not only be written but also printed. That development led to the large-scale bureaucracies we see today. The technical possibilities offered by computers and the Internet will not be less far-reaching. The appearance of a new power, a monitoring power, would seem likely. We have already witnessed this development in the form of such institutions as the Ombudsman, the National Audit Office and the National Competition Authority.

This new power, the result of social change, will have far-reaching consequences for the law, and for the functioning of the state of law and the legal profession. The growth of the executive power led to large-scale bureaucracies. Bureaucracies may be of use, but can easily lead to excesses. The systematic monitoring of those in charge of the use of surveillance technology in a democratic state is a necessity. In a globalizing and increasingly technological world democracies will need monitoring powers to supervise the use of surveillance techniques.

References

[AGAO05]   American Government Accountability Office: Information Security, Radio Frequency Identification Technology in the Federal Government, WWW, <www.gao.gov/new.items/d05551.pdf>.

[BCCM00]   Budowle, B., Carmody, G, Chakraborty, R. & Monson, K.L.: Source attribution of a forensic DNA profile. In: Forensic Science Communications, July 2000, ISSN 1528-8005.

[JeMe94]   Jensen, M.C. & Meckling, W.H: The Nature of Man. In: Journal of Applied Corporate Finance 1994-2, p. 4-19.

[JHPB97]   Jain, A.K., Hong, L, Pankanti, S & Bolle, R.: An identity authentication system using fingerprints. In: Proceedings of the IEEE 85 (9) (1997) 1365-1388.

[Muld98]   Mulder, R.V. De: The Digital Revolution: From Trias to Tetras Politica. In: Snellen, I.Th.M., Donk, W.B.H.J. van de (Eds.): Public Administration in an Information Age. Handbook, Amsterdam: IOS Press 1998, ISBN 90 5199 395 1.

[Kerr03]   Kerr, O.S.: Internet Surveillance Law After the USA Patriot Act: The Big Brother That Isn't. In: Northwestern University Law Review, Vol. 97, 2003, http://ssrn.com/abstract=317501.

[Solo01]   Solove, D.J.: Privacy and Power: Computer Databases and Metaphors for Information Privacy'. In: Stanford Law Review, 2001 Vol. 53, http://docs.law.gwu.edu/facweb/dsolove/Privacy-Power.pdf.

---

[8] [Muld98].

Index

A

B

C

F

G

H

I

J

K

L

R

S

T

Profikurse

Paul Chlebek
User Interface-orientierte Softwarearchitektur
Bauentwurfslehre für interaktive Softwareoberflächen -
Kompass für die Entwicklung dialogintensiver Anwendungen -
Leitfaden für erlebbare User Interfaces

2006. ca. XXIV, 222 S. mit 85 Abb. u. Online-Service. Br. ca. € 49,90
ISBN 3-8348-0162-3

Einführung - Funktion und Oberfläche skizzieren - UI-Beschreibung detaillie-
ren - UI-Entwicklung in der Softwarearchitektur verankern - Einbindung in das
Projektmanagement - Einbindung in die Funktionsmodellierung - Übernahme
der UI-Spezifikation als Steuerungsdaten für Prozesse - Verwertung der UI-
Beschreibung beim Testen

Jens Ferner
Profikurs PHP-Nuke
Einsatz, Anpassung und fortgeschrittene Programmierung -
PHP-Nuke vom Start bis zur strukturierten Anwendung -
Mit umfassender interner Funktionsreferenz

2., verb. u. erw. Aufl. 2004. XIV, 410 S. mit Online-Service. Br. € 34,90
ISBN 3-528-15848-4

Gottfried Wolmeringer/Thorsten Klein
Profikurs Eclipse 3
Mit Eclipse und Plugins professionell Java-Anwendungen entwickeln -
Von UML bis JUnit

2., verb. u. erw. Aufl. 2006. XIV, 215 S. mit Online-Service. Br. € 29,90
ISBN 3-8348-0007-4

Installation - CVS - Design - EMF - Rapid Prototyping - Kodierung - Extreme
Programming - Codeformating - Testphase - Aktuelle Werkzeuge - Entwicklung von eigenen Plugins

vieweg

Abraham-Lincoln-Straße 46
65189 Wiesbaden
Fax 0611.7878-400
www.vieweg.de

Stand 1.7.2006. Änderungen vorbehalten.
Erhältlich im Buchhandel oder im Verlag.

Mit Sicherheit

Heinrich Kersten/Gerhard Klett
Der IT Security Manager
Expertenwissen für jeden IT Security Manager -
Von namhaften Autoren praxisnah vermittelt
2005. VIII, 213 S. Br. € 49,90   ISBN 3-528-05900-1
Systematik der IT-Sicherheit mit vielen Beispielen - Sicherheitspoliti-
ken - Sicherheitskonzept: Theorie und Praxis - Schwachstellen-Analyse
und -Behebung - Technische, organisatorische, personelle und infra-
strukturelle Maßnahmen - Praxis des täglichen Sicherheitsmanagements

Klaus-Rainer Müller
IT-Sicherheit mit System
Sicherheitspyramide und Vorgehensmodell - Sicherheitsprozess und
Katastrophenvorsorge - Die 10 Schritte zum Sicherheitsmanagement
2., verb. u. erw. Aufl. 2005. XXIII, 328 S. mit Online-Service.
Geb. € 59,90   ISBN 3-528-15838-7
Dreidimensionale Sicherheitspyramide - Von Insellösungen zum Engi-
neering - Von der Sicherheitspolitik bis zu den Maßnahmen - Von Aus-
fällen bis zur Kontinuität - Von IT-Prozessen bis zu Personal - Compli-
ance-, Identitäts- und Risikomanagement - Firewall, Virenscanner,
Datensicherung, USB-Token - Mit Checklisten, Beispielen, Praxistipps

Hans-Peter Königs
IT-Risiko-Management mit System
Von den Grundlagen bis zur Realisierung - Ein praxisorientierter Leitfaden
2005. 296 S. mit Online-Service. Geb. € 49,90   ISBN 3-528-05875-7
Grundlagen erarbeiten - Anforderungen berücksichtigen - IT-Risiken
erkennen und bewältigen - Unternehmensprozesse meistern

vieweg

Abraham-Lincoln-Straße 46
65189 Wiesbaden
Fax 0611.7878-400   Stand 1.7.2006. Änderungen vorbehalten.
www.vieweg.de   Erhältlich im Buchhandel oder im Verlag.

Das Netzwerk der Profis

WIRTSCHAFTS INFORMATIK

Die führende Fachzeitschrift zum Thema Wirtschaftsinformatik.

Das hohe redaktionelle Niveau und der große praktische Nutzen für den Leser wird von über 30 Herausgebern - profilierte Persönlichkeiten aus Wissenschaft und Praxis - garantiert.

Profitieren Sie von der umfassenden Website unter

www.wirtschaftsinformatik.de

- Stöbern Sie im größten **Online-archiv** zum Thema Wirtschafts-informatik!
- Verpassen Sie mit dem **Newsletter** keine Neuigkeiten mehr!
- Diskutieren Sie im **Forum** und nutzen Sie das Wissen der gesamten Community!

- Sichern Sie sich weitere Fachinhalte durch die **Buchempfehlungen** und Veranstaltungshinweise!
- Binden Sie über **Content Syndication** die Inhalte der Wirtschaftsinformatik in Ihre Homepage ein!
- ... und das alles mit nur **einem Click** erreichbar.

vieweg